ALL-IN-ONE CCIE™
LAB STUDY GUIDE

All-in-One CCIE™ Lab Study Guide

Stephen Hutnik and Michael Satterlee

McGraw-Hill
New York • San Francisco • Washington, D.C. • Auckland
Bogotá • Caracas • Lisbon • London • Madrid • Mexico City
Milan • Montreal • New Delhi • San Juan • Singapore
Sydney • Tokyo • Toronto

McGraw-Hill

A Division of The **McGraw·Hill** *Companies*

2 3 4 5 6 7 8 9 0   AGM/AGM   9 0 4 3 2 1 0 9

P/N 135109-4
Part of 0-07-135108-6

*The sponsoring editor for this book was Steven Elliot and the production
supervisor was Clare Stanley. It was set in Century Schoolbook by D&G Limited LLC.*

Printed and bound by Quebecor / Martinsburg.

McGraw-Hill books are available at special quantity discounts to use as
premiums and sales promotions, or for use in corporate training programs.
For more information, please write to Director of Special Sales, McGraw-Hill,
11 West 19th Street, New York, NY 10011. Or contact your local bookstore.

 This book is printed on recycled, acid-free paper containing a minimum of 50
percent recycled de-inked fiber.

DEDICATION

To Robin, Bobby, Andrew, and Lauren for all of their love and support.

–Steve

This book is dedicated to my wife Mary Jo and my parents Jim and Gladys for their support and encouragement.

–Mike

ACKNOWLEDGMENTS

- We would like to thank our management team, especially David Mahar, Art Hautau, and Marcel Villaflor for all of their support while writing this book.
- It is a pleasure to work for a world class organization like IBM Global Services.
- Many thanks to our Editor Steve Elliot.
- We also want to thank George Kovachi from Adtran for lending us an Atlas 800 ISDN switch.

CONTENTS

Contents

LABS

ABOUT THE AUTHORS

Stephen M. Hutnik, **CCNA**, is a Senior Network Engineer at IBM Global Network Services, where he is responsible for development, testing, and training for the Global Backbone of the IBM Network. Stephen is also an adjunct professor of telecommunications at Pace University.

Stephen has extensive hands-on, design, training, and troubleshooting experience with a wide range of telecommunications equipment, including the entire line of Cisco routers (16XX through 75XX) and Cisco frame relay access devices. In recent projects, he has performed network evaluation and certification for the Cisco 1600 series of routers, and developed an MLPPP test bed for evaluating Cisco ISDN dial backup capabilities.

Stephen holds a Masters of Science in Telecommunications degree from Pace University.

Michael J. Satterlee (CCIE #3980) is a Senior Network Engineer at IBM Global Network Services, where he is responsible for managing the IBM Global Network Backbone Engineering Lab.

Michael is well-versed in IP internetworking, routing and switching, and can design, configure, install, and troubleshoot enterprise router networks with RIP, OSPF, IGRP, EIGRP and BGP. In recent projects, Michael has designed, implemented and tested the ISDN dial around the cloud Cisco solution for all IBM domestic networks. He also performed network evaluation and certification on all Cisco products before installation on the IBM domestic network.

Michael holds a Masters of Science in Telecommunications from Pace University.

TECHNICAL REVIEWERS

As the leading publisher of technical books for more than 100 years, McGraw-Hill prides itself on bringing you the most authoritative and up-to-date information available. To ensure that our books meet the highest standards of accuracy, we have asked a number of top professionals and technical experts to review the accuracy of the material you are about to read.

We take great pleasure in thanking the following technical reviewers for their insights:

Howard Berkowitz, CCSI, is Chief Technology Officer for Gett Communications, where he specializes in network architecture. He is a Certified Cisco Systems Instructor for Internetwork Design, and teaches advanced routing seminars for Cisco, Nortel, and Cisco Training Partners.

Berkowitz is the author of Designing Addressing Architectures for Routing and Switching (Macmillan 1998) and Designing Routing and Switching Architectures for Enterprise Networks (Macmillan 1999). He is also the author or co-author of several RFCs in numbering, and his current IETF work includes documents on multihoming, virtual private networks, and on OSPF network deployment.

Chad Marsh, CCNP+Voice, CCDA, is a Senior Systems Engineer for Sarcom, a Cisco Gold Partner, and works out of their Seattle, WA office. With ten years of voice and PBX communications experience, and two years of networking, he is focusing on VoIP and other Voice/Data integration solutions. He is also currently working toward CCIE certification, and is scheduled to take the CCIE lab exam in October.

Scott Morris, CCIE #4713, MCSE, oversees all Information Services (data, telco and security) systems for Tele-Tech Company, Inc. based in Lexington, KY. Tele-Tech is a telecommunications installation company doing work all across the nation. He also does network design, analysis, consulting and helps set up ISPs (in his spare time, of course)!

1

Take the Lab Once and Pass

When we started to write this book in early 1999, we wanted to write something that was unique. While there were many Cisco-related books on the market, there were no Cisco books that were 100 percent hands-on. Many of the Cisco-related books that did include configurations only included parts of the configuration and did not provide enough information so the reader could completely build and test the configuration. We feel that this book is unique. The book contains 86 fully tested and documented lab exercises, which will help the reader prepare for the CCIE lab exam.

We hope you enjoy reading this book as much as we enjoyed writing it.

CCIE Lab Exams

The CCIE lab exam is a challenging, hands-on assessment of your internetworking skills. It costs $1,000 in the United States and stretches over two days. Before you can sign up for the lab exam, you must pass the CCIE qualification exam. Unlike the computer-administered exams, CCIE lab exams are only offered through Cisco locations. CCIE Routing and Switching candidates have their choice of numerous locations. Availability of the CCIE ISP Dial and CCIE WAN Switching lab exams is much more limited. The exams are standardized among sites, and selecting the location is a matter of geographical preference.

CCIE Lab Locations

Routing and Switching Labs

San Jose, California, USA
(800) 553-NETS or (408) 526-8063
ccie_ucsa@cisco.com

Research Triangle Park, North Carolina, USA
(800) 553-NETS or (408) 527-7177
ccie_ucsa@cisco.com

Halifax, Nova Scotia, Canada
(800) 553-NETS or (902) 492-8811
ccie_ucsa@cisco.com

North Sydney, New South Wales, Australia
+61 2 9935 4128
ccie_apt@cisco.com

Brussels, Belgium
+32 2 778 46 70
ccie_emea@cisco.com

Beijing, China
+86 1 0648 92398
ccie_apt@cisco.com

Tokyo, Japan
+81 3 5219 6409
ccie@cisco.co.jp

Capetown, South Africa
+32 2 778 46 70
ccie_emea@cisco.com

ISP Dial Labs

Halifax, Nova Scotia, Canada
(800) 553-NETS or (902) 492-8811
ccie_ucsa@cisco.com

San Jose, California, USA
(800) 553-NETS or (408) 526-8063
ccie_ucsa@cisco.com

WAN Switching Labs

San Jose, California, USA
(800) 553-NETS or (408) 526-8063
ccie_ucsa@cisco.com

Stockley Park, United Kingdom
+32 2 778 46 70
ccie_emea@cisco.com

According to Jeff Buddemeier, Cisco's technical lead for the CCIE program, the lab setup incorporates five routers and a Catalyst switch. Each candidate has his own rack and patch panel. You will also receive a set of Cisco documentation to use throughout the exam. You cannot bring any other notes or documentation into the exam with you.

Your first task will be to create a network to specification. This will take up all of the first day and half of the second. Halfway through the second day, while you are out of the room, the exam proctor will insert faults into your network, and you will have to find and fix them—as well as be able to document the problems and their resolutions.

There are a total of 100 possible points on the exam. To pass, you must achieve a score of 80 or better. You must achieve a passing score on each section of the exam to be allowed to progress to the next. For example, a perfect score on the first day would be 45 points. You have to earn at least 30 of them to be allowed to return for the first part of day two.

Table 1–1 shows the scoring breakdown.

Table 1–1

CCIE Lab Exam
Scoring

Day	Task	Points	Total So Far	Minimum Score to Continue
1	build	45	45	30
2 (part I)	build	30	75	55
2 (part II)	troubleshooting	25	100	80 or better to pass

The lab starting time varies depending upon locatin, but will be somewhere between 8:00 a.m. and 9:00 a.m. each day and run for $7^1/_2$ hours. There is a half hour break for lunch. A proctor will be in the room to clarify questions and handle any emergencies that may arise, but basically you are on your own.

The failure rate for this exam is high. According to Buddmeier, only about 20% of the candidates pass it on the first attempt. On average, CCIE candidates require two to three lab exams before they earn a passing score. Think of your first time through as a learning experience, and if you manage to pass, that is a bonus. There is no limit on the number of times you can retake the exam.

As with all certification exams, lab exam content and structure are subject to change, so when you are ready to consider taking the lab exam, it's best to get the latest information from Cisco. Cisco's Web site contains specific instructions about how to prepare for each of the CCIE lab and qualification exams:

- CCIE R/S: `www.cisco.com/warp/public/625/ccie/routing.html`
- CCIE WAN Switching: `www.cisco.com/warp/public/625/ccie/cciwa_ds.htm`
- CCIE ISP Dial: `www.cisco.com/warp/public/625/ccie/isp_dial.html`

It cannot be stressed enough that you must get lots of hands-on practice if you hope to pass this exam. If you do not have equipment to practice on at work, you will have to set up a home lab or find another way to gain access to the equipment.

We picked up the preceding material from *Get Cisco Certified & Get Ahead* by Anne Martinez (McGraw-Hill, 1999).

Format of the Book

The book is geared toward a wide audience. The technology introductions at the beginning of each chapter will provide the user with a detailed explanation of networking protocols and technologies.

Students studying for their CCIE will find the 86 sample labs and over 200 router configurations a valuable study reference. Those people that are fortunate enough to have access to several routers will be able to actually go through each lab step by step.

All of the 86 labs in this book are self-contained with fully debugged configurations and step-by-step instructions. All of the labs were tested, and the output shown in each lab was actually taken from the working configurations.

Each lab was created using the least number of routers possible, so the reader who wishes to actually go through each lab can do so with the least amount of equipment. We realize that not all people have access to a world-class testing facility like we do at IBM, so we tried to keep the routers required for each lab scenario to a minimum.

Chapter Format

The format of all the chapters in this book are similar.

1. Each chapter starts with an introduction section, outlining the topic to be discussed.
2. A detailed technology overview of the topic is then presented. Readers should read through this overview to make sure that they have a thorough understanding of the topic.
3. All of the commands that are discussed in the chapter are then listed, and their use and function are then discussed.
4. The chapters labs are then presented.
5. Troubleshooting information on the topic is then presented.
6. A conclusion wraps up the chapter.

Throughout each chapter you will find the following features.

NOTE: *Notes highlight important information.*

TIP: *Tips offer guidance to help the reader better understand the material and succeed on the exam.*

Lab Format

Each of the 86 labs has the same format. All of the labs are numbered in order, starting at LAB #1 and ending at LAB #86. The format is as follows:

1. The list of equipment needed to perform the lab is reviewed.

2. The lab objectives and configuration objectives are discussed in the Configuration Overview section.

3. Any notes related to the configuration are listed.

4. A detailed drawing of the lab is shown.

5. Configurations for all routers in the lab are listed. The configurations are taken directly from the routers that were used to perform the lab while writing this book. Any interfaces that were not used to perform the lab are not shown in the configuration listing (to conserve space).

Configurations are highlighted with this icon.

6. Step-by-step monitoring and testing instructions are given to verify that the lab setup is functioning properly.

CD-ROM

The included CD-ROM contains all the configurations that are presented in this book. Readers can cut and paste the configurations into their setups, thereby saving time.

The file-naming convention for the files on the CD-ROM includes the lab number and the router name used in the lab. For example, the file `LAB75A.txt` contains the configuration for RouterA in Lab #75.

CHAPTER 2

Terminal Servers

Topics Covered in This Chapter

- Out-of-band network management
- Basic terminal server configuration
- Configuring IP host tables
- Absolute versus relative line numbers
- Changing the default escape character
- Troubleshooting a terminal server

Introduction

This chapter explores configuration and troubleshooting procedures for one of Cisco's access services—the terminal server. Cisco routers provide four "access services" which are supported on the Cisco 2500 router series: models 2509, 2510, 2511, and 2512 (Remote Node Service, Terminal Services, Protocol Translation, and Asynchronous Remote Access Routing). This chapter will discuss terminal services. The remaining access services will be covered later in the book.

The terminal server used for this configuration is a 2511RJ, which provides 16 asynchronous serial ports. The terminal server provides access to all of our test routers via reverse telnet. Reverse telnet is the process of using telnet to make a connection out an asynchronous port.

The test router's console port will be connected directly to one of the 16 asynchronous interfaces on the 2511RJ, using a standard Cisco console roll cable. The test router will be accessed using a reverse telnet connection. To make a reverse telnet connection, you telnet to any active IP address on the box followed by 20xx, where x is the port number that you wish to access (**Telnet 1.1.1.1 2001**).

Out-of-Band Network Management

Figure 2–1 depicts a hub site that does not use a terminal server to access the routers on the network. Each router requires a separate modem connection in order to be managed.

Figure 2–1
Out-of-band network management without a terminal server

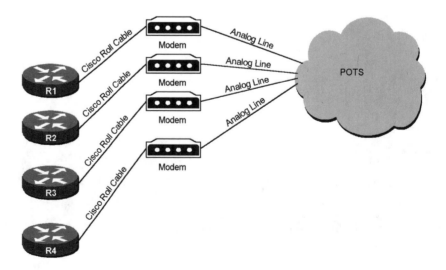

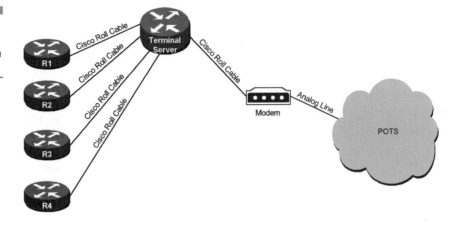

Figure 2–2
Out-of-band network
management using a
terminal server

In Figure 2–2, all devices are accessed through the terminal server. Notice that only one analog line and modem are needed to manage all of the collocated devices. Not only does this feature simplify network management, but it also greatly reduces the cost.

Commands Discussed in this Chapter

- **ip host** *name* **[tcp-port-number] address1 [address2...address8]**
- **no exec**
- **transport input {all | at | mot | nasi | none | pad | rlogin | telnet | v120}**

ip host: This Global configuration command is used to define a static host name-to-address mapping in the router's host cache.

no exec: This interface configuration command is used to disable EXEC processing for the specified line.

transport input: This interface configuration command is used to specify an incoming transport protocol. Cisco routers do not accept incoming network connections to asynchronous ports (TTY lines) by default. You have to specify an incoming transport protocol or specify transport input before the line will accept incoming connections.

Lab #1: Basic Terminal Server Configuration

Equipment Needed

The following equipment is needed to perform this lab exercise:

- Two Cisco routers, one of which is a Cisco 2511 Terminal Server
- A PC running a terminal emulation program
- One Cisco rolled cable

Connecting the Terminal Server

Connect R1's console port to the Async port 1 of the terminal server using a standard Cisco roll cable.

Basic Terminal Server Configuration

The terminal server is simple to set up and requires minimal configuration. In the following sample configuration, notice that the only commands used are **transport input all** and **no exec**. A loopback interface

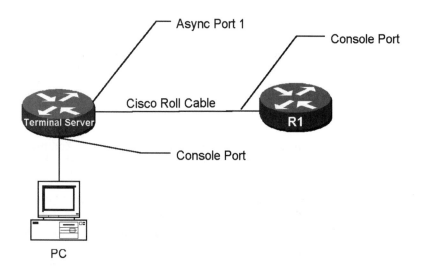

Figure 2–3
Lab #1 basic terminal server configuration

Async Port 1

Console Port

Cisco Roll Cable

Terminal Server

R1

Console Port

PC

is used because it provides a reliable interface for reverse telneting and is always up. Any active interface, however, can be used.

The command **transport input all** specifies that all protocols can be used to connect to a specific line of the router. On IOS 11.1 and later versions, the transport input is set to none—whereas prior to 11.1, the default was all. If the transport input is left to none, you will receive an error stating that the connection is refused by the remote host:

```
terminal_server# telnet 1.1.1.1 2001 ←(Reverse Telnet)
Trying 1.1.1.1, 2001 ...
% Connection refused by remote host
```

The command **no exec** allows only outgoing connections for the line. This feature prevents the terminal server from spawning an EXEC process when data is received on the port. If the port receives unsolicited data, an EXEC process starts—which makes the line unavailable. This process can be monitored by using the command **debug modem**, then showing the line that is attached to the device:

```
TTY1: EXEC creation←(Output from debug)
```

As soon as the EXEC process is created, the line becomes unavailable, as indicated by the star to the left of the line number. You will not be able to reverse telnet to the connected device.

```
terminal_server#  show line 1
  Tty Ty
    Tx/Rx    A Modem  Roty AccO AccI  Uses   Noise   Overruns
*  1 TTY   9600/9600 - -    -   - -    12    1127    871/2644
↑(Indicates the line is active)
```

Terminal Server Configuration

```
terminal_server#
Current configuration:
!
version 11.2
service timestamps log uptime
no service udp-small-servers
no service tcp-small-servers
!
hostname terminal_server
!
interface Loopback0
 ip address 1.1.1.1 255.255.255.255
!
interface Ethernet0
 ip address 2.2.2.2 255.255.255.0
!
```

```
interface Serial0
  no ip address
!
no ip classless
!
line con 0
line 1 16
 no exec←Disables EXEC processing
 transport input all←   Allows all protocols to be used to connect to line 1
                        through 16 of the router
line aux 0
line vty 0 4
 login
!
end
```

Connecting to a Port

To connect to a device attached to a terminal server, simply telnet to any active IP address on the box followed by 20xx, where xx is the port number to which you are connecting. The following example shows how you would reverse telnet to port 1 of the terminal server:

```
Telnet 1.1.1.1  2001←(01 is the port number)
         ↑(IP Address of the Loopback interface)
```

Configuring a Host Table

The Cisco IOS software maintains a table of host names and their corresponding addresses. You can statically map host names to IP address, much like you would for a DNS server. This feature is useful and saves a lot of keystrokes when you have multiple devices connected to the terminal server.

The following global configuration command defines router1 as connecting to port 1:

```
               (Port Number)
                    ↓
IP host router1 2001 1.1.1.1
         ↑              ↑
    (Host Name)    (IP Address Loopback 0)
```

After a host table entry has been added you can access a Router by typing its Host Name at the Router prompt.

Absolute Versus Relative Line Numbers

When configuring a line, you can specify an absolute line number or a relative line number. For example, on the terminal server used in Lab 1, absolute line 17 is Aux port 0. For the 16 asynchronous ports on the terminal server, the absolute and relative line numbers are the same:

```
terminal_server#show users all
                                Line         User      Host(s)   Idle Location
(Indicates an active session)→*  0 con 0               Idle      00:00:00
                                 1 tty 1                          00:00:00
                                 2 tty 2                          00:00:00
                                 3 tty 3                          00:00:00
                                 4 tty 4                          00:00:00
                                 5 tty 5                          00:00:00
                                 6 tty 6                          00:00:00
                                 7 tty 7                          00:00:00
                                 8 tty 8                          00:00:00
                                 9 tty 9                          00:00:00
                                10 tty 10                         00:00:00
                                11 tty 11                         00:00:00
                                12 tty 12                         00:00:00
                                13 tty 13                         00:00:00
                                14 tty 14                         00:00:00
                                15 tty 15                         00:00:00
                                16 tty 16                         00:00:00
        (Absolute Line Number)→ 17 aux 0  ←(Relative number) 00:00:00
                                18 vty 0                         00:00:00
```

Exiting a Reverse Telnet Session

Once you have configured your terminal server and have made a reverse telnet connection to the attached device, how do you get back to the terminal server? You type the escape character followed by x, which by default is **Ctrl-Shift-6** (written as Ctrl^), followed by x.

The escape character can be changed to any ASCII value with the **escape-character** command. For a list of possible values, see the ASCII Translation Table in Appendix A. Each line on the terminal server can have a different escape character. For example, you can specify that when you telnet to the router, the escape character is Ctrl-W—and when you are connected to the console port, the escape character is the default (Ctrl-Shift-6).

The following configuration sets the escape character on VTY 0 to Ctrl-W and the escape character on the console port to the default (Ctrl-Shift-6):

```
terminal_server#show run

Current configuration:
!
version 11.2

no service udp-small-servers
no service tcp-small-servers
!
hostname terminal_server
!
enable password cisco
!
!
interface Loopback0
 ip address 1.1.1.1 255.255.255.255
!
interface Ethernet0
 ip address 2.2.2.2 255.255.255.0
!
interface Serial0
 no ip address
!
no ip classless
!
line con 0
← default commands are not shown by the router
line 1 16
 no exec
 transport input all
 line aux 0
line vty 0
 password cisco
 login
 escape-character 23←(Escape Character Ctrl-W)
line vty 1 4
 no login
!
end
```

Figure 2–4 is a good example of when it would be necessary to use multiple escape characters on a router. User Mahar connects to the console port of RouterA and wishes to telnet to RouterB, then he wishes to reverse telnet to RouterC, which is connected to asynchronous port 1 of RouterB. The problem arises when Mahar wishes to break out of the reverse telnet. If he enters the default escape character Ctrl^x, he will be returned to RouterA—not RouterB. This result occurs because RouterA responds to the same default break character. The solution is to configure the escape character on the VTY interface on RouterB to something different.

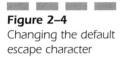

Figure 2–4
Changing the default
escape character

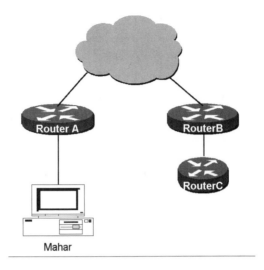

Mahar

Troubleshooting

Displaying Active Sessions

The escape sequence breaks you out of the telnet session; however, that session will still remain open. To display all open connections, use the **show sessions** command. The output from the command is shown as follows:

```
terminal_server#show sessions
Conn      Host            Address      Byte   Idle  Conn Name
*   1     routera         1.1.1.1      0      0     routera
    2     routerb         1.1.1.1      0      0     routerb
    3     routerc         1.1.1.1      0      0     routerc
```

The asterisk (*) indicates the current terminal session. If you were to hit the return key, you would be connected to RouterA. If you wanted to reestablish the connection to RouterB, you would simply type 2 (which is the connection number).

The following list describes other terms used in the example:

Conn: The connection number used to reference the session. For example, if you wished to reestablish the session to RouterC, you would type **3** at the command line.

Host: The remote host to which the router is connected through a Telnet session

Address: The IP address of the remote host. In our case, because we are reverse telneting, the address is the IP address of our loopback interface.

Byte: The number of unread bytes displayed for the user to receive

Idle: The interval (in minutes) since data was last sent on the line

Conn Name: The assigned name of the connection

Switching Between Sessions

Several concurrent sessions can be open at once. To switch between sessions by escaping one session and resuming a previously opened session, perform the following actions:

Step 1: Escape from the current session by pressing the escape sequence.

Step 2: Issue the **show sessions** command. All open sessions associated with the current terminal line are displayed.

Step 3: Enter the session number to make the connection. The following example resumes connection 2:

```
terminal_server# 2
[Resuming connection 2 to routerb ... ]
```

Disconnecting a Session

To disconnect an active reverse telnet session, use the **disconnect** command. To disconnect a session, perform the following steps:

Step 1: Issue the **show sessions** command. All open sessions associated with the current terminal line are displayed.

Step 2: Issue the command **disconnect x**, where x is the session number that you wish to terminate.

The following example disconnects session 2:

```
terminal_server# disconnect 2
Closing connection to routerb [confirm]
```

Clearing a Line

At times, it may become necessary to return a terminal line to idle state. To accomplish this task, use the command **Clear line**. The following example will clear line 1:

```
terminal_server# clear line 1
[confirm]
  [OK]
```

The following example is the output from the **debug modem** command after the **clear line** command was issued. Notice that the carrier is dropped and the line is now idle. The **debug modem** command shows the modem line activity on an access server.

```
                                      terminal_server#
(TTY1 is Line 1)→TTY1: Carrier Drop
                                      TTY1: Line reset by "TTY Daemon"
                                      TTY1: Modem: READY->READY
```

Displaying the Status of a Line

To show the status of any line, use the **show line x** command, where x is the number of the line that you wish to view. This command is useful in troubleshooting a terminal server connection.

The following sample output from the **show line** command shows that line 1 is an asynchronous terminal port with a transmit and receive rate of 9600 bps. Also shown is the modem state, terminal screen width and length, capabilities, status and much more. All significant lines are described in detail as follows:

```
terminal_server#show line 1

   Tty  Typ   Tx/Rx     A Modem Roty AccO  AccI  Uses  Noise  Overruns
 * 1    TTY   9600/9600  -  -     -    -     -     13    15     0/0
Line 1, Location: "", Type: ""
Length: 24 lines, Width: 80 columns
Baud rate (TX/RX) is 9600/9600, no parity, 2 stopbits, 8 databits
Status: Ready, Connected, Active
Capabilities: EXEC Suppressed
Modem state: Ready
Special Chars: Escape  Hold  Stop  Start Disconnect  Activation
               BREAK   none  -     -     none
Timeouts:  Idle EXEC      Idle Session   Modem Answer  Session Dispatch
           00:10:00       never                 none   not set
  Idle Session Disconnect Warning
   never
```

```
Modem type is unknown.
Session limit is not set.
Time since activation: 00:00:09
Editing is enabled.
History is enabled, history size is 10.
DNS resolution in show commands is enabled
Full user help is disabled
Allowed transports are pad v120 telnet rlogin. Preferred is telnet.
No output characters are padded
No special data dispatching characters
Modem hardware state: CTS* DSR*  DTR RTS
```

Table 2–1 shows several different fields and their descriptions.

Table 2–1

Several field names and their descriptions

Field	Description
Tty	Line number. In this case, the line number is 1.
Typ	Type of line. In this case, the type of line is a TTY-asynchronous terminal port which is active, noted by the asterisk.
Tx/Rx	The transmit rate/receive rate of the line, which is set to 9600/9600
A	Indicates whether autobaud has been configured for the line. The hyphen indicates that this option has not been configured.
Modem	Type of modem signals configured for the line. In this case, there are none.
Roty	The rotary group configured for the line. In our case, this value is none.
AccO, AccI	The number of the Output or Input access list configured on the line. In this case, there is none.
Uses	Number of connections established to or from the line since the system was restarted
Noise	Number of times noise has been detected on the line since the system restarted
Overruns	The number of overruns or overflows that have occurred on the specified line since the system was restarted
Status	The state of the line. In our case, the line is connected and is active.
Capabilities	Indicates current terminal capabilities. In this case, we are suppressing EXEC processing.
Time since activation	Time that the session has been active. Our session has been active for nine seconds.
Transport methods	The current set transport method. Our transport is set to all.

 **Conclusion**

Terminal servers permit asynchronous devices to be accessed and managed out of band.

In the past, in order to manage a group of remote devices, multiple modems and call directors were needed. Through the use of terminal servers, multiple devices can be accessed via one dialup or IP connection—which greatly reduces the complexity and cost associated with asynchronous management.

3

ISDN

Topics Covered in This Chapter

- ISDN technology overview
- ISDN configuration and switch basics
- Backup interfaces
- Floating static routes
- Dialer profiles
- ISDN PRI configuration
- Snapshot routing
- ISDN troubleshooting

■■ ■■ Introduction

ISDN is the most popular technology in use today for high-speed switched access and dial backup applications. This chapter will examine ISDN technology and will present seven hands-on ISDN labs using Cisco routers.

■■ ■■ ISDN Technology Overview

ISDN is a circuit-switched, digital data service. ISDN was originally envisioned as a way to offer enhanced voice and data services. In recent years, ISDN has been primarily used in three roles:

1. High-speed Internet access for home users—A standard ISDN BRI circuit can achieve a speed of 128K bits/second. Figure 3–1 shows three different users dialed into an ISDN network and connected to the Internet through an access server. The first user is dialed in via a V.90 analog modem. The ability to place a call from an analog phone circuit to a digital ISDN circuit is an attractive advantage of ISDN. The second user is dialed into the access server with an ISDN BRI circuit at a speed of 64K. The third user is dialed into the access server at a speed of 128K. This user is connected to two 64K channels, and his ISDN device is able to combine the two 64K circuits into a single 128K circuit (referred to as a multilink bundle).

2. Terminating circuits for large-scale dial access servers—An ISDN PRI circuit is the standard method used for terminating many dial users onto an access server. In Figure 3–1, we see an ISDN PRI circuit connecting the public network to the access server. An ISDN PRI circuit is a high-speed ISDN circuit which can accommodate up to 23 simultaneous users. Having an ISDN PRI circuit connected to the access server is more flexible and cost-effective than having 23 individual phone lines coming into the access server.

3. Dial backup—Both ISDN BRI and ISDN PRI circuits are used to provide a backup data path between routers. In Figure 3–2, we see four users connected to a Frame Relay cloud. Three of the users have Cisco 3600 access routers, while one user has a Cisco 7200 core router. Under normal conditions, all four of the routers are

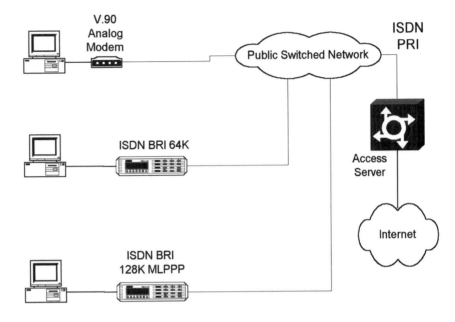

Figure 3–1
ISDN Internet access example

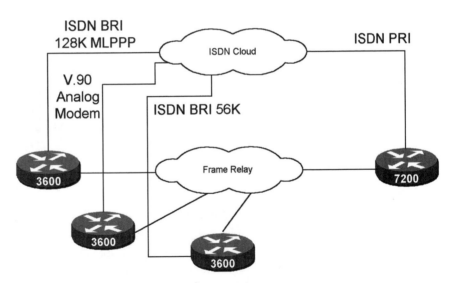

Figure 3–2
ISDN backup example

connected to the Frame Relay network. When any of the Frame Relay circuits fails on a 3600 router, that router will make an ISDN call into the 7200 router. This scenario is frequently referred to as a dial-around-the-cloud scenario, which means that all of the routers have a primary circuit that goes through the Frame Relay cloud. The backup path is an ISDN call around the Frame Relay cloud, using PPP or MLPPP.

ISDN Switches

A key component in an ISDN circuit is an ISDN switch. User equipment at both ends of a circuit connects to an ISDN switch. The ISDN switch is usually a voice switch with a special line card installed inside. The main job of the ISDN switch is to create an end-to-end data or voice circuit between two endpoints. In the case of Figure 3–3, these endpoints are RouterA and RouterB. In the United States, the most prevalent switches are built by either Lucent Technologies or Nortel. The Lucent switches are the 5ESS models, and the Nortel switches are DMS models. As shown in Figure 3–3, the D channel of the ISDN circuit only exists between the ISDN user device and the ISDN switch. This D channel is responsible for synchronization between the user and the switch as well as call setup and teardown.

The ISDN switch model does not have to be known when using an ISDN BRI circuit. A BRI circuit will use one of three types of local signaling, also referred to as call control, between the ISDN user device and the ISDN switch. This call control defines the data format for the D channel. Three call control types are used in the United States:

Figure 3–3
ISDN switch
overview

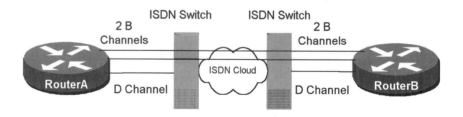

1. National ISDN—A standard call control agreed upon by all ISDN switch manufacturers. National ISDN simplifies ISDN configuration, because you no longer need to know exactly what model of switch to which you are connected. Both the Lucent 5ESS and the Nortel DMS switches support National ISDN call control.

2. Lucent—A custom Lucent call control

3. Nortel—A custom Nortel call control

People are often confused between the physical switch type and the switch signaling. A Lucent 5ESS, for example, can support both Lucent and National ISDN call signaling on the D channel.

ISDN BRI

An ISDN *Basic Rate Interface* (BRI) circuit offers a maximum data rate of 128Kbits/second. As shown in Figure 3–4, an ISDN BRI circuit consists of one or two data channels running at 56K or 64K, called bearer channels. Single B channel BRI service is referred to as 1B+D BRI. Two B channel BRI service is referred to as 2B+D service. Each of the B channels is usually assigned a unique directory number. A directory number, also referred to as a DN, is similar to a phone number. The directory number is used to dial into the BRI channel. Both B channels can also share a single directory number. This type of service is known as a hunt group, because the first incoming call will connect to the first B channel, and the second incoming call will connect to the second B channel. Each B channel can be provisioned for data only, voice only, or both voice and data.

Figure 3–4
ISDN BRI circuit

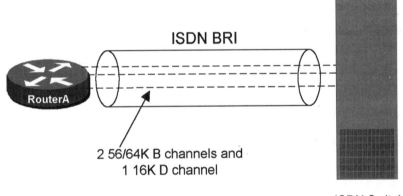

ISDN BRI

RouterA

2 56/64K B channels and
1 16K D channel

ISDN Switch

Each B channel of an ISDN BRI is also assigned a *Service Profile Identifier* (SPID). The SPID is used when the ISDN end user device initially synchronizes to the ISDN switch. The analyzer traces later in this chapter will show how the SPID is sent to the ISDN switch.

As an example, a BRI circuit ordered with 2 B channels and data only capability might be assigned the following parameters:

B Channel #	Directory Number (DN)	SPID	Capability
1	9148313510	91483135100101	Data
2	9148313511	91483135110101	Data

An ISDN BRI circuit also includes a 16K signaling channel called the D channel. The D channel is responsible for synchronization between the user and the ISDN switch, as well as for call setup and teardown. The D channel of an ISDN BRI circuit can also be used to transmit X.25 packet traffic in some applications. This type of BRI service is often referred to as 0B+D BRI.

An ISDN BRI circuit in the United States is usually delivered on a single twisted-pair wire. This circuit is referred to as a U interface ISDN circuit. In Europe and other countries, an ISDN circuit is delivered on two twisted-pair wires and is referred to as an ST interface ISDN circuit. Many of the Cisco routers with built-in ISDN interfaces have an ST interface. In order to convert the U interface circuit from the carrier to an ST interface circuit that the router can handle, an external *Network Terminating Unit* (NT1) is needed. This equipment is depicted in Figure 3–5. An ISDN circuit is usually delivered by the telco on an 8-pin RJ-45 jack.

Figure 3–5

ISDN BRI U and ST interfaces

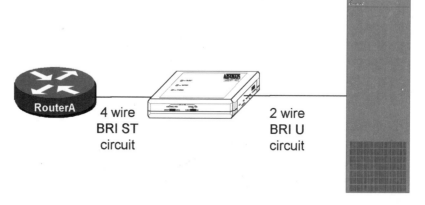

ISDN PRI

An ISDN *Primary Rate Interface* (PRI) is delivered on a T1 circuit. As shown in Figure 3–6, a PRI consists of 23 data channels (bearer channels) running at 56K or 64K each. Each B channel can be provisioned for data only, voice only, or both voice and data. A PRI also contains a single 64K signaling channel called the D channel. The D channel is responsible for synchronization between the user and the ISDN switch, as well as for call setup and teardown.

Figure 3–6
ISDN PRI

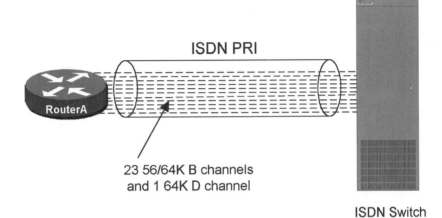

ISDN PRI

23 56/64K B channels
and 1 64K D channel

ISDN Switch

Unlike a BRI, each of the B channels on a PRI usually share the same directory number, which means that all calls coming into the PRI will be placed onto the first available B channel.

An ISDN PRI circuit does not have a SPID associated with it.

ISDN Bearer Capability

Each B (bearer) channel of an ISDN BRI or an ISDN PRI can be used in one of two modes: voice or data. If the B channel is configured to only carry data traffic, then the channel is referred to as having *Circuit Switched Data* (CSD) capability. If the B channel is configured to only carry voice traffic, then the channel is referred to as having *Circuit Switched Voice* (CSV) capability. A B channel that is configured to carry both voice and data traffic is referred to as having CSV and CSD capabilities.

ISDN Protocol Stack

As shown in Figure 3–7, ISDN provides a physical transport for upper-layer protocols. On an ISDN data circuit, you will have a layer 2 datalink encapsulation such as PPP, MLPPP, HDLC, or Frame Relay. Encapsulated in the layer 2 datalink frame will be a layer 3 Network layer protocol such as IP, IPX, or Appletalk.

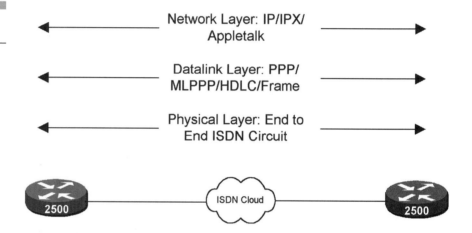

Figure 3–7
ISDN Transport

As shown in Figure 3–8, ISDN is defined as a three-layer protocol stack.

Layer 1
Layer 1 of the ISDN stack is responsible for the physical transmission of the data on the ISDN circuit.

An ISDN BRI U interface circuit is carried over a single twisted pair utilizing 2B1Q data encoding. Data is first framed in a 240-bit frame consisting of 216 data bits and 24 bits of overhead. Eight of these 240 bit frames are then combined into a 1,920 bit superframe.

An ISDN PRI circuit is carried on a T1 circuit, using the same layer 1 *Extended Super Frame* (ESF) framing and *Bipolar Eight Zero Substitution* (B8ZS) line coding as a standard, non-ISDN T1.

Layer 2
All traffic that flows on the D channel of a BRI or a PRI is encapsulated in an LAPD frame. The LAPD frame, shown in Figure 3–9, is similar in structure to an HDLC frame. The LAPD signaling is formally specified in

Figure 3–8
ISDN protocol stack

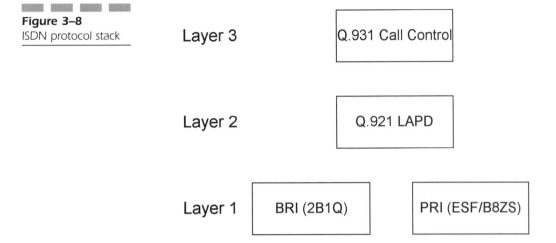

Layer 3 — Q.931 Call Control

Layer 2 — Q.921 LAPD

Layer 1 — BRI (2B1Q) | PRI (ESF/B8ZS)

the Q.921 specification. These LAPD frames can contain the following information:

- Call setup information
- Link establishment, status, and maintenance information
- X.25 packet data

As shown in Figure 3–9, a LAPD frame contains the following fields:

Figure 3–9
ISDN LAPD frame

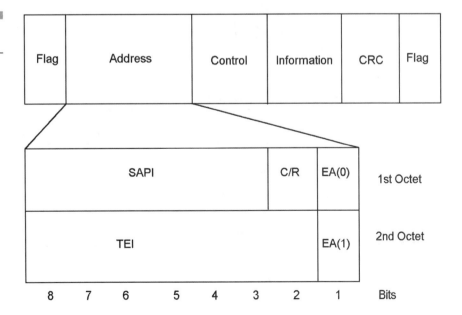

■ Flag—Every LAPD frame starts and stops with an 8-bit flag character, which is a 7E.

■ Address—This 2-byte field is used to identify whether the frame is carrying call control, management overhead, or X.25 traffic. This field also indicates whether the frame is a command frame or a response to a command.

■ Control—The control field is used to indicate whether the LAPD frame is an information frame, a supervisory frame, or an unnumbered frame.

■ Information—This field can carry up to 260 bytes of call control or address messages.

Layer 2 Link Layer Establishment

When an ISDN device is first connected to the network, a synchronization process is initiated by the user equipment to synchronize to the network. As seen in Figure 3–10, six packets are exchanged between the router and the ISDN switch to establish the link as active and to send an acceptable SPID (in the case of a BRI) to the switch. A trace of each of these packets will be discussed.

Figure 3–10
ISDN layer 2
establishment

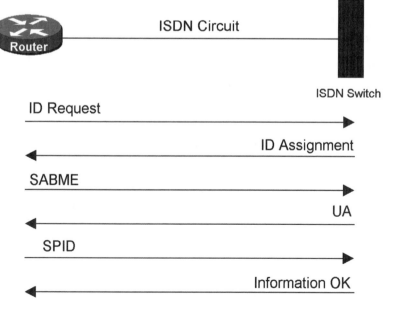

ID Request

The router sends an ID request to the switch.

```
Port A DTE ID=72, 03/02/99, 09:37:53.655500
Length=10, Good FCS
LAPD - LINK ACCESS PROCEDURE D CHANNEL
MOD 128:
Addr                                                         64767
SAPI                                       Layer 2 Management 63
Cmd/Resp                                                         0
Ext Bit                                       More Addr Octet 0
TEI                                                            127
Ext Bit                                      Final Addr Octet 1
Ctrl                                                       UI 03h
P                                                               0
TEI Management Entity ID                                       15
Reference number                                            B34Fh
Message Type                                      ID REQUEST 01h
Action Indicator                                             7Fh
Ext Bit                                                         1
FCS                                               Good EE0Dh
```

ID Assigned

The switch responds with an ID-assigned message.

```
Port A DCE ID=84, 03/02/99, 09:38:12.393575
Length=10, Good FCS
LAPD - LINK ACCESS PROCEDURE D CHANNEL
MOD 128:
Addr                                                         65279
SAPI                                       Layer 2 Management 63
Cmd/Resp                                                         1
Ext Bit                                       More Addr Octet 0
TEI                                                            127
Ext Bit                                      Final Addr Octet 1
Ctrl                                                       UI 03h
P                                                               0
TEI Management Entity ID                                       15
Reference number                                            A237h
Message Type                                     ID ASSIGNED 02h
Action Indicator                                            40h
Ext Bit                                                         1
FCS                                              Good 102Fh
```

SABME

The router responds to the switch with a SABME message.

```
Port A DTE ID=85, 03/02/99, 09:38:12.400850
Length=5, Good FCS
LAPD - LINK ACCESS PROCEDURE D CHANNEL
MOD 128:
Addr                                                             129
SAPI                                    Call Control Procedures 0
Cmd/Resp                                                           0
Ext Bit                                          More Addr Octet 0
TEI                                     Auto Assign User Eqip 64
Ext Bit                                         Final Addr Octet 1
Ctrl                                                    SABME 7Fh
P                                                                  1
FCS                                                   Good A8D8h
```

UA

The switch responds with a UA message.

```
Port A DCE ID=86, 03/02/99, 09:38:12.429075
Length=5, Good FCS
LAPD - LINK ACCESS PROCEDURE D CHANNEL
MOD 128:
Addr                                                             129
SAPI                                    Call Control Procedures 0
Cmd/Resp                                                           0
Ext Bit                                          More Addr Octet 0
TEI                                     Auto Assign User Eqip 64
Ext Bit                                         Final Addr Octet 1
Ctrl                                                       UA 73h
F                                                                  1
FCS                                                   Good C412h
```

SPID

The router can now send its SPID to the ISDN switch. This SPID must match exactly with the SPID that is entered into the database of the switch.

```
Port A DTE ID=87, 03/02/99, 09:38:12.447850
Length=22, Good FCS
LAPD - LINK ACCESS PROCEDURE D CHANNEL
MOD 128:
Addr                                                            129
SAPI                                 Call Control Procedures 0
Cmd/Resp                                                         0
Ext Bit                                       More Addr Octet 0
TEI                                  Auto Assign User Eqip 64
Ext Bit                                      Final Addr Octet 1
Ctrl                                                    I 0000h
NS                                                              0
NR                                                              0
P                                                               0
National ISDN
Protocol Discriminator                        Call Control 08h
Reference Flag                       Msg from Origination 0
Call Reference Value [len=0]                                    0
Message Type                                     INFORMATION 7Bh
INFO ELEMENT Service Profile ID [Code=58] [Len=11]
INFO ELEMENT Service Profile ID                       89953010101
                                                             ↑
                      The SPID is sent to the ISDN switch

FCS                                                   Good CAF5h
```

Information

The switch responds with an information frame to the router after the SPID has been successfully received.

```
Port A DCE ID=89, 03/02/99, 09:38:12.506075
Length=13, Good FCS
LAPD - LINK ACCESS PROCEDURE D CHANNEL
MOD 128:
Addr                                                            641
SAPI                                 Call Control Procedures 0
Cmd/Resp                                                         1
Ext Bit                                       More Addr Octet 0
TEI                                  Auto Assign User Eqip 64
Ext Bit                                      Final Addr Octet 1
Ctrl                                                    I 0002h
NS                                                              0
NR                                                              1
P                                                               0
National ISDN
Protocol Discriminator                        Call Control 08h
Reference Flag                       Msg from Origination 0
Call Reference Value [len=0]                                    0
```

```
Message Type                                        INFORMATION 7Bh
INFO ELEMENT End Point ID [Code=59] [Len=2]
EXT                                                               1
User service identifier                                          37
EXT                                                               1
Interpreter                                                       0
Interpreter terminal identifier                                   1
FCS                                                    Good 22D0h
```

Layer 2 Link Layer Status Checks

One function of ISDN Layer 2 link control is to ensure that the D channel is active. Every 10 seconds, the ISDN switch will send a *Receiver Ready* (RR) packet to the router and will expect an immediate reply. The following two packets show what this RR exchange looks like.

RR sent from the ISDN switch to the router
The ISDN switch sends an RR frame to the router.

```
Port A DCE ID=4, 03/01/99, 10:41:29.238050
Length=6, Good FCS
LAPD - LINK ACCESS PROCEDURE D CHANNEL
MOD 128:
Addr                                                            641
SAPI                                      Call Control Procedures 0
Cmd/Resp                                                          1
Ext Bit                                           More Addr Octet 0
TEI                                         Auto Assign User Eqip 64
Ext Bit                                          Final Addr Octet 1
Ctrl                                                     RR 0103h
NR                                                               1
PF                                                               1
FCS                                                    Good DBB8h
```

RR reply sent from the router to the ISDN switch
The router immediately responds with an RR frame to the ISDN switch.

```
Port A DTE ID=5, 03/01/99, 10:41:29.246300
Length=6, Good FCS
LAPD - LINK ACCESS PROCEDURE D CHANNEL
MOD 128:
Addr                                                            641
SAPI                                      Call Control Procedures 0
Cmd/Resp                                                          1
```

Ext Bit	More Addr Octet 0
TEI	Auto Assign User Eqip 64
Ext Bit	Final Addr Octet 1
Ctrl	**RR** 0103h
NR	1
PF	1
FCS	Good DBB8h

ISDN Layer 3 Signaling

The ISDN layer 3 protocols are used for establishing, maintaining, and disconnecting calls between the user equipment and the network. Various control messages are passed between the user and the network for these purposes. Figure 3–11 shows how a call is placed. As seen in Figure 3–11, some of the signaling is local (between the router and the ISDN switch on either side of the circuit), while other signaling flows end-to-end between both routers.

The following traces show a call setup and disconnect sequence between RouterA and RouterB. Refer to Figure 3–11 for a frame-by-frame explanation.

Setup message from Router to Switch

RouterA sends a setup message to RouterB. This message specifies several key parameters:

- An unrestricted digital channel is requested.
- A 64Kbits/second call is requested.
- The calling number of the router placing the call is 8995301.
- The number of the router being called is 8993601.

```
Port A DTE ID=22, 03/02/99, 16:38:08.917600
Length=37, Good FCS
LAPD - LINK ACCESS PROCEDURE D CHANNEL
MOD 128:
```

Addr	129
SAPI	Call Control Procedures 0
Cmd/Resp	0
Ext Bit	More Addr Octet 0
TEI	Auto Assign User Eqip 64
Ext Bit	Final Addr Octet 1
Ctrl	I 1216h
NS	9
NR	11
P	0

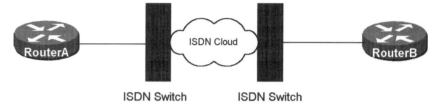

Figure 3–11
ISDN layer 3 call control

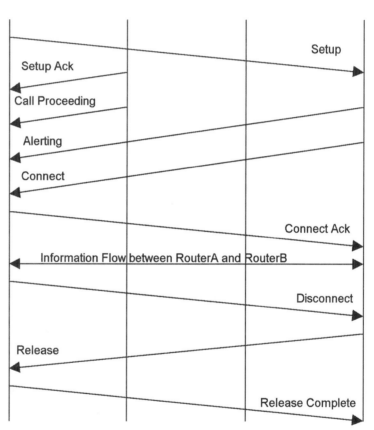

```
National ISDN
Protocol Discriminator                                        Call Control 08h
Reference Flag                                         Msg from Origination 0
Call Reference Value [len=1]                                                 1
Message Type                                                        SETUP 05h
INFO ELEMENT Bearer Capability [Code=4] [Len=2]
Coding Std                                                             CCITT 0
Transfer Capab                                         Unrestricted Digital 8
EXT                                                                          1
Transfer Mode                                                       Circuit 0
Transfer Rate (D Channel)                                           64 kb/s 16
```

```
EXT                                                                    1
INFO ELEMENT Channel ID [Code=24] [Len=1]
EXT                                                                    1
Interface ID Present                                        Implicit 0
Interface Type                                            Basic Rate 0
Pref/Excl                                             Preferred Chan 0
D-channel Ind                                                     No 0
Info Channel Select                                    Any channel 3
INFO ELEMENT Keypad [Code=44] [Len=8]
Info (IA5 Char)                                              98993601
INFO ELEMENT Calling Number [Code=108] [Len=8]
Type                                                Subscriber (Local) 4
Plan                                                ISDN - E.164/E.163 1
EXT                                                                    1
Num Digits (IA5 Char)                                          8995301
FCS                                                         Good 9BCDh
```

Setup Acknowledgment

A setup acknowledgment is sent from the local ISDN switch to RouterA.

```
Port A DCE ID=24, 03/02/99, 16:38:08.986850
Length=13, Good FCS
LAPD - LINK ACCESS PROCEDURE D CHANNEL
MOD 128:
Addr                                                                 641
SAPI                                          Call Control Procedures 0
Cmd/Resp                                                               1
Ext Bit                                              More Addr Octet 0
TEI                                           Auto Assign User Eqip 64
Ext Bit                                             Final Addr Octet 1
Ctrl                                                          I 1614h
NS                                                                   11
NR                                                                   10
P                                                                     0
National ISDN
Protocol Discriminator                              Call Control 08h
Reference Flag                                  Msg to Origination 1
Call Reference Value [len=1]                                          1
Message Type                                             SETUP ACK 0Dh
INFO ELEMENT Channel ID [Code=24] [Len=1]
EXT                                                                   1
Interface ID Present                                       Implicit 0
Interface Type                                           Basic Rate 0
Pref/Excl                                             Exclusive Chan 1
D-channel Ind                                                    No 0
Info Channel Select                                             B1 1
FCS                                                        Good 15AFh
```

Call proceeding

A call proceeding is sent from the local ISDN switch to RouterA.

```
Port A DCE ID=26, 03/02/99, 16:38:11.006325
Length=10, Good FCS
LAPD - LINK ACCESS PROCEDURE D CHANNEL
MOD 128:
Addr                                                          641
SAPI                                     Call Control Procedures 0
Cmd/Resp                                                        1
Ext Bit                                           More Addr Octet 0
TEI                                       Auto Assign User Eqip 64
Ext Bit                                          Final Addr Octet 1
Ctrl                                                     I 1814h
NS                                                             12
NR                                                             10
P                                                               0
National ISDN
Protocol Discriminator                          Call Control 08h
Reference Flag                              Msg to Origination 1
Call Reference Value [len=1]                                    1
Message Type                                CALL PROCEEDING 02h
FCS                                                  Good 6E62h
```

Alerting

An alerting message is sent from RouterB to RouterA.

```
Port A DCE ID=28, 03/02/99, 16:38:11.231825
Length=13, Good FCS
LAPD - LINK ACCESS PROCEDURE D CHANNEL
MOD 128:
Addr                                                          641
SAPI                                     Call Control Procedures 0
Cmd/Resp                                                        1
Ext Bit                                           More Addr Octet 0
TEI                                       Auto Assign User Eqip 64
Ext Bit                                          Final Addr Octet 1
Ctrl                                                     I 1A14h
NS                                                             13
NR                                                             10
P                                                               0
National ISDN
Protocol Discriminator                          Call Control 08h
Reference Flag                              Msg to Origination 1
Call Reference Value [len=1]                                    1
Message Type                                       ALERTING 01h
INFO ELEMENT Signal [Code=52] [Len=1]
INFO ELEMENT Signal                          Ring Back Tone On 01h
FCS                                                  Good D6D6h
```

Connect

A connect message is sent from RouterB to RouterA.

```
Port A DCE ID=30, 03/02/99, 16:38:11.276950
Length=13, Good FCS
LAPD - LINK ACCESS PROCEDURE D CHANNEL
MOD 128:
Addr                                                          641
SAPI                               Call Control Procedures 0
Cmd/Resp                                                       1
Ext Bit                                   More Addr Octet 0
TEI                             Auto Assign User Eqip 64
Ext Bit                                  Final Addr Octet 1
Ctrl                                                 I 1C14h
NS                                                            14
NR                                                            10
P                                                              0
National ISDN
Protocol Discriminator                  Call Control 08h
Reference Flag                    Msg to Origination 1
Call Reference Value [len=1]                                   1
Message Type                              CONNECT 07h
INFO ELEMENT Signal [Code=52] [Len=1]
INFO ELEMENT Signal                            Tones Off 3Fh
FCS                                            Good AEE1h
```

Connect Acknowledge

A connect acknowledge message is sent from RouterA to RouterB.

```
Port A DTE ID=32, 03/02/99, 16:38:11.306700
Length=10, Good FCS
LAPD - LINK ACCESS PROCEDURE D CHANNEL
MOD 128:
Addr                                                          129
SAPI                               Call Control Procedures 0
Cmd/Resp                                                       0
Ext Bit                                   More Addr Octet 0
TEI                             Auto Assign User Eqip 64
Ext Bit                                  Final Addr Octet 1
Ctrl                                                 I 141Eh
NS                                                            10
NR                                                            15
P                                                              0
National ISDN
Protocol Discriminator                  Call Control 08h
Reference Flag                  Msg from Origination 0
Call Reference Value [len=1]                                   1
Message Type                          CONNECT ACK 0Fh
FCS                                            Good 7443h
```

Once the ISDN call has been established, traffic can flow between RouterA and RouterB. The call has established a 64Kbit/sec data pipe between the two routers. The call can be terminated by either router. Call termination is initiated by one of the routers sending a disconnect message. The following disconnect sequence shows an example where RouterA initiates the disconnect sequence:

Disconnect
RouterA sends a disconnect message to RouterB.

```
Port A DTE ID=112, 03/02/99, 16:42:11.593225
Length=14, Good FCS
LAPD - LINK ACCESS PROCEDURE D CHANNEL
MOD 128:
Addr                                                              129
SAPI                                  Call Control Procedures 0
Cmd/Resp                                                           0
Ext Bit                                          More Addr Octet 0
TEI                                    Auto Assign User Eqip 64
Ext Bit                                          Final Addr Octet 1
Ctrl                                                     I 161Eh
NS                                                               11
NR                                                               15
P                                                                 0
National ISDN
Protocol Discriminator                          Call Control 08h
Reference Flag                          Msg from Origination 0
Call Reference Value [len=1]                                      1
Message Type                                        DISCONNECT 45h
INFO ELEMENT Cause [Code=8] [Len=2]
Coding Std                                                 CCITT 0
Location                                                   User 0
EXT                                                               1
Class                                           Normal Event 1
Value                                   Normal Call Clearing 16
EXT                                                               1
FCS                                                  Good 84A0h
```

Release
RouterB sends a release message to RouterA.

```
Port A DCE ID=114, 03/02/99, 16:42:11.667225
Length=10, Good FCS
LAPD - LINK ACCESS PROCEDURE D CHANNEL
MOD 128:
Addr                                                              641
SAPI                                  Call Control Procedures 0
Cmd/Resp                                                           1
Ext Bit                                          More Addr Octet 0
```

```
TEI                                      Auto Assign User Eqip 64
Ext Bit                                        Final Addr Octet 1
Ctrl                                                   I 1E18h
NS                                                           15
NR                                                           12
P                                                             0
National ISDN
Protocol Discriminator                          Call Control 08h
Reference Flag                             Msg to Origination 1
Call Reference Value [len=1]                                  1
Message Type                                      RELEASE 4Dh
FCS                                                Good 57B7h
```

Release complete

RouterA sends a release complete message to RouterB.

```
Port A DTE ID=116, 03/02/99, 16:42:11.701225
Length=10, Good FCS
LAPD - LINK ACCESS PROCEDURE D CHANNEL
MOD 128:
Addr                                                        129
SAPI                               Call Control Procedures 0
Cmd/Resp                                                     0
Ext Bit                                     More Addr Octet 0
TEI                                      Auto Assign User Eqip 64
Ext Bit                                        Final Addr Octet 1
Ctrl                                                   I 1820h
NS                                                           12
NR                                                           16
P                                                             0
National ISDN
Protocol Discriminator                          Call Control 08h
Reference Flag                           Msg from Origination 0
Call Reference Value [len=1]                                  1
Message Type                             RELEASE COMPLETE 5Ah
FCS                                                Good C1C2h
```

ISDN Configuration

When configuring ISDN on your network, you will need some basic information about the ISDN circuit which must be supplied by the carrier. For an ISDN BRI, you will need to know the following information:

- The *Directory Number* (DN) of each B channel
- The SPID of each B channel
- The D channel signaling protocol being used

For an ISDN PRI, you will need to know this information:

■ The D channel signaling protocol being used
■ The directory number of the PRI

ISDN with Non-ISDN-Equipped Routers

A router does not need an integrated BRI or PRI interface to take advantage of ISDN services. An external device known as an ISDN terminal adapter enables users to connect to an ISDN service with a router that does not have an ISDN interface. An ISDN terminal adapter has a V.35 interface on the user DTE side and one or more ISDN interfaces on the network side. The ISDN terminal adapter can be programmed to dial the far-end router in a variety of ways. The most popular dial method is usually DTR dialing. With DTR dialing, the ISDN terminal adapter will call a preprogrammed far-end number when the attached router raises the V.35 DTR interface. Figure 3–12 shows an ISDN terminal adapter network diagram.

Figure 3–12
ISDN terminal
adapter

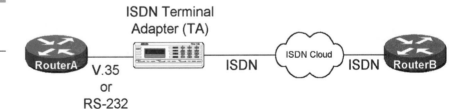

Commands Discussed in This Section

- **backup delay** *enable-delay disable-delay*
- **backup interface** *type number*
- **controller** *t1 number*
- **dialer-group** *group-number*
- **dialer idle-timeout** *seconds*
- **dialer-list** *dialer-group* **list** *access-list-number*
- **dialer-list** *dialer-group* protocol *protocol-name* {**permit** | **deny** | list *access-list-number* | *access-group*}
- **dialer load-threshold** *load* [outbound | inbound | either]
- **dialer map** *protocol next-hop-address* [**name** *hostname*] [**broadcast**] [*dial-string*]
- **dialer pool** *number*
- **dialer pool-member** *number*
- **dialer remote-name** *username*
- **dialer string** *dial-string*
- **debug isdn q921**
- **debug isdn q931**
- **debug ppp authentication**
- **interface bri** *number*
- **interface dialer** *number*
- **isdn spid1** *spid-number [ldn]*
- **isdn spid 2** *spid-number [ldn]*
- **isdn switch-type** *switch-type*
- **ppp multilink**
- **pri-group** [**timeslots** *range*]
- **show dialer**
- **show interfaces bri** *number:bchannel*
- **show isdn service**
- **show isdn status**

- **show ppp multilink**
- **show snapshot**
- **snapshot client** *active-time quiet-time* [**suppress-statechange-updates**] [**dialer**]
- **snapshot server** *active-time* [**dialer**]

Definitions

backup delay: This interface configuration command defines how much time (in seconds) will elapse before activating a backup interface when a primary interface fails. The command also specifies (in seconds) how much time will elapse before dropping the backup interface after the primary interface returns to an active state.

backup interface: This interface configuration command causes the associated interface to be defined as a backup interface. The backup interface will remain in standby mode until activated.

controller t1: This interface command defines a channelized T1 interface which is used to carry an ISDN PRI circuit.

dialer-group: This interface configuration command causes the interface to be associated with a specific dialer list.

dialer idle-timeout: This interface command specifies the idle time before the ISDN line is disconnected. Any interesting traffic will reset this timer.

dialer-list: This global command applies an access list to a specified interface, specifies which type of traffic is interesting, and initiates an ISDN call.

dialer load-threshold: This interface command defines a load threshold which must be met before the router will initiate an additional call to a destination.

dialer map: This interface command configures an ISDN interface to call a far-end device. It associates a next-hop address with an ISDN phone number.

dialer pool: This interface command can only be applied to a dialer interface. The command specifies which dialer pool to use to connect to a specific destination.

dialer pool-member: This interface command configures a physical interface to be a member of a dialer pool.

dialer remote-name: This interface command only applies to a dialer interface. The command specifies the authentication name of a router on a remote network.

dialer string: This interface configuration command specifies a phone number to be used when making an ISDN call. This command is used with dialer profiles.

debug isdn q921: This debug command causes the router to display layer 2 ISDN call control information.

debug isdn q931: This debug command causes the router to display layer 3 ISDN call control information.

debug ppp authentication: This debug command causes the router to display CHAP or PAP authentication negotiation status.

interface bri: This global command defines a BRI interface and enters interface configuration mode.

interface dialer: This global command defines a dialer interface. A dialer interface is used to apply a single interface configuration to one of more physical interfaces.

isdn spid1: This interface configuration command defines the SPID value for BRI channel B1 on a BRI interface.

isdn spid 2: This interface configuration command defines the SPID value for BRI channel B2 on a BRI interface.

isdn switch-type: This global configuration command defines the D channel signaling protocol being used on an ISDN interface.

ppp multilink: This interface configuration command causes the defined interface to try to negotiate a multilink PPP datalink protocol.

pri-group: This controller configuration command defines a channelized T1 interface to be used as an ISDN PRI circuit.

show dialer: This exec command displays diagnostic and status information for dial-on-demand interfaces.

show interfaces bri: This exec command is used to display information on an ISDN BRI D channel and B channels.

show isdn service: This exec command displays information about an ISDN PRI interface on the router.

show isdn status: This exec command displays information about the ISDN circuits defined on the router.

show ppp multilink: This exec command displays information about any multilink bundles that are active on the router.

show snapshot: This exec command displays information about snapshot routing.

snapshot client: This interface command configures a router as a snapshot client.

snapshot server: This interface command configures a router as a snapshot server.

IOS Requirements

The labs in this chapter were run with IOS 11.2. Some features, such as dialer profiles, are only available in IOS 11.2 and higher.

ISDN Switch Configuration

The Adtran Atlas 800 is being used in this chapter as our ISDN switch. The Atlas 800 can be populated with both ISDN BRI and ISDN PRI cards. The advantage of using the Atlas 800 is its ease of use and adherence to ISDN standards. In addition, Atlas' small form factor makes it a portable unit that can be set up on a desktop. The base unit of the Atlas 800 comes with two ISDN PRI circuits, additional BRI cards and PRI cards can be added. The Atlas 800 chassis can hold up to eight additional cards. Each BRI card contains eight ISDN BRI U interface circuits. Each PRI Card contains four ISDN PRI circuits.

The Atlas 800 chassis has a 10baseT Ethernet connection which is used for system management. The Atlas 800 also has a control port which can be used for local terminal access. The Atlas 800 is managed via a simple menu system. The management screens are the same, whether you telnet to the Atlas via the Ethernet port or directly connect to the unit via the rear control port. Additional information on the Atlas 800 can be found on the Adtran World Wide Web page at http://www.Adtran.com.

The Atlas 800 is simple to configure. The following information describes the System Info screen and the key configuration screens for setting up these labs. Key system information such as firmware levels and system uptime can be found on this screen.

```
CCIE LAB STUDY GUIDE/System Info
System Info       System Name          CCIE LAB STUDY GUIDE
System Status   | System Location        Adtran ATLAS 800
System Config   | System Contact         Adtran ATLAS 800
System Utility  | Firmware Revision   ATLAS 800  Rev. H 09/18/98 09:11:41
Modules         | System Uptime         0 days  1 hours  36 min  55 secs
Dedicated Maps  | Startup Mode          Power cycle
Dial Plan       | Current Time/Date (24h)  Saturday March  6  16:55:12  1999
                | Installed Memory   Flash:1048576 bytes   DRAM:8388608 bytes
                | Serial Number          847B8304
                | Boot ROM Rev           C 11/18/97
```

The Modules screen displays all active modules that are installed in the Atlas 800. We see from the following screen print that our system has four occupied slots. Slot 0 is the system controller, which is part of the base chassis. Slot 1 contains a four-port ISDN PRI card. Slot 5 contains an eight-port ISDN BRI card. Slot 8 contains a four-port V.35 card. For these labs, we will only be using the PRI and BRI cards.

```
CCIE LAB STUDY GUIDE/Modules
System Info     | Slt   Type    Menu   Alarm   Test   State   Status    Rev
System Status   | 0   Sys Ctrl  [+]    [OK]    [OFF]  ONLINE  Online     T
System Config   | 1   T1/PRI-4  [+]    [OK]    [OFF]  ONLINE  Online     A
System Utility  | 2   EMPTY                           ONLINE  Empty      -
Modules         | 3   EMPTY                           ONLINE  Empty      -
Dedicated Maps  | 4   EMPTY                           ONLINE  Empty      -
Dial Plan       | 5   UBRI-8    [+]    [OK]    [OFF]  ONLINE  Online     C
                | 6   EMPTY          ONLINE  Empty    -
                | 7   EMPTY                           ONLINE  Empty      -
                | 8   V35Nx-4   [+]    [OK]    [OFF]  ONLINE  Online     M
```

The Dial Plan screen is used to configure *Directory Numbers* (DNs) for each of the BRI circuits. We see from the following screen print that BRI #1 in slot #5 has been assigned 8995101 as its number for channel B1. BRI #2 in slot #5 has been assigned 8995201 as its number for channel B1.

```
CCIE LAB STUDY GUIDE/Dial Plan/User Term
Network Term |   #    Slot/Svc    Port/Link  Sig   In#Accept   Out#Rej   Ifc Config
User Term     |   1    5)UBRI-8    1)BRI 5/1        [8995101]    [+]      [8995101]
Global Param  |   2    5)UBRI-8    2)BRI 5/2        [8995201]    [+]      [8995201]
```

The Interface Configuration screen is used to set the switch type for each circuit. We see from the following screen that National ISDN switch type has been selected for this circuit.

```
CCIE LAB STUDY GUIDE/Dial Plan/User Term[1]/Interface Configuration
Incoming Number Accept List  | Switch Type        National ISDN
Outgoing Number Reject List  | SPID list          [8995101]
Interface Configuration      | Strip MSD          None
                             | Source ID          0
                             | Outgoing Caller ID  Send as provided
```

The SPID list screen is used to configure the SPID and call capability for each B channel. We see from the following screen print that the SPID for channel B1 has been set to 5101, while the SPID for channel B2 has been set to 5102. Each of these two B channels are enabled for 64K, 56K, audio, and speech capabilities.

```
CCIE LAB STUDY GUIDE/Dial Plan/User Term[1]/Interface Configuration/SPID list
SPID list |  #    Phone #          SPID #     Calls   D64     D56     Audio   Speech
          |  1    8995101          5101         2     Enable  Enable  Enable  Enable
          |  2    8995102          5102         2     Enable  Enable  Enable  Enable
```

Lab #2: ISDN Basics and Switch Basics

Equipment Needed

The following equipment is needed to perform this lab exercise:

■ Two Cisco routers, each of which must have a single ISDN BRI interface

- Cisco IOS 11.2 or higher
- Two ISDN BRI circuits
- A PC running a terminal emulation program for console port connection on the routers

Configuration Overview

This configuration will explore basic ISDN commands and functionality. RouterA and RouterB are connected as shown in Figure 3–13.

Figure 3–13
Lab #2

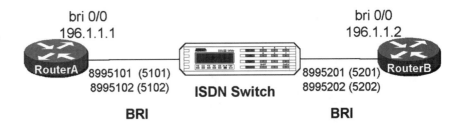

A PC running a terminal emulation program should be connected to the console port of one of the routers using a Cisco rolled cable.

ISDN Switch Setup

If you do not have access to actual ISDN circuits, you can use an ISDN desktop switch. Information on configuring an ISDN desktop switch can be found in the ISDN Switch Configuration section earlier in this chapter.

Router Configuration

The configurations for the two routers in this example are as follows (ISDN commands are highlighted in bold):

RouterA

```
RouterA#show run
Building configuration...

Current configuration:
!
version 11.2
no service udp-small-servers
no service tcp-small-servers
!
hostname RouterA
!
enable password cisco
!
username RouterB password 7 030752180500
isdn switch-type basic-ni1← Set D channel call control
!
interface Serial0/0
 no ip address
!
interface BRI0/0
 ip address 196.1.1.1 255.255.255.0
 encapsulation ppp
 isdn spid1 5101 8995101← Set SPID for both B channels
 isdn spid2 5102 8995102
 dialer idle-timeout 90← Set interesting traffic timeout
 dialer map ip 196.1.1.2 name RouterB broadcast 8995201← Define next hop
                                                         address and dial
                                                         string
 dialer load-threshold 1←  Threshold for adding additional B channels
 dialer-group 1← Associate with dialer-list 1
 no fair-queue
 ppp authentication chap
 ppp multilink← Negotiate MLPPP
!
no ip classless
dialer-list 1 protocol ip permit← Define interesting traffic
!
line con 0
 password cisco
 login
line aux 0
line vty 0 4
 login
!
end
```

RouterB

```
RouterB#show run
Building configuration...

Current configuration:
!
version 11.2
service timestamps debug datetime localtime
no service udp-small-servers
no service tcp-small-servers
!
hostname RouterB
!
enable password cisco
!
username RouterA password 7 030752180500
isdn switch-type basic-ni1← Set D channel call control
!
interface BRI0/0
 ip address 196.1.1.2 255.255.255.0
 encapsulation ppp
 isdn spid1 5201 8995201← Set the SPID for both B channels
 isdn spid2 5202 8995202
 dialer idle-timeout 90← Set interesting traffic timeout
 dialer map ip 196.1.1.1 name RouterA← Define a next hop address
 dialer-group 1← Associate with dialer-list 1
 no fair-queue
 ppp authentication chap
 ppp multilink← Negotiate MLPPP
!
no ip classless
dialer-list 1 protocol ip permit← Define interesting traffic
!
line con 0
line aux 0
line vty 0 4
 password cisco
 login
!
end
```

Monitoring and Testing the Configuration

Let's start by connecting our terminal to RouterA. Type the **show isdn status** command. This command enables you to view the operational status of the BRI circuit that is terminated on the router. The commands output displays layers 1, 2, and 3 ISDN status. We see from the following screen print that layer 1 is active on this circuit, which means that the router senses the 2B1Q line coding of the BRI circuit. Layer 2 status indicates that a TEI has been assigned for both B channels. We also see that the SPIDs for both B channels have been sent to the switch and are valid.

```
RouterA#show isdn status
The current ISDN Switchtype = basic-ni1
ISDN BRI0/0 interface
    Layer 1 Status:
       ACTIVE
    Layer 2 Status:
       TEI = 64, State = MULTIPLE_FRAME_ESTABLISHED
       TEI = 65, State = MULTIPLE_FRAME_ESTABLISHED
    Spid Status:
       TEI 64, ces = 1, state = 8(established)
           spid1 configured, spid1 sent, spid1 valid
           Endpoint ID Info: epsf = 0, usid = 70, tid = 1
       TEI 65, ces = 2, state = 8(established)
           spid2 configured, spid2 sent, spid2 valid
           Endpoint ID Info: epsf = 0, usid = 70, tid = 2
    Layer 3 Status:
       0 Active Layer 3 Call(s)
    Activated dsl 0 CCBs = 0
 Total Allocated ISDN CCBs = 0
```

Type the **show interface bri 0/0** command. We see that the interface is in an up/up (spoofing) state, which means that the D channel is active on the BRI circuit. The D channel is said to be spoofing because it is a local control circuit between the router and the ISDN switch.

```
RouterA#show interface bri 0/0
BRI0/0 is up, line protocol is up (spoofing)
   Hardware is QUICC BRI with U interface
   Internet address is 196.1.1.1/24
   MTU 1500 bytes, BW 64 Kbit, DLY 20000 usec, rely 255/255, load 1/255
   Encapsulation PPP, loopback not set
   Last input 00:00:03, output never, output hang never
   Last clearing of "show interface" counters never
   Queueing strategy: fifo
   Output queue 0/40, 0 drops; input queue 0/75, 0 drops
   5 minute input rate 0 bits/sec, 0 packets/sec
   5 minute output rate 0 bits/sec, 0 packets/sec
      1093 packets input, 4504 bytes, 0 no buffer
      Received 0 broadcasts, 0 runts, 0 giants, 0 throttles
      0 input errors, 0 CRC, 0 frame, 0 overrun, 0 ignored, 0 abort
      1092 packets output, 4558 bytes, 0 underruns
      0 output errors, 0 collisions, 6 interface resets
      0 output buffer failures, 0 output buffers swapped out
      7 carrier transitions
```

On this ISDN BRI circuit, the actual BRI interface is referenced as bri 0/0. As we saw earlier, this value refers to the D channel of the ISDN circuit. The status of each of the two B channels can also be displayed by using the **show interface bri 0/0:1** command and the **show interface bri 0/0:2** command for channels B1 and B2, respectively. We see that both of these interfaces are in the down/down state, because there are no active calls on the BRI circuit at this time.

```
RouterA#show interface bri 0/0:1
BRI0/0:1 is down, line protocol is down
  Hardware is QUICC BRI with U interface
  MTU 1500 bytes, BW 64 Kbit, DLY 20000 usec, rely 255/255, load 1/255
  Encapsulation PPP, loopback not set, keepalive set (10 sec)
  LCP Closed, multilink Closed
  Closed: IPCP, CDP
  Last input 00:00:58, output 00:00:58, output hang never
  Last clearing of "show interface" counters never
  Queueing strategy: fifo
  Output queue 0/40, 0 drops; input queue 0/75, 0 drops
  5 minute input rate 0 bits/sec, 0 packets/sec
  5 minute output rate 0 bits/sec, 0 packets/sec
     1204 packets input, 67666 bytes, 0 no buffer
     Received 0 broadcasts, 0 runts, 0 giants, 0 throttles
     0 input errors, 0 CRC, 0 frame, 0 overrun, 0 ignored, 0 abort
     1212 packets output, 69764 bytes, 0 underruns
     0 output errors, 0 collisions, 0 interface resets
     0 output buffer failures, 0 output buffers swapped out
     7 carrier transitions

RouterA#show interface bri 0/0:2
BRI0/0:2 is down, line protocol is down
  Hardware is QUICC BRI with U interface
  MTU 1500 bytes, BW 64 Kbit, DLY 20000 usec, rely 255/255, load 1/255
  Encapsulation PPP, loopback not set, keepalive set (10 sec)
  LCP Closed, multilink Closed
  Closed: IPCP, CDP
  Last input 00:01:02, output 00:01:02, output hang never
  Last clearing of "show interface" counters never
  Queueing strategy: fifo
  Output queue 0/40, 0 drops; input queue 0/75, 0 drops
  5 minute input rate 0 bits/sec, 0 packets/sec
  5 minute output rate 0 bits/sec, 0 packets/sec
     1119 packets input, 61726 bytes, 0 no buffer
     Received 0 broadcasts, 0 runts, 0 giants, 0 throttles
     0 input errors, 0 CRC, 0 frame, 0 overrun, 0 ignored, 0 abort
     1126 packets output, 62748 bytes, 0 underruns
     0 output errors, 0 collisions, 0 interface resets
     0 output buffer failures, 0 output buffers swapped out
     4 carrier transitions
```

The **show dialer** command displays the dial and timer status of each B channel that is defined on the router. We see that there have been 0 attempted calls to 8995201 since the router was last booted. We also see that each B channel will drop its call after 90 seconds of inactivity.

```
RouterA#show dialer

BRI0/0 - dialer type = ISDN

Dial String      Successes    Failures    Last called    Last status
8995201                  0           0    never                    -
0 incoming call(s) have been screened.

BRI0/0:1 - dialer type = ISDN
Idle timer (90 secs), Fast idle timer (20 secs)
Wait for carrier (30 secs), Re-enable (15 secs)
Dialer state is idle

BRI0/0:2 - dialer type = ISDN
Idle timer (90 secs), Fast idle timer (20 secs)
Wait for carrier (30 secs), Re-enable (15 secs)
Dialer state is idle
```

The show ppp multilink command will display any active MLPPP bundles on the router. Because there are no active calls, we see that there are no active bundles at this time.

```
RouterA#show ppp multi
No active bundles
```

Now, let's connect to RouterB. The BRI circuit on RouterB is also configured and active, as indicated by the **show isdn status** command:

```
RouterB#show isdn status
The current ISDN Switchtype = basic-ni1
ISDN BRI0/0 interface
    Layer 1 Status:
      ACTIVE
    Layer 2 Status:
      TEI = 64, State = MULTIPLE_FRAME_ESTABLISHED
      TEI = 65, State = MULTIPLE_FRAME_ESTABLISHED
    Spid Status:
      TEI 64, ces = 1, state = 8(established)
          spid1 configured, spid1 sent, spid1 valid
          Endpoint ID Info: epsf = 0, usid = 70, tid = 1
      TEI 65, ces = 2, state = 8(established)
          spid2 configured, spid2 sent, spid2 valid
          Endpoint ID Info: epsf = 0, usid = 70, tid = 2
```

```
     Layer 3 Status:
        0 Active Layer 3 Call(s)
     Activated dsl 0 CCBs = 0
     Number of active calls = 0
     Number of available B-channels = 2
  Total Allocated ISDN CCBs = 0
```

The **show dialer** command shows that RouterB will drop a B channel after 90 seconds of inactivity.

```
RouterB#show dialer

BRI0/0 - dialer type = ISDN

Dial String       Successes   Failures    Last called   Last status
0 incoming call(s) have been screened.

BRI0/0:1 - dialer type = ISDN
Idle timer (90 secs), Fast idle timer (20 secs)
Wait for carrier (30 secs), Re-enable (15 secs)
Dialer state is idle

BRI0/0:2 - dialer type = ISDN
Idle timer (90 secs), Fast idle timer (20 secs)
Wait for carrier (30 secs), Re-enable (15 secs)
Dialer state is idle
```

The BRI interface status for RouterB is identical to the status of the BRI interfaces that we just examined on Router A. The bri 0/0 interface refers to the D channel of the circuit, which is shown to be in an up/up (spoofing state)—indicating that the D channel is active.

```
RouterB#show interface bri 0/0
BRI0/0 is up, line protocol is up (spoofing)
   Hardware is QUICC BRI with U interface
   Internet address is 196.1.1.2/24
   MTU 1500 bytes, BW 64 Kbit, DLY 20000 usec, rely 255/255, load 1/255
   Encapsulation PPP, loopback not set
   Last input 00:00:01, output never, output hang never
   Last clearing of "show interface" counters never
   Queueing strategy: fifo
   Output queue 0/40, 0 drops; input queue 0/75, 0 drops
   5 minute input rate 0 bits/sec, 0 packets/sec
   5 minute output rate 0 bits/sec, 0 packets/sec
      1130 packets input, 4764 bytes, 0 no buffer
      Received 0 broadcasts, 0 runts, 0 giants, 0 throttles
      0 input errors, 0 CRC, 0 frame, 0 overrun, 0 ignored, 0 abort
      1121 packets output, 4585 bytes, 0 underruns
      0 output errors, 0 collisions, 6 interface resets
      0 output buffer failures, 0 output buffers swapped out
      5 carrier transitions
```

Interfaces bri 0/0:1 and bri 0/0:2 refer to the B1 and B2 channels of the BRI circuit respectively. Both of these interfaces are in the down/down state until a call is successfully placed.

```
RouterB#show interface bri 0/0:1
BRI0/0:1 is down, line protocol is down
   Hardware is QUICC BRI with U interface
   MTU 1500 bytes, BW 64 Kbit, DLY 20000 usec, rely 255/255, load 1/255
   Encapsulation PPP, loopback not set, keepalive set (10 sec)
   LCP Closed, multilink Closed
   Closed: IPCP, CDP
   Last input 00:02:33, output 00:02:33, output hang never
   Last clearing of "show interface" counters never
   Queueing strategy: fifo
   Output queue 0/40, 0 drops; input queue 0/75, 0 drops
   5 minute input rate 0 bits/sec, 0 packets/sec
   5 minute output rate 0 bits/sec, 0 packets/sec
      1212 packets input, 69764 bytes, 0 no buffer
      Received 0 broadcasts, 0 runts, 0 giants, 0 throttles
      0 input errors, 0 CRC, 0 frame, 0 overrun, 0 ignored, 0 abort
      1204 packets output, 67666 bytes, 0 underruns
      0 output errors, 0 collisions, 0 interface resets
      0 output buffer failures, 0 output buffers swapped out
      9 carrier transitions

RouterB#show interface bri 0/0:2
BRI0/0:2 is down, line protocol is down
   Hardware is QUICC BRI with U interface
   MTU 1500 bytes, BW 64 Kbit, DLY 20000 usec, rely 255/255, load 1/255
   Encapsulation PPP, loopback not set, keepalive set (10 sec)
   LCP Closed, multilink Closed
   Closed: IPCP, CDP
   Last input 00:02:36, output 00:02:36, output hang never
   Last clearing of "show interface" counters never
   Queueing strategy: fifo
   Output queue 0/40, 0 drops; input queue 0/75, 0 drops
   5 minute input rate 0 bits/sec, 0 packets/sec
   5 minute output rate 0 bits/sec, 0 packets/sec
      1126 packets input, 62748 bytes, 0 no buffer
      Received 0 broadcasts, 0 runts, 0 giants, 0 throttles
      0 input errors, 0 CRC, 0 frame, 0 overrun, 0 ignored, 0 abort
      1119 packets output, 61726 bytes, 0 underruns
      0 output errors, 0 collisions, 0 interface resets
      0 output buffer failures, 0 output buffers swapped out
      6 carrier transitions
```

Now, let's reconnect to RouterA. Try to ping the ISDN interface of RouterB at IP address 196.1.1.2. Notice that this ping causes RouterA to place two calls to RouterB.

```
RouterA#ping 196.1.1.2

Type escape sequence to abort.
Sending 5, 100-byte ICMP Echos to 196.1.1.2, timeout is 2 seconds:

%LINK-3-UPDOWN: Interface BRI0/0:1, changed state to up   ←   Call #1
%LINK-3-UPDOWN: Interface Virtual-Access1, changed state to up
%LINEPROTO-5-UPDOWN: Line protocol on Interface BRI0/0:1, changed state to up
%LINEPROTO-5-UPDOWN: Line protocol on Interface Virtual-Access1, changed state
to up
%LINK-3-UPDOWN: Interface BRI0/0:2, changed state to up   ←   Call #2
%LINEPROTO-5-UPDOWN: Line protocol on Interface BRI0/0:2, changed state to up
%ISDN-6-CONNECT: Interface BRI0/0:2 is now connected to 8995201 RouterB
```

The ping will be partially successful, because some of the ping packets will be sent when the call is being made.

```
..!!!
Success rate is 60 percent (3/5), round-trip min/avg/max = 20/21/24 ms
```

After the call has connected, another ping should be 100 percent successful.

```
RouterA#ping 196.1.1.2

Type escape sequence to abort.
Sending 5, 100-byte ICMP Echos to 196.1.1.2, timeout is 2 seconds:
!!!!!
Success rate is 100 percent (5/5), round-trip min/avg/max = 20/22/24 ms
```

The **show dialer** command will now indicate that two successful calls have been made. We see that interface bri 0/0:1 and interface bri 0/0:2 are both online. The dial reason for the call occurring on BRI channel B1 is shown as being traffic from 196.1.1.1 to 196.1.1.2. (our ping to 196.1.1.2). The dial reason for BRI channel B2 was multilink bundle overload. This overload is determined by the dialer load-threshold command in the routers configuration. The time until each B channel is disconnected is also displayed. Any interesting traffic will reset these numbers to the idle timeout value.

```
RouterA#show dialer

BRI0/0 - dialer type = ISDN

Dial String      Successes    Failures    Last called    Last status
8995201                  2           0     00:00:10       successful
0 incoming call(s) have been screened.
```

```
BRI0/0:1 - dialer type = ISDN
Idle timer (90 secs), Fast idle timer (20 secs)
Wait for carrier (30 secs), Re-enable (15 secs)
Dialer state is physical layer up
Dial reason: ip (s=196.1.1.1, d=196.1.1.2)  ←  Reason for dialing was our ping
Time until disconnect 76 secs  ←  Disconnect time
Current call connected 00:00:11
Connected to 8995201 (RouterB)

BRI0/0:2 - dialer type = ISDN
Idle timer (90 secs), Fast idle timer (20 secs)
Wait for carrier (30 secs), Re-enable (15 secs)
Dialer state is physical layer up
Dial reason: Multilink bundle overloaded
Time until disconnect 77 secs
Current call connected 00:00:12
Connected to 8995201 (RouterB)
```

Issuing the **show ppp multilink** command will now show that we have an MLPPP bundle consisting of two members. The two members are bri 0/0:1 and bri 0/0:2.

```
RouterA#show ppp multi

Bundle RouterB, 2 members, Master link is Virtual-Access1
Dialer Interface is BRI0/0
   0 lost fragments, 0 reordered, 0 unassigned, sequence 0x24/0x26 rcvd/sent
   0 discarded, 0 lost received, 1/255 load

Member Links: 2
BRI0/0:1  ←  These two interfaces make up the MLPPP bundle.
BRI0/0:2
```

The D channel of the BRI, shown as bri 0/0, will still indicate that it is in a spoofing state.

```
RouterA#show interface bri 0/0
BRI0/0 is up, line protocol is up (spoofing)
   Hardware is QUICC BRI with U interface
   Internet address is 196.1.1.1/24
   MTU 1500 bytes, BW 64 Kbit, DLY 20000 usec, rely 255/255, load 1/255
   Encapsulation PPP, loopback not set
   Last input 00:00:04, output never, output hang never
   Last clearing of "show interface" counters never
   Queueing strategy: fifo
   Output queue 0/40, 0 drops; input queue 0/75, 0 drops
   5 minute input rate 0 bits/sec, 0 packets/sec
   5 minute output rate 0 bits/sec, 0 packets/sec
      1063 packets input, 4376 bytes, 0 no buffer
      Received 0 broadcasts, 0 runts, 0 giants, 0 throttles
      0 input errors, 0 CRC, 0 frame, 0 overrun, 0 ignored, 0 abort
```

```
        1062 packets output, 4414 bytes, 0 underruns
        0 output errors, 0 collisions, 6 interface resets
        0 output buffer failures, 0 output buffers swapped out
        7 carrier transitions
```

Each of the B channels on the BRI will now be in an up/up state. Notice that both of these B channels have negotiated the multilink protocol with the far-end router.

```
RouterA#show interface bri 0/0:1
BRI0/0:1 is up, line protocol is up
  Hardware is QUICC BRI with U interface
  MTU 1500 bytes, BW 64 Kbit, DLY 20000 usec, rely 255/255, load 1/255
  Encapsulation PPP, loopback not set, keepalive set (10 sec)
  LCP Open, multilink Open   ←   MLPPP
  Last input 00:00:02, output 00:00:02, output hang never
  Last clearing of "show interface" counters never
  Queueing strategy: fifo
  Output queue 0/40, 0 drops; input queue 0/75, 0 drops
  5 minute input rate 0 bits/sec, 0 packets/sec
  5 minute output rate 0 bits/sec, 0 packets/sec
        1191 packets input, 67466 bytes, 0 no buffer
        Received 0 broadcasts, 0 runts, 0 giants, 0 throttles
        0 input errors, 0 CRC, 0 frame, 0 overrun, 0 ignored, 0 abort
        1198 packets output, 69418 bytes, 0 underruns
        0 output errors, 0 collisions, 0 interface resets
        0 output buffer failures, 0 output buffers swapped out
        6 carrier transitions

RouterA#show interface bri 0/0:2
BRI0/0:2 is up, line protocol is up
  Hardware is QUICC BRI with U interface
  MTU 1500 bytes, BW 64 Kbit, DLY 20000 usec, rely 255/255, load 1/255
  Encapsulation PPP, loopback not set, keepalive set (10 sec)
  LCP Open, multilink Open   ←   MLPPP
  Last input 00:00:02, output 00:00:02, output hang never
  Last clearing of "show interface" counters never
  Queueing strategy: fifo
  Output queue 0/40, 0 drops; input queue 0/75, 0 drops
  5 minute input rate 0 bits/sec, 0 packets/sec
  5 minute output rate 0 bits/sec, 0 packets/sec
        1107 packets input, 61542 bytes, 0 no buffer
        Received 0 broadcasts, 0 runts, 0 giants, 0 throttles
        0 input errors, 0 CRC, 0 frame, 0 overrun, 0 ignored, 0 abort
        1113 packets output, 62418 bytes, 0 underruns
        0 output errors, 0 collisions, 0 interface resets
        0 output buffer failures, 0 output buffers swapped out
        3 carrier transitions
```

The **show ppp multi, show isdn status**, and **show interface bri** commands on RouterB will display similar output with respect with what we just examined on RouterA.

After the idle timeout period (90 seconds without interesting traffic), the call will disconnect. The following screen print shows the call being brought down and both B channels on the BRI (bri 0/0:1 and bri 0/0:2) being changed to a down state.

```
%LINEPROTO-5-UPDOWN: Line protocol on Interface Virtual-Access1, changed state
to down
%LINK-3-UPDOWN: Interface Virtual-Access1, changed state to down
%ISDN-6-DISCONNECT: Interface BRI0/0:1  disconnected from 8995201 RouterB, call
lasted 99 seconds
%ISDN-6-DISCONNECT: Interface BRI0/0:2  disconnected from 8995201 RouterB, call
lasted 96 seconds
%LINK-3-UPDOWN: Interface BRI0/0:1, changed state to down
%LINK-3-UPDOWN: Interface BRI0/0:2, changed state to down
%LINEPROTO-5-UPDOWN: Line protocol on Interface BRI0/0:1, changed state to down
%LINEPROTO-5-UPDOWN: Line protocol on Interface BRI0/0:2, changed state to down
```

Lab #3: Backup Interfaces

Equipment Needed

The following equipment is needed to perform this lab exercise:

■ Two Cisco routers, each of which must have a single ISDN BRI interface, a single serial interface, and an Ethernet interface

■ Two ISDN BRI circuits

■ Cisco IOS 11.2 or higher

■ A Cisco DCE/DTE V.35 crossover cable. If a crossover cable is not available, you can use a Cisco DCE cable connected to a Cisco DTE cable.

■ A PC running a terminal emulation program for console port connection on the routers

Configuration Overview

This configuration demonstrates how to use a backup interface for ISDN dial backup. A backup interface is a designated interface which remains in standby mode until the primary interface goes down. A backup interface can be either an ISDN interface or a serial interface (such as a V.35

port). When a V.35 port acts as a backup interface, the V.35 port is usually connected to an external ISDN terminal adapter or analog modem.

The two routers are connected, as shown in Figure 3–14. RouterA and RouterB are connected to an Adtran Atlas 800 ISDN switch. When the serial connection between RouterA and RouterB is broken, RouterA will dial RouterB over the BRI circuit.

Figure 3–14
Lab #3

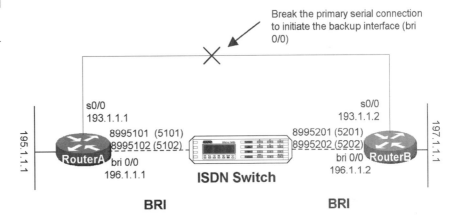

A PC running a terminal emulation program should be connected to the console port of one of the routers using a Cisco rolled cable.

NOTE: *An item to keep in mind during this lab exercise is that a drawback of backup interfaces is their testability. The only way to initiate a call from a backup interface is to bring down the primary circuit, thus affecting the customer's traffic. We will see in the next lab that floating statics allow the ISDN interface to be tested while customer traffic continues to flow.*

NOTE: *The s0/0 interface on RouterA is configured as a DCE interface and supplies clocking to the s0/0 interface of RouterB.*

ISDN Switch Setup

If you do not have access to actual ISDN circuits, you can use an ISDN desktop switch. Information on configuring an ISDN desktop switch can be found in the ISDN Switch Configuration section earlier in this chapter.

Router Configuration

The configurations for the two routers in this example are as follows (ISDN commands are highlighted in bold):

RouterA

```
RouterA#show run
Building configuration...

Current configuration:
!
version 11.2
no service udp-small-servers
no service tcp-small-servers
!
hostname RouterA
!
enable password cisco
!
username RouterB password 7 070C285F4D06
isdn switch-type basic-ni1   ←   Set D channel call control
!
interface Ethernet0/0
 ip address 195.1.1.1 255.255.255.0
 no keepalive
!
interface Serial0/0
 backup delay 5 20   ←   Go to backup 5 seconds after loss, return 20 seconds
                         after primary returns
 backup interface BRI0/0   ←   The BRI interface is the backup interface
 ip address 193.1.1.1 255.255.255.0
 encapsulation ppp
 clockrate 64000
!
interface BRI0/0
 ip address 196.1.1.1 255.255.255.0
 encapsulation ppp
 isdn spid1 5101 8995101   ←   Set SPIDs for both B channels
 isdn spid2 5102 8995102
 dialer idle-timeout 90   ←   Disconnect 90 seconds after no interesting packets
 dialer map ip 196.1.1.2 name RouterB broadcast 8995201   ←   Define next hop
                                                              address and dial
                                                              string
 dialer load-threshold 1   ←   Set threshold for adding additional B channels
 dialer-group 1   ←   Associate interface with dialer-list 1
 no fair-queue
 ppp authentication chap
```

```
 ppp multilink  ←  Try to negotiate a multilink PPP session
!
router rip
 network 195.1.1.0
 network 193.1.1.0
 network 196.1.1.0
!
no ip classless
dialer-list 1 protocol ip permit  ←  Define interesting traffic
!
line con 0
 password cisco
 login
line aux 0
line vty 0 4
 password cisco
 login
!
end
```

RouterB

```
RouterB#show run
Building configuration...

Current configuration:
!
version 11.2
service timestamps debug datetime localtime
no service udp-small-servers
no service tcp-small-servers
!
hostname RouterB
!
enable password cisco
!
username RouterA password 7 094F471A1A0A
isdn switch-type basic-ni1  ←  Set D channel call control
!
interface Ethernet0/0
 ip address 197.1.1.1 255.255.255.0
 no keepalive
!
interface Serial0/0
 ip address 193.1.1.2 255.255.255.0
 encapsulation ppp
!
interface BRI0/0
 ip address 196.1.1.2 255.255.255.0
 encapsulation ppp
 isdn spid1 5201 8995201  ←  Set the SPID value for both B channels
 isdn spid2 5202 8995202
```

```
dialer idle-timeout 90   ←  Set the interesting traffic timeout
dialer map ip 196.1.1.1 name RouterA broadcast  ←  Define a next hop address
dialer-group 1  ←  Associate this interface with dialer-list 1
no fair-queue
ppp authentication chap
ppp multilink  ←  Try to negotiate a MLPPP session
!
router rip
 network 193.1.1.0
 network 197.1.1.0
 network 196.1.1.0
!
no ip classless
dialer-list 1 protocol ip permit  ←  Define interesting traffic
!
line con 0
line aux 0
line vty 0 4
 password cisco
 login
!
end
```

Monitoring and Testing the Configuration

Let's start by connecting to RouterA. Verify that interface s 0/0 is in an up/up state. Notice that interface bri 0/0 is designated as the backup interface for s 0/0.

```
RouterA#show interface s 0/0
Serial0/0 is up, line protocol is up
  Hardware is QUICC Serial
  Internet address is 193.1.1.1/24
  Backup interface BRI0/0, kickin load not set, kickout load not set
      failure delay 5 sec, secondary disable delay 20 sec
  MTU 1500 bytes, BW 1544 Kbit, DLY 20000 usec, rely 255/255, load 1/255
  Encapsulation PPP, loopback not set, keepalive set (10 sec)
  LCP Open
  Open: IPCP, CDP
  Last input 00:00:08, output 00:00:08, output hang never
  Last clearing of "show interface" counters never
  Input queue: 0/75/0 (size/max/drops); Total output drops: 0
  Queueing strategy: weighted fair
  Output queue: 0/64/0 (size/threshold/drops)
     Conversations  0/1 (active/max active)
     Reserved Conversations 0/0 (allocated/max allocated)
  5 minute input rate 0 bits/sec, 0 packets/sec
  5 minute output rate 0 bits/sec, 0 packets/sec
     489 packets input, 63338 bytes, 0 no buffer
```

```
Received 0 broadcasts, 0 runts, 1 giants, 0 throttles
4 input errors, 1 CRC, 2 frame, 0 overrun, 0 ignored, 1 abort
518 packets output, 51626 bytes, 0 underruns
0 output errors, 0 collisions, 40 interface resets
0 output buffer failures, 0 output buffers swapped out
8 carrier transitions
DCD=up  DSR=up  DTR=up  RTS=up  CTS=up
```

We see that routes to RouterB are being learned from RIP via s 0/0 on RouterA.

```
RouterA#show ip route
Codes: C - connected, S - static, I - IGRP, R - RIP, M - mobile, B - BGP
       D - EIGRP, EX - EIGRP external, O - OSPF, IA - OSPF inter area
       N1 - OSPF NSSA external type 1, N2 - OSPF NSSA external type 2
       E1 - OSPF external type 1, E2 - OSPF external type 2, E - EGP
       i - IS-IS, L1 - IS-IS level-1, L2 - IS-IS level-2, * - candidate default
       U - per-user static route, o - ODR

Gateway of last resort is not set

     193.1.1.0/24 is variably subnetted, 2 subnets, 2 masks
C       193.1.1.0/24 is directly connected, Serial0/0
C       193.1.1.2/32 is directly connected, Serial0/0
C    195.1.1.0/24 is directly connected, Ethernet0/0
R    196.1.1.0/24 [120/1] via 193.1.1.2, 00:00:05, Serial0/0
R    197.1.1.0/24 [120/1] via 193.1.1.2, 00:00:05, Serial0/0
```

Type **show interface bri 0/0** to display the BRI interface status. Notice that the interface is in a standby mode. The BRI interface in our previous labs was in an up/up (spoofing) condition. A backup interface is treated differently and stays in standby mode until a call is made.

```
RouterA#show interface bri 0/0
BRI0/0 is standby mode, line protocol is down
  Hardware is QUICC BRI with U interface
  Internet address is 196.1.1.1/24
  MTU 1500 bytes, BW 64 Kbit, DLY 20000 usec, rely 255/255, load 1/255
  Encapsulation PPP, loopback not set
  Last input 00:05:46, output never, output hang never
  Last clearing of "show interface" counters never
  Queueing strategy: fifo
  Output queue 0/40, 0 drops; input queue 0/75, 0 drops
  5 minute input rate 0 bits/sec, 0 packets/sec
  5 minute output rate 0 bits/sec, 0 packets/sec
     279 packets input, 1465 bytes, 0 no buffer
     Received 0 broadcasts, 0 runts, 0 giants, 0 throttles
     0 input errors, 0 CRC, 0 frame, 0 overrun, 0 ignored, 0 abort
     293 packets output, 1588 bytes, 0 underruns
     0 output errors, 0 collisions, 5 interface resets
     0 output buffer failures, 0 output buffers swapped out
     4 carrier transitions
```

Both of the B channels on the BRI interface will be in a down/down state until a call is made.

```
RouterA#show interface bri 0/0:1
BRI0/0:1 is administratively down, line protocol is down ←   B channel #1
  Hardware is QUICC BRI with U interface
  MTU 1500 bytes, BW 64 Kbit, DLY 20000 usec, rely 255/255, load 1/255
  Encapsulation PPP, loopback not set, keepalive set (10 sec)
  LCP Closed, multilink Closed
  Closed: IPCP, CDP
  Last input 00:05:56, output 00:05:48, output hang never
  Last clearing of "show interface" counters never
  Queueing strategy: fifo
  Output queue 0/40, 0 drops; input queue 0/75, 0 drops
  5 minute input rate 0 bits/sec, 0 packets/sec
  5 minute output rate 0 bits/sec, 0 packets/sec
     500 packets input, 19251 bytes, 0 no buffer
     Received 0 broadcasts, 0 runts, 0 giants, 0 throttles
     0 input errors, 0 CRC, 0 frame, 0 overrun, 0 ignored, 0 abort
     512 packets output, 22556 bytes, 0 underruns
     0 output errors, 0 collisions, 0 interface resets
     0 output buffer failures, 0 output buffers swapped out
     13 carrier transitions

RouterA#show interface bri 0/0:2
BRI0/0:2 is administratively down, line protocol is down ←   B channel #2
  Hardware is QUICC BRI with U interface
  MTU 1500 bytes, BW 64 Kbit, DLY 20000 usec, rely 255/255, load 1/255
  Encapsulation PPP, loopback not set, keepalive set (10 sec)
  LCP Closed, multilink Closed
  Closed: IPCP, CDP
  Last input 00:05:59, output 00:05:59, output hang never
  Last clearing of "show interface" counters never
  Queueing strategy: fifo
  Output queue 0/40, 0 drops; input queue 0/75, 0 drops
  5 minute input rate 0 bits/sec, 0 packets/sec
  5 minute output rate 0 bits/sec, 0 packets/sec
     466 packets input, 18782 bytes, 0 no buffer
     Received 0 broadcasts, 0 runts, 0 giants, 0 throttles
     0 input errors, 0 CRC, 0 frame, 0 overrun, 0 ignored, 0 abort
     482 packets output, 21272 bytes, 0 underruns
     0 output errors, 0 collisions, 0 interface resets
     0 output buffer failures, 0 output buffers swapped out
     13 carrier transitions
```

Make sure that you can ping the far-end router (RouterB) at IP address 193.1.1.2 by using the **ping 193.1.1.2** command.

```
RouterA#ping 193.1.1.2

Type escape sequence to abort.
Sending 5, 100-byte ICMP Echos to 193.1.1.2, timeout is 2 seconds:
!!!!!
Success rate is 100 percent (5/5), round-trip min/avg/max = 28/30/32 ms
```

Now let's connect to RouterB. We see that RouterB has learned a route to the 195.1.1.0 network (RouterA) via interface S0/0.

```
RouterB#show ip route
Codes: C - connected, S - static, I - IGRP, R - RIP, M - mobile, B - BGP
       D - EIGRP, EX - EIGRP external, O - OSPF, IA - OSPF inter area
       N1 - OSPF NSSA external type 1, N2 - OSPF NSSA external type 2
       E1 - OSPF external type 1, E2 - OSPF external type 2, E - EGP
       i - IS-IS, L1 - IS-IS level-1, L2 - IS-IS level-2, * - candidate default
       U - per-user static route, o - ODR

Gateway of last resort is not set

     193.1.1.0/24 is variably subnetted, 2 subnets, 2 masks
C        193.1.1.1/32 is directly connected, Serial0/0
C        193.1.1.0/24 is directly connected, Serial0/0
R     195.1.1.0/24 [120/1] via 193.1.1.1, 00:00:02, Serial0/0
C     196.1.1.0/24 is directly connected, BRI0/0
C     197.1.1.0/24 is directly connected, Ethernet0/0
```

Make sure that S 0/0 is in an up/up state by entering the **show interface s 0/0** command.

```
RouterB#show interface s 0/0
Serial0/0 is up, line protocol is up
  Hardware is QUICC Serial
  Internet address is 193.1.1.2/24
  MTU 1500 bytes, BW 1544 Kbit, DLY 20000 usec, rely 255/255, load 1/255
  Encapsulation PPP, loopback not set, keepalive set (10 sec)
  LCP Open
  Open: IPCP, CDP
  Last input 00:00:00, output 00:00:00, output hang never
  Last clearing of "show interface" counters never
  Input queue: 0/75/0 (size/max/drops); Total output drops: 0
  Queueing strategy: weighted fair
  Output queue: 0/64/0 (size/threshold/drops)
     Conversations  0/2 (active/max active)
     Reserved Conversations 0/0 (allocated/max allocated)
  5 minute input rate 1000 bits/sec, 3 packets/sec
  5 minute output rate 2000 bits/sec, 3 packets/sec
     646 packets input, 57752 bytes, 0 no buffer
     Received 0 broadcasts, 0 runts, 0 giants, 0 throttles
     2 input errors, 0 CRC, 2 frame, 0 overrun, 0 ignored, 0 abort
     614 packets output, 73640 bytes, 0 underruns
     0 output errors, 0 collisions, 41 interface resets
```

```
         0 output buffer failures, 0 output buffers swapped out
         22 carrier transitions
DCD=up   DSR=up   DTR=up   RTS=up   CTS=up
```

We see that the BRI interface on RouterB is in an up/up (spoofing) state. Recall that the BRI interface on RouterA is in a standby mode, because RouterA is using a backup interface.

```
RouterB#show interface bri 0/0
BRI0/0 is up, line protocol is up (spoofing)  ←  D channel is active
   Hardware is QUICC BRI with U interface
   Internet address is 196.1.1.2/24
   MTU 1500 bytes, BW 64 Kbit, DLY 20000 usec, rely 255/255, load 1/255
   Encapsulation PPP, loopback not set
   Last input 00:00:02, output never, output hang never
   Last clearing of "show interface" counters never
   Queueing strategy: fifo
   Output queue 0/40, 0 drops; input queue 0/75, 0 drops
   5 minute input rate 0 bits/sec, 0 packets/sec
   5 minute output rate 0 bits/sec, 0 packets/sec
      388 packets input, 2076 bytes, 0 no buffer
      Received 0 broadcasts, 0 runts, 0 giants, 0 throttles
      0 input errors, 0 CRC, 0 frame, 0 overrun, 0 ignored, 0 abort
      376 packets output, 1756 bytes, 0 underruns
      0 output errors, 0 collisions, 5 interface resets
      0 output buffer failures, 0 output buffers swapped out
      1 carrier transitions
```

As with RouterA, both of the B channels on RouterB's BRI will be in a down/down state until a call is made.

```
RouterB#show interface bri 0/0:1
BRI0/0:1 is down, line protocol is down  ←  B channel #1
   Hardware is QUICC BRI with U interface
   MTU 1500 bytes, BW 64 Kbit, DLY 20000 usec, rely 255/255, load 1/255
   Encapsulation PPP, loopback not set, keepalive set (10 sec)
   LCP Closed, multilink Closed
   Closed: IPCP, CDP
   Last input 00:06:38, output 00:05:53, output hang never
   Last clearing of "show interface" counters never
   Queueing strategy: fifo
   Output queue 0/40, 0 drops; input queue 0/75, 0 drops
   5 minute input rate 0 bits/sec, 0 packets/sec
   5 minute output rate 0 bits/sec, 0 packets/sec
      512 packets input, 22556 bytes, 0 no buffer
      Received 0 broadcasts, 0 runts, 0 giants, 0 throttles
      0 input errors, 0 CRC, 0 frame, 0 overrun, 0 ignored, 0 abort
      508 packets output, 19579 bytes, 0 underruns
      0 output errors, 0 collisions, 0 interface resets
      0 output buffer failures, 0 output buffers swapped out
      18 carrier transitions
```

```
RouterB#show interface bri 0/0:2
BRI0/0:2 is down, line protocol is down    ←   B channel #2
  Hardware is QUICC BRI with U interface
  MTU 1500 bytes, BW 64 Kbit, DLY 20000 usec, rely 255/255, load 1/255
  Encapsulation PPP, loopback not set, keepalive set (10 sec)
  LCP Closed, multilink Closed
  Closed: IPCP, CDP
  Last input 00:06:52, output 00:05:54, output hang never
  Last clearing of "show interface" counters never
  Queueing strategy: fifo
  Output queue 0/40, 0 drops; input queue 0/75, 0 drops
  5 minute input rate 0 bits/sec, 0 packets/sec
  5 minute output rate 0 bits/sec, 0 packets/sec
     482 packets input, 21272 bytes, 0 no buffer
     Received 0 broadcasts, 0 runts, 0 giants, 0 throttles
     0 input errors, 0 CRC, 0 frame, 0 overrun, 0 ignored, 0 abort
     475 packets output, 19123 bytes, 0 underruns
     0 output errors, 0 collisions, 0 interface resets
     0 output buffer failures, 0 output buffers swapped out
     18 carrier transitions
```

Now, let's reconnect to RouterA. Turn on ISDN call control debugging with the **debug isdn q931** command.

```
RouterA#debug isdn q931
ISDN Q931 packets debugging is on
```

Turn on PPP authentication tracing with the **debug ppp authen** command.

```
RouterA#debug ppp authen
PPP authentication debugging is on
```

You can check which debug commands are enabled with the **show debug** command.

```
RouterA#show debug
PPP:
  PPP authentication debugging is on
ISDN:
  ISDN Q931 packets debugging is on
```

Now, we are going to start an extended ping between RouterA and RouterB. While the ping is running, we will pull the serial cable out of interface S0/0 of RouterA. This action will cause RouterA to activate the backup interface (bri0/0). The IP address that we will ping is 197.1.1.1, which is the Ethernet interface on RouterB. When the ping begins, the traffic will flow between RouterA and RouterB over the serial interface connecting the two routers. When the serial interface connection is broken, the traffic will start to flow over the ISDN interface.

```
RouterA#ping
Protocol [ip]:
Target IP address: 197.1.1.1
Repeat count [5]: 100000
Datagram size [100]:
Timeout in seconds [2]:
Extended commands [n]:
Sweep range of sizes [n]:
Type escape sequence to abort.
Sending 100000, 100-byte ICMP Echos to 197.1.1.1, timeout is 2 seconds:
!!!!!!!!!!!!!!!!!!!!!!!!!!!!!!!!!!!!!!!!!!!!!!!!!!!!!!!!!!!!!!!!!!!!!!!
!!!!!!!!!!!!!!!!!!!!!!!!!!!!!!!!!!!!!!!!!!!!!!!!!!!!!!!!!!!!!!!!!!!!!!!
!!!!!!!!!!!!!!!!!!!!!!!!!!!!!!!!!!!!!!!!!!!!!!!!!!!!!!........ ← Pull the cable

%LINEPROTO-5-UPDOWN: Line protocol on Interface Serial0/0, changed state to
down  ← The serial interface will be declared down
%LINK-3-UPDOWN: Interface Serial0/0, changed state to down
%LINK-3-UPDOWN: Interface BRI0/0:1, changed state to down
%LINK-3-UPDOWN: Interface BRI0/0:2, changed state to down
%LINK-3-UPDOWN: Interface BRI0/0, changed state to up  ← The backup interface
                                                          is activated
```

The following example shows the ISDN Q931 call control and CHAP
authentication that takes place between RouterA and RouterB when a
call is made:

```
ISDN BR0/0: TX ->  INFORMATION pd = 8  callref = (null)
        SPID Information i = '5101'
ISDN BR0/0: RX <-  INFORMATION pd = 8  callref = (null)
        ENDPOINT IDent i = 0xF081
ISDN BR0/0: Received EndPoint ID.
ISDN BR0/0: TX ->  SETUP pd = 8  callref = 0x0E
        Bearer Capability i = 0x8890
        Channel ID i = 0x83
        Keypad Facility i = '8995201'  ← RouterA calls RouterB on B channel
                                         #1
ISDN BR0/0: RX <-  CALL_PROC pd = 8   callref = 0x8E
        Channel ID i = 0x89
ISDN BR0/0: RX <-  CONNECT pd = 8   callref = 0x8E
        Channel ID i = 0x89
%LINK-3-UPDOWN: Interface BRI0/0:1, changed state to up
PPP BRI0/0:1: treating connection as a callout
ISDN BR0/0: TX ->  CONNECT_ACK pd = 8  callref = 0x0E
PPP BRI0/0:1: Send CHAP Challenge id=7  ← CHAP Challenge B channel #1
PPP BRI0/0:1: CHAP Challenge id=7 received from RouterB
PPP BRI0/0:1: Send CHAP Response id=7
PPP BRI0/0:1: CHAP response received from RouterB
PPP BRI0/0:1: CHAP Response id=7 received from RouterB
PPP BRI0/0:1: Send CHAP Success id=7  ← CHAP passed on B channel #1
PPP BRI0/0:1: remote passed CHAP authentication.
PPP BRI0/0:1: Passed CHAP authentication with remote
%LINK-3-UPDOWN: Interface Virtual-Access1, changed state to up
```

```
PPP Virtual-Access1: treating connection as a callin
%LINEPROTO-5-UPDOWN: Line protocol on Interface BRI0/0:1, changed state to up
%LINEPROTO-5-UPDOWN: Line protocol on Interface Virtual-Access1, changed state
to up
%ISDN-6-CONNECT: Interface BRI0/0:1 is now connected to 8995201 RouterB
ISDN BR0/0: Event: incoming ces value = 2
ISDN BR0/0: TX ->  INFORMATION pd = 8   callref = (null)
        SPID Information i = '5102'
ISDN BR0/0: RX <-  INFORMATION pd = 8   callref = (null)
        ENDPOINT IDent i = 0xF082
ISDN BR0/0: Received EndPoint ID
ISDN BR0/0: TX ->  SETUP pd = 8   callref = 0x0F
        Bearer Capability i = 0x8890
        Channel ID i = 0x83
        Keypad Facility i = '8995201'   ←  RouterA calls RouterB on B channel
                                            #2
ISDN BR0/0: RX <-  CALL_PROC pd = 8   callref = 0x8F
        Channel ID i = 0x8A
ISDN BR0/0: Event: incoming ces value = 2
ISDN BR0/0: RX <-  CONNECT pd = 8   callref = 0x8F
        Channel ID i = 0x8A
ISDN BR0/0: Event: incoming ces value = 2
%LINK-3-UPDOWN: Interface BRI0/0:2, changed state to up
PPP BRI0/0:2: treating connection as a callout
ISDN BR0/0: TX ->  CONNECT_ACK pd = 8   callref = 0x0F
PPP BRI0/0:2: Send CHAP Challenge id=7   ←  CHAP Challenge for B channel #2
PPP BRI0/0:2: CHAP Challenge id=7 received from RouterB
PPP BRI0/0:2: Send CHAP Response id=7
PPP BRI0/0:2: CHAP response received from RouterB
PPP BRI0/0:2: CHAP Response id=7 received from RouterB
PPP BRI0/0:2: Send CHAP Success id=7  ←  CHAP passed on B channel #2
PPP BRI0/0:2: remote passed CHAP authentication
PPP BRI0/0:2: Passed CHAP authentication with remote
%LINEPROTO-5-UPDOWN: Line protocol on Interface BRI0/0:2, changed state to up
%ISDN-6-CONNECT: Interface BRI0/0:2 is now connected to 8995201 RouterB
```

Once the backup interface is active, the pings will start to work again.

```
!!!!!!!!!!!!!!!!!!!!!!!!!!!!!!!!!!!!!!!!!!!!!!!!!!!!!!!!!!!!!!!!!!!!!!
!!!!!!!!!!!!!!!!!!!!!!!!!!!!!!!!!!!!!!!!!!!!!!!!!!!!!!!!!!!!!!!!!!!!!!
Success rate is 98 percent (1594/1619), round-trip min/avg/max = 20/24/40 ms
```

When the ping has completed, type the **show isdn status** command to display the call status for the router's BRI interface. Notice that there are two active layer 3 calls. These are the 2 B channels that are now connected.

```
RouterA#show isdn status
The current ISDN Switchtype = basic-ni1
ISDN BRI0/0 interface
    Layer 1 Status:
      ACTIVE
```

```
    Layer 2 Status:
      TEI = 64, State = MULTIPLE_FRAME_ESTABLISHED
      TEI = 65, State = MULTIPLE_FRAME_ESTABLISHED
    Spid Status:
      TEI 64, ces = 1, state = 5(init)
          spid1 configured, spid1 sent, spid1 valid
          Endpoint ID Info: epsf = 0, usid = 70, tid = 1
      TEI 65, ces = 2, state = 5(init)
          spid2 configured, spid2 sent, spid2 valid
          Endpoint ID Info: epsf = 0, usid = 70, tid = 2
    Layer 3 Status:
      2 Active Layer 3 Call(s)
    Activated dsl 0 CCBs = 2
      CCB:callid=8011, sapi=0, ces=1, B-chan=1
      CCB:callid=8013, sapi=0, ces=2, B-chan=2
  Total Allocated ISDN CCBs = 2
```

Type the **show ppp multilink** command to verify that the two connected B channels on the BRI have been bundled together into an MLPPP bundle. We see from the command's output that both channels bri 0/0:1 and bri 0/0:2 are connected in an MLPPP bundle.

```
RouterA#show ppp multi

Bundle RouterB, 2 members, Master link is Virtual-Access1
Dialer Interface is BRI0/0
  0 lost fragments, 11 reordered, 0 unassigned, sequence 0x99F/0x9A1 rcvd/sent
  0 discarded, 0 lost received, 29/255 load

Member Links: 2
BRI0/0:1
BRI0/0:2
```

Type the **show dialer** command to display statistics on the current ISDN call. Notice that the second B channel was brought up due to a multilink overload.

```
RouterA#show dialer

BRI0/0 - dialer type = ISDN

Dial String      Successes    Failures    Last called    Last status
8995201                 14           5     00:00:37       successful
0 incoming call(s) have been screened.

BRI0/0:1 - dialer type = ISDN
Idle timer (90 secs), Fast idle timer (20 secs)
Wait for carrier (30 secs), Re-enable (15 secs)
Dialer state is physical layer up
Dial reason: ip (s=196.1.1.1, d=255.255.255.255)
Time until disconnect 89 secs
```

```
Current call connected 00:00:38
Connected to 8995201 (RouterB)

BRI0/0:2 - dialer type = ISDN
Idle timer (90 secs), Fast idle timer (20 secs)
Wait for carrier (30 secs), Re-enable (15 secs)
Dialer state is physical layer up
```
Dial reason: Multilink bundle overloaded ← **Dialer load threshold statement determines when another channel should be brought up**

```
Time until disconnect 50 secs
Current call connected 00:00:39
Connected to 8995201 (RouterB)
```

Both of the B channels on the BRI will now be in an up/up state. Display the B channel status with the **show interface bri 0/0:1** and **show interface bri 0/0:2** commands.

```
RouterA#show interface bri 0/0:1
```
BRI0/0:1 is up, line protocol is up ← **B channel #1**
```
  Hardware is QUICC BRI with U interface
  MTU 1500 bytes, BW 64 Kbit, DLY 20000 usec, rely 255/255, load 19/255
  Encapsulation PPP, loopback not set, keepalive set (10 sec)
  LCP Open, multilink Open
  Last input 00:00:05, output 00:00:05, output hang never
  Last clearing of "show interface" counters never
  Queueing strategy: fifo
  Output queue 0/40, 0 drops; input queue 0/75, 0 drops
  5 minute input rate 5000 bits/sec, 5 packets/sec
  5 minute output rate 5000 bits/sec, 5 packets/sec
     1937 packets input, 111523 bytes, 0 no buffer
     Received 0 broadcasts, 0 runts, 0 giants, 0 throttles
     0 input errors, 0 CRC, 0 frame, 0 overrun, 0 ignored, 0 abort
     1948 packets output, 115360 bytes, 0 underruns
     0 output errors, 0 collisions, 0 interface resets
     0 output buffer failures, 0 output buffers swapped out
     14 carrier transitions

RouterA#show interface bri 0/0:2
```
BRI0/0:2 is up, line protocol is up ← **B channel #2**
```
  Hardware is QUICC BRI with U interface
  MTU 1500 bytes, BW 64 Kbit, DLY 20000 usec, rely 255/255, load 15/255
  Encapsulation PPP, loopback not set, keepalive set (10 sec)
  LCP Open, multilink Open
  Last input 00:00:00, output 00:00:08, output hang never
  Last clearing of "show interface" counters never
  Queueing strategy: fifo
  Output queue 0/40, 0 drops; input queue 1/75, 0 drops
  5 minute input rate 4000 bits/sec, 4 packets/sec
  5 minute output rate 4000 bits/sec, 4 packets/sec
     1715 packets input, 91476 bytes, 0 no buffer
```

```
Received 0 broadcasts, 0 runts, 0 giants, 0 throttles
0 input errors, 0 CRC, 0 frame, 0 overrun, 0 ignored, 0 abort
1731 packets output, 93514 bytes, 0 underruns
0 output errors, 0 collisions, 0 interface resets
0 output buffer failures, 0 output buffers swapped out
16 carrier transitions
```

Interface s0/0 is now in a down/down state. It was this interface going down that caused the backup interface, bri0/0, to go into an active state and dial the far-end router.

```
RouterA#show interface s 0/0
Serial0/0 is down, line protocol is down
  Hardware is QUICC Serial
  Internet address is 193.1.1.1/24
  Backup interface BRI0/0, kickin load not set, kickout load not set
      failure delay 5 sec, secondary disable delay 20 sec
  MTU 1500 bytes, BW 1544 Kbit, DLY 20000 usec, rely 255/255, load 1/255
  Encapsulation PPP, loopback not set, keepalive set (10 sec)
  LCP Closed
  Closed: IPCP, CDP
  Last input 00:02:20, output 00:02:20, output hang never
  Last clearing of "show interface" counters never
  Input queue: 0/75/0 (size/max/drops); Total output drops: 0
  Queueing strategy: weighted fair
  Output queue: 0/64/0 (size/threshold/drops)
     Conversations  0/1 (active/max active)
     Reserved Conversations 0/0 (allocated/max allocated)
  5 minute input rate 0 bits/sec, 0 packets/sec
  5 minute output rate 0 bits/sec, 0 packets/sec
     1075 packets input, 120020 bytes, 0 no buffer
     Received 0 broadcasts, 0 runts, 1 giants, 0 throttles
     5 input errors, 1 CRC, 3 frame, 0 overrun, 0 ignored, 1 abort
     1113 packets output, 100942 bytes, 0 underruns
     0 output errors, 0 collisions, 45 interface resets
  0 output buffer failures, 0 output buffers swapped out
     11 carrier transitions
     DCD=up  DSR=up  DTR=down  RTS=down  CTS=up
```

Let's examine the routing table with the **show ip route** command. Notice that we have now learned a RIP route to the 197.1.1.0 network via 196.1.1.2. (197.1.1.0 is the Ethernet network on RouterB, 196.1.1.2 is the IP address of the BRI interface on RouterB). Our routing table now reflects the fact that our primary serial interface, s0/0, is down, and that our backup interface, bri0/0, is now our only connection to RouterB. Routes learned via s0/0 will be deleted as soon as that interface goes down.

```
RouterA#show ip route
Codes: C - connected, S - static, I - IGRP, R - RIP, M - mobile, B - BGP
       D - EIGRP, EX - EIGRP external, O - OSPF, IA - OSPF inter area
       N1 - OSPF NSSA external type 1, N2 - OSPF NSSA external type 2
       E1 - OSPF external type 1, E2 - OSPF external type 2, E - EGP
       i - IS-IS, L1 - IS-IS level-1, L2 - IS-IS level-2, * - candidate default
       U - per-user static route, o - ODR

Gateway of last resort is not set

C    195.1.1.0/24 is directly connected, Ethernet0/0
     196.1.1.0/24 is variably subnetted, 2 subnets, 2 masks
C       196.1.1.0/24 is directly connected, BRI0/0
C       196.1.1.2/32 is directly connected, BRI0/0
R    197.1.1.0/24 [120/1] via 196.1.1.2, 00:00:05, BRI0/0
```

Now, we are going to start a ping and reconnect our serial cable to RouterB. Recall from the configuration of RouterA that the backup interface will activate five seconds after S0/0 goes down and will go inactive 20 seconds after S0/0 becomes active again.

Router A Configuration for interface S0/0

```
interface Serial0/0
 backup delay 5 20        ←  The backup interface activates 5 seconds after S0/0
                             goes down and deactivates 20 seconds after S0/0 goes
                             back up.
 backup interface BRI0/0
 ip address 193.1.1.1 255.255.255.0
 encapsulation ppp
 clockrate 64000
```

Start an extended ping to 197.1.1.1. Remember that from the IP routing table, our traffic will flow over the bri0/0 interface.

```
RouterA#ping
Protocol [ip]:
Target IP address: 197.1.1.1
Repeat count [5]: 100000
Datagram size [100]:
Timeout in seconds [2]:
Extended commands [n]:
Sweep range of sizes [n]:
Type escape sequence to abort.
Sending 100000, 100-byte ICMP Echos to 197.1.1.1, timeout is 2 seconds:
!!!!!!!!!!!!!!!!!!!!!!!!!!!!!!!!!!!!!!!!!!!!!!!!!!!!!!!!!!!!!!!!!!!!!!!!!!!!!
!!!!!!!!!!!!!!!!!!!!!!!!!!!!!!!!!!!!!!!!!!!!!!!!!!!!!!!!!!!!!!!!!!!!!!!!!!!!!
```

During the ping, reconnect the serial cable to the s0/0 interface of RouterA. You will see interface s0/0 go to an up state, and several seconds later, the bri backup interface will go down.

```
%LINK-3-UPDOWN: Interface Serial0/0, changed state to up   ←   s0/0 comes back
                                                                up
PPP Serial0/0: treating connection as a dedicated line
%LINEPROTO-5-UPDOWN: Line protocol on Interface Serial0/0, changed state to up
%LINK-3-UPDOWN: Interface BRI0/0:1, changed state to down   ←   Backup interface
                                                                goes down
%LINK-3-UPDOWN: Interface BRI0/0:2, changed state to down
%LINEPROTO-5-UPDOWN: Line protocol on Interface BRI0/0:1, changed state to down
%LINEPROTO-5-UPDOWN: Line protocol on Interface BRI0/0:2, changed state to down
%LINEPROTO-5-UPDOWN: Line protocol on Interface Virtual-Access1, changed state
to down
%ISDN-6-DISCONNECT: Interface BRI0/0:1  disconnected from unknown , call lasted
163 seconds
%ISDN-6-DISCONNECT: Interface BRI0/0:2  disconnected from unknown , call lasted
130 seconds
%LINK-3-UPDOWN: Interface Virtual-Access1, changed state to down
%LINK-5-CHANGED: Interface BRI0/0, changed state to standby mode
%LINK-3-UPDOWN: Interface BRI0/0:1, changed state to down
%LINK-3-UPDOWN: Interface BRI0/0:2, changed state to down

.!!!!!!!!!!!!!!!!!!!!!!!!!!!!!!!!!!!!!!!!!!!!!!!!!!!!!!!!!!!!!!!!!!!!
!!!!!!!!!!!!!!!!!!!!!!!!!!!!!!!!!!!!!!!!!!!!!!!!!!!!!!!!!!!!!!!!!!!!!!
!!!!!!!!!!!!!!!!!!!!!!!!!!!!!!!!!!!!!!!!!!!!!!!!!!!!!!!!!!!!!!!!!!!!!!
Success rate is 99 percent (2243/2245), round-trip min/avg/max = 20/26/64 ms
```

Verify that the ISDN call has terminated with the show isdn status command. Notice that there are no layer 3 calls currently active.

```
RouterA#show isdn status
The current ISDN Switchtype = basic-ni1
ISDN BRI0/0 interface
    Layer 1 Status:
      DEACTIVATED
    Layer 2 Status:
      TEI = 64, State = TEI_ASSIGNED
      TEI = 65, State = TEI_ASSIGNED
    Spid Status:
      TEI 64, ces = 1, state = 5(init)
          spid1 configured, spid1 sent, spid1 valid
          Endpoint ID Info: epsf = 0, usid = 70, tid = 1
      TEI 65, ces = 2, state = 5(init)
          spid2 configured, spid2 sent, spid2 valid
          Endpoint ID Info: epsf = 0, usid = 70, tid = 2
    Layer 3 Status:
      0 Active Layer 3 Call(s)   ←   The call has completed
    Activated dsl 0 CCBs = 0
 Total Allocated ISDN CCBs = 0
```

MLPPP status can be verified with the **show ppp multilink** command. Because all the ISDN BRI channels have disconnected, there will not be any active MLPPP bundles on the router.

```
RouterA#show ppp multi
No active bundles
```

Interface s0/0 should now be in an up / up state.

```
RouterA#show interface s 0/0
Serial0/0 is up, line protocol is up
  Hardware is QUICC Serial
  Internet address is 193.1.1.1/24
  Backup interface BRI0/0, kickin load not set, kickout load not set
        failure delay 5 sec, secondary disable delay 20 sec
  MTU 1500 bytes, BW 1544 Kbit, DLY 20000 usec, rely 255/255, load 1/255
  Encapsulation PPP, loopback not set, keepalive set (10 sec)
  LCP Open
  Open: IPCP, CDP
  Last input 00:00:00, output 00:00:00, output hang never
  Last clearing of "show interface" counters never
  Input queue: 0/75/0 (size/max/drops); Total output drops: 0
  Queueing strategy: weighted fair
  Output queue: 0/64/0 (size/threshold/drops)
     Conversations  0/1 (active/max active)
     Reserved Conversations 0/0 (allocated/max allocated)
  5 minute input rate 0 bits/sec, 0 packets/sec
  5 minute output rate 5000 bits/sec, 5 packets/sec
     2015 packets input, 216161 bytes, 0 no buffer
     Received 0 broadcasts, 0 runts, 1 giants, 0 throttles
     5 input errors, 1 CRC, 3 frame, 0 overrun, 0 ignored, 1 abort
     2471 packets output, 240038 bytes, 0 underruns
     0 output errors, 0 collisions, 46 interface resets
  0 output buffer failures, 0 output buffers swapped out
     14 carrier transitions
     DCD=up  DSR=up  DTR=up  RTS=up  CTS=up
```

Let's take a look at the routing table for our router. Notice that the route to the Ethernet interface (197.1.1.0) on RouterB is now being learned via 193.1.1.2, which is the serial interface on RouterB. The routes that were learned via the BRI interface on network 196.1.1.0 have now been deleted from the routing table. Routes that are learned via a specific interface are deleted if that interface goes down.

```
RouterA#show ip route
Codes: C - connected, S - static, I - IGRP, R - RIP, M - mobile, B - BGP
       D - EIGRP, EX - EIGRP external, O - OSPF, IA - OSPF inter area
       N1 - OSPF NSSA external type 1, N2 - OSPF NSSA external type 2
       E1 - OSPF external type 1, E2 - OSPF external type 2, E - EGP
       i - IS-IS, L1 - IS-IS level-1, L2 - IS-IS level-2, * - candidate default
       U - per-user static route, o - ODR

Gateway of last resort is not set
```

```
        193.1.1.0/24 is variably subnetted, 2 subnets, 2 masks
C           193.1.1.0/24 is directly connected, Serial0/0
C           193.1.1.2/32 is directly connected, Serial0/0
C       195.1.1.0/24 is directly connected, Ethernet0/0
R       196.1.1.0/24 [120/1] via 193.1.1.2, 00:00:09, Serial0/0
R       197.1.1.0/24 [120/1] via 193.1.1.2, 00:00:09, Serial0/0
```

Lab # 4: Floating Static Routes

Equipment Needed

The following equipment is needed to perform this lab exercise:

■ Two Cisco routers, each of which must have a single ISDN BRI interface, a single serial interface, and an Ethernet interface

■ Two ISDN BRI circuits

■ A Cisco V.35 DCE/DTE crossover cable. If you cannot get a crossover cable, you can use a Cisco DCE cable connected to a Cisco DTE cable.

■ Cisco IOS 11.2 or higher

■ A PC running a terminal emulation program for console port connection on the routers

Configuration Overview

This configuration demonstrates how to use a floating static route for ISDN dial backup. A floating static route is a statically defined route that has a higher administrative cost then routes learned through the dynamic routing algorithm that is being run. For example, in this lab, we will use RIP as our dynamic routing algorithm. Routes that are learned via RIP have an administrative distance of 120. In this lab, we will define a floating static route that has an administrative distance of 121. A route with a higher administrative distance then other routes will not be installed in the routing table until other routes to that same destination with lower administrative costs are removed.

ISDN backup with floating static routes uses static routes with high administrative distance in the following way: Two routes will exist to a given destination. One route will be learned dynamically via the primary leased line circuit. The second route will be defined statically and will exist via an ISDN interface. This second route will have a higher administrative distance than the first route. This static route will only take effect when the dynamic route is deleted from the routing table. When this static route takes effect, the route will cause the router to place an ISDN call. When the dynamic route is added back to the routing table, it will take precedence over the static route because it has a lower administrative distance.

The two routers are connected, as shown in Figure 3–15. RouterA and RouterB are connected to an Adtran Atlas 800 ISDN switch.

Figure 3–15
Lab #4

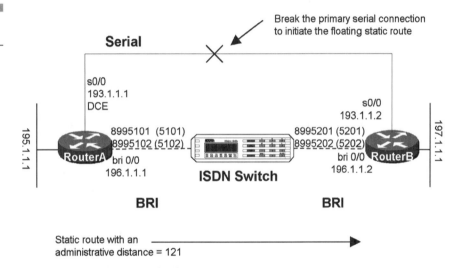

A PC running a terminal emulation program should be connected to the console port of one of the routers using a Cisco rolled cable.

NOTE: *Floating static routes have a key advantage over backup interfaces. When you use a floating static route, you can test the ISDN interface by pinging the far end of the ISDN circuit. This action can be done while customer traffic is still traversing the router. A backup interface is more difficult to test, because the primary interface has to be either brought down—or the backup statement removed.*

NOTE: *RouterA is acting as a DCE on interface s0/0, providing clocking to RouterB.*

ISDN Switch Setup

If you do not have access to actual ISDN circuits, you can use an ISDN desktop switch. Information on configuring an ISDN desktop switch can be found in the ISDN Switch Configuration section earlier in this chapter.

Router Configuration

The configurations for the two routers in this example are as follows (ISDN commands are highlighted in bold):

RouterA

```
RouterA#show run
Building configuration...

Current configuration:
!
version 11.2
no service udp-small-servers
no service tcp-small-servers
!
hostname RouterA
!
enable password cisco
!
username RouterB password 7 070C285F4D06
isdn switch-type basic-ni1   ←  Set D channel call control
!
interface Ethernet0/0
 ip address 195.1.1.1 255.255.255.0
 no keepalive
!
interface Serial0/0
 ip address 193.1.1.1 255.255.255.0
 encapsulation ppp
 clockrate 64000
!
interface BRI0/0
 ip address 196.1.1.1 255.255.255.0
 encapsulation ppp
 isdn spid1 5101 8995101   ←  Set SPID for both B channels
 isdn spid2 5102 8995102
 dialer idle-timeout 90   ←  Disconnect 90 seconds after last interesting
                             packet
 dialer map ip 196.1.1.2 name RouterB broadcast 8995201   ←  Associate next
                                                             hop address and
                                                             dialer string
```

```
 dialer load-threshold 1  ←  Define the threshold for adding additional B
                                channels
 dialer-group 1   ←  Associate interface with dialer-list 1
 no fair-queue
 ppp authentication chap
 ppp multilink
!
router rip
 network 195.1.1.0
 network 193.1.1.0
!
no ip classless
ip route 0.0.0.0 0.0.0.0 196.1.1.2 121  ←  Floating Static route pointing to
                                             the BRI interface on RouterB
dialer-list 1 protocol ip permit  ←  Define interesting traffic
!
line con 0
 password cisco
 login
line aux 0
line vty 0 4
 password cisco
 login
!
end
```

RouterB

```
RouterB#show run
Building configuration...

Current configuration:
!
version 11.2
service timestamps debug datetime localtime
no service udp-small-servers
no service tcp-small-servers
!
hostname RouterB
!
enable password cisco
!
username RouterA password 7 094F471A1A0A
isdn switch-type basic-ni1  ←  Set D channel call control
!
interface Ethernet0/0
 ip address 197.1.1.1 255.255.255.0
 no keepalive
!
interface Serial0/0
 ip address 193.1.1.2 255.255.255.0
 encapsulation ppp
```

```
!
interface BRI0/0
 ip address 196.1.1.2 255.255.255.0
 encapsulation ppp
 isdn spid1 5201 8995201   ←  Set the SPID for both B channels
 isdn spid2 5202 8995202
 dialer idle-timeout 90  ← Define the interesting traffic timeout
 dialer map ip 196.1.1.1 name RouterA  ← Define a next hop address
 dialer-group 1  ←  Associate this interface with dialer-list 1
 no fair-queue
 ppp authentication chap
 ppp multilink
!
router rip
 network 193.1.1.0
 network 197.1.1.0
!
no ip classless
dialer-list 1 protocol ip permit   ← Define interesting traffic
!
line con 0
line aux 0
line vty 0 4
 password cisco
 login
!
end
```

Monitoring and Testing the Configuration

Let's start by examining the routing table of RouterA. We see two interesting items. First, notice that RouterA has learned a route to the Ethernet interface of RouterB (197.1.1.0). This route is via 193.1.1.2, which is the serial connection between RouterA and RouterB. The route is dynamically learned via RIP and has a default administrative distance of 120. Second, there is a static default route via 196.1.1.2 with an administrative distance of 121. This route will not take effect until the first route is deleted from the routing table.

```
RouterA#show ip route
Codes: C - connected, S - static, I - IGRP, R - RIP, M - mobile, B - BGP
       D - EIGRP, EX - EIGRP external, O - OSPF, IA - OSPF inter area
       N1 - OSPF NSSA external type 1, N2 - OSPF NSSA external type 2
       E1 - OSPF external type 1, E2 - OSPF external type 2, E - EGP
       i - IS-IS, L1 - IS-IS level-1, L2 - IS-IS level-2, * - candidate default
       U - per-user static route, o - ODR

Gateway of last resort is 196.1.1.2 to network 0.0.0.0
```

```
        193.1.1.0/24 is variably subnetted, 2 subnets, 2 masks
C          193.1.1.0/24 is directly connected, Serial0/0
C          193.1.1.2/32 is directly connected, Serial0/0
C       195.1.1.0/24 is directly connected, Ethernet0/0
C       196.1.1.0/24 is directly connected, BRI0/0
R       197.1.1.0/24 [120/1] via 193.1.1.2, 00:00:12, Serial0/0
S*      0.0.0.0/0 [121/0] via 196.1.1.2  ←  Floating Static with administrative
                                                distance of 121
```

Verify that the ISDN interface is ready to place a call by typing the **show isdn status** command. Notice that RouterA has sent a SPID to the ISDN switch for each of the two B channels on the BRI interface. Also, notice that there are no active layer 3 calls.

```
RouterA#show isdn status
The current ISDN Switchtype = basic-ni1
ISDN BRI0/0 interface
    Layer 1 Status:
        ACTIVE
    Layer 2 Status:
        TEI = 64, State = MULTIPLE_FRAME_ESTABLISHED
        TEI = 65, State = MULTIPLE_FRAME_ESTABLISHED
    Spid Status:
        TEI 64, ces = 1, state = 5(init)
            spid1 configured, spid1 sent, spid1 valid  ←  SPID #1 is ok
            Endpoint ID Info: epsf = 0, usid = 70, tid = 1
        TEI 65, ces = 2, state = 5(init)
            spid2 configured, spid2 sent, spid2 valid  ←  SPID #2 is ok
            Endpoint ID Info: epsf = 0, usid = 70, tid = 2
    Layer 3 Status:
        0 Active Layer 3 Call(s)  ←  No active calls on the router
    Activated dsl 0 CCBs = 1
        CCB:callid=0, sapi=0, ces=1, B-chan=0
  Total Allocated ISDN CCBs = 1
```

Type **show interface bri 0/0** to view the status of the bri interface on the router. The up/up (spoofing) status indicates that the D channel between RouterA and the ISDN switch is active.

```
RouterA#show interface bri 0/0
BRI0/0 is up, line protocol is up (spoofing)  ←  D channel is active
   Hardware is QUICC BRI with U interface
   Internet address is 196.1.1.1/24
   MTU 1500 bytes, BW 64 Kbit, DLY 20000 usec, rely 255/255, load 1/255
   Encapsulation PPP, loopback not set
   Last input 00:00:04, output never, output hang never
   Last clearing of "show interface" counters never
   Queueing strategy: fifo
   Output queue 0/40, 0 drops; input queue 0/75, 0 drops
   5 minute input rate 0 bits/sec, 0 packets/sec
   5 minute output rate 0 bits/sec, 0 packets/sec
```

```
585 packets input, 2468 bytes, 0 no buffer
Received 0 broadcasts, 0 runts, 0 giants, 0 throttles
0 input errors, 0 CRC, 0 frame, 0 overrun, 0 ignored, 0 abort
585 packets output, 2580 bytes, 0 underruns
0 output errors, 0 collisions, 4 interface resets
0 output buffer failures, 0 output buffers swapped out
1 carrier transitions
```

The two B channels on the bri interface will be in a down/down state until a call is made. You can verify this status with the **show interface bri 0/0:1** and **show interface bri 0/0:2** commands.

```
RouterA#show interface bri 0/0:1
BRI0/0:1 is down, line protocol is down   ←   BRI Channel #1
  Hardware is QUICC BRI with U interface
  MTU 1500 bytes, BW 64 Kbit, DLY 20000 usec, rely 255/255, load 1/255
  Encapsulation PPP, loopback not set, keepalive set (10 sec)
  LCP Closed, multilink Closed
  Closed: IPCP, CDP
  Last input 00:26:59, output 00:26:59, output hang never
  Last clearing of "show interface" counters never
  Queueing strategy: fifo
  Output queue 0/40, 0 drops; input queue 0/75, 0 drops
  5 minute input rate 0 bits/sec, 0 packets/sec
  5 minute output rate 0 bits/sec, 0 packets/sec
     7248 packets input, 427881 bytes, 0 no buffer
     Received 0 broadcasts, 0 runts, 0 giants, 0 throttles
     0 input errors, 0 CRC, 0 frame, 0 overrun, 0 ignored, 0 abort
     3897 packets output, 226871 bytes, 0 underruns
     0 output errors, 0 collisions, 0 interface resets
     0 output buffer failures, 0 output buffers swapped out
     6 carrier transitions

RouterA#show interface bri 0/0:2
BRI0/0:2 is down, line protocol is down   ←   BRI Channel #2
  Hardware is QUICC BRI with U interface
  MTU 1500 bytes, BW 64 Kbit, DLY 20000 usec, rely 255/255, load 1/255
  Encapsulation PPP, loopback not set, keepalive set (10 sec)
  LCP Closed, multilink Closed
  Closed: IPCP, CDP
  Last input 00:27:02, output 00:27:02, output hang never
  Last clearing of "show interface" counters never
  Queueing strategy: fifo
  Output queue 0/40, 0 drops; input queue 0/75, 0 drops
  5 minute input rate 0 bits/sec, 0 packets/sec
  5 minute output rate 0 bits/sec, 0 packets/sec
     7229 packets input, 413782 bytes, 0 no buffer
     Received 0 broadcasts, 0 runts, 0 giants, 0 throttles
     0 input errors, 0 CRC, 0 frame, 0 overrun, 0 ignored, 0 abort
     3882 packets output, 219712 bytes, 0 underruns
     0 output errors, 0 collisions, 0 interface resets
```

```
      0 output buffer failures, 0 output buffers swapped out
      6 carrier transitions
```

Type **show dialer** to view the status of the dialer on RouterA. We see that both B channels are in an idle state. We also see that this interface will dial 8995201 to place its call.

```
RouterA#show dialer

BRI0/0 - dialer type = ISDN

Dial String      Successes    Failures    Last called    Last status
8995201                  6           0     00:28:40        successful
0 incoming call(s) have been screened.

BRI0/0:1 - dialer type = ISDN
Idle timer (90 secs), Fast idle timer (20 secs)
Wait for carrier (30 secs), Re-enable (15 secs)
Dialer state is idle

BRI0/0:2 - dialer type = ISDN
Idle timer (90 secs), Fast idle timer (20 secs)
Wait for carrier (30 secs), Re-enable (15 secs)
Dialer state is idle
```

Now let's connect to RouterB. View the routing table for RouterB with the **show ip route** command. RouterB has a route to the Ethernet interface (195.1.1.0) on RouterA via the serial 0/0 interface.

```
RouterB#show ip route
Codes: C - connected, S - static, I - IGRP, R - RIP, M - mobile, B - BGP
       D - EIGRP, EX - EIGRP external, O - OSPF, IA - OSPF inter area
       N1 - OSPF NSSA external type 1, N2 - OSPF NSSA external type 2
       E1 - OSPF external type 1, E2 - OSPF external type 2, E - EGP
       i - IS-IS, L1 - IS-IS level-1, L2 - IS-IS level-2, * - candidate default
       U - per-user static route, o - ODR

Gateway of last resort is 193.1.1.1 to network 0.0.0.0

      193.1.1.0/24 is variably subnetted, 2 subnets, 2 masks
C        193.1.1.1/32 is directly connected, Serial0/0
C        193.1.1.0/24 is directly connected, Serial0/0
R     195.1.1.0/24 [120/1] via 193.1.1.1, 00:00:07, Serial0/0
C     196.1.1.0/24 is directly connected, BRI0/0
C     197.1.1.0/24 is directly connected, Ethernet0/0
R*    0.0.0.0/0 [120/1] via 193.1.1.1, 00:00:07, Serial0/0
```

Verify that the ISDN interface on RouterB is ready to receive a call with the **show isdn status** command. We see that the SPID for both B channels has been sent, and there are no active calls on RouterB.

```
RouterB#show isdn status
The current ISDN Switchtype = basic-ni1
ISDN BRI0/0 interface
    Layer 1 Status:
      ACTIVE
    Layer 2 Status:
      TEI = 64, State = MULTIPLE_FRAME_ESTABLISHED
      TEI = 65, State = MULTIPLE_FRAME_ESTABLISHED
    Spid Status:
      TEI 64, ces = 1, state = 5(init)
          spid1 configured, spid1 sent, spid1 valid
          Endpoint ID Info: epsf = 0, usid = 70, tid = 1
      TEI 65, ces = 2, state = 5(init)
          spid2 configured, spid2 sent, spid2 valid
          Endpoint ID Info: epsf = 0, usid = 70, tid = 2
    Layer 3 Status:
      0 Active Layer 3 Call(s)
    Activated dsl 0 CCBs = 1
      CCB:callid=0, callref=0, sapi=0, ces=1, B-chan=0
    Number of active calls = 0
    Number of available B-channels = 2
  Total Allocated ISDN CCBs = 1
```

The **show dialer** command for RouterB reveals that the interface is configured to accept a call, because there is no dial string associated with the interface.

```
RouterB#show dialer

BRI0/0 - dialer type = ISDN

Dial String      Successes   Failures    Last called   Last status
0 incoming call(s) have been screened.

BRI0/0:1 - dialer type = ISDN
Idle timer (90 secs), Fast idle timer (20 secs)
Wait for carrier (30 secs), Re-enable (15 secs)
Dialer state is idle

BRI0/0:2 - dialer type = ISDN
Idle timer (90 secs), Fast idle timer (20 secs)
Wait for carrier (30 secs), Re-enable (15 secs)
Dialer state is idle
```

Verify that the D channel is active on the bri0/0 interface of RouterB with the **show interface bri 0/0** command. The up/up (spoofing) status of the interface indicates that the D channel is active.

```
RouterB#show interface bri 0/0
BRI0/0 is up, line protocol is up (spoofing)   ←   Active D channel
  Hardware is QUICC BRI with U interface
```

```
Internet address is 196.1.1.2/24
MTU 1500 bytes, BW 64 Kbit, DLY 20000 usec, rely 255/255, load 1/255
Encapsulation PPP, loopback not set
Last input 00:00:00, output never, output hang never
Last clearing of "show interface" counters never
Queueing strategy: fifo
Output queue 0/40, 0 drops; input queue 0/75, 0 drops
5 minute input rate 0 bits/sec, 0 packets/sec
5 minute output rate 0 bits/sec, 0 packets/sec
   595 packets input, 2700 bytes, 0 no buffer
   Received 0 broadcasts, 0 runts, 0 giants, 0 throttles
   0 input errors, 0 CRC, 0 frame, 0 overrun, 0 ignored, 0 abort
   589 packets output, 2446 bytes, 0 underruns
   0 output errors, 0 collisions, 5 interface resets
   0 output buffer failures, 0 output buffers swapped out
   1 carrier transitions
```

Both of the B channels on the bri interface will be in a down / down state until a call is made. You can verify this status with the **show interface bri 0/0:1** and **show interface bri 0/0:2** command.

```
RouterB#show interface bri 0/0:1
BRI0/0:1 is down, line protocol is down
   Hardware is QUICC BRI with U interface
   MTU 1500 bytes, BW 64 Kbit, DLY 20000 usec, rely 255/255, load 1/255
   Encapsulation PPP, loopback not set, keepalive set (10 sec)
   LCP Closed, multilink Closed
   Closed: IPCP, CDP
   Last input 00:28:19, output 00:28:19, output hang never
   Last clearing of "show interface" counters never
   Queueing strategy: fifo
   Output queue 0/40, 0 drops; input queue 0/75, 0 drops
   5 minute input rate 0 bits/sec, 0 packets/sec
   5 minute output rate 0 bits/sec, 0 packets/sec
      3897 packets input, 226871 bytes, 0 no buffer
      Received 0 broadcasts, 0 runts, 0 giants, 0 throttles
      0 input errors, 0 CRC, 0 frame, 0 overrun, 0 ignored, 0 abort
      7248 packets output, 427881 bytes, 0 underruns
      0 output errors, 0 collisions, 0 interface resets
      0 output buffer failures, 0 output buffers swapped out
      9 carrier transitions

RouterB#show interface bri 0/0:2
BRI0/0:2 is down, line protocol is down
   Hardware is QUICC BRI with U interface
   MTU 1500 bytes, BW 64 Kbit, DLY 20000 usec, rely 255/255, load 1/255
   Encapsulation PPP, loopback not set, keepalive set (10 sec)
   LCP Closed, multilink Closed
   Closed: IPCP, CDP
   Last input 00:28:22, output 00:28:22, output hang never
   Last clearing of "show interface" counters never
   Queueing strategy: fifo
```

```
Output queue 0/40, 0 drops; input queue 0/75, 0 drops
5 minute input rate 0 bits/sec, 0 packets/sec
5 minute output rate 0 bits/sec, 0 packets/sec
    3882 packets input, 219712 bytes, 0 no buffer
    Received 0 broadcasts, 0 runts, 0 giants, 0 throttles
    0 input errors, 0 CRC, 0 frame, 0 overrun, 0 ignored, 0 abort
    7229 packets output, 413782 bytes, 0 underruns
    0 output errors, 0 collisions, 0 interface resets
    0 output buffer failures, 0 output buffers swapped out
    9 carrier transitions
```

Let's reconnect to RouterA. Turn on PPP authentication debugging and ISDN Q931 debugging with the **debug ppp authentication** and **debug isdn q931** commands. You can verify which debug commands are enabled with the **show debug** command.

```
RouterA#show debug
PPP:
  PPP authentication debugging is on
ISDN:
  ISDN Q931 packets debugging is on
```

A major advantage of a floating static route over a backup interface is the fact that a floating static route can be tested via a ping command while traffic flows over the primary interface. Let's activate the ISDN circuit with the **ping 196.1.1.2** command. Notice that the ping command causes the ISDN interface to activate and causes both B channels to connect.

```
RouterA#ping 196.1.1.2

Type escape sequence to abort.
Sending 5, 100-byte ICMP Echos to 196.1.1.2, timeout is 2 seconds:

ISDN BR0/0: TX ->  SETUP pd = 8  callref = 0x07
        Bearer Capability i = 0x8890
        Channel ID i = 0x83
        Keypad Facility i = '8995201'
ISDN BR0/0: RX <-  CALL_PROC pd = 8  callref = 0x87
        Channel ID i = 0x89
ISDN BR0/0: RX <-  CONNECT pd = 8  callref = 0x87
        Channel ID i = 0x89
%LINK-3-UPDOWN: Interface BRI0/0:1, changed state to up   ←  Channel #1 is
                                                             active
PPP BRI0/0:1: treating connection as a callout
ISDN BR0/0: TX ->  CONNECT_ACK pd = 8  callref = 0x07
PPP BRI0/0:1: Send CHAP Challenge id=4   ←  Chap challenge for channel #1
PPP BRI0/0:1: CHAP Challenge id=4 received from RouterB
PPP BRI0/0:1: Send CHAP Response id=4
PPP BRI0/0:1: CHAP response received from RouterB
```

```
PPP 'BRI0/0:1: CHAP Response id=4 received from RouterB
PPP BRI0/0:1: Send CHAP Success id=4
PPP BRI0/0:1: remote passed CHAP authentication
PPP BRI0/0:1: Passed CHAP authentication with remote
%LINK-3-UPDOWN: Interface Virtual-Access1, changed state to up
PPP Virtual-Access1: treating connection as a callin
%LINEPROTO-5-UPDOWN: Line protocol on I.nterface BRI0/0:1, changed state to up
%LINEPROTO-5-UPDOWN: Line protocol on Interface Virtual-Access1, changed state
to up
ISDN BR0/0: TX ->  SETUP pd = 8  callref = 0x08
        Bearer Capability i = 0x8890
        Channel ID i = 0x83
        Keypad Facility i = '8995201'
ISDN BR0/0: RX <-  CALL_PROC pd = 8  callref = 0x88
        Channel ID i = 0x8A
ISDN BR0/0: Event: incoming ces value = 2
ISDN BR0/0: RX <-  CONNECT pd = 8  callref = 0x88
        Channel ID i = 0x8A
ISDN BR0/0: Event: incoming ces value = 2
%LINK-3-UPDOWN: Interface BRI0/0:2, changed state to up   ←  Channel #2 is
                                                             active
PPP BRI0/0:2: treating connection as a callout
RouterA#SDN BR0/0: TX ->  CONNECT_ACK pd = 8  callref = 0x08
PPP BRI0/0:2: Send CHAP Challenge id=4   ←  Chap challenge for channel #2
PPP BRI0/0:2: CHAP Challenge id=4 received from RouterB
PPP BRI0/0:2: Send CHAP Response id=4
PPP BRI0/0:2: CHAP response received from RouterB
PPP BRI0/0:2: CHAP Response id=4 received from RouterB
PPP BRI0/0:2: Send CHAP Success id=4
PPP BRI0/0:2: remote passed CHAP authentication
PPP BRI0/0:2: Passed CHAP authentication with remote
%LINEPROTO-5-UPDOWN: Line protocol on Interface BRI0/0:2, changed state to up
%ISDN-6-CONNECT: Interface BRI0/0:2 is now connected to 8995201 RouterB

..!!!
Success rate is 60 percent (3/5), round-trip min/avg/max = 20/22/24 ms
```

As we can see, the ping was successful. The first two ping packets were lost, because the interface was still coming up when the packets were being sent.

Let's make sure that an MLPPP bundle has been established. Type the **show ppp multilink** command. Notice that there is an active MLPPP bundle consisting of two members.

```
RouterA#show ppp multi

Bundle RouterB, 2 members, Master link is Virtual-Access1
Dialer Interface is BRI0/0
  0 lost fragments, 0 reordered, 0 unassigned, sequence 0x1A/0x1C rcvd/sent
  0 discarded, 0 lost received, 1/255 load
```

```
Member Links: 2  ←  MLPPP bundle consisting of both B channels on bri0/0
BRI0/0:1
BRI0/0:2
```

The **show isdn status** command will verify that there are two active calls on the router. Each of the B channels on the BRI is considered a separate call.

```
RouterA#show isdn status
The current ISDN Switchtype = basic-ni1
ISDN BRI0/0 interface
    Layer 1 Status:
      ACTIVE
    Layer 2 Status:
      TEI = 64, State = MULTIPLE_FRAME_ESTABLISHED
      TEI = 65, State = MULTIPLE_FRAME_ESTABLISHED
    Spid Status:
      TEI 64, ces = 1, state = 5(init)
          spid1 configured, spid1 sent, spid1 valid
          Endpoint ID Info: epsf = 0, usid = 70, tid = 1
      TEI 65, ces = 2, state = 5(init)
          spid2 configured, spid2 sent, spid2 valid
          Endpoint ID Info: epsf = 0, usid = 70, tid = 2
    Layer 3 Status:
      2 Active Layer 3 Call(s)  ←  Both B channels on the BRI are connected
    Activated dsl 0 CCBs = 3
      CCB:callid=0, sapi=0, ces=1, B-chan=0
      CCB:callid=8007, sapi=0, ces=1, B-chan=1
      CCB:callid=8008, sapi=0, ces=2, B-chan=2
  Total Allocated ISDN CCBs = 3
```

Notice that the D channel of the BRI is still in an up/up (spoofing) state, although two calls are connected.

```
RouterA#show interface bri 0/0
BRI0/0 is up, line protocol is up (spoofing)  ←  D channel status is active
  Hardware is QUICC BRI with U interface
  Internet address is 196.1.1.1/24
  MTU 1500 bytes, BW 64 Kbit, DLY 20000 usec, rely 255/255, load 1/255
  Encapsulation PPP, loopback not set
  Last input 00:00:01, output never, output hang never
  Last clearing of "show interface" counters never
  Queueing strategy: fifo
  Output queue 0/40, 0 drops; input queue 0/75, 0 drops
  5 minute input rate 0 bits/sec, 0 packets/sec
  5 minute output rate 0 bits/sec, 0 packets/sec
     622 packets input, 2644 bytes, 0 no buffer
     Received 0 broadcasts, 0 runts, 0 giants, 0 throttles
     0 input errors, 0 CRC, 0 frame, 0 overrun, 0 ignored, 0 abort
     622 packets output, 2776 bytes, 0 underruns
```

```
0 output errors, 0 collisions, 4 interface resets
0 output buffer failures, 0 output buffers swapped out
1 carrier transitions
```

Each of the two B channels on the BRI will now be in an up/up state, because we have an active call connected on each channel. Notice that there is no IP address associated with either B channel. The IP address appears under the **show interface bri 0/0** output of the D channel.

```
RouterA#show interface bri 0/0:1
BRI0/0:1 is up, line protocol is up   ←   B channel #1
  Hardware is QUICC BRI with U interface
  MTU 1500 bytes, BW 64 Kbit, DLY 20000 usec, rely 255/255, load 1/255
  Encapsulation PPP, loopback not set, keepalive set (10 sec)
  LCP Open, multilink Open
  Last input 00:00:03, output 00:00:03, output hang never
  Last clearing of "show interface" counters never
  Queueing strategy: fifo
  Output queue 0/40, 0 drops; input queue 0/75, 0 drops
  5 minute input rate 0 bits/sec, 0 packets/sec
  5 minute output rate 0 bits/sec, 0 packets/sec
     7280 packets input, 428983 bytes, 0 no buffer
     Received 0 broadcasts, 0 runts, 0 giants, 0 throttles
     0 input errors, 0 CRC, 0 frame, 0 overrun, 0 ignored, 0 abort
     3928 packets output, 228097 bytes, 0 underruns
     0 output errors, 0 collisions, 0 interface resets
     0 output buffer failures, 0 output buffers swapped out
     7 carrier transitions

RouterA#show interface bri 0/0:2
BRI0/0:2 is up, line protocol is up   ←   B channel #2
  Hardware is QUICC BRI with U interface
  MTU 1500 bytes, BW 64 Kbit, DLY 20000 usec, rely 255/255, load 1/255
  Encapsulation PPP, loopback not set, keepalive set (10 sec)
  LCP Open, multilink Open
  Last input 00:00:02, output 00:00:02, output hang never
  Last clearing of "show interface" counters never
  Queueing strategy: fifo
  Output queue 0/40, 0 drops; input queue 0/75, 0 drops
  5 minute input rate 0 bits/sec, 0 packets/sec
  5 minute output rate 0 bits/sec, 0 packets/sec
     7252 packets input, 414754 bytes, 0 no buffer
     Received 0 broadcasts, 0 runts, 0 giants, 0 throttles
     0 input errors, 0 CRC, 0 frame, 0 overrun, 0 ignored, 0 abort
     3906 packets output, 220830 bytes, 0 underruns
     0 output errors, 0 collisions, 0 interface resets
     0 output buffer failures, 0 output buffers swapped out
     7 carrier transitions
```

After the test ping has completed, RouterA will wait 90 seconds before it brings down the ISDN circuit. This 90-second period is defined by the **dialer idle-timeout 90** statement in the configuration for RouterA.

```
%LINK-3-UPDOWN: Interface Virtual-Access1, changed state to down
%ISDN-6-DISCONNECT: Interface BRI0/0:1  disconnected from 8995201 RouterB, call
lasted 210 seconds
%ISDN-6-DISCONNECT: Interface BRI0/0:2  disconnected from 8995201 RouterB, call
lasted 207 seconds
ISDN BR0/0: TX ->  DISCONNECT pd = 8  callref = 0x09 ←  Disconnect B Channel
                                                        #1
        Cause i = 0x8090 - Normal call clearing
ISDN BR0/0: TX ->  DISCONNECT pd = 8  callref = 0x0A ←  Disconnect B Channel
                                                        #2

        Cause i = 0x8090 - Normal call clearing
ISDN BR0/0: RX <-  RELEASE pd = 8  callref = 0x89
%LINK-3-UPDOWN: Interface BRI0/0:1, changed state to down
ISDN BR0/0: TX ->  RELEASE_COMP pd = 8  callref = 0x09
ISDN BR0/0: RX <-  RELEASE pd = 8  callref = 0x8A
ISDN BR0/0: Event: incoming ces value = 2
%LINK-3-UPDOWN: Interface BRI0/0:2, changed state to down
ISDN BR0/0: TX ->  RELEASE_COMP pd = 8  callref = 0x0A
%LINEPROTO-5-UPDOWN: Line protocol on Interface BRI0/0:1, changed state to down
%LINEPROTO-5-UPDOWN: Line protocol on Interface BRI0/0:2, changed state to down
```

Now, let's test the floating static route configuration. We are going to start a ping to the Ethernet interface of RouterB at IP address 197.1.1.1. After the ping starts, we will pull the serial cable connected to interface s0/0 of RouterA.

```
RouterA#ping  ←  Start an extended ping to the Ethernet interface of RouterB
Protocol [ip]:
Target IP address: 197.1.1.1
Repeat count [5]: 100000
Datagram size [100]:
Timeout in seconds [2]:
Extended commands [n]:
Sweep range of sizes [n]:
Type escape sequence to abort.
Sending 100000, 100-byte ICMP Echos to 197.1.1.1, timeout is 2 seconds:
!!!!!!!!!!!!!!!!!!!!!!!!!!!!!!!!!!!!!!!!!!!!!!!!!!!!!!!!!!!!!!!!!!!!!!!!!!
!!!!!!!!!!!!!!!!!!!!!!!!!!!!!!!!!!!!!!  ←  After the ping has started pull the
                                           cable on the s0/0 interface of
                                           RouterA


%LINEPROTO-5-UPDOWN: Line protocol on Interface Serial0/0, changed state to
down  ←  s0/0 will go down when the cable is pulled
ISDN BR0/0: TX ->  SETUP pd = 8  callref = 0x09  ←  RouterA is making a call
                                                    to RouterB on B channel
                                                    #1

        Bearer Capability i = 0x8890
        Channel ID i = 0x83
        Keypad Facility i = '8995201'
ISDN BR0/0: RX <-  CALL_PROC pd = 8  callref = 0x89
```

```
          Channel ID i = 0x89
ISDN BR0/0: RX <-  CONNECT pd = 8   callref = 0x89
          Channel ID i = 0x89
%LINK-3-UPDOWN: Interface BRI0/0:1, changed state to up
PPP BRI0/0:1: treating connection as a callout
ISDN BR0/0: TX ->  CONNECT_ACK pd = 8   callref = 0x09
PPP BRI0/0:1: Send CHAP Challenge id=5  ←  Chap challenge for B channel #1
PPP BRI0/0:1: CHAP Challenge id=5 received from RouterB
PPP BRI0/0:1: Send CHAP Response id=5
PPP BRI0/0:1: CHAP response received from RouterB
PPP BRI0/0:1: CHAP Response id=5 received from RouterB
PPP BRI0/0:1: Send CHAP Success id=5
PPP BRI0/0:1: remote passed CHAP authentication
PPP BRI0/0:1: Passed CHAP authentication with remote  ←  Chap successful for B
                                                          channel #1
%LINK-3-UPDOWN: Interface Virtual-Access1, changed state to up
PPP Virtual-Access1: treating connection as a callin
%LINK-3-UPDOWN: Interface Serial0/0, ch.anged state to down
%LINEPROTO-5-UPDOWN: Line protocol on Interface BRI0/0:1, changed state to up
%LINEPROTO-5-UPDOWN: Line protocol on Interface Virtual-Access1, changed state
to up
ISDN BR0/0: TX ->  SETUP pd = 8   callref = 0x0A  ←  RouterA is making a call
                                                     to RouterB on B channel
                                                     #2

          Bearer Capability i = 0x8890
          Channel ID i = 0x83
          Keypad Facility i = '8995201'
ISDN BR0/0: RX <-  CALL_PROC pd = 8   callref = 0x8A
          Channel ID i = 0x8A
ISDN BR0/0: Event: incoming ces value = 2
ISDN BR0/0: RX <-  CONNECT pd = 8   callref = 0x8A
          Channel ID i = 0x8A
ISDN BR0/0: Event: incoming ces value = 2
%LINK-3-UPDOWN: Interface BRI0/0:2, changed state to up
PPP BRI0/0:2: treating connection as a callout
ISDN BR0/0: TX ->  CONNECT_ACK pd = 8   callref = 0x0A
PPP BRI0/0:2: Send CHAP Challenge id=5  ←  Chap challenge for B channel #2
PPP BRI0/0:2: CHAP Challenge id=5 received from RouterB
PPP BRI0/0:2: Send CHAP Response id=5
PPP BRI0/0:2: CHAP response received from RouterB
PPP BRI0/0:2: CHAP Response id=5 received from RouterB
PPP BRI0/0:2: Send CHAP Success id=5
PPP BRI0/0:2: remote passed CHAP authentication
PPP BRI0/0:2: Passed CHAP authentication with remote  ←  Chap successful for B
                                                          channel #2
%LINEPROTO-5-UPDOWN: Line protocol on Interface BRI0/0:2, changed state to up
%ISDN-6-CONNECT: Interface BRI0/0:2 is now connected to 8995201 RouterB

!!!!!!!!!!!!!!!!!!!!!!!!!!!!!!!!!!!!!!!!!!!!!!!!!!!!!!!!!!!!!!!!!!!!!!!!!!!!!!!
!!!!!!!!!!!!!!!!!!!!!!!!!!!!!!!!!!!!!!!!!!!!!!!!!!!!!!!!!!!!!!!!!!!!!!!!!!!!!!!
!!!!!!!!!!!!!!!!!!!!!!!!!!!!!!!!!!!!!!!!!!!!!!!!!!!!!!!!!!!!!!!!!!!!!!!!!!!!!!!
!!!!!!!!!!!!!!!!!!!!!!!!!!!!!!!!!!!!!!!!!!!!!!!!!!!!!!!!!!!!!!!!!!!!!!!.
Success rate is 99 percent (2721/2725), round-trip min/avg/max = 20/23/44 ms
```

Notice that in this example, the dial backup occurred quickly. We only lost four pings between the time that interface s0/0 went down and we were able to make an ISDN backup call on interface bri0/0.

Let's view the routing table with the **show ip route** command. Notice that the RIP route to RouterB has been deleted from the routing table. This situation occurred because interface s0/0 went to a down state when the cable was pulled. Connectivity to RouterB is now being achieved via the static route, which we defined with an administrative distance of 121.

```
RouterA#show ip route
Codes: C - connected, S - static, I - IGRP, R - RIP, M - mobile, B - BGP
       D - EIGRP, EX - EIGRP external, O - OSPF, IA - OSPF inter area
       N1 - OSPF NSSA external type 1, N2 - OSPF NSSA external type 2
       E1 - OSPF external type 1, E2 - OSPF external type 2, E - EGP
       i - IS-IS, L1 - IS-IS level-1, L2 - IS-IS level-2, * - candidate default
       U - per-user static route, o - ODR

Gateway of last resort is 196.1.1.2 to network 0.0.0.0

C    195.1.1.0/24 is directly connected, Ethernet0/0
     196.1.1.0/24 is variably subnetted, 2 subnets, 2 masks
C        196.1.1.0/24 is directly connected, BRI0/0
C        196.1.1.2/32 is directly connected, BRI0/0
S*   0.0.0.0/0 [121/0] via 196.1.1.2
```

Let's type the **show ppp multilink** command to verify that we have established an MLPPP bundle between RouterA and RouterB.

```
RouterA#show ppp multi

Bundle RouterB, 2 members, Master link is Virtual-Access1
Dialer Interface is BRI0/0
  0 lost fragments, 17 reordered, 0 unassigned, sequence 0x1470/0x1474 rcvd/sent
  0 discarded, 0 lost received, 43/255 load

Member Links: 2  ←  Both B channels are in an MLPPP bundle
BRI0/0:1
BRI0/0:2
```

Let's look at the status of the dialer by typing the **show dialer** command. Notice that the dial reason is listed for each of the two B channels of the BRI. The dial reason indicates what interesting traffic caused the ISDN circuit to place a call to the far-end router. The reason that B channel #1 dialed RouterB was due to the ping. This process is written as **(s=196.1.1.1, d=197.1.1.1)** which means that traffic was sent to 197.1.1.1 (the Ethernet interface of RouterB) from 196.1.1.1 (the bri interface of RouterA). The reason that B channel #2 dialed was due to the MLPPP bundle being overloaded. This situation is determined by the **dialer load-threshold 1** statement in the configuration of RouterA.

```
RouterA#show dialer

BRI0/0 - dialer type = ISDN

Dial String       Successes    Failures    Last called   Last status
8995201                  10           0    00:01:25        successful
0 incoming call(s) have been screened.

BRI0/0:1 - dialer type = ISDN  ←  B channel #1
Idle timer (90 secs), Fast idle timer (20 secs)
Wait for carrier (30 secs), Re-enable (15 secs)
Dialer state is physical layer up
Dial reason: ip (s=196.1.1.1, d=197.1.1.1)  ←  Ping to RouterB
Time until disconnect 71 secs
Current call connected 00:01:26
Connected to 8995201 (RouterB)

BRI0/0:2 - dialer type = ISDN  ←  B channel #2
Idle timer (90 secs), Fast idle timer (20 secs)
Wait for carrier (30 secs), Re-enable (15 secs)
Dialer state is physical layer up
Dial reason: Multilink bundle overloaded  ←  Dialer load threshold
Time until disconnect 73 secs
Current call connected 00:01:27
Connected to 8995201 (RouterB)
```

Now, let's start another ping to the Ethernet interface of RouterB. This time, we will reconnect the serial cable to RouterA while the ping is running.

```
RouterA#ping  ←  Start a ping to 197.1.1.1
Protocol [ip]:
Target IP address: 197.1.1.1
Repeat count [5]: 100000
Datagram size [100]:
Timeout in seconds [2]:
Extended commands [n]:
Sweep range of sizes [n]:
Type escape sequence to abort.
Sending 100000, 100-byte ICMP Echos to 197.1.1.1, timeout is 2 seconds:

!!!!!!!!!!!!!!!!!!!!!!!!!!!!!!!!!!!!!!!!!!!!!!!!!!!!!!!!!!!!!!!!!!!!!!!!!!!
!!!!!!!!!!!!!!!!!!!!!!!!!!!!!!!!!!!!!!!!!!!!!!!!!!!!!!!!!!!!!!!!!!!!!!!!!!

%LINK-3-UPDOWN: Interface Serial0/0, changed state to up  ←  Reconnect the
                                                             serial cable
                                                             between RouterA
                                                             and RouterB


PPP Serial0/0: treating connection as a dedicated line
%LINEPROTO-5-UPDOWN: Line protocol on Interface Serial0/0, changed state to up
%LINEPROTO-5-UPDOWN: Line protocol on Interface Virtual-Access1, changed state
to down
```

```
%LINK-3-UPDOWN: Interface Virtual-Access1, changed state to down
%ISDN-6-DISCONNECT: Interface BRI0/0:1  disconnected from 8995201 RouterB, call
lasted 210 seconds
%ISDN-6-DISCONNECT: Interface BRI0/0:2  disconnected from 8995201 RouterB, call
lasted 207 seconds
ISDN BR0/0: TX ->  DISCONNECT pd = 8  callref = 0x09  ← B channel #1
                                                        disconnected
        Cause i = 0x8090 - Normal call clearing
ISDN BR0/0: TX ->  DISCONNECT pd = 8  callref = 0x0A  ← B channel #2
                                                        disconnected
        Cause i = 0x8090 - Normal call clearing
ISDN BR0/0: RX <-  RELEASE pd = 8  callref = 0x89
%LINK-3-UPDOWN: Interface BRI0/0:1, changed state to down
ISDN BR0/0: TX ->  RELEASE_COMP pd = 8  callref = 0x09
ISDN BR0/0: RX <-  RELEASE pd = 8  callref = 0x8A
ISDN BR0/0: Event: incoming ces value = 2
%LINK-3-UPDOWN: Interface BRI0/0:2, changed state to down
ISDN BR0/0: TX ->  RELEASE_COMP pd = 8  callref = 0x0A
%LINEPROTO-5-UPDOWN: Line protocol on Interface BRI0/0:1, changed state to down
%LINEPROTO-5-UPDOWN: Line protocol on Interface BRI0/0:2, changed state to down


!!!!!!!!!!!!!!!!!!!!!!!!!!!!!!!!!!!!!!!!!!!!!!!!!!!!!!!!!!!!!!!!!!!!!!!!
!!!!!!!!!.
Success rate is 99 percent (4068/4070), round-trip min/avg/max = 20/26/60 ms
```

Notice that the router quickly switched the data path back to the s0/0 interface. We only lost two pings while the ISDN line disconnected and RouterA switched back to the s0/0 interface.

Let's make sure that the routing table for RouterA reflects the fact that interface s0/0 is now up and active. Type the **show ip route** command to view the routing table for RouterA. Notice that route to 197.1.1.0, which is learned via 193.1.1.2 from RIP, has reappeared in the routing table.

```
RouterA#show ip route
Codes: C - connected, S - static, I - IGRP, R - RIP, M - mobile, B - BGP
       D - EIGRP, EX - EIGRP external, O - OSPF, IA - OSPF inter area
       N1 - OSPF NSSA external type 1, N2 - OSPF NSSA external type 2
       E1 - OSPF external type 1, E2 - OSPF external type 2, E - EGP
       i - IS-IS, L1 - IS-IS level-1, L2 - IS-IS level-2, * - candidate default
       U - per-user static route, o - ODR

Gateway of last resort is 196.1.1.2 to network 0.0.0.0

     193.1.1.0/24 is variably subnetted, 2 subnets, 2 masks
C       193.1.1.0/24 is directly connected, Serial0/0
C       193.1.1.2/32 is directly connected, Serial0/0
C    195.1.1.0/24 is directly connected, Ethernet0/0
C    196.1.1.0/24 is directly connected, BRI0/0
R    197.1.1.0/24 [120/1] via 193.1.1.2, 00:00:15, Serial0/0
S*   0.0.0.0/0 [121/0] via 196.1.1.2
```

Lab #5: Dialer Profiles

Equipment Needed

The following equipment is needed to perform this lab exercise:

■ Two Cisco routers, each of which must have a single ISDN BRI interface

■ Cisco IOS 11.2 or higher

■ A PC running a terminal emulation program for console port connection on the routers

Configuration Overview

Dialer profiles enable the configuration of physical interfaces to be separated from the logical configuration required for a call. Dialer profiles also enable the logical and physical configurations to be bound together dynamically on a per-call basis.

Dialer profiles consist of the following elements:

■ A dialer pool of physical interfaces to be used by the dialer interface

■ A dialer interface (a logical entity) configuration including one or more dial strings, each of which is used to reach one destination network

When dialer profiles are used for DDR configuration, the physical interface on the router has no configuration settings except link encapsulation, SPID information, authentication, and the dialer pools to which the interface belongs.

RouterA and RouterB are configured as shown in Figure 3–16.

ISDN Switch Setup

If you do not have access to actual ISDN circuits, you can use an ISDN desktop switch. Information on configuring an ISDN desktop switch can be found in the ISDN Switch Configuration section earlier in this chapter.

Figure 3–16
Lab #5

8995101 (5101)
8995102 (5102)
RouterA bri 0/0
196.1.1.1

ISDN Switch

8995201 (5201)
8995202 (5202)
bri 0/0 **RouterB**
196.1.1.2

BRI

BRI

Router Configuration

The configurations for the two routers in this example are as follows (ISDN commands are highlighted in bold):

RouterA

```
RouterA#show run
Building configuration...

Current configuration:
!
version 11.2
no service udp-small-servers
no service tcp-small-servers
!
hostname RouterA
!
enable password cisco
!
username RouterB password 7 070C285F4D06
isdn switch-type basic-ni1   ←   Set D channel call control
!
interface BRI0/0
 no ip address
 encapsulation ppp
 isdn spid1 5101 8995101   ←   Set SPIDs for both B channels
 isdn spid2 5102 8995102
 dialer pool-member 1   ←   This interface will be part of dialer pool #1
 no fair-queue
 ppp authentication chap
 ppp multilink   ←   Request a PPP multilink session
!
interface Dialer0
 ip address 196.1.1.1 255.255.255.0
 encapsulation ppp
 dialer remote-name RouterB   ←   Hostname of  far end router
 dialer idle-timeout 90   ←   Disconnect the call 90 seconds after the last
                              interesting packet is received
```

```
 dialer string 8995201   ←  Define number to dial to reach far end
 dialer load-threshold 1  ←  Define threshold for adding additional B channels
 dialer pool 1  ←  This is dialer pool  #1
 dialer-group 1  ←  Associate this interface with dialer-list 1
!
no ip classless
ip route 196.1.1.2 255.255.255.255 Dialer0
dialer-list 1 protocol ip permit  ←  Define interesting traffic
!
line con 0
 password cisco
 login
line aux 0
line vty 0 4
 password cisco
 login
!
end
```

RouterB

```
RouterB#show run
Building configuration...

Current configuration:
!
version 11.2
service timestamps debug datetime localtime
no service udp-small-servers
no service tcp-small-servers
!
hostname RouterB
!
enable password cisco
!
username RouterA password 7 094F471A1A0A
isdn switch-type basic-ni1  ←  Set the D channel call control
!
interface Serial0/0
 ip address 193.1.1.2 255.255.255.0
 encapsulation ppp
!
interface BRI0/0
 ip address 196.1.1.2 255.255.255.0
 encapsulation ppp
 isdn spid1 5201 8995201  ←  Set the SPID for both B channels
 isdn spid2 5202 8995202
 dialer idle-timeout 90  ←  Define the interesting traffic timeout
 dialer map ip 196.1.1.1 name RouterA  ←  Define a next hop address
 dialer-group 1  ←  Associate the interface with dialer-list 1
 no fair-queue
 ppp authentication chap
```

```
 ppp multilink
 !
no ip classless
dialer-list 1 protocol ip permit   ← Define interesting traffic
 !
line con 0
line aux 0
line vty 0 4
 password cisco
 login
 !
end
```

Monitoring and Testing the Configuration

Let's start by connecting to RouterB and verifying that the ISDN circuit is up and active. Type the **show isdn status** command to view the status of the BRI circuit on RouterB. We see that the SPID for both B channels has been sent to the ISDN switch and is valid.

```
RouterB#show isdn status
The current ISDN Switchtype = basic-ni1
ISDN BRI0/0 interface
    Layer 1 Status:
       ACTIVE
    Layer 2 Status:
       TEI = 64, State = MULTIPLE_FRAME_ESTABLISHED
       TEI = 65, State = MULTIPLE_FRAME_ESTABLISHED
    Spid Status:
       TEI 64, ces = 1, state = 5(init)
           spid1 configured, spid1 sent, spid1 valid  ←   B channel #1
           Endpoint ID Info: epsf = 0, usid = 70, tid = 1
       TEI 65, ces = 2, state = 5(init)
           spid2 configured, spid2 sent, spid2 valid  ←   B channel #2
           Endpoint ID Info: epsf = 0, usid = 70, tid = 2
    Layer 3 Status:
       0 Active Layer 3 Call(s)
    Activated dsl 0 CCBs = 1
       CCB:callid=0, callref=0, sapi=0, ces=1, B-chan=0
    Number of active calls = 0
    Number of available B-channels = 2
 Total Allocated ISDN CCBs = 1
```

Let's verify the status of the bri interface and make sure that the D channel is active between RouterB and the ISDN switch. Type **show interface bri 0/0** to view the status of the D channel. The up/up (spoofing) state indicates that the D channel is up and active.

```
RouterB#show interface bri 0/0
BRI0/0 is up, line protocol is up (spoofing) ←  Active D channel
  Hardware is QUICC BRI with U interface
  Internet address is 196.1.1.2/24
  MTU 1500 bytes, BW 64 Kbit, DLY 20000 usec, rely 255/255, load 1/255
  Encapsulation PPP, loopback not set
  Last input 00:00:04, output never, output hang never
  Last clearing of "show interface" counters never
  Queueing strategy: fifo
  Output queue 0/40, 0 drops; input queue 0/75, 0 drops
  5 minute input rate 0 bits/sec, 0 packets/sec
  5 minute output rate 0 bits/sec, 0 packets/sec
     248 packets input, 1306 bytes, 0 no buffer
     Received 0 broadcasts, 0 runts, 0 giants, 0 throttles
     0 input errors, 0 CRC, 0 frame, 0 overrun, 0 ignored, 0 abort
     241 packets output, 1121 bytes, 0 underruns
     0 output errors, 0 collisions, 5 interface resets
     0 output buffer failures, 0 output buffers swapped out
     1 carrier transitions
```

Each of the two B channels will be in a down/down state, because there are no active calls on RouterB at this time.

```
RouterB#show interface bri 0/0:1
BRI0/0:1 is down, line protocol is down
  Hardware is QUICC BRI with U interface
  MTU 1500 bytes, BW 64 Kbit, DLY 20000 usec, rely 255/255, load 1/255
  Encapsulation PPP, loopback not set, keepalive set (10 sec)
  LCP Closed, multilink Closed
  Closed: IPCP, CDP
  Last input 00:01:10, output 00:01:10, output hang never
  Last clearing of "show interface" counters never
  Queueing strategy: fifo
  Output queue 0/40, 0 drops; input queue 0/75, 0 drops
  5 minute input rate 0 bits/sec, 0 packets/sec
  5 minute output rate 0 bits/sec, 0 packets/sec
     337 packets input, 16158 bytes, 0 no buffer
     Received 0 broadcasts, 0 runts, 0 giants, 0 throttles
     0 input errors, 0 CRC, 0 frame, 0 overrun, 0 ignored, 0 abort
     309 packets output, 11474 bytes, 0 underruns
     0 output errors, 0 collisions, 0 interface resets
     0 output buffer failures, 0 output buffers swapped out
     12 carrier transitions

RouterB#show interface bri 0/0:2
BRI0/0:2 is down, line protocol is down
  Hardware is QUICC BRI with U interface
  MTU 1500 bytes, BW 64 Kbit, DLY 20000 usec, rely 255/255, load 1/255
  Encapsulation PPP, loopback not set, keepalive set (10 sec)
  LCP Closed, multilink Closed
  Closed: IPCP, CDP
  Last input 00:01:12, output 00:01:13, output hang never
  Last clearing of "show interface" counters never
```

```
Queueing strategy: fifo
Output queue 0/40, 0 drops; input queue 0/75, 0 drops
5 minute input rate 0 bits/sec, 0 packets/sec
5 minute output rate 0 bits/sec, 0 packets/sec
    264 packets input, 12174 bytes, 0 no buffer
    Received 0 broadcasts, 0 runts, 0 giants, 0 throttles
    0 input errors, 0 CRC, 0 frame, 0 overrun, 0 ignored, 0 abort
    239 packets output, 9788 bytes, 0 underruns
    0 output errors, 0 collisions, 0 interface resets
    0 output buffer failures, 0 output buffers swapped out
    9 carrier transitions
```

Now, let's connect to RouterA and verify that the BRI interface is ready to place a call. Type the **show isdn status** command to view the status of the BRI interface. We see that a SPID for B channel #1 and B channel #2 has been successfully sent to the switch.

```
RouterA#show isdn status
The current ISDN Switchtype = basic-ni1
ISDN BRI0/0 interface
    Layer 1 Status:
      ACTIVE
    Layer 2 Status:
      TEI = 64, State = MULTIPLE_FRAME_ESTABLISHED
      TEI = 65, State = MULTIPLE_FRAME_ESTABLISHED
    Spid Status:
      TEI 64, ces = 1, state = 8(established)
        spid1 configured, spid1 sent, spid1 valid  ←  B channel #1
        Endpoint ID Info: epsf = 0, usid = 70, tid = 1
      TEI 65, ces = 2, state = 8(established)
        spid2 configured, spid2 sent, spid2 valid  ←  B channel #2
        Endpoint ID Info: epsf = 0, usid = 70, tid = 2
    Layer 3 Status:
      0 Active Layer 3 Call(s)
    Activated dsl 0 CCBs = 0
  Total Allocated ISDN CCBs = 0
```

Let's verify that the D channel for the BRI interface on RouterA is active. Type the **show interface bri 0/0** command to view the D channel. The up/up (spoofing) state of the interface indicates that the D channel between RouterA and the ISDN switch is active.

```
RouterA#show interface bri 0/0
BRI0/0 is up, line protocol is up (spoofing)  ←  Active D channel
  Hardware is QUICC BRI with U interface
  MTU 1500 bytes, BW 64 Kbit, DLY 20000 usec, rely 255/255, load 1/255
  Encapsulation PPP, loopback not set
  Last input 00:00:04, output never, output hang never
  Last clearing of "show interface" counters never
  Queueing strategy: fifo
```

```
Output queue 0/40, 0 drops; input queue 0/75, 0 drops
5 minute input rate 0 bits/sec, 0 packets/sec
5 minute output rate 0 bits/sec, 0 packets/sec
    258 packets input, 1251 bytes, 0 no buffer
    Received 0 broadcasts, 0 runts, 0 giants, 0 throttles
    0 input errors, 0 CRC, 0 frame, 0 overrun, 0 ignored, 0 abort
    254 packets output, 1302 bytes, 0 underruns
    0 output errors, 0 collisions, 6 interface resets
    0 output buffer failures, 0 output buffers swapped out
    4 carrier transitions
```

As with RouterB, both B channels on the BRI will be idle. Use the **show interface bri 0/0:1** and **show interface bri 0/0:2** commands to view the status of B channels #1 and #2.

```
RouterA#show interface bri 0/0:1
BRI0/0:1 is down, line protocol is down
    Hardware is QUICC BRI with U interface
    MTU 1500 bytes, BW 64 Kbit, DLY 20000 usec, rely 255/255, load 1/255
    Encapsulation PPP, loopback not set, keepalive set (10 sec)
    LCP Closed, multilink Closed
    Closed: CDP
    Last input 00:01:37, output 00:01:37, output hang never
    Last clearing of "show interface" counters never
    Queueing strategy: fifo
    Output queue 0/40, 0 drops; input queue 0/75, 0 drops
    5 minute input rate 0 bits/sec, 0 packets/sec
    5 minute output rate 0 bits/sec, 0 packets/sec
        303 packets input, 11402 bytes, 0 no buffer
        Received 0 broadcasts, 0 runts, 0 giants, 0 throttles
        0 input errors, 0 CRC, 0 frame, 0 overrun, 0 ignored, 0 abort
        337 packets output, 16158 bytes, 0 underruns
        0 output errors, 0 collisions, 0 interface resets
        0 output buffer failures, 0 output buffers swapped out
        8 carrier transitions

RouterA#show interface bri 0/0:2
BRI0/0:2 is down, line protocol is down
    Hardware is QUICC BRI with U interface
    MTU 1500 bytes, BW 64 Kbit, DLY 20000 usec, rely 255/255, load 1/255
    Encapsulation PPP, loopback not set, keepalive set (10 sec)
    LCP Closed, multilink Closed
    Closed: CDP
    Last input 00:01:39, output 00:01:39, output hang never
    Last clearing of "show interface" counters never
    Queueing strategy: fifo
    Output queue 0/40, 0 drops; input queue 0/75, 0 drops
    5 minute input rate 0 bits/sec, 0 packets/sec
    5 minute output rate 0 bits/sec, 0 packets/sec
        233 packets input, 9716 bytes, 0 no buffer
        Received 0 broadcasts, 0 runts, 0 giants, 0 throttles
        0 input errors, 0 CRC, 0 frame, 0 overrun, 0 ignored, 0 abort
```

```
264 packets output, 12174 bytes, 0 underruns
0 output errors, 0 collisions, 0 interface resets
0 output buffer failures, 0 output buffers swapped out
10 carrier transitions
```

Let's turn on PPP authentication and ISDN call control debugging with the **debug ppp authentication** command and the **debug isdn q931** command. Active debug commands can be displayed with the **show debug** command. Remember that you also need to type the **term mon** command if you are not connected to the router's console port.

```
RouterA#show debug
PPP:
  PPP authentication debugging is on
ISDN:
  ISDN Q931 packets debugging is on
Dial on demand:
  Dial on demand events debugging is on
```

Let's ping the BRI interface on RouterB at IP address 196.1.1.2. Notice that this ping will activate the BRI interface.

```
RouterA#ping 196.1.1.2

Type escape sequence to abort.
Sending 5, 100-byte ICMP Echos to 196.1.1.2, timeout is 2 seconds:

BRI0/0: Dialing cause ip (s=196.1.1.1, d=196.1.1.2)
BRI0/0: Attempting to dial 8995201
ISDN BR0/0: TX ->  SETUP pd = 8   callref = 0x0B  ←  Placing call on B channel
                                                       #1
        Bearer Capability i = 0x8890
        Channel ID i = 0x83
        Keypad Facility i = '8995201'
ISDN BR0/0: RX <-  CALL_PROC pd = 8   callref = 0x8B
        Channel ID i = 0x89
ISDN BR0/0: RX <-  CONNECT pd = 8   callref = 0x8B
        Channel ID i = 0x89
%LINK-3-UPDOWN: Interface BRI0/0:1, changed state to up
%DIALER-6-BIND: Interface BRI0/0:1 bound to profile Dialer0
PPP BRI0/0:1: treating connection as a callout
ISDN BR0/0: TX ->  CONNECT_ACK pd = 8   callref = 0x0B
PPP BRI0/0:1: Send CHAP Challenge id=5
PPP BRI0/0:1: CHAP Challenge id=5 received from RouterB
PPP BRI0/0:1: Send CHAP Response id=5
PPP BRI0/0:1: CHAP response received from RouterB
PPP BRI0/0:1: CHAP Response id=5 received from RouterB
PPP BRI0/0:1: Send CHAP Success id=5
PPP BRI0/0:1: remote passed CHAP authentication
PPP BRI0/0:1: Passed CHAP authentication with remote
%DIALER-6-BIND: Interface Virtual-Access1 bound to profile Dialer0
```

```
%LINK-3-UPDOWN: Interface Virtual-Access1, changed state to up
PPP Virtual-Access1: treating connection as a callin
%LINEPROTO-5-UPDOWN: Line protocol on Interface BRI0/0:1, changed state to up
%LINEPROTO-5-UPDOWN: Line protocol on Interface Virtual-Access1, changed state
to up
BRI0/0: Attempting to dial 8995201
ISDN BR0/0: TX ->  SETUP pd = 8  callref = 0x0C ←  Placing call on B channel
                                                   #2
        Bearer Capability i = 0x8890
        Channel ID i = 0x83
        Keypad Facility i = '8995201'
ISDN BR0/0: RX <-  CALL_PROC pd = 8  callref = 0x8C
        Channel ID i = 0x8A
ISDN BR0/0: Event: incoming ces value = 2
ISDN BR0/0: RX <-  CONNECT pd = 8  callref = 0x8C
        Channel ID i = 0x8A
ISDN BR0/0: Event: incoming ces value = 2
%LINK-3-UPDOWN: Interface BRI0/0:2, changed state to up
%DIALER-6-BIND: Interface BRI0/0:2 bound to profile Dialer0
PPP BRI0/0:2: treating connection as a callout
ISDN BR0/0: TX ->  CONNECT_ACK pd = 8  callref = 0x0C
PPP BRI0/0:2: Send CHAP Challenge id=4
PPP BRI0/0:2: CHAP Challenge id=4 received from RouterB
PPP BRI0/0:2: Send CHAP Response id=4
PPP BRI0/0:2: CHAP response received from RouterB
PPP BRI0/0:2: CHAP Response id=4 received from RouterB
PPP BRI0/0:2: Send CHAP Success id=4
PPP BRI0/0:2: remote passed CHAP authentication.
PPP BRI0/0:2: Passed CHAP authentication with remote.
%LINEPROTO-5-UPDOWN: Line protocol on Interface BRI0/0:2, changed state to up
%ISDN-6-CONNECT: Interface BRI0/0:2 is now connected to 8995201 RouterB

..!!!
Success rate is 60 percent (3/5), round-trip min/avg/max = 20/21/24 ms
```

The **show isdn status** command will verify that we have two active calls on RouterA.

```
RouterA#show isdn status
The current ISDN Switchtype = basic-ni1
ISDN BRI0/0 interface
    Layer 1 Status:
      ACTIVE
    Layer 2 Status:
      TEI = 64, State = MULTIPLE_FRAME_ESTABLISHED
      TEI = 65, State = MULTIPLE_FRAME_ESTABLISHED
    Spid Status:
      TEI 64, ces = 1, state = 8(established)
          spid1 configured, spid1 sent, spid1 valid
          Endpoint ID Info: epsf = 0, usid = 70, tid = 1
      TEI 65, ces = 2, state = 8(established)
          spid2 configured, spid2 sent, spid2 valid
```

```
        Endpoint ID Info: epsf = 0, usid = 70, tid = 2
    Layer 3 Status:
      2 Active Layer 3 Call(s) ←   Both B channels on the BRI are active
    Activated dsl 0 CCBs = 2
       CCB:callid=800D, sapi=0, ces=1, B-chan=1
       CCB:callid=800E, sapi=0, ces=2, B-chan=2
  Total Allocated ISDN CCBs = 2
```

We see that the D channel of the BRI is still in an up/up (spoofing) state, although a call is active.

```
RouterA#show interface bri 0/0
BRI0/0 is up, line protocol is up (spoofing) ←   Active D channel
   Hardware is QUICC BRI with U interface
   MTU 1500 bytes, BW 64 Kbit, DLY 20000 usec, rely 255/255, load 1/255
   Encapsulation PPP, loopback not set
   Last input 00:00:02, output never, output hang never
   Last clearing of "show interface" counters never
   Queueing strategy: fifo
   Output queue 0/40, 0 drops; input queue 0/75, 0 drops
   5 minute input rate 0 bits/sec, 0 packets/sec
   5 minute output rate 0 bits/sec, 0 packets/sec
      275 packets input, 1347 bytes, 0 no buffer
      Received 0 broadcasts, 0 runts, 0 giants, 0 throttles
      0 input errors, 0 CRC, 0 frame, 0 overrun, 0 ignored, 0 abort
      272 packets output, 1422 bytes, 0 underruns
      0 output errors, 0 collisions, 6 interface resets
      0 output buffer failures, 0 output buffers swapped out
      4 carrier transitions
```

Both B channels will now be in an up/up state.

```
RouterA#show interface bri 0/0:1
BRI0/0:1 is up, line protocol is up
   Hardware is QUICC BRI with U interface
   MTU 1500 bytes, BW 64 Kbit, DLY 20000 usec, rely 255/255, load 1/255
   Encapsulation PPP, loopback not set, keepalive set (10 sec)
   LCP Open, multilink Open ←   MLPPP
   Last input 00:00:01, output 00:00:01, output hang never
   Last clearing of "show interface" counters never
   Queueing strategy: fifo
   Output queue 0/40, 0 drops; input queue 0/75, 0 drops
   5 minute input rate 0 bits/sec, 0 packets/sec
   5 minute output rate 0 bits/sec, 0 packets/sec
      327 packets input, 12166 bytes, 0 no buffer
      Received 0 broadcasts, 0 runts, 0 giants, 0 throttles
      0 input errors, 0 CRC, 0 frame, 0 overrun, 0 ignored, 0 abort
      360 packets output, 17052 bytes, 0 underruns
      0 output errors, 0 collisions, 0 interface resets
      0 output buffer failures, 0 output buffers swapped out
      9 carrier transitions
```

```
RouterA#show interface bri 0/0:2
BRI0/0:2 is up, line protocol is up
  Hardware is QUICC BRI with U interface
  MTU 1500 bytes, BW 64 Kbit, DLY 20000 usec, rely 255/255, load 1/255
  Encapsulation PPP, loopback not set, keepalive set (10 sec)
  LCP Open, multilink Open   ←   MLPPP
  Last input 00:00:03, output 00:00:03, output hang never
  Last clearing of "show interface" counters never
  Queueing strategy: fifo
  Output queue 0/40, 0 drops; input queue 0/75, 0 drops
  5 minute input rate 0 bits/sec, 0 packets/sec
  5 minute output rate 0 bits/sec, 0 packets/sec
     251 packets input, 10398 bytes, 0 no buffer
     Received 0 broadcasts, 0 runts, 0 giants, 0 throttles
     0 input errors, 0 CRC, 0 frame, 0 overrun, 0 ignored, 0 abort
     283 packets output, 13006 bytes, 0 underruns
     0 output errors, 0 collisions, 0 interface resets
     0 output buffer failures, 0 output buffers swapped out
     11 carrier transitions
```

The dialer status indicates that the reason for the current call on B channel #1 was our ping. This information is shown as IP traffic from a source of 196.1.1.1 (RouterA) to a destination of 196.1.1.2 (RouterB). The reason for the call on B channel #2 was the multilink bundle overload. This situation is determined by the **dialer load threshold** statement in the configuration for RouterA.

```
RouterA#show dialer

BRI0/0 - dialer type = ISDN

Dial String      Successes    Failures    Last called    Last status
0 incoming call(s) have been screened.

BRI0/0:1 - dialer type = ISDN
Idle timer (90 secs), Fast idle timer (20 secs)
Wait for carrier (30 secs), Re-enable (15 secs)
Dialer state is physical layer up
Dial reason: ip (s=196.1.1.1, d=196.1.1.2)  ←  Ping from RouterA to RouterB
Interface bound to profile Dialer0
Time until disconnect 58 secs
Current call connected 00:00:28
Connected to 8995201 (RouterB)

BRI0/0:2 - dialer type = ISDN
Idle timer (90 secs), Fast idle timer (20 secs)
Wait for carrier (30 secs), Re-enable (15 secs)
Dialer state is physical layer up
Dial reason: Multilink bundle overloaded  ←  Dialer load threshold
Interface bound to profile Dialer0
Time until disconnect 60 secs
```

```
Current call connected 00:00:29
Connected to 8995201 (RouterB)

Dialer0 - dialer type = DIALER PROFILE
Load threshold for dialing additional calls is 1
Idle timer (90 secs), Fast idle timer (20 secs)
Wait for carrier (30 secs), Re-enable (15 secs)
Dialer state is data link layer up

Dial String      Successes    Failures    Last called    Last status
8995201                  5           0     00:00:32       successful    Default
```

You can verify that RouterA and RouterB are communicating over an MLPPP bundle by typing the **show ppp multilink** command. We see that there is an active multilink bundle consisting of two B channels.

```
RouterA#show ppp multi

Bundle RouterB, 2 members, Master link is Virtual-Access1
Dialer Interface is Dialer0
  0 lost fragments, 0 reordered, 0 unassigned, sequence 0x10/0x12 rcvd/sent
  0 discarded, 0 lost received, 1/255 load

Member Links: 2  ←  2 B channels in the MLPPP bundle
BRI0/0:1
BRI0/0:2
```

Lab #6: ISDN BRI to ISDN PRI

Equipment Needed

The following equipment is needed to perform this lab exercise:

- Two Cisco routers, one of which must have a BRI interface and one which must have a PRI interface
- One ISDN PRI circuit and one ISDN BRI circuit
- Cisco IOS 11.2 or higher
- A PC running a terminal emulation program for console port connection on the routers

Configuration Overview

This configuration will demonstrate a BRI-connected router calling into a PRI-connected router. PRI-connected routers are used for large-scale access servers. A typical topology is to have spoke sites, which are BRI-connected, dialing into a hub router with a PRI interface.

The two routers are connected, as shown in Figure 3–17. RouterA and RouterB are connected to an Adtran Atlas 800 ISDN switch.

Figure 3–17
Lab #6

899-3601
899-3602

899-1000

RouterA
bri 0/0
196.1.1.1

ISDN Switch

S0:23   RouterB
196.1.1.7

BRI   **PRI**

A PC running a terminal emulation program should be connected to the console port of one of the routers using a Cisco rolled cable.

NOTE: *Keep in mind that a PRI is different from a BRI. A PRI is carried on a T1 circuit and consists of 23 B channels, each carrying 56K or 64K of user traffic. A PRI also has a 64K D channel used for signaling between the user device and the ISDN switch. A BRI, however, consists of 2 B channels, each carrying 56K or 64K of user traffic. A BRI also has a 16K D channel used for signaling between the user device and the ISDN switch.*

NOTE: *A PRI ISDN circuit does not have a SPID associated with each B channel.*

ISDN Switch Setup

If you do not have access to actual ISDN circuits, you can use an ISDN desktop switch. Information on configuring an ISDN desktop switch can be found in the ISDN Switch Configuration section earlier in this chapter.

Router Configuration

The configurations for the two routers in this example are as follows
(ISDN commands are highlighted in bold):

RouterA

```
RouterA#show run
Building configuration...

Current configuration:
!
version 11.2
no service udp-small-servers
no service tcp-small-servers
!
hostname RouterA
!
!
username RouterB password 7 121A0C041104
isdn switch-type basic-ni1  ←  Set D channel call control
!
interface BRI0/0
 ip address 196.1.1.1 255.255.255.0
 encapsulation ppp
 isdn spid1 8995101 5101  ←  Set SPID value for both B channels
 isdn spid2 8995102 5102
 dialer idle-timeout 30  ←  Define how many seconds to disconnect after last
                             interesting packet
 dialer map ip 196.1.1.7 name RouterB broadcast 8991000  ←  Associate next
                                                            hop address with
                                                            a dial string
 dialer load-threshold 1  ←  Define threshold to add additional B channels
 dialer-group 1  ←  Associate interface with dialer-list 1
 no fair-queue
 ppp authentication chap
 ppp multilink  ←  Request a PPP multilink session
!
no ip classless
dialer-list 1 protocol ip permit  ←  Define interesting traffic
!
line con 0
line aux 0
line vty 0 4
 login
!
end
```

RouterB

```
RouterB#show run
Building configuration...

Current configuration:
!
version 11.2
no service password-encryption
service udp-small-servers
service tcp-small-servers
!
hostname RouterB
!
enable password cisco
!
username RouterA password 0 cisco
isdn switch-type primary-5ess  ←  Set D channel call control for the PRI
!
controller T1 0
 framing esf  ←  Set T1 Extended Superframe Framing
 linecode b8zs  ←  Set T1 line coding
 pri-group timeslots 1-24  ←  Define entire T1 to belong to the PRI
!
interface Serial0:23  ←  D channel of the PRI
 ip address 196.1.1.7 255.255.255.0
 encapsulation ppp
 no ip mroute-cache
 isdn incoming-voice modem
 dialer idle-timeout 900  ←  Set the interesting traffic timeout
 dialer-group 1  ← Associate the interface with dialer-list 1
 no fair-queue
 no cdp enable
 ppp authentication chap
 ppp multilink
!
interface Dialer1
 no ip address
 encapsulation ppp
 dialer in-band
 dialer idle-timeout 900
 dialer-group 1
 no fair-queue
 ppp authentication chap
!
no ip classless
ip route 192.1.5.0 255.255.255.0 196.1.1.1
dialer-list 1 protocol ip permit  ← Define interesting traffic
!
line con 0
 exec-timeout 60 0
 password cisco
 login
line aux 0
line vty 0 4
 login
!
end
```

Notice that the configuration for the PRI interface on RouterB is quite different from a BRI configuration. When configuring a PRI, you must first define a T1 controller interface and specify the proper T1 framing and line coding. The PRI is configured as a serial interface:23, specifying the D channel of the PRI interface.

Monitoring and Testing the Configuration

Let's start by connecting to RouterA and verifying that the BRI circuit is up and active. Type the **show isdn status** command to display the status of the ISDN interface. We see that a SPID has been sent for both B channels to the ISDN switch and has been validated. We also see under the layer 3 status that there are no active calls on the router at this time.

```
RouterA#show isdn status
The current ISDN Switchtype = basic-ni1
ISDN BRI0/0 interface
    Layer 1 Status:
        ACTIVE
    Layer 2 Status:
        TEI = 64, State = MULTIPLE_FRAME_ESTABLISHED
        TEI = 65, State = MULTIPLE_FRAME_ESTABLISHED
    Spid Status:
        TEI 64, ces = 1, state = 5(init)
            spid1 configured, spid1 sent, spid1 valid   ←   B channel #1
            Endpoint ID Info: epsf = 0, usid = B, tid = 1
        TEI 65, ces = 2, state = 5(init)
            spid2 configured, spid2 sent, spid2 valid   ←   B channel #2
            Endpoint ID Info: epsf = 0, usid = C, tid = 1
    Layer 3 Status:
        0 Active Layer 3 Call(s)   ←   No active calls
    Activated dsl 0 CCBs = 2
        CCB:callid=0, sapi=0, ces=1, B-chan=0
        CCB:callid=0, sapi=0, ces=1, B-chan=0
    Total Allocated ISDN CCBs = 2
```

The status of the D channel of the BRI circuit can be displayed by typing **show interface bri 0/0.** We see that the interface is in an up/up (spoofing) state, which indicates that the D channel is active.

```
RouterA#show interface bri 0/0
BRI0/0 is up, line protocol is up (spoofing)    ←   D channel of BRI
  Hardware is QUICC BRI with U interface
  Internet address is 196.1.1.1/24
  MTU 1500 bytes, BW 64 Kbit, DLY 20000 usec, rely 255/255, load 1/255
  Encapsulation PPP, loopback not set
  Last input 00:00:04, output never, output hang never
  Last clearing of ìshow interfaceî counters never
  Queueing strategy: fifo
  Output queue 0/40, 0 drops; input queue 0/75, 40 drops
  5 minute input rate 0 bits/sec, 0 packets/sec
  5 minute output rate 0 bits/sec, 0 packets/sec
      272 packets input, 1670 bytes, 0 no buffer
      Received 0 broadcasts, 0 runts, 0 giants, 0 throttles
      40 input errors, 40 CRC, 0 frame, 0 overrun, 0 ignored, 24 abort
      270 packets output, 1713 bytes, 0 underruns
      0 output errors, 0 collisions, 4 interface resets
      0 output buffer failures, 0 output buffers swapped out
      3 carrier transitions
```

We see from the **show dialer** command that the BRI interface will dial 8991000 to place its calls. The idle timer is set to 30 seconds. This value is set by the **dialer idle-timeout 30** statement in the configuration for RouterA. The statement tells the router to disconnect a call 30 seconds after the last interesting packet has been transmitted.

```
RouterA#show dialer

BRI0/0 - dialer type = ISDN

Dial String      Successes    Failures    Last called    Last status
8991000                  5           0     00:07:48         successful
0 incoming call(s) have been screened.

BRI0/0:1 - dialer type = ISDN
Idle timer (30 secs), Fast idle timer (20 secs)
Wait for carrier (30 secs), Re-enable (15 secs)
Dialer state is idle

BRI0/0:2 - dialer type = ISDN
Idle timer (30 secs), Fast idle timer (20 secs)
Wait for carrier (30 secs), Re-enable (15 secs)
Dialer state is idle
```

Now, let's connect to RouterB and view some PRI statistics. We will see that monitoring a PRI ISDN circuit is slightly different then monitoring a BRI circuit. Type the **show isdn status** command. We see that although there are 23 B channels, we will only get 1 Multiple_Frame_Established message. We also see that there are no indications of valid SPIDs being sent, because an ISDN PRI circuit does not have any SPIDs associated with it.

```
RouterB#show isdn status
The current ISDN Switchtype = primary-5ess
ISDN Serial0:23 interface
    Layer 1 Status:
        ACTIVE
    Layer 2 Status:
        TEI = 0, State = MULTIPLE_FRAME_ESTABLISHED
    Layer 3 Status:
        0 Active Layer 3 Call(s)   ←   No active calls at this time
    Activated dsl 0 CCBs = 0
    Total Allocated ISDN CCBs = 0
```

A PRI ISDN interface has an additional monitoring command. Type the **show isdn service** command. This command displays the B channel status of the entire PRI circuit. The state line shows which channels are currently connected, while the channel line shows which channels can accept or make a call. Possible states are the following:

- Idle
- Busy
- Reserved
- Restart
- Maint

We see that each B channel is in an IDLE state (State=0). The last eight channels are in a state of 3, which is reserved. These channels are used for an E1 PRI, which is the European counterpart to a T1. An E1 PRI has 31 B channels, as opposed to the T1—which only has 23.

```
RouterB#show isdn service
PRI Channel Statistics:
ISDN Se0:23, Channel (1-31)
  Activated dsl 0
  State (0=Idle 1=Propose 2=Busy 3=Reserved 4=Restart 5=Maint)
  0 0 0 0 0 0 0 0 0 0 0 0 0 0 0 0 0 0 0 0 0 0 0 3 3 3 3 3 3 3 3
  Channel (1-31) Service (0=Inservice 1=Maint 2=Outofservice)
  0 0 0 0 0 0 0 0 0 0 0 0 0 0 0 0 0 0 0 0 0 0 0 0 0 0 0 0 0 0 0
```

To display the status of the D channel of the PRI, use the **show interface s 0:23** command. The **s 0** corresponds to the **controller T1 0** command in the configuration for RouterB.

```
RouterB#show interface s 0:23
Serial0:23 is up, line protocol is up (spoofing)   ←   D channel of PRI
  Hardware is DSX1   ←   T1 interface
```

```
Internet address is 196.1.1.7/24
MTU 1500 bytes, BW 64 Kbit, DLY 20000 usec, rely 255/255, load 1/255
Encapsulation PPP, loopback not set
Last input 00:00:08, output 00:00:08, output hang never
Last clearing of ìshow interfaceî counters never
Queueing strategy: fifo
Output queue 0/40, 0 drops; input queue 0/75, 0 drops
5 minute input rate 0 bits/sec, 0 packets/sec
5 minute output rate 0 bits/sec, 0 packets/sec
    1284 packets input, 5949 bytes, 0 no buffer
    Received 0 broadcasts, 0 runts, 0 giants, 0 throttles
    0 input errors, 0 CRC, 0 frame, 0 overrun, 0 ignored, 0 abort
    1285 packets output, 5541 bytes, 0 underruns
    0 output errors, 0 collisions, 5 interface resets
    0 output buffer failures, 0 output buffers swapped out
    1 carrier transitions
Timeslot(s) Used:24, Transmitter delay is 0 flags
```

The **show dialer** command will display the status of the dialer on the router. We notice some differences from how this command looks when used on a BRI interface. When used on a PRI, the command will display the status of each of the 23 B channels.

```
RouterB#show dialer

Dialer1 - dialer type = IN-BAND SYNC NO-PARITY
Idle timer (900 secs), Fast idle timer (20 secs)
Wait for carrier (30 secs), Re-enable (15 secs)

Dial String      Successes    Failures     Last called    Last status

Serial0:0 - dialer type = ISDN
Idle timer (900 secs), Fast idle timer (20 secs)
Wait for carrier (30 secs), Re-enable (15 secs)
Dialer state is idle

Serial0:1 - dialer type = ISDN
Idle timer (900 secs), Fast idle timer (20 secs)
Wait for carrier (30 secs), Re-enable (15 secs)
Dialer state is idle

    .
    .
    .
    .

Serial0:22 - dialer type = ISDN
Idle timer (900 secs), Fast idle timer (20 secs)
Wait for carrier (30 secs), Re-enable (15 secs)
Dialer state is idle
```

Serial0:23 - dialer type = ISDN

```
Dial String      Successes    Failures     Last called    Last status
0 incoming call(s) have been screened.
```

Turn on PPP authentication and ISDN Q931 call control debugging with the **debug ppp authentication** command and the **debug isdn q931** command. The status of which debug commands are active can be displayed by typing the **show debug** command. Remember to use the **term mon** command to display the debug output if you are not connected to the console port of the router.

```
RouterA#show debug
PPP:
  PPP authentication debugging is on
ISDN:
  ISDN Q931 packets debugging is on
```

Now, let's try to ping RouterB at IP address 196.1.1.7. We see that an ISDN call is made as soon as we start our ping:

```
RouterA#ping 196.1.1.7

Type escape sequence to abort.
Sending 5, 100-byte ICMP Echos to 196.1.1.7, timeout is 2 seconds:

ISDN BR0/0: TX ->  SETUP pd = 8  callref = 0x06  ←  B channel #1
        Bearer Capability I = 0x8890
        Channel ID I = 0x83
        Keypad Facility I = ě98991000í
ISDN BR0/0: RX <-  SETUP_ACK pd = 8  callref = 0x86
        Channel ID I = 0x89.
ISDN BR0/0: RX <-  CALL_PROC pd = 8  callref = 0x86
ISDN BR0/0: RX <-  CONNECT pd = 8  callref = 0x86
        Signal I = 0x3F - Tones off
%LINK-3-UPDOWN: Interface BRI0/0:1, changed state to up
PPP BRI0/0:1: treating connection as a callout
ISDN BR0/0: TX ->  CONNECT_ACK pd = 8  callref = 0x06
PPP BRI0/0:1: Send CHAP Challenge id=5
PPP BRI0/0:1: CHAP Challenge id=6 received from RouterB
PPP BRI0/0:1: Send CHAP Response id=6
PPP BRI0/0:1: Passed CHAP authentication with remote
PPP BRI0/0:1: CHAP response received from RouterB
PPP BRI0/0:1: CHAP Response id=5 received from RouterB
PPP BRI0/0:1: Send CHAP Success id=5  ←  Chap successful on B channel #1
PPP BRI0/0:1: remote passed CHAP authentication.
%LINK-3-UPDOWN: Interface Virtual-Access1, changed state to up
PPP Virtual-Access1: treating connection as a callin
%LINEPROTO-5-UPDOWN: Line protocol on Interface BRI0/0:1, changed state to up
%LINEPROTO-5-UPDOWN: Line protocol on Interface Virtual-Access1, changed state
to up
```

```
ISDN BR0/0: TX ->  SETUP pd = 8  callref = 0x07  ←  B channel #2
         Bearer Capability I = 0x8890
         Channel ID I = 0x83
         Keypad Facility I = ë98991000í
ISDN BR0/0: RX <-  SETUP_ACK pd = 8  callref = 0x87
         Channel ID I = 0x8A
ISDN BR0/0: Event: incoming ces value = 2
%ISDN-6-CONNECT: Interface BRI0/0:1 is now connected to 98991000 RouterB
ISDN BR0/0: RX <-  CALL_PROC pd = 8  callref = 0x87
ISDN BR0/0: Event: incoming ces value = 2
ISDN BR0/0: RX <-  CONNECT pd = 8  callref = 0x87
         Signal I = 0x3F - Tones off
ISDN BR0/0: Event: incoming ces value = 2
%LINK-3-UPDOWN: Interface BRI0/0:2, changed state to up
PPP BRI0/0:2: treating connection as a callout
ISDN BR0/0: TX ->  CONNECT_ACK pd = 8  callref = 0x07
PPP BRI0/0:2: Send CHAP Challenge id=2
PPP BRI0/0:2: CHAP Challenge id=3 received from RouterB
PPP BRI0/0:2: Send CHAP Response id=3
PPP BRI0/0:2: Passed CHAP authentication with remote
PPP BRI0/0:2: CHAP response received from RouterB
PPP BRI0/0:2: CHAP Response id=2 received from RouterB
PPP BRI0/0:2: Send CHAP Success id=2  ←  Chap successful on B channel #2
PPP BRI0/0:2: remote passed CHAP authentication.
%LINEPROTO-5-UPDOWN: Line protocol on Interface BRI0/0:2, changed state to up
%ISDN-6-CONNECT: Interface BRI0/0:2 is now connected to 98991000 RouterB


..!!!
Success rate is 60 percent (3/5), round-trip min/avg/max = 32/32/32 ms
RouterA#
```

Notice that the first two pings were not successful, because the router was still in the process of establishing the ISDN call. Another ping to 196.1.1.7 would be 100 percent successful.

Let's verify that we have an MLPPP bundle between RouterA and RouterB. Type the **show ppp multilink** command to view the status of the MLPPP link. We see that there are two B channels in the MLPPP bundle. These are the two B channels of the BRI.

```
RouterA#show ppp multi

Bundle RouterB, 2 members, Master link is Virtual-Access1
Dialer Interface is BRI0/0
  0 lost fragments, 0 reordered, 0 unassigned, sequence 0xA/0xA rcvd/sent
  0 discarded, 0 lost received, 1/255 load

Member Links: 2  ←  B channel #1 and B channel #2
BRI0/0:1
BRI0/0:2
```

The **show isdn status** command can also be used to verify that we have two active calls on the router.

```
RouterA#show isdn status
The current ISDN Switchtype = basic-ni1
ISDN BRI0/0 interface
    Layer 1 Status:
      ACTIVE
    Layer 2 Status:
      TEI = 64, State = MULTIPLE_FRAME_ESTABLISHED
      TEI = 65, State = MULTIPLE_FRAME_ESTABLISHED
    Spid Status:
      TEI 64, ces = 1, state = 5(init)
          spid1 configured, spid1 sent, spid1 valid
          Endpoint ID Info: epsf = 0, usid = B, tid = 1
      TEI 65, ces = 2, state = 5(init)
          spid2 configured, spid2 sent, spid2 valid
          Endpoint ID Info: epsf = 0, usid = C, tid = 1
    Layer 3 Status:
      2 Active Layer 3 Call(s) ←  Active call on both B channels
    Activated dsl 0 CCBs = 4
      CCB:callid=0, sapi=0, ces=1, B-chan=0
      CCB:callid=0, sapi=0, ces=1, B-chan=0
      CCB:callid=8006, sapi=0, ces=1, B-chan=1
      CCB:callid=8007, sapi=0, ces=2, B-chan=2
  Total Allocated ISDN CCBs = 4
```

Each of the two B channels on the BRI circuit will now be active. Using the **show interface bri 0/0:1** and **show interface bri 0/0:2** commands, verify that both interfaces are now in an up/up state. Each of these interfaces will be in a down/down state when there are no active calls.

```
RouterA#show interface bri 0/0:1
BRI0/0:1 is up, line protocol is up ←  B channel #1
  Hardware is QUICC BRI with U interface
  MTU 1500 bytes, BW 64 Kbit, DLY 20000 usec, rely 255/255, load 1/255
  Encapsulation PPP, loopback not set, keepalive set (10 sec)
  LCP Open, multilink Open
  Last input 00:00:06, output 00:00:06, output hang never
  Last clearing of "show interface" counters never
  Queueing strategy: fifo
  Output queue 0/40, 0 drops; input queue 1/75, 0 drops
  5 minute input rate 0 bits/sec, 0 packets/sec
  5 minute output rate 0 bits/sec, 0 packets/sec
    86 packets input, 3440 bytes, 0 no buffer
    Received 0 broadcasts, 0 runts, 0 giants, 0 throttles
    0 input errors, 0 CRC, 0 frame, 0 overrun, 0 ignored, 0 abort
    86 packets output, 3487 bytes, 0 underruns
    0 output errors, 0 collisions, 0 interface resets
    0 output buffer failures, 0 output buffers swapped out
    9 carrier transitions
```

```
RouterA#show interface bri 0/0:2
BRI0/0:2 is up, line protocol is up  ←  B channel #2
  Hardware is QUICC BRI with U interface
  MTU 1500 bytes, BW 64 Kbit, DLY 20000 usec, rely 255/255, load 1/255
  Encapsulation PPP, loopback not set, keepalive set (10 sec)
  LCP Open, multilink Open
  Last input 00:00:08, output 00:00:08, output hang never
  Last clearing of "show interface" counters never
  Queueing strategy: fifo
  Output queue 0/40, 0 drops; input queue 0/75, 0 drops
  5 minute input rate 0 bits/sec, 0 packets/sec
  5 minute output rate 0 bits/sec, 0 packets/sec
     59 packets input, 2378 bytes, 0 no buffer
     Received 0 broadcasts, 0 runts, 0 giants, 0 throttles
     0 input errors, 0 CRC, 0 frame, 0 overrun, 0 ignored, 0 abort
     59 packets output, 2314 bytes, 0 underruns
     0 output errors, 0 collisions, 0 interface resets
     0 output buffer failures, 0 output buffers swapped out
     3 carrier transitions
```

After the idle timeout period of 30 seconds, RouterA will disconnect the ISDN call. This period is defined by the **dialer idle-timeout 30** statement on RouterA's configuration.

```
%LINEPROTO-5-UPDOWN: Line protocol on Interface Virtual-Access1, changed state
to down
%LINK-3-UPDOWN: Interface Virtual-Access1, changed state to down
%ISDN-6-DISCONNECT: Interface BRI0/0:1  disconnected from 98991000 RouterB,
call lasted 55 seconds
%ISDN-6-DISCONNECT: Interface BRI0/0:2  disconnected from 98991000 RouterB,
call lasted 51 seconds
ISDN BR0/0: TX ->  DISCONNECT pd = 8  callref = 0x06  ←  RouterA sends a
                                                         disconnect to the
                                                         ISDN switch

         Cause i = 0x8090 - Normal call clearing
ISDN BR0/0: TX ->  DISCONNECT pd = 8  callref = 0x07  ←  RouterA sends a
                                                         disconnect to the
                                                         ISDN switch

         Cause i = 0x8090 - Normal call clearing
ISDN BR0/0: RX <-  RELEASE pd = 8  callref = 0x86
%LINK-3-UPDOWN: Interface BRI0/0:1, changed state to down
ISDN BR0/0: TX ->  RELEASE_COMP pd = 8  callref = 0x06
ISDN BR0/0: RX <-  RELEASE pd = 8  callref = 0x87
ISDN BR0/0: Event: incoming ces value = 2
%LINK-3-UPDOWN: Interface BRI0/0:2, changed state to down
ISDN BR0/0: TX ->  RELEASE_COMP pd = 8  callref = 0x07
%LINEPROTO-5-UPDOWN: Line protocol on Interface BRI0/0:1, changed state to down
%LINEPROTO-5-UPDOWN: Line protocol on Interface BRI0/0:2, changed state to down
```

Now let's connect to RouterB and see what an incoming call looks like on the ISDN PRI interface. You can either attach a second terminal to RouterB so that you can place a call on RouterA with a ping and monitor RouterB at the same time, or you can log the terminal output on RouterB to a log file.

Make sure that PPP authentication and ISDN Q931 call control debugging are enabled on RouterB by typing the **debug ppp authentication** and **debug isdn q931** commands. You can verify which debug commands are enabled on the router by typing the **show debug** command. Remember to use the **term mon** command to display the debug output if you are not connected to the console port of the router.

```
RouterB#show debug
PPP:
  PPP authentication debugging is on
ISDN:
  ISDN Q931 packets debugging is on
```

The following example shows a trace on RouterB while a call is coming in from RouterA.

The D channel of the PRI is referenced as Se0:23
                    ↓
```
ISDN Se0:23: RX <-  SETUP pd = 8  callref = 0x0C
        Bearer Capability i = 0x8890
        Channel ID i = 0xA98393
        Calling Party Number i = '!', 0x80, '8995201' ← Calling number
        Called Party Number i = 0xA1, '8991000'  ← Called number
```

                    **The first call that comes into the PRI
                    connects to channel 18**
                              ↓
```
%LINK-3-UPDOWN: Interface Serial0:18, changed state to up
Se0:18 PPP: Treating connection as a callin
ISDN Se0:23: TX ->  CALL_PROC pd = 8  callref = 0x800C
        Channel ID i = 0xA98393
ISDN Se0:23: TX ->  CONNECT pd = 8  callref = 0x800C
        Channel ID i = 0xA98393
ISDN Se0:23: RX <-  CONNECT_ACK pd = 8  callref = 0x0C
Se0:18 PPP: Phase is AUTHENTICATING, by both
Se0:18 CHAP: O CHALLENGE id 7 len 29 from "RouterB"
Se0:18 CHAP: I CHALLENGE id 6 len 28 from "RouterA"
Se0:18 CHAP: Waiting for peer to authenticate first
Se0:18 CHAP: I RESPONSE id 7 len 28 from "RouterA"
Se0:18 CHAP: O SUCCESS id 7 len 4
Se0:18 CHAP: Processing saved Challenge, id 6
Se0:18 CHAP: O RESPONSE id 6 len 29 from "RouterB"
Se0:18 CHAP: I SUCCESS id 6 len 4
%LINK-3-UPDOWN: Interface Virtual-Access1, changed state to up
```

```
Vi1 PPP: Treating connection as a callin
%LINEPROTO-5-UPDOWN: Line protocol on Interface Serial0:18, changed state to up
%LINEPROTO-5-UPDOWN: Line protocol on Interface Virtual-Access1, changed state
t
o up
ISDN Se0:23: RX <-  SETUP pd = 8  callref = 0x35
          Bearer Capability i = 0x8890
          Channel ID i = 0xA98394
          Calling Party Number i = '!', 0x80, '8995201'
          Called Party Number i = 0xA1, '8991000'
```

The second call that comes into the PRI connects to channel 19

↓

```
%LINK-3-UPDOWN: Interface Serial0:19, changed state to up
Se0:19 PPP: Treating connection as a callin
ISDN Se0:23: TX ->  CALL_PROC pd = 8  callref = 0x8035
          Channel ID i = 0xA98394
ISDN Se0:23: TX ->  CONNECT pd = 8  callref = 0x8035
          Channel ID i = 0xA98394
ISDN Se0:23: RX <-  CONNECT_ACK pd = 8  callref = 0x35
Se0:19 PPP: Phase is AUTHENTICATING, by both
Se0:19 CHAP: O CHALLENGE id 4 len 29 from "RouterB"
Se0:19 CHAP: I CHALLENGE id 3 len 28 from "RouterA"
Se0:19 CHAP: Waiting for peer to authenticate first
Se0:19 CHAP: I RESPONSE id 4 len 28 from "RouterA"
Se0:19 CHAP: O SUCCESS id 4 len 4
Se0:19 CHAP: Processing saved Challenge, id 3
Se0:19 CHAP: O RESPONSE id 3 len 29 from "RouterB"
Se0:19 CHAP: I SUCCESS id 3 len 4
%LINEPROTO-5-UPDOWN: Line protocol on Interface Serial0:19, changed state to up
%ISDN-6-CONNECT: Interface Serial0:19 is now connected to 9148993601 RouterA
```

The **show ppp multilink** command on RouterB will reveal that two B channels are active in an MLPPP bundle.

```
RouterB#show ppp multi

Bundle RouterA, 2 members, Master link is Virtual-Access1
Dialer Interface is Serial0:23
   0 lost fragments, 0 reordered, 0 unassigned, sequence 0x0/0x0 rcvd/sent
   0 discarded, 0 lost received, 1/255 load

Member Links: 2
Serial0:18
Serial0:19
```

Type the **show dialer maps** command to view the dynamic dialer map that is created when RouterA dials into RouterB.

```
RouterB#show dialer maps
Dynamic dialer map ip 196.1.1.1 name RouterA () on Serial0:23
```

The **show isdn service** command shows us that there are two active B channels on the PRI. The active channels are denoted by a 2 in the appropriate channel position of the PRI.

```
RouterB#show isdn service
PRI Channel Statistics:
ISDN Se0:23, Channel (1-31)
  Activated dsl 0
  State (0=Idle 1=Propose 2=Busy 3=Reserved 4=Restart 5=Maint)
  0 0 0 0 0 0 0 0 0 0 0 0 0 0 0 0 0 2 2 0 0 0 3 3 3 3 3 3 3 3
  Channel (1-31) Service (0=Inservice 1=Maint 2=Outofservice)
  0 0 0 0 0 0 0 0 0 0 0 0 0 0 0 0 0 0 0 0 0 0 0 0 0 0 0 0 0 0
```

When the call disconnects on the PRI, we see that channels 18 and 19 receive a disconnect message from the ISDN switch. Remember that the far-end router (RouterA) is disconnecting the call so RouterB will receive a disconnect message from the network.

```
%LINK-3-UPDOWN: Interface Virtual-Access1, changed state to down
ISDN Se0:23: RX <-  DISCONNECT pd = 8  callref = 0x0C ← Disconnect for
                                                         Channel 18
        Cause i = 0x8090 - Normal call clearing
%ISDN-6-DISCONNECT: Interface Serial0:18  disconnected from 9148993601 RouterA,
call lasted 32 seconds
%LINK-3-UPDOWN: Interface Serial0:18, changed state to down
ISDN Se0:23: TX ->  RELEASE pd = 8  callref = 0x800C
ISDN Se0:23: RX <-  DISCONNECT pd = 8  callref = 0x35 ← Disconnect for
                                                         Channel 19
        Cause i = 0x8090 - Normal call clearing
%ISDN-6-DISCONNECT: Interface Serial0:19  disconnected from 9148993601 RouterA,
call lasted 27 seconds
%LINK-3-UPDOWN: Interface Serial0:19, changed state to down
ISDN Se0:23: TX ->  RELEASE pd = 8  callref = 0x8035
ISDN Se0:23: RX <-  RELEASE_COMP pd = 8  callref = 0x0C
ISDN Se0:23: RX <-  RELEASE_COMP pd = 8  callref = 0x35
%LINEPROTO-5-UPDOWN: Line protocol on Interface Serial0:18, changed state to
down
%LINEPROTO-5-UPDOWN: Line protocol on Interface Serial0:19, changed state to
down
%LINEPROTO-5-UPDOWN: Line protocol on Interface Virtual-Access1, changed state
to down
```

Once the PRI call is disconnected, the **show isdn service** command output will reveal that there are no connected B channels on the PRI.

```
RouterB#show isdn service
PRI Channel Statistics:
ISDN Se0:23, Channel (1-31)
  Activated dsl 0
  State (0=Idle 1=Propose 2=Busy 3=Reserved 4=Restart 5=Maint)
```

```
0 0 0 0 0 0 0 0 0 0 0 0 0 0 0 0 0 0 0 0 0 0 0 3 3 3 3 3 3 3 3
Channel (1-31) Service (0=Inservice 1=Maint 2=Outofservice)
0 0 0 0 0 0 0 0 0 0 0 0 0 0 0 0 0 0 0 0 0 0 0 0 0 0 0 0 0 0 0
```

Because the PRI interface on this router contains a full T1 CSU, you can type the **show cont t 0** command to view the status of the T1 ESF registers on the interface. Data is broken into the previous 24 hours of performance information. The 24-hour statistics are broken up into 96 intervals, each representing 15 minutes of error information.

```
RouterB#show cont t 0
T1 0 is up.
  No alarms detected.
  Framing is ESF, Line Code is B8ZS, Clock Source is Line.
  Data in current interval (256 seconds elapsed):
    0 Line Code Violations, 0 Path Code Violations
    0 Slip Secs, 0 Fr Loss Secs, 0 Line Err Secs, 0 Degraded Mins
    0 Errored Secs, 0 Bursty Err Secs, 0 Severely Err Secs, 0 Unavail Secs
  Data in Interval 1: ← A single 15 minute interval
    0 Line Code Violations, 0 Path Code Violations
    0 Slip Secs, 0 Fr Loss Secs, 0 Line Err Secs, 0 Degraded Mins
    0 Errored Secs, 0 Bursty Err Secs, 0 Severely Err Secs, 0 Unavail Secs
  Data in Interval 2:
    0 Line Code Violations, 0 Path Code Violations
    0 Slip Secs, 0 Fr Loss Secs, 0 Line Err Secs, 0 Degraded Mins
    0 Errored Secs, 0 Bursty Err Secs, 0 Severely Err Secs, 0 Unavail Secs
    .
    .
    .
    .

  Total Data (last 13 15 minute intervals):
    0 Line Code Violations, 0 Path Code Violations,
    1 Slip Secs, 0 Fr Loss Secs, 0 Line Err Secs, 0 Degraded Mins,
    0 Errored Secs, 0 Bursty Err Secs, 0 Severely Err Secs, 1 Unavail Secs
```

Lab #7: Snapshot Routing

Equipment Needed

The following equipment is needed to perform this lab exercise:

■ Two Cisco routers, each of which must have a BRI interface

■ Two ISDN BRI circuits

■ Cisco IOS 11.3 or higher
■ A PC running a terminal emulation program for console port connection on the routers

Configuration Overview

This lab will demonstrate snapshot routing. Snapshot routing enables an ISDN hub and spoke network to be built without configuring and maintaining static routes. Snapshot is only supported for distance vector routing protocols, such as RIP and IGRP, for IP traffic. Without snapshot routing, running RIP on an ISDN interface would mean that every 30 seconds a call would be made (assuming a call was not already up) to exchange updates. Snapshot defines an active and quiet period. During the active period, a RIP-enabled snapshot router will exchange routing updates. If there are no active calls, the snapshot router will initiate an ISDN call during the active period to send a routing update. During the quiet period, a snapshot router will not initiate a call to send a routing update. Snapshot routing freezes entries in the routing table during the quiet period. The active and quiet periods are user-defined. The minimum active period is five minutes, and the minimum quiet period is eight minutes.

Any calls which bring up the ISDN interface will also reset the snapshot routing process to the beginning of a new active period.

The two routers are connected, as shown in Figure 3–18. RouterA and RouterB are connected to an Adtran Atlas 800 ISDN switch.

Figure 3–18
Lab #7

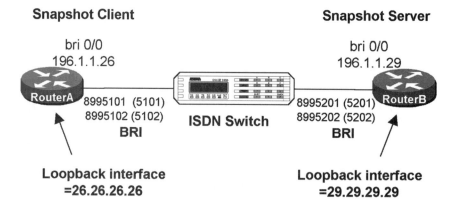

Snapshot Client

bri 0/0
196.1.1.26

RouterA 8995101 (5101)
8995102 (5102)
BRI

ISDN Switch

Snapshot Server

bri 0/0
196.1.1.29

8995201 (5201) RouterB
8995202 (5202)
BRI

**Loopback interface
=26.26.26.26**

**Loopback interface
=29.29.29.29**

A PC running a terminal emulation program should be connected to the console port of one of the routers using a Cisco rolled cable.

NOTE: *Snapshot routing does not work with MLPPP. Do not use a* **ppp multilink** *statement in your router configuration.*

ISDN Switch Setup

If you do not have access to actual ISDN circuits, you can use an ISDN desktop switch. Information on configuring an ISDN desktop switch can be found in the ISDN Switch Configuration section earlier in this chapter.

Router Configuration

The configurations for the two routers in this example are as follows (ISDN commands are highlighted in bold):

RouterA

```
RouterA#show run
Building configuration...

Current configuration:
!
version 11.3
service timestamps debug uptime
service timestamps log uptime
no service password-encryption
service udp-small-servers
service tcp-small-servers
!
hostname RouterA
!
enable password cisco
!
username RouterB password 0 cisco
isdn switch-type basic-ni ← Set the D channel call control
!
!
!
interface Loopback0
 ip address 26.26.26.26 255.255.255.0
!
interface BRI0/0
```

```
 ip address 196.1.1.26 255.255.255.0
 encapsulation ppp
```
dialer map snapshot 1 name RouterB broadcast 8995201 ← **Define the dial string**
                                                              for snapshot updates
dialer map ip 196.1.1.29 name RouterB broadcast 8995201 ← **Define next hop**
                                                                address and dial
                                                                string
dialer-group 1 ← **Associate this interface with dialer-list 1**
isdn switch-type basic-ni
isdn spid1 5101 8995101 ← **Define the SPID for both B channels**
isdn spid2 5102 8995102
snapshot client 5 8 dialer ← Define this router as a snapshot client. The
                                 active time is 5 minutes and the quiet time is
                                 8 minutes.
```
 no fair-queue
 no cdp enable
 ppp authentication chap
!
interface Serial0/0
 no ip address
!
router rip
 network 26.0.0.0
 network 196.1.1.0
!
no ip classless
!
```
dialer-list 1 protocol ip permit ← **Define interesting traffic**
```
!
line con 0
 password cisco
 login
line aux 0
line vty 0 4
 login
!
end
```

RouterB

```
RouterB#show run
Building configuration...

Current configuration:
!
version 11.3
service timestamps debug uptime
service timestamps log uptime
no service password-encryption
!
hostname RouterB
```

```
!
enable password cisco
!
username RouterA password 7 060506324F41
isdn switch-type basic-ni ← Set the D channel call control
!
!
!
interface Loopback0
 ip address 29.29.29.29 255.255.255.0
!
interface BRI0/0
 ip address 196.1.1.29 255.255.255.0
 encapsulation ppp
 dialer map ip 196.1.1.26 name RouterA broadcast ← Define the next hop address
 dialer-group 1 ← Associate this interface with dialer-list 1
 isdn switch-type basic-ni
 isdn spid1 5101 8995101 ← Define the SPID for both B channels
 isdn spid2 5102 8995102
 snapshot server 5 dialer ← Define this router as a snapshot server. The
                             active time of 5 minutes must match the active
                             time on the snapshot client
 no fair-queue
 no cdp enable
 ppp authentication chap
hold-queue 75 in
!
router rip
 network 29.0.0.0
 network 196.1.1.0
!
no ip classless
!
dialer-list 1 protocol ip permit ← Define interesting traffic
!
line con 0
 password cisco
 login
line aux 0
line vty 0 4
 password cisco
 login
!
end
```

Monitoring and Testing the Configuration

Let's start by connecting to RouterB and verifying that the ISDN circuit
is up and active. Type the **show isdn status** command to view the ISDN
BRI status information.

```
RouterB#show isdn status
Global ISDN Switchtype = basic-ni
ISDN BRI0/0 interface
        dsl 0, interface ISDN Switchtype = basic-ni
    Layer 1 Status:
        ACTIVE
    Layer 2 Status:
        TEI = 64, Ces = 1, SAPI = 0, State = MULTIPLE_FRAME_ESTABLISHED
        TEI = 65, Ces = 2, SAPI = 0, State = MULTIPLE_FRAME_ESTABLISHED
    Spid Status:
        TEI 64, ces = 1, state = 5(init)
            spid1 configured, spid1 sent, spid1 valid
            Endpoint ID Info: epsf = 0, usid = 0, tid = 1
        TEI 65, ces = 2, state = 5(init)
            spid2 configured, spid2 sent, spid2 valid
            Endpoint ID Info: epsf = 0, usid = 1, tid = 1
    Layer 3 Status:
        0 Active Layer 3 Call(s)
    Activated dsl 0 CCBs = 0
    Total Allocated ISDN CCBs = 0
```

RouterB is provisioned for snapshot routing. Type the **show snap** command to view snapshot information. We see that RouterB is a snapshot server.

```
RouterB#show snap
BRI0/0 is up, line protocol is up Snapshot server
  Options: dialer support
  Length of active period:          5 minutes
   For ip address: 196.1.1.26
    Current state: active, remaining time: 1 minute
    Connected dialer interface:
        BRI0/0:1
```

Now let's connect to RouterA. Verify that the ISDN circuit is active with the **show isdn status** command.

```
RouterA#show isdn status
Global ISDN Switchtype = basic-ni
ISDN BRI0/0 interface
        dsl 0, interface ISDN Switchtype = basic-ni
    Layer 1 Status:
        ACTIVE
    Layer 2 Status:
        TEI = 80, Ces = 1, SAPI = 0, State = MULTIPLE_FRAME_ESTABLISHED
        TEI = 89, Ces = 2, SAPI = 0, State = MULTIPLE_FRAME_ESTABLISHED
    Spid Status:
        TEI 80, ces = 1, state = 5(init)
            spid1 configured, spid1 sent, spid1 valid
            Endpoint ID Info: epsf = 0, usid = 0, tid = 1
        TEI 89, ces = 2, state = 5(init)
```

```
        spid2 configured, spid2 sent, spid2 valid
        Endpoint ID Info: epsf = 0, usid = 1, tid = 1
Layer 3 Status:
    0 Active Layer 3 Call(s)
Activated dsl 0 CCBs = 0
Total Allocated ISDN CCBs = 0
```

The **show dialer maps** command will display information about any dialer maps configured on the router. We see that RouterA has two dialer maps configured. The first dialer map is a snapshot dialer map used for snapshot routing. The second dialer map is the map used for defining the next hop address to RouterB.

```
RouterA#show dialer maps
Static dialer map snapshot 1 name RouterB broadcast (8995201) on BRI0/0
Static dialer map ip 196.1.1.29 name RouterB broadcast (8995201) on BRI0/0
```

We see from the show snap command on RouterA that RouterA is a snapshot client. RouterA is currently in the quiet state, which means that RouterA will not initiate an ISDN call to send out RIP routing updates.

```
RouterA#show snap
BRI0/0 is up, line protocol is up Snapshot client
  Options: dialer support
  Length of active period:                        5 minutes
  Length of quiet period:                         8 minutes
  Length of retry period:                         8 minutes
   For dialer address 1
    Current state: quiet, remaining: 6 minutes
```

The quiet period is defined to be eight minutes.

During the quiet period, connect to RouterB and examine its routing table. We see that the route to the loopback on RouterA (26.0.0.0/8 [120/1] via 196.1.1.26, 00:04:31, BRI0/0) is being aged but is not being deleted from the routing table. Without snapshot, the route would be deleted as soon as the BRI is disconnected. With snapshot, the route is kept in the routing table and is not deleted.

```
RouterB#show ip route
Codes: C - connected, S - static, I - IGRP, R - RIP, M - mobile, B - BGP
       D - EIGRP, EX - EIGRP external, O - OSPF, IA - OSPF inter area
       N1 - OSPF NSSA external type 1, N2 - OSPF NSSA external type 2
       E1 - OSPF external type 1, E2 - OSPF external type 2, E - EGP
       i - IS-IS, L1 - IS-IS level-1, L2 - IS-IS level-2, * - candidate default
       U - per-user static route, o - ODR

Gateway of last resort is not set
```

```
C    196.1.1.0/24 is directly connected, BRI0/0
R    26.0.0.0/8 [120/1] via 196.1.1.26, 00:04:31, BRI0/0
     29.0.0.0/24 is subnetted, 1 subnets
C       29.29.29.0 is directly connected, Loopback0
```

We see that the route ages to seven minutes and 58 seconds. Notice that the route is still in the routing table. Without snapshot, a route would have been removed from the routing table if an update had not been received for this amount of time.

```
RouterB#show ip route
Codes: C - connected, S - static, I - IGRP, R - RIP, M - mobile, B - BGP
       D - EIGRP, EX - EIGRP external, O - OSPF, IA - OSPF inter area
       N1 - OSPF NSSA external type 1, N2 - OSPF NSSA external type 2
       E1 - OSPF external type 1, E2 - OSPF external type 2, E - EGP
       i - IS-IS, L1 - IS-IS level-1, L2 - IS-IS level-2, * - candidate default
       U - per-user static route, o - ODR

Gateway of last resort is not set

C    196.1.1.0/24 is directly connected, BRI0/0
R    26.0.0.0/8 [120/1] via 196.1.1.26, 00:07:58, BRI0/0
     29.0.0.0/24 is subnetted, 1 subnets
C       29.29.29.0 is directly connected, Loopback0
```

The snapshot timers will continue to decrement. After six more minutes, the timer will show zero minutes.

```
RouterA#show snap
BRI0/0 is up, line protocol is upSnapshot client
  Options: dialer support
  Length of active period: 5 minutes
  Length of quiet period: 8 minutes
  Length of retry period: 8 minutes
   For dialer address 1
     Current state: quiet, remaining: 0 minutes
```

After the quiet period expires, snapshot will enter the active period. RouterA will now initiate an ISDN call to send out routing updates.

```
21:09:39: %LINK-3-UPDOWN: Interface BRI0/0:1, changed state to up
21:09:39: %LINK-3-UPDOWN: Interface Virtual-Access1, changed state to up
21:09:39: RT: network 196.1.1.0 is now variably masked
21:09:39: RT: add 196.1.1.29/32 via 0.0.0.0, connected metric [0/0]
21:09:39: %LINEPROTO-5-UPDOWN: Line protocol on Interface BRI0/0:1, changed
stat
e to up
21:09:39: %LINEPROTO-5-UPDOWN: Line protocol on Interface Virtual-Access1,
chang
ed state to up
```

```
21:09:45: %ISDN-6-CONNECT: Interface BRI0/0:1 is now connected to 8995201
RouterB
```

The **show snap** command now shows that RouterA is in the 5 minute active period during which it will send out RIP updates. If the ISDN circuit is not connected snapshot will initiate the ISDN circuit to place the call.

```
RouterA#show snap
BRI0/0 is up, line protocol is up Snapshot client
  Options: dialer support
  Length of active period:        5 minutes
  Length of quiet period:         8 minutes
  Length of retry period:         8 minutes
   For dialer address 1
    Current state: active, remaining/exchange time: 5/0 minutes
   Connected dialer interface:
      BRI0/0:1
    Updates received this cycle: ip
```

Now that snapshot is in the active state, reconnect to RouterB and view the routing table with the **show ip route** command. Notice that the route to RouterA is still in the table, but the route has now been updated in the last six seconds. Because snapshot is in the active state, it is now sending RIP updates again.

```
RouterB#show ip route
Codes: C - connected, S - static, I - IGRP, R - RIP, M - mobile, B - BGP
       D - EIGRP, EX - EIGRP external, O - OSPF, IA - OSPF inter area
       N1 - OSPF NSSA external type 1, N2 - OSPF NSSA external type 2
       E1 - OSPF external type 1, E2 - OSPF external type 2, E - EGP
       i - IS-IS, L1 - IS-IS level-1, L2 - IS-IS level-2, * - candidate default
       U - per-user static route, o - ODR

Gateway of last resort is not set

     196.1.1.0/24 is variably subnetted, 2 subnets, 2 masks
C       196.1.1.0/24 is directly connected, BRI0/0
C       196.1.1.26/32 is directly connected, BRI0/0
R    26.0.0.0/8 [120/1] via 196.1.1.26, 00:00:06, BRI0/0
     29.0.0.0/24 is subnetted, 1 subnets
C       29.29.29.0 is directly connected, Loopback0
```

Lab #8: ISDN Troubleshooting

Equipment Needed

The following equipment is needed to perform this lab exercise:

- Two Cisco routers, each of which must have a BRI interface
- Two ISDN BRI circuits
- Cisco IOS 11.2 or higher
- A PC running a terminal emulation program for console port connection on the routers

Configuration Overview

This lab will demonstrate key ISDN debug and troubleshooting techniques.

The two routers are connected, as shown in Figure 3–19. RouterA and RouterB are connected to an Adtran Atlas 800 ISDN switch. A PC running a terminal emulation program should be connected to the console port of one of the routers using a Cisco rolled cable.

ISDN Switch Setup

If you do not have access to actual ISDN circuits, you can use an ISDN desktop switch. Information on configuring an ISDN desktop switch can be found in the ISDN Switch Configuration section earlier in this chapter.

Figure 3–19
Lab #8

bri 0/0
196.1.1.1

RouterA 8995101 (5101)
8995102 (5102)

ISDN Switch

bri 0/0
196.1.1.2

8995201 (5201) RouterB
8995202 (5202)

BRI

BRI

Router Configuration

The configurations for the two routers in this example are as follows (ISDN commands are highlighted in bold):

RouterA

```
RouterA#show run
Building configuration...

Current configuration:
!
version 11.2
no service udp-small-servers
no service tcp-small-servers
!
hostname RouterA
!
enable password cisco
!
username RouterB password 7 070C285F4D06
isdn switch-type basic-ni1 ← Set D channel call control
!
interface Serial0/0
 no ip address
!
interface BRI0/0
 ip address 196.1.1.1 255.255.255.0
 encapsulation ppp
 isdn spid1 5101 8995101 ← Set SPID for both B channels
 isdn spid2 5102 8995102
 dialer idle-timeout 90 ← Disconnect call 90 seconds after last interesting
packet
 dialer map ip 196.1.1.2 name RouterB broadcast 8995201 ← Associate a next hop
                                                           address with dial
                                                           string
 dialer load-threshold 1 ← Threshold for adding additional B channels
 dialer-group 1 ← Associate this interface with dialer-list 1
 no fair-queue
 ppp authentication chap
 ppp multilink ← Request a PPP multilink session
!
 no ip classless
dialer-list 1 protocol ip permit ← Define interesting traffic
!
line con 0
 password cisco
 login
line aux 0
line vty 0 4
 login
!
end
```

RouterB

```
RouterB#show run
Building configuration...

Current configuration:
!
version 11.2
service timestamps debug datetime localtime
no service udp-small-servers
no service tcp-small-servers
!
hostname RouterB
!
enable password cisco
!
username RouterA password 7 094F471A1A0A
isdn switch-type basic-ni1 ← Set the D channel call control
!
interface Serial0/0
 ip address 192.1.1.1 255.255.255.0
 encapsulation frame-relay
 frame-relay lmi-type ansi
!
interface BRI0/0
 ip address 196.1.1.2 255.255.255.0
 encapsulation ppp
 isdn spid1 5201 8995201 ← Set the SPID for both B channels
 isdn spid2 5202 8995202
 dialer idle-timeout 90 ← Set the interesting traffic timeout
 dialer map ip 196.1.1.1 name RouterA ← Define a next hop address
 dialer-group 1 ← Associate this interface with dialer-list 1
 no fair-queue
 ppp authentication chap
 ppp multilink ← Request a PPP multilink session
!
router rip
 network 192.1.1.0
!
no ip classless
dialer-list 1 protocol ip permit ← Define interesting traffic
!
line con 0
line aux 0
line vty 0 4
 password cisco
 login
!
end
```

Monitoring and Testing the Configuration

The **show isdn status** command will display the condition of the ISDN circuit. This command enables you to view the layer 1, 2, and 3 status of the ISDN circuit. Layer 1 Active indicates that the router sees 2B1Q framing on the ISDN circuit. Layer 2 status should show Multiple_Frame_Established. This term indicates that the router and ISDN switch have made an initial handshake. The SPID status should show that each SPID has been sent and is valid. Remember that a 2B+D ISDN BRI circuit will usually have two SPIDs. An ISDN PRI circuit does not have any SPIDs.

```
RouterB#show isdn status
The current ISDN Switchtype = basic-ni1
ISDN BRI0/0 interface
    Layer 1 Status:
        ACTIVE
    Layer 2 Status:
        TEI = 64, State = MULTIPLE_FRAME_ESTABLISHED
        TEI = 65, State = MULTIPLE_FRAME_ESTABLISHED
    Spid Status:
        TEI 64, ces = 1, state = 5(init)
            spid1 configured, spid1 sent, spid1 valid
            Endpoint ID Info: epsf = 0, usid = 70, tid = 1
        TEI 65, ces = 2, state = 5(init)
            spid2 configured, spid2 sent, spid2 valid
            Endpoint ID Info: epsf = 0, usid = 70, tid = 2
    Layer 3 Status:
        0 Active Layer 3 Call(s)
    Activated dsl 0 CCBs = 1
        CCB:callid=0, callref=0, sapi=0, ces=1, B-chan=0
    Number of active calls = 0
    Number of available B-channels = 2
  Total Allocated ISDN CCBs = 1
```

The **show controllers** command can also be used to verify that the ISDN circuit is active.

```
RouterA#sh controllers bri 0/0
BRI unit 0:BRI unit 0 with U interface:
Layer 1 internal state is ACTIVATED

Layer 1 U interface is ACTIVATED.
ISDN Line Information:
    Last C/I from ISDN transceiver:
        AI:Activation Indication
    Last C/I to ISDN transceiver:
        AI:Activation Indication
    Current EOC commands:
        RTN - Return to normal
```

```
   Received overhead bits: AIB=1, UOA=1, FEBE=1, DEA=1, ACT=1
   Errors: Receive [NEBE]=0, Transmit [FEBE]=0

Siemens 2091 read-only registers:
   ISTA 0 MOR FF MOSR 0 CIRI 3F CIRU 33
Siemens 2091 write-only registers - last values written:
   MASK 96 STCR 15 MOX FF DWU FF ADF2 28 RSVD 0 WB1U 0 WB2U 0
   WB1I 0 WB2I 0 MOCR A0 DWI FF CIWU F3 CIWI FF ADF 10 SWST D
D Channel Information:
idb at 0x609455C4, driver data structure at 0x6097BCF0
Siemens Chip Version 0x0
```

No ISDN Signal

Let's disconnect the ISDN cable from the router. Now, type the **show isdn status** command. Notice that the layer 1 status is now deactivated. The router no longer sees the ISDN BRI signal coming from the ISDN switch.

```
RouterB#show isdn status
The current ISDN Switchtype = basic-ni1
ISDN BRI0/0 interface
    Layer 1 Status:
      DEACTIVATED ← No BRI signal from the ISDN switch
    Layer 2 Status:
      Layer 2 NOT Activated
    Spid Status:
      TEI Not Assigned, ces = 1, state = 1(terminal down)
          spid1 configured, spid1 NOT sent, spid1 NOT valid
      TEI Not Assigned, ces = 2, state = 1(terminal down)
          spid2 configured, spid2 NOT sent, spid2 NOT valid
    Layer 3 Status:
      0 Active Layer 3 Call(s)
    Activated dsl 0 CCBs = 0
    Number of active calls = 0
    Number of available B-channels = 2
  Total Allocated ISDN CCBs = 0
```

Wrong SPID

Now, let's reconnect the ISDN cable to the router. After the ISDN circuit becomes active again, we will change our SPID for both B channels to an incorrect value and see how the router reacts. Enter configuration mode with the **config term** command. Change the SPID for both B channels to an incorrect value.

```
RouterB#config term
Enter configuration commands, one per line. End with CNTL/Z.
RouterB(config)#interface bri 0/0
RouterB(config-if)#isdn spid1 6201 8995201 ← Incorrect SPID value for B
                                              channel #1
RouterB(config-if)#isdn spid2 6202 8996202 ← Incorrect SPID Value for B
                                              channel #2
RouterB(config-if)#exit
RouterB(config)#exit
```

Verify that the new SPID values have taken effect by viewing the configuration with the **show run** command.

```
RouterB#show run
Building configuration...

Current configuration:
!
version 11.2
service timestamps debug datetime localtime
no service udp-small-servers
no service tcp-small-servers
!
hostname RouterB
!
enable password cisco
!
username RouterA password 7 094F471A1A0A
isdn switch-type basic-ni1
!
interface Ethernet0/0
 no ip address
 shutdown
!
interface Serial0/0
 ip address 192.1.1.1 255.255.255.0
 encapsulation frame-relay
 frame-relay lmi-type ansi
!
interface BRI0/0
 ip address 196.1.1.2 255.255.255.0
 encapsulation ppp
 isdn spid1 6201 8995201 ← Incorrect SPID Value for B channel #1
 isdn spid2 6202 8996202 ← Incorrect SPID Value for B channel #2
 dialer idle-timeout 90
 dialer map ip 196.1.1.1 name RouterA
 dialer-group 1
 no fair-queue
 ppp authentication chap
 ppp multilink
!
```

```
router rip
 network 192.1.1.0
!
no ip classless
dialer-list 1 protocol ip permit
!
line con 0
line aux 0
line vty 0 4
 password cisco
 login
!
end
```

The router is trying to send the SPID to the ISDN switch, and the ISDN switch is rejecting the SPID—because it has the wrong value. The router will display the following message:

```
%ISDN-4-INVALID_SPID: Interface BR0/0, Spid1 was rejected
```

Type **show isdn status** to display the BRI interface status. We see that the router is reporting that it sent the SPID for B channel #1 but that it was not valid. This information is correct, because we changed the SPID for both B channels to an incorrect value.

```
RouterB#show isdn status
The current ISDN Switchtype = basic-ni1
ISDN BRI0/0 interface
    Layer 1 Status:
      ACTIVE
    Layer 2 Status:
      TEI = 64, State = MULTIPLE_FRAME_ESTABLISHED
    Spid Status:
      TEI 64, ces = 1, state = 6(not initialized)
     spid1 configured, spid1 sent, spid1 NOT valid ← ISDN switch rejected the
                                                      SPID that the router
                                                      sent
      TEI Not Assigned, ces = 2, state = 1(terminal down)
         spid2 configured, spid2 NOT sent, spid2 NOT valid
    Layer 3 Status:
      0 Active Layer 3 Call(s)
    Activated dsl 0 CCBs = 0
    Number of active calls = 0
    Number of available B-channels = 2
  Total Allocated ISDN CCBs = 0
```

Now, let's change the SPID for B channel #1 and B channel #2 back to the correct value. Type config term and change the SPIDs back to their original values as shown:

```
RouterB#config term
Enter configuration commands, one per line. End with CNTL/Z.
RouterB(config)#interface bri 0/0
RouterB(config-if)#isdn spid1 5201 8995201  ← Correct SPID Value
RouterB(config-if)#isdn spid2 5202 8995202  ← Correct SPID Value
RouterB(config-if)#exit
RouterB(config)#exit
```

Layer 2 Debugging

Now, let's look at some layer 2 debugging capabilities of the Cisco router. Enable layer 2 ISDN debugging by typing the **debug isdn q921** command. Remember to also type the **term mon** command if you are not connected to the console port of the router.

```
RouterB#debug isdn q921
ISDN Q921 packets debugging is on
```

The **debug isdn q921** command causes the router to display all layer 2 activity between itself and the ISDN switch. Recall from the ISDN technology introduction at the beginning of this chapter that layer 2 ISDN activity involves SPID and TEI negotiation, as well as periodic, 10-second "aliveness" messages (referred to as RR) that are initiated by the ISDN switch and are immediately answered by the router. In the following example, we see that the first RR message is received by the router at time 00:03:20 and is immediately answered. Notice that there are two sets of RRs being sent from the ISDN switch. The first set is for TEI=64, and the second set is for TEI=65. This value is for each of the two B channels of the BRI interface.

```
*Mar  1 00:03:20: ISDN BR0/0: RX <-  RRp sapi = 0  tei = 64 nr = 3
*Mar  1 00:03:20: ISDN BR0/0: TX ->  RRf sapi = 0  tei = 64  nr = 3

*Mar  1 00:0327: ISDN BR0/0: TX ->  Rrf sapi = 0  tei = 65  nr = 1
*Mar  1 00:0327: ISDN BR0/0: TX ->  Rrf sapi = 0  tei = 65  nr = 1

*Mar  1 00:03:30: ISDN BR0/0: RX <-  RRp sapi = 0  tei = 64 nr = 3
*Mar  1 00:03:30: ISDN BR0/0: TX ->  RRf sapi = 0  tei = 64  nr = 3

*Mar  1 00:03:37: ISDN BR0/0: RX <-  RRp sapi = 0  tei = 65 nr = 1
*Mar  1 00:03:37: ISDN BR0/0: TX ->  RRf sapi = 0  tei = 65  nr = 1
```

D Channel Monitoring

Type **show interface bri 0/0** to display the status of the D channel of the BRI interface. The physical interface that the BRI is connected to is bri 0/0. When you display this interface with the **show interface bri 0/0** command, the router displays the D channel status of the BRI circuit.

```
RouterA#show interface bri 0/0
BRI0/0 is up, line protocol is up (spoofing)  ← D channel status
   Hardware is QUICC BRI with U interface
   Internet address is 196.1.1.1/24
   MTU 1500 bytes, BW 64 Kbit, DLY 20000 usec, rely 255/255, load 1/255
   Encapsulation PPP, loopback not set
   Last input 00:00:00, output never, output hang never
   Last clearing of "show interface" counters never
   Queueing strategy: fifo
   Output queue 0/40, 0 drops; input queue 0/75, 0 drops
   5 minute input rate 0 bits/sec, 0 packets/sec
   5 minute output rate 0 bits/sec, 0 packets/sec
      156 packets input, 946 bytes, 0 no buffer
      Received 0 broadcasts, 0 runts, 0 giants, 0 throttles
      0 input errors, 0 CRC, 0 frame, 0 overrun, 0 ignored, 0 abort
      156 packets output, 1056 bytes, 0 underruns
      0 output errors, 0 collisions, 4 interface resets
      0 output buffer failures, 0 output buffers swapped out
      1 carrier transitions
```

To display the status of each individual B channel, you need to issue the **show interface bri 0/0:1** command for B channel #1 or **show interface bri 0/0:2** for B channel #2. We see that both of these interfaces are in a down/down state, because there are no active calls on the routers at this time.

```
RouterA#show interface bri 0/0:1  ← B channel #1
BRI0/0:1 is down, line protocol is down
   Hardware is QUICC BRI with U interface
   MTU 1500 bytes, BW 64 Kbit, DLY 20000 usec, rely 255/255, load 1/255
   Encapsulation PPP, loopback not set, keepalive set (10 sec)
   LCP Closed, multilink Closed
   Closed: IPCP, CDP
   Last input 00:01:04, output 00:01:04, output hang never
   Last clearing of "show interface" counters never
   Queueing strategy: fifo
   Output queue 0/40, 0 drops; input queue 0/75, 0 drops
   5 minute input rate 0 bits/sec, 0 packets/sec
   5 minute output rate 0 bits/sec, 0 packets/sec
      37 packets input, 838 bytes, 0 no buffer
      Received 0 broadcasts, 0 runts, 0 giants, 0 throttles
      0 input errors, 0 CRC, 0 frame, 0 overrun, 0 ignored, 0 abort
      38 packets output, 1116 bytes, 0 underruns
```

```
        0 output errors, 0 collisions, 0 interface resets
        0 output buffer failures, 0 output buffers swapped out
      16 carrier transitions

RouterA#show interface bri 0/0:2  ← B channel #2
BRI0/0:2 is down, line protocol is down
   Hardware is QUICC BRI with U interface
   MTU 1500 bytes, BW 64 Kbit, DLY 20000 usec, rely 255/255, load 1/255
   Encapsulation PPP, loopback not set, keepalive set (10 sec)
   LCP Closed, multilink Closed
   Closed: IPCP, CDP
   Last input 00:01:08, output 00:01:08, output hang never
   Last clearing of "show interface" counters never
   Queueing strategy: fifo
   Output queue 0/40, 0 drops; input queue 0/75, 0 drops
   5 minute input rate 0 bits/sec, 0 packets/sec
   5 minute output rate 0 bits/sec, 0 packets/sec
      30 packets input, 740 bytes, 0 no buffer
      Received 0 broadcasts, 0 runts, 0 giants, 0 throttles
       0 input errors, 0 CRC, 0 frame, 0 overrun, 0 ignored, 0 abort
      32 packets output, 1032 bytes, 0 underruns
       0 output errors, 0 collisions, 0 interface resets
       0 output buffer failures, 0 output buffers swapped out
       2 carrier transitions
```

Layer 3 Debugging

Layer 3 debugging is turned on by issuing the **debug isdn q931** command on the router. Layer 3 ISDN traffic consists of the call setup and teardown for each B channel that is either making a call or receiving a call. CHAP authentication progress and status is monitored by entering the **debug ppp authentication** command. Remember to also type the **term mon** command if you are not connected to the console port of the router.

Now that Layer 3 debugging and PPP authentication debugging are enabled, let's place a call to RouterB by pinging IP address 196.1.1.2. Because Layer 3 debugging is turned on, we will see all of the call setup and teardown. Because PPP authentication is turned on, we will see the progress of the CHAP authentication between RouterA and RouterB.

```
RouterA#ping 196.1.1.2

Type escape sequence to abort.
Sending 5, 100-byte ICMP Echos to 196.1.1.2, timeout is 2 seconds:

ISDN BR0/0: TX ->  SETUP pd = 8  callref = 0x11  ← Call placed on B channel #1
         Bearer Capability i = 0x8890
```

```
            Channel ID i = 0x83
            Keypad Facility i = '8995201'
ISDN BR0/0: RX <-  CALL_PROC pd = 8  callref = 0x91
            Channel ID i = 0x89
ISDN BR0/0: RX <-  CONNECT pd = 8  callref = 0x91 ← Connect on B channel #1
            Channel ID i = 0x89
%LINK-3-UPDOWN: Interface BRI0/0:1, changed state to up
PPP BRI0/0:1: treating connection as a callout
ISDN BR0/0: TX ->  CONNECT_ACK pd = 8  callref = 0x11
PPP BRI0/0:1: Send CHAP Challenge id=2 ← Chap challenge sent
PPP BRI0/0:1: CHAP Challenge id=2 received from RouterB
PPP BRI0/0:1: Send CHAP Response id=2
PPP BRI0/0:1: CHAP response received from RouterB
PPP BRI0/0:1: CHAP Response id=2 received from RouterB
PPP BRI0/0:1: Send CHAP Success id=2 ← CHAP success B channel #1
PPP BRI0/0:1: remote passed CHAP authentication
PPP BRI0/0:1: Passed CHAP authentication with remote
%LINK-3-UPDOWN: Interface Virtual-Access1, changed state to up
PPP Virtual-Access1: treating connection as a callin
%LINEPROTO-5-UPDOWN: Line protocol on I.nterface BRI0/0:1, changed state to up
%LINEPROTO-5-UPDOWN: Line protocol on Interface Virtual-Access1, changed state
to up
ISDN BR0/0: TX ->  SETUP pd = 8  callref = 0x12 ← Call placed on B channel #2
            Bearer Capability i = 0x8890
            Channel ID i = 0x83
            Keypad Facility i = '8995201'
ISDN BR0/0: RX <-  CALL_PROC pd = 8  callref = 0x92
            Channel ID i = 0x8A
ISDN BR0/0: Event: incoming ces value = 2
ISDN BR0/0: RX <-  CONNECT pd = 8  callref = 0x92 ← Connect on B channel #2
            Channel ID i = 0x8A
ISDN BR0/0: Event: incoming ces value = 2
%LINK-3-UPDOWN: Interface BRI0/0:2, changed state to up
PPP BRI0/0:2: treating connection as a callout
ISDN BR0/0: TX ->  CONNECT_ACK pd = 8  callref = 0x12
PPP BRI0/0:2: Send CHAP Challenge id=2 ← Chap challenge sent
PPP BRI0/0:2: CHAP Challenge id=2 received from RouterB
PPP BRI0/0:2: Send CHAP Response id=2
PPP BRI0/0:2: CHAP response received from RouterB
PPP BRI0/0:2: CHAP Response id=2 received from RouterB
PPP BRI0/0:2: Send CHAP Success id=2 ← CHAP success B channel #2
PPP BRI0/0:2: remote passed CHAP authentication.
PPP BRI0/0:2: Passed CHAP authentication with remote.
%LINEPROTO-5-UPDOWN: Line protocol on Interface BRI0/0:2, changed state to up
%ISDN-6-CONNECT: Interface BRI0/0:2 is now connected to 8995201 RouterB

..!!!
Success rate is 60 percent (3/5), round-trip min/avg/max = 20/22/24 ms
RouterA#
```

The ping was only 60 percent successful because it was started while the router was still making its ISDN call and was connecting.

The **show ppp multilink** command is used to display the status of any multilink ppp bundles on the router. We see from the following output that we have two B channels that are connected into a multilink bundle on RouterA.

```
RouterA#show ppp multilink

Bundle RouterB, 2 members, Master link is Virtual-Access1
Dialer Interface is BRI0/0
  0 lost fragments, 0 reordered, 0 unassigned, sequence 0x6/0x8 rcvd/sent
  0 discarded, 0 lost received, 1/255 load

Member Links: 2 ← 2 B channels in a multilink bundle
BRI0/0:1
BRI0/0:2
```

We see that when a call is active on the BRI interface, the D channel still shows up/up (spoofing).

```
RouterA#show interface bri 0/0
BRI0/0 is up, line protocol is up (spoofing) ← D channel will show up/up
                                                (spoofing) whether or not a
                                                call is connected

  Hardware is QUICC BRI with U interface
  Internet address is 196.1.1.1/24
  MTU 1500 bytes, BW 64 Kbit, DLY 20000 usec, rely 255/255, load 1/255
  Encapsulation PPP, loopback not set
  Last input 00:00:03, output never, output hang never
  Last clearing of "show interface" counters never
  Queueing strategy: fifo
  Output queue 0/40, 0 drops; input queue 0/75, 0 drops
  5 minute input rate 0 bits/sec, 0 packets/sec
  5 minute output rate 0 bits/sec, 0 packets/sec
     168 packets input, 1022 bytes, 0 no buffer
     Received 0 broadcasts, 0 runts, 0 giants, 0 throttles
     0 input errors, 0 CRC, 0 frame, 0 overrun, 0 ignored, 0 abort
     168 packets output, 1152 bytes, 0 underruns
     0 output errors, 0 collisions, 4 interface resets
     0 output buffer failures, 0 output buffers swapped out
     1 carrier transitions
```

We see that both B channels are now in an up/up state, because we have an active call on both channels of the BRI.

```
RouterA#show interface bri 0/0:1
BRI0/0:1 is up, line protocol is up ← B channel #1
  Hardware is QUICC BRI with U interface
  MTU 1500 bytes, BW 64 Kbit, DLY 20000 usec, rely 255/255, load 1/255
  Encapsulation PPP, loopback not set, keepalive set (10 sec)
  LCP Open, multilink Open
```

```
Last input 00:00:03, output 00:00:03, output hang never
Last clearing of "show interface" counters never
Queueing strategy: fifo
Output queue 0/40, 0 drops; input queue 0/75, 0 drops
5 minute input rate 0 bits/sec, 0 packets/sec
5 minute output rate 0 bits/sec, 0 packets/sec
    55 packets input, 1292 bytes, 0 no buffer
    Received 0 broadcasts, 0 runts, 0 giants, 0 throttles
    0 input errors, 0 CRC, 0 frame, 0 overrun, 0 ignored, 0 abort
    56 packets output, 1702 bytes, 0 underruns
    0 output errors, 0 collisions, 0 interface resets
    0 output buffer failures, 0 output buffers swapped out
    17 carrier transitions

RouterA#show interface bri 0/0:2
BRI0/0:2 is up, line protocol is up ← B channel #2
  Hardware is QUICC BRI with U interface
  MTU 1500 bytes, BW 64 Kbit, DLY 20000 usec, rely 255/255, load 1/255
  Encapsulation PPP, loopback not set, keepalive set (10 sec)
  LCP Open, multilink Open
  Last input 00:00:00, output 00:00:00, output hang never
  Last clearing of "show interface" counters never
  Queueing strategy: fifo
  Output queue 0/40, 0 drops; input queue 0/75, 0 drops
  5 minute input rate 0 bits/sec, 0 packets/sec
  5 minute output rate 0 bits/sec, 0 packets/sec
      42 packets input, 1116 bytes, 0 no buffer
      Received 0 broadcasts, 0 runts, 0 giants, 0 throttles
      0 input errors, 0 CRC, 0 frame, 0 overrun, 0 ignored, 0 abort
      45 packets output, 1554 bytes, 0 underruns
      0 output errors, 0 collisions, 0 interface resets
      0 output buffer failures, 0 output buffers swapped out
      3 carrier transitions
```

The output of the **show dialer** command will give you important information on how many successful calls and failed calls have been made. It will also show what phone number is being dialed to place calls. Under each B channel, you will also see information on how long the call has been connected, the time until the call is disconnected, what number the call actually connected to, and the reason that the call was made.

```
RouterA#show dialer

BRI0/0 - dialer type = ISDN

Dial String        Successes    Failures    Last called    Last status
8995201                    4          14     00:00:25       successful
0 incoming call(s) have been screened.

BRI0/0:1 - dialer type = ISDN
```

```
Idle timer (90 secs), Fast idle timer (20 secs)
Wait for carrier (30 secs), Re-enable (15 secs)
Dialer state is physical layer up
Dial reason: ip (s=196.1.1.1, d=196.1.1.2) ←  Reason for call
Time until disconnect 60 secs  ←  Time until disconnect
Current call connected 00:00:26  ←  Current connect time
Connected to 8995201 (RouterB)  ←  Number connected

BRI0/0:2 - dialer type = ISDN
Idle timer (90 secs), Fast idle timer (20 secs)
Wait for carrier (30 secs), Re-enable (15 secs)
Dialer state is physical layer up
Dial reason: Multilink bundle overloaded
Time until disconnect 62 secs
Current call connected 00:00:27
Connected to 8995201 (RouterB)
```

The **show dialer map** command is another important tool for troubleshooting layer 3 connectivity. This command will display all static and dynamic dialer map statements. We see that we have a static map defined on RouterA, which tells us what number to call to get to RouterB at IP address 196.1.1.2.

```
RouterA#show dialer map
Static dialer map ip 196.1.1.2 name RouterB broadcast (8995201) on BRI0/0
```

The following screen print shows what will be outputted from the router when the router disconnects an ISDN call. ISDN Q931 debugging is enabled on this trace. You can tell that the router is sending the disconnect message to the ISDN switch because the output message indicates **TX -> DISCONNECT**, which tells us that the router is transmitting a disconnect message to the ISDN switch.

```
%LINEPROTO-5-UPDOWN: Line protocol on Interface Virtual-Access1, changed state
to down
%LINK-3-UPDOWN: Interface Virtual-Access1, changed state to down
%ISDN-6-DISCONNECT: Interface BRI0/0:1  disconnected from 8995201 RouterB, call
lasted 94 seconds
%ISDN-6-DISCONNECT: Interface BRI0/0:2  disconnected from 8995201 RouterB, call
lasted 91 seconds
ISDN BR0/0: TX ->  DISCONNECT pd = 8  callref = 0x11 ← Disconnect B channel
                                                       #1
         Cause i = 0x8090 - Normal call clearing
ISDN BR0/0: TX ->  DISCONNECT pd = 8  callref = 0x12 ← Disconnect B channel
                                                       #2
         Cause i = 0x8090 - Normal call clearing
ISDN BR0/0: RX <-  RELEASE pd = 8  callref = 0x91
%LINK-3-UPDOWN: Interface BRI0/0:1, changed state to down
ISDN BR0/0: TX ->  RELEASE_COMP pd = 8  callref = 0x11
```

```
ISDN BR0/0: RX <-  RELEASE pd = 8  callref = 0x92
ISDN BR0/0: Event: incoming ces value = 2
%LINK-3-UPDOWN: Interface BRI0/0:2, changed state to down
ISDN BR0/0: TX -> RELEASE_COMP pd = 8  callref = 0x12
%LINEPROTO-5-UPDOWN: Line protocol on Interface BRI0/0:1, changed state to down
%LINEPROTO-5-UPDOWN: Line protocol on Interface BRI0/0:2, changed state to down
```

CHAP Failure

Let's force a CHAP authentication failure on our test network and see how to debug this problem. We see from our configuration that configuring CHAP involves two main steps:

1. You need the command **ppp authentication chap** under the appropriate router interface.

2. You need a username which corresponds to the far-end router's hostname, as well as a password that matches the password set on the far-end router's username statement.

Our current configuration for RouterA has the statement **username RouterB password 7 070C285F4D06**. The password is encrypted and is not visible in its clear text, but the password was set to "cisco" when the configuration was first created.

Enter configuration mode by typing **config term** at the command prompt. Enter the command **username RouterB password 0 disco**. The corresponding username statement on RouterB contains the password cisco. Having a different CHAP password on RouterA and on RouterB will create a CHAP authentication failure when the two routers attempt to authenticate.

```
RouterA#config term
Enter configuration commands, one per line. End with CNTL/Z.
RouterA(config)#username RouterB password 0 disco
RouterA(config)#exit
RouterA#
```

Make sure that PPP authentication debugging is enabled by typing **debug ppp authentication**.

```
RouterA#debug ppp authen
PPP authentication debugging is on
```

Now, let's bring up the ISDN circuit by starting a ping from RouterA to RouterB at IP address 196.1.1.2. Notice that in the debug output,

RouterA declares a CHAP failure when it is trying to authenticate with RouterB. This example demonstrates that it is crucial to enable ppp authentication debugging when a problem occurs with establishing an ISDN call.

```
RouterA#ping 196.1.1.2

Type escape sequence to abort.
Sending 5, 100-byte ICMP Echos to 196.1.1.2, timeout is 2 seconds:

%LINK-3-UPDOWN: Interface BRI0/0:1, changed state to up
PPP BRI0/0:1: treating connection as a callout
PPP BRI0/0:1: Send CHAP Challenge id=3 ← Chap sent on B channel #1
PPP BRI0/0:1: CHAP Challenge id=3 received from RouterB
PPP BRI0/0:1: Send CHAP Response id=3
PPP BRI0/0:1: CHAP response received from RouterB
PPP BRI0/0:1: CHAP Response id=3 received from RouterB
PPP BRI0/0:1: Send CHAP Failure id=3, MD compare failed ← CHAP failure on B
                                                            channel #1
%LINK-3-UPDOWN: Interface BRI0/0:1, changed state to down.
%LINK-3-UPDOWN: Interface BRI0/0:1, changed state to up
PPP BRI0/0:1: treating connection as a callout
PPP BRI0/0:1: Send CHAP Challenge id=4 ← Chap sent on B channel #1
PPP BRI0/0:1: CHAP Challenge id=4 received from RouterB
PPP BRI0/0:1: Send CHAP Response id=4
PPP BRI0/0:1: CHAP response received from RouterB
PPP BRI0/0:1: CHAP Response id=4 received from RouterB
PPP BRI0/0:1: Send CHAP Failure id=4, MD compare failed ← CHAP failure on B
                                                            channel #1
%LINK-3-UPDOWN: Interface BRI0/0:1, changed state to down.
%LINK-3-UPDOWN: Interface BRI0/0:1, changed state to up
PPP BRI0/0:1: treating connection as a callout
PPP BRI0/0:1: Send CHAP Challenge id=5 ← The far end router tries to CHAP
                                          several more times and then
                                          disconnects the call
PPP BRI0/0:1: CHAP Challenge id=5 received from RouterB
PPP BRI0/0:1: Send CHAP Response id=5
PPP BRI0/0:1: CHAP response received from RouterB
PPP BRI0/0:1: CHAP Response id=5 received from RouterB
PPP BRI0/0:1: Send CHAP Failure id=5, MD compare failed
%LINK-3-UPDOWN: Interface BRI0/0:1, changed state to down.
%LINK-3-UPDOWN: Interface BRI0/0:1, changed state to up
PPP BRI0/0:1: treating connection as a callout
PPP BRI0/0:1: Send CHAP Challenge id=6
PPP BRI0/0:1: CHAP Challenge id=6 received from RouterB
PPP BRI0/0:1: Send CHAP Response id=6
PPP BRI0/0:1: CHAP response received from RouterB
PPP BRI0/0:1: CHAP Response id=6 received from RouterB
PPP BRI0/0:1: Send CHAP Failure id=6, MD compare failed
%LINK-3-UPDOWN: Interface BRI0/0:1, changed state to down
%LINK-3-UPDOWN: Interface BRI0/0:1, changed state to up
PPP BRI0/0:1: treating connection as a callout
```

```
PPP BRI0/0:1: Send CHAP Challenge id=7
PPP BRI0/0:1: CHAP Challenge id=7 received from RouterB
PPP BRI0/0:1: Send CHAP Response id=7
PPP BRI0/0:1: CHAP response received from RouterB
PPP BRI0/0:1: CHAP Response id=7 received from RouterB
PPP BRI0/0:1: Send CHAP Failure id=7, MD compare failed
%LINK-3-UPDOWN: Interface BRI0/0:1, changed state to down  ← Call gets
                                                              disconnected
Success rate is 0 percent (0/5)
```

Now, let's change the CHAP password back to its correct value on RouterA. Enter configuration mode and type the proper username command shown as follows:

```
RouterA#config term
Enter configuration commands, one per line. End with CNTL/Z.
RouterA(config)#username RouterB password 0 cisco  ← Correct password
RouterA(config)#exit
RouterA#
```

Now, let's verify that we can make a call and pass CHAP authentication. Ping RouterB at IP address 196.1.1.2.

```
RouterA#ping 196.1.1.2

Type escape sequence to abort.
Sending 5, 100-byte ICMP Echos to 196.1.1.2, timeout is 2 seconds:

%LINK-3-UPDOWN: Interface BRI0/0:1, changed state to up
%LINK-3-UPDOWN: Interface Virtual-Access1, changed state to up
%LINEPROTO-5-UPDOWN: Line protocol on Interface BRI0/0:1, changed state to up
%LINEPROTO-5-UPDOWN: Line protocol on Interface Virtual-Access1, changed state
to up
%LINK-3-UPDOWN: Interface BRI0/0:2, changed state to up
%LINEPROTO-5-UPDOWN: Line protocol on Interface BRI0/0:2, changed state to up
%ISDN-6-CONNECT: Interface BRI0/0:2 is now connected to 8995201 RouterB

.!!!!
Success rate is 80 percent (4/5), round-trip min/avg/max = 32/33/36 ms
```

Wrong Dial Number

Now, let's see how to debug the situation where you are dialing the wrong number. Recall from the following portion of RouterA's configuration that RouterA dials the number 8995201 to call RouterB.

```
RouterA#show run
Building configuration...

interface BRI0/0
 ip address 196.1.1.1 255.255.255.0
 encapsulation ppp
 isdn spid1 5101 8995101
 isdn spid2 5102 8995102
 dialer idle-timeout 90
 dialer map ip 196.1.1.2 name RouterB broadcast 8995201 ← Dial 8995201 to call
                                                            RouterB
 dialer load-threshold 1
 dialer-group 1
 no fair-queue
 ppp authentication chap
 ppp multilink
```

Let's change the dial number in RouterA's configuration. Enter configuration mode and delete the current dialer map. Add a new dialer map that calls 8996000 instead of the correct number (8995201).

```
RouterA#config term
Enter configuration commands, one per line. End with CNTL/Z.
RouterA(config)#interface bri 0/0
RouterA(config-if)#no dialer map ip 196.1.1.2 name RouterB broadcast 8995201
RouterA(config-if)#dialer map ip 196.1.1.2 name RouterB broadcast 8996000
RouterA(config-if)#exit                                              ↑
RouterA(config)#exit                                        Incorrect number
RouterA#
```

As shown here, the configuration of RouterA will now reflect the incorrect dial number in its dialer map.

```
RouterA#show run
Building configuration...

Current configuration:
!
version 11.2
no service udp-small-servers
no service tcp-small-servers
!
hostname RouterA
!
enable password cisco
!
username RouterB password 7 01100F175804
isdn switch-type basic-ni1
!
interface Ethernet0/0
 no ip address
```

```
 shutdown
!
interface Serial0/0
 no ip address
!
interface BRI0/0
 ip address 196.1.1.1 255.255.255.0
 encapsulation ppp
 isdn spid1 5101 8995101
 isdn spid2 5102 8995102
 dialer idle-timeout 90
 dialer map ip 196.1.1.2 name RouterB broadcast 8996000 ← Incorrect number
 dialer load-threshold 1
 dialer-group 1
 no fair-queue
 ppp authentication chap
 ppp multilink
!
interface Ethernet1/0
 no ip address
 shutdown
!
interface Serial1/0
 no ip address
 shutdown
!
interface Serial1/1
 no ip address
 shutdown
!
 no ip classless
dialer-list 1 protocol ip permit
!
line con 0
 password cisco
 login
line aux 0
line vty 0 4
 login
!
end
```

Turn on ISDN layer 3 call control debugging with the **debug isdn q931** command.

```
RouterA#debug isdn q931
ISDN Q931 packets debugging is on
```

Now, let's ping RouterB at IP address 196.1.1.2. Remember that we will be dialing the wrong number to get to RouterB. Our Adtran Atlas 800 ISDN switch is not provisioned with 8996000 as a valid number.

```
RouterA#ping 196.1.1.2

Type escape sequence to abort.
Sending 5, 100-byte ICMP Echos to 196.1.1.2, timeout is 2 seconds:

ISDN BR0/0: TX ->  SETUP pd = 8  callref = 0x1A
        Bearer Capability i = 0x8890
        Channel ID i = 0x83
        Keypad Facility i = '8996000' <- RouterA is dialing 8996000
ISDN BR0/0: RX <-  CALL_PROC pd = 8  callref = 0x9A
        Channel ID i = 0x89
ISDN BR0/0: RX <-  DISCONNECT pd = 8  callref = 0x9A
        Cause i = 0x8281 - Unallocated/unassigned number <- The ISDN switch
                                                            sends an immediate
                                                            disconnect message
                                                            to RouterA. The
                                                            cause code
                                                            indicates that we
                                                            are dialing an
                                                            unassigned number.
ISDN BR0/0: TX ->  RELEASE pd = 8  callref = 0x1A
ISDN BR0/0: RX <-  RELEASE_COMP pd = 8  callref = 0x9A.
ISDN BR0/0: TX ->  SETUP pd = 8  callref = 0x1B  <- Router dialed again
        Bearer Capability i = 0x8890
        Channel ID i = 0x83
        Keypad Facility i = '8996000'
ISDN BR0/0: RX <-  CALL_PROC pd = 8  callref = 0x9B
        Channel ID i = 0x89
ISDN BR0/0: RX <-  DISCONNECT pd = 8  callref = 0x9B
        Cause i = 0x8281 - Unallocated/unassigned number
ISDN BR0/0: TX ->  RELEASE pd = 8  callref = 0x1B
ISDN BR0/0: RX <-  RELEASE_COMP pd = 8  callref = 0x9B.
ISDN BR0/0: TX ->  SETUP pd = 8  callref = 0x1C
        Bearer Capability i = 0x8890
        Channel ID i = 0x83
        Keypad Facility i = '8996000'
ISDN BR0/0: RX <-  CALL_PROC pd = 8  callref = 0x9C
        Channel ID i = 0x89
ISDN BR0/0: RX <-  DISCONNECT pd = 8  callref = 0x9C
        Cause i = 0x8281 - Unallocated/unassigned number
ISDN BR0/0: TX ->  RELEASE pd = 8  callref = 0x1C
ISDN BR0/0: RX <-  RELEASE_COMP pd = 8  callref = 0x9C.
ISDN BR0/0: TX ->  SETUP pd = 8  callref = 0x1D
        Bearer Capability i = 0x8890
        Channel ID i = 0x83
        Keypad Facility i = '8996000'
ISDN BR0/0: RX <-  CALL_PROC pd = 8  callref = 0x9D
        Channel ID i = 0x89
ISDN BR0/0: RX <-  DISCONNECT pd = 8  callref = 0x9D
        Cause i = 0x8281 - Unallocated/unassigned number
ISDN BR0/0: TX ->  RELEASE pd = 8  callref = 0x1D
ISDN BR0/0: RX <-  RELEASE_COMP pd = 8  callref = 0x9D.
ISDN BR0/0: TX ->  SETUP pd = 8  callref = 0x1E <- The router dials a total of
                                                   5 times before giving up
```

```
        Bearer Capability i = 0x8890
        Channel ID i = 0x83
        Keypad Facility i = '8996000'
ISDN BR0/0: RX <-  CALL_PROC pd = 8  callref = 0x9E
        Channel ID i = 0x89
ISDN BR0/0: RX <-  DISCONNECT pd = 8  callref = 0x9E
        Cause i = 0x8281 - Unallocated/unassigned number
ISDN BR0/0: TX ->  RELEASE pd = 8  callref = 0x1E
ISDN BR0/0: RX <-  RELEASE_COMP pd = 8  callref = 0x9E.
Success rate is 0 percent (0/5)
```

Now, let's change the dialer map for RouterA back to the correct dial number. Enter configuration mode, delete the current incorrect dialer map, and add back the correct dial map.

```
RouterA#config term
Enter configuration commands, one per line. End with CNTL/Z.
RouterA(config)#interface bri 0/0
RouterA(config-if)#no dialer map ip 196.1.1.2 name RouterB broadcast 8996000
RouterA(config-if)#dialer map ip 196.1.1.2 name RouterB broadcast 8995201
RouterA(config-if)#extit
RouterA(config)#exit
RouterA#
```

A ping to RouterB at IP address 196.1.1.2 will now be successful. Notice that from the following layer 3 trace, RouterA is now dialing the correct number (8995201).

```
RouterA#ping 196.1.1.2

Type escape sequence to abort.
Sending 5, 100-byte ICMP Echos to 196.1.1.2, timeout is 2 seconds:

ISDN BR0/0: TX ->  SETUP pd = 8  callref = 0x1F
        Bearer Capability i = 0x8890
        Channel ID i = 0x83
        Keypad Facility i = '8995201' ← Correct number
ISDN BR0/0: RX <-  CALL_PROC pd = 8  callref = 0x9F
        Channel ID i = 0x89
ISDN BR0/0: RX <-  CONNECT pd = 8  callref = 0x9F
        Channel ID i = 0x89
%LINK-3-UPDOWN: Interface BRI0/0:1, changed state to up
ISDN BR0/0: TX ->  CONNECT_ACK pd = 8  callref = 0x1F
%LINK-3-UPDOWN: Interface Virtual-Access1, changed state to up
%LINEPROTO-5-UPDOWN: Line protocol on Interface BRI0/0:1, changed state to up
%LINEPROTO-5-UPDOWN: Line protocol on Interface Virtual-Access1, changed state
to up
ISDN BR0/0: TX ->  SETUP pd = 8  callref = 0x20
        Bearer Capability i = 0x8890
        Channel ID i = 0x83
        Keypad Facility i = '8995201'
```

```
ISDN BR0/0: RX <-  CALL_PROC pd = 8  callref = 0xA0
        Channel ID i = 0x8A
ISDN BR0/0: Event: incoming ces value = 2
ISDN BR0/0: RX <-  CONNECT pd = 8  callref = 0xA0
        Channel ID i = 0x8A
ISDN BR0/0: Event: incoming ces value = 2
%LINK-3-UPDOWN: Interface BRI0/0:2, changed state to up
ISDN BR0/0: TX ->  CONNECT_ACK pd = 8  callref = 0x20
%LINEPROTO-5-UPDOWN: Line protocol on Interface BRI0/0:2, changed state to up
%ISDN-6-CONNECT: Interface BRI0/0:2 is now connected to 8995201 RouterB

.!!!!
Success rate is 80 percent (4/5), round-trip min/avg/max = 32/33/36 ms
```

Incoming Call Trace

Now, let's look at what an incoming call looks like. Unlike an outgoing call, we see that the Setup message is received by the router. We also see that the router displays the number of the calling party. Notice that the first incoming call comes from 8995101, and the second incoming call comes from 8995102.

```
*Mar  1 00:55:48: ISDN BR0/0: RX <-  SETUP pd = 8  callref = 0x0E
*Mar  1 00:55:48:          Bearer Capability i = 0x8890
*Mar  1 00:55:48:          Channel ID i = 0x89
*Mar  1 00:55:48:          Calling Party Number i = '!', 0x80, '0008995101'
*Mar  1 00:55:48:          Called Party Number i = 0xC1, '8995201'
%LINK-3-UPDOWN: Interface BRI0/0:1, changed state to up
*Mar  1 00:55:48: ISDN BR0/0: TX ->  CONNECT pd = 8  callref = 0x8E
*Mar  1 00:55:48:          Channel ID i = 0x89
*Mar  1 00:55:48: ISDN BR0/0: RX <-  CONNECT_ACK pd = 8  callref = 0x0E
*Mar  1 00:55:48: PPP BRI0/0:1: Send CHAP challenge id=10 to remote
*Mar  1 00:55:48: PPP BRI0/0:1: CHAP challenge from RouterA
*Mar  1 00:55:48: PPP BRI0/0:1: CHAP response received from RouterA
*Mar  1 00:55:48: PPP BRI0/0:1: CHAP response id=10 received from RouterA
*Mar  1 00:55:48: PPP BRI0/0:1: Send CHAP success id=10 to remote
*Mar  1 00:55:48: PPP BRI0/0:1: remote passed CHAP authentication.
*Mar  1 00:55:48: PPP BRI0/0:1: Passed CHAP authentication with remote.
%LINK-3-UPDOWN: Interface Virtual-Access1, changed state to up
%LINEPROTO-5-UPDOWN: Line protocol on Interface BRI0/0:1, changed state to up
%LINEPROTO-5-UPDOWN: Line protocol on Interface Virtual-Access1, changed state
to up
*Mar  1 00:55:50: ISDN BR0/0: RX <-  SETUP pd = 8  callref = 0x0F
*Mar  1 00:55:50:          Bearer Capability i = 0x8890
*Mar  1 00:55:50:          Channel ID i = 0x8A
*Mar  1 00:55:50:          Calling Party Number i = '!', 0x80, '0008995102'
*Mar  1 00:55:50:          Called Party Number i = 0xC1, '8995201'
%LINK-3-UPDOWN: Interface BRI0/0:2, changed state to up
```

```
*Mar  1 00:55:50: ISDN BR0/0: TX ->  CONNECT pd = 8  callref = 0x8F
*Mar  1 00:55:50:          Channel ID i = 0x8A
*Mar  1 00:55:51: ISDN BR0/0: RX <-  CONNECT_ACK pd = 8  callref = 0x0F
*Mar  1 00:55:51: PPP BRI0/0:2: Send CHAP challenge id=5 to remote
*Mar  1 00:55:51: PPP BRI0/0:2: CHAP challenge from RouterA
*Mar  1 00:55:51: PPP BRI0/0:2: CHAP response received from RouterA
*Mar  1 00:55:51: PPP BRI0/0:2: CHAP response id=5 received from RouterA
*Mar  1 00:55:51: PPP BRI0/0:2: Send CHAP success id=5 to remote
*Mar  1 00:55:51: PPP BRI0/0:2: remote passed CHAP authentication.
*Mar  1 00:55:51: PPP BRI0/0:2: Passed CHAP authentication with remote.
%ISDN-6-CONNECT: Interface BRI0/0:1 is now connected to 0008995101 RouterA
%LINEPROTO-5-UPDOWN: Line protocol on Interface BRI0/0:2, changed state to up
%ISDN-6-CONNECT: Interface BRI0/0:2 is now connected to 0008995102 RouterA
```

Conclusion

ISDN is the most popular technology in use today for high speed switched access and dial backup applications. This chapter demonstrated the ISDN capabilities of a Cisco router.

4

Frame-Relay

Topics Covered in This Chapter

- Frame Relay technology overview
- Configuring a Cisco router as a Frame Relay switch
- LMI autosense
- Configuring discard eligibility
- Frame Relay map statements
- Partial PVC mesh with full connectivity
- Frame Relay subinterfaces
- Frame Relay traffic shaping
- Troubleshooting Frame Relay

Introduction

Frame Relay is the most popular wide-area backbone networking protocol today. The Cisco IOS has extensive support for Frame Relay networking. This chapter will examine Frame Relay technology in detail as well as how the Cisco IOS supports Frame Relay with eight hands-on labs.

Frame Relay Technology Overview

Frame Relay is a connection-oriented, layer 2 transport protocol. It is closely related to X.25 but removes the error correction and retransmission built into X.25. Frame Relay assumes clean digital lines so that extensive error correction is not necessary. The following sections will take a detailed look at Frame Relay technology.

The Justification for Frame Relay

As networks grew larger during the 1980s, more and more leased lines were necessary to tie them together. These leased lines were used as point-to-point links between corporate data centers and offices. To ensure network integrity and redundancy, many sites had more than one leased line connecting it to other sites. Maximum redundancy was provided with a full mesh architecture, where every site was connected to every other site. Mathematically, a fully meshed network of n sites requires $n(n-1)/2$ leased lines. Figure 4–1 shows a sample network with five sites.

Fully meshing this network requires 10 leased lines. This number is calculated from the $n(n-1)/2$ equation, where $n=5$ as $5(5-1)/2=10$.

Figure 4–1 demonstrates the three main problems with trying to provide connectivity on a large network:

1. As the network grows, the number of leased lines and router interfaces required for a fully meshed network grows by $n(n-1)/2$. After a certain point, it becomes prohibitively expensive to implement a fully meshed network.

2. Excessive line charges are being paid, because the network owner also owns the entire links end to end (leased lines).

Figure 4–1
A fully meshed,
leased-line network

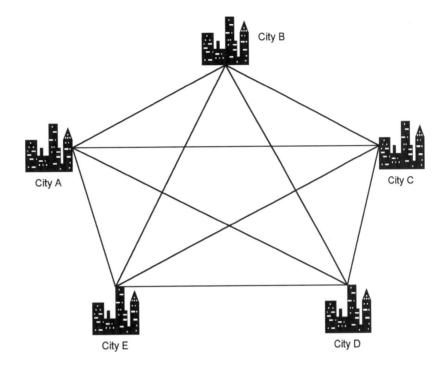

3. The network is not efficient, because statistically not all lines will be utilized at once. Each site can only be transmitting to one other site at any given time, utilizing one leased line. All other leased lines will be idle during this period.

What is Frame Relay?

Figure 4–2 shows a solution to the three problems discussed in the precious section with a fully or partially meshed network.

Each site in the network has a single leased line into the network cloud. In Figure 4–2, there are five sites and five leased lines. Notice that the number of leased lines has been cut in half with respect to a fully meshed network. Line charges are also lower, because you only pay for a circuit to the nearest Frame Relay switch instead of paying for an end-to-end leased line. This feature is the attraction of Frame Relay—the capacity to take a partially or fully meshed network of leased lines and convert it to a network with only one leased line and router interface per site.

Frame Relay is a simple and streamlined protocol. An important feature of Frame Relay to keep in mind is that Frame Relay is an access

Figure 4–2
Sample Frame Relay
network topology

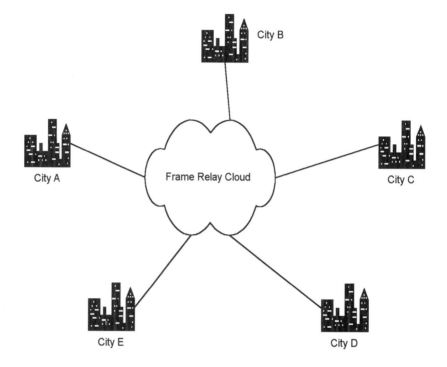

protocol, which means that Frame Relay only defines signaling and data formats between the DTE and the Frame Relay switch.

We should note an important issue at this point. It can be argued that the network depicted in Figure 4–2 is less robust then the network depicted in Figure 4–1. This reasoning occurs because the network in Figure 4–2 has only one link going to each site, while the network in Figure 4–1 has four links going to each site. This problem is addressed in modern networks by also bringing an ISDN circuit to each of the sites on the network. A combination of Frame Relay and ISDN circuits at each site can provide the same level of network integrity as a fully meshed network.

Frame Relay Terminology

Figure 4–3 shows some of the terminology used in a Frame Relay network. Two routers are connected via Frame Relay.

■ Both routers are referred to as Frame Relay DTE devices.

■ The Frame Relay switches that connect to the routers are referred to as Frame Relay DCE devices.

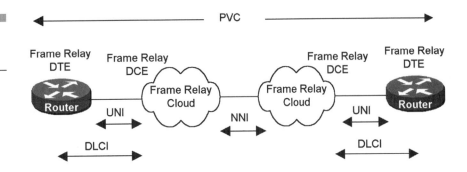

Figure 4–3
Frame Relay
terminology

- The access rate is the physical speed of the link between the user and the Frame Relay switch.

- The circuit that connects these two routers is known as a *Permanent Virtual Circuit* (PVC). This PVC consists of a unique *Data Link Connection Identifier* (DLCI) at each end of the circuit.

- Links between different Frame Relay providers' switch networks are referred to as *Network-to-Network Interfaces* (NNI) links.

- The signaling protocol between the routers and the Frame Relay switch is referred to as the *Local Management Interface* (LMI).

- The interface between the routers and the Frame Relay switches is referred to as the *User Network Interface* (UNI).

Frame Relay Addressing

Frame Relay is a layer 2, connection-oriented protocol. A Frame Relay circuit between two endpoints can either be permanent or switched. A permanent Frame Relay circuit is referred to as a PVC. A switched Frame Relay circuit is referred to as an SVC.

A point-to-point PVC connects two endpoints. Each endpoint refers to the PVC with a DLCI. These DLCI values are locally significant, which means that the DLCI value does not have to be unique between any other port on the Frame Relay network.

The primary job of a Frame Relay switch network is to receive traffic on one port—and by examining the DLCI value associated with that traffic, to send it out on the proper destination port with the proper DLCI value. The DLCI value on both sides of the circuit can be the same, or they can be different. If they are different, the Frame Relay switch network is responsible for doing the DLCI label switching.

Figure 4–4 shows an example of Frame Relay addressing. The figure shows four cities tied together via a Frame Relay network. In the diagram, there are three PVCs defined. Each PVC represents a permanent virtual circuit connection between its two endpoints.

These PVCs can be defined as follows:

■ A PVC between Denver and New York City (NYC). This PVC consists of DLCI 17 on the Denver side and DLCI 16 on the NYC side. Any traffic sent into the Denver Frame Relay switch with a DLCI value of 17 will be sent out of the NYC Frame Relay switch with a DLCI value of 16. Likewise, any traffic sent into the NYC Frame Relay switch with a DLCI value of 16 will be sent out of the Denver Frame Relay switch with a DLCI value of 17.

■ A PVC between Atlanta and NYC. This PVC consists of DLCI 100 on the Atlanta side and DLCI 100 on the NYC side. Any traffic sent into the Atlanta Frame Relay switch with a DLCI value of 100 will be sent out of the NYC Frame Relay switch with a DLCI value of 100. Likewise, any traffic sent into the NYC Frame Relay switch with a DLCI value of 100 will be sent out of the Atlanta Frame Relay switch with a DLCI value of 100. Notice that the DLCI value is 100 at both sides of the PVC. This value is allowed because a DLCI is only locally significant.

Figure 4–4
DLCI addressing
example

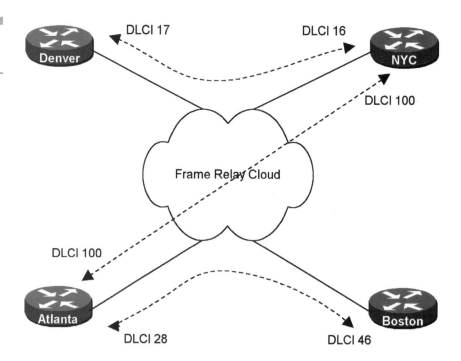

■ A PVC between Atlanta and Boston. This PVC consists of DLCI 28 on the Atlanta side and DLCI 46 on the Boston side. Any traffic sent into the Atlanta Frame Relay switch with a DLCI value of 28 will be sent out of the Boston Frame Relay switch with a DLCI value of 46. Likewise, any traffic sent into the Boston Frame Relay switch with a DLCI value of 46 will be sent out of the Atlanta Frame Relay switch with a DLCI value of 28.

Frame Relay Frame Format

One of Frame Relay's attractions is the fact that it is efficient. With only 2 bytes of address overhead, you can transmit up to 8K of data. Figure 4–5 shows the format of the Frame Relay frame.

The fields in Figure 4–5 can be explained as follows:

Flag: Each Frame Relay frame starts and ends with at least one delimiter character of 7Eh. This bit sequence enables the receiver to synchronize the start and end of a frame. A special bit destuffing algorithm exists, which ensures that this 7Eh character cannot appear in user traffic.

Address: The address field is either 2, 3, or 4 bytes long. A 2-byte address field is almost always used. The following fields are contained in a 2-byte address field:

Figure 4–5
Frame Relay
frame format

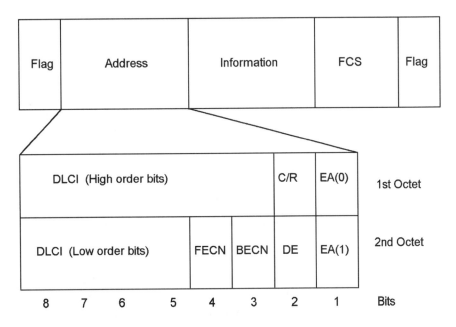

■ **DLCI:** This field is a 10-bit field which contains the Data Link Connection Identifier value that identifies a virtual circuit. For a typical 2-byte Frame Relay header, this field can take on a value between zero and 1,023. Some DLCI values such as zero and 1,023 are reserved for Frame Relay management. Valid user DLCI values range from 16 through 991. Recall from the previous section that the DLCI value tells the Frame Relay switch the proper destination of traffic sent into the Frame Relay network.

■ **CR:** This bit is known as the Command Response bit and is not used in most Frame Relay implementations.

■ **EA:** This bit is the Extended Address bit and is used to indicate whether a 2-, 3-, or 4-byte header is being used. This bit is set to 1 in the last byte of the header.

■ **FECN:** This bit is the Forward Explicit Congestion Notification bit. It is used to tell the user receiving Frame Relay frames that congestion exists in the direction that the frame was sent. FECN will be more fully discussed in a later section.

■ **BECN:** This bit is the Backward Explicit Congestion Notification bit and is used to tell the user receiving Frame Relay frames that congestion exists in the reverse direction that the frame was sent. BECN will be more fully discussed in a later section.

■ **DE:** This is the Discard Eligible bit. This bit can be set by either the Frame Relay DTE equipment (such as a router) or by the Frame Relay switch network. A frame with the DE bit set indicates that the frame can be discarded when the Frame Relay network becomes congested. Whether or not DE flagged frames are discarded depends on how the Frame Relay network has been provisioned.

User Data: This field contains the actual user payload. The default Cisco Frame Relay frame size is 1500 bytes for a synchronous serial interface. Most Frame Relay equipment can pass larger frames. The largest frame size is 8192 bytes, although many Frame Relay devices cannot pass a frame that large. The main disadvantage of using frames larger then 4KB is that the Frame Check Sequence can no longer detect many types of data errors.

Frame Check Sequence (FCS): This is a 2-byte cyclic redundancy check which is calculated on the entire frame except the flags and the two bytes of FCS. A Frame Relay network will discard any frames that have a bad FCS. The FCS is only guaranteed for Frame Relay frames of 4KB or less. Larger frames may not have their errors detected with the 2-byte CRC check that Frame Relay provides.

Frame Relay Congestion Control

Another feature of Frame Relay that makes it an efficient protocol is its simple congestion control. Three bits in the Frame Relay address field are used for congestion control: BECN, FECN, and DE. Figure 4–6 shows how the BECN and FECN bits can be set in a Frame Relay frame.

A PVC is configured between Stamford and Hawthorne. Assume that the path from Hawthorne to Stamford is not congested—but the path from Stamford to Hawthorne does become congested. The Frame Relay network will set the FECN bit to 1 in those frames that are going from Stamford to Hawthorne. The Frame Relay network will set the BECN bit to 1 in those frames that are going from Hawthorne to Stamford. A router receiving these BECN or FECN-tagged frames has no obligation to react to the fact that congestion exists in the network. Most end-user devices are not able to react. With the introduction of IOS version 11.2, Cisco added support for reacting to the BECN bit in Frame Relay frames. This

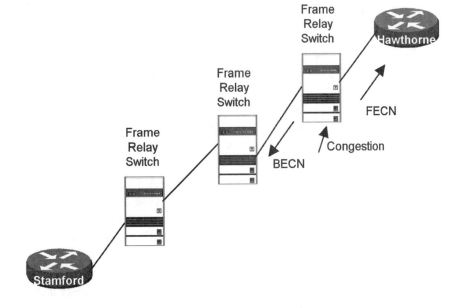

Figure 4–6
Frame Relay
congestion example

feature is enabled by default and causes the router to dynamically throttle outgoing traffic on a per PVC basis. When BECN-flagged frames stop coming into the router, the outbound traffic rate is once again increased.

The *Discard Eligibility* (DE) bit will be explained in more detail in the Frame Relay Class of Service section later in this chapter.

Frame Relay Error Handling

Frame Relay assumes that the circuits carrying the Frame Relay traffic will have low error rates. Unlike X.25, Frame Relay switches do not retransmit errored frames. If a Frame Relay switch encounters a frame with a bad *Frame Check Sequence* (FCS), that frame is simply discarded.

Retransmission is the responsibility of the hosts, not the Frame Relay switch network or the router.

Frame Relay Class of Service

Every PVC on a Frame Relay network can be quantified by a set of standard Frame Relay measurements. These measurements comprise a service contract between the Frame Relay user and the Frame Relay provider. These items are as follows:

Access Rate: The access rate is the speed of the circuit between the user and the Frame Relay network. The maximum data rate for traffic sent into the Frame Relay network is bounded by the access rate.

CIR: The *Committed Information Rate* (CIR) of a PVC is a measurement, in bits/second, of the maximum amount of traffic that the Frame Relay service provider agrees to carry through the network. The CIR value will usually be less then the access rate of the line. Keep in mind that several PVCs will be sharing the same physical link between the users equipment and the Frame Relay switch.

Bc: Bc is Committed Burst Size. Bc is defined as the maximum number of bits that the Frame Relay network agrees to carry during time interval Tc. By definition, Tc=Bc/CIR. CIR and Bc may seem similar, but notice that CIR is expressed in bits/sec—whereas Bc is expressed only in bits.

Be: Be is Excess Burst Size. It is a measurement of the maximum number of bits that the Frame Relay network will try to carry above the CIR value during time Tc.

Tc: Tc is the Committed Rate Measurement Interval. Tc, by definition, is equal to Bc/CIR. Tc is usually set to 1 second.

A Frame Relay switch needs to have a way to determine whether the service contract is being met. The value of Tc tells the Frame Relay provider to take a traffic sample every Tc seconds. Most Frame Relay switches will mark any traffic above the CIR as *Discard Eligible* (DE) and will set the DE bit.

Figure 4–7 shows a graphical description of the Frame Relay class of service parameters. In this diagram, Tc is set to 1 second. Four frames are sent during the one-second interval. The CIR is set to 16 kb/s for this circuit, and the Bc and Be are both set to 16 Kbits. The first three frames are not marked DE, because the total number of bits transmitted when any of the frames begins is less than 16 Kbits. The fourth frame is marked DE, because when the fourth frame begins, the total number of bits transmitted during the current one-second interval has already exceeded 16 Kbits.

Local Management Interface

Frame Relay provides a simple signaling protocol between the Frame Relay switch and the Frame Relay DTE (router). This signaling protocol is known as the *Local Management Interface* (LMI).

Figure 4–7
Frame Relay class
of service

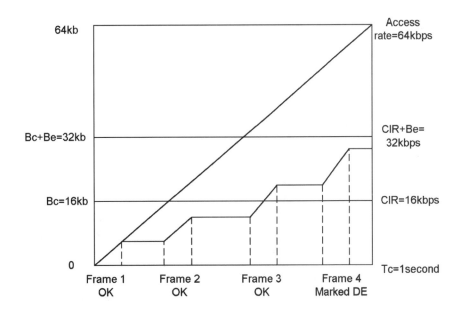

The LMI signaling protocol provides for notification of addition and deletion of PVCs, as well as periodic "keep alive" messages between the Frame Relay switch and Frame Relay DTE.

There are three types of LMI. The LMI type must be set the same on the Frame Relay switch and the attached Frame Relay DTE (router). The Frame Relay provider will usually tell the customer which of the three types will be used on their network. The three LMI types are the following:

1. ANSI Annex D—Annex D uses DLCI 0 to pass status information between the Frame Relay switch and the Frame Relay DTE. Cisco refers to this LMI type as ANSI.

2. CCITT Annex A—Annex A also uses DLCI 0 to pass status information between the Frame Relay switch and the Frame Relay DTE. Annex A signaling also provides the CIR value of each PVC that is provisioned on the Frame Relay switch port providing status. Cisco refers to this LMI type as Q933A.

3. LMI—LMI uses DLCI 1023 to pass status information between the Frame Relay switch and the Frame Relay DTE. Cisco refers to this LMI type as Cisco.

LMI works in the following manner:

1. Every 10 seconds, the DTE requests status from the Frame Relay switch. This status request will be sent to the switch over one of two reserved DLCIs—0 or 1023—depending on which of the three LMI signaling protocols has been chosen.

2. The Frame Relay switch will respond to the status request with a status response. This exchange is depicted in Figure 4–8. This exchange is referred to as a "keep alive" or "aliveness check," because its function is to tell both the DTE and the Frame Relay switch that there is still a communication path between them.

3. Every sixth status request from the DTE is sent as a full status request. A full status request is not only an aliveness check, but it also requests the Frame Relay switch to respond with a list of all DLCIs that have been defined on the port of the Frame Relay switch.

4. LThe Frame Relay switch responds with a list of all defined DLCIs on the particular Frame Relay switch port.

Both the DTE and the Frame Relay switches maintain individual sequence numbers during their exchanges. These sequence numbers can be used to determine whether an LMI sequence has been lost.

Figure 4–8
Frame Relay LMI

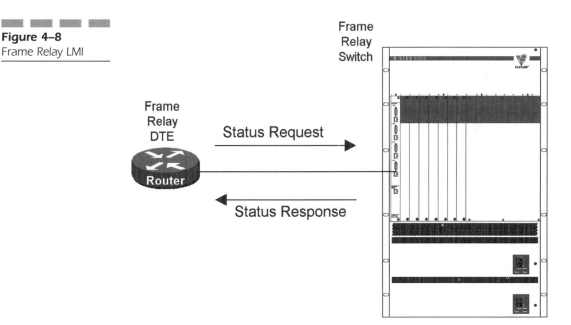

The following four frames show a typical LMI exchange between the router and a Frame Relay switch. The first frame (ID=5) is a status request from the router to the Frame Relay switch. Notice that the DLCI is 0—which, in this case, is Annex D.

The second frame (ID=6) is the reply from the switch to the first frame (ID=5). Notice from the timestamp that the reply comes within 10 milliseconds.

The next frame (ID=7) is a full status request from the router to the Frame Relay switch. The final frame (ID=8) is the reply to frame #7. The switch replies to the full status request with a listing of all DLCIs that are configured on its port.

Status request from the router to the Frame Relay switch

```
Port A RX2 ID=5, 01/19/99, 14:32:08.547325
Length=16, Good FCS
FRAME RELAY PROTOCOL
DLCI_msb                                                    00h
DLCI_lsb                                                     0h

DLCI                                            Annex D or A 0
CR                                                           0
EA                                                           0
FECN                                                         0
BECN                                                         0
```

```
DE                                                                       0
EA                                                                       1
Q.933 FRAME RELAY SVC
Control                                                       UI Frame 03h
Protocol Discriminator                                    Call Control 08h
Reference Flag                                     Msg from Origination 0
Call Reference Value [len=0]                                             0
```
Message Type   **STATUS ENQ 75h**
```
INFO ELEMENT Locking Shift [Code=18]
INFO ELEMENT Locking Shift                               (Codeset 5) 5h
IE - Annex D Report Type [Code=1] [Len=1]
IE - Annex D Report Type                          Link Verification 01h
IE - Annex D Link Integrity Ver. [Code=3] [Len=2]
Current Seq                                                            E6h
Last Rcvd Seq                                                         DAh
FCS                                                          Good FFC8h
```

Status reply from the Frame Relay switch to the router

```
Port A RX1 ID=6, 01/19/99, 14:32:08.563200
Length=16, Good FCS
FRAME RELAY PROTOCOL
DLCI_msb                                                              00h
DLCI_lsb                                                               0h
DLCI                                                     Annex D or A 0
CR                                                                      0
EA                                                                      0
FECN                                                                    0
BECN                                                                    0
DE                                                                      0
EA                                                                      1
Q.933 FRAME RELAY SVC
Control                                                       UI Frame 03h
Protocol Discriminator                                    Call Control 08h
Reference Flag                                     Msg from Origination 0
Call Reference Value [len=0]                                             0
```
Message Type   **STATUS 7Dh**
```
INFO ELEMENT Locking Shift [Code=18]
INFO ELEMENT Locking Shift                               (Codeset 5) 5h
IE - Annex D Report Type [Code=1] [Len=1]
IE - Annex D Report Type                          Link Verification 01h
IE - Annex D Link Integrity Ver. [Code=3] [Len=2]
Current Seq                                                           DBh
Last Rcvd Seq                                                         E6h
FCS                                                          Good 004Ah
```

Full Status request from the router to the Frame Relay switch

```
Port A RX2 ID=7, 01/19/99, 14:32:18.634050
Length=16, Good FCS
```

```
FRAME RELAY PROTOCOL
DLCI_msb                                                              00h
DLCI_lsb                                                               0h
DLCI                                                       Annex D or A 0
CR                                                                      0
EA                                                                      0
FECN                                                                    0
BECN                                                                    0
DE                                                                      0
EA                                                                      1
Q.933 FRAME RELAY SVC
Control                                                    UI Frame 03h
Protocol Discriminator                                  Call Control 08h
Reference Flag                                    Msg from Origination 0
Call Reference Value [len=0]                                            0

Message Type                                              STATUS ENQ 75h
INFO ELEMENT Locking Shift [Code=18]
INFO ELEMENT Locking Shift                                 (Codeset 5) 5h
IE - Annex D Report Type [Code=1] [Len=1]
```
IE - Annex D Report Type   **Full Status 00h**
```
IE - Annex D Link Integrity Ver. [Code=3] [Len=2]
Current Seq                                                          E7h
Last Rcvd Seq                                                        DBh
FCS                                                          Good EACBh
```

Full Status reply from the Frame Relay switch to the router

```
Port A RX1 ID=8, 01/19/99, 14:32:18.651225
Length=31, Good FCS
FRAME RELAY PROTOCOL
DLCI_msb                                                              00h
DLCI_lsb                                                               0h
DLCI                                                       Annex D or A 0
CR                                                                      0
EA                                                                      0
FECN                                                                    0
BECN                                                                    0
DE                                                                      0
EA                                                                      1
Q.933 FRAME RELAY SVC
Control                                                    UI Frame 03h
Protocol Discriminator                                  Call Control 08h
Reference Flag                                    Msg from Origination 0
Call Reference Value [len=0]                                            0
Message Type                                                 STATUS 7Dh
INFO ELEMENT Locking Shift [Code=18]
INFO ELEMENT Locking Shift                                 (Codeset 5) 5h
IE - Annex D Report Type [Code=1] [Len=1]
```
IE - Annex D Report Type   **Full Status 00h**
```
IE - Annex D Link Integrity Ver. [Code=3] [Len=2]
```

```
Current Seq                                                    DCh
Last Rcvd Seq                                                  E7h
IE - Annex D PVC Status [Code=7] [Len=3]
PVC DLCI MSB                                                   06h
PVC DLCI LSB                                                    9h
PVC DLCI                                                       105
N(ew)                                                       No 0h
D(eleted)                                                   No 0h
A(ctive)                                                   Yes 1h
IE - Annex D PVC Status [Code=7] [Len=3]
PVC DLCI MSB                                                   06h
PVC DLCI LSB                                                    Bh
PVC DLCI                                                       107
N(ew)                                                       No 0h
D(eleted)                                                   No 0h
A(ctive)                                                   Yes 1h
IE - Annex D PVC Status [Code=7] [Len=3]
PVC DLCI MSB                                                   07h
PVC DLCI LSB                                                    3h
PVC DLCI                                                       115
N(ew)                                                       No 0h
D(eleted)                                                   No 0h
A(ctive)                                                   Yes 1h
FCS                                                   Good 4629h
```

Asynchronous Status Updates

The previous section mentioned that Frame Relay LMI exchanges occur every 10 seconds between the router and the Frame Relay switch. The Frame Relay specification also provides for LMI updates that can be sent at any time by the Frame Relay switch to the router. These updates can be sent for a variety of reasons, such as a PVC being added or deleted. These type of updates are referred to as asynchronous updates because they are sent at any time, versus the normal LMI exchanges which are only sent at 10 second intervals. The following trace shows an asynchronous update being sent when a new PVC is added on the switch.

The first frame (ID=60) is a standard status request from the router to the Frame Relay switch. Notice that the frame occurs at time 16:40:57.56.

The second frame (ID=61) is the reply to the first frame (ID=60). This frame is sent from the Frame Relay switch to the router. Notice that this frame is sent at time 16:40:57.57—10 milliseconds after the initial request.

The third frame (ID=62) is an asynchronous update sent from the Frame Relay switch to the router. It was sent when a new DLCI

(DLCI=199) was configured on the Frame Relay switch. Notice that the update is not sent out on a 10-second boundary; rather, the update is being sent between the normal 10-second LMI exchanges.

The fourth and final frame (ID=64) is the next status request from the router to the Frame Switch. Notice that the frame occurs on the 10-second interval of the normal LMI exchanges.

Status Request from the router to the Frame Relay switch

```
Port A RX2 ID=60, 02/15/99, 16:40:57.561675
Length=16, Good FCS
FRAME RELAY PROTOCOL
DLCI_msb                                                          00h
DLCI_lsb                                                           0h
DLCI                                                  Annex D or A 0
CR                                                                 0
EA                                                                 0
FECN                                                               0
BECN                                                               0
DE                                                                 0
EA                                                                 1
Q.933 FRAME RELAY SVC
Control                                                UI Frame 03h
Protocol Discriminator                             Call Control 08h
Reference Flag                             Msg from Origination 0
Call Reference Value [len=0]                                       0
Message Type                                        STATUS ENQ 75h
INFO ELEMENT Locking Shift [Code=18]
INFO ELEMENT Locking Shift                             (Codeset 5) 5h
IE - Annex D Report Type [Code=1] [Len=1]
IE - Annex D Report Type                      Link Verification 01h
IE - Annex D Link Integrity Ver. [Code=3] [Len=2]
Current Seq                                                      B3h
Last Rcvd Seq                                                   03h
FCS                                                   Good FC2Eh
```

Status reply from the Frame Relay switch to the router

```
Port A RX1 ID=61, 02/15/99, 16:40:57.573700
Length=16, Good FCS
FRAME RELAY PROTOCOL
DLCI_msb                                                          00h
DLCI_lsb                                                           0h
DLCI                                                  Annex D or A 0
```

```
CR                                                                    0
EA                                                                    0
FECN                                                                  0
BECN                                                                  0
DE                                                                    0
EA                                                                    1
Q.933 FRAME RELAY SVC
Control                                                    UI Frame 03h
Protocol Discriminator                                  Call Control 08h
Reference Flag                                  Msg from Origination 0
Call Reference Value [len=0]                                          0
Message Type                                                  STATUS 7Dh
INFO ELEMENT Locking Shift [Code=18]
INFO ELEMENT Locking Shift                                 (Codeset 5) 5h
IE - Annex D Report Type [Code=1] [Len=1]
IE - Annex D Report Type                         Link Verification 01h
IE - Annex D Link Integrity Ver. [Code=3] [Len=2]
Current Seq                                                         04h
Last Rcvd Seq                                                       B3h
FCS                                                        Good DB93h
```

Asynchronous update from the Frame Relay switch to the router

```
Port A RX1 ID=62, 02/15/99, 16:41:01.011100
Length=17, Good FCS
FRAME RELAY PROTOCOL
DLCI_msb                                                            00h
DLCI_lsb                                                            0h
DLCI                                               Annex D or A 0
CR                                                                    0
EA                                                                    0
FECN                                                                  0
BECN                                                                  0
DE                                                                    0
EA                                                                    1
Q.933 FRAME RELAY SVC
Control                                                    UI Frame 03h
Protocol Discriminator                                  Call Control 08h
Reference Flag                                  Msg from Origination 0
Call Reference Value [len=0]                                          0
Message Type                                                  STATUS 7Dh
INFO ELEMENT Locking Shift [Code=18]
INFO ELEMENT Locking Shift                                 (Codeset 5) 5h
IE - Annex D Report Type [Code=1] [Len=1]
IE - Annex D Report Type                  Single PVC Async Status 02h
IE - Annex D PVC Status [Code=7] [Len=3]
PVC DLCI MSB                                                        0Ch
PVC DLCI LSB                                                        7h
PVC DLCI                                                            199
N(ew)                                                             No 0h
```

```
D(eleted)                                                  No 0h
A(ctive)                                                   Yes 1h
FCS                                                   Good 1320h
```

Status request from the router to the Frame Relay switch

```
Port A RX2 ID=64, 02/15/99, 16:41:07.657950
Length=16, Good FCS
FRAME RELAY PROTOCOL
DLCI_msb                                                       00h
DLCI_lsb                                                        0h
DLCI                                          Annex D or A 0
CR                                                             0
EA                                                             0
FECN                                                           0
BECN                                                           0
DE                                                             0
EA                                                             1
Q.933 FRAME RELAY SVC
Control                                          UI Frame 03h
Protocol Discriminator                       Call Control 08h
Reference Flag                       Msg from Origination 0
Call Reference Value [len=0]                                   0
Message Type                               STATUS ENQ 75h
INFO ELEMENT Locking Shift [Code=18]
INFO ELEMENT Locking Shift                      (Codeset 5) 5h
IE - Annex D Report Type [Code=1] [Len=1]
IE - Annex D Report Type                      Full Status 00h
IE - Annex D Link Integrity Ver. [Code=3] [Len=2]
Current Seq                                                  B4h
Last Rcvd Seq                                                04h
FCS                                                   Good 0F1Ch
```

Inverse Address Resolution Protocol (Inverse ARP)

Frame Relay inverse ARP provides a method to associate a far-end layer 3 network address with the local layer 2 DLCI.

When a Frame Relay circuit is initialized, a router attached to a Frame Relay switch does not have any address information except its own IP address. As shown in Figure 4–9, when the router sends a full-status LMI request to the Frame Relay switch, the switch will respond with all DLCIs that are defined on the circuit. The router needs a way to find out what the IP address of the far-end router is on the other end of the DLCI. The router does this task by sending an inverse ARP request out on each local DLCI that is defined on the circuit. The inverse ARP request travels to the far-end router, where it is received and replied to. The router which initiated the inverse ARP request receives the reply. This reply contains the IP address of the far-end router.

The following trace shows how an inverse ARP exchange takes place between a router and a Frame Relay switch.

1. The first frame (ID=6) is the inverse ARP request from the router to the Frame Relay network. Notice that the request is being sent over DLCI 100. This request will travel through the Frame Relay switch and will be terminated by the router at the far end of the circuit. Also notice that the inverse ARP frame contains the IP address (195.1.1.12) of the sending router.

2. The second frame (ID=7) is the reply packet to the original inverse ARP request (ID=6). Notice that this frame contains a new IP address. This address is the IP address of the router on the far end of the circuit (IP=195.1.1.13).

Figure 4–9
Frame Relay inverse
ARP

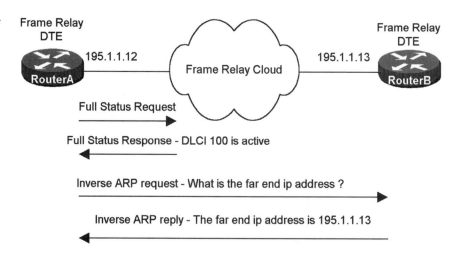

Inverse ARP request

```
Port A DTE ID=6, 01/25/99, 15:36:08.934350
Length=32, Good FCS
FRAME RELAY PROTOCOL
DLCI_msb                                                        06h
DLCI_lsb                                                         4h
DLCI                                                           100
CR                                                               0
EA                                                               0
FECN                                                             0
BECN                                                             0
DE                                                               0
EA                                                               1
NLPID - NETWORK LEVEL PROTOCOL ID
Control                                           LAPD UI Frame 03h
Pad                                                            00h
Network Level Protocol ID                                 SNAP 80h
SNAP Header OUI                              Ethertype 000000h
Ethertype                                            ARP 0806h
ARP - ADDRESS RESOLUTION PROTOCOL
Hardware Type                               Frame Relay 000Fh
Protocol Type                                    DOD IP 0800h
Hrdwr Addr Len (in bytes)                                      2
Prtcl Addr Len (in bytes)                                      4
Operation Code                           InARP Request 0008h
Sender Hardware Addr
  00000                    0000                    ..
Sender Protocol Addr                                  195.1.1.12
Target Hardware Addr
  00000                    1841                    .A
Target Protocol Addr                                     0.0.0.0
FCS                                              Good 80E9h
```

Inverse ARP reply

```
Port A DCE ID=7, 01/25/99, 15:36:08.942025
Length=32, Good FCS
FRAME RELAY PROTOCOL
DLCI_msb                                                        06h
DLCI_lsb                                                         4h
DLCI                                                           100
CR                                                               0
EA                                                               0
FECN                                                             0
BECN                                                             0
DE                                                               0
EA                                                               1
NLPID - NETWORK LEVEL PROTOCOL ID
Control                                           LAPD UI Frame 03h
Pad                                                            00h
Network Level Protocol ID                                 SNAP 80h
SNAP Header OUI                              Ethertype 000000h
```

```
Ethertype                                                       ARP 0806h
ARP - ADDRESS RESOLUTION PROTOCOL
Hardware Type                                          Frame Relay 000Fh
Protocol Type                                               DOD IP 0800h
Hrdwr Addr Len  (in bytes)                                             2
Prtcl Addr Len  (in bytes)                                             4

Operation Code                                    InARP Response 0009h
Sender Hardware Addr
  00000                     0000                 ..
Sender Protocol Addr                                         195.1.1.13
Target Hardware Addr
  00000                     1841                 .A
Target Protocol Addr                                         195.1.1.12
FCS                                                         Good 84E4h
```

Cisco Frame Relay Capabilities

The Cisco IOS includes support for the standard Frame Relay features that were discussed in the previous sections. The IOS also includes support for additional advanced features such as *Quality of Service* support (QOS), Frame Relay Switching, and Subinterfaces.

Frame Relay Switching

A Cisco router can be configured as a Frame Relay switch. This capability is usually not used in a production network; rather, it is mainly intended for use in test beds and example networks. The examples in this chapter will use a Cisco router configured as a Frame Relay switch.

IETF and Cisco Encapsulation

When a Frame Relay frame comes into a router, the router must have some way of knowing which higher layer protocol is encapsulated in the Frame Relay frame. There are two methods on a Cisco router of encapsulating higher layer traffic in a Frame Relay frame: Cisco proprietary and RFC 1490 encapsulation. Cisco proprietary encapsulation is the default encapsulation for Frame Relay traffic. IETF (RFC 1490) encapsulation should be used when the router will be communicating with another vendor's equipment. The following analyzer traces show an example of Cisco proprietary encapsulation and IETF (RFC 1490) encapsulation.

IETF ENCAPSULATION The following frame shows an example of IETF encapsulation. Notice the control and *Network-Level Protocol ID* (NLPID) bytes identifying which protocol is encapsulated in the Frame Relay frame.

```
Port A RX1 ID=7, 01/19/99, 15:26:24.045900
Length=66, Good FCS
FRAME RELAY PROTOCOL
DLCI_msb                                                        06h
DLCI_lsb                                                         Bh
DLCI                                                            107
CR                                                               0
EA                                                               0
FECN                                                             0
BECN                                                             0
DE                                                               0
EA                                                               1
NLPID - NETWORK LEVEL PROTOCOL ID
Control                                               LAPD UI Frame 03h
Network Level Protocol ID                                     IP CCh
IP - INTERNET PROTOCOL
Version                                                          4
IHL (in 32 bit words)                                           5
Precedence                                              Routine 0h
D(elay)                                                  Normal 0
T(hroughput)                                             Normal 0
R(eliability)                                            Normal 0
Total Length (in octets)                                        60
Identification                                              525Fh
D(on't) F(ragment)                                          No 0
M(ore) F(ragments)                                          No 0
Fragment Offset (in 8 octets)                                   0
Time To Live (in seconds)                                       31
Protocol                                                 ICMP 01h
Header Checksum                                             78E7h
Class A Source IP Address
Source Net ID                                                   10
Source Host ID                                              656228
Source Addr                                            10.10.3.100
Class C Destination IP Address
Destination Net ID                                         131329
Destination Host ID                                             12
Destination Addr                                       194.1.1.12
ICMP - INTERNET CONTROL MESSAGE PROTOCOL
Type                                                     Echo 08h
Code                                                          00h
Checksum                                                    2F5Ch
ID                                                          0100h
Sequence No                                                 1D00h
Dump                 00000  6162  6364  6566  6768  696A  abcdefghij
                     00010  6B6C  6D6E  6F70  7172  7374  klmnopqrst
                     00020  7576  7761  6263  6465  6667  uvwabcdefg
                     00030  6869                          hi
FCS                                                     Good D589h
```

CISCO ENCAPSULATION   The following frame shows an example of Cisco encapsulation. Notice the 2-byte Ethertype identifying which protocol is encapsulated in the Frame Relay frame.

```
Port A RX1 ID=77, 01/19/99, 14:38:02.299325
Length=66, Good FCS
FRAME RELAY PROTOCOL
DLCI_msb                                                            06h
DLCI_lsb                                                             Bh
DLCI                                                               107
CR                                                                   0
EA                                                                   0
FECN                                                                 0
BECN                                                                 0
DE                                                                   0
EA                                                                   1
NLPID - NETWORK LEVEL PROTOCOL ID
Ethertype                                                 DOD IP 0800h
IP - INTERNET PROTOCOL
Version                                                              4
IHL (in 32 bit words)                                                5
Precedence                                                  Routine 0h
D(elay)                                                       Normal 0
T(hroughput)                                                  Normal 0
R(eliability)                                                 Normal 0
Total Length (in octets)                                            60
Identification                                                   215Eh
D(on't) F(ragment)                                                No 0
M(ore) F(ragments)                                                No 0
Fragment Offset (in 8 octets)                                        0
Time To Live (in seconds)                                           31
Protocol                                                      ICMP 01h
Header Checksum                                                  A9E8h
Class A Source IP Address
Source Net ID                                                       10
Source Host ID                                                  656228
Source Addr                                                 10.10.3.100
Class C Destination IP Address
Destination Net ID                                              131329
Destination Host ID                                                 12
Destination Addr                                            194.1.1.12
ICMP - INTERNET CONTROL MESSAGE PROTOCOL
Type                                                          Echo 08h
Code                                                               00h
Checksum                                                         335Ch
ID                                                               0100h
Sequence No                                                      1900h
Dump
    00000   6162    6364    6566    6768    696A      abcdefghij
    00010   6B6C    6D6E    6F70    7172    7374      klmnopqrst
    00020   7576    7761    6263    6465    6667      uvwabcdefg
    00030   6869                                      hi
FCS                                                       Good 4264h
```

Traffic Shaping

Cisco introduced Frame Relay traffic-shaping support in IOS version 11.2. Traffic shaping enables you to define the outbound and/or inbound traffic rate on a per-PVC basis. The traffic rate can be defined in terms of either peak or average rate. This chapter includes a lab example showing how traffic shaping is configured.

DE Support

The DE bit in the Frame Relay header is used to indicate that a frame has a low priority and can be discarded when the Frame Relay network becomes congested. The Cisco IOS permits the user to specify which Frame Relay frames will have the DE bit set. The DE bit can be set based on upper-layer protocols, a specific TCP or UDP port, an access list number, a packet size, or packet fragmentation. This chapter includes a lab example showing how DE support is configured.

BECN support

Cisco introduced BECN support in IOS version 11.2. BECN support is enabled by default on the router. When the router sees BECN set on incoming frames, the router automatically throttles back outgoing traffic. Normal outgoing traffic levels are resumed when the router no longer sees incoming traffic with the BECN bit set.

Payload Compression

The Cisco IOS supports Frame Relay payload compression using the STAC compression algorithm. Payload compression differs from traditional link compression in that only the data portion of the Frame Relay frame is compressed. The Frame Relay header is left intact with payload compression.

LMI Autosense

LMI autosense support was added in IOS 11.2. This function enables the router to automatically determine which of the three LMI protocols are configured on the Frame Relay switch that is attached to the Cisco router. LMI autosense works by having the router send out an LMI full-status request to the attached Frame Relay switch in all three LMI formats: ANSI Annex D, CCITT Annex A, and LMI. When the router receives a response from the Frame Relay switch, the router will decode the response and determine which of the three LMI formats are being used. This chapter includes a lab example showing how LMI autosense is configured.

Commands Discussed in this Chapter

- **clear frame-relay-inarp**
- **debug frame-relay lmi**
- **debug frame-relay packet**
- **encapsulation frame-relay [cisco | ietf]**
- **frame-relay bc {in | out}** *bits*
- **frame-relay be {in | out}** *bits*
- **frame-relay becn-response-enable**
- **frame-relay cir {in | out}** *bps*
- **frame-relay class** *name*
- **frame-relay de-group** *group-number dlci*
- **frame-relay de-list** *list-number* {**protocol** *protocol* | **interface** *type number*} *characteristic*
- **frame-relay interface-dlci** *dlci* **[broadcast] [ietf | cisco]**
- **frame-relay intf-type [dce | dte | nni]**
- **frame-relay inverse-arp** *[protocol] [dlci]*
- **frame-relay lmi-type {ansi | cisco | q933a}**
- **frame-relay map** *protocol protocol-address dlci* **[broadcast] [ietf | cisco | payload-compress packet by packet]**
- **frame-relay mincir {in | out}** *bps*
- **frame-relay route** *in-dlci out-interface out-dlci*
- **frame-relay switching**
- **frame-relay traffic-shaping**

■ **map-group** *group-name*

■ **show frame-relay lmi** [*type number*]

■ **show frame-relay map**

■ **show frame-relay pvc** [*type number* [*dlci*]]

■ **show frame-relay route**

■ **show interfaces serial** *number*

Definitions

clear frame-relay-inarp: This exec command causes any frame-relay maps which were dynamically created through inverse arp to be cleared.

debug frame lmi: This debug command will cause the router to display all LMI transactions between itself and the attached Frame Relay switch. Remember to also enter the **term mon** command if you are not connected to the console port.

debug frame packet: This debug command causes the router to display Frame Relay packet traces for all Frame Relay traffic going through the router. Remember to also enter the **term mon** command if you are not connected to the console port.

encapsulation frame-relay: This interface command enables Frame Relay encapsulation on an interface. The router supports two types of encapsulation: RFC 1490 and Cisco proprietary.

frame-relay bc: This map-class command specifies the outgoing or incoming committed burst size in bits for a Frame Relay PVC. If neither incoming or outgoing is specified, then the command applies to both directions.

frame-relay be: This map-class command specifies the outgoing or incoming excess burst size in bits for a Frame Relay PVC. If neither incoming or outgoing is specified, then the command applies to both directions.

frame-relay becn-response-enable: This map-class command causes the router to regulate the frame transmission rate on PVCs associated with a map class. The router regulates the traffic when it sees incoming frames with the BECN bit set.

frame-relay cir: This map-class command specifies the outgoing or incoming *Committed Information Rate* (CIR) in bits per second for a Frame Relay PVC. If neither incoming or outgoing is specified, then the command applies to both directions.

frame-relay class: This interface command is used to associate a map class with an interface of a subinterface.

frame-relay de-group: This interface command is used to specify the discard eligibility group number that should be used for a particular DLCI.

frame-relay de-list: This global command defines a discard eligibility list that will specify which outgoing frames will have their DE bit set. Frames with their DE bit set can be used by a Frame Relay network to decide which traffic to discard during periods of congestion.

frame-relay interface-dlci: This interface command assigns a DLCI to a specific Frame Relay interface or subinterface on the router.

frame-relay intf-type: This interface command is used when the router will be acting as a Frame Relay switch. The command is used to define the Frame Relay switch type.

frame-relay inverse-arp: This interface command enables inverse arp on the router. Inverse arp is enabled by default.

frame-relay lmi-type: This interface command is used to set the type of *Local Management Interface* (LMI) signaling to be used on the router.

frame-relay map: This interface command is used to define a static map entry between a destination protocol address and the DLCI that is used to reach the destination protocol address.

frame-relay mincir: This map-class command specifies the outgoing or incoming minimum acceptable CIR in bits per second for a Frame Relay PVC. If neither incoming or outgoing is specified, then the command applies to both directions.

frame-relay route: This command is used to configure a Frame Relay PVC between two interfaces on a router which is configured to be a Frame Relay switch. This command is an interface command.

frame-relay switching: This global command enables a router to perform Frame Relay switching functions.

frame-relay traffic-shaping: This interface command enables Frame Relay traffic shaping for all PVCs on a Frame Relay interface.

map-class frame-relay: This command creates a Frame Relay map class which is used to define QOS parameters for a Frame Relay PVC.

show frame-relay lmi: This exec command displays detailed statistics related to the LMI between the router and the Frame Relay switch.

show frame-relay map: This exec command displays all of the statically mapped and dynamically learned DLCI to protocol mappings on the router.

show frame-relay pvc: This exec command displays statistics about the Frame Relay PVCs that are defined to the router. When this command is entered with the optional DLCI number, any defined traffic-shaping parameters will also be displayed.

show frame-relay route: This exec command is used on routers that are configured for Frame Relay switching. This command will display all configured PVCs on the router and will show their status.

show interfaces serial: This exec command will display a variety of information about the serial interfaces of the router. Several Frame Relay statistics, such as LMI status and DTE/DCE configuration, will be displayed.

IOS Requirements

All of the labs in this section used IOS version 11.2, except the Frame Relay traffic-shaping lab—which used IOS version 11.3 Cisco first supported Frame Relay with IOS 9.0.

Lab #9: Configuring a Cisco Router as a Frame Relay Switch

Equipment Needed

The following equipment is needed to perform this lab exercise:

■ Three Cisco routers, one of which must have two serial ports. The other two routers can have one serial port.

■ Cisco IOS 11.2 or higher

■ A PC running a terminal emulation program for console port connection on the routers

■ Two Cisco DTE/DCE crossover cables. If no crossover cables are available, you can make a crossover cable by connecting a standard Cisco DTE cable to a standard Cisco DCE cable.

NOTE: The DCE side of the V.35 crossover cables must connect to the router FrameSwitch.

Configuration Overview

This configuration will demonstrate how to configure a Cisco router as a Frame Relay DTE and as a Frame Relay switch.

The three routers are connected, as shown in Figure 4–10. RouterA and RouterB are configured as Frame Relay DTE devices. These two routers are connected to the router FrameSwitch, which is acting as a Frame Relay switch. Router FrameSwitch is also configured to supply clock to both RouterA and RouterB. This task is accomplished via the use of a Cisco DCE cable and the **clock rate** statement in the router configuration.

A PC running a terminal emulation program should be connected to the console port of one of the three routers using a Cisco rolled cable.

NOTE: Keep in mind that although a Cisco router can act as a Frame Relay switch, this feature is typically only used in test and demonstration situations—such as this lab.

Figure 4–10
Basic Frame
Relay switching

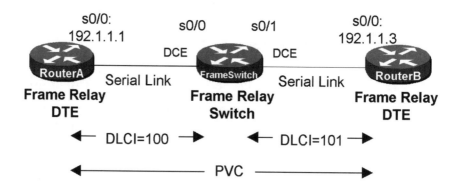

Router Configuration

The configurations for the three routers in this example are as follows (Frame Relay commands are highlighted in bold):

RouterA (Frame Relay DTE)

```
Current configuration:
!
version 11.2
service timestamps debug datetime localtime
no service udp-small-servers
no service tcp-small-servers
!
hostname RouterA
!
enable password cisco
!
interface Serial0/0
 ip address 192.1.1.1 255.255.255.0
 encapsulation frame-relay←Configure interface for Frame Relay Encapsulation
 frame-relay lmi-type ansi←Set LMI type to ANSI Annex D
!
router rip
 network 192.1.1.0
!
no ip classless
!
line con 0
line aux 0
line vty 0 4
 password cisco
 login
!
end
```

RouterB (Frame Relay DTE)

```
Current configuration:
!
version 11.2
no service udp-small-servers
no service tcp-small-servers
!
hostname RouterB
!
enable password cisco
!
interface Serial0/0
 ip address 192.1.1.3 255.255.255.0
 encapsulation frame-relay←Set the interface to Frame Relay encapsulation
```

```
frame-relay lmi-type ansi←Set the LMI type to Annex D
!
no ip classless
!
line con 0
line aux 0
line vty 0 4
 password cisco
 login
!
end
```

The configuration for Routers A and B demonstrate a basic Frame Relay configuration on a Cisco router. You will need to set the interface for Frame Relay encapsulation via the **encapsulation frame-relay** command. You will also need to specify the type of LMI signalling between the router and the Frame Relay switch via the **frame-relay LMI-type** command.

FrameSwitch (Frame Relay Switch)

```
Current configuration:
!
version 11.2
no service udp-small-servers
no service tcp-small-servers
!
hostname FrameSwitch
!
!
frame-relay switching←Enable Frame Relay switching on the router
!
interface Serial0/0
 no ip address
 encapsulation frame-relay
 clockrate 38400←Generate a 38,400 bps clock to the DTE
 frame-relay lmi-type ansi←Set LMI to Annex D
 frame-relay intf-type dce←Set the interface type to a Frame Relay DCE
 frame-relay route 100 interface Serial0/1 101←Define PVC between ports S0/0 and S0/1
!
interface Serial0/1
 no ip address
 encapsulation frame-relay
 clockrate 19200
 frame-relay lmi-type ansi
 frame-relay intf-type dce
 frame-relay route 101 interface Serial0/0 100
!
no ip classless
!
line con 0
line aux 0
line vty 0 4
 login
!
end
```

Notice that in this example, the router FrameSwitch is acting as a Frame Relay switch. This feature is particularly useful in testing situations such as these hands-on labs.

Frame Relay switching is enabled on the router by the global command **frame-relay switching**. In addition to the standard configuration commands defining Frame Relay encapsulation and LMI signaling, each interface on the router that will support switching needs to be defined as a Frame Relay DCE via the **frame-relay intf-type dce** command.

Frame Relay PVCs are defined with the **frame-relay route** command. As an example, let's look at interface S0/0 of router FrameSwitch. We see the command **frame-relay route 100 interface Serial0/1 101**. As shown in Figure 4–11, this command tells the router that any Frame Relay traffic coming into interface S0/0 with DLCI 100 should be sent out interface S0/1 with DLCI 101. Similarly, interface S0/1 has the command **frame-relay route 101 interface Serial0/0 100**. This command tells

Figure 4–11
Frame Relay label
switching example

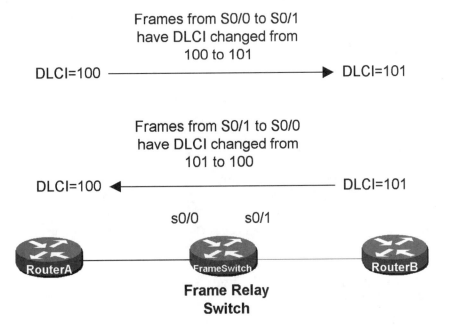

the router that any Frame Relay traffic coming into interface S0/1 with DLCI 101 should be sent out interface S0/0 with DLCI 100. These two **frame-relay route** commands create a Frame Relay PVC between ports S0/0 and S0/1 of the router FrameSwitch. The local DLCI on port S0/0 is DLCI 100, and the local DLCI on port S0/1 is DLCI 101.

Monitoring and Testing the Configuration

We can start to verify our configuration by connecting to router FrameSwitch. The **show frame pvc** command is used to display all PVCs that are passing through the router. Several items in the output of the **show frame pvc** command indicate that the router FrameSwitch is acting as a Frame Relay switch. These items are shown in bold in the following screen print. The PVC statistics indicate that S0/0 and S0/1 are acting as Frame Relay DCE interfaces. DLCI usage is indicated as Switched. Finally, the indication Num Pkts Switched shows how many frames have been switched through the interface.

```
FrameSwitch#sh frame pvc

PVC Statistics for interface Serial0/0 (Frame Relay DCE)

DLCI = 100, DLCI USAGE = SWITCHED, PVC STATUS = ACTIVE, INTERFACE = Serial0/0

    input pkts 7              output pkts 1            in bytes 340
    out bytes 30             dropped pkts 0           in FECN pkts 0
    in BECN pkts 0           out FECN pkts 0          out BECN pkts 0
    in DE pkts 0             out DE pkts 0
    pvc create time 00:07:57, last time pvc status changed 00:02:13
    Num Pkts Switched 7


PVC Statistics for interface Serial0/1 (Frame Relay DCE)

DLCI = 101, DLCI USAGE = SWITCHED, PVC STATUS = ACTIVE, INTERFACE = Serial0/1

    input pkts 1              output pkts 7            in bytes 30
    out bytes 340           dropped pkts 0           in FECN pkts 0
    in BECN pkts 0           out FECN pkts 0          out BECN pkts 0
    in DE pkts 0             out DE pkts 0
    pvc create time 00:07:06, last time pvc status changed 00:04:49
    Num Pkts Switched 1
```

Notice that the output of the **show frame pvc** command displays how many frames were sent/received with the FECN bit, BECN bit, or DE bit set. These performance parameters are key to determining whether your Frame Relay network is experiencing congestion.

The **show frame pvc** command also displays how many frames have been sent into and out of an interface, as well as how long the PVC has existed and when its status was last changed.

The **show frame lmi** command displays the status of the LMI interface between the router FrameSwitch and both directly connected routers—RouterA and RouterB. Again, we see that the router FrameSwitch is acting as a Frame Relay switch. The indication is the Frame Relay DCE message on the command output. Notice that the **show frame lmi** command displays information for all interfaces on the router that are set for Frame Relay encapsulation. In the case of the router FrameSwitch, these are interfaces S0/0 and S0/1.

```
FrameSwitch#sh frame lmi

LMI Statistics for interface Serial0/0 (Frame Relay DCE) LMI TYPE = ANSI
   Invalid Unnumbered info 0      Invalid Prot Disc 0
   Invalid dummy Call Ref 0       Invalid Msg Type 0
   Invalid Status Message 0       Invalid Lock Shift 0
   Invalid Information ID 0       Invalid Report IE Len 0
   Invalid Report Request 0       Invalid Keep IE Len 0
   Num Status Enq. Rcvd 32        Num Status msgs Sent 32
   Num Update Status Sent 0       Num St Enq. Timeouts 13


LMI Statistics for interface Serial0/1 (Frame Relay DCE) LMI TYPE = ANSI
   Invalid Unnumbered info 0      Invalid Prot Disc 0
   Invalid dummy Call Ref 0       Invalid Msg Type 0
   Invalid Status Message 0       Invalid Lock Shift 0
   Invalid Information ID 0       Invalid Report IE Len 0
   Invalid Report Request 0       Invalid Keep IE Len 0
   Num Status Enq. Rcvd 15        Num Status msgs Sent 15
   Num Update Status Sent 0       Num St Enq. Timeouts 20
```

The **show frame route** command is used when a router is configured as a Frame Relay switch. The command will display all DLCIs that are configured on the router. The following sample output from the router FrameSwitch shows that two DLCIs are configured on the router. The output of the command can be read as follows: Traffic coming into interface S0/0 with a DLCI value of 100 will get switched to interface S0/1 and will be given a DLCI value of 101. Traffic coming into interface S0/1 with a DLCI value of 101 will be switched to interface S0/0 and will be given a DLCI value of 100. The **show frame route** output also indicates that both of these DLCIs are currently in an active state.

```
FrameSwitch#sh frame route
Input Intf                      Input Dlci   Output Intf   Output Dlci  Status
Serial0/0                       100          Serial0/1     101          active
Serial0/1                       101          Serial0/0     100          active
```

The output of the **show interface** command for the two Frame Relay encapsulated interfaces (S0/0 and S0/1) on the router FrameSwitch indicates several important items. We see that the interface is up and the line protocol is up, telling us that the Frame Relay protocol is running properly on this interface. Other important Frame Relay-related status information supplied in the output of the show interface command includes the following:

■ Confirmation that the interface is set for Frame Relay encapsulation

■ A summary of the LMI exchanges between the router and the Frame switch

■ Indications that the router interface is acting as a Frame Relay switch. These indications are highlighted in bold in the following screen prints.

■ Verification that the LMI signaling type is ANSI Annex D

```
FrameSwitch#sh int s 0/0
Serial0/0 is up, line protocol is up
  Hardware is QUICC Serial
  MTU 1500 bytes, BW 1544 Kbit, DLY 20000 usec, rely 255/255, load 1/255
  Encapsulation FRAME-RELAY, loopback not set, keepalive set (10 sec)
  LMI enq sent   0, LMI stat recvd 0, LMI upd recvd 0
  LMI enq recvd 34, LMI stat sent  34, LMI upd sent   0, DCE LMI up
  LMI DLCI 0   LMI type is ANSI Annex D   frame relay DCE
  Broadcast queue 0/64, broadcasts sent/dropped 0/0, interface broadcasts 0
  Last input 00:00:00, output 00:00:00, output hang never
  Last clearing of "show interface" counters never
  Input queue: 0/75/0 (size/max/drops); Total output drops: 0
  Queueing strategy: weighted fair
  Output queue: 0/64/0 (size/threshold/drops)
     Conversations   0/3 (active/max active)
     Reserved Conversations 0/0 (allocated/max allocated)
  5 minute input rate 0 bits/sec, 0 packets/sec
  5 minute output rate 0 bits/sec, 0 packets/sec
     42 packets input, 872 bytes, 0 no buffer
     Received 0 broadcasts, 0 runts, 0 giants, 0 throttles
     0 input errors, 0 CRC, 0 frame, 0 overrun, 0 ignored, 0 abort
     49 packets output, 1423 bytes, 0 underruns
     0 output errors, 0 collisions, 39 interface resets
     0 output buffer failures, 0 output buffers swapped out
     42 carrier transitions
     DCD=up  DSR=up  DTR=up  RTS=up  CTS=up
```

```
FrameSwitch#sh int s 0/1
Serial0/1 is up, line protocol is up
  Hardware is QUICC Serial
  MTU 1500 bytes, BW 1544 Kbit, DLY 20000 usec, rely 255/255, load 1/255
  Encapsulation FRAME-RELAY, loopback not set, keepalive set (10 sec)
  LMI enq sent  0, LMI stat recvd 0, LMI upd recvd 0
  LMI enq recvd 17, LMI stat sent  17, LMI upd sent  0, DCE LMI up
  LMI DLCI 0  LMI type is ANSI Annex D  frame relay DCE
  Broadcast queue 0/64, broadcasts sent/dropped 0/0, interface broadcasts 0
  Last input 00:00:03, output 00:00:03, output hang never
  Last clearing of "show interface" counters never
  Input queue: 0/75/0 (size/max/drops); Total output drops: 0
  Queueing strategy: weighted fair
  Output queue: 0/64/0 (size/threshold/drops)
     Conversations  0/2 (active/max active)
     Reserved Conversations 0/0 (allocated/max allocated)
  5 minute input rate 0 bits/sec, 0 packets/sec
  5 minute output rate 0 bits/sec, 0 packets/sec
     18 packets input, 268 bytes, 0 no buffer
     Received 0 broadcasts, 0 runts, 0 giants, 0 throttles
     0 input errors, 0 CRC, 0 frame, 0 overrun, 0 ignored, 0 abort
     37 packets output, 1553 bytes, 0 underruns
     0 output errors, 0 collisions, 14 interface resets
     0 output buffer failures, 0 output buffers swapped out
     36 carrier transitions
     DCD=up  DSR=up  DTR=up  RTS=up  CTS=up
```

Now, connect your terminal emulator to RouterA. RouterA is a Frame Relay DTE. The **show frame pvc** command indicates that DLCI 100 is active on interface S0/0. This command also indicates that interface S0/0 is acting like a Frame Relay DTE. Notice that there is no indication of Num Pkts Switched, because this router is not emulating a Frame Switch.

```
RouterA#sh frame pvc

PVC Statistics for interface Serial0/0 (Frame Relay DTE)

DLCI = 100, DLCI USAGE = LOCAL, PVC STATUS = ACTIVE, INTERFACE = Serial0/0

  input pkts 1            output pkts 11      in bytes 30
  out bytes 590      dropped pkts 0      in FECN pkts 0
  in BECN pkts 0     out FECN pkts 0     out BECN pkts 0
  in DE pkts 0       out DE pkts 0
  pvc create time 00:07:14, last time pvc status changed 00:04:31
```

By default, a Cisco router will attempt to inverse arp to resolve the DLCI(s) active on a given interface to the IP address on the other end of the PVC. The **show frame map** command shows the results of the inverse arp. We will see in a future lab that static entries can also be made to the Frame Relay map table. The output for the **show frame relay** map command for RouterA is shown as follows. The output indicates that DLCI 100 is active on interface S0/0, and it shows that the IP address of the interface on the far end of the PVC is 192.1.1.3. This address is the IP address for the S0/0 interface of RouterB. The command output also indicates that this DLCI-to-IP address resolution occurred dynamically, as opposed to a static Frame Relay map—which will be discussed in a later lab.

```
RouterA#sh frame map
Serial0/0 (up): ip 192.1.1.3 dlci 100(0x64,0x1840), dynamic,
         broadcast,, status defined, active
```

Now verify that the LMI between RouterA and the Frame Relay switch is active with the **show frame lmi** command.

```
RouterA#sh frame lmi

LMI Statistics for interface Serial0/0 (Frame Relay DTE) LMI TYPE = ANSI
    Invalid Unnumbered info 0        Invalid Prot Disc 0
    Invalid dummy Call Ref 0         Invalid Msg Type 0
    Invalid Status Message 0         Invalid Lock Shift 0
    Invalid Information ID 0         Invalid Report IE Len 0
    Invalid Report Request 0         Invalid Keep IE Len 0
    Num Status Enq. Sent 173         Num Status msgs Rcvd 44
    Num Update Status Rcvd 0         Num Status Timeouts 129
```

Verify that the serial interface of RouterA is in an up state with the show interface s0/0 command. The interface should be in an up/up state. This status indicates that the interface is receiving carrier detect from the Frame Switch and that Frame Relay LMI is active between RouterA and the switch. Notice that the LMI is DTE LMI, which means that RouterA is a Frame Relay DTE.

```
RouterA#sh int s 0/0
Serial0/0 is up, line protocol is up
  Hardware is QUICC Serial
  Internet address is 192.1.1.1/24
  MTU 1500 bytes, BW 1544 Kbit, DLY 20000 usec, rely 255/255, load 1/255
  Encapsulation FRAME-RELAY, loopback not set, keepalive set (10 sec)
  LMI enq sent  168, LMI stat recvd 39, LMI upd recvd 0, DTE LMI up
  LMI enq recvd 0, LMI stat sent  0, LMI upd sent  0
  LMI DLCI 0  LMI type is ANSI Annex D  frame relay DTE
  Broadcast queue 0/64, broadcasts sent/dropped 8/0, interface broadcasts 8
  Last input 00:00:03, output 00:00:03, output hang never
  Last clearing of "show interface" counters never
  Input queue: 0/75/0 (size/max/drops); Total output drops: 0
```

```
Queueing strategy: weighted fair
Output queue: 0/64/0 (size/threshold/drops)
    Conversations  0/1 (active/max active)
    Reserved Conversations 0/0 (allocated/max allocated)
5 minute input rate 0 bits/sec, 0 packets/sec
5 minute output rate 0 bits/sec, 0 packets/sec
    306 packets input, 11113 bytes, 0 no buffer
    Received 3 broadcasts, 0 runts, 0 giants, 0 throttles
    4 input errors, 0 CRC, 4 frame, 0 overrun, 0 ignored, 0 abort
    293 packets output, 9685 bytes, 0 underruns
    0 output errors, 0 collisions, 55 interface resets
    0 output buffer failures, 0 output buffers swapped out
    80 carrier transitions
    DCD=up  DSR=up  DTR=up  RTS=up  CTS=up
```

Ping RouterB at 192.1.1.3 to verify end to end connectivity.

```
RouterA#ping 192.1.1.3

Type escape sequence to abort.
Sending 5, 100-byte ICMP Echos to 192.1.1.3, timeout is 2 seconds:
!!!!!
Success rate is 100 percent (5/5), round-trip min/avg/max = 134/136/141 ms
```

Now, let's connect to RouterB and verify that RouterB has a Frame Relay map entry to RouterA. Notice that the map entry is dynamic, indicating that the entry was learned via Inverse ARP.

```
RouterB#sh frame map
Serial0/0 (up): ip 192.1.1.1 dlci 100(0x64,0x1840), dynamic,
                broadcast,, status defined, active
```

Use the **show frame-relay pvc** command to verify that DLCI 100 is active on the S0/0 interface of RouterB.

```
RouterB#sh frame pvc

PVC Statistics for interface Serial0/0 (Frame Relay DTE)

DLCI = 100, DLCI USAGE = LOCAL, PVC STATUS = ACTIVE, INTERFACE = Serial0/0

    input pkts 13              output pkts 1              in bytes 702
    out bytes 30               dropped pkts 0             in FECN pkts 0
    in BECN pkts 0             out FECN pkts 0            out BECN pkts 0
    in DE pkts 0               out DE pkts 0
    pvc create time 00:05:21, last time pvc status changed 00:05:21
```

Verify that you can reach RouterA at 192.1.1.1 with a ping command.

```
RouterB#ping 192.1.1.1

Type escape sequence to abort.
Sending 5, 100-byte ICMP Echos to 192.1.1.1, timeout is 2 seconds:
!!!!!
Success rate is 100 percent (5/5), round-trip min/avg/max = 136/138/140 ms
```

Lab #10: Configuring LMI Autosense

Equipment Needed

The following equipment is needed to perform this lab exercise:

■ Two Cisco routers, each of which must have at least one serial port

■ Cisco IOS 11.2 or higher

■ A PC running a terminal emulation program for console port connection on the routers

■ One Cisco DTE/DCE crossover cable. If no crossover cables are available, you can make a crossover cable by connecting a standard Cisco DTE cable to a standard Cisco DCE cable.

Configuration Overview

This configuration will demonstrate how a Cisco router running IOS 11.2 or greater can autoconfigure its LMI signaling protocol.

The two routers are connected, as shown in Figure 4–12. RouterB is configured as a Frame Relay DTE device. Router FrameSwitch is configured as a Frame Relay switch. Router FrameSwitch is configured for Cisco LMI, and RouterB is configured for LMI autosense. The router configured as a Frame Relay switch is also configured to supply clock to the DTE router. This task is accomplished via the use of a Cisco DCE cable and a clock rate statement in the router configuration.

Figure 4-12
LMI autosense

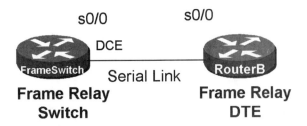

 NOTES: *Keep in mind that although a Cisco router can act as a Frame Relay switch, this feature is typically only used in test and demonstration situations (such as this lab).*

Frame Relay autoconfigure is supported in IOS version 11.2 and higher.

The DCE side of the V.35 cable must connect to router FrameSwitch.

Router Configuration

Start the lab by configuring both routers for Frame Relay encapsulation. The router FrameSwitch should be configured as a Frame Relay switch, and RouterB should be configured as a Frame Relay DTE. Configure the FrameSwitch router for Cisco LMI by typing the command **frame-relay lmi-type cisco** under interface s0/0, and configure RouterB without a **frame-relay lmi-type** statement. Not including an LMI statement will cause the router to go into autoconfigure mode.

Frameswitch

```
Current configuration:
!
version 11.2
no service udp-small-servers
no service tcp-small-servers
!
hostname FrameSwitch
!
!
frame-relay switching←Enable Frame Relay switching on this router
!
interface Serial0/0
 no ip address
 encapsulation frame-relay
 clockrate 64000←Generate a 64,000 bps clock to the DTE
 frame-relay intf-type dce←Define this interface as a Frame Relay DCE
!
```

```
no ip classless
!
line con 0
line aux 0
line vty 0 4
 login
!
end
```

Note that the **frame-relay lmi-type cisco** statement does not appear in the configuration for the router FrameSwitch. Because this is the default LMI type, it is not shown in the router configuration.

Router B

```
Current configuration:
!
version 11.2
no service udp-small-servers
no service tcp-small-servers
!
hostname RouterB
!
interface Serial0/0←Do not set an LMI type. The router can autoconfig its LMI setting
 ip address 195.1.1.33 255.255.255.0
 encapsulation frame-relay
!
no ip classless
!
line con 0
line aux 0
line vty 0 4
 login
!
end
```

Monitoring and Testing the Configuration

The **show interface s0/0** command output issued on the router FrameSwitch is shown as follows. This command verifies that the LMI type is Cisco, as shown in bold.

```
FrameSwitch#sh int s 0/0
Serial0/0 is up, line protocol is up
  Hardware is QUICC Serial
  MTU 1500 bytes, BW 1544 Kbit, DLY 20000 usec, rely 255/255, load 1/255
  Encapsulation FRAME-RELAY, loopback not set, keepalive set (10 sec)
  LMI enq sent  1, LMI stat recvd 0, LMI upd recvd 0
  LMI enq recvd 273, LMI stat sent  265, LMI upd sent  0, DCE LMI up
  LMI DLCI 1023  LMI type is CISCO  frame relay DCE
```

```
    Broadcast queue 0/64, broadcasts sent/dropped 0/0, interface broadcasts 0
    Last input 00:00:03, output 00:00:03, output hang never
    Last clearing of "show interface" counters never
    Input queue: 0/75/0 (size/max/drops); Total output drops: 0
    Queueing strategy: weighted fair
    Output queue: 0/64/0 (size/threshold/drops)
        Conversations   0/1 (active/max active)
        Reserved Conversations 0/0 (allocated/max allocated)
    5 minute input rate 0 bits/sec, 0 packets/sec
    5 minute output rate 0 bits/sec, 0 packets/sec
        273 packets input, 3602 bytes, 0 no buffer
        Received 0 broadcasts, 0 runts, 0 giants, 0 throttles
        5 input errors, 0 CRC, 4 frame, 0 overrun, 0 ignored, 1 abort
        265 packets output, 3495 bytes, 0 underruns
        0 output errors, 0 collisions, 99 interface resets
        0 output buffer failures, 0 output buffers swapped out
        51 carrier transitions
        DCD=up   DSR=up   DTR=up   RTS=up   CTS=up
```

Now connect to RouterB. We will change the encapsulation from Frame Relay to PPP so that we can restart the LMI autoconfiguration process and capture it with a debug trace. Once you are in enabled mode, enter the command **config term**.

```
RouterB#config term
Enter configuration commands, one per line. End with CNTL/Z.
```

Under interface s0/0, you should shut down the interface and change its encapsulation to ppp:

```
RouterB(config)#int s 0/0
RouterB(config-if)#shut
RouterB(config-if)#encap ppp
RouterB(config)#exit
```

After exiting out of the configuration, verify that interface s0/0 is in a shutdown state and that its encapsulation is set to ppp by issuing the **show run** command:

```
Current configuration:
!
version 11.2
no service udp-small-servers
no service tcp-small-servers
!
hostname RouterB
!
!
!
interface Ethernet0/0
 no ip address
 shutdown
!
```

```
interface Serial0/0
 ip address 195.1.1.33 255.255.255.0
 encapsulation ppp←The encapsulation for interface s0/0 has now been set to ppp
          shutdown←The interface has been shut down
!
interface BRI0/0
 no ip address
 shutdown
!
no ip classless
!
line con 0
line aux 0
line vty 0 4
 login
!
end
```

Turn on Frame Relay LMI debugging via the **debug frame-relay lmi** command. Remember to also type the **term mon** command if you are not connected to the console port.

```
RouterB#debug frame-relay lmi
Frame Relay LMI debugging is on
Displaying all Frame Relay LMI data
```

Now, enter configuration mode and activate interface s0/0 by changing its encapsulation to Frame Relay.

```
RouterB#config term
Enter configuration commands, one per line. End with CNTL/Z.
```

Under interface s0/0, change the router's encapsulation to Frame Relay and take the interface out of shutdown mode.

```
RouterB(config)#int s 0/0
RouterB(config-if)#encap frame-relay
RouterB(config-if)#no shut
RouterB(config-if)#exit
RouterB(config)#exit
```

A few seconds after exiting configuration mode you will see four debug messages display on the screen. The first three messages are a result of RouterB sending out three LMI requests using Annex D, AnnexA, and Cisco LMI signaling. Notice that the first three debug outputs are indicated as being in the direction "out," which means that they are originating on RouterB and being sent towards router FrameSwitch.

```
Serial0/0(out): StEnq, myseq 1, yourseen 0, DTE up←Annex D request from router
to Frame switch
datagramstart = 0xD31EF4, datagramsize = 14
FR encap = 0x00010308
00 75 95 01 01 00 03 02 01 00

Serial0/0(out): StEnq, myseq 1, yourseen 0, DTE up←Annex A request from router
to Frame switch
datagramstart = 0xD31DB4, datagramsize = 13
FR encap = 0x00010308
00 75 51 01 00 53 02 01 00

Serial0/0(out): StEnq, myseq 1, yourseen 0, DTE up←Cisco LMI request from
router to Frame switch
datagramstart = 0xD31EF4, datagramsize = 13
FR encap = 0xFCF10309
00 75 01 01 00 03 02 01 00
```

After sending all three LMI requests to the router FrameSwitch, a response is sent back. Recall that the router FrameSwitch is set for LMI type Cisco, so the router answers the third and last request from RouterB. The direction is indicated as "in," meaning that this packet came from router FrameSwitch into RouterB.

```
Serial0/0(in): Status, myseq 1←Frame switch reply to Cisco LMI status request.
RT IE 1, length 1, type 0
KA IE 3, length 2, yourseq 1 , myseq 1
```

Demonstrating the Configuration

Figure 4–13 shows a TTC Fireberd 500 Internetwork Analyzer connected between routers FrameSwitch and RouterB. The TTC 500 was configured to trace all Frame Relay transactions between the two routers. The following traces show RouterB sending out three status inquiries spaced approximately 2 milliseconds apart. The first status is in the Annex D format; the second is in the Annex A format; and the third is in the Cisco LMI format. Because router FrameSwitch is set for Cisco LMI format, it does not respond until it receives the last LMI request—which is in the Cisco LMI format.

Figure 4–13
Monitoring LMI
autosense

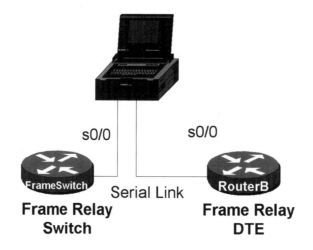

Annex D request from RouterB to FrameSwitch

```
Port A DTE ID=24, 02/05/99, 16:39:54.153700

Length=16, Good FCS
FRAME RELAY PROTOCOL
DLCI_msb                                                              00h
DLCI_lsb                                                               0h
DLCI                                                  Annex D or A 0
CR                                                                   0
EA                                                                   0
FECN                                                                 0
BECN                                                                 0
DE                                                                   0
EA                                                                   1
Q.933 FRAME RELAY SVC
Control                                                   UI Frame 03h
Protocol Discriminator                                Call Control 08h
Reference Flag                                   Msg from Origination 0
Call Reference Value [len=0]                                         0
Message Type                                           STATUS ENQ 75h
INFO ELEMENT Locking Shift [Code=18]
INFO ELEMENT Locking Shift                            (Codeset 5) 5h
IE - Annex D Report Type [Code=1] [Len=1]
IE - Annex D Report Type                            Full Status 00h
IE - Annex D Link Integrity Ver. [Code=3] [Len=2]
Current Seq                                                       01h
Last Rcvd Seq                                                    00h
FCS                                                    Good FD1Eh
```

Annex A request from RouterB to FrameSwitch

```
Port A DTE ID=25, 02/05/99, 16:39:54.155825
Length=15, Good FCS
```

```
FRAME RELAY PROTOCOL
DLCI_msb                                                            00h
DLCI_lsb                                                             0h
DLCI                                                   Annex D or A 0
CR                                                                   0
EA                                                                   0
FECN                                                                 0
BECN                                                                 0
DE                                                                   0
EA                                                                   1
Q.933 FRAME RELAY SVC
Control                                                   UI Frame 03h
Protocol Discriminator                                Call Control 08h
Reference Flag                              Msg from Origination 0
Call Reference Value [len=0]                                         0
Message Type                                          STATUS ENQ 75h
INFO ELEMENT Report Type [Code=81] [Len=1]
INFO ELEMENT Report Type                             Full Status 00h
INFO ELEMENT Link Integrity Ver. [Code=83] [Len=2]
Current Seq                                                        01h
Last Rcvd Seq                                                      00h
FCS                                                       Good B677h
```

Cisco LMI request from RouterB to FrameSwitch

```
Port A DTE ID=26, 02/05/99, 16:39:54.158000
Length=15, Good FCS
FRAME RELAY PROTOCOL
DLCI_msb                                                            3Fh
DLCI_lsb                                                             Fh
DLCI                                                LMI or CLLM 1023
CR                                                                   0
EA                                                                   0
FECN                                                                 0
BECN                                                                 0
DE                                                                   0
EA                                                                   1
LMI - LOCAL MANAGEMENT INTERFACE
Control                                                   UI Frame 03h
Protocol Discriminator                                        LMI 09h
Call Reference                                                    00h
Message Type                                      Status Enquiry 75h
Report Type IE [Code=1] [Len=1]
Report Type IE                                       Full Status 0
Keep Alive Sequence IE [Code=3] [Len=2]
Current Seq                                                        01h
Last Rcvd Seq                                                      00h
FCS                                                       Good DF4Ah
```

FrameSwitch Response to RouterB Cisco LMI Status Request

```
Port A DCE ID=33, 02/05/99, 16:39:54.164325
Length=15, Good FCS
FRAME RELAY PROTOCOL
DLCI_msb                                                              3Fh
DLCI_lsb                                                               Fh
DLCI                                                  LMI or CLLM 1023
CR                                                                      0
EA                                                                      0
FECN                                                                    0
BECN                                                                    0
DE                                                                      0
EA                                                                      1
LMI - LOCAL MANAGEMENT INTERFACE
Control                                                     UI Frame 03h
Protocol Discriminator                                           LMI 09h
Call Reference                                                       00h
Message Type                                                  Status 7Dh
Report Type IE [Code=1] [Len=1]
Report Type IE                                            Full Status 0
Keep Alive Sequence IE [Code=3] [Len=2]
Current Seq                                                          01h
Last Rcvd Seq                                                        01h
FCS                                                         Good EA76h
```

Lab #11: Configuring Cisco Discard Eligibility Support

Equipment Needed

The following equipment is needed to perform this lab exercise:

- Three Cisco routers. Two must have at least one serial port, and one must have two serial ports.

- Cisco IOS 11.2 or higher

- A PC running a terminal emulation program used for console port connection to the routers

- Two Cisco DTE/DCE crossover cables. If no crossover cables are available, you can make a crossover cable by connecting a standard Cisco DTE cable to a standard Cisco DCE cable.

Configuration Overview

This configuration will demonstrate Cisco IOS support for setting the Discard Eligible bit on outgoing traffic. RouterB will be configured to set the DE bit on outgoing frames that are greater then 512 bytes in length.

The three routers are connected, as shown in Figure 4–14. Two of the routers are configured as Frame Relay DTE devices. The third router is configured as a Frame Relay switch. The router configured as a Frame Relay switch is also configured to supply clock to the DTE routers. This task is accomplished via the use of a Cisco DCE cable and a clock rate statement in the router configuration.

NOTES: *Keep in mind that although a Cisco router can act as a Frame Relay switch, this feature is typically only used in test and demonstration situations—such as in this lab.*

The DCE side of the V.35 cable must be on the router FrameSwitch.

Figure 4–14
Cisco Discard
Eligibility support

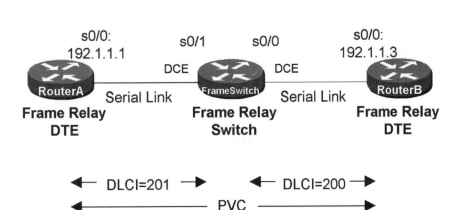

Router Configuration

The configurations for the three routers in this example are as follows (Key Frame Relay commands are in bold):

FrameSwitch (Frame Relay Switch)

```
Current configuration:
!
version 11.2
no service udp-small-servers
no service tcp-small-servers
!
hostname FrameSwitch
!
!
frame-relay switching  ←Configure Frame Relay switching on this router
!
interface Serial0/0
 no ip address
 encapsulation frame-relay
 clockrate 64000  ←Generate a 64,000 bps clock to the DTE
 frame-relay lmi-type ansi  ←Set LMI to Annex D
 frame-relay intf-type dce  ←Set the interface type to a Frame Relay DCE
 frame-relay route 200 interface Serial0/1 201←Define a PVC between S0/0 and S0/1
!
interface Serial0/1
 no ip address
 encapsulation frame-relay
 clockrate 64000
 frame-relay lmi-type ansi
 frame-relay intf-type dce
 frame-relay route 201 interface Serial0/0 200
!
no ip classless
!
line con 0
line aux 0
line vty 0 4
 login
!
end
```

RouterA (Frame Relay DTE)

```
Current configuration:
!
version 11.2
no service udp-small-servers
no service tcp-small-servers
!
hostname RouterA
```

```
!
!
interface Serial0/0
 ip address 192.1.1.1 255.255.255.0
 encapsulation frame-relay←Set the interface encapsulation to Frame Relay
 frame-relay lmi-type ansi←Set the LMI type to Annex D
!
no ip classless
!
line con 0
line aux 0
line vty 0 4
 login
!
end
```

RouterB (Frame Relay DTE)

```
Current configuration:
!
version 11.2
no service udp-small-servers
no service tcp-small-servers
!
hostname RouterB
!
!
frame-relay de-list 3 protocol ip gt 512←Create a Frame Relay DE list.
!                                          Any IP traffic greater then 512 bytes
                                           will be marked.
interface Serial0/0
 ip address 192.1.1.3 255.255.255.0
 encapsulation frame-relay
 frame-relay de-group 3 200←Apply the DE list to this interface for DLCI 200.
 frame-relay lmi-type ansi
!
no ip classless
!
line con 0
line aux 0
line vty 0 4
 login
!
end
```

Notice that the configuration for RouterB has two statements which will cause the DE bit to be set on outgoing traffic: **frame-relay de-list 3 protocol ip gt 512** and **frame-relay de-group 3 200**.

Monitoring and Testing the Configuration

Let's begin by connecting to router FrameSwitch and verifying that it is working properly. Issue the **show frame pvc** command to display all DLCIs that are passing through the router. We see that DLCI 200 is active on port S0/0, and DLCI 201 is active on port S0/1. Several items indicate that ports S0/0 and S0/1 are acting as Frame Relay switch ports. These include the DLCI usage being referenced as Switched, the interface being referred to as a Frame Relay DCE, and the indication of Num Pkts Switched. The PVC status should indicate Active.

```
FrameSwitch#sh frame pvc

PVC Statistics for interface Serial0/0 (Frame Relay DCE)

DLCI = 200, DLCI USAGE = SWITCHED, PVC STATUS = ACTIVE, INTERFACE = Serial0/0

   input pkts 845         output pkts 850        in bytes 143231
   out bytes 143751       dropped pkts 1         in FECN pkts 0
   in BECN pkts 0         out FECN pkts 0        out BECN pkts 0
   in DE pkts 50          out DE pkts 0
   pvc create time 1d00h, last time pvc status changed 1d00h
   Num Pkts Switched 845
 PVC Statistics for interface Serial0/1 (Frame Relay DCE)

DLCI = 201, DLCI USAGE = SWITCHED, PVC STATUS = ACTIVE, INTERFACE = Serial0/1

   input pkts 851         output pkts 845        in bytes 143781
   out bytes 143231       dropped pkts 0         in FECN pkts 0
   in BECN pkts 0         out FECN pkts 0        out BECN pkts 0
   in DE pkts 0           out DE pkts 0
   pvc create time 1d00h, last time pvc status changed 1d00h
   Num Pkts Switched 850
```

Next, issue the **show frame route** command. This command will display all active PVCs that are defined on the router. We see that two DLCIs are configured on this router: 200 and 201. The Frame Relay route table can be interpreted as follows: Any traffic coming into interface S0/0 with a DLCI of 200 will be sent out interface S0/1 with a DLCI of 201. Any traffic coming into interface S0/1 with a DLCI of 201 will be sent out interface S0/0 with a DLCI of 200. The status of both DLCIs should be active.

```
FrameSwitch#sh frame route
Input Intf        Input Dlci    Output Intf    Output Dlci    Status
Serial0/0         200           Serial0/1      201            active
Serial0/1         201           Serial0/0      200            active
```

The **show interface s0/0** and **show interface s0/1** commands will display the status of the serial interfaces on the router. Several important Frame Relay parameters are displayed by this command including the following: the interface encapsulation (Frame-Relay), the LMI status (LMI up), the fact that this port is acting as a Frame Relay DCE, the LMI signaling type (ANSI Annex D), and the LMI exchange counters.

```
FrameSwitch#sh int s 0/0
Serial0/0 is up, line protocol is up
  Hardware is QUICC Serial
  MTU 1500 bytes, BW 1544 Kbit, DLY 20000 usec, rely 255/255, load 1/255
  Encapsulation FRAME-RELAY, loopback not set, keepalive set (10 sec)
  LMI enq sent  1, LMI stat recvd 0, LMI upd recvd 0
  LMI enq recvd 34644, LMI stat sent  33688, LMI upd sent  0, DCE LMI up
  LMI DLCI 0   LMI type is ANSI Annex D  frame relay DCE
  Broadcast queue 0/64, broadcasts sent/dropped 0/0, interface broadcasts 0
  Last input 00:00:09, output 00:00:09, output hang never
  Last clearing of "show interface" counters never
  Input queue: 0/75/0 (size/max/drops); Total output drops: 0
  Queueing strategy: weighted fair
  Output queue: 0/64/0 (size/threshold/drops)
     Conversations  0/1 (active/max active)
     Reserved Conversations 0/0 (allocated/max allocated)
  5 minute input rate 0 bits/sec, 0 packets/sec
  5 minute output rate 0 bits/sec, 0 packets/sec
     35490 packets input, 603366 bytes, 0 no buffer
     Received 0 broadcasts, 0 runts, 0 giants, 0 throttles
     83 input errors, 0 CRC, 82 frame, 0 overrun, 0 ignored, 1 abort
     34539 packets output, 597803 bytes, 0 underruns
     0 output errors, 0 collisions, 425 interface resets
     0 output buffer failures, 0 output buffers swapped out
     701 carrier transitions
     DCD=up  DSR=up  DTR=up  RTS=up  CTS=up

FrameSwitch#sh int s 0/1
Serial0/1 is up, line protocol is up
  Hardware is QUICC Serial
  MTU 1500 bytes, BW 1544 Kbit, DLY 20000 usec, rely 255/255, load 1/255
  Encapsulation FRAME-RELAY, loopback not set, keepalive set (10 sec)
  LMI enq sent  0, LMI stat recvd 0, LMI upd recvd 0
  LMI enq recvd 8735, LMI stat sent  8735, LMI upd sent  0, DCE LMI up
  LMI DLCI 0   LMI type is ANSI Annex D  frame relay DCE
  Broadcast queue 0/64, broadcasts sent/dropped 0/0, interface broadcasts 0
  Last input 00:00:05, output 00:00:05, output hang never
  Last clearing of "show interface" counters never
  Input queue: 0/75/0 (size/max/drops); Total output drops: 0
```

```
Queueing strategy: weighted fair
Output queue: 0/64/0 (size/threshold/drops)
   Conversations   0/1 (active/max active)
   Reserved Conversations 0/0 (allocated/max allocated)
5 minute input rate 0 bits/sec, 0 packets/sec
5 minute output rate 0 bits/sec, 0 packets/sec
   9586 packets input, 266071 bytes, 0 no buffer
   Received 0 broadcasts, 0 runts, 0 giants, 0 throttles
   0 input errors, 0 CRC, 0 frame, 0 overrun, 0 ignored, 0 abort
   9581 packets output, 273105 bytes, 0 underruns
   0 output errors, 0 collisions, 61 interface resets
   0 output buffer failures, 0 output buffers swapped out
   18 carrier transitions
   DCD=up   DSR=up   DTR=up   RTS=up   CTS=up
```

Now, let's connect to RouterA. Display the results of the router's inverse arp with the **show frame map** command. Notice how the router has resolved its local DLCI of 201 to an address of 192.1.1.3 at the far end of the PVC. Recall that 192.1.1.3 is the IP address of the S0/0 interface of RouterB.

```
RouterA#sh fra map
Serial0/0 (up): ip 192.1.1.3 dlci 201(0xC9,0x3090), dynamic,
            broadcast,, status defined, active
```

Verify end to end connectivity between RouterA and RouterB by pinging Router B at 192.1.1.3:

```
RouterA#ping 192.1.1.3

Type escape sequence to abort.
Sending 5, 100-byte ICMP Echos to 192.1.1.3, timeout is 2 seconds:
!!!!!
Success rate is 100 percent (5/5), round-trip min/avg/max = 56/56/60 ms
```

For the sake of completeness, the output of the **show frame pvc, show frame lmi**, and **show interface s0/0** commands are shown as follows for RouterA. These three commands are important troubleshooting tools. Any problems with the ping between RouterA and RouterB could be investigated by issuing these commands and examining their outputs.

```
RouterA#sh frame pvc

PVC Statistics for interface Serial0/0 (Frame Relay DTE)

DLCI = 201, DLCI USAGE = LOCAL, PVC STATUS = ACTIVE, INTERFACE = Serial0/0

   input pkts 272              output pkts 272            in bytes 70953
   out bytes 70953             dropped pkts 0             in FECN pkts 0
   in BECN pkts 0              out FECN pkts 0            out BECN pkts 0
   in DE pkts 35               out DE pkts 0
```

```
     pvc create time 1d00h, last time pvc status changed 1d00h

RouterA#sh frame lmi

LMI Statistics for interface Serial0/0 (Frame Relay DTE) LMI TYPE = ANSI
   Invalid Unnumbered info 0            Invalid Prot Disc 0
   Invalid dummy Call Ref 0        Invalid Msg Type 0
   Invalid Status Message 0        Invalid Lock Shift 0
   Invalid Information ID 0        Invalid Report IE Len 0
   Invalid Report Request 0        Invalid Keep IE Len 0
   Num Status Enq. Sent 218        Num Status msgs Rcvd 218
   Num Update Status Rcvd 0        Num Status Timeouts 0

RouterA#sh int s 0/0
Serial0/0 is up, line protocol is up
   Hardware is QUICC Serial
   Internet address is 192.1.1.1/24
   MTU 1500 bytes, BW 1544 Kbit, DLY 20000 usec, rely 255/255, load 1/255
   Encapsulation FRAME-RELAY, loopback not set, keepalive set (10 sec)
   LMI enq sent  218, LMI stat recvd 218, LMI upd recvd 0, DTE LMI up
   LMI enq recvd 0, LMI stat sent  0, LMI upd sent  0
   LMI DLCI 0  LMI type is ANSI Annex D  frame relay DTE
   Broadcast queue 0/64, broadcasts sent/dropped 0/0, interface broadcasts 0
   Last input 00:00:08, output 00:00:08, output hang never
   Last clearing of "show interface" counters 00:36:23
   Input queue: 0/75/0 (size/max/drops); Total output drops: 0
   Queueing strategy: weighted fair
   Output queue: 0/64/0 (size/threshold/drops)
      Conversations  0/1 (active/max active)
      Reserved Conversations 0/0 (allocated/max allocated)
   5 minute input rate 0 bits/sec, 0 packets/sec
   5 minute output rate 0 bits/sec, 0 packets/sec
      490 packets input, 74185 bytes, 0 no buffer
      Received 0 broadcasts, 0 runts, 0 giants, 0 throttles
      0 input errors, 0 CRC, 0 frame, 0 overrun, 0 ignored, 0 abort
      490 packets output, 74005 bytes, 0 underruns
      0 output errors, 0 collisions, 0 interface resets
      0 output buffer failures, 0 output buffers swapped out
      0 carrier transitions
      DCD=up  DSR=up  DTR=up  RTS=up  CTS=up
```

Now, let's connect to RouterB. The **show frame map** command should display an entry for RouterA's S0/0 interface at ip address 192.1.1.1.

```
RouterB#sh frame map
Serial0/0 (up): ip 192.1.1.1 dlci 200(0xC8,0x3080), dynamic,
            broadcast,, status defined, active
```

Verify end-to-end connectivity by pinging Router A at 192.1.1.1.

```
RouterB#ping 192.1.1.1

Type escape sequence to abort.
```

```
Sending 5, 100-byte ICMP Echos to 192.1.1.1, timeout is 2 seconds:
!!!!!
```
Success rate is 100 percent (5/5), round-trip min/avg/max = 56/56/60 ms

Clear the interface counters with the clear counters command.

```
RouterB#clear counters
Clear "show interface" counters on all interfaces [confirm]
%CLEAR-5-COUNTERS: Clear counter on all interfaces by console
```

Verify that all counters are cleared by typing the **show frame pvc** command. Notice how all packet counters have been reset to 0.

```
RouterB#sh frame pvc

PVC Statistics for interface Serial0/0 (Frame Relay DTE)

DLCI = 200, DLCI USAGE = LOCAL, PVC STATUS = ACTIVE, INTERFACE = Serial0/0

    input pkts 0                output pkts 0          in bytes 0
    out bytes 0                 dropped pkts 0         in FECN pkts 0
    in BECN pkts 0              out FECN pkts 0        out BECN pkts 0
    in DE pkts 0                out DE pkts 0
    pvc create time 00:39:11, last time pvc status changed 00:39:11
```

Do another ping to RouterA at ip address 192.1.1.1. Remember that a standard ping will issue five packets.

```
RouterB#ping 192.1.1.1

Type escape sequence to abort.
Sending 5, 100-byte ICMP Echos to 192.1.1.1, timeout is 2 seconds:
!!!!!
Success rate is 100 percent (5/5), round-trip min/avg/max = 56/56/60 ms
```

Now, type the **show frame pvc** command again. Notice how the input and output packets are now 5. This number represents the five ping packets that were just sent.

```
RouterB#sh frame pvc

PVC Statistics for interface Serial0/0 (Frame Relay DTE)

DLCI = 200, DLCI USAGE = LOCAL, PVC STATUS = ACTIVE, INTERFACE = Serial0/0
```
input pkts 5   **output pkts 5**   in bytes 520
```
    out bytes 520               dropped pkts 0         in FECN pkts 0
    in BECN pkts 0              out FECN pkts 0        out BECN pkts 0
    in DE pkts 0                out DE pkts 0
    pvc create time 00:39:19, last time pvc status changed 00:39:19
```

Now, let's issue an extended ping with 10 ping packets sent, each ping packet being 500 bytes.

```
RouterB#ping
Protocol [ip]:
Target IP address: 192.1.1.1
Repeat count [5]: 10
Datagram size [100]: 500
Timeout in seconds [2]:
Extended commands [n]:
Sweep range of sizes [n]:
Type escape sequence to abort.
Sending 10, 500-byte ICMP Echos to 192.1.1.1, timeout is 2 seconds:
!!!!!!!!!!
Success rate is 100 percent (10/10), round-trip min/avg/max = 256/257/260 ms
```

The **show frame pvc** command will now show 15 input and output packets. This number is 10 more that the last time we examined the values. Remember that our extended ping was 10 packets. Notice that the command output shows no input or output DE packets.

```
RouterB#sh frame pvc

PVC Statistics for interface Serial0/0 (Frame Relay DTE)

DLCI = 200, DLCI USAGE = LOCAL, PVC STATUS = ACTIVE, INTERFACE = Serial0/0

  input pkts 15          output pkts 15         in bytes 5560
  out bytes 5560         dropped pkts 0         in FECN pkts 0
  in BECN pkts 0         out FECN pkts 0        out BECN pkts 0
  in DE pkts 0           out DE pkts 0
  pvc create time 00:39:39, last time pvc status changed 00:39:39
```

Now let's do another extended ping. Ping the far-end address of RouterA at 192.1.1.1. This time, we will use a datagram size of 512 bytes.

```
RouterB#ping
Protocol [ip]:
Target IP address: 192.1.1.1
Repeat count [5]: 10
Datagram size [100]: 512
Timeout in seconds [2]:
Extended commands [n]:
Sweep range of sizes [n]:
Type escape sequence to abort.
Sending 10, 512-byte ICMP Echos to 192.1.1.1, timeout is 2 seconds:
!!!!!!!!!!
Success rate is 100 percent (10/10), round-trip min/avg/max = 260/263/264 ms
```

Now type the show frame pvc command. Notice that our input and output packets have increased by 10, from 15 to 25. Also notice that we now have 10 output DE packets. This result occurred because we exceeded our 512 byte limit for non-DE frames going out of the router.

```
RouterB#sh frame pvc

PVC Statistics for interface Serial0/0 (Frame Relay DTE)


DLCI = 200, DLCI USAGE = LOCAL, PVC STATUS = ACTIVE, INTERFACE = Serial0/0

    input pkts 25            output pkts 25          in bytes 10720
    out bytes 10720          dropped pkts 0          in FECN pkts 0
    in BECN pkts 0           out FECN pkts 0         out BECN pkts 0
    in DE pkts 0             out DE pkts 10
    pvc create time 00:39:58, last time pvc status changed 00:39:58
```

The following analyzer trace shows what a frame looks like that has its DE bit set.

```
Port A DTE ID=54, 01/25/99, 16:19:25.718925


Length=106, Good FCS
FRAME RELAY PROTOCOL
DLCI_msb                                                          06h
DLCI_lsb                                                           4h
DLCI                                                              100
CR                                                                  0
EA                                                                  0
FECN                                                                0
BECN                                                                0
DE                                                                  1
EA                                                                  1
NLPID - NETWORK LEVEL PROTOCOL ID
Ethertype                                                DOD IP 0800h
IP - INTERNET PROTOCOL
Version                                                             4
IHL (in 32 bit words)                                               5
Precedence                                                  Routine 0h
D(elay)                                                      Normal 0
T(hroughput)                                                 Normal 0
R(eliability)                                                Normal 0
Total Length (in octets)                                          100
Identification                                                  0212h
D(on't) F(ragment)                                               No 0
M(ore) F(ragments)                                               No 0
Fragment Offset (in 8 octets)                                       0
Time To Live (in seconds)                                         255
Protocol                                                     ICMP 01h
Header Checksum                                                  316Bh
Class C Source IP Address
Source Net ID                                                  196865
Source Host ID                                                     12
```

```
Source Addr                                                   195.1.1.12
Class C Destination IP Address
Destination Net ID                                                196865
Destination Host ID                                                    13
Destination Addr                                              195.1.1.13
ICMP - INTERNET CONTROL MESSAGE PROTOCOL
Type                                                             Echo 08h
Code                                                                  00h
Checksum                                                            AA4Dh
ID                                                                 0004h
Sequence No                                                        23FFh
Dump
  00000               0000  0000  6BF1  4408  ABCD         ....k.D...
  00010               ABCD  ABCD  ABCD  ABCD  ABCD         ..........
  00020               ABCD  ABCD  ABCD  ABCD  ABCD         ..........
  00030               ABCD  ABCD  ABCD  ABCD  ABCD         ..........
  00040               ABCD  ABCD  ABCD  ABCD  ABCD         ..........
  00050               ABCD  ABCD  ABCD  ABCD  ABCD         ..........
  00060               ABCD  ABCD  ABCD  ABCD  ABCD         ..........
  00070               ABCD                                          ..
FCS                                                          Good 2834h
```

Lab #12: Frame Relay Map Statements

Equipment Needed

The following equipment is needed to perform this lab exercise:

- Three Cisco routers, two of which must have at least one serial port and one of which must have two serial ports
- Cisco IOS 11.2 or higher
- A PC running a terminal emulation program for console port connection to the routers
- Two Cisco DTE/DCE crossover cables. If no crossover cables are available, you can make a crossover cable by connecting a standard Cisco DTE cable to a standard Cisco DCE cable.

Configuration Overview

This configuration will demonstrate the use of the Frame Relay map statement. A Frame Relay map is used when connecting to a device that

Figure 4–15
Frame Relay
map statements

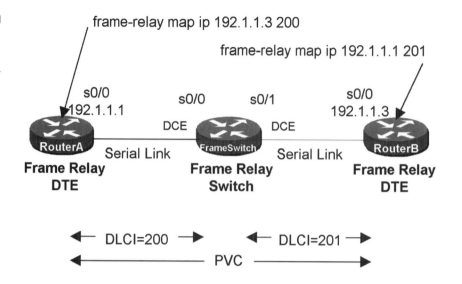

does not respond to an inverse arp request. Because the device does not respond to inverse arp, the router cannot automatically resolve the local DLCI to the far-end IP address. Configuring a Frame Relay map statement causes the router to install a static mapping to the far-end device. This static mapping contains the local DLCI and the far-end IP address. Frame Relay maps can be used for many other protocols, such as IPX.

The three routers are connected, as shown in Figure 4–15. Two of the routers are configured as Frame Relay DTE devices. The third router is configured as a Frame Relay switch. The router configured as a Frame Relay switch is also configured to supply clock to the DTE routers. This task is accomplished via the use of a Cisco DCE cable and a clock rate statement in the router's configuration.

NOTES: Keep in mind that although a Cisco router can act as a Frame Relay switch, this feature is typically only used in test and demonstration situations (such as this lab).

The DCE side of the V.35 crossover cables must be connected to the router FrameSwitch.

Router Configuration

The initial configurations for the three routers in this example are as follows (Key Frame Relay commands are in bold):

FrameSwitch (Frame Relay Switch)

```
Current configuration:
!
version 11.2
no service udp-small-servers
no service tcp-small-servers
!
hostname FrameSwitch
!
!
frame-relay switching ←Configure Frame Relay Switching on this router
!
interface Serial0/0
 no ip address
 encapsulation frame-relay ←Set the interface encapsulation to Frame Relay
 clockrate 64000
 frame-relay lmi-type ansi ←Set the LMI type to Annex D
 frame-relay intf-type dce ←Set the interface type to a DCE
 frame-relay route 200 interface Serial0/1 201←Define a PVC between S0/0 and S0/1
!
interface Serial0/1
 no ip address
 encapsulation frame-relay
 clockrate 64000
 frame-relay lmi-type ansi
 frame-relay intf-type dce
 frame-relay route 201 interface Serial0/0 200
!
no ip classless
!
line con 0
line aux 0
line vty 0 4
 login
!
end
```

RouterA (Frame Relay DTE)

```
Current configuration:
!
version 11.2
service timestamps debug datetime localtime
no service udp-small-servers
no service tcp-small-servers
!
hostname RouterA
!
enable password cisco
!
interface Serial0/0
 ip address 192.1.1.1 255.255.255.0
```

```
 encapsulation frame-relay
 no frame-relay inverse-arp←Disable Frame Relay inverse arp support on this
interface
 frame-relay lmi-type ansi
!
router rip
 network 192.1.1.0
!
no ip classless
!
line con 0
line aux 0
line vty 0 4
 password cisco
 login
!
end
```

RouterB (Frame Relay DTE)

```
Current configuration:
!
version 11.2
no service udp-small-servers
no service tcp-small-servers
!
hostname RouterB
!
enable password cisco
!
interface Serial0/0
 ip address 192.1.1.3 255.255.255.0
 encapsulation frame-relay
 no frame-relay inverse-arp←Disable Frame Relay inverse arp support on this
                            interface
 frame-relay lmi-type ansi
!
no ip classless
!
line con 0
line aux 0
line vty 0 4
 password cisco
 login
!
end
```

Notice that RouterA and RouterB both have the statement **no frame-relay inverse-arp** under their serial 0/0 interface. This command will stop the router from sending out an inverse arp request on its local DLCIs. Some networking devices do not respond to inverse arp requests, so another way must be used to tell the router what far-end IP address corresponds to each local DLCI.

Monitoring and Testing the Configuration

Let's begin by connecting to router FrameSwitch and verifying that it is working properly. Issue the **show frame pvc** command to display all DLCIs that are passing through the router.

```
FrameSwitch#sh frame pvc

PVC Statistics for interface Serial0/0 (Frame Relay DCE)

DLCI = 200, DLCI USAGE = SWITCHED, PVC STATUS = ACTIVE, INTERFACE = Serial0/0

   input pkts 0            output pkts 0          in bytes 0
   out bytes 0            dropped pkts 0          in FECN pkts 0
   in BECN pkts 0         out FECN pkts 0         out BECN pkts 0
   in DE pkts 0           out DE pkts 0
   pvc create time 00:03:24, last time pvc status changed 00:02:40
   Num Pkts Switched 0

PVC Statistics for interface Serial0/1 (Frame Relay DCE)

DLCI = 201, DLCI USAGE = SWITCHED, PVC STATUS = ACTIVE, INTERFACE = Serial0/1

   input pkts 0            output pkts 0          in bytes 0
   out bytes 0            dropped pkts 0          in FECN pkts 0
   in BECN pkts 0         out FECN pkts 0         out BECN pkts 0
   in DE pkts 0           out DE pkts 0
   pvc create time 00:02:45, last time pvc status changed 00:02:41
   Num Pkts Switched 0
```

We see that DLCI 200 is active on port S0/0 and DLCI 201 is active on port S0/1. Several items indicate that ports S0/0 and S0/1 are acting as Frame Relay switch ports. These include the DLCI usage being referred to as switched, the interface being referred to as a Frame Relay DCE, and the indication of Num Pkts Switched. The PVC status should indicate Active.

Next, issue the **show frame route** command. This command will display all active PVCs that are defined on the router.

```
FrameSwitch#sh frame route
Input Intf      Input Dlci     Output Intf     Output Dlci     Status
Serial0/0       200            Serial0/1       201             active
Serial0/1       201            Serial0/0       200             active
```

We see that two DLCIs are configured on this router: 200 and 201. The Frame Relay route table can be interpreted as follows: Any traffic coming into interface S0/0 with a DLCI of 200 will be sent out interface S0/1 with a DLCI of 201. Any traffic coming into interface S0/1 with a DLCI of 201 will be sent out interface S0/0 with a DLCI of 200. The status of both DLCIs should be active.

The **show interface s0/0** and **show interface s0/1** commands will display the status of the serial interfaces on the router. Several important Frame Relay parameters are displayed by this command including: The interface encapsulation (Frame-Relay); the LMI status (LMI up); the fact that this port is acting as a Frame Relay DCE; the LMI signaling type (ANSI Annex D); and the LMI exchange counters.

```
FrameSwitch#sh int s 0/0
Serial0/0 is up, line protocol is up
  Hardware is QUICC Serial
  MTU 1500 bytes, BW 1544 Kbit, DLY 20000 usec, rely 255/255, load 1/255
  Encapsulation FRAME-RELAY, loopback not set, keepalive set (10 sec)
  LMI enq sent   0, LMI stat recvd 0, LMI upd recvd 0
  LMI enq recvd 297, LMI stat sent   297, LMI upd sent   0, DCE LMI up
  LMI DLCI 0  LMI type is ANSI Annex D  frame relay DCE
  Broadcast queue 0/64, broadcasts sent/dropped 0/0, interface broadcasts 0
  Last input 00:00:06, output 00:00:06, output hang never
  Last clearing of "show interface" counters 00:50:00
  Input queue: 0/75/0 (size/max/drops); Total output drops: 0
  Queueing strategy: weighted fair
  Output queue: 0/64/0 (size/threshold/drops)
     Conversations  0/1 (active/max active)
     Reserved Conversations 0/0 (allocated/max allocated)
  5 minute input rate 0 bits/sec, 0 packets/sec
  5 minute output rate 0 bits/sec, 0 packets/sec
     344 packets input, 8392 bytes, 0 no buffer
     Received 0 broadcasts, 0 runts, 0 giants, 0 throttles
     1 input errors, 0 CRC, 1 frame, 0 overrun, 0 ignored, 0 abort
     334 packets output, 8143 bytes, 0 underruns
     0 output errors, 0 collisions, 3 interface resets
     0 output buffer failures, 0 output buffers swapped out
     2 carrier transitions
     DCD=up  DSR=up  DTR=up  RTS=up  CTS=up

FrameSwitch#sh int s 0/1
Serial0/1 is up, line protocol is up
  Hardware is QUICC Serial
  MTU 1500 bytes, BW 1544 Kbit, DLY 20000 usec, rely 255/255, load 1/255
  Encapsulation FRAME-RELAY, loopback not set, keepalive set (10 sec)
  LMI enq sent   0, LMI stat recvd 0, LMI upd recvd 0
  LMI enq recvd 301, LMI stat sent   301, LMI upd sent   0, DCE LMI up
  LMI DLCI 0  LMI type is ANSI Annex D  frame relay DCE
  Broadcast queue 0/64, broadcasts sent/dropped 0/0, interface broadcasts 0
  Last input 00:00:01, output 00:00:01, output hang never
  Last clearing of "show interface" counters 00:50:07
  Input queue: 0/75/0 (size/max/drops); Total output drops: 0
  Queueing strategy: weighted fair
  Output queue: 0/64/0 (size/threshold/drops)
     Conversations  0/1 (active/max active)
     Reserved Conversations 0/0 (allocated/max allocated)
  5 minute input rate 0 bits/sec, 0 packets/sec
```

```
5 minute output rate 0 bits/sec, 0 packets/sec
   338 packets input, 7914 bytes, 0 no buffer
   Received 0 broadcasts, 0 runts, 0 giants, 0 throttles
   0 input errors, 0 CRC, 0 frame, 0 overrun, 0 ignored, 0 abort
   347 packets output, 8693 bytes, 0 underruns
   0 output errors, 0 collisions, 1 interface resets
   0 output buffer failures, 0 output buffers swapped out
   0 carrier transitions
   DCD=up  DSR=up  DTR=up  RTS=up  CTS=up
```

Now, let's connect to RouterA. Verify that RouterA uses DLCI 200 as its local DLCI:

```
RouterA#sh frame pvc

PVC Statistics for interface Serial0/0 (Frame Relay DTE)

DLCI = 200, DLCI USAGE = UNUSED, PVC STATUS = ACTIVE, INTERFACE = Serial0/0

   input pkts 0           output pkts 0          in bytes 0
   out bytes 0            dropped pkts 0         in FECN pkts 0
   in BECN pkts 0         out FECN pkts 0        out BECN pkts 0
   in DE pkts 0           out DE pkts 0
   pvc create time 00:02:03, last time pvc status changed 00:01:23
   Num Pkts Switched 0
```

Display the results of the routers inverse arp with the **show frame map** command.

```
RouterA#sh fra map
RouterA#
```

Notice how there is no output from the router, because we have disabled inverse arp on this router. Although the router learns about new DLCIs from the switch, the router will still not inverse arp on these DLCIs to learn the far-end IP address. In the case of RouterA, the router will not inverse arp on DLCI 200.

Now, turn on Frame Relay packet debugging on RouterA. Remember that debug messages only appear on the console. If you have a telnet connection into the router or are connected to the AUX port, you will also need to issue the **term mon** command.

```
RouterA#debug frame packet
Frame Relay packet debugging is on
```

Verify which debug items are enabled by typing the **show debug** command.

```
RouterA#sh debug
Frame Relay:
  Frame Relay packet debugging is on
```

Now, try to ping RouterB at its address of 192.1.1.3. The ping to 192.1.1.3 fails.

```
RouterA#ping 192.1.1.3

Type escape sequence to abort.
Sending 5, 100-byte ICMP Echos to 192.1.1.3, timeout is 2 seconds:

*Mar  1 00:52:56: Serial0/0:Encaps failed—no map entry link 7(IP)
*Mar  1 00:52:58: Serial0/0:Encaps failed—no map entry link 7(IP)
*Mar  1 00:53:00: Serial0/0:Encaps failed—no map entry link 7(IP)
*Mar  1 00:53:02: Serial0/0:Encaps failed—no map entry link 7(IP)
*Mar  1 00:53:04: Serial0/0:Encaps failed—no map entry link 7(IP)
Success rate is 0 percent (0/5)
```

Let's examine the output of the debug command. The ping command attempted to send five ICMP echo packets to 192.1.1.3. Each packet that was sent generated a debug statement, saying that there was an encapsulation failure with no map entry link. The router cannot send the ping packet to 192.1.1.3, because the router does not have a Frame Relay map to 192.1.1.3.

Now, let's connect to RouterB. Verify that there is no Frame Relay map with the **show frame map** command.

```
RouterB#sh frame map
```

The **show frame pvc** command will verify that DLCI 201 is being used as the local DLCI. Remember that the router will not inverse arp on this DLCI, because inverse arp has been disabled.

```
RouterB#sh frame pvc

PVC Statistics for interface Serial0/0 (Frame Relay DTE)

DLCI = 201, DLCI USAGE = UNUSED, PVC STATUS = ACTIVE, INTERFACE = Serial0/0

   input pkts 0            output pkts 0          in bytes 0
   out bytes 0             dropped pkts 0         in FECN pkts 0
   in BECN pkts 0          out FECN pkts 0        out BECN pkts 0
   in DE pkts 0            out DE pkts 0
   pvc create time 00:03:09, last time pvc status changed 00:03:09
   Num Pkts Switched 0
```

Turn on Frame Relay packet debugging on RouterB with the **debug frame packet** command.

```
RouterB#debug frame packet
Frame Relay packet debugging is on
```

Attempt to ping RouterA at IP address 192.1.1.1.

```
RouterB#ping 192.1.1.1
```

Notice that RouterB has the same problem as RouterA. Neither router knows how to reach the far-end router.

```
Type escape sequence to abort.
Sending 5, 100-byte ICMP Echos to 192.1.1.1, timeout is 2 seconds:

Serial0/0:Encaps failed—no map entry link 7(IP).
Serial0/0:Encaps failed—no map entry link 7(IP).
Serial0/0:Encaps failed—no map entry link 7(IP).
Serial0/0:Encaps failed—no map entry link 7(IP).
Serial0/0:Encaps failed—no map entry link 7(IP).
Success rate is 0 percent (0/5)
```

The problem of RouterA not being able to see RouterB and RouterB not being able to see Router A can be fixed by adding a Frame Relay map in the configurations of RouterA and RouterB. Enter configuration mode, and under interface s 0/0, type the command **frame-relay map ip 192.1.1.1 201.** This command tells RouterB that to reach the IP address of 192.1.1.1, it should encapsulate its Frame Relay traffic in DLCI 201 and send it out interface s 0/0.

```
RouterB#config term
Enter configuration commands, one per line. End with CNTL/Z.
RouterB(config)#int s 0/0
RouterB(config-if)#frame-relay map ip 192.1.1.1 201
RouterB(config-if)#exit
RouterB(config)#exit
```

The configuration of RouterB should now appear as follows (notice the frame relay map command under interface s 0/0):

```
Current configuration:
!
version 11.2
no service udp-small-servers
no service tcp-small-servers
!
hostname RouterB
!
enable password cisco
!
!
interface Ethernet0/0
 no ip address
 shutdown
!
```

```
interface Serial0/0
 ip address 192.1.1.3 255.255.255.0
 encapsulation frame-relay
 frame-relay map ip 192.1.1.1 201←Configure a static Frame Relay map
 no frame-relay inverse-arp
 frame-relay lmi-type ansi
!
 interface Serial0/1
 no ip address
 shutdown
!
no ip classless
!
line con 0
line aux 0
line vty 0 4
 password cisco
 login
!
end
```

Display the current frame relay maps with the **show frame map** command. Remember that most changes on the router take effect immediately. Notice how there is now a mapping between 192.1.1.1 and DLCI 201. Notice also that this map is a static map. The map is static because it was manually added in the configuration.

```
RouterB#sh fra map
Serial0/0 (up): ip 192.1.1.1 dlci 201(0xC9,0x3090), static,
                CISCO, status defined, active
```

Now, let's try to ping RouterA at 192.1.1.1. Before typing the ping command, turn on Frame Relay packet debugging so we can see the results of the ping.

```
RouterB#debug frame packet
Frame Relay packet debugging is on

RouterB#ping 192.1.1.1

Type escape sequence to abort.
Sending 5, 100-byte ICMP Echos to 192.1.1.1, timeout is 2 seconds:

Serial0/0(o): dlci 201(0x3091), pkt type 0x800(IP), datagramsize 104.
Serial0/0(o): dlci 201(0x3091), pkt type 0x800(IP), datagramsize 104.
Serial0/0(o): dlci 201(0x3091), pkt type 0x800(IP), datagramsize 104.
Serial0/0(o): dlci 201(0x3091), pkt type 0x800(IP), datagramsize 104.
Serial0/0(o): dlci 201(0x3091), pkt type 0x800(IP), datagramsize 104.
Success rate is 0 percent (0/5)
```

The ping was not a success. None of the five ICMP echo packets sent to RouterA were returned. But notice the output of the debug trace. Each of the five ICMP packets sent to RouterA were encapsulated in DLCI 201. This process is correct, because we now have a Frame Relay map that associates the IP address of RouterA (192.1.1.1) with DLCI 201. Why, then, did the ping not work? RouterB knows how to get to RouterA. Why did the ICMP packets not get returned? The answer is that although RouterB has a Frame Relay map to RouterA, RouterA does not know how to get back to RouterB. When the ping is sent from RouterB to RouterA, it is being sent to RouterA via DLCI 201 as per the Frame Relay map. But when RouterA has to send the ICMP packet back to RouterB, it does not know how to send it. The solution is to also add a Frame Relay map statement to RouterA so that a return path to RouterB exists.

Connect to RouterA and go into configuration mode. Enter the command **frame-relay map ip 192.1.1.3 200** under interface s 0/0.

```
RouterA#config term
Enter configuration commands, one per line. End with CNTL/Z.
RouterA(config)#int s 0/0
RouterA(config-if)#frame-relay map ip 192.1.1.3 200
RouterA(config-if)#exit
RouterA(config)#exit
```

The configuration for RouterA should now appear as follows. Make sure that the Frame Relay map is under interface s 0/0.

```
Current configuration:
!
version 11.2
service timestamps debug datetime localtime
no service udp-small-servers
no service tcp-small-servers
!
hostname RouterA
!
enable password cisco
!
!
interface Ethernet0/0
 no ip address
 shutdown
!
interface Serial0/0
 ip address 192.1.1.1 255.255.255.0
 encapsulation frame-relay
 frame-relay map ip 192.1.1.3 200←Frame Relay map statement
 no frame-relay inverse-arp
 frame-relay lmi-type ansi
!
interface Serial0/1
```

```
 no ip address
 shutdown
!
router rip
 network 192.1.1.0
!
no ip classless
!
line con 0
line aux 0
line vty 0 4
 password cisco
 login
!
end
```

Display the current Frame Relay map table with the show frame map command.

```
RouterA#sh frame map
Serial0/0 (up): ip 192.1.1.3 dlci 200(0xC8,0x3080), static,
              CISCO, status defined, active
```

This map tells RouterA that to get to 192.1.1.3 (which is the address of RouterB), it must send traffic out of interface s 0/0 encapsulated in DLCI 200.

Now, try to ping RouterB from RouterA. The ping is successful. Both RouterA and RouterB have a defined path to each other.

```
RouterA#ping 192.1.1.3

Type escape sequence to abort.
Sending 5, 100-byte ICMP Echos to 192.1.1.3, timeout is 2 seconds:
!!!!!
Success rate is 100 percent (5/5), round-trip min/avg/max = 56/56/60 ms
```

A ping from RouterB to RouterA should also now be successful:

```
RouterB#ping 192.1.1.1

Type escape sequence to abort.
Sending 5, 100-byte ICMP Echos to 192.1.1.1, timeout is 2 seconds:
!!!!!
Success rate is 100 percent (5/5), round-trip min/avg/max = 56/56/60 ms
```

Lab #13: Full Connectivity with a Partial PVC Mesh and Frame Relay Map Statements

Equipment Needed

The following equipment is needed to perform this lab exercise:

- Four Cisco routers, three of which must have at least one serial port and one of which must have three serial ports
- Cisco IOS 11.2 or higher
- A PC running a terminal emulation program for console port connection to the routers
- Three Cisco DTE/DCE crossover cables. If no crossover cables are available, you can make a crossover cable by connecting a standard Cisco DTE cable to a standard Cisco DCE cable.

NOTE: *The DCE side of the V.35 crossover cables must be connected to the router FrameSwitch.*

Configuration Overview

This configuration will demonstrate a method of achieving full mesh connectivity in a network that does not have a full mesh of PVCs. The configuration for this lab is shown in Figure 4–16. Most network protocols assume transitivity, which means that if RouterB can communicate with RouterA—and if RouterC can communicate with RouterA—then RouterB can communicate with RouterC. This process does not apply with Frame Relay.

This issue poses a problem in configuring Frame Relay networks. As depicted in Figure 4–16, the configuration only has two PVCs. A company purchasing PVCs from a Frame Relay provider would ideally like to be able to communicate from RouterB to RouterC without having to purchase a third PVC between RouterB and RouterC.

Figure 4–16
Full connectivity with
partial PVC mesh

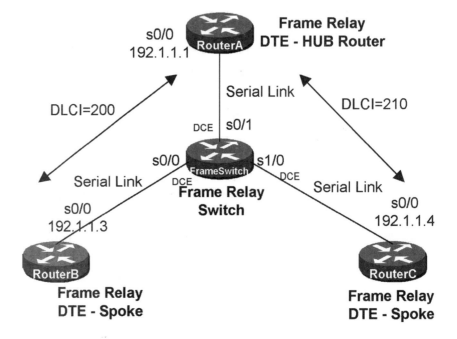

Figure 4–16
Full connectivity with
partial PVC mesh

The four routers are connected, as shown in Figure 4–16. Three of the routers are configured as Frame Relay DTE devices. The fourth router is configured as a Frame Relay switch. The router configured as a Frame Relay switch is also configured to supply clock to the DTE router. This task is accomplished via the use of a Cisco DCE cable and a clock rate statement in the router's configuration.

NOTE: Keep in mind that although a Cisco router can act as a Frame Relay switch, this feature is typically only used in test and demonstration situations (such as this lab).

Router Configuration

The initial configurations for the four routers in this example are as follows (Key Frame Relay commands are highlighted in bold):

FrameSwitch (Frame Relay Switch)

```
Current configuration:
!
version 11.2
no service udp-small-servers
```

```
no service tcp-small-servers
!
hostname FrameSwitch
!
!
frame-relay switching←Configure Frame Relay switching on this interface
!
interface Serial0/0
 no ip address
 encapsulation frame-relay
 clockrate 64000  ←Clock the DTE at 64,000 bps
 frame-relay lmi-type ansi  ←Set the LMI type to Annex D
 frame-relay intf-type dce  ←Set the interface type to a DCE
 frame-relay route 200 interface Serial0/1 200  ←Define a PVC between interface
S0/0 and S0/1
!
interface Serial0/1
 no ip address
 encapsulation frame-relay
 clockrate 64000
 frame-relay lmi-type ansi
 frame-relay intf-type dce
 frame-relay route 200 interface Serial0/0 200
 frame-relay route 210 interface Serial1/0 210
!
interface Serial1/0
 no ip address
 encapsulation frame-relay
 clockrate 64000
 frame-relay lmi-type ansi
 frame-relay intf-type dce
 frame-relay route 210 interface Serial0/1 210
!
no ip classless
!
line con 0
line aux 0
line vty 0 4
 login
!
end
```

RouterA (Frame Relay DTE)

```
Current configuration:
!
version 11.2
no service udp-small-servers
no service tcp-small-servers
!
hostname RouterA
```

```
!
interface Serial0/0
 ip address 192.1.1.1 255.255.255.0
 encapsulation frame-relay←Set the interface encapsulation to Frame Relay
 frame-relay lmi-type ansi←Set the LMI type to Annex D
!
no ip classless
!
line con 0
line aux 0
line vty 0 4
 login
!
end
```

RouterB (Frame Relay DTE)

```
Current configuration:
!
version 11.2
no service udp-small-servers
no service tcp-small-servers
!
hostname RouterB
!
interface Serial0/0
 ip address 192.1.1.3 255.255.255.0
 encapsulation frame-relay
 frame-relay lmi-type ansi
!
no ip classless
!
line con 0
line aux 0
line vty 0 4
 login
!
end
```

RouterC (Frame Relay DTE)

```
Current configuration:
!
version 11.2
no service password-encryption
no service udp-small-servers
no service tcp-small-servers
!
hostname RouterC
!
```

```
interface Serial0/0
 ip address 192.1.1.4 255.255.255.0
 encapsulation frame-relay
 frame-relay lmi-type ansi
!
no ip classless
!
!
line con 0
line aux 0
line vty 0 4
 login
!
end
```

Monitoring and Testing the Configuration

Let's begin by connecting to router FrameSwitch and verifying that it is working properly. Issue the **show frame pvc** command to display all DLCIs that are passing through the router. The PVC configuration is more complex for this lab than for the previous labs. There are now two PVCs that are configured on this router. Several items indicate that these ports are acting as Frame Relay switch ports. These include the DLCI usage being referenced as switched, the interface being referred to as a Frame Relay DCE, and the indication of Num Pkts Switched. The PVC status should indicate Active.

```
FrameSwitch#sh frame pvc

PVC Statistics for interface Serial0/0 (Frame Relay DCE)

DLCI = 200, DLCI USAGE = SWITCHED, PVC STATUS = ACTIVE, INTERFACE = Serial0/0

    input pkts 16          output pkts 17         in bytes 1590
    out bytes 1620         dropped pkts 0         in FECN pkts 0
    in BECN pkts 0         out FECN pkts 0        out BECN pkts 0
    in DE pkts 0           out DE pkts 0
    pvc create time 00:47:35, last time pvc status changed 00:46:33
    Num Pkts Switched 16

PVC Statistics for interface Serial0/1 (Frame Relay DCE)

DLCI = 200, DLCI USAGE = SWITCHED, PVC STATUS = ACTIVE, INTERFACE = Serial0/1

    input pkts 17          output pkts 16         in bytes 1620
    out bytes 1590         dropped pkts 0         in FECN pkts 0
    in BECN pkts 0         out FECN pkts 0        out BECN pkts 0
    in DE pkts 0           out DE pkts 0
    pvc create time 00:46:41, last time pvc status changed 00:46:40
    Num Pkts Switched 17
```

```
DLCI = 210, DLCI USAGE = SWITCHED, PVC STATUS = ACTIVE, INTERFACE = Serial0/1

    input pkts 40          output pkts 36          in bytes 3790
    out bytes 3670         dropped pkts 0          in FECN pkts 0
    in BECN pkts 0         out FECN pkts 0         out BECN pkts 0
    in DE pkts 0           out DE pkts 0
    pvc create time 00:46:30, last time pvc status changed 00:15:12
    Num Pkts Switched 40

PVC Statistics for interface Serial1/0 (Frame Relay DCE)

DLCI = 210, DLCI USAGE = SWITCHED, PVC STATUS = ACTIVE, INTERFACE = Serial1/0

    input pkts 36          output pkts 40          in bytes 3670
    out bytes 3790         dropped pkts 0          in FECN pkts 0
    in BECN pkts 0         out FECN pkts 0         out BECN pkts 0
    in DE pkts 0           out DE pkts 0
    pvc create time 00:47:07, last time pvc status changed 00:46:24
    Num Pkts Switched 36
```

Next, issue the **show frame route** command. This command will display all active PVCs that are defined on the router. There are four DLCIs configured on this router. RouterA is acting as a hub router. All DLCIs terminate on this router. RouterB and RouterC are acting as spoke routers, each having a PVC terminating on RouterA.

```
FrameSwitch#sh frame route
Input Intf      Input Dlci      Output Intf     Output Dlci    Status
Serial0/0       200             Serial0/1       200            active
Serial0/1       200             Serial0/0       200            active
Serial0/1       210             Serial1/0       210            active
Serial1/0       210             Serial0/1       210            active
```

The show interface command will display the status of the serial interfaces on the router. Several important Frame Relay parameters are displayed by this command including the following: the interface encapsulation (Frame-Relay); the LMI status (LMI up); the fact that this port is acting as a Frame Relay DCE; the LMI signaling type (ANSI Annex D); and the LMI exchange counters.

```
FrameSwitch#sh int s 0/0
Serial0/0 is up, line protocol is up
  Hardware is QUICC Serial
  MTU 1500 bytes, BW 1544 Kbit, DLY 20000 usec, rely 255/255, load 1/255
  Encapsulation FRAME-RELAY, loopback not set, keepalive set (10 sec)
  LMI enq sent   0, LMI stat recvd 0, LMI upd recvd 0
  LMI enq recvd 297, LMI stat sent  297, LMI upd sent  0, DCE LMI up
  LMI DCLI 0  LMI type is ANSI Annex D  frame relay DCE
  Broadcast queue 0/64, broadcasts sent/dropped 0/0, interface broadcasts 0
  Last input 00:00:06, output 00:00:06, output hang never
```

```
Last clearing of "show interface" counters 00:50:00
Input queue: 0/75/0 (size/max/drops); Total output drops: 0
Queueing strategy: weighted fair
Output queue: 0/64/0 (size/threshold/drops)
    Conversations   0/1 (active/max active)
    Reserved Conversations 0/0 (allocated/max allocated)
5 minute input rate 0 bits/sec, 0 packets/sec
5 minute output rate 0 bits/sec, 0 packets/sec
    344 packets input, 8392 bytes, 0 no buffer
    Received 0 broadcasts, 0 runts, 0 giants, 0 throttles
    1 input errors, 0 CRC, 1 frame, 0 overrun, 0 ignored, 0 abort
    334 packets output, 8143 bytes, 0 underruns
    0 output errors, 0 collisions, 3 interface resets
    0 output buffer failures, 0 output buffers swapped out
    2 carrier transitions
    DCD=up  DSR=up  DTR=up  RTS=up  CTS=up
```

Let's start by connecting to RouterC. Type the **show frame map** command to display the current Frame Relay map.

```
RouterC#sh frame map
Serial0/0 (up): ip 192.1.1.1 dlci 210(0xD2,0x3420), dynamic,
            broadcast,, status defined, active
```

We see that RouterC has resolved the IP address of RouterA (192.1.1.1) via inverse arp. Notice that RouterC has not resolved the address of RouterB, because RouterC only has a PVC to RouterA—not to RouterB. In general, a spoke router (such as RouterC) will inverse arp to the hub router (such as RouterA) but will not inverse arp to other spoke routers. Verify that you can ping from RouterC to RouterA:

```
RouterC#ping 192.1.1.1

Type escape sequence to abort.
Sending 5, 100-byte ICMP Echos to 192.1.1.1, timeout is 2 seconds:
!!!!!
Success rate is 100 percent (5/5), round-trip min/avg/max = 56/56/56 ms
```

Verify that DLCI 210 is active on interface s0/0 of RouterC:

```
RouterC#sh frame pvc

PVC Statistics for interface Serial0/0 (Frame Relay DTE)

DLCI = 210, DLCI USAGE = LOCAL, PVC STATUS = ACTIVE, INTERFACE = Serial0/0

    input pkts 33            output pkts 31          in bytes 3210
    out bytes 3150           dropped pkts 2          in FECN pkts 0
    in BECN pkts 0           out FECN pkts 0         out BECN pkts 0
    in DE pkts 0             out DE pkts 0
    out bcast pkts 1         out bcast bytes 30
    pvc create time 00:10:44, last time pvc status changed 00:09:44
```

Now, let's connect to RouterB. The **show frame map** command will verify that RouterB has resolved the IP address of RouterA via inverse arp. Again, notice that RouterB does not have a mapping to RouterC.

```
RouterB#sh frame map
Serial0/0 (up): ip 192.1.1.1 dlci 200(0xC8,0x3080), dynamic,
            broadcast,, status defined, active
```

Verify that you can ping RouterA from RouterB:

```
RouterB#ping 192.1.1.1

Type escape sequence to abort.
Sending 5, 100-byte ICMP Echos to 192.1.1.1, timeout is 2 seconds:
!!!!!
Success rate is 100 percent (5/5), round-trip min/avg/max = 56/56/60 ms
```

Verify that DLCI 200 is active on interface s0/0 of RouterB:

```
RouterB#sh frame pvc

PVC Statistics for interface Serial0/0 (Frame Relay DTE)

DLCI = 200, DLCI USAGE = LOCAL, PVC STATUS = ACTIVE, INTERFACE = Serial0/0

   input pkts 12          output pkts 11          in bytes 1100
   out bytes 1070         dropped pkts 1          in FECN pkts 0
   in BECN pkts 0         out FECN pkts 0         out BECN pkts 0
   in DE pkts 0           out DE pkts 0
   pvc create time 00:43:35, last time pvc status changed 00:42:35
```

Now, connect to RouterA. The **show frame pvc** command should report two DLCIs coming into RouterA. Both DLCIs are assigned to interface s0/0. As we can see from Figure 4–16, one of these DLCIs connects RouterA to RouterB (DLCI 200), and the second DLCI connects RouterA to RouterC (DLCI 210).

```
RouterA#sh frame pvc

PVC Statistics for interface Serial0/0 (Frame Relay DTE)

DLCI = 200, DLCI USAGE = LOCAL, PVC STATUS = ACTIVE, INTERFACE = Serial0/0

   input pkts 16          output pkts 16          in bytes 1590
   out bytes 1590         dropped pkts 0          in FECN pkts 0
   in BECN pkts 0         out FECN pkts 0         out BECN pkts 0
   in DE pkts 0           out DE pkts 0
   pvc create time 00:44:41, last time pvc status changed 00:44:41

DLCI = 210, DLCI USAGE = LOCAL, PVC STATUS = ACTIVE, INTERFACE = Serial0/0
```

```
input pkts 36          output pkts 39          in bytes 3670
out bytes 3760         dropped pkts 0          in FECN pkts 0
in BECN pkts 0         out FECN pkts 0         out BECN pkts 0
in DE pkts 0           out DE pkts 0
pvc create time 00:44:32, last time pvc status changed 00:13:12
```

The **show frame map** command will reveal that RouterA has resolved both of its DLCIs to a far-end IP address. DLCI 200 has been resolved to 192.1.1.3 (RouterB), and DLCI 210 has been resolved to 192.1.1.4 (RouterC).

```
RouterA#sh fra map
Serial0/0 (up): ip 192.1.1.3 dlci 200(0xC8,0x3080), dynamic,
          broadcast,, status defined, active
Serial0/0 (up): ip 192.1.1.4 dlci 210(0xD2,0x3420), dynamic,
          broadcast,, status defined, active
```

Verify that you can reach both RouterB and RouterC with the ping command:

```
RouterA#ping 192.1.1.3

Type escape sequence to abort.
Sending 5, 100-byte ICMP Echos to 192.1.1.3, timeout is 2 seconds:
!!!!!
Success rate is 100 percent (5/5), round-trip min/avg/max = 56/57/60 ms

RouterA#ping 192.1.1.4

Type escape sequence to abort.
Sending 5, 100-byte ICMP Echos to 192.1.1.4, timeout is 2 seconds:
!!!!!
Success rate is 100 percent (5/5), round-trip min/avg/max = 56/56/60 ms
```

Now, let's reconnect to RouterC. Verify that RouterC still has a Frame Relay map to RouterA with the **show frame map** command.

```
RouterC#sh frame map
Serial0/0 (up): ip 192.1.1.1 dlci 210(0xD2,0x3420), dynamic,
          broadcast,, status defined, active
```

Enable Frame Relay packet debugging with the **debug frame packet** command.

```
RouterC#debug frame packet
Frame Relay packet debugging is on
```

Verify that our hub router (RouterA) is still reachable at IP address 192.1.1.1.

```
RouterC#ping 192.1.1.1

Type escape sequence to abort.
Sending 5, 100-byte ICMP Echos to 192.1.1.1, timeout is 2 seconds:
!!!!!
Success rate is 100 percent (5/5), round-trip min/avg/max = 56/57/60 ms
```

The ping should be successful. The following screen print shows what the output from the **debug frame packet** command will look like. Notice that the outgoing pings are sent on DLCI 210. The incoming responses also come in on DLCI 210. RouterC knows how to reach RouterA, because it has a Frame Relay map entry to RouterA. Notice that there are five outgoing packets and five incoming packets.

```
Serial0/0(o): dlci 210(0x3421), pkt type 0x800(IP), datagramsize 104
Serial0/0(i): dlci 210(0x3421), pkt type 0x800, datagramsize 104
Serial0/0(o): dlci 210(0x3421), pkt type 0x800(IP), datagramsize 104
Serial0/0(i): dlci 210(0x3421), pkt type 0x800, datagramsize 104
Serial0/0(o): dlci 210(0x3421), pkt type 0x800(IP), datagramsize 104
Serial0/0(i): dlci 210(0x3421), pkt type 0x800, datagramsize 104
Serial0/0(o): dlci 210(0x3421), pkt type 0x800(IP), datagramsize 104
Serial0/0(i): dlci 210(0x3421), pkt type 0x800, datagramsize 104
Serial0/0(o): dlci 210(0x3421), pkt type 0x800(IP), datagramsize 104
Serial0/0(i): dlci 210(0x3421), pkt type 0x800, datagramsize 104
```

Now let's try to ping RouterB at IP address 192.1.1.3.

```
RouterC#ping 192.1.1.3

Type escape sequence to abort.
Sending 5, 100-byte ICMP Echos to 192.1.1.3, timeout is 2 seconds:

Serial0/0:Encaps failed—no map entry link 7(IP).
Serial0/0:Encaps failed—no map entry link 7(IP).
Serial0/0:Encaps failed—no map entry link 7(IP).
Serial0/0:Encaps failed—no map entry link 7(IP).
Serial0/0:Encaps failed—no map entry link 7(IP).
Success rate is 0 percent (0/5)
```

The ping failed. The output of the **debug frame packet** shows that RouterC does not know how to encapsulate the ping that is destined for RouterB. This problem is caused by RouterC not having a Frame Relay mapping to RouterB.

The solution is to tell RouterC how to get to RouterB with a Frame Relay map statement. Enter configuration mode and enter the command **frame-relay map ip 192.1.1.3 210** under interface s 0/0. This command will tell RouterC that if it has traffic for RouterB, it should send that traffic out on DLCI 210. This information will be enough to get the traffic to

RouterA. RouterA then has its own Frame Relay map to RouterB, so the traffic will be able to find its destination.

```
RouterC#config term
Enter configuration commands, one per line. End with CNTL/Z.
RouterC(config)#int s 0/0
RouterC(config-if)#frame-relay map ip 192.1.1.3 210
RouterC(config-if)#exit
RouterC(config)#exit
```

The resulting configuration for RouterC with the new Frame Relay map should appear as follows:

```
Current configuration:
!
version 11.2
no service password-encryption
no service udp-small-servers
no service tcp-small-servers
!
hostname RouterC
!
!
partition slot0: 2 4 4
!
!
interface Ethernet0/0
 no ip address
 shutdown
!
interface Serial0/0
 ip address 192.1.1.4 255.255.255.0
 encapsulation frame-relay
 frame-relay map ip 192.1.1.3 210←Define a static map to 192.1.1.3 via DLCI 210
 frame-relay lmi-type ansi
!
interface BRI0/0
 no ip address
 shutdown
!
interface Ethernet1/0
 no ip address
 shutdown
!
interface Serial1/0
 no ip address
 shutdown
!
interface BRI1/0
 no ip address
 shutdown
!
no ip classless
```

```
!
!
line con 0
line aux 0
line vty 0 4
 login
!
end
```

Verify that the new Frame Relay map has taken effect by typing the **show frame map** command. Notice how the map to RouterA is dynamic while the map to RouterB is static, because the map to RouterA (192.1.1.1) was discovered via inverse arp—while the map to RouterB (192.1.1.3) was manually entered into the RouterC's configuration.

```
RouterC#sh frame map
Serial0/0 (up): ip 192.1.1.1 dlci 210(0xD2,0x3420), dynamic,
             broadcast,, status defined, active
Serial0/0 (up): ip 192.1.1.3 dlci 210(0xD2,0x3420), static,
             CISCO, status defined, active
```

Make sure that Frame Relay packet debugging is still enabled by typing the **show debug** command. Now, try to ping RouterB at IP address 192.1.1.3.

```
RouterC#ping 192.1.1.3

Type escape sequence to abort.
Sending 5, 100-byte ICMP Echos to 192.1.1.3, timeout is 2 seconds:

Serial0/0(o): dlci 210(0x3421), pkt type 0x800(IP), datagramsize 104
Serial0/0(o): dlci 210(0x3421), pkt type 0x800(IP), datagramsize 104.
Serial0/0(o): dlci 210(0x3421), pkt type 0x800(IP), datagramsize 104.
Serial0/0(o): dlci 210(0x3421), pkt type 0x800(IP), datagramsize 104.
Serial0/0(o): dlci 210(0x3421), pkt type 0x800(IP), datagramsize 104.
Success rate is 0 percent (0/5)
```

Notice that the ping still fails. The output from the debug command is now different from the first time we tried to ping 192.1.1.3. The first time we tried the ping, we had not added a static Frame Relay map to 192.1.1.3—and the debug output showed encapsulation failures. Now, the debug shows that the router knows to encapsulate the ICMP packets in DLCI 210. Why, then, does the ping fail? When the ping traffic gets to RouterB, RouterB does not have a path back to RouterC. We must now go to RouterB and add an equivalent Frame Relay map statement.

Connect to RouterB and display the current Frame Relay map with the show frame map command. Verify that only a single dynamic map exists to RouterA at IP address 192.1.1.1.

```
RouterB#sh frame map
Serial0/0 (up): ip 192.1.1.1 dlci 200(0xC8,0x3080), dynamic,
                broadcast,, status defined, active
```

> Enter configuration mode and add the statement **frame-relay map ip 192.1.1.4 200** under interface s 0/0. This command will tell RouterB that if it has traffic for 192.1.1.4 (RouterC), then it should send the traffic out on DLCI 200. Encapsulating the traffic on DLCI 200 will send it to RouterA. RouterA then has a Frame Relay map to RouterC and will know how to get the traffic there.

```
RouterB#config term
Enter configuration commands, one per line. End with CNTL/Z.
RouterB(config)#int s 0/0
RouterB(config-if)#frame-relay map ip 192.1.1.4 200
RouterB(config-if)#exit
RouterB(config)#exit
```

> The resulting configuration for RouterB should appear as follows. Notice the Frame Relay map statement under interface s 0/0.

```
Current configuration:
!
version 11.2
no service udp-small-servers
no service tcp-small-servers
!
hostname RouterB
!
!
!
interface Ethernet0/0
 no ip address
 shutdown
!
interface Serial0/0
 ip address 192.1.1.3 255.255.255.0
 encapsulation frame-relay
 frame-relay map ip 192.1.1.4 200←Define a static map to 192.1.1.4 via DLCI 200
 frame-relay lmi-type ansi
!
interface Serial0/1
 no ip address
 shutdown
!
no ip classless
!
line con 0
line aux 0
line vty 0 4
 login
!
end
```

Verify that there are now two Frame Relay maps for RouterB. The first map to RouterA (192.1.1.1) is a dynamic map, because it was discovered via inverse arp. The second map to RouterC is a static map, because it was manually entered in the router's configuration.

```
RouterB#sh frame map
Serial0/0 (up): ip 192.1.1.1 dlci 200(0xC8,0x3080), dynamic,
          broadcast,, status defined, active
Serial0/0 (up): ip 192.1.1.4 dlci 200(0xC8,0x3080), static,
          CISCO, status defined, active
```

You should now be able to successfully ping RouterC (at IP address 192.1.1.4) from RouterB.

```
RouterB#ping 192.1.1.4

Type escape sequence to abort.
Sending 5, 100-byte ICMP Echos to 192.1.1.4, timeout is 2 seconds:
!!!!!
Success rate is 100 percent (5/5), round-trip min/avg/max = 112/113/120 ms
```

Connect to RouterC and verify that you can now successfully ping RouterB at IP address 192.1.1.3.

```
RouterC#ping 192.1.1.3

Type escape sequence to abort.
Sending 5, 100-byte ICMP Echos to 192.1.1.3, timeout is 2 seconds:
!!!!!
Success rate is 100 percent (5/5), round-trip min/avg/max = 112/112/112 ms
```

Lab #14: Full Connectivity with a Partial PVC Mesh and Subinterfaces

Equipment Needed

The following equipment is needed to perform this lab exercise:

- Four Cisco routers, three of which must have at least one serial port and one of which must have three serial ports
- Cisco IOS 11.2 or higher

A PC running a terminal emulation program for console port connection to the routers

Three Cisco DTE/DCE crossover cables. If no crossover cables are available, you can make a crossover cable by connecting a standard Cisco DTE cable to a standard Cisco DCE cable.

NOTE: *The DCE side of the crossover cables must connect to the router FrameSwitch.*

Configuration Overview

This configuration will demonstrate a method of achieving full mesh connectivity in a network that does not have a full mesh of PVCs by using subinterfaces. A subinterface is a way to treat a physical interface as multiple virtual interfaces, each having its own network layer address. The configuration for this lab is shown in Figure 4–17. Most network protocols assume transitivity, which means that if RouterB can communicate with RouterA and RouterC can communicate with RouterA, then RouterB can communicate with RouterC. This statement does not apply with Frame Relay.

Figure 4–17
Subinterfaces

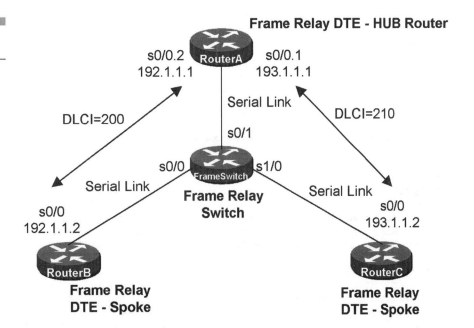

This issue poses a problem in configuring Frame Relay networks. As depicted in Figure 4–17, the configuration has only two PVCs. A company purchasing PVCs from a Frame Relay provider would ideally like to be able to communicate from RouterB to RouterC without having to purchase a third PVC between RouterB and RouterC.

The four routers are connected, as shown in Figure 4–17. Three of the routers are configured as Frame Relay DTE devices. The fourth router is configured as a Frame Relay switch. The router configured as a Frame Relay switch is also configured to supply clock to the DTE router. This task is accomplished via the use of a Cisco DCE cable and a clock rate statement in the router's configuration.

NOTE: Keep in mind that although a Cisco router can act as a Frame Relay switch, this feature is typically only used in test and demonstration situations (such as this lab).

Router Configuration

The configurations for the four routers in this example are as follows (Frame Relay specific commands are highlighted in bold):

FrameSwitch (Frame Relay Switch)

```
Current configuration:
!
version 11.2
no service udp-small-servers
no service tcp-small-servers
!
hostname FrameSwitch
!
!
frame-relay switching ←Define Frame Relay switching on this router
!
interface Serial0/0
 no ip address
 encapsulation frame-relay
 clockrate 64000 ←Clock the DTE at a speed of 64,000 bps
 frame-relay lmi-type ansi ←Set the LMI type to Annex D
 frame-relay intf-type dce ←Set the interface type a DCE
 frame-relay route 200 interface Serial0/1 200←Define a PVC between port s0/0 and s0/1
!
interface Serial0/1
 no ip address
 encapsulation frame-relay
 clockrate 64000
```

```
 frame-relay lmi-type ansi
 frame-relay intf-type dce
 frame-relay route 200 interface Serial0/0 200←This interface will terminate two PVCs
 frame-relay route 210 interface Serial1/0 210
!
interface Serial1/0
 no ip address
 encapsulation frame-relay
 clockrate 64000
 frame-relay lmi-type ansi
 frame-relay intf-type dce
 frame-relay route 210 interface Serial0/1 210
!
no ip classless
!
line con 0
line aux 0
line vty 0 4
 login
!
end
```

RouterA (Frame Relay DTE)

```
Current configuration:
!
version 11.2
no service udp-small-servers
no service tcp-small-servers
!
hostname RouterA
!
interface Serial0/0
 no ip address
 encapsulation frame-relay←Set the interface to Frame Relay encapsulation
 frame-relay lmi-type ansi←Set the LMI type to Annex D
!
interface Serial0/0.1 point-to-point
 ip address 193.1.1.1 255.255.255.0
 frame-relay interface-dlci 210←Assign DLCI 210 to subinterface s0/0.1
!
interface Serial0/0.2 point-to-point
 ip address 192.1.1.1 255.255.255.0
 frame-relay interface-dlci 200←Assign DLCI 200 to subinterface s0/0.2
!
router rip
 network 193.1.1.0
 network 192.1.1.0
!
no ip classless
!
line con 0
line aux 0
line vty 0 4
 login
!
end
```

RouterB (Frame Relay DTE)

```
Current configuration:
!
version 11.2
no service udp-small-servers
no service tcp-small-servers
!
hostname RouterB
!
!
frame-relay de-list 3 protocol ip gt 512
!
interface Serial0/0
 ip address 192.1.1.2 255.255.255.0
 encapsulation frame-relay←Set the interface to Frame Relay encapsulation
 frame-relay lmi-type ansi←Set the LMI type to Annex D
!
router rip
 network 192.1.1.0
!
no ip classless
!
line con 0
line aux 0
line vty 0 4
 login
!
end
```

RouterC (Frame Relay DTE)

```
Current configuration:
!
version 11.2
no service password-encryption
no service udp-small-servers
no service tcp-small-servers
!
hostname RouterC
!
interface Serial0/0
 ip address 193.1.1.2 255.255.255.0
 encapsulation frame-relay←Set the interface to Frame Relay encapsulation
 frame-relay lmi-type ansi←Set the LMI type to Annex D
!
router rip
 network 193.1.1.0
!
no ip classless
!
```

```
!
line con 0
line aux 0
line vty 0 4
 login
!
end
```

Monitoring and Testing the Configuration

Let's begin by connecting to router FrameSwitch and verifying that it is working properly. Issue the **show frame pvc** command to display all DLCIs that are passing through the router. The PVC configuration is more complex for this lab than for the previous labs. There are now two PVCs that are configured on this router. Several items indicate that these ports are acting as Frame Relay switch ports. These include the DLCI usage being referenced as Switched, the interface being referred to as a Frame Relay DCE, and the indication of Num Pkts Switched. The PVC status should indicate Active.

```
FrameSwitch#sh frame pvc

PVC Statistics for interface Serial0/0 (Frame Relay DCE)

DLCI = 200, DLCI USAGE = SWITCHED, PVC STATUS = ACTIVE, INTERFACE = Serial0/0

    input pkts 165          output pkts 178         in bytes 15902
    out bytes 19810         dropped pkts 0          in FECN pkts 0
    in BECN pkts 0          out FECN pkts 0         out BECN pkts 0
    in DE pkts 0            out DE pkts 0
    pvc create time 02:56:16, last time pvc status changed 02:55:15
    Num Pkts Switched 165

PVC Statistics for interface Serial0/1 (Frame Relay DCE)

DLCI = 200, DLCI USAGE = SWITCHED, PVC STATUS = ACTIVE, INTERFACE = Serial0/1

    input pkts 178          output pkts 165         in bytes 19810
    out bytes 15902         dropped pkts 0          in FECN pkts 0
    in BECN pkts 0          out FECN pkts 0         out BECN pkts 0
    in DE pkts 0            out DE pkts 0
    pvc create time 02:55:23, last time pvc status changed 02:55:22
    Num Pkts Switched 178

DLCI = 210, DLCI USAGE = SWITCHED, PVC STATUS = ACTIVE, INTERFACE = Serial0/1
```

```
input pkts 181          output pkts 161         in bytes 19874
out bytes 15652         dropped pkts 0          in FECN pkts 0
in BECN pkts 0          out FECN pkts 0         out BECN pkts 0
in DE pkts 0            out DE pkts 0
pvc create time 02:55:11, last time pvc status changed 02:23:53
Num Pkts Switched 181

PVC Statistics for interface Serial1/0 (Frame Relay DCE)

DLCI = 210, DLCI USAGE = SWITCHED, PVC STATUS = ACTIVE, INTERFACE = Serial1/0

input pkts 161          output pkts 181         in bytes 15652
out bytes 19874         dropped pkts 0          in FECN pkts 0
in BECN pkts 0          out FECN pkts 0         out BECN pkts 0
in DE pkts 0            out DE pkts 0
pvc create time 02:55:48, last time pvc status changed 02:55:05
Num Pkts Switched 161
```

Next, issue the **show frame route** command. This command will display all active PVCs that are defined on the router. There are four DLCIs configured on this router. RouterA is acting as a hub router. All DLCIs terminate on this router. RouterB and RouterC are acting as spoke routers, each having a PVC terminating on RouterA.

```
FrameSwitch#sh frame route
Input Intf      Input Dlci      Output Intf     Output Dlci     Status
Serial0/0       200             Serial0/1       200             active
Serial0/1       200             Serial0/0       200             active
Serial0/1       210             Serial1/0       210             active
Serial1/0       210             Serial0/1       210             active
```

The **show interface** command will display the status of the serial interfaces on the router. Several important Frame Relay parameters are displayed by this command and are highlighted in bold, the interface encapsulation (Frame-Relay); the LMI status (LMI up); the fact that this port is acting as a Frame Relay DCE; the LMI signaling type (ANSI Annex D); and the LMI exchange counters.

```
FrameSwitch#sh int s 0/0
Serial0/0 is up, line protocol is up
  Hardware is QUICC Serial
  MTU 1500 bytes, BW 1544 Kbit, DLY 20000 usec, rely 255/255, load 1/255
  Encapsulation FRAME-RELAY, loopback not set, keepalive set (10 sec)
  LMI enq sent  3, LMI stat recvd 0, LMI upd recvd 0
  LMI enq recvd 1106, LMI stat sent  1103, LMI upd sent  0, DCE LMI up
  LMI DLCI 0  LMI type is ANSI Annex D  frame relay DCE
  Broadcast queue 0/64, broadcasts sent/dropped 0/0, interface broadcasts 0
  Last input 00:00:08, output 00:00:08, output hang never
  Last clearing of "show interface" counters never
  Input queue: 0/75/0 (size/max/drops); Total output drops: 0
```

```
Queueing strategy: weighted fair
Output queue: 0/64/0 (size/threshold/drops)
    Conversations  0/1 (active/max active)
    Reserved Conversations 0/0 (allocated/max allocated)
5 minute input rate 0 bits/sec, 0 packets/sec
5 minute output rate 0 bits/sec, 0 packets/sec
    1452 packets input, 33982 bytes, 0 no buffer
    Received 0 broadcasts, 0 runts, 0 giants, 0 throttles
    17 input errors, 0 CRC, 17 frame, 0 overrun, 0 ignored, 0 abort
    1463 packets output, 40475 bytes, 0 underruns
    0 output errors, 0 collisions, 71 interface resets
    0 output buffer failures, 0 output buffers swapped out
    124 carrier transitions
    DCD=up  DSR=up  DTR=up  RTS=up  CTS=up
```

Let's start by connecting to RouterA.

```
interface Serial0/0
 no ip address
 encapsulation frame-relay
 frame-relay lmi-type ansi
!
interface Serial0/0.1 point-to-point
 ip address 193.1.1.1 255.255.255.0
 frame-relay interface-dlci 210
!
interface Serial0/0.2 point-to-point
 ip address 192.1.1.1 255.255.255.0
 frame-relay interface-dlci 200
```

This screen print above contains a portion of the configuration for RouterA. This configuration uses two subinterfaces, which are bolded. The physical interface s0/0 is being made to appear as two different physical interfaces: s0/0.1 and s0/0.2. Both s0/0.1 and s0/0.2 are referred to as subinterfaces. Because each subinterface appears as a separate interface, it can have its own IP address. Notice that s0/0.1 and s0/0.2 have IP addresses that are on different networks. Because of this fact, the router can route between these two subinterfaces. This feature will enable us to achieve full connectivity without having to have a static Frame Relay map statement added on any of the routers (as we had to do in our previous configuration). The advantage is that this configuration is totally dynamic and does not depend on any statically mapped parameters.

Under each subinterface, there is a **frame-relay interface dlci** command. This command tells each subinterface which DLCI is assigned to it.

Verify that both DLCI 210 and DLCI 200 are active on RouterA with the show frame pvc command.

```
RouterA#sh frame pvc

PVC Statistics for interface Serial0/0 (Frame Relay DTE)

DLCI = 200, DLCI USAGE = LOCAL, PVC STATUS = ACTIVE, INTERFACE = Serial0/0.2

    input pkts 115          output pkts 119         in bytes 10980
    out bytes 13961         dropped pkts 0          in FECN pkts 0
    in BECN pkts 0          out FECN pkts 0         out BECN pkts 0
    in DE pkts 0            out DE pkts 0
    pvc create time 00:23:55, last time pvc status changed 00:23:55

DLCI = 210, DLCI USAGE = LOCAL, PVC STATUS = ACTIVE, INTERFACE = Serial0/0.1

    input pkts 81           output pkts 97          in bytes 7610
    out bytes 11524         dropped pkts 0          in FECN pkts 0
    in BECN pkts 0          out FECN pkts 0         out BECN pkts 0
    in DE pkts 0            out DE pkts 0
    pvc create time 00:23:57, last time pvc status changed 00:23:57
```

Display the Frame Relay map for RouterA with the **show frame map** command.

```
RouterA#sh frame map
Serial0/0.1 (up): point-to-point dlci, dlci 210(0xD2,0x3420), broadcast
          status defined, active
Serial0/0.2 (up): point-to-point dlci, dlci 200(0xC8,0x3080), broadcast
          status defined, active
```

Notice how the command output shows us which DLCI is associated with which subinterface. DLCI 200 and 210 are assigned to subinterfaces s0/0.2 and s0/0.1, respectively. Remember that this interface is defined by the **frame-relay interface-dlci** command in the configuration for RouterA.

Because a subinterface acts as a separate interface and has its own IP address, we need to examine the routing table of the routers in order to understand how this configuration works. Use the **show ip route** command to display the contents of the routers routing table. RouterA sees two networks as being directly connected: 192.1.1.0 and 193.1.1.0.

```
RouterA#sh ip route
Codes: C - connected, S - static, I - IGRP, R - RIP, M - mobile, B - BGP
       D - EIGRP, EX - EIGRP external, O - OSPF, IA - OSPF inter area
       N1 - OSPF NSSA external type 1, N2 - OSPF NSSA external type 2
       E1 - OSPF external type 1, E2 - OSPF external type 2, E - EGP
       i - IS-IS, L1 - IS-IS level-1, L2 - IS-IS level-2, * - candidate default
       U - per-user static route, o - ODR

Gateway of last resort is not set

C    192.1.1.0/24 is directly connected, Serial0/0.2
C    193.1.1.0/24 is directly connected, Serial0/0.1
```

Verify that both RouterB (192.1.1.2) and RouterC (193.1.1.2) can be reached via the ping command.

```
RouterA#ping 192.1.1.2

Type escape sequence to abort.
Sending 5, 100-byte ICMP Echos to 192.1.1.2, timeout is 2 seconds:
!!!!!
Success rate is 100 percent (5/5), round-trip min/avg/max = 56/56/60 ms

RouterA#ping 193.1.1.2

Type escape sequence to abort.
Sending 5, 100-byte ICMP Echos to 193.1.1.2, timeout is 2 seconds:
!!!!!
Success rate is 100 percent (5/5), round-trip min/avg/max = 56/56/60 ms
```

Now, let's connect to RouterC. Verify that DLCI 210 is active by typing the **show frame pvc** command.

```
RouterC#sh frame pvc

PVC Statistics for interface Serial0/0 (Frame Relay DTE)

DLCI = 210, DLCI USAGE = LOCAL, PVC STATUS = ACTIVE, INTERFACE = Serial0/0

    input pkts 60              output pkts 57          in bytes 6469
    out bytes 5686             dropped pkts 0          in FECN pkts 0
    in BECN pkts 0             out FECN pkts 0         out BECN pkts 0
    in DE pkts 0               out DE pkts 0
    out bcast pkts 7           out bcast bytes 486
    pvc create time 00:02:45, last time pvc status changed 00:02:45
```

Use the **show frame map** command to check that RouterC has a Frame Relay map to RouterA (193.1.1.1) via DLCI 210.

```
RouterC#sh frame map
Serial0/0 (up): ip 193.1.1.1 dlci 210(0xD2,0x3420), dynamic,
             broadcast,, status defined, active
```

Use the ping command to verify that RouterC can ping RouterA.

```
RouterC#ping 193.1.1.1

Type escape sequence to abort.
Sending 5, 100-byte ICMP Echos to 193.1.1.1, timeout is 2 seconds:
!!!!!
Success rate is 100 percent (5/5), round-trip min/avg/max = 56/56/60 ms
```

Now, let's take a look at the routing table for RouterC.

```
RouterC#sh ip route
Codes: C - connected, S - static, I - IGRP, R - RIP, M - mobile, B - BGP
       D - EIGRP, EX - EIGRP external, O - OSPF, IA - OSPF inter area
       N1 - OSPF NSSA external type 1, N2 - OSPF NSSA external type 2
       E1 - OSPF external type 1, E2 - OSPF external type 2, E - EGP
       i - IS-IS, L1 - IS-IS level-1, L2 - IS-IS level-2, * - candidate
default
       U - per-user static route, o - ODR

Gateway of last resort is not set

R      192.1.1.0/24 [120/1] via 193.1.1.1, 00:00:04, Serial0/0
C      193.1.1.0/24 is directly connected, Serial0/0
```

Notice that RouterC has a directly connected route to the 193.1.1.0 network. This network is the one that is connected to the s0/0 interface of RouterC, so it appears as a directly connected network. Also notice that there is a route learned via RIP that has the 192.1.1.0 network as its destination. 192.1.1.0 is the network on which RouterB resides. RouterC has learned about a route to RouterB. Keep in mind that this process is all automatic. We did not have to enter any static configurations into any of our routers.

Try to ping subinterface s0/0.2 of RouterA at IP address 192.1.1.1. The ping should be successful. Although RouterC only has a Frame Relay map to 193.1.1.1, the router has learned a RIP route to 192.1.1.1 via the next-hop address of 193.1.1.1. RouterC, therefore, knows that the ping to 192.1.1.1 should be encapsulated in DLCI 210.

```
RouterC#ping 192.1.1.1

Type escape sequence to abort.
Sending 5, 100-byte ICMP Echos to 192.1.1.1, timeout is 2 seconds:
!!!!!
Success rate is 100 percent (5/5), round-trip min/avg/max = 56/56/60 ms
```

Now, try to ping the s0/0 interface of RouterB at IP address 192.1.1.2. Again, the ping should be successful. RouterC has a RIP route to the 192.1.1.0 network with a next-hop address of 193.1.1.1. RouterC knows how to get to 193.1.1.1, because it has a Frame Relay map to that address.

```
RouterC#ping 192.1.1.2

Type escape sequence to abort.
Sending 5, 100-byte ICMP Echos to 192.1.1.2, timeout is 2 seconds:
!!!!!
Success rate is 100 percent (5/5), round-trip min/avg/max = 108/109/112 ms
```

Now, let's connect to RouterB. Verify that DLCI 200 is active by typing the **show frame pvc** command.

```
RouterB#sh frame pvc

PVC Statistics for interface Serial0/0 (Frame Relay DTE)

DLCI = 200, DLCI USAGE = LOCAL, PVC STATUS = ACTIVE, INTERFACE = Serial0/0

    input pkts 100          output pkts 97          in bytes 11661
    out bytes 9146          dropped pkts 0          in FECN pkts 0
    in BECN pkts 0          out FECN pkts 0         out BECN pkts 0
    in DE pkts 0            out DE pkts 0
    pvc create time 00:23:53, last time pvc status changed 00:23:53
```

Display the Frame Relay map with the **show frame map** command. Notice that RouterB only has a Frame Relay map to RouterA's subinterface s0/0.2 at IP address 192.1.1.1.

```
RouterB#sh frame map
Serial0/0 (up): ip 192.1.1.1 dlci 200(0xC8,0x3080), dynamic,
              broadcast,, status defined, active
```

Display the routing table with the **show ip route** command. Notice that there are two routes in the table. The first route entry is for the directly connected 192.1.1.0 network. The second route is learned via RIP. This route is to the 193.1.1.0 network (RouterC) with a next-hop address of 192.1.1.1.

```
RouterB#sh ip route
Codes: C - connected, S - static, I - IGRP, R - RIP, M - mobile, B - BGP
       D - EIGRP, EX - EIGRP external, O - OSPF, IA - OSPF inter area
       N1 - OSPF NSSA external type 1, N2 - OSPF NSSA external type 2
       E1 - OSPF external type 1, E2 - OSPF external type 2, E - EGP
       i - IS-IS, L1 - IS-IS level-1, L2 - IS-IS level-2, * - candidate default
       U - per-user static route, o - ODR
Gateway of last resort is not set

C    192.1.1.0/24 is directly connected, Serial0/0
R    193.1.1.0/24 [120/1] via 192.1.1.1, 00:00:04, Serial0/0
```

Ping the s0/0.1 subinterface (193.1.1.1) on RouterA.

```
RouterB#ping 193.1.1.1

Type escape sequence to abort.
Sending 5, 100-byte ICMP Echos to 193.1.1.1, timeout is 2 seconds:
!!!!!
Success rate is 100 percent (5/5), round-trip min/avg/max = 56/57/60 ms
```

The ping should be successful. RouterB knows how to get to the 193.1.1.0 network because there is a RIP route in the routing table—which tells us that the 193.1.1.0 network is reachable via the 192.1.1.0 network. RouterB has a Frame Relay map to 192.1.1.1, so it knows how to send traffic to 193.1.1.1.

Finally, verify that you can ping RouterC at IP address 193.1.1.2.

```
RouterB#ping 193.1.1.2

Type escape sequence to abort.
Sending 5, 100-byte ICMP Echos to 193.1.1.2, timeout is 2 seconds:
!!!!!
Success rate is 100 percent (5/5), round-trip min/avg/max = 108/109/112 ms
```

We have demonstrated that it is possible to achieve a fully connected Frame Relay network without having to have a full mesh of PVCs using subinterfaces.

Lab #15: Frame Relay Traffic Shaping

Equipment Needed

The following equipment is needed to perform this lab exercise:

■ Three Cisco routers, two of which must have at least one serial port and one of which must have two serial ports

■ Cisco IOS 11.3 or higher

■ A PC running a terminal emulation program for console port connection to the routers

■ Two Cisco DTE/DCE crossover cables. If no crossover cables are available, you can make a crossover cable by connecting a standard Cisco DTE cable to a standard Cisco DCE cable.

NOTE: *The DCE side of the crossover cables must be connected to the router FrameSwitch.*

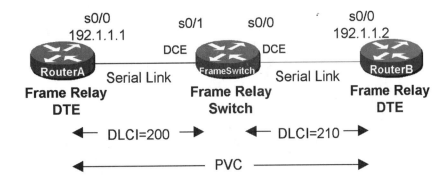

Figure 4-18
Frame Relay
traffic shaping

Configuration Overview

This configuration will demonstrate the Frame Relay traffic shaping capabilities of a Cisco Router. Frame Relay traffic shaping was introduced with IOS 11.2. Frame Relay traffic shaping enables QOS parameters to be assigned to each Frame Relay circuit on a per-PVC basis.

The three routers are connected, as shown in Figure 4–18. Two of the routers are configured as Frame Relay DTE devices. The third router is configured as a Frame Relay switch. The router configured as a Frame Relay switch is also configured to supply clock to the DTE router. This task is accomplished via the use of a Cisco DCE cable and a clock rate statement in the router's configuration.

NOTE: *Keep in mind that although a Cisco router can act as a Frame Relay switch, this feature is typically only used in test and demonstration situations (such as this lab).*

Router Configuration

The configurations for the three routers in this example are as follows (Key Frame Relay commands are shown in bold):

FrameSwitch (Frame Relay Switch)

```
Current configuration:
!
version 11.2
no service udp-small-servers
no service tcp-small-servers
```

```
!
hostname FrameSwitch
!
!
frame-relay switching ←Enable Frame Relay switching on this router
!
interface Serial0/0
 no ip address
 encapsulation frame-relay
 clockrate 64000 ←Clock the DTE at a rate of 64,000 bps
 frame-relay lmi-type ansi ←Set the LMI type to Annex D
 frame-relay intf-type dce ←Set the interface type to a DCE
 frame-relay route 210 interface Serial0/1 200←Define a PVC between interface S0/0 and S0/1
!
interface Serial0/1
 no ip address
 encapsulation frame-relay
 clockrate 64000
 frame-relay lmi-type ansi
 frame-relay intf-type dce
 frame-relay route 200 interface Serial0/0 210
!
no ip classless
!
line con 0
line aux 0
line vty 0 4
 login
!
end
```

RouterA (Frame Relay DTE)

```
Current configuration:
!
version 11.2
no service udp-small-servers
no service tcp-small-servers
!
hostname RouterA
!
interface Serial0/0
 ip address 192.1.1.1 255.255.255.0
 encapsulation frame-relay←Set the interface to Frame Relay encapsulation
 frame-relay lmi-type ansi←Set the LMI type to Annex D
!
interface Serial0/1
 no ip address
 shutdown
!
router rip
 network 193.1.1.0
```

```
 network 192.1.1.0
!
no ip classless
!
line con 0
line aux 0
line vty 0 4
 login
!
end
```

RouterB (Frame Relay DTE)

```
Current configuration:
!
version 11.3
no service password-encryption
!
hostname RouterB
!
enable password cisco
!
interface Serial0/0
 ip address 192.1.1.2 255.255.255.0
 encapsulation frame-relay
 no fair-queue
 frame-relay traffic-shaping←Enable traffic shaping on this interface
 frame-relay class first←Associate a map class to this interface
 frame-relay lmi-type ansi
!
no ip classless
!
map-class frame-relay first←Define a map class on this router
 frame-relay adaptive-shaping becn←Enable BECN flow control
 frame-relay cir 56000←Define CIR value for traffic shaping
 frame-relay bc 1100←Define a Bc value for traffic shaping
 frame-relay mincir 1000←Define a minimum CIR value for traffic shaping
!
line con 0
line aux 0
line vty 0 4
 login
!
end
```

Monitoring and Testing the Configuration

Let's start by connecting to router FrameSwitch and verifying that it is functioning properly. Use the **show frame route** command to display the current active DLCIs on the router. The following example shows what the output should look like. The Frame route tells us that any traffic coming into interface s0/0 with a DLCI value of 210 will be sent out of interface s0/1 with a DLCI value of 200. Any traffic coming into interface s0/1 with a DLCI value of 200 will be sent out of interface s0/0 with a DLCI value of 210. Both DLCIs should show a status of active.

```
FrameSwitch#sh frame route
Input Intf       Input Dlci     Output Intf      Output Dlci    Status
Serial0/0        210            Serial0/1        200            active
Serial0/1        200            Serial0/0        210            active
```

The **show frame pvc** command should indicate that two DLCIs—210 and 200—are active.

```
FrameSwitch#sh frame pvc

PVC Statistics for interface Serial0/0 (Frame Relay DCE)

DLCI = 210, DLCI USAGE = SWITCHED, PVC STATUS = ACTIVE, INTERFACE = Serial0/0

    input pkts 5293          output pkts 6931          in bytes 801309
    out bytes 667933         dropped pkts 0            in FECN pkts 0
    in BECN pkts 0           out FECN pkts 0           out BECN pkts 0
    in DE pkts 0             out DE pkts 0
    pvc create time 2d00h, last time pvc status changed 2d00h
    Num Pkts Switched 5292

PVC Statistics for interface Serial0/1 (Frame Relay DCE)

DLCI = 200, DLCI USAGE = SWITCHED, PVC STATUS = ACTIVE, INTERFACE = Serial0/1

    input pkts 6931          output pkts 5292          in bytes 667933
    out bytes 801279         dropped pkts 0            in FECN pkts 0
    in BECN pkts 0           out FECN pkts 0           out BECN pkts 0
    in DE pkts 0             out DE pkts 0
    pvc create time 2d00h, last time pvc status changed 03:50:05
    Num Pkts Switched 6931
```

We see that this router is acting like a Frame Relay switch—because the DLCI usage is indicated to be switched, the serial interface is referred to as a Frame Relay DCE, and there is an indication of the number of packets switched.

Verify that both serial interfaces of the router FrameSwitch are up using the **show interface** command.

```
FrameSwitch#sh int s 0/0
Serial0/0 is up, line protocol is up
  Hardware is QUICC Serial
  MTU 1500 bytes, BW 1544 Kbit, DLY 20000 usec, rely 255/255, load 1/255
```

Encapsulation FRAME-RELAY, loopback not set, keepalive set (10 sec)
LMI enq sent   0, LMI stat recvd 0, LMI upd recvd 0
LMI enq recvd 34, LMI stat sent   34, LMI upd sent   0, **DCE LMI up**
LMI DLCI 0 LMI type is ANSI Annex D **frame relay DCE**
Broadcast queue 0/64, broadcasts sent/dropped 0/0, interface broadcasts 0
Last input 00:00:00, output 00:00:00, output hang never
Last clearing of "show interface" counters never
Input queue: 0/75/0 (size/max/drops); Total output drops: 0
Queueing strategy: weighted fair
Output queue: 0/64/0 (size/threshold/drops)
    Conversations   0/3 (active/max active)
    Reserved Conversations 0/0 (allocated/max allocated)
5 minute input rate 0 bits/sec, 0 packets/sec
5 minute output rate 0 bits/sec, 0 packets/sec
    42 packets input, 872 bytes, 0 no buffer
    Received 0 broadcasts, 0 runts, 0 giants, 0 throttles
    0 input errors, 0 CRC, 0 frame, 0 overrun, 0 ignored, 0 abort
    49 packets output, 1423 bytes, 0 underruns
    0 output errors, 0 collisions, 39 interface resets
    0 output buffer failures, 0 output buffers swapped out
    42 carrier transitions
    DCD=up DSR=up DTR=up RTS=up CTS=up

FrameSwitch#sh int s 0/1
Serial0/1 is up, line protocol is up
  Hardware is QUICC Serial
  MTU 1500 bytes, BW 1544 Kbit, DLY 20000 usec, rely 255/255, load 1/255
  Encapsulation FRAME-RELAY, loopback not set, keepalive set (10 sec)
  LMI enq sent   0, LMI stat recvd 0, LMI upd recvd 0
  LMI enq recvd 17, LMI stat sent   17, LMI upd sent   0, **DCE LMI up**
  LMI DLCI 0 LMI type is ANSI Annex D **frame relay DCE**
  Broadcast queue 0/64, broadcasts sent/dropped 0/0, interface broadcasts 0
  Last input 00:00:03, output 00:00:03, output hang never
  Last clearing of "show interface" counters never
  Input queue: 0/75/0 (size/max/drops); Total output drops: 0
  Queueing strategy: weighted fair
  Output queue: 0/64/0 (size/threshold/drops)
      Conversations   0/2 (active/max active)
      Reserved Conversations 0/0 (allocated/max allocated)
  5 minute input rate 0 bits/sec, 0 packets/sec
  5 minute output rate 0 bits/sec, 0 packets/sec
      18 packets input, 268 bytes, 0 no buffer
      Received 0 broadcasts, 0 runts, 0 giants, 0 throttles
      0 input errors, 0 CRC, 0 frame, 0 overrun, 0 ignored, 0 abort
      37 packets output, 1553 bytes, 0 underruns
      0 output errors, 0 collisions, 14 interface resets
      0 output buffer failures, 0 output buffers swapped out
      36 carrier transitions
      DCD=up DSR=up DTR=up RTS=up CTS=up

Now, connect to RouterA. Verify that DLCI 200 is up and active by typing the **show frame pvc** command. The PVC status should be active.

```
RouterA#sh frame pvc

PVC Statistics for interface Serial0/0 (Frame Relay DTE)

DLCI = 200, DLCI USAGE = LOCAL, PVC STATUS = ACTIVE, INTERFACE = Serial0/0

   input pkts 380          output pkts 871         in bytes 106424
   out bytes 133998        dropped pkts 0          in FECN pkts 0
   in BECN pkts 0          out FECN pkts 0         out BECN pkts 0
   in DE pkts 0            out DE pkts 0
   pvc create time 03:49:28, last time pvc status changed 03:49:18
```

Show the current Frame Relay map with the **show frame map** command. Make sure that RouterA sees RouterB (IP address 192.1.1.2) at the far end of the circuit.

```
RouterA#sh frame map
Serial0/0 (up): ip 192.1.1.2 dlci 200(0xC8,0x3080), dynamic,
               broadcast,, status defined, active
```

Verify connectivity end-to-end by pinging RouterB at IP address 192.1.1.2. The ping should be successful.

```
RouterA#ping 192.1.1.2

Type escape sequence to abort.
Sending 5, 100-byte ICMP Echos to 192.1.1.2, timeout is 2 seconds:
!!!!!
Success rate is 100 percent (5/5), round-trip min/avg/max = 56/597/768 ms
```

Now, let's connect to RouterB. You can see from the router configuration at the beginning of this chapter that RouterB is configured for Frame Relay traffic shaping. Start by typing the **show frame pvc** command and verifying that DLCI 210 is up and active on RouterB.

```
RouterB#sh frame pvc

PVC Statistics for interface Serial0/0 (Frame Relay DTE)

DLCI = 210, DLCI USAGE = LOCAL, PVC STATUS = ACTIVE, INTERFACE = Serial0/0

   input pkts 39           output pkts 30          in bytes 3624
   out bytes 3120          dropped pkts 0          in FECN pkts 0
   in BECN pkts 0          out FECN pkts 0         out BECN pkts 0
   in DE pkts 0            out DE pkts 0
   out bcast pkts 0        out bcast bytes 0
   Shaping adapts to BECN
   pvc create time 02:41:15, last time pvc status changed 02:41:15
```

Now, type the **show frame pvc** command—but include DLCI 210 at the end of the command by typing **show frame pvc 210**.

```
RouterB#sh frame pvc 210

PVC Statistics for interface Serial0/0 (Frame Relay DTE)

DLCI = 210, DLCI USAGE = LOCAL, PVC STATUS = ACTIVE, INTERFACE = Serial0/0

   input pkts 39              output pkts 30           in bytes 3624
   out bytes 3120            dropped pkts 0            in FECN pkts 0
   in BECN pkts 0            out FECN pkts 0           out BECN pkts 0
   in DE pkts 0              out DE pkts 0
   out bcast pkts 0          out bcast bytes 0
   Shaping adapts to BECN
   pvc create time 02:41:21, last time pvc status changed 02:41:21
   cir 56000      bc 1100      be 0        limit 137    interval 19
   mincir 1000     byte increment 137    BECN response yes
   pkts 30         bytes 3120     pkts delayed 0        bytes delayed 0
   shaping inactive
   Serial0/0 dlci 210 is first come first serve default queueing

   Output queue 0/40, 0 drop, 92 dequeued
```

We see that the command's output is different. The output now shows the CIR, Bc, Be, MinCIR, and traffic-shaping statistics for this PVC. One of the most important indications in this output is the packets delayed. This information shows how many Frame Relay packets have been buffered and delayed due to traffic shaping being activated.

Verify that RouterB has resolved the IP address of RouterA (192.1.1.1) by typing the **show frame map** command.

```
RouterB#sh frame map
Serial0/0 (up): ip 192.1.1.1 dlci 210(0xD2,0x3420), dynamic,
          broadcast,, status defined, active
```

Ping RouterA at IP address 192.1.1.1. The ping should be successful.

```
RouterB#ping 192.1.1.1

Type escape sequence to abort.
Sending 5, 100-byte ICMP Echos to 192.1.1.1, timeout is 2 seconds:
!!!!!
Success rate is 100 percent (5/5), round-trip min/avg/max = 56/58/60 ms
```

Now, show the status of the traffic and traffic shaping for DLCI 210 with the **show frame pvc 210** command.

```
RouterB#sh frame pvc 210

PVC Statistics for interface Serial0/0 (Frame Relay DTE)

DLCI = 210, DLCI USAGE = LOCAL, PVC STATUS = ACTIVE, INTERFACE = Serial0/0

    input pkts 50              output pkts 40            in bytes 4720
    out bytes 4160            dropped pkts 0            in FECN pkts 0
    in BECN pkts 0            out FECN pkts 0           out BECN pkts 0
    in DE pkts 0              out DE pkts 0
    out bcast pkts 0          out bcast bytes 0
    Shaping adapts to BECN
    pvc create time 02:41:42, last time pvc status changed 02:41:42
    cir 56000      bc 1100      be 0          limit 137     interval 19
    mincir 1000       byte increment 137   BECN response yes
    pkts 40           bytes 4160      pkts delayed 0          bytes delayed 0
    shaping inactive
    Serial0/0 dlci 210 is first come first serve default queueing

Output queue 0/40, 0 drop, 92 dequeued
```

Notice that the packet and byte count have incremented since they were last displayed. Packets delayed are still 0, because our CIR is set to 56000 on a 64000 bit/sec link. The five pings that were sent did not generate enough traffic to exceed the CIR value of 56000 bits/sec.

Let's lower the traffic-shaping threshold by decreasing the CIR from 56000 bits/sec to 1100 bits/sec. We can do this by entering configuration mode and typing the command **frame-relay cir 1100** as shown here.

```
RouterB#config term
Enter configuration commands, one per line. End with CNTL/Z.
RouterB(config)#map-class frame-relay first
RouterB(config-map-class)#frame-relay cir 1100
RouterB(config-map-class)#exit
RouterB(config)#exit
```

The configuration should now appear as follows. Notice that the CIR is now set to 1100.

```
Current configuration:
!
version 11.3
no service password-encryption
!
hostname RouterB
!
boot system flash c3620-is-mz_113-3a_T.bin
enable password cisco
!
!
```

```
interface Ethernet0/0
 no ip address
 shutdown
!
interface Serial0/0
 ip address 192.1.1.2 255.255.255.0
 encapsulation frame-relay
 no fair-queue
 frame-relay traffic-shaping
 frame-relay class first
 frame-relay lmi-type ansi
!
interface Serial0/1
 no ip address
 shutdown
!
no ip classless
!
map-class frame-relay first
 frame-relay adaptive-shaping becn
 frame-relay cir 1100←CIR is now set to 1100 bits/sec
 frame-relay bc 1100
 frame-relay mincir 1000
!
line con 0
line aux 0
line vty 0 4
 login
!
end
```

The output of the **show frame pvc 210** command will now indicate that the CIR is set to 1100 bits/sec.

```
RouterB#sh frame pvc 210

PVC Statistics for interface Serial0/0 (Frame Relay DTE)

DLCI = 210, DLCI USAGE = LOCAL, PVC STATUS = ACTIVE, INTERFACE = Serial0/0

    input pkts 68          output pkts 40        in bytes 5728
    out bytes 4160         dropped pkts 0        in FECN pkts 0
    in BECN pkts 0         out FECN pkts 0       out BECN pkts 0
    in DE pkts 0           out DE pkts 0
    out bcast pkts 0       out bcast bytes 0
    Shaping adapts to BECN
    pvc create time 02:50:11, last time pvc status changed 02:50:11
    cir 1100       bc 1100      be 0           limit 15      interval 125
    mincir 1000       byte increment 18     BECN response yes
    pkts 40        bytes 4160       pkts delayed 0         bytes delayed 0
    shaping inactive
    Serial0/0 dlci 210 is first come first serve default queueing

    Output queue 0/40, 0 drop, 0 dequeued
```

Now, ping RouterA at IP address 192.1.1.1.

```
RouterB#ping 192.1.1.1

Type escape sequence to abort.
Sending 5, 100-byte ICMP Echos to 192.1.1.1, timeout is 2 seconds:
!!!!!
Success rate is 100 percent (5/5), round-trip min/avg/max = 60/600/768 ms
```

Display the traffic-shaping statistics for DLCI 210 with the **show frame pvc 210** command. Notice that the packets delayed is now four. The CIR is now set low enough so that the ping generates enough traffic to exceed the CIR and activate traffic shaping on the router.

```
RouterB#sh frame pvc 210

PVC Statistics for interface Serial0/0 (Frame Relay DTE)

DLCI = 210, DLCI USAGE = LOCAL, PVC STATUS = ACTIVE, INTERFACE = Serial0/0

    input pkts 73              output pkts 45           in bytes 6248
    out bytes 4680             dropped pkts 0           in FECN pkts 0
    in BECN pkts 0             out FECN pkts 0          out BECN pkts 0
    in DE pkts 0               out DE pkts 0
    out bcast pkts 0           out bcast bytes 0
    Shaping adapts to BECN
    pvc create time 02:50:27, last time pvc status changed 02:50:27
    cir 1100       bc 1100       be 0            limit 15      interval 125
    mincir 1000       byte increment 18    BECN response yes
    pkts 49          bytes 5096      pkts delayed 4           bytes delayed 416
    shaping inactive
    Serial0/0 dlci 210 is first come first serve default queueing

    Output queue 0/40, 0 drop, 4 dequeued
```

Lab #16: Monitoring and Troubleshooting Frame Relay Connections

Equipment Needed

The following equipment is needed to perform this lab exercise:

- Three Cisco routers, two of which must have at least one serial port and one of which must have two serial ports
- Cisco IOS 11.2 or higher

■ A PC running a terminal emulation program for console port connection to the routers

■ Two Cisco DTE/DCE crossover cables. If no crossover cables are available, you can make a crossover cable by connecting a standard Cisco DTE cable to a standard Cisco DCE cable.

NOTE: *The DCE side of the crossover cables must be connected to the router FrameSwitch.*

Configuration Overview

This lab will review the important monitoring and troubleshooting techniques for Frame Relay configurations.

The three routers are connected, as shown in Figure 4–19. Two of the routers are configured as Frame Relay DTE devices. The third router is configured as a Frame Relay switch. The router configured as a Frame Relay switch is also configured to supply clock to the DTE router. This task is accomplished via the use of a Cisco DCE cable and a clock rate statement in the router's configuration.

NOTE: *Keep in mind that although a Cisco router can act as a Frame Relay switch, this feature is typically only used in test and demonstration situations—such as this lab.*

Figure 4–19
Monitoring
Frame Relay

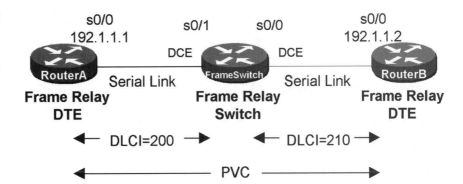

Router Configuration

The configurations for the three routers in this example are as follows (Key Frame Relay commands are highlighted in bold):

FrameSwitch (Frame Relay Switch)

```
Current configuration:
!
version 11.2
no service udp-small-servers
no service tcp-small-servers
!
hostname FrameSwitch
!
!
frame-relay switching ←Enable Frame Relay switching on this router
!
interface Serial0/0
 no ip address
 encapsulation frame-relay
 clockrate 64000 ←Generate a 64,000 bps clock to the DTE
 frame-relay lmi-type ansi ←Set the LMI type to Annex D
 frame-relay intf-type dce ←Set the interface type to a DCE
 frame-relay route 210 interface Serial0/1 200←Define a PVC between S0/0 and S0/1
!
interface Serial0/1
 no ip address
 encapsulation frame-relay
 clockrate 64000
 frame-relay lmi-type ansi
 frame-relay intf-type dce
 frame-relay route 200 interface Serial0/0 210
!
no ip classless
!
line con 0
line aux 0
line vty 0 4
 login
!
end
```

RouterA (Frame Relay DTE)

```
Current configuration:
!
version 11.2
no service udp-small-servers
```

```
no service tcp-small-servers
!
hostname RouterA
!
interface Serial0/0
 ip address 192.1.1.1 255.255.255.0
encapsulation frame-relay←Set the interface to Frame Relay encapsulation
 frame-relay lmi-type ansi←Set the LMI type to Annex D
!
router rip
 network 193.1.1.0
 network 192.1.1.0
!
no ip classless
!
line con 0
line aux 0
line vty 0 4
 login
!
end
```

RouterB (Frame Relay DTE)

```
Current configuration:
!
version 11.2
no service udp-small-servers
no service tcp-small-servers
!
hostname RouterB
!
!
interface Serial0/0
 ip address 192.1.1.2 255.255.255.0
encapsulation frame-relay←Set the interface to Frame Relay encapsulation
 frame-relay lmi-type ansi←Set the LMI type to Annex D
!
router rip
 network 192.1.1.0
!
no ip classless
!
line con 0
line aux 0
line vty 0 4
 login
!
end
```

Monitoring and Testing the Configuration

There are several important show commands that can be used to verify
that a Cisco router acting as a Frame Relay switch is operating properly.
The **show frame route** command will display all PVCs that are configured on the router. The following screen print can be explained as follows:
Any traffic coming into interface s0/0 with a DLCI value of 210 will be
sent out on interface s0/1 on DLCI 200. Any traffic coming into interface
s0/1 on DLCI 200 will be sent out on interface s0/0 on DLCI 210. Both of
the DLCIs are active.

```
FrameSwitch#sh frame route
Input Intf       Input Dlci      Output Intf      Output Dlci      Status
Serial0/0        210             Serial0/1        200              active
Serial0/1        200             Serial0/0        210              active
```

The show frame pvc command will display the status of all DLCIs passing through the router.

```
FrameSwitch#sh frame pvc

PVC Statistics for interface Serial0/0 (Frame Relay DCE)

DLCI = 210, DLCI USAGE = SWITCHED, PVC STATUS = ACTIVE, INTERFACE = Serial0/0

    input pkts 35            output pkts 28          in bytes 2650
    out bytes 2945           dropped pkts 0          in FECN pkts 0
    in BECN pkts 0           out FECN pkts 0         out BECN pkts 0
    in DE pkts 0             out DE pkts 0
    pvc create time 00:07:07, last time pvc status changed 00:06:32
    Num Pkts Switched 34

PVC Statistics for interface Serial0/1 (Frame Relay DCE)

DLCI = 200, DLCI USAGE = SWITCHED, PVC STATUS = ACTIVE, INTERFACE = Serial0/1

    input pkts 28            output pkts 34          in bytes 2945
    out bytes 2620           dropped pkts 0          in FECN pkts 0
    in BECN pkts 0           out FECN pkts 0         out BECN pkts 0
    in DE pkts 0             out DE pkts 0
    pvc create time 00:06:33, last time pvc status changed 00:06:29
    Num Pkts Switched 28
```

We see here that DLCI 210 is active. We see several indications here
that this router is acting like a Frame Relay switch. The interface is
referred to as a Frame Relay DCE. Also, there is an indication of number
of packets switched.

Both of the serial interfaces on the router Frameswitch should be in the up state. This status can be verified with the show interface command.

```
FrameSwitch#sh int s 0/0
Serial0/0 is up, line protocol is up
  Hardware is QUICC Serial
  MTU 1500 bytes, BW 1544 Kbit, DLY 20000 usec, rely 255/255, load 1/255
  Encapsulation FRAME-RELAY, loopback not set, keepalive set (10 sec)
  LMI enq sent  0, LMI stat recvd 0, LMI upd recvd 0
  LMI enq recvd 34, LMI stat sent  34, LMI upd sent  0, DCE LMI up
  LMI DLCI 0  LMI type is ANSI Annex D  frame relay DCE
  Broadcast queue 0/64, broadcasts sent/dropped 0/0, interface broadcasts 0
  Last input 00:00:00, output 00:00:00, output hang never
  Last clearing of "show interface" counters never
  Input queue: 0/75/0 (size/max/drops); Total output drops: 0
  Queueing strategy: weighted fair
  Output queue: 0/64/0 (size/threshold/drops)
     Conversations  0/3 (active/max active)
     Reserved Conversations 0/0 (allocated/max allocated)
  5 minute input rate 0 bits/sec, 0 packets/sec
  5 minute output rate 0 bits/sec, 0 packets/sec
     42 packets input, 872 bytes, 0 no buffer
     Received 0 broadcasts, 0 runts, 0 giants, 0 throttles
     0 input errors, 0 CRC, 0 frame, 0 overrun, 0 ignored, 0 abort
     49 packets output, 1423 bytes, 0 underruns
     0 output errors, 0 collisions, 39 interface resets
     0 output buffer failures, 0 output buffers swapped out
     42 carrier transitions
     DCD=up  DSR=up  DTR=up  RTS=up  CTS=up

FrameSwitch#sh int s 0/1
Serial0/1 is up, line protocol is up
  Hardware is QUICC Serial
  MTU 1500 bytes, BW 1544 Kbit, DLY 20000 usec, rely 255/255, load 1/255
  Encapsulation FRAME-RELAY, loopback not set, keepalive set (10 sec)
  LMI enq sent  0, LMI stat recvd 0, LMI upd recvd 0
  LMI enq recvd 17, LMI stat sent  17, LMI upd sent  0, DCE LMI up
  LMI DLCI 0  LMI type is ANSI Annex D  frame relay DCE
  Broadcast queue 0/64, broadcasts sent/dropped 0/0, interface broadcasts 0
  Last input 00:00:03, output 00:00:03, output hang never
  Last clearing of "show interface" counters never
  Input queue: 0/75/0 (size/max/drops); Total output drops: 0
  Queueing strategy: weighted fair
  Output queue: 0/64/0 (size/threshold/drops)
     Conversations  0/2 (active/max active)
     Reserved Conversations 0/0 (allocated/max allocated)
  5 minute input rate 0 bits/sec, 0 packets/sec
  5 minute output rate 0 bits/sec, 0 packets/sec
     18 packets input, 268 bytes, 0 no buffer
     Received 0 broadcasts, 0 runts, 0 giants, 0 throttles
     0 input errors, 0 CRC, 0 frame, 0 overrun, 0 ignored, 0 abort
     37 packets output, 1553 bytes, 0 underruns
```

```
0 output errors, 0 collisions, 14 interface resets
0 output buffer failures, 0 output buffers swapped out
36 carrier transitions
DCD=up   DSR=up   DTR=up   RTS=up   CTS=up
```

Now, let's examine some troubleshooting and debug commands for a router acting like a standard Frame Relay DTE. The first thing to check is the status of the interface that is connected to the Frame Relay network. In the case of RouterA, this interface is the s0/0 interface. You can display the status of this interface with the **show int s 0/0** command.

```
RouterA#sh int s 0/0
Serial0/0 is up, line protocol is up
  Hardware is QUICC Serial
  Internet address is 192.1.1.1/24
  MTU 1500 bytes, BW 1544 Kbit, DLY 20000 usec, rely 255/255, load 1/255
  Encapsulation FRAME-RELAY, loopback not set, keepalive set (10 sec)
  LMI enq sent  16, LMI stat recvd 16, LMI upd recvd 0, DTE LMI up
  LMI enq recvd 0, LMI stat sent  0, LMI upd sent  0
  LMI DLCI 0   LMI type is ANSI Annex D  frame relay DTE
  Broadcast queue 0/64, broadcasts sent/dropped 5/0, interface broadcasts 5
  Last input 00:00:02, output 00:00:02, output hang never
  Last clearing of "show interface" counters 00:02:38
  Input queue: 0/75/0 (size/max/drops); Total output drops: 0
  Queueing strategy: weighted fair
  Output queue: 0/64/0 (size/threshold/drops)
     Conversations  0/2 (active/max active)
     Reserved Conversations 0/0 (allocated/max allocated)
  5 minute input rate 0 bits/sec, 0 packets/sec
  5 minute output rate 0 bits/sec, 0 packets/sec
     27 packets input, 1095 bytes, 0 no buffer
     Received 0 broadcasts, 0 runts, 0 giants, 0 throttles
     0 input errors, 0 CRC, 0 frame, 0 overrun, 0 ignored, 0 abort
     26 packets output, 1024 bytes, 0 underruns
     0 output errors, 0 collisions, 0 interface resets
     0 output buffer failures, 0 output buffers swapped out
     0 carrier transitions
     DCD=up   DSR=up   DTR=up   RTS=up   CTS=up
```

The interface is shown being in the up, up state. This state is the ideal condition for the interface. If the interface is in the up, down state, there is a problem with the encapsulation settings. Verify that the encapsulation is Frame Relay.

The **show interface** output also contains important information on the status of the Frame Relay link. We see from the following command output that the number of LMI requests sent is 16 and that it matches the number of LMI status messages received. The number of requests should always match the number of messages received. This situation may sometimes not be the case when the router is in the process of being configured. Use the **clear counters** command to reset the counters after the router is up and running to reset these indications.

The output of the **show interface** command also displays the LMI signaling protocol and the DTE/DCE status of the Frame Relay link. We see that this router is configured for Annex D LMI signaling and is acting like a Frame Relay DTE.

The middle portion of the **show interface** commands output displays information on the packet rates on the interface, as well as information on the number of transmission- and reception-errored packets.

The last line of the commands output displays the status of the V.35 control leads. DCD (carrier detect) must be high in order for the interface to be in an up state.

The **show frame pvc** command appears slightly different on a Frame DTE then it does on a router acting like a Frame Relay switch.

```
RouterB#sh frame pvc

PVC Statistics for interface Serial0/0 (Frame Relay DTE)

DLCI = 210, DLCI USAGE = LOCAL, PVC STATUS = ACTIVE, INTERFACE = Serial0/0

   input pkts 34           output pkts 39          in bytes 3521
   out bytes 3166          dropped pkts 0          in FECN pkts 0
   in BECN pkts 0          out FECN pkts 0         out BECN pkts 0
   in DE pkts 0            out DE pkts 0
   pvc create time 00:07:25, last time pvc status changed 00:06:55
```

The commands output provides important information on the number of packets sent and received on the router's interface. Congestion notification is reported for BECN, FECN, and DE bits. The last line of the output shows how long the PVC has been active and also shows the last time that the PVC status changed.

The **show frame lmi** command is used to verify proper communication between the router and the Frame Relay switch. Some of this information is contained in the show interface command, but the **show frame lmi** output contains more detailed statistics.

```
RouterB#sh frame lmi

LMI Statistics for interface Serial0/0 (Frame Relay DTE) LMI TYPE = ANSI
   Invalid Unnumbered info 0      Invalid Prot Disc 0
   Invalid dummy Call Ref 0       Invalid Msg Type 0
   Invalid Status Message 0       Invalid Lock Shift 0
   Invalid Information ID 0       Invalid Report IE Len 0
   Invalid Report Request 0       Invalid Keep IE Len 0
   Num Status Enq. Sent 51368     Num Status msgs Rcvd 51120
   Num Update Status Rcvd 0       Num Status Timeouts 248
```

If the router appears to not receive LMI updates, you can use the **debug frame lmi** command to see what exchanges are taking place with the Frame Relay switch. Remember to also use the **term mon** command if you are not connected to the console port of the router.

```
RouterA#debug frame lmi
Frame Relay LMI debugging is on
Displaying all Frame Relay LMI data


Serial0/0(out): StEnq, myseq 132, yourseen 131, DTE up
datagramstart = 0xD2A9D4, datagramsize = 14
FR encap = 0x00010308
00 75 95 01 01 01 03 02 84 83

Serial0/0(in): Status, myseq 132
RT IE 1, length 1, type 1
KA IE 3, length 2, yourseq 132, myseq 132

Serial0/0(out): StEnq, myseq 133, yourseen 132, DTE up
datagramstart = 0xD2A9D4, datagramsize = 14
FR encap = 0x00010308
00 75 95 01 01 00 03 02 85 84

Serial0/0(in): Status, myseq 133
RT IE 1, length 1, type 0
KA IE 3, length 2, yourseq 133, myseq 133
PVC IE 0x7 , length 0x3 , dlci 200, status 0x2←Full Status Response from the
                                                switch telling the router that
                                                DLCI 200 is active

Serial0/0(out): StEnq, myseq 134, yourseen 133, DTE up
datagramstart = 0xD2A9D4, datagramsize = 14
FR encap = 0x00010308
00 75 95 01 01 01 03 02 86 85

Serial0/0(in): Status, myseq 134
RT IE 1, length 1, type 1
KA IE 3, length 2, yourseq 134, myseq 134
```

The **show frame map** command displays the results of the router's inverse arp on known DLCIs. When the router requests full status from the Frame Relay switch, the switch responds with a list of all configured DLCIs. The router will inverse arp on each of these DLCIs and will resolve a far-end IP address from the inverse arp.

```
RouterB#sh frame map
Serial0/0 (up): ip 192.1.1.1 dlci 210(0xD2,0x3420), dynamic,
                broadcast,, status defined, active
```

The sample Frame Relay map tells us that the far-end router's IP address on the PVC associated with the local DLCI 210 is 192.1.1.1. We also see that the map is dynamic, which means that the mapping was learned dynamically through an inverse arp. If the map were shown as static, that would have meant that the map was configured manually in the router's configuration.

Once the far-end IP address is known, it should be checked for reachability with the ping command.

```
RouterB#ping 192.1.1.1

Type escape sequence to abort.
Sending 5, 100-byte ICMP Echos to 192.1.1.1, timeout is 2 seconds:
!!!!!
Success rate is 100 percent (5/5), round-trip min/avg/max = 56/57/60 ms
```

If the ping is not successful, you can enable frame packet debug with the **debug frame packet** command. Remember to use the **term mon** command if you are not connected to the console port. The output of the following failed ping shows that the encapsulation has failed on interface s 0/0. This situation is usually caused by the lack of a Frame Relay map statement to the far end.

```
RouterA#debug frame packet
Frame Relay packet debugging is on

RouterA#ping 192.1.1.1

Type escape sequence to abort.
Sending 5, 100-byte ICMP Echos to 192.1.1.1, timeout is 2 seconds:

Serial0/0:Encaps failed—no map entry link 7(IP)
Serial0/0:Encaps failed—no map entry link 7(IP).
Serial0/0:Encaps failed—no map entry link 7(IP).
Serial0/0:Encaps failed—no map entry link 7(IP)
Serial0/0: broadcast search
Serial0/0:Encaps failed—no map entry link 7(IP).
Success rate is 0 percent (0/5)
```

A successful ping will show the proper encapsulation when monitoring with the **debug frame packet** command. Notice in the following successful ping that the traffic to IP address 192.1.1.2 is being encapsulated on DLCI 200.

```
RouterA#ping 192.1.1.2

Type escape sequence to abort.
Sending 5, 100-byte ICMP Echos to 192.1.1.2, timeout is 2 seconds:
!!!!!
Success rate is 100 percent (5/5), round-trip min/avg/max = 56/56/60 ms
```

```
Serial0/0(o): dlci 200(0x3081), pkt type 0x800(IP), datagramsize 104
Serial0/0(i): dlci 200(0x3081), pkt type 0x800, datagramsize 104
Serial0/0(o): dlci 200(0x3081), pkt type 0x800(IP), datagramsize 104
Serial0/0(i): dlci 200(0x3081), pkt type 0x800, datagramsize 104
Serial0/0(o): dlci 200(0x3081), pkt type 0x800(IP), datagramsize 104
Serial0/0(i): dlci 200(0x3081), pkt type 0x800, datagramsize 104
Serial0/0(o): dlci 200(0x3081), pkt type 0x800(IP), datagramsize 104
Serial0/0(i): dlci 200(0x3081), pkt type 0x800, datagramsize 104
Serial0/0(o): dlci 200(0x3081), pkt type 0x800(IP), datagramsize 104
Serial0/0(i): dlci 200(0x3081), pkt type 0x800, datagramsize 104
```

The **show controllers** command is useful in doing a debug. The command will show you which kind of cable is connected to a particular interface. The command also tells you whether the interface sees a clock signal.

```
RouterA#sh cont s 0/0
Interface Serial0/0
Hardware is Quicc 68360
DTE V.35 TX and RX clocks detected.←V.35 DTE cable detected. Router sees an
                                       incoming clock
```

Conclusion

Frame Relay is the most popular wide-area-networking protocol. We have seen that there are several reasons for the wide acceptance of Frame Relay in the networking world.

The Cisco IOS features extensive support for Frame Relay networking. This chapter contained eight labs which explore Cisco's support for Frame Relay networks.

Asynchronous Transfer Mode (ATM)

Topics Covered in This Chapter

- ATM technology overview
- Cisco 4500 ATM configuration
- Cisco ATM loopbacks
- ATM troubleshooting

Introduction

Asynchronous Transfer Mode (ATM) is an exciting *Wide Area Network* (WAN) technology that has been the focus of much attention during the last few years. Cisco has extensive support for ATM networking. This chapter will examine ATM technology in detail and will then explore how the Cisco IOS supports ATM with two hands-on labs.

ATM Overview

ATM is a standard for cell switching, where traffic for multiple types of services such as data, voice, and video are transmitted in fixed-size, 53-byte cells. As shown in Figures 5–1 and 5–2, ATM differs from other networking protocols in that ATM is the only protocol which keeps the same cell format and protocol end to end.

ATM also differs from other protocols in that it is a switched protocol. All ATM end-user devices are directly connected to a switch.

In Figure 5–1, we see a traditional LAN/WAN architecture. Ethernet-connected workstations reside on shared Ethernet LANs and are connected to a router. Two routers are connected together via a Frame Relay link, and two routers are connected together via an HDLC link. With this architecture, the data link encapsulation of the traffic traveling between the two Ethernet LANs changes at every router hop. Traffic starts out on an Ethernet LAN with 802.3 encapsulation and leaves the first router

Figure 5–1
Traditional Local Area Network (LAN)/ WAN network

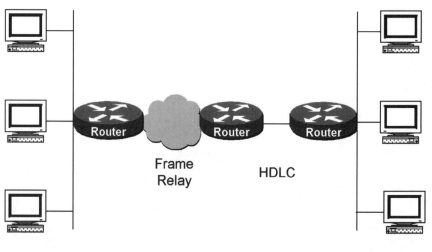

Ethernet   Ethernet

Figure 5–2
ATM network

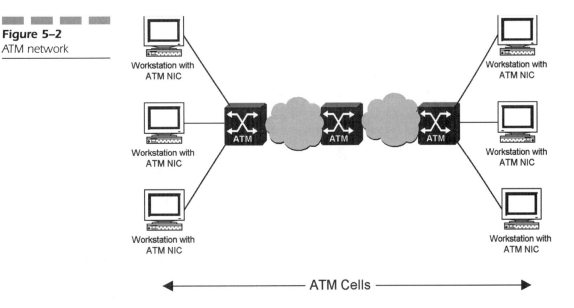

encapsulated in Frame Relay. Data leaves the second router encapsulated in HDLC. Finally, data leaves the third router encapsulated once again in 802.3 Ethernet. This traditional LAN/WAN architecture has the disadvantage of adding overhead to perform the hop-by-hop encapsulation/de-encapsulation/encapsulation as traffic passes from one datalink format to the next.

Figure 5–2 shows an ATM network. In this scenario, data leaves the workstations as ATM traffic and travels across the entire network using the same ATM format. No overhead is lost in any kind of encapsulation/de-encapsulation at each hop.

ATM is a cell-switching and multiplexing technology that combines the benefits of circuit switching (guaranteed capacity and constant transmission delay) with those of packet switching (flexibility and efficiency for intermittent traffic).

ATM is referred to as asynchronous, because data can be sent in any available time slot—as opposed to TDM, where each user is assigned to a specific time slot. If a TDM user has no data to send, then that user's time slot will remain empty. The source of the traffic is identified by addressing information in the header of each ATM cell.

ATM networks are connection-oriented, meaning that a virtual circuit must be set up across the ATM network prior to any data transfer. These virtual circuits can be either permanent or switched.

ATM Protocol Stack

As shown in Figure 5–3, ATM does not use the standard seven-layer OSI protocol reference model; instead, it uses its own protocol stack.

The ATM protocol stack is composed of the following components:

- **Physical layer**: The ATM physical layer manages the medium-dependent transmission.
  - Converting the 53-byte ATM cell into an outgoing bitstream and converting an incoming bitstream to a 53-byte ATM cell
  - Keeping track of the ATM cell boundaries
  - Electrical and physical specifications
- **ATM layer**: The ATM layer is responsible for establishing connections and passing cells through the ATM network. To do this task, the layer uses information in the header of each ATM cell. The layer performs such tasks as the following:
  - VPI and VCI switching
  - Cell multiplexing and demultiplexing
  - Flow Control
  - Header error control
  - *Cell Loss Priority* (CLP) processing
  - QOS support
- *ATM Adaptation Layer* (**AAL**): The AAL is responsible for isolating higher-layer protocols from the details of the ATM processes. The AAL performs such tasks as:
  - Segmentation and reassembly of the data
  - Payload error control
  - End-to-end timing

Figure 5–3
ATM protocol stack

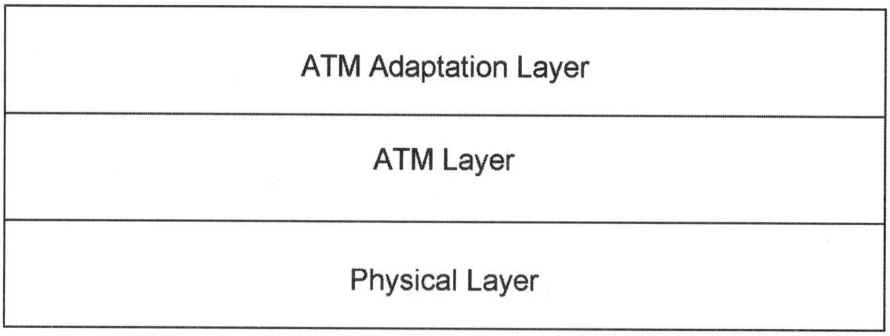

ATM Adaptation Layer

ATM Layer

Physical Layer

ATM Cell Basic Format

ATM transfers information in fixed-size units called cells. As shown in Figure 5–4, each cell consists of 53 bytes. The first five bytes contain cell-header information, and the remaining 48 bytes contain the user information or payload. Small, fixed-size cells are advantageous in that they prevent larger cells from causing large latency delays. A fixed-size cell can also be switched in hardware, making ATM switching extremely fast. One of ATM's advantages is being able to transmit isochronous traffic, meaning traffic with a well-defined delay between successive cells. Isochronous traffic is important for real-time applications, such as video and voice.

ATM Cell Header

Figure 5–5 shows the structure of an ATM cell header. The 5-byte ATM cell header contains information needed to switch the ATM cell to its next destination. The ATM cell header is examined and updated on a switch-by-switch basis.

The fields in the ATM cell header can be explained as follows:

- *Generic Flow Control* (GFC)—A 4-bit field which is typically not used

- *Virtual Path Identifier* (VPI)—An 8-bit field that along with the VCI identifies the next destination of a cell as it passes through an ATM network toward its final destination

- *Virtual Channel Identifier* (VCI)—This 16 bit field, along with the VPI, identifies the next destination of a cell as it passes through an ATM network toward its final destination.

- *Payload Type Identifier* (PT)—This 3-bit field indicates whether the cell contains user data or control data. The field is also used to indicate congestion.

Figure 5–4
ATM Cell Format

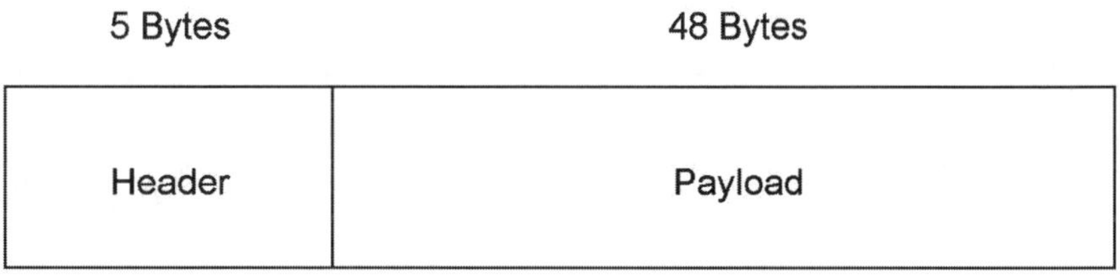

5 Bytes	48 Bytes
Header	Payload

■ *Cell Loss Priority* (CLP)—This 1-bit field indicates whether the cell should be discarded if it encounters extreme congestion as it moves through the network.

■ *Header Error Control* (HEC)—The HEC calculates a checksum on the header of the ATM cell only. There is no checksum on the ATM cell payload. The HEC is capable of detecting and correcting single-bit errors. Multiple-bit errors are detected, and the ATM cell is discarded.

Both the VPI and VCI value can be changed every time the cell passes through a switch. As with Frame Relay, there are several preassigned VPI/VCI pairs that are reserved for uses such as signaling, broadcasting, and operations and maintenance use.

There are two types of ATM cell header formats: *User Network Interface* (UNI) and *Network Network Interface* (NNI).

The UNI header, shown in Figure 5–5, is used for communication between ATM end-user devices and ATM switches.

The NNI header, shown in Figure 5–6, is used for communication between ATM switches. The ATM NNI cell header differs from the ATM UNI cell header in several ways:

■ The NNI header does not include the *Generic Flow Control* (GFC) field.

■ The NNI header has a *Virtual Path Identifier* (VPI) field that occupies the first 12 bits, allowing for larger trunks between public ATM switches.

Figure 5–5
ATM UNI header

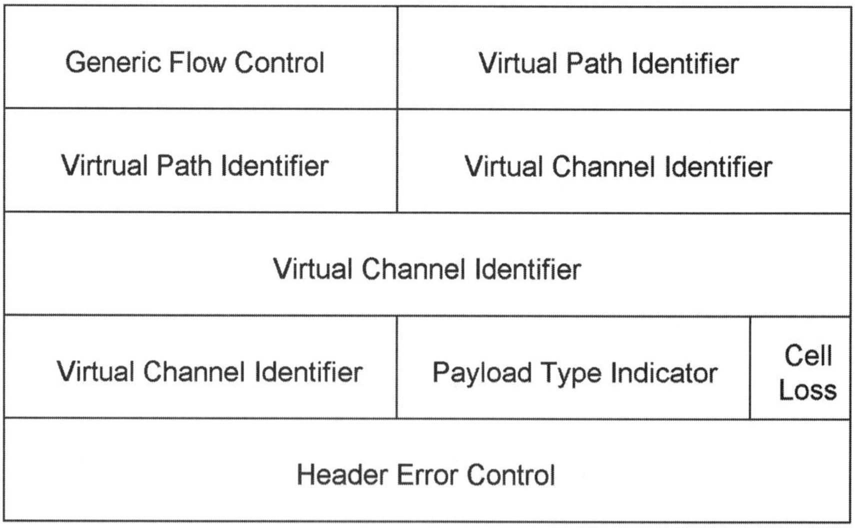

Generic Flow Control	Virtual Path Identifier	
Virtrual Path Identifier	Virtual Channel Identifier	
Virtual Channel Identifier		
Virtual Channel Identifier	Payload Type Indicator	Cell Loss
Header Error Control		

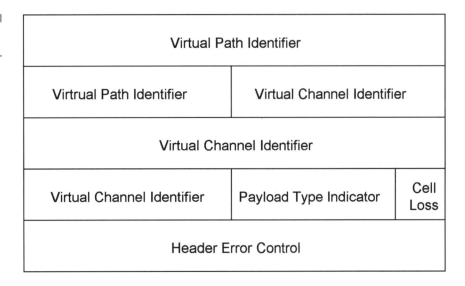

Figure 5–6
ATM NNI header

ATM Addressing

An ATM circuit is based on a connection-oriented, end-to-end link. Addressing information is contained in the ATM cell header in the form of a VPI and a VCI.

As shown in Figure 5–7, a virtual channel can be thought of as a transport of cells. A virtual path is a bundle of virtual channels.

Components of an ATM Network

ATM networks are made up of ATM switches and ATM end-user equipment.

An ATM switch is responsible for transmitting ATM cells through an ATM network. The ATM switch takes an incoming cell and reads and

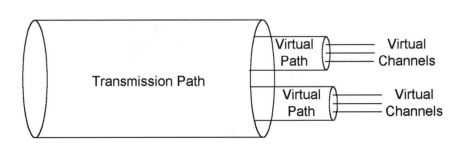

Figure 5–7
VPI, VCI, and transmission paths

updates the cell-header information. For example, the VPI and VCI values may change. The switch then switches the cell towards its final destination.

An ATM end-user device connects to an ATM switch and is responsible for generating and sending ATM traffic into the network.

As shown in Figure 5–8, an ATM network consists of a set of ATM switches interconnected by point-to-point ATM links, often referred to as trunks. ATM switches support two primary types of interfaces: *User-Network Interface* (UNI) and *Network-Network Interface* (NNI). The UNI connects ATM end-systems (such as hosts and routers) to an ATM switch. The NNI connects two ATM switches.

ATM Physical Interfaces

ATM is supported on a variety of physical interfaces, from T1 to SONET speeds. Although ATM can function over a low speed circuit such as a T1, ATM is not too efficient at these speeds—due to the high overhead that the combination of the T1 framing and the ATM cell overhead imposes. Some popular ATM interfaces include the following:

- T1 (1.544Mb/s)
- 25Mb/sec
- DS-3 (44.7Mb/s)
- OC-3 (155Mb/s)
- OC-12 (622MB/s)
- OC-48 (2448Mb/s)

Figure 5–8
ATM UNI and
NNI interfaces

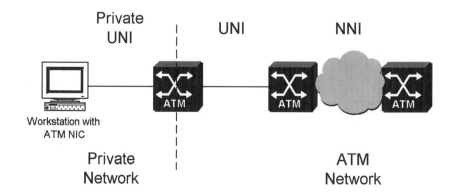

ATM Call Types

ATM supports both PVCs and SVCs.

A PVC is similar to a Frame Relay PVC in that it defines an end-to-end circuit whose path can be rerouted in the event of an intermediate node failure.

An SVC is a switched ATM circuit which is established, maintained, and released by signaling between the ATM end-user device and the ATM switch. This signaling occurs over a dedicated VPI/VCI pair. UNI signaling requests are carried in a well-known default connection: VPI=0 and VPI=5. When an ATM device wants to establish a connection with another ATM device, it sends a signaling request packet to its directly connected ATM switch. This request contains the ATM address of the desired ATM endpoint, as well as any QOS parameters required for the connection. The ATM UNI specification is based on the Q.2931 public network signaling protocol. The Q.2931 signaling standard is similar to the ISDN Q.931 signaling standard and contains commands such as Setup, Call Proceeding, Connect, and Release, which are used to establish and tear down an ATM connection.

ATM Switching Operation

The basic operation of an ATM switch is shown in Figure 5–9. An ATM cell is received across a link on a known VPI/VCI value. The switch looks up the connection value in a local translation table to determine the outgoing port (or ports) of the connection and the new VPI/VCI value of the connection on that link. The switch then retransmits the cell on that outgoing link with the appropriate VPI and VCI. Because all VPIs and VCIs have only local significance across a particular link, these values are remapped as necessary at each switch.

Two types of ATM connections exist: virtual paths, which are identified by *Virtual Path Identifiers* (VPI); and virtual channels, which are identified by the combination of a VPI and a *Virtual Channel Identifier* (VCI).

Figure 5–9
ATM switching
example

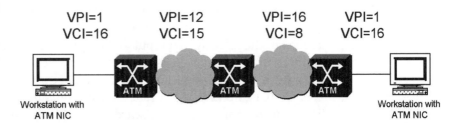

A virtual path is a bundle of virtual channels, all of which are switched transparently across the ATM network on the basis of the common VPI. All VCIs and VPIs, however, have only local significance across a particular link and are remapped, as appropriate, at each switch.

ATM Classes of Service

One of ATM's major advantages is its capability to handle multiple types of traffic, referred to as classes of service, on a single network. The ATM adaptation layer is responsible for mapping these classes of services into actual ATM traffic. Let's look at each of these classes of service and their characteristics:

Constant Bit Rate (CBR)   CBR specifies a connection-oriented, synchronous traffic stream. This class of service emulates traditional leased-line circuits and appears to the end user as a point-to-point circuit. CBR requires an end-to-end timing relationship.

Variable Bit Rate Real Time (VBR-RT)   VBR-RT supports real-time, connection-oriented, synchronous traffic. VBR-RT requires an end-to-end timing relationship.

Available Bit Rate (ABR)   ABR supports variable-bit rate, asynchronous traffic streams for services such as Frame Relay and X.25 over ATM. ABR does not require an end-to-end timing relationship.

Unspecified Bit Rate (UBR)   UBR supports connectionless packet data. No guarantees are made as to loss, delay, or available user bandwidth. UBR does not require an end-to-end timing relationship.

ATM Quality of Service (QoS)

ATM has extensive QoS support. A QOS contract can specify values for such items as peak bandwidth, average sustained bandwidth, cell delay variation, and burst size—among others. These QOS parameters are guaranteed through the use of traffic shaping. Traffic shaping uses queues in the ATM switch input and output buffers to limit the data rate and to control "bursty" data—so that the traffic profile will closely match the agreed-upon QOS parameters. The ATM switch can set the *Cell-Loss Priority* (CLP) bit for those cells that are outside of the traffic contract. This feature makes the cell discard eligible during periods of congestion.

ATM with a Non-ATM Device

Routers without native ATM interfaces can still take advantage of ATM networking. As specified in RFC 1483, a serial interface on a Cisco router can be configured for ATM-DXI encapsulation.

RFC 1483 describes two methods of transporting multi-protocol traffic over an ATM network. The first method enables multiplexing of multiple protocols over a single PVC. The second method can use a different PVC to carry each protocol. Cisco supports both methods of DXI encapsulation. Cisco can transport the following protocols over a DXI encapsulated interface:

- Apollo Domain
- Appletalk
- Banyan VINES
- DECnet
- IP
- Novell IPX
- ISO CLNS
- XNS traffic

As shown in Figure 5–10, ATM-DXI works by connecting the DXI-encapsulated serial interface of the router to an ATM DSU, which is referred to as an ADSU. At the ADSU, the DXI header is stripped off, and the data is segmented into cells for transport over an ATM network.

Cisco ATM Capabilities

Cisco sells both ATM switches and ATM-enabled routers. Cisco routers from the 2600 up to the 12000 can support a variety of ATM interfaces.

Figure 5–10
ATM ADSU example

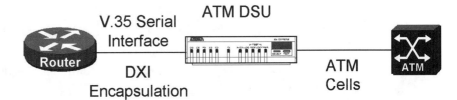

Commands Discussed in This Chapter

- **atm pvc** *vcd vpi vci aal-encap*
- *protocol protocol-address* **atm vc** *vcd* [**broadcast**]
- **debug atm packet**
- **loopback diagnostic**
- **loopback line**
- **map-group** *name*
- **map-list** *name*
- **show atm map**
- **show atm traffic**
- **show atm vc** [*vcd*]
- **show interface atm** *number*

Definitions

atm pvc: This interface configuration command creates a PVC on the ATM interface of a Cisco router. The *vcd* number describes a unique VPI, VCI pair to the router.

atm vc: This map-list configuration command defines a map statement for an ATM PVC. This command is used with the **map-list** command.

debug atm packet: This debug command will display all ATM cells going into and out of the router.

loopback diagnostic: This interface command places the ATM interface in a loopback mode, where all ATM cells leaving an interface are sent back toward the same interface.

loopback line: This interface command places the ATM interface in a loopback mode, where all ATM cells coming into an interface are sent back toward the interface that sent the traffic.

map-group: This interface configuration command associates an ATM map list to an ATM interface.

map-list: This global configuration command defines a map statement for a PVC or an SVC.

show atm map: This exec command will cause all configured ATM static maps to be displayed.

show atm traffic: This exec command will display incoming and outgoing traffic information for all ATM interfaces on a router.

show atm vc: This exec command will display information on all active virtual circuits (PVCs and SVCs). When issued with the optional *vcd* argument, this command will display traffic information for individual virtual circuits (PVCs and SVCs).

show interface: This exec command displays information on the status of the ATM interface. Various status information, such as total traffic transmitted and received on the interface, is displayed.

IOS Requirements

The labs in the chapter were done with IOS 11.2. Most ATM commands discussed in this chapter were introduced in IOS 10.0.

Lab #17: ATM Configuration on a Cisco 4500

Equipment Needed

The following equipment is needed to perform this lab exercise:

- Two Cisco routers, each having an ATM OC-3 interface, running IOS 11.2
- Two Multimode fiber cables
- A Cisco rolled cable for console port connection to the routers
- An ATM switch. (This lab can also be done by connecting the two ATM interfaces directly using a single fiber cable.)

Configuration Overview

This lab will demonstrate a basic ATM configuration on a Cisco 4500 OC-3 Multi-mode 155Mb/s ATM interface. This lab can be performed in one of two ways. As shown in Figure 5–11, if an ATM switch is available, then the two routers can be connected to the ATM switch. This method is the preferred way, because it is how ATM switching works in the real world. As shown in Figure 5–12, if an ATM switch is not available, then the two routers can be directly connected with a multi-mode fiber. The IP addressing scheme is as shown in these figures.

NOTE: *The configurations in this lab will not change whether you are directly connected between the two routers or are connected through an ATM switch.*

Figure 5–11
configuration with an ATM switch

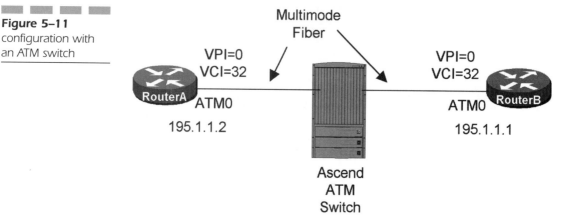

Figure 5–12
configuration without an ATM switch

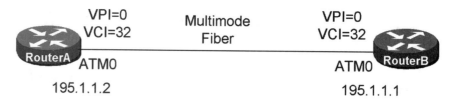

Router Configuration

The configurations for the router in this example are as follows (key ATM commands are highlighted in bold):

RouterA

```
Current configuration:
!
version 11.2
no service udp-small-servers
no service tcp-small-servers
!
hostname RouterA
!
```

```
enable password cisco
!
no ip domain-lookup
!
interface ATM0
 ip address 195.1.1.2 255.255.255.0
 atm pvc 1 0 32 aal5nlpid←define an ATM PVC using the vcd, vpi and vci
 map-group 1←associate this interface with map-list 1
!
no ip classless
!
map-list 1
 ip 195.1.1.1 atm-vc 1 broadcast←this statement maps the layer 3 next hop
                                  address to the layer 2 ATM PVC
!
line con 0
 exec-timeout 0 0
line aux 0
line vty 0 4
 password cisco
 login
!
end
```

RouterB

```
RouterB#sh run
Building configuration...

Current configuration:
!
version 11.2
no service password-encryption
no service udp-small-servers
no service tcp-small-servers
!
hostname RouterB
!
interface ATM0
 ip address 195.1.1.1 255.255.255.0
 atm pvc 1 0 32 aal5nlpid←define an ATM PVC using the vcd, vpi and vci
 map-group 1←associate this interface with map-list 1
!
no ip classless
!
map-list 1
 ip 195.1.1.2 atm-vc 1 broadcast←this statement maps the layer 3 next hop
                                  address to the layer 2 ATM PVC
!
!
line con 0
line aux 0
line vty 0 4
 login
!
end
```

We see that in both routers' configurations, we have to manually define which VPI/VCI combination will be present on the ATM interface. In the case of this lab, we have defined VPI=0/VCI=32 on the ATM interface of each router. A static map must also be created. This static map defines the IP address at the far end of the ATM PVC.

Monitoring and Testing the Configuration

Let's start by connecting to RouterA and examining the status of the ATM interface with the **show interface atm 0** command. We see that the interface is an up/up condition.

```
RouterA#show interface atm 0
ATM0 is up, line protocol is up←Interface status
   Hardware is ATMizer BX-50
   Internet address is 195.1.1.2/24
   MTU 4470 bytes, sub MTU 4470, BW 156250 Kbit, DLY 100 usec, rely 10/255, load
1/255
   Encapsulation ATM, loopback not set, keepalive set (10 sec)
   Encapsulation(s): AAL5 AAL3/4, PVC mode
   1024 maximum active VCs, 1024 VCs per VP, 1 current VCCs
   VC idle disconnect time: 300 seconds
   Last input 00:09:56, output 00:09:56, output hang never
   Last clearing of "show interface" counters never
   Queueing strategy: fifo
   Output queue 0/40, 0 drops; input queue 0/75, 0 drops
   5 minute input rate 0 bits/sec, 0 packets/sec
   5 minute output rate 0 bits/sec, 0 packets/sec
      25 packets input, 2650 bytes, 0 no buffer
      Received 0 broadcasts, 0 runts, 0 giants, 0 throttles
      0 input errors, 0 CRC, 0 frame, 0 overrun, 0 ignored, 0 abort
      25 packets output, 2650 bytes, 0 underruns
      0 output errors, 0 collisions, 1 interface resets
      0 output buffer failures, 0 output buffers swapped out
```

The **show controller atm 0** command can also be used to verify that the ATM network module is installed and is properly functioning.

```
RouterA#show controller atm 0
ATM Unit 0, Slot 2, Type ATMizer BX-50, Hardware Version 1
   ATM Xilinx Code, Version 2, ATMizer Firmware, Version 3.0
   Public SRAM 65536 bytes, Private SRAM 524288 bytes, I/O Base Addr 0x3C200000
   PLIM Type OC-3 Multi-Mode Fiber, Version 3
```

```
Network Transmit Clock
NIM IS Operational, Configuration OK
DMA Read 12, DMA Write 12
```

Now, connect to RouterB and verify that the ATM interface is in an up/up state.

```
RouterB#show interface atm 0
ATM0 is up, line protocol is up←Interface status
   Hardware is ATMizer BX-50
   Internet address is 195.1.1.1/24
   MTU 4470 bytes, sub MTU 4470, BW 155520 Kbit, DLY 100 usec, rely 15/255, load
1/255
   Encapsulation ATM, loopback not set, keepalive not supported
   Encapsulation(s): AAL5 AAL3/4, PVC mode
   1024 maximum active VCs, 1024 VCs per VP, 1 current VCCs
   VC idle disconnect time: 300 seconds
   Last input 00:00:43, output 00:00:43, output hang never
   Last clearing of "show interface" counters never
   Queueing strategy: fifo
   Output queue 0/40, 0 drops; input queue 0/75, 0 drops
   5 minute input rate 0 bits/sec, 0 packets/sec
   5 minute output rate 0 bits/sec, 0 packets/sec
      30 packets input, 3180 bytes, 0 no buffer
      Received 0 broadcasts, 0 runts, 0 giants, 0 throttles
      0 input errors, 0 CRC, 0 frame, 0 overrun, 0 ignored, 0 abort
      30 packets output, 3180 bytes, 0 underruns
      0 output errors, 0 collisions, 5 interface resets
      0 output buffer failures, 0 output buffers swapped out
```

Reconnect to RouterA. Use the **show atm vc** command to display the status of all virtual circuits that are configured on the router. We see that our PVC (VPI=0/VCI=32) is active on interface ATM0.

```
RouterA#show atm vc
                           AAL /            Peak    Avg. Burst
Interface    VCD   VPI   VCI  Type  Encapsulation  Kbps   Kbps  Cells Status
ATM0          1     0    32   PVC   AAL5-NLPID    155000 155000   94  ACTIVE
```

Entering the **show atm vc** command with the virtual circuit descriptor for the PVC will show detailed information about the PVC. Type **show atm vc 1** to display detailed information on our PVC.

```
RouterA#sh atm vc 1
ATM0: VCD: 1, VPI: 0, VCI: 32, etype:0x2, AAL5 - NLPID, Flags: 0xC31
PeakRate: 155000, Average Rate: 155000, Burst Cells: 94, VCmode: 0x1
OAM DISABLED, InARP DISABLED
InPkts: 5, OutPkts: 5, InBytes: 530, OutBytes: 530
InPROc: 5, OutPROc: 5, Broadcasts: 0
InFast: 0, OutFast: 0, InAS: 0, OutAS: 0
OAM F5 cells sent: 0, OAM cells received: 0
Status: ACTIVE
```

The **show atm map** command displays any ATM maps that have been configured on the router. We see that we have one ATM map. This map is to IP address 195.1.1.1 and is associated with map list 1, which points to IP address 195.1.1.1 at the far end of the ATM PVC.

```
RouterA#show atm map
Map list 1 : PERMANENT
ip 195.1.1.1 maps to VC 1←VC #1 is our PVC of VPI=0/VCI=32
        , broadcast
```

The **show atm traffic** command will show how many packets have been sent and received on each ATM interface.

```
RouterA#sh atm traffic
25 Input packets
25 Output packets
0 Broadcast packets
0 Packets received on non-existent VC
0 Packets attempted to send on non-existent VC
0 OAM cells received
0 OAM cells sent
```

Verify that you can ping RouterB at IP address 195.1.1.1.

```
RouterA#ping 195.1.1.1

Type escape sequence to abort.
Sending 5, 100-byte ICMP Echos to 195.1.1.1, timeout is 2 seconds:
!!!!!
Success rate is 100 percent (5/5), round-trip min/avg/max = 4/4/4 ms
```

After the ping is completed, type the **show atm traffic** command again. Notice that there are now 30 input and output packets.

```
RouterA#show atm traffic
30 Input packets←5 more packets then before the ping
30 Output packets
0 Broadcast packets
0 Packets received on non-existent VC
0 Packets attempted to send on non-existent VC
0 OAM cells received
0 OAM cells sent
```

Now, connect to RouterB and type the **show atm vc** command. Verify that our PVC is active on RouterB.

```
RouterB#show atm vc
                                    AAL /           Peak   Avg.  Burst
Interface   VCD   VPI   VCI Type Encapsulation  Kbps   Kbps   Cells  Status
0           1     0     32  PVC  AAL5-NLPID     155000 155000   94   ACTIVE
```

Enable ATM packet debugging with the **debug atm packet** command.

```
RouterA#debug atm packet
ATM packets debugging is on
Displaying all ATM packets
```

Now, ping RouterA at IP address 195.1.1.2. Each ping packet that is sent out of RouterB will be marked with an (O), and each ping packet that is received back from RouterA will be marked with an (I).

```
RouterB#ping 195.1.1.2

Type escape sequence to abort.
Sending 5, 100-byte ICMP Echos to 195.1.1.2, timeout is 2 seconds:
!!!!!
Success rate is 100 percent (5/5), round-trip min/avg/max = 1/1/1 ms
```

ATM0(O):←**The (O) indicates that the packet is being sent out of RouterB**

This is our vcd number we defined for this PVC
↓
```
VCD:0x1 DM:0x100 NLPID:0x03CC Length:0x6A
4500 0064 0046 0000 FF01 334D C301 0101 C301 0102 0800 3924 0114 05EC 0000
0000 0096 3D90 ABCD ABCD ABCD ABCD ABCD ABCD ABCD ABCD ABCD ABCD ABCD ABCD
ABCD ABCD ABCD ABCD ABCD ABCD ABCD ABCD ABCD ABCD ABCD ABCD ABCD ABCD ABCD
```

ATM0(I):←**The (I) indicates that the packet is being received from RouterA**

This is our vcd number we defined for this PVC
↓
```
VCD:0x1 Type:0x2 NLPID:0x03CC Length:0x6A
4500 0064 0046 0000 FF01 334D C301 0102 C301 0101 0000 4124 0114 05EC 0000
0000 0096 3D90 ABCD ABCD ABCD ABCD ABCD ABCD ABCD ABCD ABCD ABCD ABCD ABCD
ABCD ABCD ABCD ABCD ABCD ABCD ABCD ABCD ABCD ABCD ABCD ABCD ABCD ABCD ABCD
```

The output of the debug atm packet has been truncated here. The actual output would contain five pairs of output and input packet traces.

Lab #18: ATM Loopbacks on a Cisco 4500

Equipment Needed

The following equipment is needed to perform this lab exercise:

■ Two Cisco routers, each having an ATM OC-3 interface running IOS 11.2

■ Two Multimode fiber cables

■ A Cisco rolled cable for console port connection to the routers

■ An ATM switch. (This lab can also be done by connecting the two ATM interfaces together, back to back.)

Configuration Overview

This lab will demonstrate the loopback capabilities of the ATM OC-3 interface on a Cisco 4500.

This lab can be performed in one of two ways. As shown in Figure 5–13, if an ATM switch is available, then the two routers can be connected to the ATM switch. This way is the preferred method, because this method is how ATM switching works in the real world. As shown in Figure 5–14, if an ATM switch is not available, then the two routers can be directly connected with a multi-mode fiber.

Loopbacks are an important element of network testability. They provide well-defined test points that can be used when a circuit is down, and troubleshooting is required to determine the exact point of failure.

The ATM interface on the Cisco 4500 has two loopback modes. Figure 5–15 shows the Loopback Diagnostic mode. You enter this loopback mode by entering the **loopback diagnostic** command under the ATM interface of the router that will be put into a loop. This loopback mode will cause any traffic being sent out of the router's ATM interface to be sent back to the router that generated the traffic. The router interface will go from an up/up state to an up/up (looped) state.

Figure 5–13
configuration with
an ATM switch

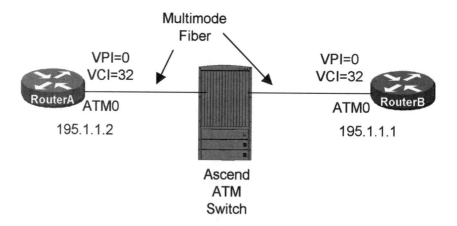

Figure 5–14
configuration
without an
ATM switch

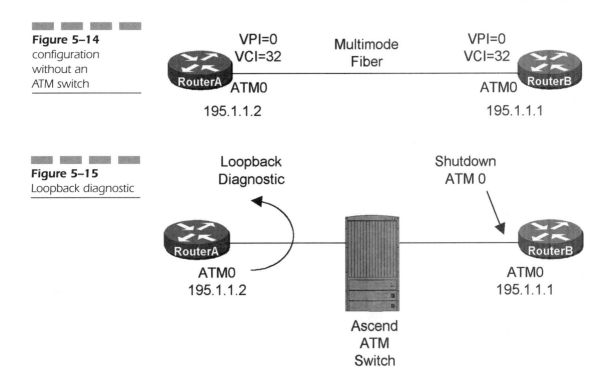

Figure 5–15
Loopback diagnostic

Figure 5–16 shows the Loopback Line mode. You enter this loopback mode by entering the **loopback line** command under the ATM interface of the router that will be put into a loop. This loopback mode causes any traffic that is coming into the router to be sent back to the network.

Figure 5–16
Loopback line

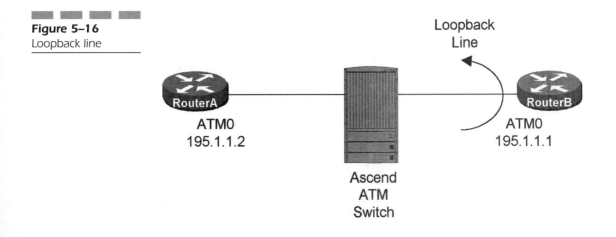

NOTE: The configurations in this lab will not change whether you are directly connected between the two routers or are connected through an ATM switch.

Router Configuration

The starting configurations for the routers in this example are as follows (key ATM commands are highlighted in bold):

RouterA

```
Current configuration:
!
version 11.2
no service udp-small-servers
no service tcp-small-servers
!
hostname RouterA
!
enable password cisco
!
no ip domain-lookup
!
interface ATM0
 ip address 195.1.1.2 255.255.255.0
 atm pvc 1 0 32 aal5nlpid←define an ATM PVC using the vcd, vpi and vci
 map-group 1←associate this interface with map-list 1
!
no ip classless
!
map-list 1
 ip 195.1.1.1 atm-vc 1 broadcast←this statement maps the layer 3 next hop
                                 address to the layer 2 ATM PVC
!
line con 0
 exec-timeout 0 0
line aux 0
line vty 0 4
 password cisco
 login
!
end
```

RouterB

```
Current configuration:
!
version 11.2
no service password-encryption
no service udp-small-servers
no service tcp-small-servers
!
```

```
hostname RouterB
!
interface ATM0
 ip address 195.1.1.1 255.255.255.0
 atm pvc 1 0 32 aal5nlpid←define an ATM PVC using the vcd, vpi and vci
 map-group 1←associate this interface with map-list 1
!
no ip classless
!
map-list 1
 ip 195.1.1.2 atm-vc 1 broadcast←this statement maps the layer 3 next hop
                                  address to the layer 2 ATM PVC
!
!
line con 0
line aux 0
line vty 0 4
 login
!
end
```

We see that in both configurations, we have to manually define what VPI/VCI combination will be present on the ATM interface. In the case of this lab, we have defined VPI=0/VCI=32 on the ATM interface of each router. A static map must also be created. This static map defines the IP address at the far end of the ATM PVC.

Monitoring and Testing the Configuration

Loopback Line

Let's start by connecting to RouterA and verifying that the ATM interface is in an up/up state by typing the **show interface atm 0** command.

```
RouterA#show interface atm 0
ATM0 is up, line protocol is up←Interface status
  Hardware is ATMizer BX-50
  Internet address is 195.1.1.2/24
  MTU 4470 bytes, sub MTU 4470, BW 156250 Kbit, DLY 100 usec, rely 164/255, load 1/255
  Encapsulation ATM, loopback not set, keepalive set (10 sec)
  Encapsulation(s): AAL5 AAL3/4, PVC mode
  1024 maximum active VCs, 1024 VCs per VP, 1 current VCCs
  VC idle disconnect time: 300 seconds
  Last input 00:00:02, output 00:00:02, output hang never
  Last clearing of "show interface" counters never
  Queueing strategy: fifo
  Output queue 0/40, 0 drops; input queue 0/75, 0 drops
```

```
    5 minute input rate 0 bits/sec, 1 packets/sec
    5 minute output rate 0 bits/sec, 1 packets/sec
        193 packets input, 15058 bytes, 0 no buffer
        Received 0 broadcasts, 0 runts, 0 giants, 0 throttles
        0 input errors, 0 CRC, 0 frame, 0 overrun, 0 ignored, 0 abort
        198 packets output, 15588 bytes, 0 underruns
        0 output errors, 0 collisions, 3 interface resets
        0 output buffer failures, 0 output buffers swapped out
```

Now, connect to RouterB and verify that its interface is in an up/up state by typing the **show interface atm 0** command.

```
RouterB#show interface atm 0
ATM0 is up, line protocol is up←Interface status
    Hardware is ATMizer BX-50
    Internet address is 195.1.1.1/24
    MTU 4470 bytes, sub MTU 4470, BW 155520 Kbit, DLY 100 usec, rely 15/255, load
1/255
    Encapsulation ATM, loopback not set, keepalive not supported
    Encapsulation(s): AAL5 AAL3/4, PVC mode
    1024 maximum active VCs, 1024 VCs per VP, 1 current VCCs
    VC idle disconnect time: 300 seconds
    Last input 00:00:43, output 00:00:43, output hang never
    Last clearing of "show interface" counters never
    Queueing strategy: fifo
    Output queue 0/40, 0 drops; input queue 0/75, 0 drops
    5 minute input rate 0 bits/sec, 0 packets/sec
    5 minute output rate 0 bits/sec, 0 packets/sec
        30 packets input, 3180 bytes, 0 no buffer
        Received 0 broadcasts, 0 runts, 0 giants, 0 throttles
        0 input errors, 0 CRC, 0 frame, 0 overrun, 0 ignored, 0 abort
        30 packets output, 3180 bytes, 0 underruns
        0 output errors, 0 collisions, 5 interface resets
        0 output buffer failures, 0 output buffers swapped out
```

Let's reconnect to RouterA and ping RouterB at IP address 195.1.1.1. The ping should be 100 percent successful.

```
RouterA#ping 195.1.1.1

Type escape sequence to abort.
Sending 5, 100-byte ICMP Echos to 195.1.1.1, timeout is 2 seconds:
!!!!!
Success rate is 100 percent (5/5), round-trip min/avg/max = 1/1/4 ms
```

Now, connect to RouterB. We are going to disable the ATM interface on RouterB by entering the **shutdown** command under the ATM 0 interface.

```
RouterB#config term
Enter configuration commands, one per line. End with CNTL/Z.
RouterB(config)#int atm 0
RouterB(config-if)#shutdown
RouterB(config)#exit
```

After entering the shutdown command on the **ATM** interface, the interface will
change to an administratively down state.
   ↓
%LINEPROTO-5-UPDOWN: Line protocol on Interface ATM0, changed state to down
%LINK-5-CHANGED: Interface ATM0, changed state to administratively down

> Verify that the ATM interface on RouterB is in a down state by typing the **show interface atm 0** command.

```
RouterB#show interface atm 0
```
ATM0 is administratively down, line protocol is down←**The interface has been shutdown**
```
   Hardware is ATMizer BX-50
   Internet address is 195.1.1.1/24
   MTU 4470 bytes, sub MTU 4470, BW 155520 Kbit, DLY 100 usec, rely 255/255, load
1/255
   Encapsulation ATM, loopback not set, keepalive not supported
   Encapsulation(s): AAL5 AAL3/4, PVC mode
   1024 maximum active VCs, 1024 VCs per VP, 0 current VCCs
   VC idle disconnect time: 300 seconds
   Last input 00:00:31, output 00:00:31, output hang never
   Last clearing of "show interface" counters never
   Queueing strategy: fifo
   Output queue 0/40, 0 drops; input queue 0/75, 0 drops
   5 minute input rate 0 bits/sec, 0 packets/sec
   5 minute output rate 0 bits/sec, 0 packets/sec
      52784 packets input, 2750708 bytes, 0 no buffer
      Received 0 broadcasts, 0 runts, 0 giants, 0 throttles
      0 input errors, 0 CRC, 0 frame, 0 overrun, 0 ignored, 0 abort
      52794 packets output, 2751768 bytes, 0 underruns
      0 output errors, 0 collisions, 8 interface resets
      0 output buffer failures, 0 output buffers swapped out
```

> Now reconnect to RouterA. Enable ATM packet debugging with the **debug atm packet** command.

```
RouterA#debug atm packet
ATM packets debugging is on
Displaying all ATM packets
```

> Now, ping RouterB at IP address 195.1.1.1. The ping will fail, because the ATM interface on RouterB has been shut down.

```
RouterA#ping 195.1.1.1

Type escape sequence to abort.
Sending 5, 100-byte ICMP Echos to 195.1.1.1, timeout is 2 seconds:
```
ATM0(O):←**There will be five output, (O), ping packets sent out from RouterA.**
      Since the ping fails there will not be any returned packets.

```
VCD:0x1 DM:0x100 NLPID:0x03CC Length:0x6A
4500 0064 0064 0000 FF01 332F C301 0102 C301 0101 0800 CEA5 0000 0B0B 0000
0000 0041 A458 ABCD ABCD ABCD ABCD ABCD ABCD ABCD ABCD ABCD ABCD ABCD ABCD
ABCD ABCD ABCD ABCD ABCD ABCD ABCD ABCD ABCD ABCD ABCD ABCD ABCD ABCD ABCD
```

The other three ping packets are not shown here, but they are identical to the others.

```
ATM0(O):←Last of 5 output ping packets
VCD:0x1 DM:0x100 NLPID:0x03CC Length:0x6A
4500 0064 0068 0000 FF01 332B C301 0102 C301 0101 0800 AF61 0004 0B0B 0000
0000 0041 C398 ABCD ABCD ABCD ABCD ABCD ABCD ABCD ABCD ABCD ABCD ABCD ABCD
ABCD ABCD ABCD ABCD ABCD ABCD ABCD ABCD ABCD ABCD ABCD ABCD ABCD ABCD ABCD
.
Success rate is 0 percent (0/5)←The ping will fail because the ATM interface
on RouterB is shutdown
```

Enter configuration mode on RouterA by typing the **config term** command. Enter the **loopback diagnostic** command under the ATM interface of RouterA.

```
RouterA#config term
Enter configuration commands, one per line. End with CNTL/Z.
RouterA(config)#int atm 0
RouterA(config-if)#loopback diagnostic
RouterA(config-if)#exit
RouterA(config)#exit
```

Type the show run command to view the router's configuration. Notice that the **loopback diagnostic** command is now under the ATM 0 interface configuration for the router.

```
Current configuration:
!
version 11.2
no service udp-small-servers
no service tcp-small-servers
!
hostname RouterA
!
enable password cisco
!
no ip domain-lookup
!
```

```
interface ATM0
 ip address 195.1.1.2 255.255.255.0
 loopback diagnostic←The loopback diagnostic command will appear under the
                        interface of the router
 atm pvc 1 0 32 aal5nlpid
 map-group 1
!
no ip classless
!
map-list 1
 ip 195.1.1.1 atm-vc 1 broadcast
!
line con 0
 exec-timeout 0 0
line aux 0
line vty 0 4
 password cisco
 login
!
end
```

Ping RouterB at IP address 195.1.1.1. We see that the ping fails, but the debug output shows us that each packet being sent out is being received back. This situation occurs because we have a loopback on the ATM interface of RouterA.

```
RouterA#ping 195.1.1.1

Type escape sequence to abort.
Sending 5, 100-byte ICMP Echos to 195.1.1.1, timeout is 2 seconds:

ATM0(O):←Output packet from RouterA to RouterB
VCD:0x1 DM:0x100 NLPID:0x03CC Length:0x6A
4500 0064 005F 0000 FF01 3334 C301 0102 C301 0101 0800 5F48 0000 1241 0000
0000 0041 0C80 ABCD ABCD ABCD ABCD ABCD ABCD ABCD ABCD ABCD ABCD ABCD ABCD
ABCD ABCD ABCD ABCD ABCD ABCD ABCD ABCD ABCD ABCD ABCD ABCD ABCD ABCD

ATM0(I):←Loopback response
VCD:0x1 Type:0x2 NLPID:0x03CC Length:0x6A
4500 0064 005F 0000 FF01 3334 C301 0102 C301 0101 0800 5F48 0000 1241 0000
0000 0041 0C80 ABCD ABCD ABCD ABCD ABCD ABCD ABCD ABCD ABCD ABCD ABCD ABCD
ABCD ABCD ABCD. ABCD ABCD ABCD ABCD ABCD ABCD ABCD ABCD ABCD ABCD ABCD ABCD
 .
 .
```

There will be a total of 5 output packets and 5 input packets displayed. Only
the first output and input packet are shown here.
.
.
RouterA# Success rate is 0 percent (0/5)

Loopback Line

Now, let's disable the loopback we entered on RouterA. Enter router configuration mode and enter the command **no loopback diagnostic** under
the ATM 0 interface.

```
RouterA#config term
Enter configuration commands, one per line. End with CNTL/Z.
RouterA(config)#int atm 0
RouterA(config-if)#no loopback diagnostic←Disable the loopback diagnostic on
                                             the interface
RouterA(config-if)#exit
RouterA(config)#exit
```

Connect to RouterB and enable the ATM interface. Remember that we
had put the interface into a shutdown state to demonstrate the **loopback
diagnostic** command. While in interface configuration mode, type the
command **loopback line**. Recall from Figure 5–16 that this command
will cause RouterB to loop all traffic that comes into its ATM interface
back toward the network.

```
RouterB#config term
Enter configuration commands, one per line. End with CNTL/Z.
RouterB(config)#int atm 0
RouterB(config-if)#no shut←Reactivate the interface
RouterB(config-if)#loopback line←Enable the line loopback on RouterB. All
                                  traffic that comes into RouterB will be
                                  looped back towards the network.
RouterB(config-if)#exit
RouterB(config)#exit

%LINK-3-UPDOWN: Interface ATM0, changed state to up←The ATM interface will go
                                                     back to an up state as
                                                     soon as the shutdown
                                                     statement is removed
%LINEPROTO-5-UPDOWN: Line protocol on Interface ATM0, changed state to up
```

Type the **show interface atm 0** command on RouterB to display the
status of the ATM interface. The interface should be in an up/up (looped)
state.

```
RouterB#show int atm 0
ATM0 is up, line protocol is up (looped)←The interface is looped because we
                                          have enabled a line loopback on the
                                          Router.
  Hardware is ATMizer BX-50
  Internet address is 195.1.1.1/24
  MTU 4470 bytes, sub MTU 4470, BW 155520 Kbit, DLY 100 usec, rely 255/255, load
  1/255

                        The interface is looped
                                 ↓
  Encapsulation ATM, loopback set, keepalive not supported
  Encapsulation(s): AAL5 AAL3/4, PVC mode
  1024 maximum active VCs, 1024 VCs per VP, 1 current VCCs
  VC idle disconnect time: 300 seconds
  Last input 00:04:16, output 00:04:16, output hang never
  Last clearing of "show interface" counters never
  Queueing strategy: fifo
  Output queue 0/40, 0 drops; input queue 0/75, 0 drops
  5 minute input rate 0 bits/sec, 0 packets/sec
  5 minute output rate 0 bits/sec, 0 packets/sec
     52784 packets input, 2750708 bytes, 0 no buffer
     Received 0 broadcasts, 0 runts, 0 giants, 0 throttles
     0 input errors, 0 CRC, 0 frame, 0 overrun, 0 ignored, 0 abort
     52794 packets output, 2751768 bytes, 0 underruns
     0 output errors, 0 collisions, 10 interface resets
     0 output buffer failures, 0 output buffers swapped out
```

Connect to RouterA. Enable ATM packet debugging by typing the **debug atm packet** command.

```
RouterA#debug atm packet
ATM packets debugging is on
Displaying all ATM packets
```

Ping RouterB at IP address 195.1.1.1. We see that the ping fails, because all traffic coming into RouterB is looped back to the network before entering the Router. Notice that the ping packets are returned from the loopback on RouterB. Five output packets are sent, and five input packets are received.

```
RouterA#ping 195.1.1.1

Type escape sequence to abort.
Sending 5, 100-byte ICMP Echos to 195.1.1.1, timeout is 2 seconds:

ATM0(O):←Ping packet from RouterA to RouterB
VCD:0x1 DM:0x100 NLPID:0x03CC Length:0x6A
4500 0064 006E 0000 FF01 3325 C301 0102 C301 0101 0800 AB35 0000 076D 0000
0000 0043 CB64 ABCD ABCD ABCD ABCD ABCD ABCD ABCD ABCD ABCD ABCD ABCD ABCD
ABCD ABCD ABCD ABCD ABCD ABCD ABCD ABCD ABCD ABCD ABCD ABCD ABCD ABCD ABCD
```

```
ATM0(I):←Packet returned from the line loopback on RouterB
VCD:0x1 Type:0x2 NLPID:0x03CC Length:0x6A
4500 0064 006E 0000 FF01 3325 C301 0102 C301 0101 0800 AB35 0000 076D 0000
0000 0043 CB64 ABCD ABCD ABCD ABCD ABCD ABCD ABCD ABCD ABCD ABCD ABCD ABCD
ABCD ABCD ABCD. ABCD ABCD ABCD ABCD ABCD ABCD ABCD ABCD ABCD ABCD ABCD ABCD
```
```
 .
 .
There will be a total of 5 output packets and 5 input packets. Only the first
output and input packet are shown here
 .
 .
RouterA# Success rate is 0 percent (0/5)←
```

The ping fails because all traffic being sent to RouterB is looped back to the network before being sent into the Router. All the ping packets are returned back to RouterA since RouterB has a line loopback enabled.

Troubleshooting ATM

This section will discuss important commands that can be used to monitor and troubleshoot an ATM configuration.

{**show interface atm**} This command will display information on the status of the ATM interface on a router.

```
RouterA#show interface atm 0
ATM0 is up, line protocol is up←Interface status
   Hardware is ATMizer BX-50
   Internet address is 195.1.1.2/24
   MTU 4470 bytes, sub MTU 4470, BW 156250 Kbit, DLY 100 usec, rely 10/255, load
1/255
   Encapsulation ATM, loopback not set, keepalive set (10 sec)
   Encapsulation(s): AAL5 AAL3/4, PVC mode
   1024 maximum active VCs, 1024 VCs per VP, 1 current VCCs
   VC idle disconnect time: 300 seconds
   Last input 00:09:56, output 00:09:56, output hang never
   Last clearing of "show interface" counters never
   Queueing strategy: fifo
   Output queue 0/40, 0 drops; input queue 0/75, 0 drops
   5 minute input rate 0 bits/sec, 0 packets/sec
   5 minute output rate 0 bits/sec, 0 packets/sec
       25 packets input, 2650 bytes, 0 no buffer
       Received 0 broadcasts, 0 runts, 0 giants, 0 throttles
       0 input errors, 0 CRC, 0 frame, 0 overrun, 0 ignored, 0 abort
```

```
25 packets output, 2650 bytes, 0 underruns
0 output errors, 0 collisions, 1 interface resets
0 output buffer failures, 0 output buffers swapped out
```

{show controller atm}   This command can be used to verify that the ATM network module is installed and is functioning properly.

```
RouterA#show controller atm 0
ATM Unit 0, Slot 2, Type ATMizer BX-50, Hardware Version 1
   ATM Xilinx Code, Version 2, ATMizer Firmware, Version 3.0
   Public SRAM 65536 bytes, Private SRAM 524288 bytes, I/O Base Addr 0x3C200000
   PLIM Type OC-3 Multi-Mode Fiber, Version 3
   Network Transmit Clock
   NIM IS Operational, Configuration OK
   DMA Read 12, DMA Write 12
```

{show atm vc}   This command will provide a summary of all active PVCs on a router.

```
RouterA#show atm vc
                                    AAL /            Peak   Avg. Burst
Interface     VCD   VPI   VCI Type  Encapsulation    Kbps   Kbps  Cells Status
ATM0           1     0     32 PVC   AAL5-NLPID       155000 155000  94  ACTIVE
```

Entering the **show atm vc** command with the virtual circuit descriptor for the PVC will show detailed information on the PVC.

```
RouterA#sh atm vc 1
ATM0: VCD: 1, VPI: 0, VCI: 32, etype:0x2, AAL5 - NLPID, Flags: 0xC31
PeakRate: 155000, Average Rate: 155000, Burst Cells: 94, VCmode: 0x1
OAM DISABLED, InARP DISABLED
InPkts: 5, OutPkts: 5, InBytes: 530, OutBytes: 530
InPRoc: 5, OutPRoc: 5, Broadcasts: 0
InFast: 0, OutFast: 0, InAS: 0, OutAS: 0
OAM F5 cells sent: 0, OAM cells received: 0
Status: ACTIVE
```

{show atm map}
This command displays any ATM maps that have been configured on the router.

```
RouterA#show atm map
Map list 1 : PERMANENT
ip 195.1.1.1 maps to VC 1, broadcast
```

{show atm traffic}   This command will show how many packets have been sent and received on each ATM interface.

```
RouterA#sh atm traffic
25 Input packets
25 Output packets
0 Broadcast packets
0 Packets received on non-existent VC
0 Packets attempted to send on non-existent VC
0 OAM cells received
0 OAM cells sent
```

Conclusion

This chapter has explored the technology of ATM. We have seen that ATM has many advantages over traditional network protocols. Our hands-on labs have demonstrated some of Cisco's ATM capabilities.

6

Routing Information Protocol (RIP)

Topics Covered in This Chapter

- Detailed technology overview
- Mechanisms to prevent routing loops
- RIP message format
- Basic RIP configuration
- Configuring RIP timers
- Configuring Unicast RIP updates
- Detailed troubleshooting

Introduction

Routing Information Protocol (RIP) is a distance vector protocol used to exchange routing information among gateways (routers) and hosts. RIP is based on the Bellham-Ford (distance vector) algorithm, which was originally used in computer routing in 1969 by ARPANET. Xerox, however, originally developed the protocol "RIP" as we know it today in the late-1970s as part of their *Xerox Networking Services* (NXS) protocol suite.

Despite its technical limitations, RIP is one of the most widely used *Interior Gateway Protocols* (IGP) designed for medium-size homogeneous networks. RIP owes its widespread-installed base to the fact that Berkeley distributed routed software along with their popular 4BSD UNIX. Routed software used RIP to provide consistent routing and reachability information for machines on local networks. TCP/IP sites started using RIP to provide local-area routing and eventually began using this system in the wide area.

Technology Overview

RIP uses two packet types to convey information, updates and requests. Each RIP-enabled router on the network broadcasts update messages every 30 seconds using UDP port 520 to all directly connected neighbors. Update messages reflect the complete routing database which currently exists in the router. Each entry in the database consists of two elements: the IP address of the network that can be reached and the distance to that network. Request messages are used by the router to discover other RIP-speaking devices on the network.

RIP uses hop count as the metric to measure the distance to a network. Each router adds its internal distance (1) to the route before advertising the route to its neighbors. In Figure 6–1, RouterC is directly connected to NetworkC. When it advertises network 152.1.0.0 to RouterB, it increments the metric by 1. Likewise, RouterB increases the metric to two and advertises the route to RouterA. RouterB and RouterA are said to be one and two hops, respectively, from 152.1.0.0.

As per Figure 6–1, the number of hops to get to a given destination is the number of routers that a datagram must pass through to get to that

Figure 6–1
RIP metrics

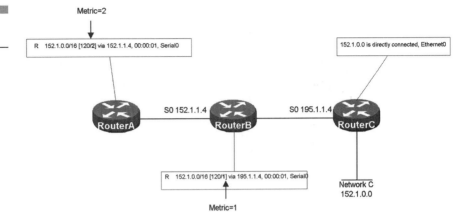

destination network. Using hop count for path determination does not always provide the best path, however. For example, in Figure 6–2, to get from RouterA to NetworkB, RIP will prefer the one 56Kbps link over the two 1.5Mbps links. The hop count of one across a 56Kbps serial circuit, however, will be substantially slower then a path with a hop count of two that crosses two 1.5Mbps serial circuits.

Figure 6–2
Hop count

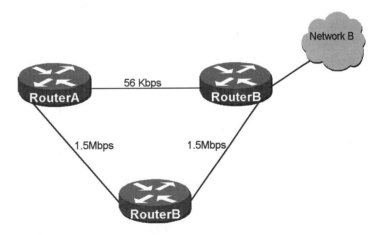

Routing Loops

The problem with any Distance Vector routing protocol such as RIP is that each router does not have a complete view of the network. Routers must rely on the neighboring routers for network reachability information. The distance vector routing algorithm creates a slow convergence problem in which inconsistencies arise, because routing update messages propagate slowly across the network. To reduce the likelihood of routing loops caused by inconsistencies across the network, RIP uses the following mechanisms: count-to-infinity, split horizons, poison reverse updates, hold-down counters, and triggered updates.

Count-to-Infinity Problem   RIP permits a maximum hop count of 15. Any destination that is more than 15 hops away is considered unreachable. This number, while severely limiting the size of a network, prevents a problem called count-to-infinity—as illustrated in Figure 6–3.

1. Count-to-infinity works as follows: RouterA loses its Ethernet interface and generates a triggered update, which is sent to RouterB and RouterC. The triggered update tells RouterB and RouterC that RouterA no longer has a route to NetworkA. The update is delayed during transmission to RouterB (busy CPU, congested link, etc.) but arrives at RouterC. RouterC removes the route to NetworkA from its routing table.

2. RouterB still has not received the triggered update from RouterA

Figure 6–3
Count-to-infinity
problem

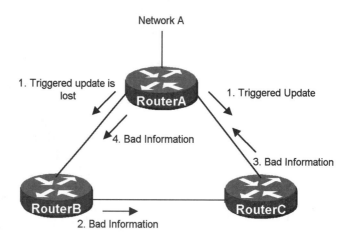

and sends its regular routing update, advertising NetworkA as reachable with a hop count of 2. RouterC receives the update and thinks a new route exists to NetworkA.

3. RouterC then advertises to RouterA that it can reach NetworkA with a hop count of 3.

4. RouterA then advertises to RouterB that that it can reach NetworkA with a hop count of 4.

5. This loop will continue until the hop count reaches infinity, which is defined by RIP as 16. Once a route reaches infinity (16), the route is declared unusable and is deleted from the routing table.

With the count-to-infinity problem, the routing information will continue to pass from router to router, incrementing the hop count by one. This problem, and the routing loop, will continue indefinitely—or until some limit is reached. That limit is RIP's maximum hop count. When the hop count of a route exceeds 15, the route is marked unreachable. Over time, the route is eventually removed from the routing table.

Split Horizons   The rule of split horizon states that it is never useful for a router to advertise a route back in the direction from which it came. When split horizons is enabled on a router's interface, the router records the interface over which a route was received and does not propagate information about that route back to that interface.

The Cisco router enables you to disable split horizons on a per-interface basis. This feature is sometimes necessary in *Non Broadcast Multiple Access* (NBMA) hub-and-spoke environments. In Figure 6–4, RouterB is connected to RouterC and RouterA via Frame Relay, and both PVCs are terminating on one physical interface on RouterB.

In Figure 6–4, if split horizon is not disabled on RouterB's serial interface, then RouterC will not receive RouterA's routing advertisements (and vise-versa). Use the **no ip split-horizon** interface subcommand to disable split horizons.

Poison Reverse   Split horizon is a scheme used by the router to avoid problems caused by advertising routes back to the router from which they were learned. The split horizon scheme omits routes learned from one neighbor in updates sent to that neighbor. Split horizon with poisoned reverse includes the routes in updates, but this process sets their metrics to 16 (infinity).

By setting the hop count to infinity and advertising the route back to

Figure 6-4
Split horizons

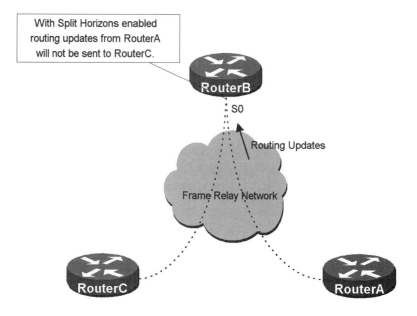

With Split Horizons enabled routing updates from RouterA will not be sent to RouterC.

its source, it is possible to immediately break a routing loop. Otherwise, the inaccurate route will stay in the routing table until it times out. The disadvantage of poison reverse is that it increases the size of the routing updates.

Holddown   Holddown timers prevent the router from accepting routing information about a network for a fixed period of time after the route has been removed from the routing table. The idea is to make sure that all routers have received the information and that no router sends out an invalid route. For example, in Figure 6-3, RouterB advertised bad information to RouterC because of the delay in the routing update. With holddown counters, this situation would not happen—because RouterC would not install a new route to NetworkA for 180 seconds. By then, RouterB would have converged with the proper routing information.

Triggered Updates   Split horizons with poison reverse breaks any loop between two routers. Loops containing three or more routers can still occur, ending only when infinity (16) is reached. Triggered updates are an attempt to speed up convergence time. Whenever the metric of a route changes, the router immediately sends an update message regardless of when the regular update message is scheduled to be sent.

RIP Message Format

Figure 6–5 shows the format of a RIP message. After the 32-bit header, the message contains a sequence of pairs. The pairs contain the network IP address and an integer reflecting the distance to reach the network.

Commands: The command is generally either a RIP request (1) or a RIP response (2). Commands 3 and 4 are obsolete, and command 5 is reserved for Sun Microsystems internal use.

Version: This field contains the protocol version number. There are two versions of RIP.

Address Family Identifier: RIP was designed to carry routing information for multiple protocols. This field specifies the family of the protocol that is being carried. The address family identifier for IP is 2.

IP Address: This field contains the IP address, which is stored as a four octet number.

Must Be Zero: RIP can carry network addresses that are up to 12 octets long. Because an IP address only uses four of the 12 octets, the remaining eight octets are padded with zeros.

Distance to Net: This field contains an integer count of the distance to the specified network and contains a value of 16 if the network is unreachable.

Figure 6–5
RIP message format

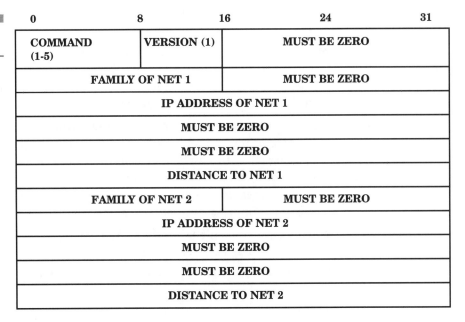

Commands Discussed in This Chapter

- **clear ip route**
- **debug ip rip events**
- **network** {network-number}
- **passive-interface** {type number}
- **router rip**
- **timers basic** {update invalid holddown flush}
- **show ip protocol**
- **show ip route rip**

Definitions

clear ip route: This exec command removes one or more routes from the routing table. The command enables you to enter a specific route or use an asterisk (*) to remove all routes.

debug ip rip events: This exec command displays information on RIP routing transactions and displays all RIP routing updates that are sent or received by the router.

network: This router configuration command specifies which interfaces will receive and send RIP routing updates. The command also specifies which networks will be advertised. If a network is not specified, it will not be advertised in a RIP update.

passive-interface: This router configuration command disables the sending of routing updates on a given interface. If you disable the sending of routing updates on an interface, the particular subnet will continue to be advertised out other RIP-enabled interfaces—and request packets will still be sent out the interface. Routes received by a passive interface will still be processed.

router rip: This global configuration command enables the RIP routing process on the router.

timers basic: This router configuration command enables the user to set the update, invalid, holddown, and flush timers for the RIP process. Following is an explanation of the use of each timer:

■ **update**:   The update timer sets the rate in seconds at which routing updates are sent by the router. The default is 30 seconds.

■ **invalid**:   The invalid timer sets the interval of time in seconds after which a route is declared invalid. The timer is started if the route is not present in the regular update message. The default is 180 seconds.

■ **holddown**:   The holddown timer sets the interval in seconds during which routing information regarding better paths is suppressed. The idea is to make sure that all routers have received the information and that no router sends out an invalid route. The default is 180 seconds.

■ **flush**:   The flush timer sets in seconds the amount of time that must pass before a route is removed from the routing table. The default is 240 seconds.

show ip protocol: This exec command displays the current state of any active routing protocol process.

show ip route rip: This exec command displays all RIP-learned routes.

IOS Requirements

RIP first became available in IOS 10.0.

LAB #19: Basic RIP Configuration

Equipment Needed

The following equipment is needed to perform this lab exercise:

■ Two Cisco routers with one Ethernet port and one serial port
■ One Cisco router with two serial ports
■ Cisco IOS 10.0 or higher

- A PC running a terminal emulation program
- Two Cisco DTE/DCE crossover cables
- One Cisco rolled cable

Configuration Overview

This configuration will demonstrate basic routing using RIP. As per Figure 6–6, RouterA, RouterB, and RouterC will use RIP to advertise routing information.

RouterA, RouterB, and RouterC are connected serially via a crossover cable. RouterB will act as the DCE supplying clock to RouterA and RouterC. The IP addresses are assigned as per Figure 6–6. All routers will be configured for RIP and will advertise all connected networks.

Router Configurations

The configurations for the three routers in this example are as follows (key RIP configurations are highlighted in bold):

RouterA#

```
Current configuration:
!
version 11.2
no service udp-small-servers
no service tcp-small-servers
!
```

Figure 6–6
Basic RIP

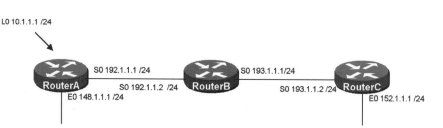

```
hostname RouterA
!
interface Loopback0←Defines a virtual interface that will be used as a test
                    point.
 ip address 10.1.1.1 255.255.255.0
!
interface Ethernet0
 ip address 148.1.1.1 255.255.255.0
 no keepalive←Disables the keepalive on the Ethernet interface, allows the
              interface to stay up when it is not attached to a hub.
!
interface Serial0
 ip address 192.1.1.1 255.255.255.0
!
!
router rip←Enables the RIP routing process on the router.
 network 10.0.0.0←Specifies what interfaces will receive and send RIP routing
                  updates. It also specifies what networks will be advertised.
 network 148.1.0.0
 network 192.1.1.0
!
no ip classless
!
!line con 0
line aux 0
line vty 0 4
 login
!
end
```

RouterB

```
!
version 11.2
service udp-small-servers
service tcp-small-servers
!
hostname RouterB
!
interface Ethernet0
 no ip address
 shutdown
!
interface Serial0
 ip address 192.1.1.2 255.255.255.0
 no fair-queue
 clockrate 500000←Acts as DCE providing clock
!
```

```
interface Serial1
  ip address 193.1.1.2 255.255.255.0
  clockrate 500000←Acts as DCE providing clock
!
```
router rip←Enables the RIP routing process on the router.
network 192.1.1.0←Specifies what interfaces will receive and send RIP routing
                     updates. It also specifies what networks will be advertised.
network 193.1.1.0
```
!
!
line con 0
line aux 0
line vty 0 4
  login
```

RouterC

```
!
version 11.2
service udp-small-servers
service tcp-small-servers
!
hostname RouterC
!
interface Ethernet0
  ip address 152.1.1.1 255.255.255.0
  no the keepalive on the Ethernet interface, allows the interface to stay up
when it is not attached to a hub.
!
!
interface Serial0
  ip address 193.1.1.1 255.255.255.0
!
```
router rip←Enables the RIP routing process on the router.
network 152.1.0.0←Specifies what interfaces will receive and send RIP routing
                     updates. It also specifies what networks will be advertised.
network 193.1.1.0
```
!
no ip classless
!
!
line con 0
line aux 0
line vty 0 4
  login
!
end
```

Monitoring and Testing the Configuration

RIP is a simple protocol to configure and troubleshoot. Show the IP routing table on RouterA with the **show ip route** command. The following example shows the output from this command. Notice that two networks were learned via RIP: 152.1.0.0 and 193.1.1.0.

```
RouterA#show ip route
Codes: C - connected, S - static, I - IGRP, R - RIP, M - mobile, B - BGP
       D - EIGRP, EX - EIGRP external, O - OSPF, IA - OSPF inter area
       N1 - OSPF NSSA external type 1, N2 - OSPF NSSA external type 2
       E1 - OSPF external type 1, E2 - OSPF external type 2, E - EGP
       i - IS-IS, L1 - IS-IS level-1, L2 - IS-IS level-2, * - candidate default
       U - per-user static route, o - ODR

Gateway of last resort is not set

     10.0.0.0/24 is subnetted, 1 subnets
C       10.1.1.0 is directly connected, Loopback0
     148.1.0.0/24 is subnetted, 1 subnets
C       148.1.1.0 is directly connected, Ethernet0
R    152.1.0.0/16 [120/2] via 192.1.1.2, 00:00:20, Serial0
C    192.1.1.0/24 is directly connected, Serial0
R    193.1.1.0/24 [120/1] via 192.1.1.2, 00:00:20, Serial0
```

From RouterA, monitor the routing updates being passed using the **debug ip rip** command. The following example shows the output from this command. Notice that on interface serial 0, the router does not advertise the networks it learns from RouterB (152.1.0.0 and 193.1.1.0)— but on all other interfaces, these networks are advertised. This situation shows split horizons at work. Remember that when split horizons is enabled, the router will never advertise a route back in the direction from which it came.

```
RouterA#debug ip rip
RIP: sending v1 update to 255.255.255.255 via Ethernet0 (148.1.1.1)
     network 10.0.0.0, metric 1
     network 152.1.0.0, metric 3
     network 192.1.1.0, metric 1
     network 193.1.1.0, metric 2
RIP: sending v1 update to 255.255.255.255 via Loopback0 (10.1.1.1)
     network 148.1.0.0, metric 1
     network 152.1.0.0, metric 3
     network 192.1.1.0, metric 1
     network 193.1.1.0, metric 2
RIP: sending v1 update to 255.255.255.255 via Serial0 (192.1.1.1)
     network 10.0.0.0, metric 1
     network 148.1.0.0, metric 1
```

Now, disable split horizons on RouterA using the interface configuration command **no ip split horizons**.

```
RouterA(config)#int s0
RouterA(config-if)#no ip split-horizon
```

From RouterA, monitor the routing updates being passed using the **debug ip rip** command. The following example shows the output from this command. Notice now all routes are being advertised out serial 0, including the routes learned form RouterB on serial 0.

```
RouterA#debug ip rip
IP: sending v1 update to 255.255.255.255 via Ethernet0 (148.1.1.1)
      network 10.0.0.0, metric 1
      network 152.1.0.0, metric 3
      network 192.1.1.0, metric 1
      network 193.1.1.0, metric 2
RIP: sending v1 update to 255.255.255.255 via Loopback0 (10.1.1.1)
      network 148.1.0.0, metric 1
      network 152.1.0.0, metric 3
      network 192.1.1.0, metric 1
      network 193.1.1.0, metric 2
RIP: sending v1 update to 255.255.255.255 via Serial0 (192.1.1.1)
      network 10.0.0.0, metric 1
      network 148.1.0.0, metric 1
      network 152.1.0.0, metric 3
      network 192.1.1.0, metric 1
      network 193.1.1.0, metric 2
```

LAB #20: Passive Interface Configuration

Equipment Needed

The following equipment is needed to perform this lab exercise:

- Two Cisco routers with one Ethernet port and one serial port
- One Cisco router with two serial ports
- Cisco IOS 10.0 or higher
- A PC running a terminal emulation program

■ One Cisco DTE/DCE crossover cable

■ One Cisco rolled cable

Configuration Overview

This configuration will demonstrate the use of the passive-interface command, which provides RIP-enabled routers the capacity to listen to, but not send, routing updates out a particular interface. The passive-interface router configuration command is typically used when the network router configuration command configures more interfaces than is desirable.

RIP is a classful routing protocol that does not carry subnet information. When enabling RIP on a router, you specify which classful network on which the protocol will be run. For example, in Figure 6–7, there are three subnets on RouterA: 10.1.1.0/24, 10.1.2.0/24, and 10.1.3.0/24. When enabling RIP, the user specifies which network RIP will run under—in this case, network 10.0.0.0—which encompasses all three subnets.

The reason that RIP changes the network entry from 10.1.1.0 to 10.0.0.0 is because RIP is considered a "classful" protocol. This term means that RIP recognizes the IP address class of the network address that you type and assumes the proper mask. For a Class A network like this one, the mask is 255.0.0.0, yielding 10.0.0.0 (no matter what you actually type as the last two octets). The network statement tells the routing protocol to route on the interfaces where the network address matches the one specified in the network statement.

In this scenario, the user only wishes to send RIP updates out network 10.1.2.0, so interface E0 (10.1.1.0) and S1 (10.1.3.0) are made passive interfaces.

RouterA, RouterB, and RouterC are connected serially via a crossover cable. RouterB will act as the DCE supplying clock to RouterA and RouterC. The IP addresses are assigned as per Figure 6–8. All routers will be configured for RIP, and RouterB and RouterC will advertise all connected networks. RouterA's interface S0 will be passive and will not advertise any routing information; however, it will still receive routing updates.

Figure 6–7
Passive interface

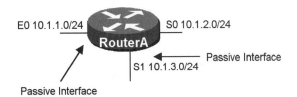

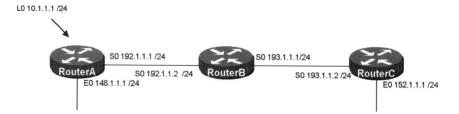

Figure 6–8
RIP passive interface
configuration

Router Configurations

The configurations for the three routers in this example are as follows
(key RIP configurations are highlighted in bold):

RouterA

```
Current configuration:
!
version 11.2
no service udp-small-servers
no service tcp-small-servers
!
hostname RouterA
!
interface Loopback0←Defines a virtual interface that will be used as a test point.
 ip address 10.1.1.1 255.255.255.0
!
interface Ethernet0
 ip address 148.1.1.1 255.255.255.0
 no keepalive←Disables the keepalive on the Ethernet interface, allows the
               interface to stay up when it is not attached to a hub.
!
interface Serial0
 ip address 192.1.1.1 255.255.255.0
!
!
router rip←Enables the RIP routing process on the router.
passive-interface Serial0←Disables the sending of RIP updates on interface
                          Serial 0.
```

```
 network 10.0.0.0←Specifies what interfaces will receive and send RIP routing
                  updates. It also specifies what networks will be advertised.
 network 148.1.0.0
 network 192.1.1.0
!
no ip classless
!
!line con 0
line aux 0
line vty 0 4
 login
!
end
```

RouterB

```
!
version 11.0
service udp-small-servers
service tcp-small-servers
!
hostname RouterB
!
!
interface Serial0
 ip address 192.1.1.2 255.255.255.0
 no fair-queue
 clockrate 500000←Acts as DCE providing clock

!
interface Serial1
 ip address 193.1.1.2 255.255.255.0
 clockrate 500000←Acts as DCE providing clock
!
router rip←Enables the RIP routing process on the router.
network 192.1.1.0←Specifies what interfaces will receive and send RIP routing
                  updates. It also specifies what networks will be advertised.
 network 193.1.1.0
!
!
line con 0
line aux 0
line vty 0 4
 login
```

RouterC

```
!
version 11.1
service udp-small-servers
service tcp-small-servers
!
hostname RouterC
!
interface Ethernet0
  ip address 152.1.1.1 255.255.255.0
  no keepalive←Disables the keepalive on the Ethernet interface, allows the
               interface to stay up when it is not attached to a hub.
!
!
interface Serial0
  ip address 193.1.1.1 255.255.255.0
!
!
router rip←Enables the RIP routing process on the router.
network 152.1.0.0←Specifies what interfaces will receive and send RIP routing
                  updates. It also specifies what networks will be advertised.
network 193.1.1.0
!
no ip classless
!
!
line con 0
line aux 0
line vty 0 4
  login
!
end
```

Monitoring and Testing the Configuration

The following example shows the output from the **debug ip rip** command on RouterA. Notice that RIP updates are only being sent out interface Ethernet 0 and Loopback 0. Also note that interface S0 is still receiving RIP updates.

```
RouterA#debug ip rip
RIP: received v1 update from 192.1.1.2 on Serial0
      152.1.0.0 in 2 hops
      193.1.1.0 in 1 hops
RIP: sending v1 update to 255.255.255.255 via Ethernet0 (148.1.1.1)
      network 10.0.0.0, metric 1
      network 152.1.0.0, metric 3
```

```
       network 192.1.1.0, metric 1
       network 193.1.1.0, metric 2
RIP: sending v1 update to 255.255.255.255 via Loopback0 (10.1.1.1)
       network 148.1.0.0, metric 1
       network 152.1.0.0, metric 3
       network 192.1.1.0, metric 1
       network 193.1.1.0, metric 2
```

The following example shows the output from the **show ip route** command on RouterA and RouterC. Note that RouterA has learned all of the routes from RouterC, but RouterC has no routes from RouterA.

```
RouterA#show ip route
Codes: C - connected, S - static, I - IGRP, R - RIP, M - mobile, B - BGP
       D - EIGRP, EX - EIGRP external, O - OSPF, IA - OSPF inter area
       N1 - OSPF NSSA external type 1, N2 - OSPF NSSA external type 2
       E1 - OSPF external type 1, E2 - OSPF external type 2, E - EGP
       i - IS-IS, L1 - IS-IS level-1, L2 - IS-IS level-2, * - candidate default
       U - per-user static route, o - ODR

Gateway of last resort is not set
       10.0.0.0/24 is subnetted, 1 subnets
C         10.1.1.0 is directly connected, Loopback0
       148.1.0.0/24 is subnetted, 1 subnets
C         148.1.1.0 is directly connected, Ethernet0
R      152.1.0.0/16 [120/2] via 192.1.1.2, 00:00:13, Serial0
C      192.1.1.0/24 is directly connected, Serial0
R      193.1.1.0/24 [120/1] via 192.1.1.2, 00:00:13, Serial0

RouterC#show ip route
Codes: C - connected, S - static, I - IGRP, R - RIP, M - mobile, B - BGP
       D - EIGRP, EX - EIGRP external, O - OSPF, IA - OSPF inter area
       N1 - OSPF NSSA external type 1, N2 - OSPF NSSA external type 2
       E1 - OSPF external type 1, E2 - OSPF external type 2, E - EGP
       i - IS-IS, L1 - IS-IS level-1, L2 - IS-IS level-2, * - candidate default
       U - per-user static route, o - ODR

Gateway of last resort is not set

       152.1.0.0/24 is subnetted, 1 subnets
C         152.1.1.0 is directly connected, Ethernet0
R      192.1.1.0/24 [120/1] via 193.1.1.2, 00:00:20, Serial0
C      193.1.1.0/24 is directly connected, Serial0
```

LAB #21: RIP Timer Configurations

Equipment Needed

The following equipment is need to perform this lab exercise:

■ Two Cisco routers with one Ethernet port and one serial port
■ One Cisco router with two serial ports
■ Cisco IOS 10.0 or higher
■ A PC running a terminal emulation program
■ One Cisco DTE/DCE crossover cable
■ One Cisco rolled cable

Configuration Overview

This configuration will demonstrate using the timer basic command to set the four configurable RIP timers (update, invalid, holddown, and flush timers). Depending on the network topology, it may become necessary to change the update timers, which control the rate in seconds that routing updates are sent. For example, if the access link is 56Kbps, generating RIP updates every 30 seconds might not be the most efficient use of bandwidth. By increasing the update timer, however, you also increase the convergence time of the network.

The three other RIP timers are all dependent on the value of the update timer. The invalid timer should be at least three times the value of update timer, the holddown timer should be at least three times the value of update timer, and the flush timer must be at least the sum of invalid and holddown timers. So, if the update timer is changed, then the invalid, holddown, and flush timers must also be changed.

Each time a route is updated, which is dependent on the update interval, the invalid timer is reset. If a route is not seen in an update for 180 seconds, the route is put in holddown—which means that the router will use the route to route packets but will not announce the route in its updates. This also means that the router will not install any another route to this destination until the holddown counter expires. This result happens after 180 seconds; in which case, the route is removed from the routing table.

Figure 6–9
RIP timer
configuration

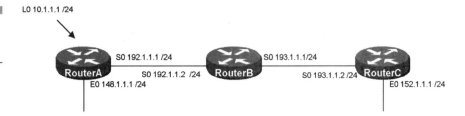

RouterA, RouterB, and RouterC are connected serially via a crossover cable. RouterB will act as the DCE supplying clock to RouterA and RouterC. The IP addresses are assigned as per Figure 6–9. All routers will be configured for RIP. RouterA, RouterB, and RouterC will advertise all connected networks. The timers on each router will be as follows:

- Update 5
- Invalid=15
- Holddown=15
- Flush=30

With these timers, updates are broadcast every five seconds. If a route is not heard from in 15 seconds, the route is declared unusable (invalid). Any information received in routing updates about this particular network is suppressed for an additional 15 seconds (holddown). At the end of the suppression period, the route is flushed from the routing table.

NOTE: *The update interval must be the same value on neighboring routers.*

Router Configurations

The configurations for the three routers in this example are as follows (key RIP configurations are highlighted in bold):

RouterA

```
Current configuration:
!
version 11.2
```

```
no service udp-small-servers
no service tcp-small-servers
!
hostname RouterA
!
interface Loopback0←Defines a virtual interface that will be used as a test
                    point.
 ip address 10.1.1.1 255.255.255.0
!
interface Ethernet0
 ip address 148.1.1.1 255.255.255.0
 no the keepalive←Disables the keepalive on the Ethernet interface, allows the
                  interface to stay up when it is not attached to a hub.
!
interface Serial0
 ip address 192.1.1.1 255.255.255.0
!
router rip←Enables the RIP routing process on the router.
timers basic 5 15 15 30←Updates are broadcast every 5 seconds. If a router is
                        not heard from in 15 seconds, the route is declared
                        unusable. Further information is suppressed for an
                        additional 15 seconds. At the end of the suppression
                        period, the route is flushed from the routing table.
network 10.0.0.0←Specifies what interfaces will receive and send RIP routing
                 updates. It also specifies what networks will be advertised.
 network 148.1.0.0
 network 192.1.1.0
!
no ip classless
!
!line con 0
line aux 0
line vty 0 4
 login
!
end
```

RouterB

```
!
version 11.0
service udp-small-servers
service tcp-small-servers
!
hostname RouterB
!
interface Ethernet0
 no ip address
 shutdown
```

```
!
interface Serial0
 ip address 192.1.1.2 255.255.255.0
 no fair-queue
 clockrate 500000←Acts as DCE providing clock

!
interface Serial1
 ip address 193.1.1.2 255.255.255.0
 clockrate 500000←Acts as DCE providing clock
!
router rip←Enables the RIP routing process on the router.
timers basic 5 15 15 30←Updates are broadcast every 5 seconds. If a router is
                        not heard from in 15 seconds, the route is declared
                        unusable. Further information is suppressed for an
                        additional 15 seconds. At the end of the suppression
                        period, the route is flushed from the routing table.
network 192.1.1.0←Specifies what interfaces will receive and send RIP routing
                  updates. It also specifies what networks will be advertised.
  network 193.1.1.0
!
!
line con 0
line aux 0
line vty 0 4
 login
```

RouterC

```
!
version 11.1
service udp-small-servers
service tcp-small-servers
!
hostname RouterC
!
interface Ethernet0
 ip address 152.1.1.1 255.255.255.0
 no keepalive←Disables the keepalive on the Ethernet interface, allows the
              interface to stay up when it is not attached to a hub.
!
!
interface Serial0
 ip address 193.1.1.1 255.255.255.0
!
!
router rip←Enables the RIP routing process on the router.
timers basic 5 15 15 30←Updates are broadcast every 5 seconds. If a router is
                        not heard from in 15 seconds, the route is declared
                        unusable. Further information is suppressed for an
                        additional 15 seconds. At the end of the suppression
                        period, the route is flushed from the routing table.
```

network 152.1.0.0←Specifies what interfaces will receive and send RIP routing
                   updates. It also specifies what networks will be advertised.
network 193.1.1.0
```
!
no ip classless
!
!
line con 0
line aux 0
line vty 0 4
 login
!
```

Monitoring and Testing the Configuration

The following example shows the output from the **show ip protocols**
command. Note that the timers have been changed.

```
RouterA#show ip protocols
Routing Protocol is "rip"
  Sending updates every 5 seconds, next due in 3 seconds
  Invalid after 15 seconds, hold down 15, flushed after 30
  Outgoing update filter list for all interfaces is not set
  Incoming update filter list for all interfaces is not set
  Redistributing: rip
  Default version control: send version 1, receive any version
    Interface         Send   Recv   Key-chain
    Ethernet0          1      12
    Loopback0          1      1 2
    Serial0            1      1 2
  Routing for Networks:
    10.0.0.0
    192.1.1.0
    148.1.0.0
  Routing Information Sources:
    Gateway          Distance      Last Update
    192.1.1.2            120       01:13:39
  Distance: (default is 120)
```

Now, lets examine how these timers work when a route is lost. Perform
the following steps:

1. Add the service timestamps command to RouterA's configuration:

```
RouterA(config)#service timestamps
```

2. On RouterA, monitor the routing table changes with the **debug ip routing** command:

```
RouterA#debug ip routing
```

3. Disconnect the serial line between RouterB and RouterC.

The following example shows the output from the debug command. Note that after the route was declared invalid, the route was placed in holddown. Approximately 30 seconds later, the route was cleared from the table.

```
07:03:18: RT: delete route to 152.1.0.0 via 192.1.1.2, rip metric [120/2]←Route
is declared invalid.
07:03:18: RT: no routes to 152.1.0.0, entering holddown←Route is placed in
                                                         holddown
07:03:18:        193.1.1.0 in 16 hops (inaccessible)
07:03:18: RT: delete route to 193.1.1.0 via 192.1.1.2, rip metric [120/1]
07:03:18: RT: no routes to 193.1.1.0, entering holddown
07:03:45: RT: garbage collecting entry for 152.1.0.0←Route is removed from the
                                                      routing table.
07:03:45: RT: garbage collecting entry for 193.1.1.0
```

Next is the snapshot of the routing table after the route was declared invalid but before the route was flushed from the table. At this time, the route is marked down and is advertised out to all neighbors with a hop count of 16. After the route is flushed from the table, it is no longer advertised to neighboring routers.

```
RouterA#sho ip route
Codes: C - connected, S - static, I - IGRP, R - RIP, M - mobile, B - BGP
       D - EIGRP, EX - EIGRP external, O - OSPF, IA - OSPF inter area
       N1 - OSPF NSSA external type 1, N2 - OSPF NSSA external type 2
       E1 - OSPF external type 1, E2 - OSPF external type 2, E - EGP
       i - IS-IS, L1 - IS-IS level-1, L2 - IS-IS level-2, * - candidate default
       U - per-user static route, o - ODR

Gateway of last resort is not set

     10.0.0.0/24 is subnetted, 1 subnets
C       10.1.1.0 is directly connected, Loopback0
     148.1.0.0/24 is subnetted, 1 subnets
C       148.1.1.0 is directly connected, Ethernet0
R    152.1.0.0/16 is possibly down, routing via 192.1.1.2, Serial0
C    192.1.1.0/24 is directly connected, Serial0
R    193.1.1.0/24 is possibly down, routing via 192.1.1.2, Serial0
```

The following example shows the output from the **debug ip rip** command taken during the transition from the invalid to holddown to flushed state.

```
07:03:18: RIP: received v1 update from 192.1.1.2 on Serial0
07:03:18:     152.1.0.0 in 16 hops (inaccessible)
07:03:18: RIP: sending v1 update to 255.255.255.255 via Ethernet0 (148.1.1.1)
07:03:18:     network 10.0.0.0, metric 1
07:03:18:     network 152.1.0.0, metric 16
07:03:18:     network 192.1.1.0, metric 1
07:03:45: RIP: sending v1 update to 255.255.255.255 via Ethernet0 (148.1.1.1)
07:03:45:     network 10.0.0.0, metric 1
07:03:45:     network 192.1.1.0, metric 1
```

Let's examine all of the data in chronological order using the time stamps. At 07:03:18, the route is declared invalid, and the holddown counter begins. At this time, the route is advertised to all neighbors during the normal update period with a metric of 16. At 07:03:45, approximately 30 seconds after the route was declared invalid, the route is removed from the routing table and is no longer advertised in the normal routing updates.

LAB #22: Configuring Unicast RIP Updates

Equipment Needed

The following equipment is need to perform this lab exercise:

- One Cisco router with one Ethernet port
- Cisco IOS 10.0 or higher
- A PC running a terminal emulation program
- One Cisco rolled cable

Configuration Overview

The RIP neighbor command permits the point-to-point (nonbroadcast) exchange of routing information. This command can be used in combination with the passive-interface router configuration command to exchange information between a subset of routers and access servers all connected to the same LAN.

Figure 6–10
RIP Unicast updates

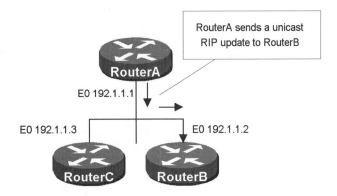

For example, in Figure 6–10, RouterA wishes to only send routing updates to RouterB on the Ethernet LAN. Because RIP is a broadcast protocol, by default updates will be sent to all devices on the Ethernet LAN. To prevent this process from taking place, RouterA's Ethernet interface is configured as passive. In this case, however, a neighbor router configuration command is included. This command permits the sending of routing updates to a specific neighbor. One copy of the routing update is generated per defined neighbor.

Router Configurations

The configuration for RouterA is as follows (key RIP configurations are highlighted in bold):

RouterA

```
Building configuration...

Current configuration:
!
version 11.2
no service password-encryption
no service udp-small-servers
no service tcp-small-servers
!
hostname RouterA
!
interface Loopback0
 ip address 1.1.1.1 255.255.255.0
!
interface Ethernet0
 ip address 192.1.1.1 255.255.255.0
 no keepalive←Disables the keepalive on the Ethernet interface,  allows the
             interface to stay up when it is not attached to a hub.
```

```
!
!
router rip←Enables the RIP routing process on the router.
passive-interface Ethernet0←Disables the sending of RIP updates on interface
                      Ethernet 0.

network 192.1.1.0←Specifies what interfaces will receive and send RIP routing
                      updates. It also specifies what networks will be advertised.
network 1.1.1.1
neighbor 192.1.1.2←permits the point-to-point (nonbroadcast) exchange of
                      routing information.
!
no ip classless
!
line con 0
line aux 0
line vty 0 4
 login
!
end
```

Monitoring and Testing the Configuration

The following example shows the output from the **debug ip rip** command. Note that RIP updates are being sent only to the Unicast address 192.1.1.2 on Ethernet 0 but are still being sent to the broadcast address 255.255.255.255 on interface loopback 0.

```
RouterA#debug ip rip
RIP: sending v1 update to 255.255.255.255 via Loopback0 (1.1.1.1)
      network 192.1.1.0, metric 1
RIP: sending v1 update to 192.1.1.2 via Ethernet0 (192.1.1.1)
      network 1.0.0.0, metric 1
```

Troubleshooting RIP

The Cisco IOS provides many tools for troubleshooting routing protocols. The following paragraphs show a list of key commands, along with a sample output from each, that will aid in troubleshooting RIP.

{debug ip rip}   This exec command displays information on RIP routing transactions. The output shows whether the router is sending or receiving an update, the networks contained in the update, and the metric or hop count for each.

```
RIP: sending v1 update to 255.255.255.255 via Ethernet0 (148.1.1.1)
 network 10.0.0.0, metric 1
 network 192.1.1.0, metric 1
network 148.1.0.0, metric 1
RIP: received v1 update from 192.1.1.2 on Serial0
193.1.1.0 in 1 hops
```

{debug ip routing } This exec command displays information on routing table updates. The output shows what routes have been added or deleted—and for the distance vector routing protocols, what routes are in holddown.

```
RT: delete route to 152.1.0.0 via 192.1.1.2, rip metric [120/2]
 RT: no routes to 152.1.0.0, entering holddown
 RT: delete route to 193.1.1.0 via 192.1.1.2, rip metric [120/1]
 RT: no routes to 193.1.1.0, entering holddown
RT: add 193.1.1.0/24 via 192.1.1.2, rip metric [120/1]
```

{show ip protocol} This exec command displays the parameters and current state of the active routing protocol process. The output shows the routing protocol used, timer information, inbound and outbound filter information, protocols being redistributed, and the networks for which the protocol is routing. This command is useful for troubleshooting a router that is sending bad router updates.

```
RouterA#show ip protocols
Routing Protocol is "rip"
  Sending updates every 5 seconds, next due in 0 seconds
  Invalid after 15 seconds, hold down 15, flushed after 30
  Outgoing update filter list for all interfaces is not set
  Incoming update filter list for all interfaces is not set
  Redistributing: rip
  Default version control: send version 1, receive any version
    Interface      Send  Recv  Key-chain
    Ethernet0      1     1     2
    Loopback0      1     1     2
    Serial0        1     1     2
  Routing for Networks:
    10.0.0.0
    192.1.1.0
    148.1.0.0
  Routing Information Sources:
    Gateway         Distance      Last Update
    192.1.1.2           120        00:00:01
  Distance: (default is 120)
```

{ show ip route rip}   This exec command quickly displays all of the routes learned via RIP. This method is a quick way to verify that a router is receiving RIP updates.

```
RouterA#show ip route rip
R    152.1.0.0/16 [120/2] via 192.1.1.2, 00:00:00, Serial0
R    193.1.1.0/24 [120/1] via 192.1.1.2, 00:00:00, Serial0
```

Conclusion

RIP is the most widely used *Interior Gateway routing Protocol* (IGP) in large organizations today, especially in organizations that have a large Unix-based routing environment. It is worth noting the limitations one faces when deploying a large RIP network, however.

■ RIP uses a four-bit metric to count router hops to destinations. This method limits the size of a RIP network, which can not contain more than 15 hops to a destination. This limitation is severe when trying to implement a typical, modern, large-scale network.

■ RIP uses hop count as a routing metric, which does provide the most optimal path selection. More advanced protocols such as IGRP use complex metrics to determine the optimal path.

■ RIP was deployed prior to subnetting and has no direct subnet support. RIP assumes that all interfaces on the network have the same mask.

■ RIP broadcasts a complete list of networks it can reach every 30 seconds. This feature can produce a significant amount of traffic—especially on low-speed links.

■ RIP has no security features built in. A RIP-enabled device will accept RIP updates from any other device on the network. More modern routing protocols such as OSPF enable the router to authenticate updates.

Interior Gateway Routing Protocol (IGRP)

Topics Covered in This Chapter

- Detailed technology overview
- Mechanisms to prevent routing loops
- IGRP route types
- Basic IGRP configuration
- IGRP unequal-cost load balancing
- IGRP timer configurations
- Detailed troubleshooting examples

Introduction

Interior Gateway Routing Protocol (IGRP) is a Cisco proprietary Distance Vector Routing protocol developed in 1986 to address the limitations of RIP. Although RIP works quite well in small, homogenous internetworks, its small hop count (16) severely limits the size of the network—and its single metric (hop count) does not provide the routing flexibility needed in complex networks. IGRP addresses the shortcomings of RIP by enabling the network to grow up to 255 hops and by providing a wide range of metrics (link reliability, bandwidth, internetwork delay, and load) to provide routing flexibility in today's complex networks.

Technology Overview

Routing Loops

The problem with a **first or second generation** Distance Vector routing protocol such as IGRP is that each router does not have a complete view of the network. Routers must rely on the neighboring routers for network reachability information, which creates a slow convergence problem where inconsistencies arise (because routing update messages propagate slowly across the network). To reduce the likelihood of routing loops caused by inconsistencies across the network, IGRP uses the following mechanisms: split horizons, poison reverse updates, hold-down counters, and flash updates.

Split Horizons

The rule of split horizon states that it is never useful for a router to advertise a route back in the direction from which it came. When split horizons is enabled on a router's interface, the router records the interface over which a route was received and does not propagate information about that route back out that interface.

The Cisco router enables you to disable split horizons on a per-interface basis. This feature is sometimes necessary in *Non Broadcast Multiple Access* (NBMA) hub-and-spoke environments. In Figure 7–1, RouterB is connected to RouterC and RouterA via Frame Relay, and both PVCs are terminating on one physical interface on RouterB.

In Figure 7–1, if split horizon is not disabled on RouterB's Serial interface, then RouterC will not receive RouterA's routing advertisements (and vice-versa). Use the **no ip split-horizon interface** subcommand to disable split horizons.

Poison Reverse

Split horizon is a scheme used by the router to avoid problems caused by advertising routes back to the router from which they were learned. The split horizon scheme omits routes learned from one neighbor in updates sent to that neighbor. Split horizon with poisoned reverse includes the routes in updates but sets the metric to 4294967295.

When a router sees increases in routing metrics, it generally indicates a routing loop. The router then sends poison reverse updates to remove the route and place it in holddown. In Cisco's implementation of IGRP, poison reverse updates are sent if a route metric has increased by a factor of 1.1 or greater.

By setting the hop count to the maximum value and advertising the route back to its source, it is possible to immediately break a routing loop. Otherwise, the inaccurate route will stay in the routing table until it times out. The disadvantage to poison reverse is that it increases the size of the routing updates.

Figure 7–1
Split horizons

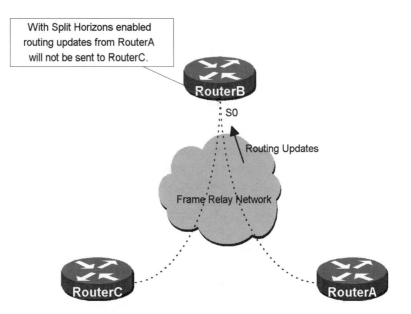

With Split Horizons enabled routing updates from RouterA will not be sent to RouterC.

Holddown

Holddown timers prevent the router from accepting routing information about a network for a fixed period of time after the route has been removed from the routing table. The idea is to make sure all routers have received the information and that no router sends out an invalid route. For example, in Figure 7–2, RouterB advertises bad information to RouterC because of the delay in the routing update. Holddown counters would prevent this situation from happening, because RouterC would not install a new route to NetworkA for 280 seconds. By then, RouterB would have converged with the proper routing information.

Flash Updates

Flash updates are an attempt to speed up convergence time. Whenever the metric of a route changes, the router must send an update message immediately. A flash update message is sent immediately, regardless of when the regular update message is scheduled to be sent.

IGRP Routes

IGRP advertises three types of routes, as seen in Figure 7–3: interior, system, and exterior. Interior routes are routes between subnets that are

Figure 7–2
Routing loop

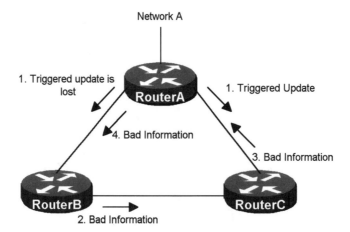

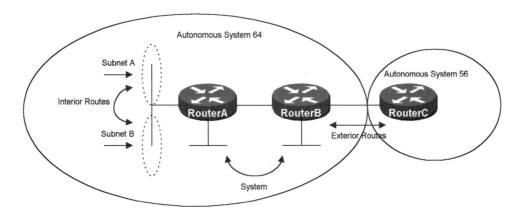

Figure 7–3
IGRP route types

attached to the same router interface. System routes are routes to networks that are in the same autonomous system, and exterior routes are routes to networks outside the autonomous system.

Commands Discussed in this Chapter

- clear ip route
- debug ip igrp events
- debug ip igrp transaction
- neighbor (ip-address)
- network (network-number)
- router igrp (autonomous-system number)
- show ip route igrp
- show ip protocol
- timers basic
- traffic-share {balanced | min}
- variance (multiplier)

Definitions

clear ip route: This exec command removes one or more routes from the routing table. The command enables you to enter a specific route or use an asterisk (*) to remove all routes.

debug ip igrp events: This exec command displays information on IGRP-routing transactions and displays all IGRP routing updates that are sent or received by the router.

debug ip igrp transaction: This exec command displays transaction information on *Interior Gateway Routing Protocol* (IGRP) routing transactions.

neighbor: This router configuration command permits the point-to-point (nonbroadcast) exchange of routing information. By default, IGRP routing advertisements are sent as broadcast traffic. The neighbor command enables advertisements to be sent to define neighbors as Unicast traffic.

network: This router configuration command specifies a list of networks on which the IGRP routing process will run. This command sends IGRP updates to the interfaces that are specified. If an interface's network is not specified, it will not be advertised in any IGRP update.

router igrp: This global command enables the IGRP routing process on the router. The autonomous system number used is a routing domain identifier, not a true ASN as defined in RFC 1930.

show ip route igrp: This exec command displays all IGRP-learned routes.

show ip protocol: This exec command displays the current state of the active routing protocol process.

timers basic: This router configuration command enables the user to tune the IGRP timers.

update: The update timer sets the rate in seconds at which routing updates are sent. The default is 90 seconds.

invalid: The invalid timer sets the interval of time in seconds after which a route is declared invalid. The timer is started if the route is not present in the regular update message. The default is 270 seconds.

holddown: The holddown timer sets the interval in seconds during which routing information regarding better paths is suppressed. The idea is to make sure that all routers have received the information and that no router sends out an invalid route. The default is 280 seconds.

flush: The flush timer sets in seconds the amount of time that must pass before a route is removed from the routing table. The default is 630 seconds.

traffic-share: This router configuration command controls how traffic is distributed among routes when there are multiple routes to the same destination network that have different costs. The traffic can be distributed proportionately to the ratios of the metrics or can be set to only use routes that have minimum costs.

variance: This router configuration command controls the load balancing over two IGRP paths and also enables the administrator to load balance across multiple paths—even if the metric of the paths is different. By default, the amount of variance is set to one (equal-cost load balancing). The variance command enables you to define how much worse an alternate path can be before that path is allowed to be used. For example, if the variance is set to four, the router will load balance across paths that are up to four times as bad as the best route.

IOS Requirements

IGRP first became available in IOS 10.0.

LAB #23: Basic IGRP Configuration

Equipment Needed

The following equipment is needed to perform this lab exercise:

- Two Cisco routers with one Ethernet port and one serial port
- One Cisco router with two serial ports
- Cisco IOS 10.0 or higher
- A PC running a terminal emulation program
- Two Cisco DTE/DCE crossover cables
- One Cisco rolled cable for accessing the console port of the router

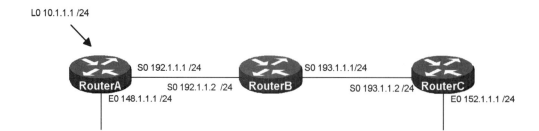

LO 10.1.1.1 /24

SO 192.1.1.1 /24   SO 193.1.1.1/24

RouterA   SO 192.1.1.2 /24   **RouterB**   SO 193.1.1.2 /24   **RouterC**

EO 148.1.1.1 /24   EO 152.1.1.1 /24

Figure 7–4
Basic IGRP

Configuration Overview

This configuration will demonstrate basic routing using IGRP. As per Figure 7–4, RouterA, RouterB, and RouterC will use IGRP to advertise routing information.

RouterA, RouterB, and RouterC are connected serially via a crossover cable. RouterB will act as the DCE supplying clock to RouterA and RouterC. The IP addresses are assigned as per Figure 7–4. All routers will be configured for IGRP and will advertise all connected networks.

Router Configurations

The configurations for the three routers in this example are as follows (key IGRP configurations are highlighted in bold):

RouterA

```
Current configuration:
!
version 11.2
no service udp-small-servers
no service tcp-small-servers
!
hostname RouterA
!
```

```
interface Loopback0←Defines a virtual interface that will be used as a test
                    point.
 ip address 10.1.1.1 255.255.255.0
!
interface Ethernet0
 ip address 148.1.1.1 255.255.255.0
 no keepalive←Disables the keepalive on the Ethernet interface, allows the
              interface to stay up when it is not attached to a hub.
!
interface Serial0
 ip address 192.1.1.1 255.255.255.0
!
router IGRP 64←Enables the IGRP routing process on the router.
 network 10.0.0.0←Specifies what interfaces will receive and send IGRP routing
                  updates. It also specifies what networks will be advertised.
 network 148.1.0.0
 network 192.1.1.0
!
no ip classless
!
!line con 0
line aux 0
line vty 0 4
 login
!
end
```

RouterB

```
!
version 11.0
service udp-small-servers
service tcp-small-servers
!
hostname RouterB
!
!
interface Serial0
 ip address 192.1.1.2 255.255.255.0
 no fair-queue
 clockrate 500000←Acts as DCE providing clock

!
interface Serial1
 ip address 193.1.1.2 255.255.255.0
 clockrate 500000←Acts as DCE providing clock
!
router igrp 64←Enables the IGRP routing process on the router.
network 192.1.1.0←Specifies what interfaces will receive and send IGRP routing
                  updates. It also specifies what networks will be advertised.
 network 193.1.1.0
!
!
```

```
line con 0
line aux 0
line vty 0 4
 login
```

RouterC

```
!
version 11.1
service udp-small-servers
service tcp-small-servers
!
hostname RouterC
!
interface Ethernet0
 ip address 152.1.1.1 255.255.255.0
 no keepalive←Disables the keepalive on the Ethernet interface, allows the
              interface to stay up when it is not attached to a hub.
!
!
interface Serial0
 ip address 193.1.1.1 255.255.255.0
!
!
router igrp 64←Enables the IGRP routing process on the router.
network 152.1.0.0←Specifies what interfaces will receive and send IGRP routing
                  updates. It also specifies what networks will be advertised.
network 193.1.1.0
!
no ip classless
!
!
line con 0
line aux 0
line vty 0 4
 login
!
end
```

Monitoring and Testing the Configuration

Like RIP, IGRP is a simple protocol to configure and troubleshoot. Show the IP routing table on RouterA with the **show ip route** command. The following example shows the output from this command. Notice that two networks were learned via IGRP: 152.1.0.0 and 193.1.1.0.

```
RouterA#show ip route
Codes: C - connected, S - static, I - IGRP, R - RIP, M - mobile, B - BGP
       D - EIGRP, EX - EIGRP external, O - OSPF, IA - OSPF inter area
       N1 - OSPF NSSA external type 1, N2 - OSPF NSSA external type 2
       E1 - OSPF external type 1, E2 - OSPF external type 2, E - EGP
       i - IS-IS, L1 - IS-IS level-1, L2 - IS-IS level-2, * - candidate default
       U - per-user static route, o - ODR

Gateway of last resort is not set

     10.0.0.0/24 is subnetted, 1 subnets
C        10.1.1.0 is directly connected, Loopback0
     148.1.0.0/24 is subnetted, 1 subnets
C        148.1.1.0 is directly connected, Ethernet0
I    152.1.0.0/16 [100/10576] via 192.1.1.2, 00:00:40, Serial0
C    192.1.1.0/24 is directly connected, Serial0
I    193.1.1.0/24 [100/10476] via 192.1.1.2, 00:00:40, Serial0
```

From RouterA, monitor the routing updates being passed using the **debug ip igrp transactions** command. The following example shows the output from this command. Notice that on interface serial 0, the router does not advertise the networks it learns from RouterB (152.1.0.0 and 193.1.1.0)—but on all other interfaces, these networks are advertised. This situation shows split horizons at work. Remember, when split horizons is enabled, the router will never advertise a route back in the direction from which it came.

```
RouterA#debug ip igrp transactions
IGRP: sending update to 255.255.255.255 via Ethernet0 (148.1.1.1)
       network 10.0.0.0, metric=501
       network 152.1.0.0, metric=10576
       network 192.1.1.0, metric=8476
       network 193.1.1.0, metric=10476
IGRP: sending update to 255.255.255.255 via Loopback0 (10.1.1.1)
       network 148.1.0.0, metric=1100
       network 152.1.0.0, metric=10576
       network 192.1.1.0, metric=8476
       network 193.1.1.0, metric=10476
IGRP: sending update to 255.255.255.255 via Serial0 (192.1.1.1)
       network 10.0.0.0, metric=501
       network 148.1.0.0, metric=1100
```

Now, disable split horizons on RouterA using the interface configuration command **no ip split horizons**.

```
RouterA(config)#int s0
RouterA(config-if)#no ip split-horizon
```

From RouterA, monitor the routing updates being passed using the **debug ip igrp transactions** command. The following example shows the output from this command. Notice how all routes are being advertised out serial 0—including the routes learned from RouterB on serial 0.

```
RouterA# debug ip igrp transactions
IGRP: sending update to 255.255.255.255 via Ethernet0 (148.1.1.1)
      network 10.0.0.0, metric=501
      network 152.1.0.0, metric=10576
      network 192.1.1.0, metric=8476
      network 193.1.1.0, metric=10476
IGRP: sending update to 255.255.255.255 via Loopback0 (10.1.1.1)
      network 148.1.0.0, metric=1100
      network 152.1.0.0, metric=10576
      network 192.1.1.0, metric=8476
      network 193.1.1.0, metric=10476
IGRP: sending update to 255.255.255.255 via Serial0 (192.1.1.1)
      network 10.0.0.0, metric=501
      network 148.1.0.0, metric=1100
      network 152.1.0.0, metric=10576
      network 192.1.1.0, metric=8476
      network 193.1.1.0, metric=10476
```

From RouterA, delete the IGRP process and add a new process using autonomous system 56 with the following commands:

```
RouterA#configure terminal
RouterA(config)#no router igrp 64
RouterA(config)#router igrp 56
RouterA(config-router)#network 10.0.0.0
RouterA(config-router)# network 148.1.0.0
RouterA(config-router)# network 192.1.1.0
```

Show the IP routing table on RouterA with the **show ip route** command. The following example shows the output from this command. Notice that no networks are being learned via IGRP because the autonomous system numbers are different. The autonomous system number must match, or the routers will not exchange routing information.

```
RouterA#show ip route
Codes: C - connected, S - static, I - IGRP, R - RIP, M - mobile, B - BGP
       D - EIGRP, EX - EIGRP external, O - OSPF, IA - OSPF inter area
       N1 - OSPF NSSA external type 1, N2 - OSPF NSSA external type 2
       E1 - OSPF external type 1, E2 - OSPF external type 2, E - EGP
       i - IS-IS, L1 - IS-IS level-1, L2 - IS-IS level-2, * - candidate default
       U - per-user static route, o - ODR

Gateway of last resort is not set

     10.0.0.0/24 is subnetted, 1 subnets
C       10.1.1.0 is directly connected, Loopback0
     148.1.0.0/24 is subnetted, 1 subnets
C       148.1.1.0 is directly connected, Ethernet0
C    192.1.1.0/24 is directly connected, Serial0
```

LAB #24: Passive Interface Configuration

Equipment Needed

The following equipment is needed to perform this lab exercise:

- Two Cisco routers with one Ethernet port and one serial port
- One Cisco router with two serial ports
- Cisco IOS 10.0 or higher
- A PC running a terminal emulation program
- Two Cisco DTE/DCE crossover cables
- One Cisco rolled cable for accessing the console port of the router

Configuration Overview

This configuration will demonstrate the use of the passive-interface command, which permits IGRP-enabled routers to listen, but not send, routing updates out a particular interface. The passive-interface router configuration command is typically used when the network router configuration command configures more interfaces than desirable. For example, in Figure 7–5, RouterA has three defined subnets: 10.1.1.0/24, 10.1.2.0/24, and 10.1.3.0/24. Because IGRP is a classful protocol, when enabled it is turned on for the classful network of 10.0.0.0. This network encompasses all three subnets. The passive-interface command enables the user to turn off IGRP advertisements on a particular interface (subnet).

The reason that IGRP changes the network entry from 10.1.1.0 to 10.0.0.0 is because IGRP is considered a "classful" protocol. This term means that the protocol recognizes the IP address class of the network

Figure 7–5
The passive-interface command

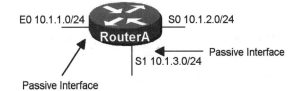

address that you type and assumes the proper mask. For a Class A network like this one, the mask is 255.0.0.0, yielding 10.0.0.0 (no matter what you actually type as the last two octets). The network statement tells the routing protocol to route on the interfaces where the network address matches the one specified in the network statement.

In this lab scenario, the user only wishes to send IGRP updates out interface L0(10.1.1.1) and E0(148.1.1.1) so interface S0(192.1.1.1) is made passive.

RouterA, RouterB, and RouterC are connected serially via a crossover cable. RouterB will act as the DCE supplying clock to RouterA and RouterC. The IP addresses are assigned as per Figure 7–6. All routers will be configured for IGRP, and RouterB and RouterC will advertise all connected networks. RouterA's interface S0 will be passive and will not advertise any routing information; however, the interface will still receive routing updates.

Router Configurations

The configurations for the three routers in this example are as follows (key IGRP configurations are highlighted in bold):

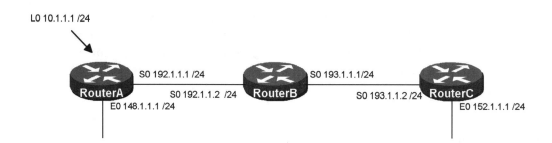

Figure 7–6
IGRP passive-interface configuration

RouterA

```
Current configuration:
!
version 11.2
no service udp-small-servers
no service tcp-small-servers
!
hostname RouterA
!
interface Loopback0←Defines a virtual interface that will be used as a test
                    point.
 ip address 10.1.1.1 255.255.255.0
!
interface Ethernet0
 ip address 148.1.1.1 255.255.255.0
 no keepalive←Disables the keepalive on the Ethernet interface,  allows the
              interface to stay up when it is not attached to a hub.
!
interface Serial0
 ip address 192.1.1.1 255.255.255.0
!
!
router IGRP 64←Enables the IGRP routing process on the router.
passive-interface Serial0←Disables the sending of IGRP updates on interface
                          Serial 0.
network 10.0.0.0←Specifies what interfaces will receive and send IGRP routing
                 updates. It also specifies what networks will be advertised.
 network 148.1.0.0
 network 192.1.1.0
!
no ip classless
!
!line con 0
line aux 0
line vty 0 4
 login
!
end
```

RouterB

```
!
version 11.0
service udp-small-servers
service tcp-small-servers
!
hostname RouterB
!
!
interface Serial0
```

```
 ip address 192.1.1.2 255.255.255.0
 no fair-queue
 clockrate 500000←Acts as DCE providing clock

!
interface Serial1
 ip address 193.1.1.2 255.255.255.0
 clockrate 500000←Acts as DCE providing clock
!
router igrp 64←Enables the IGRP routing process on the router.
network 192.1.1.0←Specifies what interfaces will receive and send IGRP routing
                  updates. It also specifies what networks will be advertised.
 network 193.1.1.0
!
!
line con 0
line aux 0
line vty 0 4
 login
```

RouterC

```
!
version 11.1
service udp-small-servers
service tcp-small-servers
!
hostname RouterC
!
interface Ethernet0
 ip address 152.1.1.1 255.255.255.0
 no keepalive←Disables the keepalive on the Ethernet interface,  allows the
              interface to stay up when it is not attached to a hub.
!
!
interface Serial0
 ip address 193.1.1.1 255.255.255.0
!
!
router igrp 64←Enables the IGRP routing process on the router.
network 152.1.0.0←Specifies what interfaces will receive and send IGRP routing
                  updates. It also specifies what networks will be advertised.
network 193.1.1.0
!
no ip classless
!
!
line con 0
line aux 0
line vty 0 4
 login
!
end
```

Monitoring and Testing the Configuration

Display the routing protocol information with the command **show ip protocols**. Notice that RouterA's serial interface is passive.

```
RouterA#show ip protocols
Routing Protocol is "igrp 64"
  Sending updates every 90 seconds, next due in 31 seconds
  Invalid after 270 seconds, hold down 280, flushed after 630
  Outgoing update filter list for all interfaces is not set
  Incoming update filter list for all interfaces is not set
  Default networks flagged in outgoing updates
  Default networks accepted from incoming updates
  IGRP metric weight K1=1, K2=0, K3=1, K4=0, K5=0
  IGRP maximum hopcount 100
  IGRP maximum metric variance 1
  Redistributing: igrp 64
  Routing for Networks:
    10.0.0.0
    148.1.0.0
    192.1.1.0
  Passive Interface(s):
    Serial0
  Routing Information Sources:
    Gateway          Distance       Last Update
    192.1.1.2             100       00:00:48
  Distance: (default is 100)
```

The following example shows the output from the **debug ip igrp transactions** command on RouterA. Notice that IGRP updates are only being sent out interface Ethernet 0 and Loopback 0. Also note that interface S0 is still receiving IGRP updates.

```
RouterA#debug ip igrp transactions

IGRP: sending update to 255.255.255.255 via Ethernet0 (148.1.1.1)
      network 10.0.0.0, metric=501
      network 152.1.0.0, metric=10576
      network 192.1.1.0, metric=8476
      network 193.1.1.0, metric=10476
IGRP: sending update to 255.255.255.255 via Loopback0 (10.1.1.1)
      network 148.1.0.0, metric=1100
      network 152.1.0.0, metric=10576
      network 192.1.1.0, metric=8476
      network 193.1.1.0, metric=10476
IGRP: received update from 192.1.1.2 on Serial0
      network 152.1.0.0, metric 10576 (neighbor 8576)
      network 193.1.1.0, metric 10476 (neighbor 8476)
```

The following example shows the output from the **show ip route** command on RouterA and RouterC. Note that RouterA has learned all of the routes from RouterC, but RouterC has no routes from RouterA.

```
RouterA#show ip route
Codes: C - connected, S - static, I - IGRP, R - RIP, M - mobile, B - BGP
       D - EIGRP, EX - EIGRP external, O - OSPF, IA - OSPF inter area
       N1 - OSPF NSSA external type 1, N2 - OSPF NSSA external type 2
       E1 - OSPF external type 1, E2 - OSPF external type 2, E - EGP
       i - IS-IS, L1 - IS-IS level-1, L2 - IS-IS level-2, * - candidate default
       U - per-user static route, o - ODR

Gateway of last resort is not set

     10.0.0.0/24 is subnetted, 1 subnets
C       10.1.1.0 is directly connected, Loopback0
     148.1.0.0/24 is subnetted, 1 subnets
C       148.1.1.0 is directly connected, Ethernet0
I    152.1.0.0/16 [100/10576] via 192.1.1.2, 00:00:29, Serial0
C    192.1.1.0/24 is directly connected, Serial0
I    193.1.1.0/24 [100/10476] via 192.1.1.2, 00:00:29, Serial0

RouterC#show ip route
Codes: C - connected, S - static, I - IGRP, R - RIP, M - mobile, B - BGP
       D - EIGRP, EX - EIGRP external, O - OSPF, IA - OSPF inter area
       N1 - OSPF NSSA external type 1, N2 - OSPF NSSA external type 2
       E1 - OSPF external type 1, E2 - OSPF external type 2, E - EGP
       i - IS-IS, L1 - IS-IS level-1, L2 - IS-IS level-2, * - candidate default
       U - per-user static route, o - ODR

Gateway of last resort is not set

     152.1.0.0/24 is subnetted, 1 subnets
C       152.1.1.0 is directly connected, Ethernet0
I    192.1.1.0/24 [100/10476] via 193.1.1.2, 00:00:13, Serial0←Route from
                                                                      RouterB
C    193.1.1.0/24 is directly connected, Serial0
```

LAB #25: IGRP Unequal-Cost Load Balancing

Equipment Needed

The following equipment is needed to perform this lab exercise:

- Two Cisco routers with one Ethernet port and one serial port
- One Cisco router with two serial ports and one Ethernet port

- Cisco IOS 10.0 or higher
- A PC running a terminal emulation program
- Two Ethernet cables
- One Ethernet hub
- Two Cisco DTE/DCE crossover cables
- One Cisco rolled cable for accessing the console port of the router

Overview

IGRP can be configured to load balance on up to four unequal cost paths to a given destination. This feature is known as unequal-cost load balancing and is set using the variance command. By default, the router will load balance across up to four equal cost paths. The variance command lets you set how much worse an alternate path can be (in terms of metrics) and still be used to load balance across.

For example, if RouterA has two routes to network 3.0.0.0—one with a cost of four and one with a cost of eight—by default, the route will only use the path with a cost of four when sending packets to 3.0.0.0. If a variance of two is set, however, the router will load balance across both paths. This situation occurs because the route with the cost of eight is within the variance, which in this case can be up to two times as bad as the preferred route (4(preferred route) * 2 = 8).

Configuration Overview

This configuration will demonstrate the use of the variance command, which permits IGRP-enabled routers to load balance across unequal-cost paths. The variance command will be set on RouterA so that both paths to network 3.0.0.0 are used.

RouterA, RouterB, and RouterC are connected serially via a crossover cable, and RouterA and RouterB are also connected via an Ethernet hub. RouterB will act as the DCE supplying clock to RouterA and RouterC. The IP addresses are assigned as per Figure 7–7. All routers will be configured for IGRP. RouterA will be configured to load-balance traffic that is destined for Host 3.3.3.3 over two unequal cost paths.

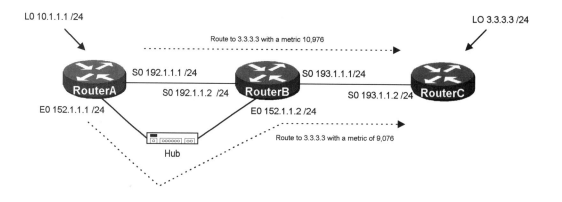

Figure 7–7
IGRP unequal-cost load balancing

Router Configurations

The configurations for the three routers in this example are as follows (key IGRP configurations are highlighted in bold):

RouterA

```
Current configuration:
!
version 11.2
no service udp-small-servers
no service tcp-small-servers
!
hostname RouterA
!
interface Loopback0←Defines a virtual interface that will be used as a test
                    point.
 ip address 10.1.1.1 255.255.255.0
!
interface Ethernet0
 ip address 152.1.1.1 255.255.255.0
 keepalive
!
interface Serial0
 ip address 192.1.1.1 255.255.255.0
!
!
router IGRP 64←Enables the IGRP routing process on the router.
```

```
variance 2
 network 10.0.0.0←Specifies what interfaces will receive and send IGRP routing
                 updates. It also specifies what networks will be advertised.
 network 152.1.0.0
 network 192.1.1.0
!
no ip classless
!
!
line con 0
line aux 0
line vty 0 4
 login
!
end
```

RouterB

```
!
version 11.0
service udp-small-servers
service tcp-small-servers
!
hostname RouterB
!
interface Ethernet0
 no ip address
ip address 152.1.1.2 255.255.255.0
!
interface Serial0
 ip address 192.1.1.2 255.255.255.0
 no fair-queue
 clockrate 500000←Acts as DCE providing clock

!
interface Serial1
 ip address 193.1.1.2 255.255.255.0
 clockrate 500000←Acts as DCE providing clock
!
router igrp 64←Enables the IGRP routing process on the router.
network 192.1.1.0←Specifies what interfaces will receive and send IGRP routing
                 updates. It also specifies what networks will be advertised.
network 193.1.1.0
network 152.1.0.0

!
!
line con 0
line aux 0
line vty 0 4
 login
```

RouterC

```
!
version 11.1
service udp-small-servers
service tcp-small-servers
!
hostname RouterC
!
interface Loopback0
 ip address 3.3.3.3 255.255.255.0
!
!
interface Serial0
 ip address 193.1.1.1 255.255.255.0
!
!
router igrp 64←Enables the IGRP routing process on the router.

network 193.1.1.0←Specifies what interfaces will receive and send IGRP routing
                  updates. It also specifies what networks will be advertised.

network 3.0.0.0
!
no ip classless
!
!
line con 0
line aux 0
line vty 0 4
 login
!
end
```

Monitoring and Testing the Configuration

Display the routing table on RouterA with the command **show ip route**.
Notice that there are two routes to network 3.0.0.0: one via the Ethernet
interface and one via the serial interface. The cost to reach the network
over each path is different; however, because the variance is set to two, as
long as the cost of the second path is not greater than two times the preferred path, then the route will be used.

Let's take a closer look at this situation. The best route to network
3.0.0.0 is via the Ethernet interface, with a cost of 9,076. Because the variance is set to two, as long as the cost on any other route to network 3.0.0.0
is below 18,152 (9,076*2), then the route will be used. Because the cost of
the route via the serial interface is 10,976 which is lower than 18,152, the
route is used.

```
RouterA#show ip route

Codes: C - connected, S - static, I - IGRP, R - RIP, M - mobile, B - BGP
       D - EIGRP, EX - EIGRP external, O - OSPF, IA - OSPF inter area
       N1 - OSPF NSSA external type 1, N2 - OSPF NSSA external type 2
       E1 - OSPF external type 1, E2 - OSPF external type 2, E - EGP
       i - IS-IS, L1 - IS-IS level-1, L2 - IS-IS level-2, * - candidate default
       U - per-user static route, o - ODR

Gateway of last resort is not set

I     3.0.0.0/8 [100/9076] via 152.1.1.1, 00:00:04, Ethernet0
                [100/10976] via 192.1.1.2, 00:00:04, Serial0
10.0.0.0/24 is subnetted, 1 subnets
C        10.1.1.0 is directly connected, Loopback0
      152.1.0.0/24 is subnetted, 1 subnets
C        152.1.1.0 is directly connected, Ethernet0
C     192.1.1.0/24 is directly connected, Serial0
I     193.1.1.0/24 [100/10476] via 192.1.1.2, 00:00:27, Serial0
                   [100/8576] via 152.1.1.1, 00:00:27, Ethernet0
```

From RouterA, display the route to host 3.3.3.3 with the command **show ip route 3.3.3.3**. Notice that both routes are shown; however, there is an asterisk next to the first route. The asterisk indicates that the next packet leaving RouterA destined for host 3.3.3.3 will use this route.

```
RouterA#show ip route 3.3.3.3
Routing entry for 3.0.0.0/8
  Known via "igrp 64", distance 100, metric 9076
  Redistributing via igrp 64
  Advertised by igrp 64 (self originated)
  Last update from 192.1.1.2 on Serial0, 00:00:18 ago
  Routing Descriptor Blocks:
  * 152.1.1.1, from 152.1.1.1, 00:00:18 ago, via Ethernet0
      Route metric is 9076, traffic share count is 1
      Total delay is 26000 microseconds, minimum bandwidth is 1544 Kbit
      Reliability 255/255, minimum MTU 1500 bytes
      Loading 1/255, Hops 1
    192.1.1.2, from 192.1.1.2, 00:00:18 ago, via Serial0
      Route metric is 10976, traffic share count is 1
      Total delay is 45000 microseconds, minimum bandwidth is 1544 Kbit
      Reliability 255/255, minimum MTU 1500 bytes
      Loading 1/255, Hops 1
```

From RouterA, ping host 3.3.3.3.

```
RouterA#ping 3.3.3.3

Type escape sequence to abort.
Sending 5, 100-byte ICMP Echos to 3.3.3.3, timeout is 2 seconds:
!!!!!
```

Now, from RouterA, display the route to host 3.3.3.3 with the command **show ip route 3.3.3.3**. Notice that the asterisk is now by the second route. This situation occurs because the router is load-balancing the traffic destined for network 3.0.0.0 over both links.

```
RouterA#show ip route 3.3.3.3
Routing entry for 3.0.0.0/8
  Known via "igrp 64", distance 100, metric 9076
  Redistributing via igrp 64
  Advertised by igrp 64 (self originated)
  Last update from 192.1.1.2 on Serial0, 00:00:06 ago
  Routing Descriptor Blocks:
    152.1.1.1, from 152.1.1.1, 00:00:06 ago, via Ethernet0
      Route metric is 9076, traffic share count is 1
      Total delay is 26000 microseconds, minimum bandwidth is 1544 Kbit
      Reliability 255/255, minimum MTU 1500 bytes
      Loading 1/255, Hops 1
  * 192.1.1.2, from 192.1.1.2, 00:00:07 ago, via Serial0
      Route metric is 10976, traffic share count is 1
      Total delay is 45000 microseconds, minimum bandwidth is 1544 Kbit
      Reliability 255/255, minimum MTU 1500 bytes
      Loading 1/255, Hops 1
```

Remove the variance command on RouterA with the router configuration command **no variance**.

```
outerA#configure terminal
RouterA(config)#router igrp 64
RouterA(config-router)#no variance
```

From RouterA, display the route to host 3.3.3.3 with the command **show ip route 3.3.3.3**. Notice that only one route is being used (the route with the lowest metric, where no load balancing is being performed).

LAB #26: IGRP Timer Configurations

Equipment Needed

The following equipment is need to perform this lab exercise:

- Two Cisco routers with one Ethernet port and one serial port
- One Cisco router with two serial ports
- Cisco IOS 10.0 or higher

- A PC running a terminal emulation program
- Two Cisco DTE/DCE crossover cables
- One Cisco rolled cable for console port access

Configuration Overview

This configuration will demonstrate using the timer basic command to set the four configurable IGRP timers (update, invalid, holddown, and flush timers). Depending on the network topology, it may become necessary to change the update timers, which control the rate in seconds that routing updates are sent. For example, if the access link is 56Kbps, generating IGRP updates every 90 seconds might not be the most efficient use of bandwidth. By increasing the update timer, however, you also increase the convergence time of the network.

The three other IGRP timers are all dependent on the value of the update timer. The invalid timer should be at least three times the value of the update timer; the holddown timer should be at least three times the value of the update timer; and the flush timer must be at least the sum of invalid and holddown timers.

Each time a route is updated (which is dependent on the update interval), the invalid timer is reset. By default, if a route is not seen in an update for 270 seconds, the route is put in holddown—which means that the router will use the route-to-route packets but will not announce the route in its updates. Also, the router will not install any other route to this destination until the holddown counter expires. This event happens after 630 seconds, at which time the route is flushed from the routing table.

NOTE: *The update interval must be the same value on neighboring routers.*

RouterA, RouterB, and RouterC are connected serially via a crossover cable. RouterB will act as the DCE supplying clock to RouterA and RouterC. The IP addresses are assigned as per Figure 7–8. All routers will be configured for IGRP. RouterA, RouterB, and RouterC will advertise all connected networks. The timers on each router will be as follows:

- Update 5
- Invalid=15
- Holddown=15
- Flush=30

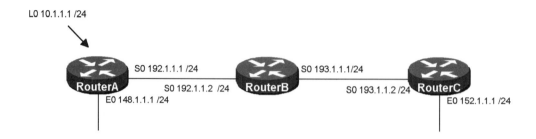

Figure 7–8
IGRP timer configuration

With these timers set, updates are broadcast every five seconds. If a route is not heard from in 15 seconds, the route is declared unusable (invalid). Any information received in routing updates about this particular network is suppressed for an additional 15 seconds (holddown). At the end of the suppression period, the route is flushed from the routing table.

Router Configurations

The configurations for the three routers in this example are as follows (key IGRP configurations are highlighted in bold):

RouterA

```
Current configuration:
!
version 11.2
no service udp-small-servers
no service tcp-small-servers
!
hostname RouterA
!
interface Loopback0←Defines a virtual interface that will be used as a test
                    point.
 ip address 10.1.1.1 255.255.255.0
!
interface Ethernet0
 ip address 148.1.1.1 255.255.255.0
```

```
 no keepalive←Disables the keepalive on the Ethernet interface,  allows the
                interface to stay up when it is not attached to a hub.
!
interface Serial0
 ip address 192.1.1.1 255.255.255.0
!
!
router igrp 64←Enables the IGRP routing process on the router.
 timers basic 5 15 15 30←Updates are broadcast every 5 seconds. If a router
                          is not heard from in 15 seconds, the route is
                          declared unusable. Further information is suppressed
                          for an additional 15 seconds. At the end of the
                          suppression period, the route is flushed from the
                          routing table.

network 10.0.0.0←Specifies what interfaces will receive and send IGRP routing
                  updates. It also specifies what networks will be advertised.
 network 148.1.0.0
 network 192.1.1.0
!
no ip classless
!
!line con 0
line aux 0
line vty 0 4
 login
!
end
```

RouterB

```
!
version 11.0
service udp-small-servers
service tcp-small-servers
!
hostname RouterB
!
!
interface Serial0
 ip address 192.1.1.2 255.255.255.0
 no fair-queue
 clockrate 500000←Acts as DCE providing clock

!
interface Serial1
 ip address 193.1.1.2 255.255.255.0
 clockrate 500000←Acts as DCE providing clock
!
router igrp 64←Enables the IGRP routing process on the router.
```

timers basic 5 15 15 30←Updates are broadcast every 5 seconds. If a router is
                    not heard from in 15 seconds, the route is declared
                    unusable. Further information is suppressed for an
                    additional 15 seconds. At the end of the suppression
                    period, the route is flushed from the routing table.

network 192.1.1.0←Specifies what interfaces will receive and send IGRP routing
                    updates. It also specifies what networks will be advertised.
 network 193.1.1.0
!
!
line con 0
line aux 0
line vty 0 4
 login

RouterC

!
version 11.1
service udp-small-servers
service tcp-small-servers
!
hostname RouterC
!
interface Ethernet0
 ip address 152.1.1.1 255.255.255.0
 no keepalive←Disables the keepalive on the Ethernet interface, allows the
              interface to stay up when it is not attached to a hub.
!
!
interface Serial0
 ip address 193.1.1.1 255.255.255.0
!
!
router igrp 64←Enables the IGRP routing process on the router.
timers basic 5 15 15 30←Updates are broadcast every 5 seconds. If a router is
                    not heard from in 15 seconds, the route is declared
                    unusable. Further information is suppressed for an
                    additional 15 seconds. At the end of the suppression
                    period, the route is flushed from the routing table.

network 152.1.0.0←Specifies what interfaces will receive and send IGRP routing
                    updates. It also specifies what networks will be advertised.
network 193.1.1.0
!
no ip classless
!
!

```
line con 0
line aux 0
line vty 0 4
 login
!
end
```

Monitoring and Testing the Configuration

The following example shows the output from the **show ip protocols** command on RouterA. Note that the timers have been changed.

```
RouterA#show ip protocols
Routing Protocol is "igrp 64"
  Sending updates every 5 seconds, next due in 1 seconds
  Invalid after 15 seconds, hold down 15, flushed after 30
  Outgoing update filter list for all interfaces is not set
  Incoming update filter list for all interfaces is not set
  Default networks flagged in outgoing updates
  Default networks accepted from incoming updates
  IGRP metric weight K1=1, K2=0, K3=1, K4=0, K5=0
  IGRP maximum hopcount 100
  IGRP maximum metric variance 1
  Redistributing: igrp 64
  Routing for Networks:
    10.0.0.0
    148.1.0.0
    192.1.1.0
  Routing Information Sources:
    Gateway          Distance      Last Update
    192.1.1.2             100      00:01:14
  Distance: (default is 100)
```

LAB #27: Configuring Unicast IGRP Updates

Equipment Needed

The following equipment is need to perform this lab exercise:

■ One Cisco router with one Ethernet port

■ Cisco IOS 10.0 or higher

■ A PC running a terminal emulation program

■ One Cisco rolled cable for console port access

▬▬ ▬▬ ▬▬ ▬▬

Figure 7–9
IGRP Unicast updates

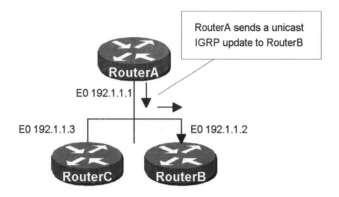

RouterA sends a unicast
IGRP update to RouterB

EO 192.1.1.1

EO 192.1.1.3

EO 192.1.1.2

The IGRP neighbor command permits the point-to-point (non-broadcast) exchange of routing information. This command can be used in combination with the passive-interface router configuration command to exchange information between a subset of routers and access servers all connected to the same LAN.

For example, in Figure 7–9, RouterA wishes to only send routing updates to RouterB on the Ethernet LAN. Because IGRP is a broadcast protocol, by default it will send updates to all devices on the Ethernet LAN. To prevent this situation from happening, RouterA's Ethernet interface is configured as passive. In this case, however, a neighbor router configuration command is included. This command permits the sending of routing updates to a specific neighbor. One copy of the routing update is generated per defined neighbor.

Router Configurations

The configuration for RouterA is as follows (key IGRP configurations for RouterA are highlighted in bold):

RouterA

```
Building configuration...

Current configuration:
!
version 11.2
```

```
no service password-encryption
no service udp-small-servers
no service tcp-small-servers
!
hostname RouterA
!
interface Loopback0
 ip address 1.1.1.1 255.255.255.0
!
interface Ethernet0
 ip address 192.1.1.1 255.255.255.0
 no keepalive←Disables the keepalive on the Ethernet interface, allows the
               interface to stay up when it is not attached to a hub.
!
!
router igrp 64←Enables the IGRP routing process on the router.
passive-interface Ethernet0←Disables the sending of IGRP updates on interface
                Ethernet 0.

network 192.1.1.0←Specifies what interfaces will receive and send IGRP routing
                  updates. It also specifies what networks will be advertised.
network 1.1.1.1
neighbor 192.1.1.2←permits the point-to-point (nonbroadcast) exchange of
                   routing information.
!
no ip classless
!
line con 0
line aux 0
line vty 0 4
 login
!
end
```

Monitoring and Testing the Configuration

The following example shows the output from the **debug ip igrp events** command. Note that IGRP updates are being sent to the Unicast address 192.1.1.2 on Ethernet 0 and the broadcast address 255.255.255.255 on interface loopback 0.

```
RouterA#debug ip igrp events
IGRP: sending update to 255.255.255.255 via Loopback0 (10.1.1.1)
IGRP: Update contains 0 interior, 1 system, and 0 exterior routes.
IGRP: Total routes in update: 1
IGRP: sending update to 192.1.1.2 via Ethernet0 (192.1.1.1)
IGRP: Update contains 0 interior, 1 system, and 0 exterior routes.
```

Troubleshooting IGRP

The Cisco IOS provides many tools for troubleshooting routing protocols. The following example shows a list of key commands, along with a sample output from each, that will aid in troubleshooting IGRP.

{debug ip igrp events}   This exec command displays summary information on IGRP routing messages. The information contains the source and destination of each routing update and the type of routes contained in the update (system, exterior, and interior), as well as the number of routes in each update.

```
RouterA#debug ip igrp events
IGRP: sending update to 255.255.255.255 via Ethernet0 (148.1.1.1)
IGRP: Update contains 0 interior, 2 system, and 0 exterior routes.
IGRP: Total routes in update: 2
IGRP: sending update to 255.255.255.255 via Loopback0 (10.1.1.1)
IGRP: Update contains 0 interior, 2 system, and 0 exterior routes.
IGRP: Total routes in update: 2
IGRP: sending update to 255.255.255.255 via Serial0 (192.1.1.1)
IGRP: Update contains 0 interior, 2 system, and 0 exterior routes.
IGRP: Total routes in update: 2
```

{debug ip igrp transactions}   This exec command displays transaction information on IGRP routing transactions. The information contains the source and destination of each update, the routes that are received or being advertised, and the metric of each route.

```
RouterA#debug ip igrp transactions
IGRP: sending update to 255.255.255.255 via Ethernet0 (148.1.1.1)
      network 10.0.0.0, metric=501
      network 152.1.0.0, metric=10576
      network 192.1.1.0, metric=8476
      network 193.1.1.0, metric=10476
IGRP: sending update to 255.255.255.255 via Loopback0 (10.1.1.1)
      network 148.1.0.0, metric=1100
      network 152.1.0.0, metric=10576
      network 192.1.1.0, metric=8476
      network 193.1.1.0, metric=10476
IGRP: sending update to 255.255.255.255 via Serial0 (192.1.1.1)
      network 10.0.0.0, metric=501
      network 148.1.0.0, metric=1100
IGRP: received update from 192.1.1.2 on Serial0
      network 152.1.0.0, metric 10576 (neighbor 8576)
      network 193.1.1.0, metric 10476 (neighbor 8476)
```

{debug ip routing} This exec command displays information on routing table updates. The output shows which routes have been added or deleted—and for the distance vector routing protocols, which routes are in holddown.

```
RouterA#debug ip routing
RT: add 148.1.1.0/24 via 0.0.0.0, connected metric [0/0]
RT: add 10.1.1.0/24 via 0.0.0.0, connected metric [0/0]
RT: add 192.1.1.0/24 via 0.0.0.0, connected metric [0/0]
```

{show ip protocol} This exec command displays the parameters and current state of the active routing protocol process. The output shows the routing protocol used, timer information, inbound and outbound filter information, protocols being redistributed, and the networks for which the protocol is routing. This command is useful for troubleshooting a router that is sending bad router updates.

```
RouterA#show ip protocols
Routing Protocol is "igrp 64"
  Sending updates every 5 seconds, next due in 1 seconds
  Invalid after 15 seconds, hold down 15, flushed after 30
  Outgoing update filter list for all interfaces is not set
  Incoming update filter list for all interfaces is not set
  Default networks flagged in outgoing updates
  Default networks accepted from incoming updates
  IGRP metric weight K1=1, K2=0, K3=1, K4=0, K5=0
  IGRP maximum hopcount 100
  IGRP maximum metric variance 1
  Redistributing: igrp 64
  Routing for Networks:
    10.0.0.0
    148.1.0.0
    192.1.1.0
  Routing Information Sources:
    Gateway         Distance      Last Update
    192.1.1.2            100      00:16:28
  Distance: (default is 100)
```

{show ip route igrp} This exec command quickly displays all of the routes learned via IGRP. This method is a quick way to verify that a router is receiving IGRP updates.

```
RouterA#show ip route igrp
I     152.1.0.0/16 [100/10576] via 192.1.1.2, 00:00:00, Serial0
I     193.1.1.0/24 [100/10476] via 192.1.1.2, 00:00:00, Serial0
```

Conclusion

Because IGRP is a distance vector protocol, IGRP suffers from some of the same limitations as RIP—namely slow convergence. Unlike RIP, however, IGRP can scale across large networks. IGRPs maximum hop count of 255 enables the protocol to be run in even the largest networks. Also, because IGRP uses four metrics (Internetwork delay, bandwidth, reliability, and load) instead of one (hop count) to calculate route feasibility, this intuitive route selection provides optimal performance in even the most complex networks.

CHAPTER 8

Open Shortest Path First (OSPF)

Topics Covered in This Chapter

- Detailed technology overview
- OSPF terminology
- OSPF protocol packets
- Basic OSPF configuration
- Configuring OSPF priority "DR Election"
- Configuring OSPF virtual links
- Configuring OSPF neighbor authentication
- Configuring OSPF on NBMA network "Non-Broadcast Model"
- Configuring OSPF on NBMA network "Broadcast Model"
- Configuring OSPF on NBMA network "Point-to-Multipoint"
- Configure OSPF interface parameters
- Detailed troubleshooting examples

Introduction

Open Shortest Path First (OSPF) is a link state routing protocol developed for IP networks. OSPF was developed to be used within a single Autonomous System to distribute routing information. The following chapter will discuss terminology, key concepts, configuration issues, and troubleshooting techniques for OSPF-enabled networks.

OSPF Terminology

When dealing with OSPF, you should understand the terminology being used.

Autonomous System (**AS**): A group of routers that are under the control of a single administrative entity; for example, all of the routers belonging to a particular corporation.

Link State Advertisement (**LSA**): LSA is used to describe the local state of the router. The LSAs contain information about the state of the router's interfaces and the state of any adjacencies that are formed. The LSAs are flooded through the network. The information contained in the LSA sent by each router in the domain is used to form the router's topological database. From this information, a shortest path is calculated to each destination.

Area: An area is a collection of routers that has an identical topological database. OSPF uses areas to break an AS into multiple link-state domains. Because the topology of an area is invisible to another area, no flooding leaves an area. This feature greatly reduces the amount of routing traffic within an AS. Areas are used to contain link-state updates and to enable administrators to build hierarchical networks.

Cost: The metric that the router uses to compare routes to the same destination. The lower the cost, the more preferred the route. OSPF calculates the cost of using a link based on bandwidth. The higher the bandwidth, the lower the cost—and the more preferable the route.

Router ID: The router ID is a 32-bit number assigned to each OSPF-enabled router which is used to uniquely identify the router within an AS. The router ID calculated at boot time is the highest loopback address on the router. If no loopback interfaces are configured, the highest IP address on the router is used.

Adjacency: OSPF forms adjacencies between neighboring routers in order to exchange routing information. On a multi-access network, each router forms an adjacency with the designated router.

***Designated Router* (DR):** Used to reduce the number of adjacencies that need to be formed on a multi-access network such as Ethernet, Token Ring, or Frame Relay. The reduction in the amount of adjacencies formed greatly reduces the size of the topological database. The DR becomes adjacent with all other routers on the multi-access network. The routers send their LSAs to the DR, and the DR is responsible for forwarding them throughout the network. The idea behind a DR is that routers have a central point to which information is sent, versus every router exchanging information with every other router on the network.

***Backup Designated Router* (BDR):** Is formed on a multi-access network and is responsible for taking over for the DR if it should fail

Inter-Area Route: A route that is generated in an area other than the local one, inside the current OSPF routing domain

Intra-Area Route: A route that is within one area

Neighbor: Neighbors are routers that share a common network. For example, two routers on an Ethernet interface are said to be neighbors.

Flooding: A technique used to distribute LSAs between routers

Hello: A hello packet is used to establish and maintain neighbor relationships. The hello packet is also used to elect a DR for the network.

Technology Overview

Let's start with a brief introduction to OSPF before going into more detail. OSPF uses a link state algorithm to calculate the shortest path to all destinations in each area. When a router is first enabled, or if any routing changes occur, the router configured for OSPF floods LSAs to all routers in the same hierarchical area. The LSAs contain information about the state of the router's links and the router's relationship to its neighboring routers. From the collection of LSAs, the router forms what is called a link state database. All routers in an area have an identical database describing the area's topology.

The router then runs the Dijkstra algorithm using the link state database to form a shortest path tree to all destinations inside the area. From this shortest path tree, the IP routing table is formed. Any changes that occur on the network are flooded via link state packets and will cause the router to recalculate the shortest path tree using the new information.

Link State Routing Protocol

OSPF uses a link state algorithm to calculate the shortest path to all known destinations. Link state refers to the state of a router's interface (up, down, IP address, type of network, etc.) and the router's relationship to its neighbors (how the routers are connected on the network). The link states advertisements are flooded to each router and are used to create a topological database.

The Dijkstra algorithm is run on each router using the topological database, which is created by all LSAs received from all the routers in the area. The algorithm places each router at the root of the tree and calculates the shortest path to each destination based on the cost to reach that network.

Flooding

Flooding is the process of distributing link state advertisements between adjacent routers. The flooding procedure carries the LSA one hop further from its point of origin.

Because all routers in an OSPF domain are interconnected via adjacencies, the information disseminates throughout the network. To make this process reliable, each link state advertisement must be acknowledged.

Dijkstra Algorithm

The Dijkstra Algorithm is the heart of OSPF. Once the router receives all link state advertisements, the router then uses the Dijkstra Algorithm to calculate the shortest path to each destination inside the area (based on the cumulative cost to reach that destination). Each router will have a complete view of the network topology inside the area. The router builds a tree with itself as the root and has the entire path to any destination network or host.

The view of the topology from one router will be different from that of another, however, because each router uses itself as the root of the tree. The Dijkstra Algorithm is run any time a router receives a new link state advertisement.

Areas

OSPF uses areas to segment the AS and contain link state updates, as shown in Figure 8–1. LSAs are only flooded within an area, so separating the areas reduces the amount of routing traffic on a network.

Each router within an area has an identical topological database as all other routers in the same area. A router in multiple areas has a separate topological database for each area to which the router is connected.

Routers that have all of their interfaces within the same area are called *internal routers* (IR). Routers that connect areas within the same AS are called *Area Border Routers* (ABRs), and routers that act as gateways—redistributing routing information from one AS to another AS—are called *Autonomous System Border Routers* (ASBRs).

Figure 8–1
OSPF areas

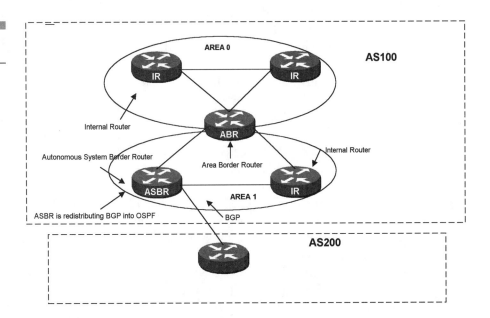

Backbone Area 0

OSPF has a concept of a backbone area, referred to as area 0. If multiple areas are configured, one of these areas must be configured as area 0. The backbone (area 0) is the center for all areas (i.e., all areas must have a connection to the backbone). In cases where an area does not have direct physical connectivity to the backbone, a virtual link must be configured. Virtual links will be discussed later in this chapter.

All areas inject routing information into the backbone area (area 0), and the backbone propagates routing information back to each area.

Designated Router (DR)

All multi-access networks with two or more attached routers elect a DR. The DR concept enables a reduction in the number of adjacencies that need to be formed on a network. In order for OSPF-enabled routers to exchange routing information, they must form an adjacency. If a DR was not used, then each router on a multi-access network would need to form an adjacency with every other router (because link state databases are synchronized across adjacencies). This process would result in N-1 adjacencies.

Instead, all routers on a multi-access network form adjacencies only with the DR and BDR. Each router sends the DR and BDR routing information, and the DR is responsible for flooding this information to all adjacent routers and originating a network link advertisement on behalf of the network. The backup DR is used in case the DR fails.

The reduction in adjacencies reduces the volume of routing protocol traffic, as well as the size of the topological database.

The DR is elected using the hello protocol, which was described earlier in this chapter. The election of the DR is determined by the router priority, which is carried in the hello packet. The router with the highest priority will be elected as the DR. If a tie occurs, the router with the highest router ID is selected.

The router ID is the IP address of the loopback interface. If no loopback is configured, the router ID is the highest IP address on the router. The router priority can be configured on the router interface with the **ip ospf priority** command.

When a router first becomes active on a multi-access network, the router checks to see whether there is currently a DR for the network. If a DR is present, the router accepts the DR regardless of its priority. Once a DR is elected, no other router can become the DR unless the DR fails.

If there is no DR present on the network, then the routers negotiate the DR based on router priority.

OSPF Protocol Packets

The OSPF protocol runs directly over IP protocol 89 and begins with the same 24-byte header (shown as follows):

0	8	16	24	31
Version Number	OSPF packet type	Packet length		
ROUTER ID				
AREA ID				
CHECKSUM		AUTHENTICATION TYPE		
AUTHENTICATION				
AUTHENTICATION				

There are five OSPF packet types:

Type	Packet Name	Protocol Function
1	Hello	Discover and maintain neighbors
2	Database Description	Summarize database contents
3	Link State Request	Request for database information
4	Link State Update	Database update
5	Link State Acknowledgment	Acknowledgment

Hello packets: The hello protocol is responsible for discovering neighbors and maintaining the neighbor relationship. Hello packets are sent periodically out the router's interface, depending on the network type. The hello protocol is also responsible for electing a DR on multi-access networks. The role of the DR was discussed earlier in this chapter.

Database Description Packets: Database description packets are OSPF type 2 packets. These packets are responsible for describing the contents of the Link State Database of the router and are one of the first steps to forming an adjacency. Database descriptor packets are sent in a poll response manner. One router is designated the master, and the other is designated as the slave. The master sends database polls which are acknowledged by the database descriptor packets, which are sent by the slave.

Link State Request Packets: Link state request packets are OSPF type 3 packets. Once the complete databases are exchanged between routers using the data base description packets, the routers compare the database of their neighbor with their own database. At this point, the router may find that parts of the neighbor's database may be more up-to-date than its own. If so, the router requests these pieces using the link state request packet.

Link State Update Packet: Link state update packets are OSPF packet type 4. The router uses a flooding technique to pass LSA. There are multiple LSA types (Router, Network, Summary, and External), which are described in detail later in this chapter.

Link State Acknowledgment Packet: Link state acknowledgments are OSPF type 4 packets, which are used to acknowledge the receipt of LSAs. This acknowledgment makes the OSPF flooding procedure reliable.

Link State Advertisements

Each of the router types mentioned in Figure 8–1 generates a different type of link state advertisements. Although there are more LSA types, we will only be discussing the four major LSAs.

All link state advertisements begin with the same 20-byte header (as follows):

0	16	24	31
LS age		Options	LS type
link state ID			
advertising router			
LS sequence number			
LS checksum		Length	

LS age: The time in seconds since the link state advertisement originated

Options: The optional capabilities supported by the router

LS type: The type of link state advertisement

Link State ID: This field identifies the portion of the Internet environment that is being described by the advertisement.

Advertising Router: The router ID of the router that originated the packet

LS sequence number: Used to detect old or duplicate link state advertisements

LS checksum: The checksum of the complete contents of the link state advertisement

Length: The length in bytes of the link state advertisement, including the 20-byte header

Router Link

Each router in the area generates a router LSA (type 1 LSA). This advertisement describes the state and cost of the router's interfaces to that area. All of the router's links to the area must be described in a single-router LSA. The router LSAs are only flooded throughout a single area.

Network Link

Network link advertisements are type 2 LSAs. The DR for each multi-access network that has more than one attached router originates a network advertisement. The advertisement describes all of the routers attached to the network, as well as the DR itself.

Summary Link

Summary LSAs are Type 3 and Type 4 LSAs. The ABR generates Summary LSAs, which describe a route to a single destination. The summary LSA is advertised within the single area, and the destination described is external to the area—yet is still part of the same AS. Only intra-area routes are advertised in the backbone.

External Link

The ASBR generates an external type 5 LSA, which advertises each destination known to the router that is external to the AS. AS external type 5 LSAs are used to advertise default routes into the AS.

There are two types of external routes: external type 1 and external type 2. The difference between the two is the way the cost or metric of the route is calculated. External type 1 routes use the external cost plus the internal cost of reaching a route. External type 2 only uses the external cost of reaching the route. Type 2 routes are always preferred over type 1 routes and are the default type for any route that is redistributed into OSPF.

How it Works

When an OSPF-enabled router first comes online, the router sends a hello packet to the multicast address 224.0.0.5. Then the packet is periodically sent out over all OSPF-enabled interfaces, depending on the interface type. For broadcast media such as Ethernet, Token Ring, or Point-to-Point interfaces, the hello packet is sent every 10 seconds. On a NBMA such as Frame Relay or ATM, the hello packet is sent out every 30 seconds.

The hello packets are not only used to build neighbor relationships and discover which neighbors are on the same wire, but they are also used to describe any optional capabilities of the router—such as whether the router is in a regular or stub area. The hello packet is also used to elect the DR on multi-access networks.

After the neighbor is discovered, bidirectional communication is assured, and a designated router is elected (on a multi-access media), the router attempts to form an adjacency with the neighboring router.

To form an adjacency, the routers must synchronize their databases. To complete this task, each router describes its databases to the other by sending a sequence of database description packets. This process is called the Database Exchange process and will be covered in more detail later in the chapter.

During the Database Exchange Process, the two routers form a master/slave relationship. Each database description packet sent by the master contains a sequence number. The slave acknowledges receipt of the packet by echoing the sequence number.

During the database exchange process, each router checks its own database to see whether any of the link state advertisements received by its neighbor are more recent than its own database copy. If any are, the router makes note of this fact, and after the database exchange process is over, the router requests updated LSAs using a link state request packet. Each router responds to the link state request using a link state update. When the requesting router receives the updated LSA, the router acknowledges the packet. When the database description process is complete and all link state requests have been updated, the databases are synchronized.

How an Adjacency is Formed

In order for a router to exchange link state database information with another router, an adjacency must be formed. This process is a key part of OSPF and therefore needs to be completely understood.

On a Cisco router, you can check the status of the adjacency using the **show ip ospf neighbor** command. The following example shows the output from this command. Notice that the state of the adjacency is full, which means that RouterB's database is synchronized with neighbor 1.1.1.1, which is RouterA.

```
RouterB#show ip ospf neighbor

Neighbor ID  Pri    State       Dead Time    Address       Interface
1.1.1.1       1     FULL/BDR    0:00:37      10.10.3.1     Ethernet0
```

There are five states that neighbor routers go through before fully forming an adjacency or having a full neighbor state. Figure 8–2 shows an example of how an adjacency is formed between two neighboring routers on a broadcast media. RouterA and RouterB both connect to an Ethernet network, and RouterB is configured with a higher DR priority.

When RouterA and RouterB first come online, they both initialize and begin sending hello packets. At this point in time, neither router knows of the presence of the other router on the network, and no DR is selected. RouterB hears the hello from RouterA, changing the state of the adjacency from down to Initializing (Init). This process can be seen from the **show ip ospf neighbor** command on RouterB.

```
RouterB#show ip ospf neighbor

Neighbor ID  Pri    State          Dead Time    Address       Interface
1.1.1.1       1     INIT/DROTHER   0:00:39      10.10.3.1     Ethernet0
```

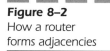

Figure 8–2
How a router
forms adjacencies

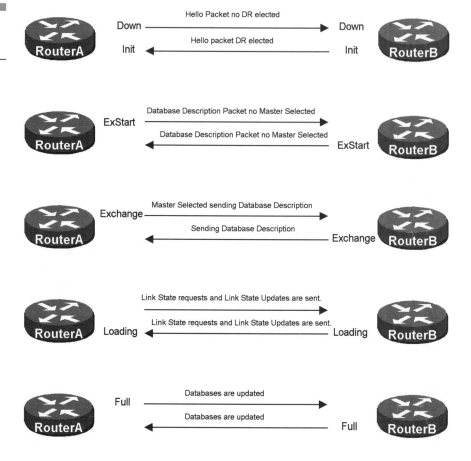

At this point, the routers have seen themselves in the hello packet from their neighbors, and bidirectional communication is established. The adjacency changes from Initializing to 2way. This process can be seen from the **show ip ospf neighbor** command on RouterB.

At the end of this stage, the DR and BDR is elected for the network, and the router then decides whether to form an adjacency with its neighbor. On a multi-access network, routers will only form adjacencies with the DR and BDR on the network.

```
Routerb#show ip ospf neighbor

Neighbor ID   Pri   State          Dead Time   Address      Interface
1.1.1.1       1     2WAY/DROTHER   0:00:3      10.10.3.1    Ethernet0
```

RouterB in the next hello packet indicates to RouterA that it is the DR for the link. At this point, the state of the adjacency changes from Initializing to Exchange (Exstart). This process can be seen from the **show ip ospf neighbor** command on RouterB. During the Exstart state, a master and slave relationship is formed between the two routers, and the slave router adopts the master's *Database Description* (DD) sequence number.

```
routerb#show ip ospf neighbor

Neighbor ID    Pri    State         Dead Time    Address       Interface
1.1.1.1        1      EXSTART/BDR   0:00:32      10.10.3.1
                              ↑RouterA is the Backup DR
```

After the master slave relationship is formed and the routers agree on a common DD sequence number, the routers begin to exchange database description packets. At this point, the state of the adjacency changes from Exstart to Exchange. This change can be seen from the **show ip ospf neighbor** command on RouterB.

```
routerb#show ip ospf neighbor

Neighbor ID    Pri    State          Dead Time    Address       Interface
1.1.1.1        1      EXCHANGE/DR    0:00:38      10.10.3.1     Ethernet0
```

After the complete databases are exchanged between routers using the DD packets, the routers compare the database of their neighbor with their own database. At this point, the router may find that parts of the neighbor's database may be more up-to-date than its own. If so, the router requests these pieces using a link state request packet. At this point, the state of the adjacency is loading. This process can be seen from the **show ip ospf neighbor** command on RouterB.

```
routerb#show ip ospf neighbor

Neighbor ID    Pri    State         Dead Time    Address       Interface
1.1.1.1        1      LOADING/DR    0:00:38      10.10.3.1     Ethernet0
```

After the link state update requests have all been satisfied, RouterA and RouterB databases are deemed synchronized—and the routers are fully adjacent. This process can be seen from the **show ip ospf neighbor** command on RouterB.

```
RouterB#show ip ospf neighbor

Neighbor ID    Pri    State       Dead Time    Address       Interface
1.1.1.1        1      FULL/BDR    0:00:37      10.10.3.1     Ethernet0
```

Figure 8–3
Database
synchronize process

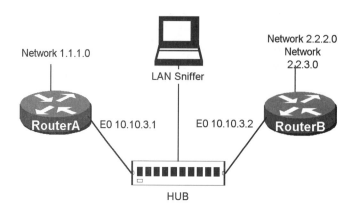

Sniffer Trace of Database Synchronization

Using a sniffer on an Ethernet LAN lets you examine how the database
synchronization process between two routers works. Figure 8–3 depicts
the setup.

Step 1: RouterA and RouterB send out hello packets. Notice that in the
first two packets, no DR is elected. In the third hello packet, RouterB is
elected the DR.

```
Hello From RouterA

Open Shortest Path First Protocol
        Version = 2, Type = Hello (1), Message len = 44
        Source gateway IP address = 1.1.1.1←Router ID of RouterA
        Area ID = 0.0.0.0←AREA of advertising Interface
        Checksum = 0xFA9C
        Authentication type = 0 (None), Value = 0000000000000000
        Network mask = 255.255.255.0
        Interval = 10 second(s)←Hello Interval
        Optional capabilities = 0X02
            .... ..1. = external routing capability
            .... ...0 = no Type of Service routing capability
        Router priority = 1←Priority used to select DR.
        Router dead interval = 40 second(s)←If the Router does not receive a
                                        Hello in 40 seconds, the neighbor
                                        is declared dead.
        Designated router = 0.0.0.0←No DR is elected.

Hello From RouterB

Open Shortest Path First Protocol
        Version = 2, Type = Hello (1), Message len = 44
        Source gateway IP address = 2.2.3.2←Router ID of RouterB
```

```
        Area ID = 0.0.0.0←AREA of advertising Interface
        Checksum = 0xF79A
        Authentication type = 0 (None), Value = 0000000000000000
        Network mask = 255.255.255.0
        Interval = 10 second(s)←Hello Interval
        Optional capabilities = 0X02
             .... ..1. = external routing capability
             .... ...0 = no Type of Service routing capability
        Router priority = 1←Priority used to select DR
        Router dead interval = 40 second(s)←If the Router does not receive a
                                            Hello in 40 seconds, the neighbor
                                            is declared dead.
        Designated router = 0.0.0.0←No DR is elected.
```

Hello From RouterB

```
Open Shortest Path First Protocol
        Version = 2, Type = Hello (1), Message len = 48
        Source gateway IP address = 2.2.3.2
        Area ID = 0.0.0.0
        Checksum = 0xDB7D
        Authentication type = 0 (None), Value = 0000000000000000
        Network mask = 255.255.255.0
        Interval = 10 second(s)
        Optional capabilities = 0X02
             .... ..1. = external routing capability
             .... ...0 = no Type of Service routing capability
        Router priority = 1
        Router dead interval = 40 second(s)
        Designated router = 2.2.3.2←RouterB is elected DR.
```

> **Step 2**: RouterB was selected as the designated router, and now the routers exchange database description packets. The first packet is just an initialization packet and contains no database information. RouterB becomes the master because it has the higher router ID.

Database Description Packet From RouterB

```
Open Shortest Path First Protocol
        Version = 2, Type = Database Desp. (2), Message len = 32
        Source gateway IP address = 2.2.3.2
        Area ID = 0.0.0.0
        Checksum = 0xD519
        Authentication type = 0 (None), Value = 0000000000000000
          Optional capabilities = 0X02
             .... ..1. = external routing capability
             .... ...0 = no Type of Service routing capability
        Init = 1, More = 1, Master←RouterB is the Master.
        ↑
        This is an Initialization packet.
     DD Sequence number = 8633←The sequence number is 8633.
```

Step 3: RouterA and RouterB continue to send database description packets, with polls coming from the master and responses coming from the slave. Both the polls from the master and responses from the slave contain summaries of the link state database. This exchange is done when both the poll from the master and the response from the slave have the *More bit* (M-bit) off or set to zero.

```
Database Description Packet From RouterA

Open Shortest Path First Protocol
        Version = 2, Type = Database Desp. (2), Message len = 52
        Source gateway IP address = 1.1.1.1
        Area ID = 0.0.0.0
        Checksum = 0x5199
        Authentication type = 0 (None), Value = 0000000000000000
          Optional capabilities = 0X02
            .... ..1. = external routing capability
            .... ...0 = no Type of Service routing capability
        Init = 0, More = 1, Slave
        DD Sequence number = 8633
        Link state advertisement #1:
          LS age = 40 seconds
        Optional capabilities = 0X22
            .... ..1. = external routing capability
            .... ...0 = no Type of Service routing capability
          LS type = Router links
          Link state ID = 1.1.1.1
          Advertising router = 1.1.1.1
          LS Sequence number = 2147483650,    LS checksum = 0xE013,
          Length = 48

Database Description Packet From RouterB

Open Shortest Path First Protocol
        Version = 2, Type = Database Desp. (2), Message len = 52
        Source gateway IP address = 2.2.3.2
        Area ID = 0.0.0.0
        Checksum = 0x7A7B
        Authentication type = 0 (None), Value = 0000000000000000
          Optional capabilities = 0X02
            .... ..1. = external routing capability
            .... ...0 = no Type of Service routing capability
        Init = 0, More = 1, Master
        DD Sequence number = 8634
        Link state advertisement #1:
          LS age = 40 seconds←This is the age of the LSA.
        Optional capabilities = 0X02
            .... ..1. = external routing capability
            .... ...0 = no Type of Service routing capability
          LS type = Router links
          Link state ID = 2.2.3.2
          Advertising router = 2.2.3.2
```

```
     LS Sequence number = 2147483651,    LS checksum = 0xCE1C,
     Length = 60
```

Database Description Packet From RouterA

```
Open Shortest Path First Protocol
        Version = 2, Type = Database Desp. (2), Message len = 32
        Source gateway IP address = 1.1.1.1
        Area ID = 0.0.0.0
        Checksum = 0xD821
        Authentication type = 0 (None), Value = 0000000000000000
          Optional capabilities = 0X02
          .... ..1. = external routing capability
          .... ...0 = no Type of Service routing capability
      Init = 0, More = 0, Slave←The M-bit is set to zero this is the end of
                              the database exchange.
        DD Sequence number = 8634
```

Step 4: Now that RouterA and RouterB have exchanged database information, each router looks at its own database and compares that information with the information it just received for its neighbor. If the information in its database is not as current as the information received from the neighbor, the router will request that this information be sent. This process is done using a link state request packet.

Link State Request From RouterB

```
Open Shortest Path First Protocol
        Version = 2, Type = LS Req. (3), Message len = 36
        Source gateway IP address = 2.2.3.2
        Area ID = 0.0.0.0
        Checksum = 0xF4CF
        Authentication type = 0 (None), Value = 0000000000000000
        Link state advertisement #1:
          LS type = Router links
          LS ID = 1.1.1.1
          Advertising router = 1.1.1.1
```

Link State Request From RouterA

```
Open Shortest Path First Protocol
        Version = 2, Type = LS Req. (3), Message len = 36
        Source gateway IP address = 1.1.1.1
        Area ID = 0.0.0.0
        Checksum = 0xF1CD
        Authentication type = 0 (None), Value = 0000000000000000
        Link state advertisement #1:
          LS type = Router links
          LS ID = 2.2.3.2
          Advertising router = 2.2.3.2
```

Step 5: After the router receives a link state request packet from its neighbor, the router sends the piece of the database that is requested. When the router receives the update, the router sends an acknowledgment packet back to the sender acknowledging receipt of the packet.

Link State Update from RouterA

```
Open Shortest Path First Protocol
        Version = 2, Type = LS Upd. (4), Message len = 76
        Source gateway IP address = 1.1.1.1
        Area ID = 0.0.0.0
        Checksum = 0x611E
        Authentication type = 0 (None), Value = 0000000000000000
        Number of advertisements = 1
        Link state advertisement #1:
          LS age = 41 seconds
        Optional capabilities = 0X22
            .... ..1. = external routing capability
            .... ...0 = no Type of Service routing capability
          LS type = Router links
          Link state ID = 1.1.1.1
          Advertising router = 1.1.1.1
          LS Sequence number = 2147483650,    LS checksum = 0xE013,
          Length = 48
          Router type flag = Unknown (0x00)
          Number of router links = 2
          Router link #1:
            Link ID = 10.10.3.0
            Link data = 255.255.255.0
            Link type = Connection to a stub network
            Number of TOS = 0, TOS 0 metric = 10
          Router link #2:
            Link ID = 1.1.1.1
            Link data = BROADCAST
            Link type = Connection to a stub network
            Number of TOS = 0, TOS 0 metric = 1
        Link state advertisement #2:
```

Link State Update from RouterB

```
Open Shortest Path First Protocol
        Version = 2, Type = LS Upd. (4), Message len = 88
        Source gateway IP address = 2.2.3.2
        Area ID = 0.0.0.0
        Checksum = 0x7FEE
        Authentication type = 0 (None), Value = 0000000000000000
        Number of advertisements = 1
      Link state advertisement #1:
          LS age = 41 seconds
        Optional capabilities = 0X02
            .... ..1. = external routing capability
            .... ...0 = no Type of Service routing capability
          LS type = Router links
```

```
          Link state ID = 2.2.3.2
          Advertising router = 2.2.3.2
          LS Sequence number = 2147483651,    LS checksum = 0xCE1C,
          Length = 60
          Router type flag = Unknown (0x00)
          Number of router links = 3
          Router link #1:
            Link ID = 2.2.2.2
            Link data = BROADCAST
            Link type = Connection to a stub network
            Number of TOS = 0, TOS 0 metric = 1
          Router link #2:
            Link ID = 2.2.3.2
            Link data = BROADCAST
            Link type = Connection to a stub network
            Number of TOS = 0, TOS 0 metric = 1
          Router link #3:
            Link ID = 10.10.3.0
            Link data = 255.255.255.0
            Link type = Connection to a stub network
            Number of TOS = 0, TOS 0 metric = 10
       Link state advertisement #2:
```

Link State Acknowledgment from RouterA

```
Open Shortest Path First Protocol
        Version = 2, Type = LS Ack. (5), Message len = 64
        Source gateway IP address = 1.1.1.1
        Area ID = 0.0.0.0
        Checksum = 0x7F58
        Authentication type = 0 (None), Value = 0000000000000000
        Link state advertisement #1:
          LS age = 41 seconds
        Optional capabilities = 0X02
            .... ..1. = external routing capability
            .... ...0 = no Type of Service routing capability
          LS type = Router links
          Link state ID = 2.2.3.2
          Advertising router = 2.2.3.2
          LS Sequence number = 2147483651,    LS checksum = 0xCE1C,
          Length = 60
        Link state advertisement #2:
          LS age = 1 seconds
        Optional capabilities = 0X02
            .... ..1. = external routing capability
            .... ...0 = no Type of Service routing capability
          LS type = Network links
          Link state ID = 10.10.3.2
          Advertising router = 2.2.3.2
          LS Sequence number = 2147483649,    LS checksum = 0x8D9D,
          Length = 32
```

Link State Acknowledgment from RouterB

```
Open Shortest Path First Protocol
```

```
Version = 2, Type = LS Ack. (5), Message len = 44
Source gateway IP address = 2.2.3.2
Area ID = 0.0.0.0
Checksum = 0x52B2
Authentication type = 0 (None), Value = 0000000000000000
Link state advertisement #1:
  LS age = 6 seconds
Optional capabilities = 0X22
    .... ..1. = external routing capability
    .... ...0 = no Type of Service routing capability
  LS type = Router links
  Link state ID = 1.1.1.1
  Advertising router = 1.1.1.1
  LS Sequence number = 2147483651,    LS checksum = 0xFFD9,
  Length = 48
```

Step 6: All link state requests have been fulfilled, the databases are synchronized, and the routers are fully adjacent.

OSPF Network Types

OSPF has four network types or models (broadcast, non-broadcast, point-to-point, and point-to-multipoint). Depending on the network type, OSPF works differently. Understanding how OSPF works on each network model is essential in designing a stable and robust OSPF network.

Broadcast

The broadcast network type is the default type on LANs (Token Ring, Ethernet, and FDDI). Any interface, however, can be configured as broadcast using the **ip ospf network** interface command.

- On a broadcast model, both a DR and BDR are elected, and all routers form adjacencies with the DR and BDR. This achieves optimal flooding, because all LSAs are sent to the DR—and the DR floods them to each individual router on the network.

- Neighbors do not need to be defined.

- All routers are on the same subnet.

- Care must be taken if the broadcast model is used on NBMA networks, such as Frame Relay or ATM. Since a DR is elected, all routers must have physical connectivity to the DR. A full, meshed environment should be used, or the DR should be statically configured using the priority command to assure physical connectivity.

■ The hello timer is 10 seconds, the dead interval is 40 seconds, and the wait interval is 40 seconds.

In Figure 8–4, RouterA and RouterC are connected via Frame Relay to RouterB. The network is a hub-and-spoke environment configured as an OSPF network-type broadcast.

Because RouterB is the only router that has logical connectivity to each router on the network, this router must be elected the DR.

If a broadcast model is used on an NBMA network, all routers should be fully meshed—or care should be taken on which router is elected DR. In a hub-and-spoke environment, the hub should be configured as the DR.

The following example shows the output from the command **show ip ospf interface**. Note that the command shows the network type, along with other key OSPF parameters.

```
Routerb#show ip ospf interface e0
Ethernet0 is up, line protocol is up
   Internet Address 10.10.3.2 255.255.255.0, Area 0
   Process ID 64, Router ID 2.2.3.2, Network Type BROADCAST, Cost: 10
   Transmit Delay is 1 sec, State BDR, Priority 1
   Designated Router (ID) 9.9.21.9, Interface address 10.10.3.1
   Backup Designated router (ID) 2.2.3.2, Interface address 10.10.3.2
   Timer intervals configured, Hello 10, Dead 40, Wait 40, Retransmit 5
```

Figure 8–4
NBMA using a network-type broadcast

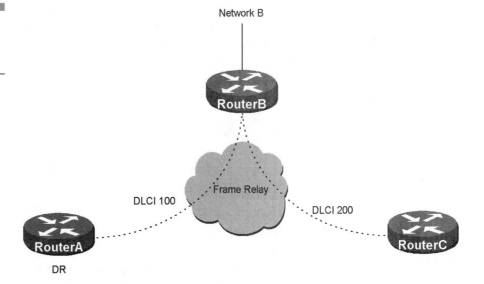

```
Hello due in 0:00:07
Neighbor Count is 1, Adjacent neighbor count is 1
  Adjacent with neighbor 9.9.21.9  (Designated Router)
```

Non-Broadcast

The non-broadcast network type is the default type on serial interfaces configured for Frame Relay encapsulation. Any interface can be configured as non-broadcast, however, using the **ip ospf network interface** command.

- With the non-broadcast model, a DR and BDR are elected, and all routers form adjacencies with the DR and BDR. This alliance achieves optimized flooding, because all LSAs are sent to the DR—and the DR floods them to each individual router on the network.
- Due to the lack of broadcast capabilities, neighbors must be defined using the neighbor command.
- All routers are on the same subnet.
- Similar to the broadcast model, a DR is elected. Care must be taken to assure that the DR has logical connectivity to all routers on the network.
- The hello timer is 30 seconds, the dead interval is 120 seconds, and the wait interval is 120 seconds.

The following example shows the output from the command **show ip ospf interface serial 0**, which is configured for Frame Relay encapsulation. Note that the command shows the network type, along with other key OSPF parameters.

```
Serial0 is up, line protocol is down
  Internet Address 193.1.1.1 255.255.255.0, Area 0
  Process ID 64, Router ID 2.2.3.2, Network Type NON_BROADCAST, Cost: 64
  Transmit Delay is 1 sec, State DOWN, Priority 1
  No designated router on this network
  No backup designated router on this network
  Timer intervals configured, Hello 30, Dead 120, Wait 120, Retransmit 5
```

Point-to-Point

The network type point-to-point is the default type on serial interfaces that are not using Frame Relay encapsulation or can be selected as a subinterface type point-to-point. A sub-interface is a logical way of defining an interface. The same physical interface can be split into multiple logical interfaces. This concept was originally created to deal with issues caused by split horizons on NBMA networks.

The point-to-point model can be configured on any interface using the **ip ospf network point-to-point** interface command.

- With a point-to-point model, neither a DR nor a BDR are elected, and directly connected routers form adjacencies.

- Each point-to-point link requires a separate subnet.

- The hello timer is 10 seconds, the dead interval is 40 seconds, and the wait interval is 40 seconds.

The following example shows the output from the command **show ip ospf interface serial 0**, which is not configured for Frame Relay encapsulation. Note that the command shows the network type, along with other key OSPF parameters.

```
Routerb#show ip ospf interface s0
Serial0 is up, line protocol is down
   Internet Address 193.1.1.1 255.255.255.0, Area 0
   Process ID 64, Router ID 2.2.3.2, Network Type POINT_TO_POINT, Cost: 64
   Transmit Delay is 1 sec, State DOWN,
   Timer intervals configured, Hello 10, Dead 40, Wait 40, Retransmit 5
```

Point-to-Multipoint

The network type point-to-multipoint can be configured on any interface using the **ip ospf network point-to-multipoint** interface command.

- No DR is elected.

- Neighbors do not need to be defined, because additional LSAs are used to convey neighbor router connectivity.

- One subnet is used for the whole network.

- The hello timer is 30 seconds, the dead interval is 120 seconds, and the wait interval is 120 seconds.

The following example shows the output from the command **show ip ospf interface serial 0**. Notice that the command shows the network type, along with other key OSPF parameters.

```
routerb#show ip ospf interface s0
Serial0 is up, line protocol is down
```

```
Internet Address 193.1.1.1 255.255.255.0, Area 0
Process ID 64, Router ID 2.2.3.2, Network Type POINT_TO_MULTIPOINT, Cost: 64
Transmit Delay is 1 sec, State DOWN,
Timer intervals configured, Hello 30, Dead 120, Wait 120, Retransmit 5
```

Commands Discussed in This Chapter

- **area** area-id **authentication** [message-digest]
- **area** area-id **range** address mask
- **debug ip ospf events**
- **debug ip ospf packet**
- **ip ospf authentication-key** password
- **ip ospf cost** cost
- **ip ospf dead-interval** seconds
- **ip ospf hello-interval** seconds
- **ip ospf message-digest-key** keyid **md5** key
- **ip ospf network** {broadcast | non-broadcast | point-to-multipoint}
- **ip ospf priority** number
- **neighbor** ip-address [priority number] [poll-interval seconds]
- **network** *address wildcard-mask* **area** *area-id*
- **passive-interface** type number
- **router ospf** process-id
- **show ip ospf** [process-id]
- **show ip ospf** [process-id area-id] database
- **show ip ospf interface** [type number]
- **show ip ospf neighbor** [type number] [neighbor-id] detail
- **show ip ospf virtual-links**

Definitions

area authentication: This router configuration command enables authentication for an OSPF area. Authentication assures that the routing information being received by the router is from a trusted source.

area range: This router configuration command consolidates and summarizes routes at an area boundary.

debug ip ospf events: The output for this Exec command displays OSPF information such as adjacencies, flooding information, designated router selection, and *shortest path first* (SPF) calculations.

debug ip ospf packet: The output from this Exec command displays detailed OSPF information for all OSPF packets received by the router.

ip ospf authentication-key: This interface configuration command is used to assign a password that will be used by neighboring routers if simple password authentication is configured on the router.

ip ospf cost: This interface configuration command sets the OSPF cost for sending a packet out that particular interface. Cisco uses bandwidth as a metric for best path selection; i.e., an Ethernet interface is preferred over a T1 interface. This command would be used if the administrator wished to change the default cost of an interface or show preference for one identical interface over another. The path cost is calculated using the following formula: cost=100,000,000/bandwidth in bits per second. The cost is inversely proportional to the bandwidth of the link. The higher the bandwidth, the lower the cost.

ip ospf dead-interval: This interface configuration command sets the amount of time in seconds that a router will wait before declaring a neighbor router dead after not receiving a hello packet.

ip ospf hello-interval: This interface configuration command sets the interval in seconds that OSPF hello packets are sent out the router interface.

ip ospf message-digest-key: This interface configuration command enables OSPF MD5 authentication.

ip ospf network: This interface configuration command will change the OSPF network type to a type other than the default for a given media.

ip ospf priority: This interface configuration command is used to set the priority of the router interface, which is used for DR election. The router with the highest priority will be elected the DR for the multi-access network. If two routers have the same OSPF priority, the router with the highest router ID will be elected the DR. A router with a priority of zero is ineligible to become the DR or BDR. In some cases, particularly on NBMAs such as Frame Relay or ATM, it is necessary to specify which router becomes the DR for the network. In Figure 8–5, because RouterB is the only router that has full logical connectivity (meaning that RouterB is the only router with a PVC to every router on the network) to all the routers on the network, it is essential that this router is elected the DR. If Router A was elected DR, RouterC and RouterD would not be able to form an adjacency with RouterA, because they do not have logical connectivity.

neighbor: This router configuration command is used on non-broadcast networks (due to the lack of broadcast capabilities) to define OSPF neighbors. On broadcast networks, this command is not needed, because neighbors are found using the hello protocol. On NBMA networks, the neighbor commands must be defined on any router that has the potential of becoming the DR or BDR. The neighbor command has two optional parameters associated with it: OSPF neighbor priority and the poll interval. The OPSF neighbor priority is an 8-bit number indicating the priority value of the non-broadcast neighbor associated with the IP address specified. The OSPF priority is used in DR and BDR election. The router with the highest priority will be elected the DR. A router with an OSPF priority of zero is not eligible for DR election. The poll interval is used if a neighboring router has become inactive (when hello packets have not been seen for a period of time which exceeds the router's dead interval). It may still be necessary to send hello packets to the

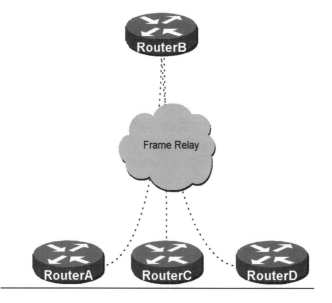

Figure 8–5
Designated router
on NBMA network

dead neighbor. In this case, the hello packets will be sent at a reduced rate—which is the defined poll interval. It is recommended that the poll interval should be larger than the hello interval. The default is 120 seconds.

network: This router configuration command defines what interface OSPF will run on and what OSPF area in which the interface will reside. A wild card mask is used in conjunction with the IP address, which enables the user to specify one or more interfaces in an area using only a single command. When using a wild card mask, a 0 means "must match," while a 1 means "does not matter." In the following example, OSPF process 64 is defined. The first line only enables OSPF on one interface: 192.1.1.1. Line 2 enables OSPF on any interface with an IP address 132.10.x.x, and line 3 enables OSPF on all interfaces on the router.

```
router ospf 64
network 192.1.1.1  0.0.0.0 area 1
                   ↑Wild Card Mask of all zero specifies one particular
                   address
network 132.10.0.0  0.0.255.255 area 2
                   ↑This Wild Card Mask specifies that only the first two
                   Octets must match.
network 0.0.0.0  255.255.255.255 area 0
                   ↑A wild card mask of all ones specifies any interface on
                   the router.
```

passive-interface: This router configuration command disables the sending and receiving of OSPF router information. The specified interface address appears as a stub network in the OSPF domain.

router ospf: This global configuration command enables an OSPF process on the router. The OSPF process number is an internally used identification parameter. Multiple OSPF processes can be defined on the same router.

show ip ospf interface: This exec command displays information about all OSPF-configured interfaces.

show ip ospf: This exec command displays information about the OSPF process.

show ip ospf neighbor: This exec command displays information about all OPSF neighbors.

show ip ospf virtual-links: This exec command displays information about the current state of any configured virtual links.

IOS Requirements

OSPF first appeared in IOS 10.0; however, some of the commands described in this chapter require later IOS versions.

Lab #28: Basic OSPF Configuration

Equipment Needed

The following equipment is needed to perform this lab exercise:

- Two Cisco routers, each having one serial port
- Cisco IOS 10.0 or higher
- A PC running a terminal emulation program
- One Cisco DTE/DCE crossover cable
- A Cisco rolled cable for console port access

Configuration Overview

This configuration will demonstrate basic OSPF configuration on a Cisco router. As per Figure 8–6, RouterA and RouterB will be running OSPF to advertise routing information.

RouterA and RouterB are connected serially via a crossover cable. RouterB will act as the DCE, supplying clock to RouterA. The IP addresses are assigned as per Figure 8–6. RouterA and RouterB have loopback interfaces defined to provide a test point.

Enabling OSPF

There are two steps to enabling OSPF on a router. First, an OSPF process is defined, and then an interface is added to the process. The command to start an OSPF process is **Router OSPF [Process #]**. The process number is used internally by the router. Multiple OSPF routing processes can be configured on one router.

Figure 8.6
Basic OSPF
configuration

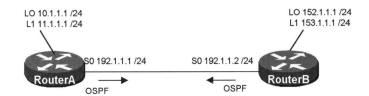

The following command enables OSPF process 64 on the router and assigns all interfaces on the router to area 0:

```
router ospf 64
network 0.0.0.0 255.255.255.255 area 0
```

Router Configurations

The configurations for the two routers in this example are as follows (key OSPF configurations are highlighted in bold):

RouterA

```
version 11.2
no service udp-small-servers
no service tcp-small-servers
!
hostname RouterA
!
interface Loopback0←Defines a virtual interface that will be used as a test point
 ip address 10.1.1.1 255.255.255.0
 !

interface Loopback1←Defines a virtual interface that will be used as a test point
 ip address 11.1.1.1 255.255.255.0

 !
 !
interface Serial0/0
 ip address 192.1.1.1 255.255.255.0
 no fair-queue
 !
```

```
!
```
router ospf 64←Enables OSPF process 64 on the router.
               ↓Wild Card Mask can be used to specify multiple
               interfaces with one command.
  network 192.1.1.1 0.0.0.0 area 0←Specifies what interface OSPF will be run
      ↑   and what area the interface will be in.
The IP address of the interface that OSPF will run on in this case interface
S0.

network 10.1.1.1 0.0.0.0 area 0

```
!
no ip classless
!
!
line con 0
line aux 0
line vty 0 4
 login
!
end
```

RouterB

```
version 11.2

no service udp-small-servers
no service tcp-small-servers
!
hostname RouterB
!
!
!
```
interface Loopback0←Defines a virtual interface that will be used as a test
point
```
 ip address 152.1.1.1 255.255.255.0
!
```

interface Loopback1←Defines a virtual interface that will be used as a test
point
```
 ip address 153.1.1.1 255.255.255.0

!
interface Serial0/0
 ip address 192.1.1.2 255.255.255.0
 no fair-queue
```
 clockrate 500000←Acts as DCE providing clock
```
!
interface Serial1
 no ip address
 shutdown
```

```
!
router ospf 64←Enables OSPF process 64 on the router.

        ↓An IP address of all zeros and a  Wild Card Mask of all ones
          enables OSPF on all interfaces.
network 0.0.0.0 255.255.255.255 area 0←Specifies what interface OSPF will be
                                        run on and what area the interface will
                                        be in.
!
no ip classless
!
!
line con 0
line aux 0
line vty 0 4
 login
!
end
```

Monitoring and Testing the Configuration

Show the IP routing table on RouterA with the command **show ip route**. The following example shows the output from this command. Notice that two host-specific routes were learned via OSPF: 152.1.1.1 and 153.1.1.1. This situation occurred because loopback interfaces are treated as stub hosts.

```
RouterA#show ip route
Codes: C - connected, S - static, I - IGRP, R - RIP, M - mobile, B - BGP
       D - EIGRP, EX - EIGRP external, O - OSPF, IA - OSPF inter area
       N1 - OSPF NSSA external type 1, N2 - OSPF NSSA external type 2
       E1 - OSPF external type 1, E2 - OSPF external type 2, E - EGP
       i - IS-IS, L1 - IS-IS level-1, L2 - IS-IS level-2, * - candidate default
       U - per-user static route, o - ODR

Gateway of last resort is not set

     10.0.0.0/24 is subnetted, 1 subnets
C       10.1.1.0 is directly connected, Loopback0
     11.0.0.0/24 is subnetted, 1 subnets
C       11.1.1.0 is directly connected, Loopback1
     153.1.0.0/32 is subnetted, 1 subnets
O       153.1.1.1 [110/65] via 192.1.1.2, 00:00:41, Serial0/0
     152.1.0.0/32 is subnetted, 1 subnets
O       152.1.1.1 [110/65] via 192.1.1.2, 00:00:41, Serial0/0
C    192.1.1.0/24 is directly connected, Serial0/0
```

Show the IP routing table on RouterB with the command **show ip route**. The following example shows the output from the command. Notice that only one host-specific route was learned via OSPF: 10.1.1.1.

```
RouterB#show ip route
Codes: C - connected, S - static, I - IGRP, R - RIP, M - mobile, B - BGP
       D - EIGRP, EX - EIGRP external, O - OSPF, IA - OSPF inter area
       N1 - OSPF NSSA external type 1, N2 - OSPF NSSA external type 2
       E1 - OSPF external type 1, E2 - OSPF external type 2, E - EGP
       i - IS-IS, L1 - IS-IS level-1, L2 - IS-IS level-2, * - candidate default
       U - per-user static route, o - ODR

Gateway of last resort is not set

     10.0.0.0/32 is subnetted, 1 subnets
O        10.1.1.1 [110/65] via 192.1.1.1, 00:17:16, Serial0/0
     153.1.0.0/24 is subnetted, 1 subnets
C        153.1.1.0 is directly connected, Loopback1
     152.1.0.0/24 is subnetted, 1 subnets
C        152.1.1.0 is directly connected, Loopback0
     C       192.1.1.0/24 is directly connected, Serial0/0
```

The numbers after the destination address [110/65] are the administrative distance and the routing metric, respectively. The administrative distance is used by the router to compare routes learned from multiple routing protocols. For example, if the router learned about network 10.1.1.0 from OSPF and RIP, the router would prefer the route learned via OPSF—because OSPF has a lower administrative distance than RIP (110 versus 120).

The second number is the metric or cost of using the route, which is inversely proportional to the bandwidth of a link. The router uses the metric to compare routes, which are learned via the same routing protocol. For example, if the router learned about network 10.1.1.0 from two separate routers running OSPF, it would prefer the route with the lower metric.

From RouterA, use the command **show ip ospf interface** to display the interfaces on which OSPF is configured. The following example shows the output from this command. Notice that on RouterA, interface s0/0 and interface loopback 0 are configured for OSPF and are in area 0. The command also shows the network type, timer intervals, and adjacent neighbors.

```
RouterA#show ip ospf interface
Ethernet0/0 is administratively down, line protocol is down
   OSPF not enabled on this interface
Serial0/0 is up, line protocol is up
   Internet Address 192.1.1.1/24, Area 0
   Process ID 64, Router ID 11.1.1.1, Network Type POINT_TO_POINT, Cost: 64
   Transmit Delay is 1 sec, State POINT_TO_POINT,
   Timer intervals configured, Hello 10, Dead 40, Wait 40, Retransmit 5
     Hello due in 00:00:03
   Neighbor Count is 1, Adjacent neighbor count is 1
     Adjacent with neighbor 152.1.1.1
   Suppress hello for 0 neighbor(s)
Serial0/1 is administratively down, line protocol is down
   OSPF not enabled on this interface
```

```
Loopback0 is up, line protocol is up
   Internet Address 10.1.1.1/24, Area 0
   Process ID 64, Router ID 11.1.1.1, Network Type LOOPBACK, Cost: 1
   Loopback interface is treated as a stub Host
Loopback1 is up, line protocol is up
     OSPF not enabled on this interface
```

From RouterB, use the command **show ip ospf neighbors** to display the status of the router's neighbors. The following example shows the output from the command. Notice that the neighbor ID is 11.1.1.1. This number is the IP address of the loopback interface. The loopback interface is always used as the router ID. If no loopback interface is configured, then the highest IP address on the router is used.

```
RouterB#show ip ospf neighbor

Neighbor ID     Pri   State     Dead Time   Address     Interface
11.1.1.1        1     FULL/-    00:00:37    192.1.1.1   Serial0/0
```

The state of the adjacency is [Full/-], which means that RouterA's and RouterB's databases are synchronized and that the routers are fully adjacent. Full is the last state of forming an adjacency. The other states are described in detail earlier in the chapter. The — indicates that there is no DR or BDR and appears on point-to-point interfaces, where there is no concept of DR or BDR.

Lab #29: Configuring OSPF Priority "DR Election"

Equipment Needed

The following equipment is needed to perform this lab exercise:

- Four Cisco routers with Ethernet interfaces
- Cisco IOS 10.0 or higher
- A PC running a terminal emulation program
- Four Ethernet cables and one Ethernet hub
- A Cisco rolled cable for console port access

Configuration Overview

This configuration will demonstrate configuring OSPF priority on an interface to influence the selection of the DR and BDR. As per Figure 8–7,

Figure 8–7
DR election

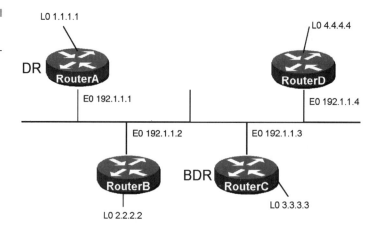

four routers are connected to an Ethernet hub and are all running OSPF to advertise routing information.

RouterA will be set with an OSPF priority of 100, which will be the highest priority on the network—so RouterA will be selected as the DR. RouterC will have the second-highest priority (2) and will be elected the BDR. RouterB will be set for a priority of zero, which means that it not eligible for becoming the DR. RouterD has no priority set and defaults to a priority of 1.

The IP addresses are assigned as per Figure 8–7. All routers have loop-back interfaces defined for test purposes.

Router Configurations

The configurations for the two routers in this example are as follows (key OSPF configurations are highlighted in bold):

RouterA

```
!
version 11.2
no service udp-small-servers
no service tcp-small-servers
!
hostname RouterA
!
!
!
```

```
interface Loopback0←Defines a virtual interface that will be used as a test
                    point
 ip address 1.1.1.1 255.255.255.0
!
interface Ethernet0/0
 ip address 192.1.1.1 255.255.255.0
 ip ospf priority 100←Sets the priority used by the router in DR election for
                    a particular interface
!
interface Serial0/0
 no ip address
 shutdown
!


!
router ospf 64←Enables OSPF process 64 on the router
 network 192.1.1.0 0.0.0.255 area 0←Specifies what interface OSPF will be run
                                   and what area the I interface will be in

   network 1.1.1.1 0.0.0.0 area 0
!
no ip classless
!
!
line con 0
line aux 0
line vty 0 4
 login
!
end
```

RouterB

```
Current configuration:
!
version 11.2
no service udp-small-servers
no service tcp-small-servers
!
hostname RouterB
!
interface Loopback0←Defines a virtual interface that will be used as a test
                    point
 ip address 2.2.2.2 255.255.255.0
!
interface Ethernet0/0
 ip address 192.1.1.2 255.255.255.0
 ip ospf priority 0←Sets the priority used by the router in DR election for a
                    particular interface. An OSPF priority of zero means that
                    the router is ineligible in the DR election process.
```

```
!
!
router ospf 64←Enables OSPF process 64 on the router
 network 192.1.1.0 0.0.0.255 area 0←Specifies what interface OSPF will be run
                                    and what area the I interface will be in.

 network 2.2.2.2 0.0.0.0 area 0
!
no ip classless
!
!
line con 0
line aux 0
line vty 0 4
 login
!
end
```

RouterC

```
Current configuration:
!
version 11.2
no service udp-small-servers
no service tcp-small-servers
!
hostname RouterC
!
interface Loopback0←Defines a virtual interface that will be used as a test
                    point
 ip address 3.3.3.3 255.255.255.0
!
interface Ethernet0/0
 ip address 192.1.1.3 255.255.255.0
 ip ospf priority 2←Sets the priority used by the router in DR election for a
                    particular interface.

!
!
router ospf 64←Enables OSPF process 64 on the router
 network 3.3.3.3 0.0.0.0 area 0←Specifies what interface OSPF will be run on
                                and what area the interface will be in.
network 192.1.1.0 0.0.0.255 area 0
!
no ip classless
!
!
line con 0
line aux 0
```

```
line vty 0 4
 login
!
end
```

RouterD

```
Current configuration:
!
version 11.2
no service udp-small-servers
no service tcp-small-servers
!
hostname RouterD
!
!
interface Loopback0←Defines a virtual interface that will be used as a test
                    point
 ip address 4.4.4.4 255.255.255.0
!
interface Ethernet0/0
 ip address 192.1.1.4 255.255.255.0
!
interface Serial0/0
 no ip address
 shutdown
 no fair-queue
!
!
router ospf 64←Enables OSPF process 64 on the router
 network 192.1.1.0 0.0.0.255 area 0←Specifies what interface OSPF will be run
                                    and what area the I interface will be in.
 network 4.4.4.4 0.0.0.0 area 0
!
no ip classless
!
!
line con 0
line aux 0
line vty 0 4
 login
!
end
```

Monitoring and Testing the Configuration

From RouterA, display the OSPF neighbors with the **show ip ospf neighbor** command. Notice that RouterA has three OSPF neighbors:

4.4.4.4, 3.3.3.3, and 2.2.2.2. These neighbor IDs are the router IDs. OSPF uses the highest loopback interfaces as its router ID. If no loopback interface is configured on the router, the highest IP address is used.

```
RouterA#show ip ospf neighbor

Neighbor ID   Pri   State          Dead Time   Address     Interface
4.4.4.4       1     FULL/DROTHER   00:00:35    192.1.1.4   Ethernet0/0
3.3.3.3       2     FULL/BDR       00:00:39    192.1.1.3   Ethernet0/0
2.2.2.2       0     FULL/DROTHER   00:00:34    192.1.1.2   Ethernet0/0
```

The state of each neighbor is full, meaning that RouterA has formed an adjacency with each one of its neighbors. Only the DR and BDR form adjacencies with all of the routers on the network. RouterA is the DR for the network, and neighbor 3.3.3.3 is the BDR for the network. All other neighbors are DROTHER, which means that they are neither the BDR or DR for the network.

From RouterB, display the OSPF neighbors with the **show ip ospf neighbor** command. Notice that the state of neighbor 4.4.4.4 is 2WAY and not full. This situation occurs because 4.4.4.4 is not the DR or BDR for the network, so an adjacency is not formed between the two routers.

RouterA (1.1.1.1) is the DR for the network, and RouterC (3.3.3.3) is the BDR for the network.

```
RouterB#show ip ospf neighbor

Neighbor ID   Pri   State          Dead Time   Address     Interface
4.4.4.4       1     2WAY/DROTHER   00:00:32    192.1.1.4   Ethernet0/0
3.3.3.3       2     FULL/BDR       00:00:36    192.1.1.3   Ethernet0/0
1.1.1.1       100   FULL/DR        00:00:35    192.1.1.1   Ethernet0/0
```

From RouterC, display the OSPF neighbors with the **show ip ospf neighbor** command. Notice that the state of all of the neighbors is full, because RouterC is the BDR for the link.

```
RouterC#sho ip ospf neighbor

Neighbor ID   Pri   State          Dead Time   Address     Interface
4.4.4.4       1     FULL/DROTHER   00:00:36    192.1.1.4   Ethernet0/0
1.1.1.1       100   FULL/DR        00:00:39    192.1.1.1   Ethernet0/0
2.2.2.2       0     FULL/DROTHER   00:00:35    192.1.1.2   Ethernet0/0
```

From RouterD, display the OSPF neighbors with the **show ip ospf neighbor** command. Notice that the state of the neighbor 2.2.2.2 is 2WAY and not full—remember that adjacencies are only formed with the DR or BDR. RouterB (2.2.2.2) is neither the DR or BDR for the link.

```
RouterD#show ip ospf neighbor

Neighbor ID   Pri    State           Dead Time   Address       Interface
2.2.2.2       0      2WAY/DROTHER    00:00:36    192.1.1.2     Ethernet0/0
3.3.3.3       2      FULL/BDR        00:00:32    192.1.1.3     Ethernet0/0
1.1.1.1       100    FULL/DR         00:00:30    192.1.1.1     Ethernet0/0
```

The DR and BDR are selected for the link depending on Router priority; however, once a DR is selected for a network, the router remains the DR until it goes down. On RouterB's Ethernet interface, change the OSPF priority to 200.

```
RouterB(config)#INT E0/0
RouterB(config-if)#IP OSPF priority 200
```

From RouterA, display the OSPF neighbors with the **show ip ospf neighbor** command. Notice that neighbor 2.2.2.2 (RouterB) priority has changed to 200; however, it has not become the DR.

```
RouterA#show ip ospf neighbor

Neighbor ID   Pri    State           Dead Time   Address       Interface
4.4.4.4       1      FULL/DROTHER    00:00:31    192.1.1.4     Ethernet0/0
3.3.3.3       2      FULL/BDR        00:00:35    192.1.1.3     Ethernet0/0
2.2.2.2       200    FULL/DROTHER    00:00:30    192.1.1.2     Ethernet0/0
```

The DR will only change if the present DR is no longer on the network. Power down RouterA and display the OSPF neighbors on RouterD with the **show ip ospf neighbor** command. Notice that the BDR RouterC has become the DR, and RouterB is now the BDR.

```
RouterD#show ip ospf neighbor

Neighbor ID   Pri    State           Dead Time   Address       Interface
2.2.2.2       200    FULL/BDR        00:00:31    192.1.1.2     Ethernet0/0
3.3.3.3       2      FULL/DR         00:00:36    192.1.1.3     Ethernet0/0
```

If all routers were removed from the network and then were added again, RouterB would then be elected the DR (OSPF priority 200), and the BDR would be RouterA (OSPF priority 100).

Power all of the routers down and restart them. This action will force a new DR/BDR election. Display the OSPF neighbors on RouterD with the **show ip ospf neighbor** command. Notice that RouterB is the DR, and RouterA is the BDR.

```
RouterD#show ip ospf neighbor

Neighbor ID  Pri   State        Dead Time   Address      Interface
1.1.1.1      100   FULL/BDR     00:00:33    192.1.1.1    Ethernet0/0
3.3.3.3      2     2WAY/DROTHER 00:00:33    192.1.1.3    Ethernet0/0
2.2.2.2      200   FULL/DR      00:00:30    192.1.1.2    Ethernet0/0
```

Lab #30: Configuring OSPF Virtual Links

Equipment Needed

The following equipment is needed to perform this lab exercise:

- Two Cisco routers, each having one Ethernet port and one serial port
- One Cisco router with one Ethernet port and two serial ports
- Cisco IOS 10.0 or higher
- A PC running a terminal emulation program
- Two Ethernet cables and one Ethernet hub
- One Cisco DTE/DCE crossover cable
- A Cisco rolled cable for console port access

Configuration Overview

This configuration will demonstrate the process of configuring an OSPF virtual circuit. In Figure 8–8, area 4 does not have a direct connection to area 0. Area 1 is used as a transport area to connect area 4 to area 0. A virtual link is configured between RouterB and RouterC. The IP addresses are assigned as per Figure 8–8, and loopback interfaces are configured on each router.

The virtual link is configured under the router process using the following command:

area [area-id] **virtual-link** [RID]

The area-id is the transit area. For this example, the transit area is area 1. The RID is the router ID of the router at the other end of the virtual link. The router ID is the highest loopback address on the router. If no loopback is configured, then the router ID is the highest IP address.

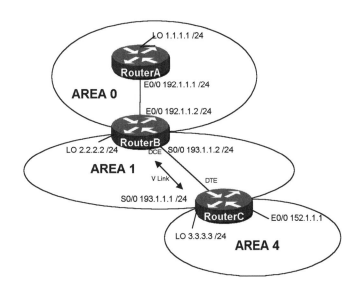

Figure 8–8
0 OSPF virtual circuits

Router Configurations

The configurations for the routers in this example are as follows (key OSPF configurations are highlighted in bold):

RouterA

```
!
version 11.2
no service udp-small-servers
no service tcp-small-servers
!
hostname RouterA
!
interface Loopback0←Defines a virtual interface the IP address is used as the
router ID.
 ip address 1.1.1.1 255.255.255.0
!
interface Ethernet0/0
 ip address 192.1.1.1 255.255.255.0
!
router ospf 64←Enables OSPF process 64 on the router
 network 192.1.1.0 0.0.0.255 area 0←Specifies what interface OSPF will be run
                                    and what area that interface will be in.
!
no ip classless
```

```
!
!
line con 0
line aux 0
line vty 0 4
 login
!
end
```

RouterB

```
!
version 11.2
no service udp-small-servers
no service tcp-small-servers
!
hostname RouterB
!
interface Loopback0←Defines a virtual interface the IP address is used as the
                    router ID
 ip address 2.2.2.2 255.255.255.0
!
interface Ethernet0/0
 ip address 192.1.1.2 255.255.255.0
!
interface Serial0/0
 ip address 193.1.1.2 255.255.255.0
 clockrate 500000
!
!
router ospf 64←Enables OSPF process 64 on the router
 network 192.1.1.0 0.0.0.255 area 0←Specifies what interface OSPF will be run
                                    and what area that interface will be in.
!

 network 193.1.1.0 0.0.0.255 area 1

 area 1 virtual-link 3.3.3.3←Defines the virtual link across area 1 to 3.3.3.3
                             which is the router ID of RouterC.
!
no ip classless
!
!
line con 0
line aux 0
line vty 0 4
 login
!
end
```

RouterC

```
version 11.2
no service udp-small-servers
no service tcp-small-servers
!
hostname RouterC
!
!
!
interface Loopback0←Defines a virtual interface the IP address is used as the
                    router ID
 ip address 3.3.3.3 255.255.255.0
!
interface Ethernet0/0
 ip address 152.1.1.1 255.255.255.0
 no keepalive←Disables the keepalive on the ethernet interface, allows the
              interface to stay up when it is not attached to a hub.

!
interface Serial0/0
 ip address 193.1.1.1 255.255.255.0
!
!
router ospf 64←Enables OSPF process 64 on the router
 network 193.1.1.0 0.0.0.255 area 1←Specifies what interface OSPF will be run
                                    and what area that interface will be in.
 network 152.1.1.0 0.0.0.255 area 4
 area 1 virtual-link 2.2.2.2←Defines the virtual link across area 1 to 2.2.2.2
                             which is the router ID of RouterB.

!
no ip classless
!
!
line con 0
line aux 0
line vty 0 4
 login
```

Monitoring and Testing the Configuration

From RouterC and RouterB, verify that the virtual link is up with the command **show ip ospf virtual-links**. The following example shows the output from this command:

```
RouterC#show ip ospf virtual-links
Virtual Link OSPF_VL0 to router 2.2.2.2 is up
  Run as demand circuit
  DoNotAge LSA allowed.
  Transit area 1, via interface Serial0/0, Cost of using 64
  Transmit Delay is 1 sec, State POINT_TO_POINT,
  Timer intervals configured, Hello 10, Dead 40, Wait 40, Retransmit 5
    Hello due in 00:00:07
    Adjacency State FULL (Hello suppressed)

RouterB#show ip ospf virtual-links
Virtual Link OSPF_VL0 to router 3.3.3.3 is up
  Run as demand circuit
  DoNotAge LSA allowed.
  Transit area 1, via interface Serial0/0, Cost of using 64
  Transmit Delay is 1 sec, State POINT_TO_POINT,
  Timer intervals configured, Hello 10, Dead 40, Wait 40, Retransmit 5
    Hello due in 00:00:07
    Adjacency State FULL (Hello suppressed)
```

Display the routing table on RouterA with the command **show ip route**. Notice that RouterA has a route to the 152.1.1.0 network, which is attached to RouterC.

```
RouterA#show ip route
Codes: C - connected, S - static, I - IGRP, R - RIP, M - mobile, B - BGP
       D - EIGRP, EX - EIGRP external, O - OSPF, IA - OSPF inter area
       N1 - OSPF NSSA external type 1, N2 - OSPF NSSA external type 2
       E1 - OSPF external type 1, E2 - OSPF external type 2, E - EGP
       i - IS-IS, L1 - IS-IS level-1, L2 - IS-IS level-2, * - candidate default
       U - per-user static route, o - ODR

Gateway of last resort is not set

     1.0.0.0/24 is subnetted, 1 subnets
C        1.1.1.0 is directly connected, Loopback0
   152.1.0.0/24 is subnetted, 1 subnets
O IA   152.1.1.0 [110/84] via 192.1.1.2, 00:00:26, Ethernet0/0
C    192.1.1.0/24 is directly connected, Ethernet0/0
O IA 193.1.1.0/24 [110/74] via 192.1.1.2, 00:00:26, Ethernet0/0
```

Remove the virtual link statement from RouterB and RouterC.

```
RouterB#configure terminal
RouterB(config)#router ospf 64
RouterB(config-router)#no area 1 virtual-link 3.3.3.3

RouterC#configure terminal
RouterC(config)#router ospf 64
RouterC(config-router)#no area 1 virtual-link 2.2.2.2
```

Display the routing table on RouterA with the command **show ip route**. Notice that RouterA no longer has a route to the 152.1.1.0 network, which is attached to RouterC.

```
RouterA#show ip route
Codes: C - connected, S - static, I - IGRP, R - RIP, M - mobile, B - BGP
       D - EIGRP, EX - EIGRP external, O - OSPF, IA - OSPF inter area
       N1 - OSPF NSSA external type 1, N2 - OSPF NSSA external type 2
       E1 - OSPF external type 1, E2 - OSPF external type 2, E - EGP
       i - IS-IS, L1 - IS-IS level-1, L2 - IS-IS level-2, * - candidate default
       U - per-user static route, o - ODR

Gateway of last resort is not set

     1.0.0.0/24 is subnetted, 1 subnets
C       1.1.1.0 is directly connected, Loopback0
C     192.1.1.0/24 is directly connected, Ethernet0/0
O IA 193.1.1.0/24 [110/74] via 192.1.1.2, 00:36:05, Ethernet0/0
```

Add the virtual link statement back to RouterB and RouterC.

```
RouterB# configure terminal
RouterB(config)#router ospf 64
RouterB(config-router)#area 1 virtual-link 3.3.3.3

RouterC# configure terminal
RouterC(config)#router ospf 64
RouterC(config-router)#area 1 virtual-link 2.2.2.2
```

Verify that the virtual link is up with the command **show ip ospf virtual-links**. Add another loopback interface to RouterB using IP address 5.5.5.5 with a 24-bit mask.

```
RouterB#configure terminal
RouterB(config)#interface loopback 1
RouterB(config-if)#ip address 5.5.5.5 255.255.255.0
```

Verify once again that the virtual link is up. Now, reload RouterB, and make sure that the configuration is written to memory.

Log into RouterC, and you will see the following error message:

```
RouterC#
%OSPF-4-ERRRCV: Received invalid packet: mismatch area ID, from backbone area
               must be virtual-link but not found from 193.1.1.2, Serial0/0
```

The virtual link is not found, because the Router ID of RouterB has changed. Remember that the router ID is the highest loopback interface on the router. If no loopback interface is defined, the router ID is the highest IP address. The router ID is only calculated at boot time or any time the OSPF process is restarted, which is why the virtual link was up after we added the new loopback but went down after the router was reloaded. When virtual links are configured, care must be taken when adding IP address or loopback interfaces to the router (because the router ID may change).

Display the OSPF neighbors on RouterC with the command **show ip ospf neighbor**. Notice that the router ID of RouterB has changed from 2.2.2.2 to 5.5.5.5, which is why the error message is seen on RouterC.

```
RouterC#show ip ospf neighbor

Neighbor ID  Pri   State        Dead Time     Address        Interface
5.5.5.5      1     FULL/  -     00:00:30      193.1.1.2      Serial0/0
```

Lab #31: Configuring OSPF Neighbor Authentication

Equipment Needed

The following equipment is needed to perform this lab exercise:

- One Cisco router having one Ethernet port
- One Cisco router having one serial port and one Ethernet port
- Cisco IOS 10.0 or higher
- A PC running a terminal emulation program
- Two Ethernet cables and one Ethernet hub
- A Cisco rolled cable for console port access

Overview

Neighbor authentication enables the router to authenticate the source of each routing update received. An authentication key or password is exchanged between routers. If the keys do not match, the routing update is rejected.

Cisco uses two types of neighbor authentication: *plain text* and *Message Digest Algorithm Version 5* (MD5). Plain-text authentication sends a key over the wire. Because the key is passed in plain text, it can be read during transit (and therefore, is not recommended).

MD5 authentication sends a message digest instead of the key. The MD5 algorithm is used to produce a "hash" of the key, and this hash is what is sent. For additional information about the MD5 algorithm, reference RFC1321.

Configuration Overview

This configuration will demonstrate neighbor authentication using both plain-text authentication and MD5 authentication. RouterA will be configured to use plain-text authentication when exchanging routing updates with RouterB and MD5 authentication when exchanging routing updates with RouterC.

RouterA's Ethernet interface and RouterB's Ethernet interface are in OSPF area 0. Both Routers have plain-text neighbor authentication configured for area 0. RouterA's serial interface and RouterB's serial interface are both in area 1, and both routers have MD5 authentication configured for area 1.

RouterA is connected to RouterB via an Ethernet network and is connected to RouterC via a V35 crossover cable. RouterA will act as the DCE and will supply clock. The IP addresses are assigned as per Figure 8–9.

There are two steps in enabling neighbor authentication on a router. First, authentication is enabled for a particular area under the routing process:

Figure 8–9
OSPF neighbor
authentication

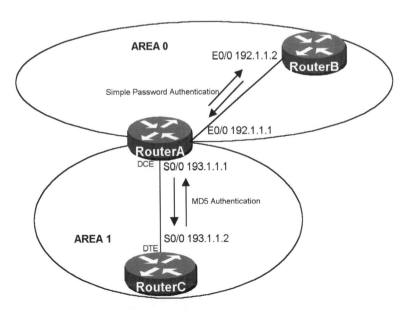

Plain text neighbor authentication
```
RouterA#configure terminal
RouterA(config)#router ospf 64
RouterA(config-router)#area 0 authentication
```

MD5 neighbor authentication
```
RouterA#configure terminal
RouterA(config)#router ospf 64
RouterA(config-router)#area 0 authentication
RouterA(config-router)#area 0 authentication message-digest
```

The next step is to define the authentication key under the interface:

Plain text neighbor authentication
```
RouterA#configure terminal
RouterA(config)#interface e0/0
RouterA(config-if)#ip ospf authentication-key cisco
```

 NOTE: The authentication password for all OSPF routers on a network must be the same if the routers are to communicate with each other via OSPF.

MD5 neighbor authentication
```
RouterA#configure terminal
RouterA(config)#interface e0/0
RouterA(config-if)#ip ospf message-digest-key 1 md5 cisco
```

 NOTE: When using MD5 authentication, the key identifier must be the same on neighbor routers.

 # Router Configurations

The configurations for the routers in this example are as follows (key OSPF neighbor authentication commands are highlighted in bold):

RouterA

```
version 11.2
no service udp-small-servers
no service tcp-small-servers
!
hostname RouterA
```

```
!
!
interface Ethernet0/0
 ip address 192.1.1.1 255.255.255.0
 ip ospf authentication-key cisco←Assigns a password to be used by neighboring
                                   routers that are using OSPF's simple
                                   password authentication
!
interface Serial0/0
 ip address 193.1.1.1 255.255.255.0
 ip ospf message-digest-key 1 md5 cisco←Assigns a password and MD5 key to be
                                         used by neighboring routers that are
                                         using OSPF's MD5 authentication
 clockrate 500000
!
!
router ospf 64
 network 192.1.1.0 0.0.0.255 area 0
 network 193.1.1.0 0.0.0.255 area 1
 area 0 authentication←Enables plain text neighbor authentication for OSPF
                       area 0.
 area 1 authentication message-digest←Enables MD5 authentication for OSPF
                                       area 1.

!
no ip classless
!
!
line con 0
line aux 0
line vty 0 4
 login
!
end
```

RouterB

```
!
version 11.2
no service udp-small-servers
no service tcp-small-servers
!
hostname RouterB
!
!
!
!
interface Ethernet0/0
 ip address 192.1.1.2 255.255.255.0
 ip ospf authentication-key cisco←Assigns a password to be used by neighboring
                                   routers that are using OSPF's simple
                                   password authentication
```

```
!
!
router ospf 64←Enables OSPF process 64 on the router
 network 192.1.1.0 0.0.0.255 area 0←Specifies what interface OSPF will be run
                                    and what area that interface will be in

 area 0 authentication←Enables plain text neighbor authentication for  OSPF area
0.
!
no ip classless
ip ospf name-lookup
!
!
line con 0
line aux 0
line vty 0 4
 login
!
end
```

RouterC

```
!
version 11.2
no service udp-small-servers
no service tcp-small-servers
!
hostname RouterC
!
interface Ethernet0/0
 no ip address
 shutdown
!
interface Serial0/0
 ip address 193.1.1.2 255.255.255.0
 ip ospf message-digest-key 1 md5 cisco←Assigns a password and MD5 key to be
                                        used by neighboring routers that are
                                        using OSPF's MD5 authentication

!
interface Serial0/1
 no ip address
 shutdown
!
router ospf 64
 network 193.1.1.0 0.0.0.255 area 1
 area 1 authentication message-digest←Enables MD5 authentication for  OSPF
                                      area 1.

!
no ip classless
!
!
```

```
line con 0
line aux 0
line vty 0 4
 login
!
end
```

Monitoring and Testing the Configuration

From RouterC, display the OSPF parameters with the command **show ip ospf interface s0/0**. Notice that MD5 is enabled on the interface, and the key is 1. This information is important, because keys must match in each router.

```
RouterC#show ip ospf interface s0/0
Serial0/0 is up, line protocol is up
  Internet Address 193.1.1.2/24, Area 1
  Process ID 64, Router ID 193.1.1.2, Network Type POINT_TO_POINT, Cost: 64
  Transmit Delay is 1 sec, State POINT_TO_POINT,
  Timer intervals configured, Hello 10, Dead 40, Wait 40, Retransmit 5
    Hello due in 00:00:01
  Neighbor Count is 1, Adjacent neighbor count is 1
    Adjacent with neighbor 193.1.1.1
  Suppress hello for 0 neighbor(s)
  Message digest authentication enabled
    Youngest key id is 1
```

From RouterC, display the state of the OSPF neighbors with the command **show ip ospf neighbor**. Notice that RouterC has formed an adjacency with neighbor 193.1.1.1 (RouterA).

```
RouterC#show ip ospf neighbor

Neighbor ID  Pri   State       Dead Time   Address      Interface
193.1.1.1    1     FULL/  -    00:00:33    193.1.1.1    Serial0/0
```

Change the message digest key on RouterC from 1 to 5.

```
RouterC#configure term
RouterC(config)#interface s0/0
RouterC(config-if)#no ip ospf message-digest-key 1 md5 cisco
RouterC(config-if)#ip ospf message-digest-key 5 md5 cisco
```

Monitor the OSPF events on RouterC with the command **debug ip ospf events**. The following example shows the output from the command. Notice that RouterC is receiving an MD key of 1 and is sending an MD key of 5, causing an authentication key mismatch. Because the neighbor authentication does not match, RouterC simply disregards the OSPF packets from RouterA.

The authentication key and the md5 password must match, or the routers will not exchange OSPF information.

```
OSPF: Send with youngest Key 5
OSPF: Rcv pkt from 193.1.1.1, Serial0/0 : Mismatch Authentication Key - No
                                   message digest key 1 on interface
```

Lab #32: Configuring OSPF on an NBMA Network "Non-Broadcast" Model

Equipment Needed

The following equipment is needed to perform this lab exercise:

■ Three Cisco routers, each having one serial port

■ One Cisco router with three serial ports acting as a Frame-Relay switch

■ Cisco IOS 10.0 or higher

■ A PC running a terminal emulation program

■ Three Cisco V35 DCE/DTE crossover cables

■ A Cisco rolled cable for console port access

Overview

When configuring OSPF on NBMA networks such as Frame-Relay or ATM, care must be taken as to which router becomes the DR and BDR for the network. The DR and BDR require full logical connectivity with all routers on the network.

Also, depending on which one of the four network types is used (Broadcast, Non-Broadcast, Point-Point, or Point-to-Multipoint), additional configuration may be necessary.

This lab will address OSPF over a NBMA frame-relay network using the Non-Broadcast network type. This type is the default network type for physical interfaces configured for Frame Relay. On the Non-Broadcast network type, a DR/BDR is elected for the network; however, due to the lack of broadcast capabilities, the DR and BDR must have a static list of

Figure 8–10
Configuring OSPF on
an NBMA network

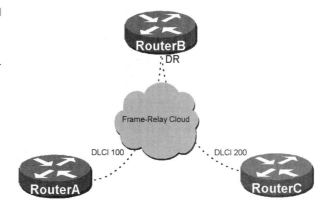

Figure 8–10
Configuring OSPF on
an NBMA network

all routers attached to the frame-relay cloud. This task is achieved by using the neighbor command under the OSPF process.

For this lab, RouterB must be elected the DR—because it is the only router that has full physical connectivity with all other routers on the network, as shown in Figure 8–10.

Configuration Overview

This lab will demonstrate the configuration process of OSPF over Frame-Relay using the Non-Broadcast network type. RouterA, RouterB, and RouterC will connect serially via a crossover cable to a Cisco router (FrameSwitch), which will act as a Frame-Relay switch.

The FrameSwitch will act as the DCE, supplying clock for all attached routers. Detailed documentation on configuring a Cisco router as a Frame-Relay switch can be found in Chapter 4, "Frame Relay."

The IP addresses are as per Figure 8–11. RouterA's and RouterC's serial interfaces will be configured with an OSPF priority of 0. This configuration will ensure that RouterB becomes the DR for the network. Neighbor statements for each router will be configured on RouterB.

Figure 8–11
Physical connectivity

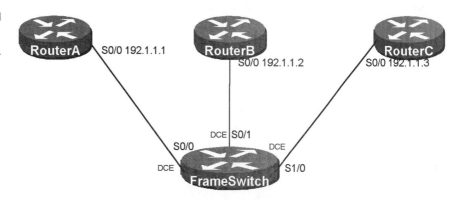

Router Configurations

The configurations for the routers in this example are as follows (key OSPF commands are highlighted in bold):

FrameSwitch

```
!
version 11.2
no service udp-small-servers
no service tcp-small-servers
!
hostname FrameSwitch
!
!
frame-relay switching
!
interface Ethernet0/0
 no ip address
 shutdown
!
interface Serial0/0
 no ip address
 encapsulation frame-relay IETF
 no fair-queue
 clockrate 500000
 frame-relay lmi-type ansi
 frame-relay intf-type dce
 frame-relay route 100 interface Serial0/1 100
!
interface Serial0/1
 no ip address
 encapsulation frame-relay IETF
 clockrate 500000
 frame-relay lmi-type ansi
 frame-relay intf-type dce
 frame-relay route 100 interface Serial0/0 100
 frame-relay route 200 interface Serial1/0 200
!
interface Ethernet1/0
 no ip address
 shutdown
!
interface Serial1/0
 no ip address
 encapsulation frame-relay IETF
 clockrate 500000
 frame-relay lmi-type ansi
 frame-relay intf-type dce
 frame-relay route 200 interface Serial0/1 200
```

```
!
no ip classless
!
!
line con 0
line aux 0
line vty 0 4
 login
!
end
```

RouterA

```
!
version 11.2

no service udp-small-servers
no service tcp-small-servers
!
hostname RouterA
!
!
interface Loopback0←Defines a virtual interface the IP address is used as the
                    router ID
 ip address 1.1.1.1 255.255.255.0
!
interface Ethernet0/0
 no ip address
 shutdown
!
interface Serial0/0
 ip address 192.1.1.1 255.255.255.0
 encapsulation frame-relay IETF
ip ospf priority 0←Sets the priority used by the router in DR election for a
                   particular interface. An OSPF priority of zero means that
                   the router is ineligible in the DR election process.
 frame-relay map ip 192.1.1.2 100 broadcast
 frame-relay map ip 192.1.1.3 100 broadcast
 frame-relay lmi-type ansi
!
!
router ospf 64←Enables OSPF process 64 on the router

 network 192.1.1.0 0.0.0.255 area 0←Specifies what interface OSPF will be run
                                    on and what area the interface will be in
network 1.1.1.1 0.0.0.0 area 0
!
no ip classless
!
line con 0
line aux 0
```

```
line vty 0 4
 login
!
end
```

RouterB

```
!
version 11.2
no service udp-small-servers
no service tcp-small-servers
!
hostname RouterB
!
!
interface Loopback0←Defines a virtual interface the IP address is used as the
                    router ID
 ip address 2.2.2.2 255.255.255.0

!
interface Ethernet0/0
 no ip address
 shutdown
!
interface Serial0/0
 ip address 192.1.1.2 255.255.255.0
 encapsulation frame-relay IETF
 frame-relay map ip 192.1.1.1 100 broadcast
 frame-relay map ip 192.1.1.3 200 broadcast
 frame-relay lmi-type ansi
!
!
router ospf 64←Enables OSPF process 64 on the router

network 192.1.1.0 0.0.0.255 area 0←Specifies what interface OSPF will be run
                                    on and what area the interface will be in

network 2.2.2.2 0.0.0.0 area 0
neighbor 192.1.1.1←Used to define the neighbor on a Non-broadcast network
neighbor 192.1.1.3
!
no ip classless
!
!
line con 0
line aux 0
line vty 0 4
 login
!
end
```

RouterC

```
!
version 11.2
no service udp-small-servers
no service tcp-small-servers
!
hostname RouterC
!
!
interface Loopback0←Defines a virtual interface the IP address is used as the
                    router ID
  ip address 3.3.3.3   255.255.255.0

!
interface Ethernet0/0
 no ip address
 shutdown
!
interface Serial0/0
 ip address 192.1.1.3 255.255.255.0
 encapsulation frame-relay IETF

 ip ospf priority 0←Sets the priority used by the router in DR election for a
                    particular interface. An OSPF priority of zero means that
                    the router is ineligible for the DR election process.

 frame-relay map ip 192.1.1.1 200 broadcast
 frame-relay map ip 192.1.1.2 200 broadcast
 frame-relay lmi-type ansi
!
interface Serial0/1
 no ip address
 shutdown
!
!
router ospf 64←Enables OSPF process 64 on the router

 network 192.1.1.0 0.0.0.255 area 0
 network 3.3.3.3 0.0.0.0 area 0

!
no ip classless
!
!
line con 0
line aux 0
line vty 0 4
 login
!
end
```

Monitoring and Testing the Configuration

From RouterA, show the OSPF interface statistics with the command **show ip ospf interface s0/0**. Notice that the interface is network-type Non-Broadcast, which means that a DR is elected and the router and OSPF neighbors must be configured manually.

The priority of the interface is 0, which means that it is ineligible for being elected the DR or BDR for the network.

```
RouterA#show ip ospf interface s0/0
Serial0/0 is up, line protocol is up
  Internet Address 192.1.1.1/24, Area 0
  Process ID 64, Router ID 1.1.1.1, Network Type NON_BROADCAST, Cost: 64
  Transmit Delay is 1 sec, State DROTHER, Priority 0
  Designated Router (ID) 192.1.1.2, Interface address 192.1.1.2
  No backup designated router on this network
  Timer intervals configured, Hello 30, Dead 120, Wait 120, Retransmit 5
    Hello due in 00:00:13
  Neighbor Count is 1, Adjacent neighbor count is 1
    Adjacent with neighbor 192.1.1.2  (Designated Router)
  Suppress hello for 0 neighbor(s)
```

Show the status of the OSPF neighbors on RouterA with the command **show ip ospf neighbor**. Notice that RouterA is fully adjacent with RouterB (2.2.2.2), which is the DR for the network.

```
RouterA#show ip ospf neighbor

Neighbor ID   Pri   State      Dead Time    Address      Interface
2.2.2.2       1     FULL/DR    00:01:42     192.1.1.2    Serial0/0
```

Show the IP routing table on RouterA with the command **show ip route**, and note that RouterA has a route to the loopback addresses on RouterB and RouterC.

After the destination address are two numbers: 110/65. The 110 is the administrative distance for OSPF, which is used to compare multiple routes to the same destination. The lower the administrative distance, the more trustworthy the route. For example, RIP has an administrative distance of 120, so if RouterA learned the same route from RIP and OSPF, the OSPF route is preferred—because it has the lower administrative distance.

The second number, 65, is the metric or cost of using the route. This cost is used to compare routes that are learned via the same routing protocol. The route with the lowest cost is preferred.

```
RouterA#show ip route
Codes: C - connected, S - static, I - IGRP, R - RIP, M - mobile, B - BGP
       D - EIGRP, EX - EIGRP external, O - OSPF, IA - OSPF inter area
       N1 - OSPF NSSA external type 1, N2 - OSPF NSSA external type 2
       E1 - OSPF external type 1, E2 - OSPF external type 2, E - EGP
       i - IS-IS, L1 - IS-IS level-1, L2 - IS-IS level-2, * - candidate default
       U - per-user static route, o - ODR

Gateway of last resort is not set

     1.0.0.0/24 is subnetted, 1 subnets
C       1.1.1.0 is directly connected, Loopback0
     2.0.0.0/32 is subnetted, 1 subnets
O       2.2.2.2 [110/65] via 192.1.1.2, 00:02:22, Serial0/0
     3.0.0.0/32 is subnetted, 1 subnets
O       3.3.3.3 [110/65] via 192.1.1.3, 00:02:22, Serial0/0
C    192.1.1.0/24 is directly connected, Serial0/0
```

Display the status of the OSPF neighbors on RouterB with the command **show ip ospf neighbor**. Notice that RouterB has two neighbors, RouterA (1.1.1.1) and RouterC (3.3.3.3), and has formed a full adjacency with each. RouterB was elected DR for the network because it has the highest priority. The DR and BDR form full adjacencies with every other router. On a Non-Broadcast network, the DR and BDR are the only routers that need to define neighbors.

```
RouterB#show ip ospf neighbor

Neighbor ID  Pri   State         Dead Time   Address      Interface
3.3.3.3      0     FULL/DROTHER  00:01:55    192.1.1.3    Serial0/0
1.1.1.1      0     FULL/DROTHER  00:01:43    192.1.1.1    Serial0/0
```

Display the status of the OSPF neighbors on RouterC with the command **show ip ospf neighbor**. Notice that RouterC has only one neighbor, RouterB, which is the DR for the network. No BDR was elected for the network, because RouterB was the only router that had a non-zero OSPF priority. If the OSPF priority of a router is zero, then the router cannot be elected the DR or BDR.

```
RouterC#show ip ospf neighbor

Neighbor ID  Pri   State     Dead Time   Address      Interface
192.1.1.2    3     FULL/DR   00:01:37    192.1.1.2    Serial0/0
```

In an NBMA network, care must be taken to assure a full mesh topology or static selection of the DR using interface priority. For this lab topology, it is imperative that RouterB's serial interface should become the DR, because it is the only router that has full connectivity to all other routers.

Let's see what would happen when RouterA becomes the DR for the network. Change the OSPF priority on RouterB and remove the neighbor statements with the following commands:

```
RouterB#configure terminal
RouterB(config)#interface s0/0
RouterB(config-if)#ip ospf priority 0
RouterB(config-if)#router ospf 64
RouterB(config-router)#no neighbor 192.1.1.1
RouterB(config-router)#no neighbor 192.1.1.3
```

Change the OSPF priority of RouterA's serial interface to 10, and add a neighbor statement for RouterB and RouterC with the following command:

```
RouterA#configure terminal
RouterA(config)#interface s0
RouterA(config-if)#ip ospf priority 10
RouterA(config-if)#router ospf 64
RouterA(config-router)#neighbor 192.1.1.2
RouterA(config-router)#neighbor 192.1.1.3
```

Make sure that the configurations are written to NVRAM, and reload the routers. The reason the routers need to be reloaded is because once a DR is elected for the network, no other router can become the DR until the DR is dead.

From RouterA, show the OSPF interface statistics with the command **show ip ospf interface s0/0**. Notice that RouterA (1.1.1.1) is now the DR for the network.

```
RouterA#show ip  ospf interface s0
Serial0 is up, line protocol is up
  Internet Address 192.1.1.1/24, Area 0
  Process ID 64, Router ID 1.1.1.1, Network Type NON_BROADCAST, Cost: 64
  Transmit Delay is 1 sec, State DR, Priority 10
  Designated Router (ID) 1.1.1.1, Interface address 192.1.1.1
  No backup designated router on this network
  Timer intervals configured, Hello 30, Dead 120, Wait 120, Retransmit 5
    Hello due in 00:00:01
  Neighbor Count is 1, Adjacent neighbor count is 1
    Adjacent with neighbor 2.2.2.2
```

Display the status of the OSPF neighbors on RouterC with the command **show ip ospf neighbor**. Notice that RouterA has only formed an adjacency with RouterB (2.2.2.2) but not RouterC, because it only has physical connectivity to RouterB. The DR must have physical connectivity to all routers on the network.

```
RouterA#show ip ospf neighbor

Neighbor ID  Pri  State            Dead Time  Address    Interface
N/A          0    ATTEMPT/DROTHER  -          192.1.1.3  Serial0
2.2.2.2      0    FULL/DROTHER     00:01:55   192.1.1.2  Serial0
```

Display the routing table on RouterC. Notice that there are no routes, because RouterC was unable to form an adjacency with the DR.

```
RouterC#show ip route
Codes: C - connected, S - static, I - IGRP, R - RIP, M - mobile, B - BGP
       D - EIGRP, EX - EIGRP external, O - OSPF, IA - OSPF inter area
       N1 - OSPF NSSA external type 1, N2 - OSPF NSSA external type 2
       E1 - OSPF external type 1, E2 - OSPF external type 2, E - EGP
       i - IS-IS, L1 - IS-IS level-1, L2 - IS-IS level-2, * - candidate default
       U - per-user static route, o - ODR

Gateway of last resort is not set

     3.0.0.0/24 is subnetted, 1 subnets
C       3.3.3.0 is directly connected, Loopback0
C    192.1.1.0/24 is directly connected, Serial0
```

Lab #33: Configuring OSPF on an NBMA Network "Broadcast" Model

Equipment Needed

The following equipment is needed to perform this lab exercise:

- Three Cisco routers, each having one serial port
- One Cisco router with three serial ports acting as a Frame-Relay switch
- Cisco IOS 10.0 or higher
- A PC running a terminal emulation program
- Three Cisco V35 DCE/DTE crossover cables
- A Cisco rolled cable for console port access

Overview

The broadcast network type is a work-around for having to define all neighbors statically. When an interface is configured for broadcast, the interface will behave as if connected to a LAN. A DR and BDR will still be elected for the network, so care must be taken to assure that the router-elected DR/BDR has physical connectivity to all routers on the network.

Configuration Overview

This lab will demonstrate configuring OSPF over Frame-Relay using the Broadcast network type. RouterA, RouterB, and RouterC will connect serially via a crossover cable to a Cisco router (FrameSwitch), which will act as a Frame-Relay switch.

The FrameSwitch will act as the DCE, supplying clock for all attached routers. Detailed documentation on configuring a Cisco router as a Frame-Relay switch can be found in Chapter 4.

The network type will be set on all routers using the interface command **ip ospf network broadcast**. The IP addresses are as per Figure 8–12. RouterA and RouterC serial interfaces will be configured with an OSPF priority of 0, which will ensure that RouterB becomes the DR for the network.

Router Configurations

The configurations for the routers in this example are as follows (key OSPF commands are highlighted in bold):

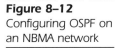

Figure 8–12
Configuring OSPF on an NBMA network

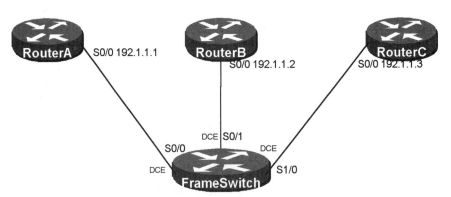

FrameSwitch

```
:
!
version 11.2
no service udp-small-servers
no service tcp-small-servers
!
hostname FrameSwitch
!
!
frame-relay switching
!
interface Ethernet0/0
 no ip address
 shutdown
!
interface Serial0/0
 no ip address
 encapsulation frame-relay IETF
 no fair-queue
 clockrate 500000
 frame-relay lmi-type ansi
 frame-relay intf-type dce
 frame-relay route 100 interface Serial0/1 100
!
interface Serial0/1
 no ip address
 encapsulation frame-relay IETF
 clockrate 500000
 frame-relay lmi-type ansi
 frame-relay intf-type dce
 frame-relay route 100 interface Serial0/0 100
 frame-relay route 200 interface Serial1/0 200
!
interface Ethernet1/0
 no ip address
 shutdown
!
interface Serial1/0
 no ip address
 encapsulation frame-relay IETF
 clockrate 500000
 frame-relay lmi-type ansi
 frame-relay intf-type dce
 frame-relay route 200 interface Serial0/1 200
!
no ip classless
!
!
line con 0
line aux 0
line vty 0 4
 login
!
end
```

RouterA

```
version 11.2
no service udp-small-servers
no service tcp-small-servers
!
hostname RouterA
!
!
interface Loopback0←Defines a virtual interface the IP address is used as the
                     router ID
 ip address 1.1.1.1 255.255.255.0
!
interface Ethernet0/0
 no ip address
 shutdown
!
interface Serial0/0
 ip address 192.1.1.1 255.255.255.0
 encapsulation frame-relay IETF
ip ospf network broadcast←Defines the network type as broadcast.
ip ospf priority 0←Sets the priority used by the router in DR election for a
                     particular interface. An OSPF priority of zero means that
                     the router is ineligible for the DR election process.
 frame-relay map ip 192.1.1.2 100 broadcast
 frame-relay map ip 192.1.1.3 100 broadcast
 frame-relay lmi-type ansi
!
interface Serial1/0
 no ip address
 shutdown
!
!
router ospf 64←Enables OSPF process 64 on the router

 network 192.1.1.0 0.0.0.255 area 0←Specifies what interface OSPF will be run
                                     on and what area the interface will be in
network 1.1.1.1 0.0.0.0 area 0
!
no ip classless
!
line con 0
line aux 0
line vty 0 4
 login
!
end
```

RouterB

```
version 11.2
no service udp-small-servers
no service tcp-small-servers
!
hostname RouterB
!
interface Loopback0←Defines a virtual interface the IP address is used as the
                     router ID
 ip address 2.2.2.2 255.255.255.0


!
interface Ethernet0/0
 no ip address
 shutdown
!
interface Serial0/0
 ip address 192.1.1.2 255.255.255.0
 encapsulation frame-relay IETF
ip ospf network broadcast←Defines the network type as broadcast.

 frame-relay map ip 192.1.1.1 100 broadcast
 frame-relay map ip 192.1.1.3 200 broadcast
 frame-relay lmi-type ansi
!
interface Serial0/1
 no ip address
 shutdown
!
router ospf 64←Enables OSPF process 64 on the router

network 192.1.1.0 0.0.0.255 area 0←Specifies what interface OSPF will be run
                                     on and what area the interface will be in
network 2.2.2.2 0.0.0.0 area 0
!
no ip classless
!
!
line con 0
line aux 0
line vty 0 4
 login
!
end
```

RouterC

```
!
version 11.2
no service udp-small-servers
no service tcp-small-servers
!
hostname RouterC
!
!
interface Loopback0←Defines a virtual interface the IP address is used as the
                        router ID
 ip address 3.3.3.3   255.255.255.0

!
interface Ethernet0/0
 no ip address
 shutdown
!
interface Serial0/0
 ip address 192.1.1.3 255.255.255.0
 encapsulation frame-relay IETF
ip ospf network broadcast←Defines the network type as broadcast.
 ip ospf priority 0←Sets the priority used by the router in DR election for a
                        particular interface. An OSPF priority of zero means that
                        the router is ineligible for the DR election process.
 frame-relay map ip 192.1.1.1 200 broadcast
 frame-relay map ip 192.1.1.2 200 broadcast
 frame-relay lmi-type ansi
!
interface Serial0/1
 no ip address
 shutdown
!
!
router ospf 64←Enables OSPF process 64 on the router
network 192.1.1.0 0.0.0.255 area 0
network 3.3.3.3 0.0.0.0 area 0

!
no ip classless
!
!
line con 0
line aux 0
line vty 0 4
 login
!
end
```

Monitoring and Testing the Configuration

From RouterA, show the OSPF interface statistics with the command **show ip ospf interface s0/0**. Notice that the interface is network-type Broadcast, which means that a DR is elected. Because the network is broadcast, no neighbors need to be defined.

The priority of the interface is 0, which means that the router is ineligible for being elected the DR or BDR for the network.

```
RouterA#show ip ospf interface s0/0
Serial0 is up, line protocol is up
  Internet Address 192.1.1.1/24, Area 0
  Process ID 64, Router ID 1.1.1.1, Network Type BROADCAST, Cost: 64
  Transmit Delay is 1 sec, State DROTHER, Priority 0
  Designated Router (ID) 2.2.2.2, Interface address 192.1.1.2
  No backup designated router on this network
  Timer intervals configured, Hello 10, Dead 40, Wait 40, Retransmit 5
    Hello due in 00:00:01
  Neighbor Count is 1, Adjacent neighbor count is 1
    Adjacent with neighbor 2.2.2.2  (Designated Router)
```

Show the status of the OSPF neighbors on RouterA with the command **show ip ospf neighbor**. Notice that RouterA is fully adjacent with RouterB (2.2.2.2), which is the DR for the network.

```
RouterA#show ip ospf neighbor

Neighbor ID  Pri   State       Dead Time   Address     Interface
2.2.2.2      1     FULL/DR     00:00:34    192.1.1.2   Serial0
```

Show the status of the OSPF neighbors on RouterB with the command **show ip ospf neighbor**. Notice that RouterB is fully adjacent with RouterA (1.1.1.1) and RouterC (3.3.3.3). Both routers are DROTHER, which means that they are neither the DR or BDR for the network.

```
RouterB#show ip ospf neighbor

Neighbor ID  Pri   State           Dead Time   Address     Interface
3.3.3.3      0     FULL/DROTHER    00:00:34    192.1.1.3   Serial0
1.1.1.1      0     FULL/DROTHER    00:00:35    192.1.1.1   Serial0
```

Let's see what would happen when RouterA becomes the DR and RouterB becomes the BDR for the network. Change the OSPF priority on RouterB with the following command:

```
RouterB#configure terminal
RouterB(config)#interface s0/0
RouterB(config-if)#ip ospf priority 1
```

Change the OSPF priority of RouterA's serial interface to 10 with the following command:

```
RouterA#configure terminal
RouterA(config)#interface s0
RouterA(config-if)#ip ospf priority 10
```

Make sure the configurations are written to NVRAM, and reload the routers. The reason the routers need to be reloaded is because once a DR is elected for the network, no other router can become the DR until the DR is dead.

From RouterA, show the OSPF interface statistics with the command **show ip ospf interface s0/0**. Notice that RouterA is now the DR, and RouterB is the BDR for the network.

```
RouterA#show ip ospf interface s0
Serial0 is up, line protocol is up
  Internet Address 192.1.1.1/24, Area 0
  Process ID 64, Router ID 1.1.1.1, Network Type BROADCAST, Cost: 64
  Transmit Delay is 1 sec, State DR, Priority 10
  Designated Router (ID) 1.1.1.1, Interface address 192.1.1.1
  Backup Designated router (ID) 2.2.2.2, Interface address 192.1.1.2
  Timer intervals configured, Hello 10, Dead 40, Wait 40, Retransmit 5
    Hello due in 00:00:05
  Neighbor Count is 1, Adjacent neighbor count is 1
    Adjacent with neighbor 2.2.2.2   (Backup Designated Router)
```

Show the status of the OSPF neighbors on RouterB with the command **show ip ospf neighbor**. Notice that RouterB is fully adjacent with RouterA (1.1.1.1) and RouterC (3.3.3.3). RouterA is the DR for the network, and RouterC is DROTHER.

```
RouterB#show ip ospf neighbor

Neighbor ID  Pri   State         Dead Time   Address     Interface
3.3.3.3      0     FULL/DROTHER  00:00:34    192.1.1.3   Serial0
1.1.1.1      10    FULL/DR       00:00:36    192.1.1.1   Serial0
```

Show the status of the OSPF neighbors on RouterC with the command **show ip ospf neighbor**. Notice that RouterC thinks that RouterB is the DR for the network, because RouterC does not have a physical connection to RouterA.

```
RouterC#show ip ospf neighbor

Neighbor ID  Pri   State         Dead Time   Address     Interface
2.2.2.2      1     FULL/DR       00:00:31    192.1.1.2   Serial0
```

Let's take a look at the OSPF database on RouterC with the command **show ip ospf database**. This command shows the table of link state advertisements the router uses as input to the Diskjtra algorithm to determine the routing table. Notice that RouterC has the links 1.1.1.1 and 2.2.2.2, which are the loopback interfaces on RouterA and RouterB, respectively.

```
RouterC#show ip ospf database

        OSPF Router with ID (3.3.3.3) (Process ID 64)

            Router Link States (Area 0)

Link ID        ADV Router     Age   Seq#          Checksum Link count
1.1.1.1        1.1.1.1        663   0x80000003    0xB4B8   2
2.2.2.2        2.2.2.2        662   0x80000003    0xC27D   2
3.3.3.3        3.3.3.        665   0x80000003    0xC869   2

            Net Link States (Area 0)

Link ID        ADVRouter      Age   Seq#          Checksum
192.1.1.1      1.1.1.1        663   0x80000001    0xFE87
```

Show the routing table on RouterC with the command **show ip route**. Notice that there is not a route to 1.1.1.1 or 2.2.2.2.

```
RouterC#show ip route
Codes: C - connected, S - static, I - IGRP, R - RIP, M - mobile, B - BGP
       D - EIGRP, EX - EIGRP external, O - OSPF, IA - OSPF inter area
       N1 - OSPF NSSA external type 1, N2 - OSPF NSSA external type 2
       E1 - OSPF external type 1, E2 - OSPF external type 2, E - EGP
       i - IS-IS, L1 - IS-IS level-1, L2 - IS-IS level-2, * - candidate default
       U - per-user static route, o - ODR

Gateway of last resort is not set

     3.0.0.0/24 is subnetted, 1 subnets
C       3.3.3.0 is directly connected, Loopback0
C    192.1.1.0/24 is directly connected, Serial0
```

This situation occurs because the advertising router (the DR) for the broadcast network (RouterA) is not reachable. This situation can be seen from the command **show ip ospf database router** on RouterC.

```
RouterC#show ip ospf database router

        OSPF Router with ID (3.3.3.3) (Process ID 64)


            Router Link States (Area 0)
```

```
Adv Router is not-reachable
LS age: 63
Options: (No TOS-capability, No DC)
LS Type: Router Links
Link State ID: 1.1.1.1
Advertising Router: 1.1.1.1
LS Seq Number: 80000004
Checksum: 0xB2B9
Length: 48
 Number of Links: 2

  Link connected to: a Stub Network
    (Link ID) Network/subnet number: 1.1.1.1
    (Link Data) Network Mask: 255.255.255.255
     Number of TOS metrics: 0
      TOS 0 Metrics: 1

  Link connected to: a Transit Network
    (Link ID) Designated Router address: 192.1.1.1
    (Link Data) Router Interface address: 192.1.1.1
     Number of TOS metrics: 0
      TOS 0 Metrics: 64
```

Lab #34: Configuring OSPF on an NBMA Network "Point-to-Multipoint" Model

Equipment Needed

The following equipment is needed to perform this lab exercise:

■ Three Cisco routers, each having one serial port

■ One Cisco router with three serial ports acting as a Frame-Relay switch

■ Cisco IOS 10.0 or higher

■ A PC running a terminal emulation program

■ Three Cisco V35 DCE/DTE crossover cables

■ A Cisco rolled cable for console port access

Overview

A Point-to-Multipoint network type is treated as a numbered point-to-point interface having one or more neighbors. When an interface is configured for Point-to-Multipoint, no DR/BDR is elected, and neighbors do not need to be defined—which greatly simplifies configuring OSPF over an NBMA network.

Configuration Overview

This lab will demonstrate configuring OSPF over Frame-Relay using the Point-to-Multipoint network type. RouterA, RouterB, and RouterC will connect serially via a crossover cable to a Cisco router (FrameSwitch), which will act as a Frame-Relay switch.

The FrameSwitch will act as the DCE, supplying clock for all attached routers. Detailed documentation on configuring a Cisco router as a Frame-Relay switch can be found in Chapter 4.

The network type will be set on all routers using the interface command **ip ospf network point-to-multipoint**. The IP addresses are as per Figure 8–13. No neighbors need to be defined, and OSPF priorities do not need to be set, because DR/BDR is not elected for the network.

Router Configurations

The configurations for the routers in this example are as follows (key OSPF commands are highlighted in bold):

Figure 8–13
Physical connectivity
for Lab

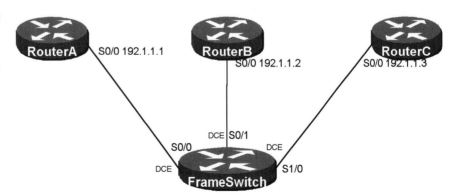

FrameSwitch

```
version 11.2
no service udp-small-servers
no service tcp-small-servers
!
hostname FrameSwitch
!
!
frame-relay switching
!
interface Ethernet0/0
 no ip address
 shutdown
!
interface Serial0/0
 no ip address
 encapsulation frame-relay IETF
 no fair-queue
 clockrate 500000
 frame-relay lmi-type ansi
 frame-relay intf-type dce
 frame-relay route 100 interface Serial0/1 100
!
interface Serial0/1
 no ip address
 encapsulation frame-relay IETF
 clockrate 500000
 frame-relay lmi-type ansi
 frame-relay intf-type dce
 frame-relay route 100 interface Serial0/0 100
 frame-relay route 200 interface Serial1/0 200
!
interface Ethernet1/0
 no ip address
 shutdown
!
interface Serial1/0
 no ip address
 encapsulation frame-relay IETF
 clockrate 500000
 frame-relay lmi-type ansi
 frame-relay intf-type dce
 frame-relay route 200 interface Serial0/1 200
!
no ip classless
!
!
line con 0
line aux 0
line vty 0 4
```

```
 login
 !
 end
```

RouterA

```
version 11.2
no service udp-small-servers
no service tcp-small-servers
!
hostname RouterA
!
!
interface Loopback0←Defines a virtual interface the IP address is used as the
                        router ID
 ip address 1.1.1.1 255.255.255.0
!
interface Ethernet0/0
 no ip address
 shutdown
!
interface Serial0/0
 ip address 192.1.1.1 255.255.255.0
 encapsulation frame-relay IETF
ip ospf network point-to-multipoint←Defines the network type as point-to-
                                      multipoint.
frame-relay map ip 192.1.1.2 100 broadcast
 frame-relay map ip 192.1.1.3 100 broadcast
 frame-relay lmi-type ansi
!
interface Serial1/0
 no ip address
 shutdown
!
!
router ospf 64←Enables OSPF process 64 on the router

 network 192.1.1.0 0.0.0.255 area 0←Specifies what interface OSPF will be run
                                     on and what area the interface will be in
network 1.1.1.1 0.0.0.0 area 0
!
no ip classless
!
line con 0
line aux 0
line vty 0 4
 login
!
end
```

RouterB

```
version 11.2
no service udp-small-servers
no service tcp-small-servers
!
hostname RouterB
!
!
interface Loopback0←Defines a virtual interface the IP address is used as the
                    router ID
 ip address 2.2.2.2 255.255.255.0

!
interface Ethernet0/0
 no ip address
 shutdown
!
interface Serial0/0
 ip address 192.1.1.2 255.255.255.0
 encapsulation frame-relay IETF
ip ospf network point-to-multipoint←Defines the network type as point-to-
                                    multipoint.
 frame-relay map ip 192.1.1.1 100 broadcast
 frame-relay map ip 192.1.1.3 200 broadcast
 frame-relay lmi-type ansi
!
interface Serial0/1
 no ip address
 shutdown
!
router ospf 64←Enables OSPF process 64 on the router

network 192.1.1.0 0.0.0.255 area 0←Specifies what interface OSPF will be run
                                   on and what area the interface will be in
network 2.2.2.2 0.0.0.0 area 0
!
no ip classless
!
!
line con 0
line aux 0
line vty 0 4
 login
!
end
```

RouterC

```
!
version 11.2
no service password-encryption
no service udp-small-servers
no service tcp-small-servers
!
hostname RouterC
!
!
interface Loopback0←Defines a virtual interface the IP address is used as the
                    router ID
 ip address 3.3.3.3   255.255.255.0

!
interface Ethernet0/0
 no ip address
 shutdown
!
interface Serial0/0
 ip address 192.1.1.3 255.255.255.0
 encapsulation frame-relay IETF
 ip ospf network point-to-multipoint←Defines the network type as point-to-
                                     multipoint.
 frame-relay map ip 192.1.1.1 200 broadcast
 frame-relay map ip 192.1.1.2 200 broadcast
 frame-relay lmi-type ansi
!
interface Serial0/1
 no ip address
 shutdown
!
!
router ospf 64←Enables OSPF process 64 on the router
network 192.1.1.0 0.0.0.255 area 0
network 3.3.3.3 0.0.0.0 area 0

!
no ip classless
!
!
line con 0
line aux 0
line vty 0 4
 login
!
end
```

Monitoring and Testing the Configuration

From RouterA, show the OSPF interface statistics with the command **show ip ospf interface s0/0**. Notice that the interface is network type POINT_TO_MULTIPOINT, which means that a DR/BDR is elected and no neighbors need to be defined.

```
RouterA#show ip ospf interface s0/0
Serial0 is up, line protocol is up
  Internet Address 192.1.1.1/24, Area 0
  Process ID 64, Router ID 1.1.1.1, Network Type POINT_TO_MULTIPOINT, Cost: 64
  Transmit Delay is 1 sec, State POINT_TO_MULTIPOINT,
  Timer intervals configured, Hello 30, Dead 120, Wait 120, Retransmit 5
    Hello due in 00:00:01
  Neighbor Count is 1, Adjacent neighbor count is 1
    Adjacent with neighbor 2.2.2.2
```

Display the neighbor state on RouterA with the command show ip ospf neighbor. Notice that RouterA is fully adjacent with RouterB (2.2.2.2), but there is no concept of DR. The link is treated as a point-to-point link; however, the difference is that all routers can be on the same subnet.

```
RouterA#show ip ospf neighbor

Neighbor ID  Pri   State      Dead Time    Address       Interface
2.2.2.2      1     FULL/  -   00:01:59     192.1.1.2     Serial0/0
```

Lab #35: Configuring OSPF Interface Parameters

Equipment Needed

The following equipment is needed to perform this lab exercise:

- Three Cisco routers, each having one serial port and one Ethernet port
- Cisco IOS 10.0 or higher
- A PC running a terminal emulation program
- Two Cisco V35 DCE/DTE crossover cables
- One Ethernet hub and two Ethernet cables
- A Cisco rolled cable for console port access

Overview

The Cisco IOS enables the administrator to alter certain interface-specific OSPF parameters. This lab will deal with three of the more commonly used ones (cost, hello interval, and dead interval).

The cost parameter sets the cost of OSPF sending a packet over a particular interface. By default, the cost is calculated using the formula (100,000,000/bandwidth of the link). So, by default, the cost of using an Ethernet interface is 100 million divided by 10 million, which equals 10. The OSPF cost parameter is useful in manipulating the flow of traffic—especially if you prefer a slower link to a faster link.

The OSPF hello interval is the length of time (in seconds) between sending hello packets on a particular interface. The hello interval must be consistent across all routers in an attached network. The hello interval will vary based on the Interface Network type (Broadcast=10, Non-Broadcast=30, Point-to-Point=10, and Point-to-Multipoint=30).

The OSPF dead interval is the length of time in seconds that a hello packet must not be seen from a neighboring router before the neighbor is declared down. The dead interval must be consistent across all routers in an attached network. According to the interface network type, the dead interval will vary (Broadcast=40, Non-Broadcast=120, Point-to-Point=40, and Point-to-Multipoint=120).

Configuration Overview

This lab will demonstrate configuring OSPF interface-specific parameters (cost, hello interval, and dead interval). The serial interface between RouterA and RouterB will be configured for a cost of 66, which is two higher than the default of the serial link connecting RouterB and RouterC. The OSPF hello interval will be set to 20, and the dead interval will be set to 120 on the serial interface connecting RouterA and RouterB.

RouterA and RouterC will attach to RouterB via a V35 crossover cable. RouterB will act as the DCE, supplying clock. RouterA and RouterC will also be attached via an Ethernet hub. All IP addresses are as per Figure 8–14.

Router Configurations

The configurations for the routers in this example are as follows (key OSPF commands are highlighted in bold):

Figure 8–14
Configuration of
OSPF interface
parameters

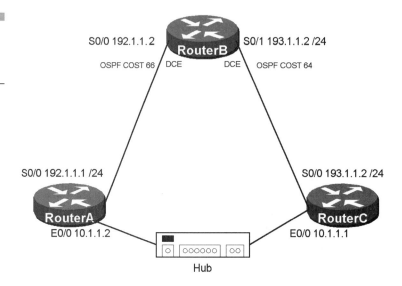

RouterA

```
!
version 11.2
no service udp-small-servers
no service tcp-small-servers
!
hostname RouterA
!
!
interface Loopback0←Defines a virtual interface the IP address is used as the
                    router ID
 ip address 1.1.1.1 255.255.255.0
!
interface Ethernet0/0
  ip address 10.1.1.2 255.255.255.0
 !
interface Serial0/0
 ip address 192.1.1.1 255.255.255.0
 ip ospf cost 66
 ip ospf hello-interval 20
ip ospf dead-interval 120
!
interface Serial1/0
 no ip address
 shutdown
!
!
router ospf 64←Enables OSPF process 64 on the router
```

```
network 192.1.1.0 0.0.0.255 area 0←Specifies what interface OSPF will be run
                                on and what area the interface will be in
network 1.1.1.1 0.0.0.0 area 0
network 10.1.1.0 0.0.0.0.255 area 0

!
no ip classless
!
line con 0
line aux 0
line vty 0 4
 login
!
end
```

RouterB

```
version 11.2
no service udp-small-servers
no service tcp-small-servers
!
hostname RouterB
!
!
interface Loopback0←Defines a virtual interface the IP address is used as the
                    router ID
 ip address 2.2.2.2 255.255.255.0

!
interface Ethernet0/0
 no ip address
 shutdown
!
interface Serial0/0
 ip address 192.1.1.2 255.255.255.0
 ip ospf cost 66
 ip ospf hello-interval 20
 ip ospf dead-interval 120
 clockrate 500000
 !
interface Serial0/1
ip address 193.1.1.2 255.255.255.0
  clockrate 500000
!
router ospf 64←Enables OSPF process 64 on the router

network 192.1.1.0 0.0.0.255 area 0←Specifies what interface OSPF will be run
                                on and what area the interface will be in
network 2.2.2.2 0.0.0.0 area 0
network 193.1.1.0 0.0.0.255 area 0
```

```
!
no ip classless
!
!
line con 0
line aux 0
line vty 0 4
 login
!
end
```

RouterC

```
!
version 11.2
no service udp-small-servers
no service tcp-small-servers
!
hostname RouterC
!
!
interface Loopback0←Defines a virtual interface the IP address is used as the
                    router ID
  ip address 3.3.3.3   255.255.255.0

!
interface Ethernet0/0
  ip address 10.1.1.2 255.255.255.0
 !
interface Serial0/0
  ip address 193.1.1.1 255.255.255.0
 !
interface Serial0/1
 no ip address
 shutdown
!
!
router ospf 64←Enables OSPF process 64 on the router
network 192.1.1.0 0.0.0.255 area 0
network 3.3.3.3 0.0.0.0 area 0
network 10.1.1.0 0.0.0.255 area 0

!
no ip classless
!
!
line con 0
line aux 0
line vty 0 4
 login
!
end
```

Monitoring and Testing the Configuration

From RouterA, show the OSPF interface statistics with the command **show ip ospf interface s0/0**. Notice that the hello and dead intervals have been changed, and the OSPF cost of sending a packet out the interface has changed to 66.

```
RouterA#show ip ospf int s0/0
Serial0 is up, line protocol is up
  Internet Address 192.1.1.1/24, Area 0
  Process ID 64, Router ID 192.1.1.1, Network Type POINT_TO_POINT, Cost: 66
  Transmit Delay is 1 sec, State POINT_TO_POINT,
  Timer intervals configured, Hello 20, Dead 120, Wait 120, Retransmit 5
    Hello due in 00:00:08
  Neighbor Count is 1, Adjacent neighbor count is 1
    Adjacent with neighbor 193.1.1.2
  Suppress hello for 0 neighbor(s)
```

Display the routing table on RouterA with the command **show ip route**. Notice that the cost of reaching the loopback interface on RouterC (3.3.3.3) is 11. The reason for the cost being 11 is that the cost of the Ethernet is 10, and the cost of a loopback interface is 1. This can be seen from the following output.

```
RouterA#show ip route
Codes: C - connected, S - static, I - IGRP, R - RIP, M - mobile, B - BGP
       D - EIGRP, EX - EIGRP external, O - OSPF, IA - OSPF inter area
       N1 - OSPF NSSA external type 1, N2 - OSPF NSSA external type 2
       E1 - OSPF external type 1, E2 - OSPF external type 2, E - EGP
       i - IS-IS, L1 - IS-IS level-1, L2 - IS-IS level-2, * - candidate default
       U - per-user static route, o - ODR

Gateway of last resort is not set

     1.0.0.0/24 is subnetted, 1 subnets
C       1.1.1.0 is directly connected, Loopback0
     2.0.0.0/32 is subnetted, 1 subnets
O       2.2.2.2 [110/67] via 192.1.1.2, 00:15:08, Serial0
     3.0.0.0/32 is subnetted, 1 subnets
O       3.3.3.3 [110/11] via 10.1.1.2, 00:15:08, Ethernet0
     10.0.0.0/24 is subnetted, 1 subnets
C       10.1.1.0 is directly connected, Ethernet0
C    192.1.1.0/24 is directly connected, Serial0
     193.1.1.0/24 [110/74] via 10.1.1.2, 00:15:08, Ethernet0
```

Notice that the cost of reaching the loopback interface on RouterC (3.3.3.3) is 11. The reason: OSPF's cost of sending a packet out the Ethernet on RouterA is 10, and the cost of sending a packet out the loopback interface on RouterC is 1. This information can be seen by displaying th

OSPF statistics on RouterA's Ethernet interface and RouterC's loopback interface.

```
RouterA#show ip ospf interface e0/0
Ethernet0 is up, line protocol is up
  Internet Address 10.1.1.1/24, Area 0
  Process ID 64, Router ID 192.1.1.1, Network Type BROADCAST, Cost: 10
  Transmit Delay is 1 sec, State DR, Priority 1
  Designated Router (ID) 192.1.1.1, Interface address 10.1.1.1
  Backup Designated router (ID) 3.3.3.3, Interface address 10.1.1.2
  Timer intervals configured, Hello 10, Dead 40, Wait 40, Retransmit 5
    Hello due in 00:00:09
  Neighbor Count is 1, Adjacent neighbor count is 1
    Adjacent with neighbor 3.3.3.3   (Backup Designated Router)
  Suppress hello for 0 neighbor(s)

RouterC#show ip ospf int loopback 0
Loopback0 is up, line protocol is up
  Internet Address 3.3.3.3/24, Area 0
  Process ID 64, Router ID 3.3.3.3, Network Type LOOPBACK, Cost: 1
  Loopback interface is treated as a stub Host
```

Change the OSPF cost of RouterA's Ethernet interface to 200.

```
RouterA#configure terminal
RouterA(config)#interface e0/0
RouterA(config-if)#ip ospf cost 200
```

Display the routing table on RouterA with the command **show ip route**. Notice that the route to 3.3.3.3 has now changed. RouterA now uses the path over the serial interface, which has a cost of 131 and is now lower than the new cost of using the Ethernet interface.

```
RouterA#show ip route
Codes: C - connected, S - static, I - IGRP, R - RIP, M - mobile, B - BGP
       D - EIGRP, EX - EIGRP external, O - OSPF, IA - OSPF inter area
       N1 - OSPF NSSA external type 1, N2 - OSPF NSSA external type 2
       E1 - OSPF external type 1, E2 - OSPF external type 2, E - EGP
       i - IS-IS, L1 - IS-IS level-1, L2 - IS-IS level-2, * - candidate default
       U - per-user static route, o - ODR

Gateway of last resort is not set

     1.0.0.0/24 is subnetted, 1 subnets
C       1.1.1.0 is directly connected, Loopback0
     2.0.0.0/32 is subnetted, 1 subnets
O       2.2.2.2 [110/67] via 192.1.1.2, 00:03:20, Serial0
     3.0.0.0/32 is subnetted, 1 subnets
O       3.3.3.3 [110/131] via 192.1.1.2, 00:03:20, Serial0
     10.0.0.0/24 is subnetted, 1 subnets
```

Now, lets take a look and see what happens when the hello intervals do not match on routers connected to the same network. On RouterA's serial interface, change the hello interval to 30 seconds.

```
RouterA#configure terminal
RouterA(config)#interface s0/0
RouterA(config-if)#ip ospf hello-interval 30
```

Display the status of the OSPF neighbors on RouterA with the command **show ip ospf neighbor**. The neighbor relationship with RouterB is gone.

```
RouterA#show ip ospf neighbor

Neighbor ID   Pri   State       Dead Time   Address    Interface
3.3.3.3       1     FULL/BDR    00:00:37    10.1.1.2   Ethernet0
```

Monitor the OSPF events on RouterA with the command **debug ip ospf events**. Notice that RouterA is receiving an OSPF packet from RouterB and that the hello intervals do not match. If either the hello interval or the dead interval do not match, then the router will not form an adjacency with its neighbor.

```
RouterA#
OSPF: Mismatched hello parameters from 192.1.1.2
```

Troubleshooting OSPF

The Cisco IOS provides many tools for troubleshooting OSPF. The following example shows a list of key commands, along with sample output from each.

{**show ip ospf**}   This exec command displays general information about OSPF routing processes. This command can display information about a specific routing process by entering the process number after the command. If no process number is entered, the command will display all OSPF processes on the router.

```
RouterA#show ip ospf
 Routing Process "ospf 64" with ID 192.1.1.1
 Supports only single TOS(TOS0) routes
 SPF schedule delay 5 secs, Hold time between two SPFs 10 secs
 Number of DCbitless external LSA 0
 Number of DoNotAge external LSA 0
```

```
Number of areas in this router is 1. 1 normal 0 stub 0 nssa
    Area BACKBONE(0)
          Number of interfaces in this area is 3
          Area has no authentication
          SPF algorithm executed 16 times
          Area ranges are
          Link State Update Interval is 00:30:00 and due in 00:05:11
          Link State Age Interval is 00:20:00 and due in 00:15:10
          Number of DCbitless LSA 1
          Number of indication LSA 0
          Number of DoNotAge LSA 0
```

{**show ip ospf interface**}   This exec command displays information about all OSPF-configured interfaces. The command also can be used to display information about only a particular interface by specifying the interface after the command. If no interface is specified, the command will display OSPF information for all interfaces on the router.

This one command will tell you the status of the interface, the IP address, the area to which it is attached, the router ID, the interface network type, the interval timers, and more. When troubleshooting an OSPF network, this command should be one of the first commands you use.

```
RouterA#show ip ospf interface s0
Serial0 is up, line protocol is up
 Internet Address 192.1.1.1/24, Area 0
 Process ID 64, Router ID 192.1.1.1, Network Type POINT_TO_POINT, Cost: 66
 Transmit Delay is 1 sec, State POINT_TO_POINT,
 Timer intervals configured, Hello 30, Dead 120, Wait 120, Retransmit 5
  Hello due in 00:00:22
  Neighbor Count is 0, Adjacent neighbor count is 0
  Suppress hello for 0 neighbor(s)
```

{**show ip ospf neighbor**}   This exec command displays OSPF neighbor information for the router. This command can be used to display information about a particular neighbor when specifying the neighbor's router ID after the command. If no router ID is specified, the command will display information about all OSPF neighbors.

The most important information this command gives is the state of the adjacency with the neighbor. When troubleshooting an OSPF network, this command should be the second command you use.

```
RouterA#show ip ospf neighbor

Neighbor ID     Pri    State        Dead Time     Address       Interface
3.3.3.3          1     FULL/BDR     00:00:36      10.1.1.2      Ethernet0
```

{show ip ospf database} This exec command displays information related to the OSPF database for a specific router.

```
RouterA#show ip ospf database

        OSPF Router with ID (192.1.1.1) (Process ID 64)

            Router Link States (Area 0)

Link ID         ADV Router      Age         Seq#            Checksum Link count
3.3.3.3         3.3.3.3         1594        0x80000008      0x7174      4
192.1.1.1       192.1.1.1       1751        0x8000000C      0x573D      3
193.1.1.2       193.1.1.2       140         0x8000000A      0x610B      4

            Net Link States (Area 0)

Link ID         ADV Router      Age         Seq#            Checksum
10.1.1.1        192.1.1.1       1751        0x80000004      0x1185
```

{show ip ospf virtual-links} This exec command displays information about the virtual links configured on the router.

```
RouterC#show ip ospf virtual-links
Virtual Link OSPF_VL0 to router 2.2.2.2 is up
  Run as demand circuit
  DoNotAge LSA allowed.
  Transit area 1, via interface Serial0/0, Cost of using 64
  Transmit Delay is 1 sec, State POINT_TO_POINT,
  Timer intervals configured, Hello 10, Dead 40, Wait 40, Retransmit 5
    Hello due in 00:00:07
    Adjacency State FULL (Hello suppressed)
```

{debug ip ospf events} This exec command displays information about OSPF-related events, such as the forming of adjacencies, flooding information, designated router selection, and *shortest path first* (SPF) calculation. The following output debug command shows the steps that the router goes through while attempting to form adjacencies.

```
RouterC#debug ip ospf events
OSPF: 2 Way Communication to 193.1.1.2 on Serial0, state 2WAY
OSPF: Send DBD to 193.1.1.2 on Serial0 seq 0x1 opt 0x2 flag 0x7 len 32
OSPF: Rcv DBD from 193.1.1.2 on Serial0 seq 0x1CCD opt 0x2 flag 0x7 len 32 state
 EXSTART
OSPF: NBR Negotiation Done. We are the SLAVE
OSPF: Send DBD to 193.1.1.2 on Serial0 seq 0x1CCD opt 0x2 flag 0x2 len 72
```

```
OSPF: Rcv DBD from 193.1.1.2 on Serial0 seq 0x1CCE opt 0x2 flag 0x3 len 72 state
  EXCHANGE
OSPF: Send DBD to 193.1.1.2 on Serial0 seq 0x1CCE opt 0x2 flag 0x0 len 32
OSPF: Rcv DBD from 193.1.1.2 on Serial0 seq 0x1CCF opt 0x2 flag 0x1 len 32 stat
```

{debug ip ospf packet} This exec command displays information about every OSPF packet that is received by the router, such as OSPF version, OSPF packet type, packet length, router ID, area ID, authentication type, and authentication key.

```
RouterC#debug ip ospf packets
OSPF: rcv. v:2 t:1 l:48 rid:193.1.1.2
         aid:0.0.0.0 chk:3437 aut:0 auk: from Serial0
```

Using Figure 8–15, we can tell that RouterC received an OSPF version 2 hello packet that is 48 bytes long. The router ID of the sending router is 193.1.1.2, which is attached to area 0. There is no authentication used on this packet.

Figure 8–15
Debug IP
OSPF packet

Field	Description
v:	OSPF version.
t:	OSPF packet type. Possible packet types follow: 1—Hello 2—Data description 3—Link state request 4—Link state update 5—Link state acknowledgment
l:	OSPF packet length in bytes.
rid:	OSPF router ID.
aid:	OSPF area ID.
chk:	OSPF checksum.
aut:	OSPF authentication type. Possible authentication types follow: 0—No authentication 1—Simple password 2—MD5
auk:	OSPF authentication key.
keyid:	MD5 key ID.
seq:	Sequence number.

■ ■ **Conclusion**

As you can see from this chapter, a network that is based on a link state protocol such as OSPF is considerably more complex to configure, design, and troubleshoot than a network based on a distance vector protocol such as RIP. OSPF, however, provides the following advantages over RIP Version 1:

- No limitation on hop count
- Faster convergence than RIP, because routing changes are instantly flooded throughout the network
- Security. OSPF supports router authentication, while RIP does not.
- OSPF has the concept of route-tagging external routes that are injected into the AS. This feature enables the protocol to keep track of external routes that are injected by other protocols, such as BGP.
- OSPF is classless; RIP is classful.
- OSPF uses the available bandwidth more effectively by only sending routing updates when a change exists.
- OSPF uses multicast packets versus broadcast packets to send LSAs. This feature ensures that routers that are not configured for OSPF do not have to process the packet.

CHAPTER

9

Enhanced Interior Gateway Routing Protocol (EIGRP)

Topics Covered in This Chapter

- Detailed technology overview
- EIGRP terminology
- EIGRP metrics explained
- Basic EIGRP configuration
- EIGRP unequal-cost load balancing
- EIGRP timer configuration
- Configuring EIGRP on an NBMA network
- Detailed troubleshooting examples

Introduction

Enhanced Interior Gateway Routing Protocol (EIGRP) is a Cisco proprietary advanced Distance Vector Routing protocol which was first released in 1994 (IOS 9.21) to address the limitations of traditional Distance Vector and Link State protocols.

Traditional Distance Vector protocols such as RIP forward routing updates to all attached neighbors, which in turn forward the updates to their neighbors. This hop-by-hop propagation of routing information creates large convergence times and looped topology problems.

Link State protocols such as OSPF have been offered as an alternative to the traditional Distance Vector protocols. The problem with Link State protocols is that they solve the convergence problems of traditional Distance Vector protocols by replicating the topology information across the entire domain. This replication becomes undesirable in large networks and greatly affects CPU utilization (due to the number of SPF calculations that need to be run).

EIGRP Terminology

When dealing with EIGRP, you should understand the terminology used.

Successor: The successor is the directly connected neighboring router that has the best route to reach a particular destination. This route is used by the router to forward packets to a given destination. In order for a neighbor to become the successor for a particular destination, the neighbor must first meet the feasibility condition. The feasibility condition states that the route must be advertised from a neighbor that is downstream (with respect to the destination), and the cost to reach the destination must be less than or equal to the cost of the route that is currently being used by the routing table. For example, in Figure 9–1, RouterB's successor to reach NetworkA is RouterA, because the cost to reach NetworkA is two—which is lower than going through RouterC, which is three. If the metric of the link between RouterA and RouterB changed from one to 20, however, then RouterC would meet the feasibility condition and would become the successor.

Feasible Successor: The feasible successor is a neighboring router through which the destination can be reached. This router is not used, however, because the cost to reach the destination is higher than via a different router. The feasible successor can be thought of

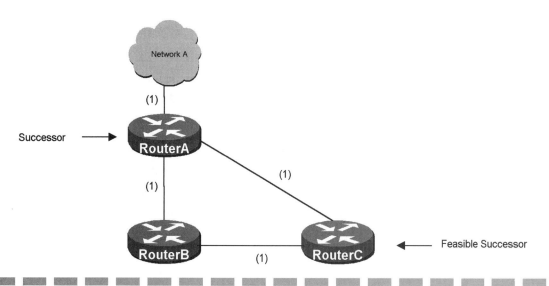

Figure 9–1
EIGRP terminology

as having the next-best route to a destination. Feasible successors are kept in the topology table and are used as backup routes. For example, in Figure 9–1, RouterB's feasible successor to reach NetworkA is RouterC. RouterC has a route to NetworkA; however, this route is not the least-cost path. Therefore, this route is not used to forward data.

Feasibility Condition: The feasibility condition is used to prevent routing loops. In order for the feasibility condition to be met, the route must be advertised from a neighbor that is downstream (with respect to the destination). The cost to reach the destination must be less than or equal to the cost of the route that is currently being used in the routing table. If the feasibility condition is met, then the neighbor becomes the successor. For example, in Figure 9–1, if the link between RouterB and RouterA were to fail, RouterA would no longer be the successor. RouterC would move from being the feasible successor to the successor. If the link between RouterA and RouterB became active again, RouterA would take over as successor because it meets the feasibility condition. RouterA is downstream from NetworkA, and its cost to reach NetworkA is less than RouterC's cost to reach NetworkA.

Active State: When the router loses its route to a destination and no feasible successor is available, the router goes into active state. While in active state, the router sends out queries to all neighbors in order to find a route to the destination. At this time, the router must run the routing algorithm to recompute a new route to the destination.

Passive State: When the router loses its successor but has a feasible successor, the router goes into passive state.

Hello: Hello packets are exchanged between neighboring routers. As long as hello packets are received, the router can determine that the neighbor is alive and functioning.

Acknowledgment Packets (ACKs): ACKs are sent by the router to acknowledge the receipt of update packets.

Update: Update packets are used by the router to send routing information between neighbors. Update messages are sent if the metric of a route changes or when a router first comes up.

Query: When the router loses its route to a destination and no feasible successor is available, the router goes into active state. While in this active state, the router sends out query packets to all neighbors for a particular destination. The router waits for a response from all neighbors before starting the computation for a new successor.

Replies: Replies are sent in response to queries. The reply contains information about how to reach a destination. If the queried neighbor does not have the information requested, the neighbor sends queries to all its neighbors.

Technology Overview

When an EIGRP-enabled router first comes online, it sends hello packets out all EIGRP-enabled interfaces using Multicast address 224.0.0.10. The hello packets are used for two purposes: discovering neighboring routers, and after the neighbors are discovered, determining whether a neighbor has become unreachable or inoperative.

Once a new neighbor is discovered via the hello packet, the router records the IP address and interface on which the neighbor was discovered. The router then sends an update to the neighbor containing all of its known routes, and the neighbor does the same. This information is stored in the EIGRP topology table.

Subsequently, hello packets are sent out every five seconds (or every 60 seconds on low-speed NBMA networks). The hello packets enable the router to dynamically and quickly discover the loss of its neighbor. If a hello packet is not received from the neighbor router before the expiration of the Holdtimer, then the neighbor is declared down. At this point, the neighbor adjacency is deleted, and all routes associated with that neighbor are removed.

The topology table includes the router's and neighbor's metric to reach the destination. The DUAL algorithm uses the topology table to find the lowest metric loop-free path to each destination. The next-hop router for the lowest-cost path is referred to as the Successor and is the next-hop IP address loaded in the routing table. The DUAL algorithm also tries to find a Feasible Successor (or the next-best route), which is kept in the topology database.

If the router loses its Successor and a Feasible Successor is available, no route recomputation is necessary. The router simply makes the Feasible Successor the Successor and adds the new route to the routing table, remaining in a passive state. If no Feasible Successor is available, however, then the router goes into active state for the destination network, and recomputation for the route is necessary.

While the router is in active state, the router sends a query packet out all EIGRP-enabled interfaces—except the interface on which the Successor resides—and inquires whether the neighbor has a route to the given destination. The neighbors respond, notifying the sender that they do or do not have a route to the destination. Once all replies are received, the router can then calculate a new Successor. If the neighbor receiving the query packet was using the sender to reach the destination network (as its Successor), the neighbor will query all of its neighbors for a route to the destination. The queried neighbors go through the same process, which creates a cascading of queries through the network that search for a path to the destination.

As long as EIGRP has a Feasible Successor, no recomputation is necessary. This situation prevents the router from having to use CPU cycles and also speeds up convergence. Routers that are not affected by topology changes are not involved in recomputations.

EIGRP Metrics

The EIGRP metric is a 32-bit number which is calculated using bandwidth, delay, reliability, loading, and MTU. Calculating the metric for a route is a two-step process using five different characteristics of the link and the K values. The K values are configurable, but this is not recommended. The default K values are: K1 = 1, K2 = 0, K3 = 1, K4 = 0, and K5 = 0.

The EIGRP metric is calculated as:

1. **Metric** = K1 * Bandwidth + (K2 * Bandwidth) / (256-load) + K3 * Delay

2. If K5 is not equal to zero, take the Metric from step 1 and multiply it by [K5 / (reliability + K4)]. If K5 is zero, ignore step 2.

As shown earlier, Cisco sets K2, K4, and K5 to zero. This situation leaves only two variables to compute the EIGRP metric (bandwidth and delay). Because three of the K values are zero, the formula reduces to the following:

```
Metric = Bandwidth + Delay
```

The bandwidth is derived by finding the smallest of all bandwidths in the path to the destination and dividing 10,000,000 by that number.

The delay is found by adding all of the delays along the paths and dividing that number by 10. The sum of the two numbers is then multiplied by 256. This equation can be written as follows:

```
Metric = [(10,000,000 / minimum bandwidth) + (SUM (interface delay) / 10)] * 256
```

Let's look at Figure 9–2 and determine what the metric is to reach network 1.0.0.0 from RouterB.

Use the **show interface** command on each router to determine the bandwidth and delay for each interface.

```
RouterB#show interfaces S0/0
Serial0/0 is up, line protocol is up
  Hardware is QUICC Serial
  Internet address is 192.1.1.1/24
  MTU 1500 bytes, BW 1544 Kbit, DLY 20000 usec, rely 255/255, load 1/255
  Encapsulation HDLC, loopback not set, keepalive set (10 sec)
  Last input 00:00:02, output 00:00:02, output hang never
  Last clearing of "show interface" counters never
```

Figure 9–2
EIGRP metric

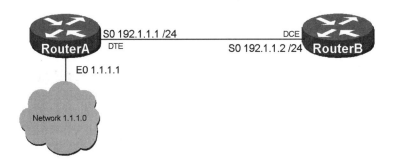

```
Input queue: 0/75/0 (size/max/drops); Total output drops: 0
Queueing strategy: weighted fair
Output queue: 0/64/0 (size/threshold/drops)
    Conversations  0/3 (active/max active)
    Reserved Conversations 0/0 (allocated/max allocated)
5 minute input rate 0 bits/sec, 1 packets/sec
5 minute output rate 0 bits/sec, 1 packets/sec
    155 packets input, 10368 bytes, 0 no buffer
    Received 80 broadcasts, 0 runts, 1 giants, 0 throttles
    5 input errors, 1 CRC, 2 frame, 0 overrun, 0 ignored, 1 abort
    246 packets output, 13455 bytes, 0 underruns
    0 output errors, 0 collisions, 910 interface resets
    0 output buffer failures, 0 output buffers swapped out
    154 carrier transitions
    DCD=up  DSR=up  DTR=up  RTS=up  CTS=up

RouterA#show interfaces e0/0
Ethernet0/0 is up, line protocol is up
  Hardware is AmdP2, address is 00e0.1e5b.25a1 (bia 00e0.1e5b.25a1)
  MTU 1500 bytes, BW 10000 Kbit, DLY 1000 usec, rely 243/255, load 1/255
  Encapsulation ARPA, loopback not set, keepalive not set
  ARP type: ARPA, ARP Timeout 04:00:00
  Last input never, output 00:00:08, output hang never
  Last clearing of "show interface" counters never
  Queueing strategy: fifo
  Output queue 0/40, 0 drops; input queue 0/75, 0 drops
  5 minute input rate 0 bits/sec, 0 packets/sec
  5 minute output rate 0 bits/sec, 0 packets/sec
    0 packets input, 0 bytes, 0 no buffer
    Received 0 broadcasts, 0 runts, 0 giants, 0 throttles
    0 input errors, 0 CRC, 0 frame, 0 overrun, 0 ignored, 0 abort
    0 input packets with dribble condition detected
    6 packets output, 1071 bytes, 0 underruns
    6 output errors, 0 collisions, 2 interface resets
    0 babbles, 0 late collision, 0 deferred
    6 lost carrier, 0 no carrier
    0 output buffer failures, 0 output buffers swapped out
```

To reach network 1.1.1.0 from RouterB, a packet will cross the serial interface between RouterA and RouterB and the Ethernet interface on RouterA. Because the lowest bandwidth is used for the calculation, the bandwidth of the serial interface is used.

```
Metric = [(10,000,000 / BW Serial link) + ((delay on serial link + delay on
                                      the Ethernet link) / 10)] * 256
Metric = [(10,000,000 / 1544) + ((20000 + 1000) / 10)] * 256
Metric = 2195456
```

Lets take a look at the routing table on RouterB and see if our calculations are correct.

```
RouterB#show ip route
Codes: C - connected, S - static, I - IGRP, R - RIP, M - mobile, B - BGP
       D - EIGRP, EX - EIGRP external, O - OSPF, IA - OSPF inter area
       N1 - OSPF NSSA external type 1, N2 - OSPF NSSA external type 2
       E1 - OSPF external type 1, E2 - OSPF external type 2, E - EGP
       i - IS-IS, L1 - IS-IS level-1, L2 - IS-IS level-2, * - candidate default
       U - per-user static route, o - ODR

Gateway of last resort is not set

D    1.0.0.0/8 [90/2195456] via 192.1.1.1, 00:21:50, Serial0/0
C    192.1.1.0/24 is directly connected, Serial0/0
```

IOS Requirements

EIGRP first became available in IOS 9.21; however, EIGRP was significantly enhanced in releases 10.3.(11), 11.0(8), and 11.1(3). All of our labs
were performed using IOS 11.2.

Commands Discussed in This Chapter

- **debug eigrp fsm**
- **debug eigrp packet**
- **debug ip eigrp**
- **ip hello-interval eigrp** autonomous-system-number seconds
- **ip hold-time eigrp** autonomous-system-number seconds
- **network** (network-number)
- **no ip split-horizon eigrp** autonomous-system-number
- **passive-interface** type number
- **router eigrp** (autonomous-system number)
- **show ip eigrp interfaces** [interface] [as-number]
- **show ip eigrp neighbors** (type number)
- **show ip eigrp topology** (autonomous-system-number)
- **show ip eigrp traffic** (autonomous-system-number)
- **show ip protocols**

■ **traffic-share** {balanced | min}

■ **variance** (multiplier)

Definitions

debug eigrp fsm: This debug command displays information about EIGRP *Feasible Successor Metrics* (FSM).

debug eigrp packet: This debug command displays information about any EIGRP messages traveling between the routers.

debug ip eigrp: This debug command displays information about any EIGRP packets that are sent or received by the router.

ip hello-interval eigrp: This interface configuration command sets the hello interval in seconds for the EIGRP routing process. The default hello timer is 60 seconds for low-speed (any network that is T1 or slower) NBMA networks. For all other networks, the default is five seconds.

ip hold-time eigrp: This interface configuration command sets the hold time in seconds for an EIGRP process. The default hold time is 180 seconds for low-speed (any network that is T1 or slower) NBMA networks. For all other networks, the default is 15 seconds.

network: This router configuration command specifies a list of networks on which the EIGRP routing process will run. This command sends EIGRP updates to the interfaces that are specified. If an interface's network is not specified, it will not be advertised in any EIGRP updates.

no ip split-horizon eigrp: This interface configuration command disables split horizons on a particular interface. Spilt-horizons blocks the sending of routing information out the same interface from which it was received. This behavior is used to prevent routing loops; however, in the case of NBMA networks such as Frame-Relay or ATM, this behavior can prevent routing information from being passed to spoke routers.

passive-interface: This router configuration command disables the sending of routing updates on a given interface. If you disable the sending of routing updates on an interface, the particular network will continue to be advertised out other EIGRP-enabled interfaces. Any routing updates received by the router on a passive interface will still be processed.

router eigrp: This global command enables the EIGRP routing process on the router.

show ip eigrp interfaces: This exec command displays information about all interfaces configured for EIGRP.

show ip eigrp neighbors: This exec command displays information about all neighbors that are discovered by EIGRP. This command is helpful in determining when neighbors become active or inactive.

show ip eigrp topology: This exec command displays the EIGRP topology table and is useful in debugging problems with the DUAL algorithm.

show ip eigrp traffic: This exec command displays the number of EIGRP packets sent and received by the router.

show ip protocols: This exec command displays the current state of all active routing protocol processes.

traffic-share: This router configuration command controls how traffic is distributed across routes when there are multiple routes to the same destination network that have different costs. The traffic can be distributed proportionately to the ratios of the metrics—or can be set to only use routes that have minimum costs.

variance: This router configuration command controls load balancing over multiple EIGRP paths. This command enables the administrator to load balance across multiple paths, even if the metric of the paths is different. By default, the amount of variance is set to one (equal-cost load balancing). The variance command enables the user to define how much worse the metric of an alternate path can be and still be used to route packets to a given destination. For example, if the variance is set to two, the router will load balance across up to four paths—as long as the metric is lower than twice the metric of the best route. This concept will be explained in more detail in Lab #38.

LAB #36: Basic EIGRP Configuration

Equipment Needed

The following equipment is needed to perform this lab exercise:

- Two Cisco routers with one Ethernet port and one serial port
- One Cisco router with two serial ports
- Cisco IOS 10.0 or higher
- A PC running a terminal emulation program for connecting to the console port of the router
- One Ethernet hub and two Ethernet cables
- Two Cisco DTE/DCE crossover cables
- One Cisco rolled cable

Configuration Overview

This configuration will demonstrate basic routing using EIGRP. All routers will be configured for EIGRP.

RouterA and RouterB are connected via an Ethernet hub, and RouterC is connected to RouterA and RouterB serially via a crossover cable. RouterC will act as the DCE, supplying clock to RouterA and RouterB. The IP addresses are assigned as per Figure 9–3. All routers will be configured for EIGRP and will advertise all connected networks.

Router Configurations

The configurations for the three routers in this example are as follows (key EIGRP configurations are highlighted in bold):

RouterA

```
version 11.2
no service udp-small-servers
no service tcp-small-servers
!
```

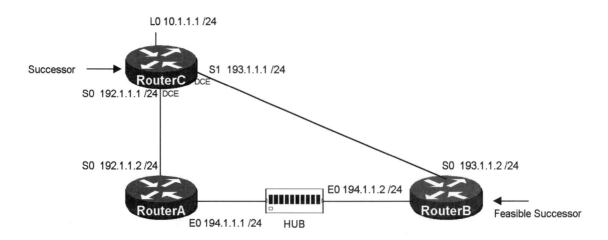

Figure 9–3
EIGRP Basic Configuration

```
hostname RouterA
!
!
interface Ethernet0
 ip address 194.1.1.1 255.255.255.0
!
interface Serial0
 ip address 192.1.1.2 255.255.255.0
!
interface Serial1
 no ip address
 shutdown
!
!
```
router eigrp 64←Enables the EIGRP routing process on the router.
network 192.1.1.0←Specifies what interfaces will receive and send EIGRP
                    routing updates. It also specifies what networks will be
                    advertised

 network 194.1.1.0
```
!
no ip classless
!
!line con 0
line aux 0
line vty 0 4
 login
!
end
```

RouterB

```
!
version 11.0
service udp-small-servers
service tcp-small-servers
!
hostname RouterB
!
interface Ethernet0
 ip address 194.1.1.2 255.255.255.0
!
interface Serial0
 ip address 193.1.1.2 255.255.255.0
 no fair-queue
 !
!
router eigrp 64←Enables the EIGRP routing process on the router.
network 193.1.1.0←Specifies what interfaces will receive and send IGRP routing
                 updates. It also specifies what networks will be advertised.
 network 194.1.1.0
!
!
line con 0
line aux 0
line vty 0 4
 login
```

RouterC

```
!
version 11.1
service udp-small-servers
service tcp-small-servers
!
hostname RouterC
!
interface Loopback0
 ip address 10.1.1.1 255.255.255.0
!
interface Ethernet0
 no ip address
shutdown
!
interface Serial0
 ip address 192.1.1.1 255.255.255.0
clockrate 500000←Acts as DCE providing clock
!
interface Serial1
```

```
 ip address 193.1.1.1 255.255.255.0
 clockrate 500000←Acts as DCE providing clock
!
router eigrp 64←Enables the EIGRP routing process on the router.
network 10.0.0.0←Specifies what interfaces will receive and send IGRP routing
                  updates. It also specifies what networks will be advertised.
network 193.1.1.0
network 192.1.1.0
!
no ip classless
!
!
line con 0
line aux 0
line vty 0 4
 login
!
end
```

Monitoring and Testing the Configuration

Like IGRP, EIGRP is a simple protocol to configure and troubleshoot. Show the IP routing table on RouterA with the **show ip route** command. The following example shows the output from this command. Notice that two networks were learned via EIGRP: 10.0.0.0 and 193.1.1.0. EIGRP routing table entries are identified by the letters "D" and "EX." A "D" is a route that is within the same AS, and an "EX" is a route that has been received from a different AS. EIGRP internal routes have an administrative distance of 90, and EIGRP external routes have a administrative distance of 170.

```
RouterA#show ip route
Codes: C - connected, S - static, I - IGRP, R - RIP, M - mobile, B - BGP
       D - EIGRP, EX - EIGRP external, O - OSPF, IA - OSPF inter area
       N1 - OSPF NSSA external type 1, N2 - OSPF NSSA external type 2
       E1 - OSPF external type 1, E2 - OSPF external type 2, E - EGP
       i - IS-IS, L1 - IS-IS level-1, L2 - IS-IS level-2, * - candidate default
       U - per-user static route, o - ODR

Gateway of last resort is not set

D    10.0.0.0/8 [90/2297856] via 192.1.1.1, 00:22:19, Serial0
C    192.1.1.0/24 is directly connected, Serial0
D    193.1.1.0/24 [90/2195456] via 194.1.1.2, 00:22:20, Ethernet0
C    194.1.1.0/24 is directly connected, Ethernet0
```

The network 10.0.0.0 appears as a classful network in RouterA's routing table instead of 10.1.1.0, which is the subnet on RouterC. The reason for this situation is that by default, automatic summarization is performed when there are two or more network router configuration commands configured for the IP EIGRP process. To disable automatic summarization, use the command **no auto-summary**.

Display the information about EIGRP with the command **show ip protocols**. Notice that on RouterC, automatic summarization is on, and the router is summarizing network 10.0.0.0.

```
RouterC#show ip protocols
Routing Protocol is "eigrp 64"
  Outgoing update filter list for all interfaces is not set
  Incoming update filter list for all interfaces is not set
  Default networks flagged in outgoing updates
  Default networks accepted from incoming updates
  EIGRP metric weight K1=1, K2=0, K3=1, K4=0, K5=0
  EIGRP maximum hopcount 100
  EIGRP maximum metric variance 1
  Redistributing: eigrp 64
      Automatic network summarization is in effect
      10.0.0.0/8 for Serial 0
      Summarizing with metric 2297856
  Routing for Networks:
    10.0.0.0
    1.0.0.0
  Passive Interface(s):
    Serial1
  Routing Information Sources:
    Gateway         Distance      Last Update
    (this router)          5      00:00:03
    Gateway         Distance      Last Update
    10.1.3.2              90      00:41:18
    10.1.2.2              90      00:00:14
  Distance: internal 90 external 170
```

Let's see what happens when auto summary is disabled on RouterC. From RouterC, enter the command **no auto summary** under the EIGRP routing process.

```
RouterC#configure terminal
Enter configuration commands, one per line. End with CNTL/Z.
RouterC(config)#router eigrp 64
RouterC(config-router)#no auto-summary
```

Display the information about EIGRP with the command **show ip protocols**. Notice that on RouterC, automatic network summarization is now off.

```
RouterC#show ip protocols
Routing Protocol is "eigrp 64"
  Outgoing update filter list for all interfaces is not set
  Incoming update filter list for all interfaces is not set
  Default networks flagged in outgoing updates
```

```
Default networks accepted from incoming updates
EIGRP metric weight K1=1, K2=0, K3=1, K4=0, K5=0
EIGRP maximum hopcount 100
EIGRP maximum metric variance 1
Redistributing: eigrp 64
Automatic network summarization is not in effect
Routing for Networks:
   10.0.0.0
```

Display the contents of the routing table on RouterA with the command **show ip route**. Notice that the subnet 10.1.1.0 is now in the routing table.

```
RouterA#show ip route
Codes: C - connected, S - static, I - IGRP, R - RIP, M - mobile, B - BGP
       D - EIGRP, EX - EIGRP external, O - OSPF, IA - OSPF inter area
       N1 - OSPF NSSA external type 1, N2 - OSPF NSSA external type 2
       E1 - OSPF external type 1, E2 - OSPF external type 2, E - EGP
       i - IS-IS, L1 - IS-IS level-1, L2 - IS-IS level-2, * - candidate default
       U - per-user static route, o - ODR

Gateway of last resort is not set

10.0.0.0/24 is subnetted, 1 subnets
D        10.1.1.0 [90/2297856] via 192.1.1.1, 00:13:00, Serial0
C     192.1.1.0/24 is directly connected, Serial0
D     193.1.1.0/24 [90/2195456] via 194.1.1.2, 00:13:00, Ethernet0
C     194.1.1.0/24 is directly connected, Ethernet0
```

From RouterA, monitor the hello exchanges being passed between neighbors using the **debug eigrp packets** command. The following example shows the output from this command. Notice the hello packets being sent between neighbors. Hello packets are sent periodically between neighboring routers, enabling the router to quickly and dynamically discover the loss of a neighbor.

```
RouterA#debug eigrp packets
EIGRP Packets debugging is on
    (UPDATE, REQUEST, QUERY, REPLY, HELLO, IPXSAP, PROBE, ACK)
RouterA#
EIGRP: Received HELLO on Serial0 nbr 192.1.1.1
  AS 64, Flags 0x0, Seq 0/0 idbQ 0/0 iidbQ un/rely 0/0 peerQ un/rely 0/0
EIGRP: Sending HELLO on Ethernet0
  AS 64, Flags 0x0, Seq 0/0 idbQ 0/0 iidbQ un/rely 0/0
EIGRP: Sending HELLO on Serial0
  AS 64, Flags 0x0, Seq 0/0 idbQ 0/0 iidbQ un/rely 0/0
EIGRP: Received HELLO on Ethernet0 nbr 194.1.1.2
  AS 64, Flags 0x0, Seq 0/0 idbQ 0/0 iidbQ un/rely 0/0 peerQ un/rely 0/0
```

Display RouterA's EIGRP neighbors with the command **show ip eigrp neighbors**. The following example shows the output from the command.

Notice that RouterA has two neighbors, 192.1.1.1 (RouterC) and 194.1.1.2 (RouterB). The command displays information about the Autonomous system number, how long the neighbor has been up, and the interface on which the neighbor resides.

```
RouterA#show ip eigrp neighbors
IP-EIGRP neighbors for process 64
H   Address      Interface   Hold    Uptime     SRTT   RTO    Q     Seq
                             (sec)              (ms)          Cnt   Num
0   192.1.1.1  Se0          13      00:13:14   15     200    0     31
1   194.1.1.2  Et0          10      00:57:17   35     210    0     38
```

From RouterA, display the EIGRP topology database with the command **show ip eigrp topology**. Notice the letter (P) preceding the destination address. This letter indicates that the router is in passive state for the particular destination. When a router is in the passive state, no EIGRP recomputations are being performed for this destination. The router will only perform a recomputation if the router has lost its successor (and no feasible successor is available).

For destination network 10.0.0.0, RouterA can reach the network in two ways: via 192.1.1.1 or via 194.1.1.2. The successor is the route via 192.1.1.1, because the cost to reach network 10.0.0.0 is less via 192.1.1.1 than via 194.1.1.2. Because network 10.0.0.0 can be reached via 194.1.1.2, however, this route becomes the feasible successor.

```
RouterA#show ip eigrp topology
IP-EIGRP Topology Table for process 64

Codes: P - Passive, A - Active, U - Update, Q - Query, R - Reply,
       r - Reply status

P 10.0.0.0/8, 1 successors, FD is 2297856
        via 192.1.1.1 (2297856/128256), Serial0
P 192.1.1.0/24, 1 successors, FD is 2169856
        via Connected, Serial0
P 193.1.1.0/24, 1 successors, FD is 2195456
        via 194.1.1.2 (2195456/2169856), Ethernet0
        via 192.1.1.1 (2681856/2169856), Serial0
P 194.1.1.0/24, 1 successors, FD is 281600
        via Connected, Ethernet0
```

Let's see what happens when RouterA loses its primary route (successor) to destination network 10.0.0.0. From RouterA, shut down the serial interface 0.

```
RouterA#conf terminal
Enter configuration commands, one per line. End with CNTL/Z.
RouterA(config)#interface s0
RouterA(config-if)#shutdown
```

Display the EIGRP topology on RouterA with the command **show ip eigrp topology**. Notice that the successor for network 10.0.0.0 is now 194.1.1.2, which is RouterB's Ethernet interface. Also note that the router's state for this destination is still *passive* (P). The router will only become active if it loses its successor (and no feasible successor is available).

```
RouterA#show ip eigrp topology
IP-EIGRP Topology Table for process 64

Codes: P - Passive, A - Active, U - Update, Q - Query, R - Reply,
       r - Reply status

P 10.0.0.0/8, 1 successors, FD is 2323456
         via 194.1.1.2 (2323456/2297856), Ethernet0
P 193.1.1.0/24, 1 successors, FD is 2195456
         via 194.1.1.2 (2195456/2169856), Ethernet0
P 194.1.1.0/24, 1 successors, FD is 281600
         via Connected, Ethernet0
```

From RouterB, delete the IGRP process, and add a new process using autonomous system 56 with the following commands:

```
RouterB#configure terminal
RouterB(config)#no router eigrp 64
RouterB(config)#router eigrp 56
RouterB(config-router)#network 193.1.1.0
RouterB(config-router)# network 194.1.1.0
```

Show the EIGRP neighbors on RouterA with the command **show ip eigrp neighbors**.

```
RouterA#show ip eigrp neighbors
IP-EIGRP neighbors for process 64
H   Address     Interface   Hold    Uptime    SRTT    RTO    Q    Seq
                            (sec)             (ms)           nt   Num
1   192.1.1.1   Se0         11      00:06:31  43      258    0    55
```

Notice that RouterB is no longer a neighbor, and no networks are being learned via EIGRP for RouterB. This situation occurs because the autonomous system numbers are different. The autonomous system number must match, or the routers will not exchange routing information.

LAB #37: Passive Interface Configuration

Equipment Needed

The following equipment is needed to perform this lab exercise:

- Two Cisco routers with one serial port
- One Cisco router with two serial ports
- Cisco IOS 10.0 or higher
- A PC running a terminal emulation program
- Two Cisco DTE/DCE crossover cables
- One Cisco rolled cable for accessing the console port of the router

Configuration Overview

This configuration will demonstrate the use of the passive-interface command, which permits EIGRP-enabled routers to disable the sending of EIGRP packets on a particular interface.

The passive-interface router configuration command is typically used when the network router configuration command configures more interfaces than desirable. For example, in Figure 9–4, RouterA has three defined subnets: 10.1.1.0/24, 10.1.2.0/24, and 10.1.3.0/24. When EIGRP is enabled, EIGRP is turned on for the classful network 10.0.0.0. This area encompasses all three subnets. The passive-interface command enables the user to turn off EIGRP advertisements on a particular interface (subnet).

In this lab scenario, shown in Figure 9–5 the user only wishes to send EIGRP updates out network 10.1.2.0, so interfaces S1 (10.1.3.0) is made passive.

Figure 9–4
The passive-interface command

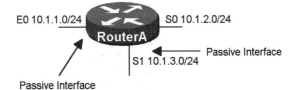

Figure 9–5

EIGRP passive-
interface
configuration

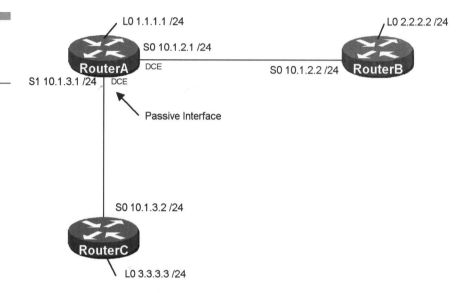

RouterA is connected to RouterB and RouterC via a serial crossover cable. RouterA will act as the DCE, supplying clock to RouterB and RouterC. The IP addresses are assigned as per Figure 9–5. All routers will be configured for EIGRP. RouterB and RouterC will advertise all connected networks. RouterA's interface S1 will be passive and will not advertise any routing information.

Router Configurations

The configurations for the three routers in this example are as follows (key EIGRP configurations are highlighted in bold):

RouterA

```
version 11.1
service udp-small-servers
service tcp-small-servers
!
hostname RouterA
!
interface Loopback0
 ip address 1.1.1.1 255.255.255.0
!
```

```
interface Ethernet0
 no ip address
shutdown
!
interface Serial0
 ip address 10.1.2.1 255.255.255.0
 clockrate 500000←Acts as DCE providing clock
!
interface Serial1
 ip address 10.1.3.1 255.255.255.0
 clockrate 500000←Acts as DCE providing clock
!
router eigrp 64←Enables the EIGRP routing process on the router
 network 10.0.0.0←Specifies what interfaces will receive and send EIGRP
                  routing updates. It also specifies what networks will be
                  advertised.
 network 1.0.0.0
 no auto-summary←Turns off automatic summarization of subnet routes into
                  network-level routes
!
no ip classless
!
line con 0
line aux 0
line vty 0 4
 login
!
end
```

RouterB

```
version 11.2
no service udp-small-servers
no service tcp-small-servers
!
hostname RouterB
!
interface Loopback0
 ip address 2.2.2.2 255.255.255.0
!
interface Ethernet0
 no ip address
 shutdown
!
interface Serial0
 ip address 10.1.2.2 255.255.255.0
!
router eigrp 64←Enables the EIGRP routing process on the router
```

```
 network 10.0.0.0←Specifies what interfaces will receive and send EIGRP
                 routing updates. It also specifies what networks will be
                 advertised.
 network 2.0.0.0
 no auto-summary←Turns off automatic summarization of subnet routes into
                 network-level routes
!
no ip classless
!
line con 0
line vty 0 4
 login
!
end
```

RouterC

```
Current configuration:
!
version 11.2
no service udp-small-servers
no service tcp-small-servers
!
hostname RouterC
!
interface Loopback0
 ip address 3.3.3.3 255.255.255.0
!
interface Ethernet0
 no ip address
 shutdown
!
interface Serial0
 ip address 10.1.3.2 255.255.255.0
!
router eigrp 64←Enables the EIGRP routing process on the router
 network 3.0.0.0
 network 10.0.0.0←Specifies what interfaces will receive and send EIGRP
                 routing updates. It also specifies what networks will be
                 advertised.

 no auto-summary←Turns off automatic summarization of subnet routes into
                 network-level routes
!
no ip classless
!
line con 0
line vty 0 4
 login
!
end
```

Monitoring and Testing the Configuration

When EIGRP is enabled on the router, the classful network number is used—just like with RIP or IGRP. If you enter a subnet with the network command, the router converts it back to the classful network. For example, if you try to enable EIGRP on sub-network 10.1.1.0, the router converts it to its natural network number (which is 10.0.0.0). Therefore, this process enables EIGRP on any sub-network of 10.0.0.0. EIGRP updates can be disabled on an per interface basis through the use of the passive interface command.

Let's look at RouterA and see which interfaces EIGRP is configured on with the command **show ip eigrp interfaces**. Notice that EIGRP is configured on S0 and S1, which are both subnets of 10.0.0.0.

```
RouterA#show ip eigrp interfaces
IP-EIGRP interfaces for process 64
                        Xmit Queue    Mean    Pacing Time   Multicast    Pending
Interface    Peers      Un/Reliable   SRTT    Un/Reliable   Flow Timer   Routes
Se0          1          0/0           94      0/15          479          0
Lo0          0          0/0           0       0/10          0            0
Se1          1          0/0           12      0/15          50           0
```

Show the routing table on RouterA with the command **show ip route**. Note that RouterA has a route to network 3.3.3.0, which is on RouterC.

```
RouterA#show ip route
Codes: C - connected, S - static, I - IGRP, R - RIP, M - mobile, B - BGP
       D - EIGRP, EX - EIGRP external, O - OSPF, IA - OSPF inter area
       E1 - OSPF external type 1, E2 - OSPF external type 2, E - EGP
       i - IS-IS, L1 - IS-IS level-1, L2 - IS-IS level-2, * - candidate default
       U - per-user static route

Gateway of last resort is not set

     1.0.0.0/24 is subnetted, 1 subnets
C       1.1.1.0 is directly connected, Loopback0
     2.0.0.0/24 is subnetted, 1 subnets
D       2.2.2.0 [90/2297856] via 10.1.2.2, 00:18:07, Serial0
     3.0.0.0/24 is subnetted, 1 subnets
D       3.3.3.0 [90/2297856] via 10.1.3.2, 00:18:08, Serial1
     10.0.0.0/24 is subnetted, 2 subnets
C       10.1.3.0 is directly connected, Serial1
C       10.1.2.0 is directly connected, Serial0
```

Now, let's add the passive interface command on RouterA and see what happens.

```
RouterA#configure terminal
Enter configuration commands, one per line. End with CNTL/Z.
RouterA(config-if)#router eigrp 64
RouterA(config-router)#passive-interface s1
```

Display the information about EIGRP with the command **show ip protocols**. Notice that RouterA's interface (S1) is now passive.

```
RouterA#show ip protocols
Routing Protocol is "eigrp 64"
  Outgoing update filter list for all interfaces is not set
  Incoming update filter list for all interfaces is not set
  Default networks flagged in outgoing updates
  Default networks accepted from incoming updates
  EIGRP metric weight K1=1, K2=0, K3=1, K4=0, K5=0
  EIGRP maximum hopcount 100
  EIGRP maximum metric variance 1
  Redistributing: eigrp 64
  Automatic network summarization is not in effect
  Routing for Networks:
    10.0.0.0
    1.0.0.0
  Passive Interface(s):
    Serial1
  Routing Information Sources:
    Gateway          Distance      Last Update
    (this router)        5         01:20:53
    10.1.3.2            90         00:38:50
    10.1.2.2            90         00:18:36
  Distance: internal 90 external 170
```

Display the EIGRP neighbor table on RouterA with the command **show ip eigrp neighbors**. Notice that RouterC (10.1.3.2) is no longer a neighbor.

```
RouterA#show ip eigrp neighbors
IP-EIGRP neighbors for process 64
H   Address      Interface    Hold    Uptime    SRTT    RTO    Q     Seq
                              (sec)              (ms)           Cnt   Num
0   10.1.2.2     Se0          14      01:01:10   64      384    0     19
```

When an EIGRP-enabled interface is made passive, no EIGRP packets are sent out that interface. Because EIGRP uses hello packets to form adjacencies with neighbors, no adjacencies will be formed.

Show the routing table on RouterA with the command **show ip route**. Notice that the route to 3.3.3.0 has been removed. Unlike RIP or IGRP (where updates are received but are not sent), when the passive interface command is used with EIGRP, routing updates are neither received or sent—because no neighbor relationship is formed.

```
RouterA#show ip route
Codes: C - connected, S - static, I - IGRP, R - RIP, M - mobile, B - BGP
       D - EIGRP, EX - EIGRP external, O - OSPF, IA - OSPF inter area
       E1 - OSPF external type 1, E2 - OSPF external type 2, E - EGP
       i - IS-IS, L1 - IS-IS level-1, L2 - IS-IS level-2, * - candidate default
       U - per-user static route

Gateway of last resort is not set

     1.0.0.0/24 is subnetted, 1 subnets
C       1.1.1.0 is directly connected, Loopback0
     2.0.0.0/24 is subnetted, 1 subnets
D       2.2.2.0 [90/2297856] via 10.1.2.2, 00:29:40, Serial0
     10.0.0.0/24 is subnetted, 2 subnets
C       10.1.3.0 is directly connected, Serial1
C       10.1.2.0 is directly connected, Serial0
```

LAB #38: EIGRP Unequal-Cost Load Balancing

Equipment Needed

The following equipment is needed to perform this lab exercise:

- One Cisco router with one Ethernet port and two serial ports
- One Cisco router with one Ethernet port and one serial port
- One Cisco router with one serial port
- Cisco IOS 10.0 or higher
- A PC running a terminal emulation program
- Two Ethernet cables
- One Ethernet hub
- Two Cisco DTE/DCE crossover cables
- One Cisco rolled cable for accessing the console port of the router

Overview

EIGRP can be configured to load balance on up to four unequal cost paths to a given destination. This feature is known as unequal-cost load balancing and is set using the variance command. By default, the router will load balance across up to four equal cost paths. The variance command lets you set how much worse an alternate path can be (in terms of metrics) and still be used to load balance across.

For example, if RouterA has two routes to network 3.3.3.0, one with a cost of four and one with a cost of eight, by default the route will only use the path with a cost of four when sending packets to 3.3.3.3. If a variance of two is set, however, the router will load balance across both paths. This situation occurs because the route with the cost of eight is within the variance, which in this case can be up to two times as bad as the preferred route (4 (preferred route) * 2 = 8).

Configuration Overview

This configuration will demonstrate the use of the variance command, which permits EIGRP enabled routers to load balance across unequal-cost paths. The variance command will be set on RouterA, so that both paths to network 3.3.3.3 are used.

RouterA, RouterB, and RouterC are connected serially via a crossover cable, and RouterA and RouterB are also connected via an Ethernet hub. RouterB will act as the DCE, supplying clock to RouterA and RouterC. The IP addresses are assigned as per Figure 9–6. All routers will be configured for EIGRP. RouterA will be configured to load balance traffic that is destined for 3.3.3.3 over two unequal-cost paths.

Router Configurations

The configurations for the three routers in this example are as follows (key EIGRP configurations are highlighted in bold):

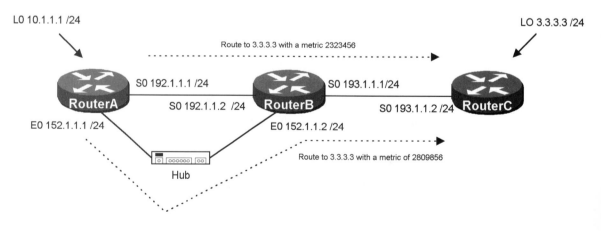

Figure 9–6
EIGRP unequal-cost load balancing

RouterA

```
version 11.2
no service udp-small-servers
no service tcp-small-servers
!
hostname RouterA
!
interface Loopback0←Defines a virtual interface that will be used as a test
                    point.
 ip address 10.1.1.1 255.255.255.0
!
interface Ethernet0
 ip address 152.1.1.1 255.255.255.0
 keepalive
!
interface Serial0
 ip address 192.1.1.1 255.255.255.0
!
router eigrp 64←Enables the EIGRP routing process on the router
variance 2
 network 10.0.0.0←Specifies what interfaces will receive and send EIGRP
                 routing updates. It also specifies what networks will be
                 advertised.
 network 152.1.0.0
 network 192.1.1.0
!
no ip classless
!
!line con 0
line aux 0
line vty 0 4
 login
!
end
```

RouterB

```
!
version 11.2
service udp-small-servers
service tcp-small-servers
!
hostname RouterB
!
interface Ethernet0
 no ip address
ip address 152.1.1.2 255.255.255.0
!
```

```
interface Serial0
 ip address 192.1.1.2 255.255.255.0
 no fair-queue
 clockrate 500000←Acts as DCE providing clock


!
interface Serial1
 ip address 193.1.1.2 255.255.255.0
 clockrate 500000←Acts as DCE providing clock
!
```
router eigrp 64←Enables the IGRP routing process on the router
network 192.1.1.0←Specifies what interfaces will receive and send IGRP routing
                    updates. It also specifies what networks will be advertised.
  network 193.1.1.0
network 152.1.0.0

```
!
!
line con 0
line aux 0
line vty 0 4
 login
```

RouterC

```
!
version 11.1
service udp-small-servers
service tcp-small-servers
!
hostname RouterC
!
interface Loopback0
 ip address 3.3.3.3 255.255.255.0
!
interface Ethernet0
 no ip address
shutdown
!
interface Serial0
 ip address 193.1.1.1 255.255.255.0
!
interface Serial1
 no ip address
 shutdown
!
```
router eigrp 64←Enables the IGRP routing process on the router.

network 193.1.1.0←Specifies what interfaces will receive and send IGRP routing
                    updates. It also specifies what networks will be advertised.

```
network 3.0.0.0
!
no ip classless
!
!
line con 0
line aux 0
line vty 0 4
 login
!
end
```

Monitoring and Testing the Configuration

Display the routing table on RouterA with the command **show ip route**. Notice that there are two routes to network 3.0.0.0: one via the Ethernet interface, and one via the serial interface. The cost to reach the network over each path is different; however, because the variance is set to two, as long as the cost of the second path is not greater than two times the preferred path, then the route will be used.

Let's take a closer look at this situation. The best route to network 3.0.0.0 is via the Ethernet interface, with a cost of 2,323,456. Because the variance is set to two, as long as the cost of any other route to network 3.0.0.0 is less than 4,646,912 (2,323,456 * 2), then the route will be used. Because the cost of the route via the serial interface is 2,809,856, which is lower than 4,646,912, then the route is used.

```
RouterA#show ip route
Codes: C - connected, S - static, I - IGRP, R - RIP, M - mobile, B - BGP
       D - EIGRP, EX - EIGRP external, O - OSPF, IA - OSPF inter area
       N1 - OSPF NSSA external type 1, N2 - OSPF NSSA external type 2
       E1 - OSPF external type 1, E2 - OSPF external type 2, E - EGP
       i - IS-IS, L1 - IS-IS level-1, L2 - IS-IS level-2, * - candidate default
       U - per-user static route, o - ODR

Gateway of last resort is not set

D      3.0.0.0/8 [90/2323456] via 152.1.1.2, 00:00:09, Ethernet0
                 [90/2809856] via 192.1.1.2, 00:00:10, Serial0
       10.0.0.0/8 is variably subnetted, 2 subnets, 2 masks
D         10.0.0.0/8 is a summary, 00:00:10, Null0
C         10.1.1.0/24 is directly connected, Loopback0
       152.1.0.0/16 is variably subnetted, 2 subnets, 2 masks
C         152.1.1.0/24 is directly connected, Ethernet0
D         152.1.0.0/16 is a summary, 00:00:10, Null0
C      192.1.1.0/24 is directly connected, Serial0
D      193.1.1.0/24 [90/2195456] via 152.1.1.2, 00:00:10, Ethernet0
                    [90/2681856] via 192.1.1.2, 00:00:10, Serial0
```

From RouterA, display the route to host 3.3.3.3 with the command **show ip route 3.3.3.3**. Notice that both routes are shown; however, there is an asterisk next to the first route. The asterisk indicates that the next packet leaving RouterA destined for host 3.3.3.3 will use this route.

```
RouterA#show ip route 3.3.3.3
Routing entry for 3.0.0.0/8
  Known via "eigrp 64", distance 90, metric 2323456, type internal
  Redistributing via eigrp 64
  Last update from 192.1.1.2 on Serial0, 00:09:05 ago
  Routing Descriptor Blocks:
  * 152.1.1.2, from 152.1.1.2, 00:09:05 ago, via Ethernet0
      Route metric is 2323456, traffic share count is 1
      Total delay is 26000 microseconds, minimum bandwidth is 1544 Kbit
      Reliability 255/255, minimum MTU 1500 bytes
      Loading 1/255, Hops 2
    192.1.1.2, from 192.1.1.2, 00:09:06 ago, via Serial0
      Route metric is 2809856, traffic share count is 1
      Total delay is 45000 microseconds, minimum bandwidth is 1544 Kbit
      Reliability 252/255, minimum MTU 1500 bytes
      Loading 1/255, Hops 2
```

From RouterA, ping host 3.3.3.3.

```
RouterA#ping 3.3.3.3

Type escape sequence to abort.
Sending 5, 100-byte ICMP Echos to 3.3.3.3, timeout is 2 seconds:
!!!!!
```

Now, from RouterA, display the route to host 3.3.3.3 with the command **show ip route 3.3.3.3**. Notice that the asterisk is now by the second route, because the router is load balancing the traffic destined for network 3.0.0.0 over both links.

```
RouterA#show ip route 3.3.3.3
Routing entry for 3.0.0.0/8
  Known via "eigrp 64", distance 90, metric 2323456, type internal
  Redistributing via eigrp 64
  Last update from 192.1.1.2 on Serial0, 00:10:09 ago
  Routing Descriptor Blocks:
    152.1.1.2, from 152.1.1.2, 00:10:09 ago, via Ethernet0
      Route metric is 2323456, traffic share count is 1
      Total delay is 26000 microseconds, minimum bandwidth is 1544 Kbit
      Reliability 255/255, minimum MTU 1500 bytes
      Loading 1/255, Hops 2
  * 192.1.1.2, from 192.1.1.2, 00:10:10 ago, via Serial0
      Route metric is 2809856, traffic share count is 1
      Total delay is 45000 microseconds, minimum bandwidth is 1544 Kbit
      Reliability 252/255, minimum MTU 1500 bytes
      Loading 1/255, Hops 2
```

Remove the variance command on RouterA with the router configuration command **no variance**.

```
RouterA#configure terminal
RouterA(config)#router eigrp 64
RouterA(config-router)#no variance
```

From RouterA, display the route to host 3.3.3.3 with the command **show ip route 3.3.3.3**. Notice that only one route is being used. This route is the route with the lowest metric, and no load balancing is being performed.

```
RouterA#show ip route 3.3.3.3
Routing entry for 3.0.0.0/8
  Known via "eigrp 64", distance 90, metric 2323456, type internal
  Redistributing via eigrp 64
  Last update from 152.1.1.2 on Ethernet0, 00:00:01 ago
  Routing Descriptor Blocks:
  * 152.1.1.2, from 152.1.1.2, 00:00:01 ago, via Ethernet0
      Route metric is 2323456, traffic share count is 1
      Total delay is 26000 microseconds, minimum bandwidth is 1544 Kbit
      Reliability 255/255, minimum MTU 1500 bytes
      Loading 1/255, Hops 2
```

LAB #39: EIGRP Timer Configuration

Equipment Needed

The following equipment is needed to perform this lab exercise:
- Two Cisco routers with one serial port
- Cisco IOS 10.0 or higher
- A PC running a terminal emulation program
- Two Cisco DTE/DCE crossover cables
- One Cisco rolled cable for accessing the console port of the router

Overview

EIGRP uses hello packets to discover neighbors and to learn when their neighbors become unreachable or inoperative. By default, hello packets are sent out every five seconds—or every 60 seconds on low-speed (T1 or less) NBMA media. The hello interval is configurable and may require tweaking, depending on the network topology.

Hello packets carry a holdtime, which is the amount of time in which a router receiving the hello will consider the sender of the hello packet reachable. The default hold time is three times the hello interval, or 15 seconds. For slow-speed NBMA networks, the default holdtime is 180 seconds. If the router does not receive another hello packet within the holdtime, the neighbor is considered down.

Configuration Overview

This configuration will demonstrate how to change EIGRP hello and holdtime intervals. The hello interval will be changed from the default of five seconds to 10 seconds. The holdtime will be set to three times the hello interval, or 30 seconds.

RouterA will be connected to RouterB via a serial crossover cable. RouterB will act as the DCE, supplying clock. The IP addresses are shown in Figure 9–7.

Router Configurations

The configurations for the two routers in this example are as follows (key EIGRP configurations are highlighted in bold):

RouterA

```
version 11.2
no service udp-small-servers
no service tcp-small-servers
!
hostname RouterA
!
```

Figure 9–7
EIGRP timers

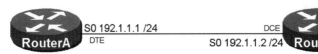

```
!
!
interface Ethernet0
 no ip address
 shutdown
!
interface Serial0
 ip address 192.1.1.1 255.255.255.0
 ip hello-interval eigrp 64 10←EIGRP uses hello packets to discover neighbors
                               and to learn when their neighbors become
                               unreachable or inoperative. This command sets
                               the interval at which hello packets are sent
                               to, 10 seconds.
 ip hold-time eigrp 64 30←The Holdtime is the amount of time in which a
                           router receiving the hello packet will consider the
                           sender of the hello packet reachable. If the router
                           does not receive another hello packet within the
                           holdtime, the neighbor is considered down. This
                           command sets the holdtime to 30 seconds, which is
                           three times the hello interval.
!
router eigrp 64←Enables the EIGRP routing process on the router.
network 192.1.1.0←Specifies what interfaces will receive and send EIGRP
                  routing updates. It also specifies what networks will be
                  advertised.


!
no ip classless
!
line con 0
line vty 0 4
 login
!
end
```

RouterB

```
Current configuration:
!
version 11.1
service udp-small-servers
service tcp-small-servers
!
hostname RouterB
!
!
interface Ethernet0
 no ip address
```

```
 shutdown
!
interface Serial0
 ip address 192.1.1.2 255.255.255.0
 ip hello-interval eigrp 64 10←EIGRP uses hello packets to discover neighbors
                         and to learn when their neighbors become
                         unreachable or inoperative. This command sets
                         the interval at which hello packets are sent
                         to, 10 seconds.
 ip hold-time eigrp 64 30←The Holdtime is the amount of time in which a
                         router receiving the hello packet will consider the
                         sender of the hello packet unreachable. If the
                         router does not receive another hello packet within
                         the holdtime, the neighbor is considered down. This
                         command sets the holdtime to 30 seconds, which is
                         three times the hello interval.
 no fair-queue
 clockrate 500000←Acts as DCE providing clock
!
interface Serial1
 no ip address
 shutdown
!
router eigrp 64←Enables the EIGRP routing process on the router
 network 192.1.1.0←Specifies what interfaces will receive and send EIGRP
                         routing updates. It also specifies what networks will be
                         advertised.

!
no ip classless
!
line con 0
line aux 0
line vty 0 4
 login
!
end
```

Monitoring and Testing the Configuration

On RouterA, enable time stamping on the output of the debug command. Time stamping marks each packet generated from the debug command with the time the event occurred. This feature is useful when trying to determine the order of events. By default, debug messages are not time stamped. You can enable time stamping by performing the following task in global configuration mode:

```
RouterA(config)#service timestamps debug
```

On RouterA, enable debugging of EIGRP packets with the command **debug eigrp packets**. The following example shows the output from this command. Notice that the hello packets are now being sent every 10 seconds.

```
→02:54:54: EIGRP: Sending HELLO on Serial0
   02:54:54:  AS 64, Flags 0x0, Seq 0/0 idbQ 0/0 iidbQ un/rely 0/0
   02:54:55: EIGRP: Received HELLO on Serial0 nbr 192.1.1.2
   02:54:55:  AS 64, Flags 0x0, Seq 0/0 idbQ 0/0 iidbQ un/rely 0/0 peerQ un/rely 0/0
→02:55:04: EIGRP: Sending HELLO on Serial0
   02:55:03:  AS 64, Flags 0x0, Seq 0/0 idbQ 0/0 iidbQ un/rely 0/0
```

Display the EIGRP neighbor table on RouterB with the command **show ip eigrp neighbors**. Notice that RouterB has one neighbor—RouterA (192.1.1.1).

```
RouterB#show ip eigrp neighbors
IP-EIGRP neighbors for process 64
H   Address     Interface    Hold     Uptime    SRTT    RTO    Q     Seq
                             (sec)    (ms)                     Cnt   Num
0   192.1.1.1  Se0          27 00:   29:00     0       3000   0     28
```

Now, change the hello interval on RouterA to 60 seconds.

```
RouterA#configure terminal
RouterA(config)#interface s0
RouterA(config-if)#ip hello-interval eigrp 64 60
```

Display the neighbor table on RouterB using the **show ip eigrp neighbors** command. Note that RouterB no longer has any neighbors. The reason is because RouterA is only sending hello packets every 60 seconds, but the router is still telling RouterB that its holdtimer is 30 seconds. After RouterB receives the first hello packet, RouterB declares the neighbor 192.1.1.1 (RouterA) down, because the router does not receive another hello packet within 30 seconds. Remember, the holdtimer is sent within the hello packet, so if you change the hello interval, you must also change the holdtimer. The holdtimer should be three times greater than the hello interval.

```
RouterB#show ip eigrp neighbors
IP-EIGRP neighbors for process 64
```

Now, change the holdtimer on RouterA to 180 seconds.

```
RouterA#conf terminal
Enter configuration commands, one per line. End with CNTL/Z.
RouterA(config)#interface s0
RouterA(config-if)#ip hold-time eigrp 64 180
```

Display the neighbor table on RouterB. Note that the neighbor is back, and the holdtimer is now counting down from 180 seconds—not 30.

```
RouterB#show ip eigrp neighbors
IP-EIGRP neighbors for process 64
H   Address    Interface   Hold    Uptime    SRTT   RTO    Q     Seq
                           (sec)   (ms)                    Cnt   Num
0   192.1.1.1  Se0         179     00:00:00  0      2000   1     0
```

LAB #40: Configuring EIGRP on an NBMA Network

Equipment Needed

The following equipment is needed to perform this lab exercise:

■ Three Cisco routers with one serial port

■ One Cisco router with three serial ports

■ Cisco IOS 10.0 or higher

■ A PC running a terminal emulation program

■ Three Cisco DTE/DCE crossover cables

■ One Cisco rolled cable for accessing the console port of the router

Overview

This lab will address the issue of split-horizons when enabling EIGRP on a NBMA network, such as Frame-Relay. The network is a typical hub-and-spoke environment. RouterB acts as the hub and has a PVC defined to each spoke. All routers are on the same subnet. The problem is that the rule of split-horizons prevents RouterB from advertising routing information out the same physical interface on which the information was received. Because the PVCs from RouterA and RouterC terminate on the same physical interface of RouterB, split-horizons prevents RouterA from receiving the routing updates from RouterC (and vice-versa).

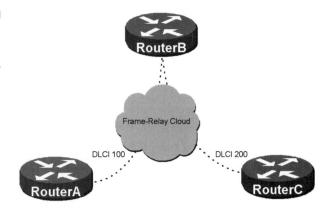

Figure 9–8
Logical connectivity
for NBMA Lab

Configuration Overview

This lab will demonstrate how to configure EIGRP over Frame-Relay. RouterA, RouterB, and RouterC will connect serially via a crossover cable to a Cisco router (FrameSwitch), which will act as a Frame-Relay switch.

The FrameSwitch will act as the DCE, supplying clock for all attached routers. Detailed documentation on configuring a Cisco router as a Frame-Relay switch can be found in Chapter 4. The IP addresses are as per Figure 9–9.

Router Configurations

The configurations for the routers in this example are as follows (key EIGRP commands are highlighted in bold):

Figure 9–9
EIGRP a NBMA
Network

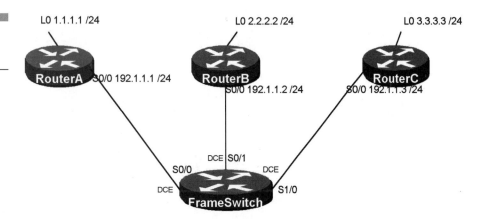

FrameSwitch

```
!
version 11.2
no service password-encryption
no service udp-small-servers
no service tcp-small-servers
!
hostname FrameSwitch
!
!
frame-relay switching
!
interface Ethernet0/0
 no ip address
 shutdown
!
interface Serial0/0
 no ip address
 encapsulation frame-relay IETF
 no fair-queue
 clockrate 500000
 frame-relay lmi-type ansi
 frame-relay intf-type dce
 frame-relay route 100 interface Serial0/1 100
!
interface Serial0/1
 no ip address
 encapsulation frame-relay IETF
 clockrate 500000
 frame-relay lmi-type ansi
 frame-relay intf-type dce
 frame-relay route 100 interface Serial0/0 100
 frame-relay route 200 interface Serial1/0 200
!
interface Ethernet1/0
 no ip address
 shutdown
!
interface Serial1/0
 no ip address
 encapsulation frame-relay IETF
 clockrate 500000
 frame-relay lmi-type ansi
 frame-relay intf-type dce
 frame-relay route 200 interface Serial0/1 200
!
no ip classless
!
!
line con 0
```

```
line aux 0
line vty 0 4
 login
!
end
```

RouterA

```
version 11.2
no service udp-small-servers
no service tcp-small-servers
!
hostname RouterA
!
!
interface Loopback0←Defines a virtual interface
 ip address 1.1.1.1 255.255.255.0
!
interface Ethernet0/0
 no ip address
 shutdown
!
interface Serial0/0
 ip address 192.1.1.1 255.255.255.0
 encapsulation frame-relay IETF
frame-relay map ip 192.1.1.2 100 broadcast
 frame-relay map ip 192.1.1.3 100 broadcast
 frame-relay lmi-type ansi
!
interface Serial1/0
 no ip address
 shutdown
!
!
router eigrp 64←Enables EIGRP routing  process
network 192.1.1.0
network 1.0.0.0
!
no ip classless
!
line con 0
line aux 0
line vty 0 4
 login
!
end
```

RouterB

```
version 11.2
no service udp-small-servers
no service tcp-small-servers
!
hostname RouterB
!
interface Loopback0←Defines a virtual interface.
 ip address 2.2.2.2 255.255.255.0
!
interface Ethernet0/0
 no ip address
 shutdown
!
interface Serial0/0
 ip address 192.1.1.2 255.255.255.0
 encapsulation frame-relay IETF
 frame-relay map ip 192.1.1.1 100 broadcast
 frame-relay map ip 192.1.1.3 200 broadcast
 frame-relay lmi-type ansi
!
interface Serial0/1
 no ip address
 shutdown
!
router eigrp 64←Enables EIGRP routing process

network 192.1.1.0
network 2.0.0.0
!
no ip classless
!
!
line con 0
line aux 0
line vty 0 4
 login
!
end
```

RouterC

```
version 11.2
no service password-encryption
no service udp-small-servers
no service tcp-small-servers
```

```
!
hostname RouterC
!
!
interface Loopback0←Defines a virtual interface
 ip address 3.3.3.3   255.255.255.0

!
interface Ethernet0/0
 no ip address
 shutdown
!
interface Serial0/0
 ip address 192.1.1.3 255.255.255.0
 encapsulation frame-relay IETF

frame-relay map ip 192.1.1.1 200 broadcast
 frame-relay map ip 192.1.1.2 200 broadcast
 frame-relay lmi-type ansi
!
!
router eigrp 64

network 192.1.1.0
network 3.0.0.0

!
no ip classless
!
line con 0
line aux 0
line vty 0 4
 login
!
end
```

Monitoring and Testing the Configuration

Display RouterA's routing table with the command **show ip route**. Note that RouterA has not received any information about network 3.0.0.0, due to split-horizons. RouterB will not advertise a route out the same interface on which it was received.

```
RouterA#show ip route
Codes: C - connected, S - static, I - IGRP, R - RIP, M - mobile, B - BGP
       D - EIGRP, EX - EIGRP external, O - OSPF, IA - OSPF inter area
       N1 - OSPF NSSA external type 1, N2 - OSPF NSSA external type 2
       E1 - OSPF external type 1, E2 - OSPF external type 2, E - EGP
       i - IS-IS, L1 - IS-IS level-1, L2 - IS-IS level-2, * - candidate default
       U - per-user static route, o - ODR
```

```
Gateway of last resort is not set

     1.0.0.0/8 is variably subnetted, 2 subnets, 2 masks
C        1.1.1.0/24 is directly connected, Loopback0
D     2.0.0.0/8 [90/2297856] via 192.1.1.2, 00:11:06, Serial0/0
C     192.1.1.0/24 is directly connected, Serial0/0
```

Disable split-horizons on RouterB with the command **no ip split-horizon eigrp 64**.

```
RouterB#configure terminal
RouterB(config)#int
RouterB(config)#interface s0/0
RouterB(config-if)#no ip split-horizon eigrp 64
```

Now, display the routing table on RouterA. Note that RouterA now has a route to network 3.0.0.0.

```
RouterA#show ip route
Codes: C - connected, S - static, I - IGRP, R - RIP, M - mobile, B - BGP
       D - EIGRP, EX - EIGRP external, O - OSPF, IA - OSPF inter area
       N1 - OSPF NSSA external type 1, N2 - OSPF NSSA external type 2
       E1 - OSPF external type 1, E2 - OSPF external type 2, E - EGP
       i - IS-IS, L1 - IS-IS level-1, L2 - IS-IS level-2, * - candidate default
       U - per-user static route, o - ODR

Gateway of last resort is not set

     1.0.0.0/8 is variably subnetted, 2 subnets, 2 masks
C        1.1.1.0/24 is directly connected, Loopback0
D     2.0.0.0/8 [90/2297856] via 192.1.1.2, 00:00:57, Serial0/0
D     3.0.0.0/8 [90/2809856] via 192.1.1.2, 00:00:57, Serial0/0
C     192.1.1.0/24 is directly connected, Serial0/0
```

Troubleshooting EIGRP

The Cisco IOS provides many tools for troubleshooting routing protocols. The following example shows a list of key commands, along with a sample output from each command that will aid in troubleshooting EIGRP.

{show ip eigrp neighbor}   This exec command displays information about all neighbors that are discovered by EIGRP. This command is helpful in determining whether the router has any neighbors. The command also shows the amount of time the neighbor has been active and the amount of time remaining on the holdtimer.

```
RouterB#show ip eigrp neighbors
IP-EIGRP neighbors for process 64
H   Address      Interface    Hold   Uptime     SRTT  RTO    Q     Seq
                              (sec)  (ms)              Cnt   Num
1   192.1.1.3    Se0/0        163    00:08:30   12    200    0     21
0   192.1.1.1    Se0/0        163    00:08:39   8     200    0     21
```

{show ip protocol} This exec command displays the parameters and current state of the active routing protocol process. The output shows the routing protocol used, timer information, inbound and outbound filter information, protocols being redistributed, and the networks for which the protocol is routing.

```
RouterB#show ip protocols
Routing Protocol is "eigrp 64"
  Outgoing update filter list for all interfaces is not set
  Incoming update filter list for all interfaces is not set
  Default networks flagged in outgoing updates
  Default networks accepted from incoming updates
  EIGRP metric weight K1=1, K2=0, K3=1, K4=0, K5=0
  EIGRP maximum hopcount 100
  EIGRP maximum metric variance 1
  Redistributing: eigrp 64
  Automatic network summarization is in effect
  Automatic address summarization:
    2.0.0.0/8 for Serial0/0
      Summarizing with metric 128256
    192.1.1.0/24 for Loopback0
  Routing for Networks:
    2.0.0.0
    192.1.1.0
  Routing Information Sources:
    Gateway         Distance      Last Update
    (this router)         5       1d01h
    192.1.1.1            90       00:06:30
    192.1.1.3            90       00:06:30
  Distance: internal 90 external 170
```

{show ip eigrp topology} This exec command displays the EIGRP topology table, which shows the state of the *Diffusing Update Algorithm* (DUAL)—which is helpful in identifying possible DUAL problems.

```
RouterB#show ip eigrp topology
IP-EIGRP Topology Table for process 64

Codes: P - Passive, A - Active, U - Update, Q - Query, R - Reply,
       r - Reply status

P 1.0.0.0/8, 1 successors, FD is 2297856
```

```
         via 192.1.1.1 (2297856/128256), Serial0/0
P 2.0.0.0/8, 1 successors, FD is 128256
         via Summary (128256/0), Null0
P 2.2.2.0/24, 1 successors, FD is 128256
         via Connected, Loopback0
P 3.0.0.0/8, 1 successors, FD is 2297856
         via 192.1.1.3 (2297856/128256), Serial0/0
P 192.1.1.0/24, 1 successors, FD is 2169856
         via Connected, Serial0/0
```

{show ip eigrp interfaces} This exec command displays information about all EIGRP-enabled interfaces. The command can be used as a quick reference to verify that EIGRP is configured on a particular interface in a particular AS.

```
RouterB#show ip eigrp interfaces
IP-EIGRP interfaces for process 64
            Xmit      Queue        Mean   Pacing Time   Multicast    Pending
Interface   Peers     Un/Reliable  SRTT   Un/Reliable   Flow Timer   Routes
Lo0         0         0/0          0      0/10          0            0
Se0/0       2         0/0          10     0/15          50           0
```

{debug eigrp packet} This exec command displays information about any EIGRP packet that comes into or leaves the router. This command is useful for analyzing the messages traveling between neighbor routers.

```
RouterB#
EIGRP: Sending HELLO on Loopback0
  AS 64, Flags 0x0, Seq 0/0 idbQ 0/0 iidbQ un/rely 0/0
EIGRP: Received HELLO on Loopback0 nbr 2.2.2.2
  AS 64, Flags 0x0, Seq 0/0 idbQ 0/0
```

{show ip eigrp traffic} This exec command displays the type and number of EIGRP packets sent and received by the router.

```
RouterB#show ip eigrp traffic
IP-EIGRP Traffic Statistics for process 64
   Hellos sent/received: 12139/12128
   Updates sent/received: 4/1
   Queries sent/received: 0/0
   Replies sent/received: 0/0
   Acks sent/received: 0/2
   Input queue high water mark 1, 0 drops
```

Conclusion

EIGRP is an enhanced version of IGRP. It uses the same distance vector algorithm and distance information as IGRP. EIGRP has been enhanced, making it converge faster and operate more efficiently than IGRP.
EIGRP also provides the following benefits:

■ Fast convergence through use of the DUAL (Diffusing Update Algorithm)

■ It sends partial updates for routes that have changed, instead of sending the entire routing table

■ Supports variable-length subnet masking

■ The EIGRP metric is large enough to support thousands of hops.

10

Border Gateway Protocol (BGP)

Topics Covered in This Chapter

- Detailed technology overview
- BGP terminology
- Synchronization within an AS
- BGP message format
- BGP path attributes
- BGP route summarization
- BGP route aggregation
- BGP route reflectors
- Manipulating BGP path selection
- AS path manipulation
- Route filtering based on network number
- BGP soft configuration
- Regular expressions
- Filtering based on AS path
- Detailed troubleshooting examples

Introduction

Border Gateway Protocol (BGP) is a path vector, inter-Autonomous System routing protocol that is based on Distance Vector algorithms. (For the purposes of this chapter, "inter-" means routing between entities, and "intra-" means routing within an entity.) An *Autonomous System* (AS) is a collection of routers or end stations that are under the same administrative control and are viewed as a single entity. The reason that BGP is called a path vector protocol is that the BGP routing information carries a sequence of AS numbers, which indicate the path the route has traversed. This information is used to construct a graph of AS connectivity, from which routing loops can be pruned.

In previous chapters, we looked at interior gateway routing protocols (RIP, OSPF, IGRP, and EIGRP) that were designed to operate in a single AS, under a single administrative control. BGP was introduced to facilitate a loop-free exchange of routing information between autonomous systems while controlling the expansion of routing tables through *Classless Inter-Domain Routing* (CIDR). It is also designed to provide a structured view of the Internet through the use of autonomous systems.

In a sense, the Internet could have been a large OSPF network. If this situation had occurred, then all organizations that participated in the Internet would have to adhere to the same administrative policies. By segregating the Internet into multiple autonomous systems, we are able to create one large network consisting of smaller, more manageable networks. Within these smaller networks, called autonomous systems, an organization's unique rules and administrative policies can be applied. Each AS is identified by a unique number that is assigned by an Internet registry.

In Figure 10–1, we have two Internet service providers—Xnet and Ynet—each of which consist of multiple networks running multiple IGPs. Each service provider is assigned an AS number by an Internet registry,

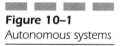

Figure 10–1
Autonomous systems

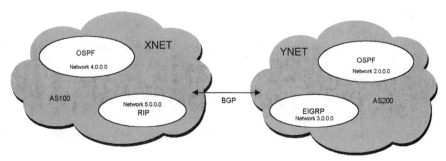

which represents its entire network. When company Xnet and Ynet wish to exchange routing information, they do so using BGP.

Company Ynet advertises networks 2.0.0.0 and 3.0.0.0 to company Xnet. The routes are marked as originating from AS 200. Company Xnet does not need to have a full topological view of company Ynet, nor does it need to understand Ynet's internal routing or policies. Xnet simply knows that networks 2.0.0.0 and 3.0.0.0 are in AS 200.

BGP Terminology

Before diving into the intricate details of BGP, you should have a clear understanding of key terms and concepts—some of which are used interchangeably.

EBGP versus IBGP: Although BGP was designed to be used between autonomous systems (EBGP), BGP is often used within an AS (IBGP) to carry information between border routers running EBGP to other autonomous systems. This process enables all BGP path attributes to be maintained across the AS, as shown in Figure 10–2.

By definition, an external BGP neighbor is a router whose administrative and policy control is outside your AS. An internal BGP neighbor is a router that is under the same administrative control.

CIDR: CIDR was developed to handle the explosive growth of IP addresses present in IP routing tables on Internet routers and the exhaustion of IP address space. CIDR is an address allocation scheme, which eliminates the concept of network class within BGP. In CIDR, an IP network is represented by a prefix—which is the IP address and a number that indicates the left-most contiguous significant bits in the address. For example, in Figure 10–3, there are a number of Class C networks that are present on Service Provider A's network. Without CIDR,

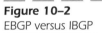

Figure 10–2
EBGP versus IBGP

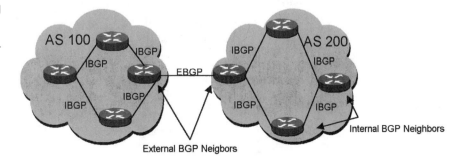

Figure 10–3
Network
advertisement
without CIDR

the service provider must advertise each network individually. With CIDR, Figure 10–4, service provider A can advertise all of these networks with one classless advertisement (200.10.0.0 / 16).

Supernet: A supernet is a network advertisement whose prefix boundary contains fewer bits than the network's natural mask. For example, in Figure 10–4, the natural network mask for the Class C network 200.10.1.0 is 255.255.255.0. When we represent the address as 200.10.0.0 / 16, however, the mask is 16—which is less then 24. Hence, a supernet.

IP prefix: An IP prefix is an IP network address along with an indication of the number of bits that make up the network number. The IP prefix is what is present in the routing table. 10.0.0.0 / 8 is an IP prefix.

***Network Layer Reachability Information* (NLRI)**:   NLRI is how BGP supports classless routing (CIDR). The NLRI is part of the BGP update message and is used to list a set of destinations that are reachable. The NLRI field in the BGP update message contains 2-tuples <length, prefix>. The length is the number of bits in the mask, and the prefix is the IP address. The two combined represent the network number. For example, the network 10.0.0.0 / 8 would be advertised in the NLRI field of a BGP update message as <8,10.0.0.0>.

AS: An AS is a group of routers or hosts that are under the same administrative control and policies. AS numbers are assigned by an Internet registry.

Synchronization: Before BGP can announce a route, the route must be present in the IP routing table. In other words, BGP and IGP must be in sync before the networks can be advertised. Cisco permits BGP to override the synchronization requirement with the command **no synchronization**. This feature enables BGP to announce routes which are known via BGP but are not in the routing table. The reason that this rule exists is because the AS must be consistent with the routes it advertises.

Figure 10–4
Network
advertisement
with CIDR

For example, in Figure 10–5, RouterA and RouterB are the only routers running IBGP. If synchronization is disabled on RouterB, the router will advertise network 1.0.0.0 / 8 to AS 200 even though the Route is not in its IP forwarding table. When RouterD wishes to send traffic to network 1.0.0.0, the router sends the packet to RouterB, which does a recursive lookup in its IP routing table and forwards the packet to RouterC. Because RouterC is not running IBGP, the router has no visibility to network 1.0.0.0—and therefore drops the packet. This situation is why BGP requires synchronization between BGP and IGP. Care must be taken when disabling synchronization. If an AS is a transit AS, all routers should be running fully meshed IBGP before synchronization is disabled.

Technology Overview

BGP is an inter-Autonomous System routing protocol whose primary function is to exchange network reachability information with other BGP speakers. A BGP speaker is any device configured for BGP. BGP uses TCP as its transport protocol (port 179), which provides reliable data transfer.

Two BGP routers form a transport protocol connection. The two routers are called neighbors, or peers. Once the transport connection is formed,

Figure 10–5
Synchronization within an AS

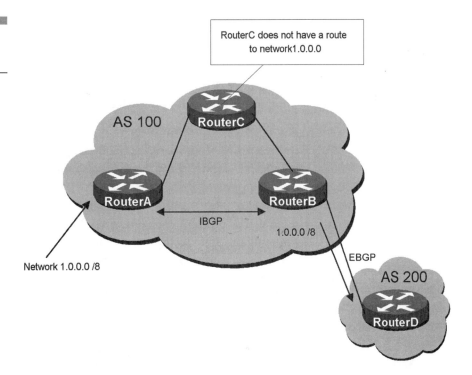

the peer routers exchange messages to open and confirm connection parameters. In this stage, the routers exchange information on BGP version number, AS number, holdtime, BGP identifier, and other optional parameters. If the peers disagree on any of the parameters, a notification error is sent—and the peer connection is not established.

If the parameters are agreed upon by the peer routers, then the entire BGP routing table is exchanged using UPDATE messages. The UPDATE messages contain a list of destinations reachable via each system (Network Layer Reachability Information), along with path attributes for each route. The path attributes contain information such as ORIGIN of the route and degree of preference. Path attributes will be covered in detail later in this chapter.

The BGP table is valid for each peer for the duration of the BGP connection. If any routing information changes, the neighbor router uses incremental updates to convey this information. BGP does not require that routing information be refreshed. If no routing changes occur, then BGP peers only exchange keepalive packets. The keepalive messages are sent periodically to ensure that the connection is kept active.

BGP Neighbor Negotiation

Before BGP speakers can exchange network layer reachability information (networks being advertised), a BGP session must be established. Figure 10–6 illustrates the states that BGP neighbor negotiation goes through before a connection becomes fully established.

Idle: Initially, BGP is in an idle state until an operator initiates a start event, which is usually caused by establishing or restarting a BGP session.

Connect: In this state, BGP is waiting for the transport protocol connection to be completed. If the transport protocol connection succeeds, an Open message is sent to the peer router, and the BGP state changes to OpenSent. If the connection fails, the local system changes to active state and continues to listen for connections.

Active State: In this state, BGP is trying to acquire a peer by initiating a transport protocol connection. If the connection is successful, an OPEN message is sent to the peer router. If the connection retry timer expires, the BGP state changes to connect and continues to listen for connections that may be initiated by the remote BGP peer.

OpenSent State: In this state, BGP is waiting for an OPEN message from its peer. When an OPEN message is received, all fields are checked for correctness. If an error is detected, the local system sends a NOTIFI-

Figure 10–6
BGP neighbor
negotiation

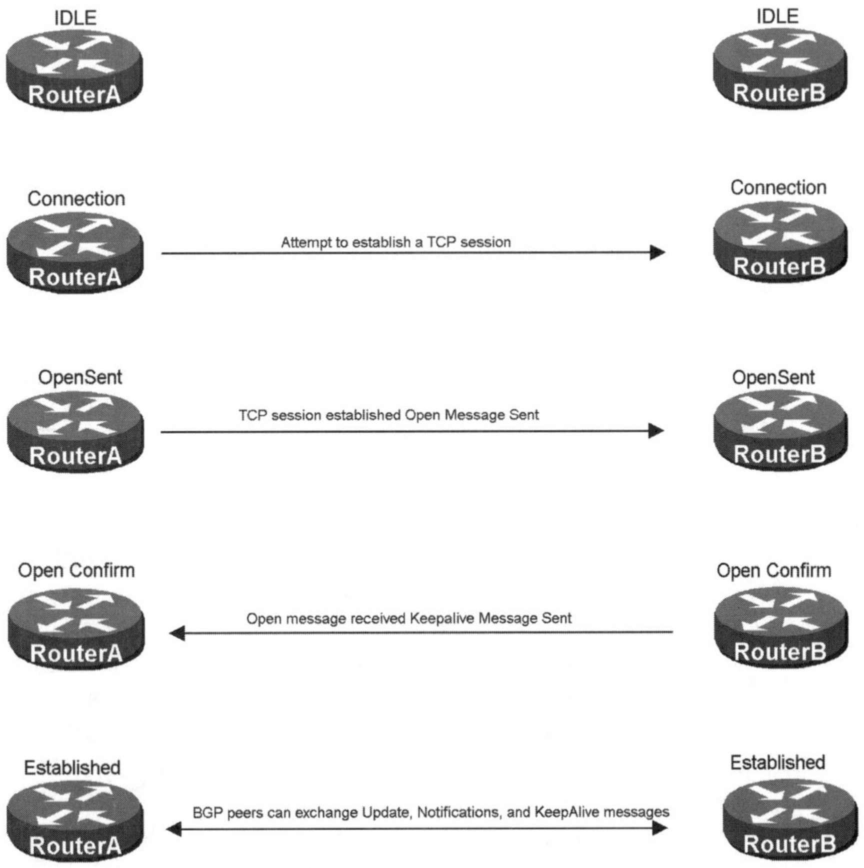

CATION message and changes its state to Idle. If there are no errors, BGP
starts sending keepalive messages to its peer.

OpenConfirm: In this state, BGP waits for a KeepAlive or notification message. If the local system receives a keepalive message, the system changes its state to established. If the Hold timer expires before a
keepalive message is received, the local system sends a notification message and changes its state to Idle.

Established: This stage is the final stage of the neighbor negotiation. In the established state, BGP peers can exchange Update, Notifica-
tions, and KeepAlive messages.

BGP Message Format

All BGP messages use the same fixed size header as follows:

0	15	23	31
MARKER			
MARKER			
MARKER			
MARKER			
LENGTH		TYPE	

Marker: A 16-byte field which is used to either authenticate incoming BGP messages or to detect loss of synchronization between BGP peers. If the type of message is OPEN, or if the OPEN message carries no authentication information, then the marker is all ones. Otherwise, the marker field is computed based on the authentication being used.

Length: The length field is a 2-byte field which indicates the total length of the message. The smallest permitted length is 19 bytes, and the largest is 4,096.

Type: The type field is a 1-byte field that indicates the type of BGP message. There are four BGP message types:

- OPEN
- UPDATE
- KEEPALIVE
- NOTIFICATION

Open Message Format

BGP cannot exchange routing information until neighbor negotiation is complete. After the transport connection is established, the first message sent is an OPEN message. This message contains information on BGP version number, AS number, Hold time, BGP identifier, and other optional parameters. If the peers disagree on any of the parameters, a notification error is sent, and the peer connection is not established.

If the OPEN message is acceptable, meaning that the peer router agrees on the parameters, then a KEEPALIVE message is sent to confirm the OPEN message.

In addition to the fixed-size BGP header, the OPEN message contains the following fields:

0	15	23	31
FIXED SIZE BGP HEADER			
			Version
My Autonomous System		Hold Time	
BGP Identifier			
Opt Parm Len	Variable length field that indicates a list of Optional Parameters		

Version: The version field is a 1-byte field which indicates the version of the BGP protocol. During the neighbor negotiation, peer routers agree on the BGP version number to be used. The highest version that both routers support is usually used.

My Autonomous System: This field is two bytes long and indicates the AS number of the sending router.

Hold Time: This field is two bytes long and indicates the maximum time in seconds that may elapse between the receipt of a successive KEEPALIVE and/or UPDATE message. If the hold time is exceeded, the neighbor is considered dead.

The hold time is negotiated between neighbors and is set to the lowest value. The router that receives the open message must calculate the hold time by using the smaller of its configured hold time and the hold time received in the open message.

BGP Identifier: This field is four bytes long and indicates the BGP identifier of the sending router. This field is the router ID, which is the highest loopback address or the highest IP address on the router at BGP session startup.

Optional Parameter Length: This field is one byte long and indicates the total length (in bytes) of the optional parameter field. If n⁻ optional parameters are present, the field is set to 0.

Optional Parameters: This field is a variable-length field that indicates the list of optional parameters used in BGP neighbor session negotiation.

Update Message Format

The update message is the primary message used to communicate information between BGP peers. When a BGP speaker advertises or withdraws a route from a peer router, an UPDATE message is used. The UPDATE message always includes the fixed-length BGP header and can optionally include the following:

Field	Length
Unfeasible Routes Length	2 bytes
Withdrawn Routes	Variable
Total Path Attribute Length	2 bytes
Path Attributes	Variable
Network Layer Reachability Information	Variable

Unfeasible Routes Length: This 2-byte field indicates the total length (in octets) of the withdrawn routes field. If the value is zero, no routes are being withdrawn from service.

Withdrawn Routes: This variable-length field contains a list of IP address prefixes of the routes that are being withdrawn from service.

Total Path Attribute Length: This 2-byte field indicates the total length in octets of the Path Attributes field.

Path Attributes: This variable-length field contains a list of BGP attributes associated with the prefixes in the Network Layer Reachability field. The path attributes give information on the prefixes that are being advertised, such as degree of preference or origin of the prefix. This information is used for filtering and in the route decision process. The path attributes fall into four categories:

1. *Well-Known Mandatory*: An attribute that has to exist in the BGP update and must be recognized by all BGP vendor implementations. ORIGIN, AS_PATH, and Next_Hop are three examples of well-known mandatory attributes.

ORIGIN: The ORIGIN attribute is an example of a well-known mandatory attribute, which indicates the origin of the routing update with respect to the AS that originated the update. This attribute tells how the original route was put into the BGP table. A route could be learned via an IGP such as OSPF, which was redistributed into BGP. This attribute is learned through external routing protocol (EGP) or through something other than an IGP or EGP (such as a static route).

There are three possible origins: IGP, EGP, and INCOMPLETE. The router uses this information in its decision process when choosing between multiple routes. The router prefers the path with the lowest ORIGIN Type. IGP is lower than EGP, and EGP is lower than INCOMPLETE.

AS_PATH: AS_PATH is a well-known mandatory attribute, which indicates the autonomous systems through which routing information contained in this UPDATE message have passed. In Figure 10–7, prefix 1.0.0.0 / 8 is advertised to AS 300 and AS 200. When AS 300 passes the prefix to AS 200, it appends its AS number to the AS_PATH. When AS 200 receives the UPDATE from AS300, it knows that 1.0.0.0 originated in AS100 and then passed through AS300.

NEXT_HOP: This attribute defines the IP address of the border router that should be used as the next-hop to the destinations listed in the UPDATE message. For example, in Figure 10–8, RouterB learns route 1.0.0.0 / 8 via 192.1.1.1, which is the IP

Figure 10–7
AS_PATH attribute

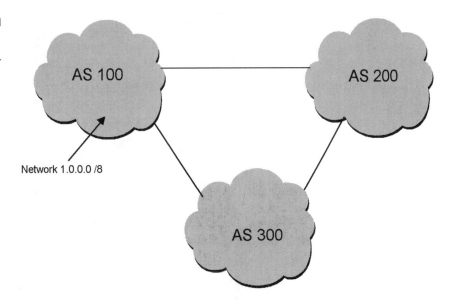

Network 1.0.0.0 /8

Figure 10–8
BGP next-hop
attribute

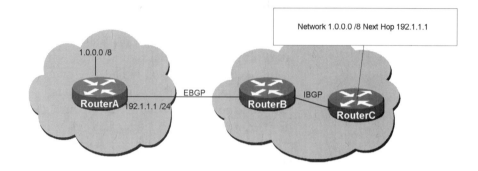

address of its EBGP peer. When RouterB advertises this route to RouterC, it includes the next-hop information (unaltered). RouterC will receive an IBGP update for network 1.0.0.0 / 8 with a next-hop of 192.1.1.1.

2. **Well-Known Discretionary**: An attribute that must be recognized by all BGP implementations but may or may not be sent in a BGP update

Figure 10–9
BGP local preference
attribute

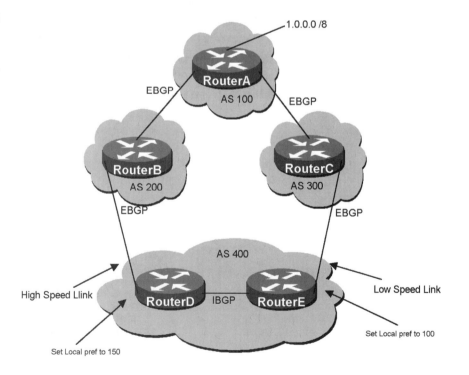

LOCAL_PREF: The local preference attribute is a degree of preference given to a route to compare it with other routes to the same destination. The higher local preference is the more preferred route. Local preference is not included in update messages that are sent to BGP neighbors outside the AS. If the attribute is contained in an update received from a BGP neighbor in a different AS, the update is ignored.

In Figure 10–9, we see where the local preference attribute would be used. RouterB and RouterC are both advertising network 1.0.0.0 / 8 into AS 400; however, because the link between RouterB and Rou-terD is a high-speed link, we would like traffic destined for network 1.0.0.0 / 8 to use this route. The Local Preference Attribute will be used to manipulate the flow of traffic within AS 400. RouterD gives routes coming from RouterB a local preference of 150, and RouterE gives routes coming from RouterC a local preference of 100. Because RouterD and RouterE are exchanging routes via IBGP, they both will use the route with the highest local preference. In this case, all traffic destined for network 1.0.0.0 / 8 will be routed over the high-speed link between RouterB and RouterD.

ATOMIC_AGGREGATE: The atomic aggregator attribute indicates that information has been lost. When routes are aggregated, this process causes a loss of information, because the aggregate is coming from different sources that have different attributes. If a router sends an aggregate that causes loss of information, the router is required to attach the atomic aggregate attribute to the route.

3. ***Optional Transitive***: An optional transitive attribute is not required to be supported by all BGP implementations. If the attribute is not recognized by the BGP process, however, it will look at the transitive flag. If the flag is set, the BGP implementation should accept the attribute and pass it along to other BGP speakers.

   AGGREGATOR: This attribute identifies the BGP speaker (IP address) and AS number which performed the route aggregation.

4. ***Optional Nontransitive***: An optional nontransitive attribute is not required to be supported by all BGP implementations. If the attribute is not recognized by the BGP process, however, it will look at the transitive flag. If the flag is not set, the attribute should be quietly ignored and not passed along to other BGP peers.

MULTI_EXIT_DISC (**MED**): MED is used by the BGP speakers to discriminate between multiple-exit points to a neighboring AS. A lower Med is preferred over a higher one. The MED attribute is exchanged between autonomous systems, but a MED attribute that comes into an AS does not leave the AS (nontransitive). This process differs from the Local preference attribute, where external routers can influence the path selection of another AS. With Local preference, you can only influence the route selection within your own AS.

In Figure 10–10, the MED attribute is used to influence the path that RouterA uses to reach network 1.0.0.0 / 8. Both RouterB and RouterC are advertising network 1.0.0.0 / 8 to RouterA; however, because RouterC is closer to this network, we would like for all traffic destined to network 1.0.0.0 / 8 from RouterA to be routed through RouterC. To achieve this task, we set the MED on route 1.0.0.0 / 8 advertised from RouterC to 100 and the MED on route 1.0.0.0 / 8 advertised from RouterB to 200. Because the MED coming from RouterC is lower, RouterA will prefer this route.

Network Layer Reachability: This variable-length field contains a list of IP address prefixes that are reachable via the sender. All path attributes contained in a given update message apply to the destinations

Figure 10–10
BGP Multi-Exit
Discriminator (MED)

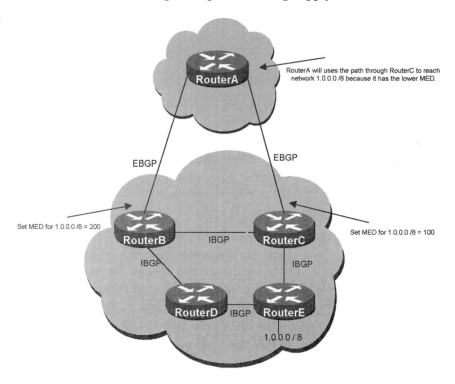

carried in the Network Layer Reachability information field of the update message.

KeepAlive Message Format

KeepAlive messages are exchanged periodically between peers to determine whether peers are reachable. KeepAlive messages are exchanged between peers often enough to prevent the Hold timer from expiring.

Notification Message Format

A notification message is sent whenever an error condition is detected. The BGP connection is closed immediately after sending the message. In addition to the fixed-size BGP header, the notification message contains the following fields:

Field	Length
Error code	1 byte
Error subcode	1 byte
Data	Variable

Error Code: This one-byte field indicates the type of notification. The following codes are possible:

Error Code	Symbolic Name
1	Message Header Error
2	OPEN Message Error
3	UPDATE Message Error
4	Hold Timer Expired
5	Finite State Machine Error
6	Cease

Error Subcode: This one-byte field provides more specific information about the nature of the reported error. Each error code may have one or more error subcodes associated with it. The following list shows the error subcodes:

Error Code	Error Subcode
1—Message Header Error	—Connection Not Synchronized —Bad Message Length —Bad Message Type
2—OPEN Message Error subcodes	—Unsupported Version Number —Bad Peer AS —Bad BGP Identifier —Unsupported Optional Parameter —Authentication Failure —Unacceptable Hold Time
3—UPDATE Message Error subcodes	—Malformed Attribute List —Unrecognized Well-Known Attribute —Missing Well-Known Attribute —Attribute Flags Error —Attribute Length Error —Invalid ORIGIN Attribute —AS Routing Loop —Invalid Next_HOP Attribute —Optional Attribute Error —Invalid Network Field —Malformed AS_Path
4—Hold Timer Expired	Not applicable
5—Finite State Machine Error	Not applicable
6—Cease	Not applicable

Data: This variable-length field is used to diagnose the reason for the notification. The contents of the Data field depend upon the Error Code and Error Subcode.

Commands Discussed in This Chapter

- **aggregate-address** address mask
- **clear ip bgp**
- **debug ip bgp**
- **ip as-path access-list**
- **neighbor**{ip-address | peer-group-name}**distribute-list**
- **neighbor** ip-address **filter-list**
- **neighbor** {ip-address | peer-group-name} **next-hop-self**
- **neighbor** {ip-address} **remote-as number**
- **neighbor** {ip-address | peer-group-name} **route-map**
- **neighbor** ip-address **route-reflector-client**
- **network** (network-number)
- **no auto-summary**
- **no synchronization**
- **route-map** map-tag [permit | deny] [sequence-number]
- **router bgp** autonomous-system
- **show ip bgp**
- **show ip bgp filter-list**
- **show ip bgp neighbor**
- **show ip bgp summary**

Definitions

aggregate-address: This router configuration command creates an aggregate entry in the BGP routing table (if there are any more-specific BGP routes available that fall into the aggregate range). For example, if a router had routes to networks 192.1.24.0 / 24, 192.1.25.0 / 24, 192.1.26.0 / 24, and 192.1.27.0 / 24, all of these networks could be advertised in one aggregate route: 192.1.24.0/22.

Figure 10–11 shows the concept of route aggregation, also referred to as supernetting. Four Class C networks, each using a standard 24-bit mask, are shown in the following diagram:

■ 192.1.24.0/24

■ 192.1.25.0/24

■ 192.1.26.0/24

■ 192.1.27.0/24

Without supernetting, a router advertising these four networks would need to send a separate route update for each of these networks. Supernetting enables a router to advertise more then one network with a single advertisement. In the case of our four networks, a router can advertise the 192.1.24.0 network with a 22-bit mask. Notice that the default 24-bit mask has been shortened to 22 bits. Supernetting works by reducing the number of subnet bits in a routing advertisement. This process has the effect of matching several networks with a single routing update.

In Figure 10–11, we see that all four networks have an exact match for their first 22 bits. The remaining two bits of the original 24-bit mask are now part of the supernet. Notice that the .24, .25, .26, and .27 networks use all four combinations of the two remaining bits. Thus, a 22-bit subnet mask can be used to advertise four Class C networks with a single advertisement of 192.1.24.0 / 22.

Figure 10–11
Supernetting

First 22 Bits Match

	↓	↓
192.1.**24**.0	11000000.00000001.**000110**	**00**.00000000
192.1.**25**.0	11000000.00000001.**000110**	**01**.00000000
192.1.**26**.0	11000000.00000001.**000110**	**10**.00000000
192.1.**27**.0	11000000.00000001.**000110**	**11**.00000000
255.255.**252**.0 Supernet Mask	11111111.11111111.**111111**	**00**.00000000

If this command is used with no additional arguments, the aggregate will be advertised as originating from the aggregating router and will have the atomic aggregate attribute set to show that information might be missing. The more specific routes will also be advertised along with the aggregate. This command has several optional arguments:

as-set: The as-set keyword creates an aggregate entry whose path consists of all elements contained in all the paths that are being summarized.

summary-only: The summary-only keyword suppresses advertisements of more-specific routes to all neighbors.

suppress-map: The suppress-map keyword creates the aggregate route but suppresses advertisement of specified routes. The route map can be used to selectively suppress some more specific routes of the aggregate and to permit others.

clear ip bgp: This exec command is used to reset the BGP connection. When a configuration change is made to an established BGP peer, the BGP session must be reset using this command.

debug ip bgp: This exec command is used to display BGP events as the events occur. These events include state messages, routing updates, etc.

ip as-path access-list: This global configuration command enables the user to define an access list filter on both inbound and outbound BGP routes. The filter is an access list based on regular expressions. If the regular expression matches the representation of the AS path of the route as an ASCII string, then the permit or deny condition applies.

neighbor distribute-list: This router configuration command applies a distribute list to either inbound or outbound routes to a particular neighbor. Using distribute lists is one of two ways to filter BGP advertisements. The other way is to use an AS-path filter with the **neighbor filter list** command.

neighbor filter-list: This router configuration command applies the BGP filters to inbound and outbound BGP routes to or from a specified neighbor.

neighbor next-hop-self: This router configuration command forces the router to advertise itself, rather than the external peer, as the next-hop to reach the route.

neighbor remote-as: This router configuration command adds a BGP neighbor to the neighbor table. The router will only exchange information with neighboring routers. If the specified neighbor is in the same AS as the AS specified in the global router bgp configuration command, the neighbor is internal to the AS (IBGP neighbor). Otherwise, the neighbor is external to the AS (EBGP neighbor).

neighbor route-map: This router configuration command applies a route map to incoming or outgoing routes to or from a particular neighbor.

neighbor route-reflector-client: This router configuration command configures the router as a BGP route reflector and configures the specified neighbor as the route-reflector-client.

network: This router configuration command specifies a network address that should be included in the BGP update.

no auto-summary: This router configuration command disables the summarization of subnet routes into network level routes.

no synchronization: This router configuration command disables the synchronization between BGP and IGP. A BGP speaker will not advertise a route to an external neighbor unless the route is local or exists in the IGP routing table. The **no synchronization** command enables the router to advertise a network route without first having that route present in the IGP routing table.

route-map: This global configuration command is used with BGP to control and modify routing information and to define the conditions by which routes are redistributed between routing domains.

The route-map uses a ***map tag***, which is a name that identifies the route map, and a ***sequence number***, which indicates the position a new route map is to have in the list of route maps already configured with the same name.

The following is an example of a route map:

```
                   ↓map tag
route-map localpref 10←sequence number (First)
match ip address 1←match criteria—the conditions that must be met
set local-preference 200←set actions—the actions to perform
route-map localpref permit 20←sequence number (Second)
set local-preference 100
```

When BGP applies route-map localpref to routing updates, it applies the lowest sequence number first (in this case, 10). If the first set of conditions are not met, then the second sequence is applied. This process goes on until a match condition is found or there are no more conditions to apply. For this particular example, if the route matches the IP address defined in access-list 1, then the local preference is set to 200. If the route does not match, sequence 20 is used—which applies a local preference of 100.

router bgp: This global configuration command enables the BGP routing process on the router.

show ip bgp: This exec command is used to display entries in the BGP routing table.

show ip bgp filter-list: This exec command is used to display routes that conform to a specified filter list.

show ip bgp neighbors: This exec command is used to display information about the TCP and BGP connections to neighbors.

show ip bgp summary: This exec command is used to display the status of all BGP connections.

IOS Requirements

BGP first became available in IOS 10.0; however, all labs were performed using IOS 11.2.

LAB #41: BGP Configuration

Equipment Needed

The following equipment is needed to perform this lab exercise:

- One Cisco router with one serial port
- One Cisco router with one Ethernet port
- One Cisco router with one serial port and one Ethernet port
- Cisco IOS 10.0 or higher
- A PC running a terminal emulation program for connecting to the console port of the router
- One Ethernet hub and two Ethernet cables
- One Cisco DTE/DCE crossover cable
- One Cisco rolled cable

Configuration Overview

This configuration will demonstrate basic routing using BGP. All routers will be configured for BGP, and no IGP will be run. RouterA is in AS 100 and will be external BGP neighbors with RouterB in AS 200. RouterC is also in AS 200 and will be internal BGP neighbors with RouterB.

RouterA and RouterB are connected serially via a crossover cable, and RouterC is connected to RouterB via an Ethernet hub. RouterA will act as the DCE, supplying clock to RouterB. The IP addresses are assigned as per Figure 10–12. All routers are configured for BGP and have loop-back addresses defined. RouterA will advertise network 1.0.0.0.

Router Configurations

The configurations for the three routers in this example are as follows (key BGP configuration statements are highlighted in bold):

Figure 10–12
Basic BGP
configuration.

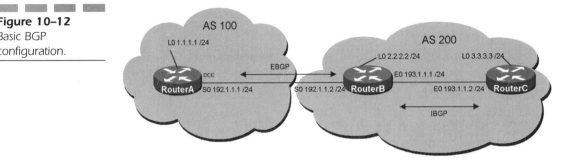

RouterA

```
version 11.2
no service udp-small-servers
no service tcp-small-servers
!
hostname RouterA
!
interface Loopback0
 ip address 1.1.1.1 255.255.255.0
!
interface Ethernet0/0
 no ip address
!
interface Serial0/0
 ip address 192.1.1.1 255.255.255.0
 clockrate 500000←Acts as DCE providing clock

!
!
router bgp 100←Configures a BGP process for autonomous system 100.
 neighbor 192.1.1.2 remote-as 200←Specifies the neighboring router and the
                                  autonomous system it is in
no ip classless
!
line con 0
line aux 0
line vty 0 4
 login
!
end
```

RouterB

```
!
version 11.2
no service udp-small-servers
no service tcp-small-servers
!
```

```
hostname RouterB
!
!interface Loopback0
 ip address 2.2.2.2 255.255.255.0
!
interface Ethernet0/0
 ip address 193.1.1.1 255.255.255.0
!
interface Serial0/0
 ip address 192.1.1.2 255.255.255.0
!
!
```
router bgp 200←Configures a BGP process for autonomous system 200.
 neighbor 192.1.1.1 remote-as 100←Specifies the neighboring router and the
                                   autonomous system it is in

 neighbor 193.1.1.2 remote-as 200←IBGP neighbor
```
!
no ip classless
!
line con 0
line aux 0
line vty 0 4
 login
!
end
```

RouterC

```
version 11.2
no service password-encryption
no service udp-small-servers
no service tcp-small-servers
!
hostname RouterC
!
!
interface Loopback0
 ip address 3.3.3.3 255.255.255.0
!
interface Ethernet0/0
 ip address 193.1.1.2 255.255.255.0
!
interface Serial0/0
 ip address 194.1.1.1 255.255.255.0
!
!
```
router bgp 200←Configures a BGP process for autonomous system 200.

 neighbor 193.1.1.1 remote-as 200←Specifies the neighboring router and the
                                   autonomous system it is in

```
!
no ip classless
!
!
line con 0
line aux 0
line vty 0 4
 login
!
end
```

Monitoring and Testing the Configuration

From RouterA, display the BGP neighbors with the command **show ip bgp neighbors.** The following example shows the output from this command, which has been truncated. Notice that RouterA has one external BGP neighbor, RouterB (192.1.1.2), in AS 200. The router ID of this neighbor is 2.2.2.2, which is the loopback address on RouterB.

To identify itself to its neighbors, the BGP process uses a router ID (which is an IP address). This address is either the loopback address or the highest IP address of an active interface on the router. The router ID is calculated at boot time and will remain until the BGP process is removed or the router is reloaded.

One of the most important pieces of information shown by the command **show ip bgp neighbors** is the line BGP state =. This line shows the state of the BGP connection. Remember that from earlier discussion, there are five possible states. The state should be established, which means that the session between the BGP peers is up and running. If any other state is shown, there is a problem.

```
RouterA#show ip bgp neighbors
BGP neighbor is 192.1.1.2, remote AS 200, external link
  Index 1, Offset 0, Mask 0x2
    BGP version 4, remote router ID 2.2.2.2
    BGP state = Established, table version = 1, up for 00:10:12
    Last read 00:00:12, hold time is 180, keepalive interval is 60 seconds
    Minimum time between advertisement runs is 30 seconds
    Received 13 messages, 0 notifications, 0 in queue
    Sent 13 messages, 0 notifications, 0 in queue
    Connections established 1; dropped 0
Connection state is ESTAB, I/O status: 1, unread input bytes: 0
Local host: 192.1.1.1, Local port: 11000
Foreign host: 192.1.1.2, Foreign port: 179
```

Now, from RouterA, we will advertise network 1.0.0.0 via BGP to RouterB. In order for a router to advertise a network to another BGP speaker, two conditions must be met:

- The BGP process must be aware of the route, either through the use of the network command or by redistribution.

- The network to be advertised must be present in the IP routing table.

For the purposes of this lab, we will be using the network command under the BGP process. This command takes care of the first rule, making the BGP process aware of the route. The network command gives you better control of what is being redistributed from the IGP into BGP, enabling the user to individually list the prefixes that need to be advertised via BGP. The maximum number of network statements that can be configured on a Cisco router is 200. If you have more than 200 networks to advertise, dynamic redistribution must be used.

The second rule is met because network 1.0.0.0 is a directly connected network; therefore, the network is in the IP routing table.

Display the IP routing table on RouterA. Notice that network 1.0.0.0 is in the IP routing table.

```
RouterA#show ip route
Codes: C - connected, S - static, I - IGRP, R - RIP, M - mobile, B - BGP
       D - EIGRP, EX - EIGRP external, O - OSPF, IA - OSPF inter area
       N1 - OSPF NSSA external type 1, N2 - OSPF NSSA external type 2
       E1 - OSPF external type 1, E2 - OSPF external type 2, E - EGP
       i - IS-IS, L1 - IS-IS level-1, L2 - IS-IS level-2, * - candidate default
       U - per-user static route, o - ODR

Gateway of last resort is not set
     1.0.0.0/24 is subnetted, 1 subnets
C       1.1.1.0 is directly connected, Loopback0
C    192.1.1.0/24 is directly connected, Serial0/0
```

On RouterA, add the command **network 1.0.0.0** under the BGP process.

```
RouterA#configure terminal
RouterA(config)#router bgp 100
RouterA(config-router)#network 1.0.0.0
```

Display the IP BGP table on RouterB with the command **show ip bgp.** The following example shows the output from the command. Notice that network 1.0.0.0 was learned via the next-hop address of 192.1.1.1, which is the serial interface of RouterA. Also note that the entry is valid (indicated by the asterisk (*) before the network number), and the entry is the best one to use for that network (indicated by the greater-than sign (>) before the network number). The route entry originated from IGP and was advertised with a network router configuration command. This information is indicated by the (i) after the AS path.

```
RouterB#show ip bgp
BGP table version is 2, local router ID is 2.2.2.2
Status codes: s suppressed, d damped, h history, * valid, > best, i - internal
Origin codes: i - IGP, e - EGP, ? - incomplete

   Network        Next Hop      Metric      LocPrf       Weight        Path
*> 1.0.0.0        192.1.1.1     0           0                          100 i
```

From RouterB, display the IP routing table with the command **show ip route.** The output from the command is shown as follows. Note that the router has a route to network 1.0.0.0 via 192.1.1.1, which is RouterA's serial interface.

```
RouterB#show ip route
Codes: C - connected, S - static, I - IGRP, R - RIP, M - mobile, B - BGP
       D - EIGRP, EX - EIGRP external, O - OSPF, IA - OSPF inter area
       N1 - OSPF NSSA external type 1, N2 - OSPF NSSA external type 2
       E1 - OSPF external type 1, E2 - OSPF external type 2, E - EGP
       i - IS-IS, L1 - IS-IS level-1, L2 - IS-IS level-2, * - candidate default
       U - per-user static route, o - ODR

Gateway of last resort is not set

B      1.0.0.0/8 [20/0] via 192.1.1.1, 00:12:01
       2.0.0.0/24 is subnetted, 1 subnets
C         2.2.2.0 is directly connected, Loopback0
C      192.1.1.0/24 is directly connected, Serial0/0
C      193.1.1.0/24 is directly connected, Ethernet0/0
```

Display the IP BGP table on RouterC with the command **show ip bgp**. The following example shows the output from the command. Note that network 1.0.0.0 is in the BGP table with a next-hop of 192.1.1.1. The route is valid, indicated by the asterisk (*), and was learned via an internal BGP session. This status is indicated by the letter (i) preceding the network number.

```
RouterC#show ip bgp
BGP table version is 1, local router ID is 3.3.3.3
Status codes: s suppressed, d damped, h history, * valid, > best, i - internal
Origin codes: i - IGP, e - EGP, ? - incomplete

   Network        Next Hop      Metric      LocPrf       Weight        Path
*  i1.0.0.0       192.1.1.1     0           100          0             100 i
```

From RouterC, display the IP routing table with the command **show ip route**. The output from the command is shown as follows. Note that the router has no route to network 1.0.0.0.

```
RouterC#show ip route
Codes: C - connected, S - static, I - IGRP, R - RIP, M - mobile, B - BGP
       D - EIGRP, EX - EIGRP external, O - OSPF, IA - OSPF inter area
       N1 - OSPF NSSA external type 1, N2 - OSPF NSSA external type 2
       E1 - OSPF external type 1, E2 - OSPF external type 2, E - EGP
       i - IS-IS, L1 - IS-IS level-1, L2 - IS-IS level-2, * - candidate default
       U - per-user static route, o - ODR

Gateway of last resort is not set

     3.0.0.0/24 is subnetted, 1 subnets
C       3.3.3.0 is directly connected, Loopback0
C    193.1.1.0/24 is directly connected, Ethernet0/0
```

The reason that the route to network 1.0.0.0 is not in the IP routing table is two-fold. First, the next-hop to reach network 1.0.0.0 is via 192.1.1.1, which is not in RouterC's routing table. Remember from earlier discussions that the next-hop address is the IP address of the EBGP neighbor from which the route was learned. When routes are injected into the AS via EBGP, the next-hop learned from EBGP is carried unaltered into IBGP.

The second reason is that by default, BGP and IGP must be in sync. Because the 1.0.0.0 network is not being learned via an IGP, meaning that the BGP-learned routes on RouterB are not being redistributed into an IGP, the two are not in sync.

Let's fix the next-hop address problem first. Force RouterB to advertise itself as the next-hop for all BGP updates being sent to RouterC. To do this task, add the command **neighbor 193.1.1.2 next-hop-self** under the BGP routing process on RouterB.

```
RouterB#configure terminal
RouterB(config)#router bgp 200
RouterB(config-router)#neighbor 193.1.1.2 next-hop-self
```

NOTE: *There would be no need for this command if RouterB and RouterC were advertising connected networks to each other via an IGP. This command is useful in non-meshed networks (such as Frame-Relay or X.25), where BGP neighbors may not have direct access to all other neighbors on the same IP subnet.*

When a configuration change is made to an established BGP peer, the session must be reset. From RouterC, reset the BGP connection with the command **clear ip bgp 193.1.1.1**. This command will reset only the specific neighbor. If you want to reset all BGP neighbors, you could use the command **clear ip bgp ***.

Display the IP BGP table on RouterC with the command **show ip bgp.** The following example shows the output from the command. Notice that the next-hop IP address is now 193.1.1.1, which is RouterB's Ethernet interface.

```
RouterC#show ip bgp
BGP table version is 2, local router ID is 3.3.3.3
Status codes: s suppressed, d damped, h history, * valid, > best, i - internal
Origin codes: i - IGP, e - EGP, ? - incomplete

   Network      Next Hop       Metric    LocPrf    Weight    Path
*>i1.0.0.0      193.1.1.1        0        100        0       100 I
```

On RouterC, disable synchronization with the command **no synchronization** under the BGP routing process.

```
RouterC#conf terminal
RouterC(config)#router bgp 200
RouterC(config-router)#no synchronization
```

From RouterC, display the IP routing table with the command **show ip route**. The output from the command is shown as follows. Note that the router now has a route to network 1.0.0.0 in its IP routing table.

```
RouterC#show ip route
Codes: C - connected, S - static, I - IGRP, R - RIP, M - mobile, B - BGP
       D - EIGRP, EX - EIGRP external, O - OSPF, IA - OSPF inter area
       N1 - OSPF NSSA external type 1, N2 - OSPF NSSA external type 2
       E1 - OSPF external type 1, E2 - OSPF external type 2, E - EGP
       i - IS-IS, L1 - IS-IS level-1, L2 - IS-IS level-2, * - candidate default
       U - per-user static route, o - ODR

Gateway of last resort is not set

B      1.0.0.0/8 [200/0] via 193.1.1.1, 00:00:03
       3.0.0.0/24 is subnetted, 1 subnets
C         3.3.3.0 is directly connected, Loopback0
C      193.1.1.0/24 is directly connected, Ethernet0/0
C      194.1.1.0/24 is directly connected, Serial0/0
```

BGP Summarization

In this section, let's take a look at how BGP can summarize multiple contiguous networks into one advertisement. The router advertises what is called a supernet, which is a network advertisement whose prefix contains fewer bits than the network's natural mask. For example, if RouterA contained network 192.1.24.0 / 24, 192.1.25.0 / 24 , 192.1.26.0 / 24, and 192.1.27.0 / 24, these routes could all be advertised using the supernet 192.1.24.0/22.

Figure 10–13 shows the concept of route aggregation, also referred to as supernetting. Four Class C networks, each using a standard 24-bit mask, are shown in the diagram:

- 192.1.24.0/24
- 192.1.25.0/24
- 192.1.26.0/24
- 192.1.27.0/24

Without supernetting, a router advertising these four networks would need to send a separate route update for each of these networks. Supernetting enables a router to advertise more than one network with a single advertisement. In the case of our four networks, a router can advertise the 192.1.24.0 network with a 22-bit mask. Notice that the default 24-bit mask has been shortened to 22 bits. Supernetting works by reducing the number of subnet bits in a routing advertisement. This process has the effect of matching several networks with a single routing update.

In Figure 10–13, we see that all four networks have an exact match for their first 22 bits. The remaining two bits of the original 24-bit mask are now part of the supernet. Notice that the .24, .25, .26, and .27 networks use all four combinations of the two remaining bits. Thus, a 22-bit subnet mask can be used to advertise four Class C networks with a single advertisement of 192.1.24.0 / 22.

On RouterA, add four loopback interfaces with the following IP addresses: 192.1.24.1, 192.1.25.1, 192.1.26.1, and 192.1.27.1.

Figure 10–13
Supernetting

	First 22 Bits Match	
	↓	↓
192.1.**24**.0	11000000.00000001.**000110**	**00**.00000000
192.1.**25**.0	11000000.00000001.**000110**	**01**.00000000
192.1.**26**.0	11000000.00000001.**000110**	**10**.00000000
192.1.**27**.0	11000000.00000001.**000110**	**11**.00000000
255.255.**252**.0 Supernet Mask	11111111.11111111.**111111**	**00**.00000000

```
RouterA#configure terminal
RouterA(config)#interface loopback 1
RouterA(config-if)#ip add 192.1.24.1 255.255.255.0
RouterA(config)#interface loopback 2
RouterA(config-if)#ip add 192.1.25.1 255.255.255.0
RouterA(config)#interface Loopback 3
RouterA(config-if)#ip address 192.1.26.1 255.255.255.0
RouterA(config)#interface Loopback 4
RouterA(config-if)#ip address 192.1.27.1 255.255.255.0
```

Normally, each network would need to be advertised under the BGP process; however, because we are summarizing all four networks into one announcement, only one network statement is needed. This network statement will contain the mask that we wish to advertise.

On RouterA, add the following command: **network 192.1.24.0 mask 255.255.252.0**. Notice that the mask is a 22-bit mask (smaller than the natural 24-bit mask), creating a supernet.

```
RouterA#configure terminal
RouterA(config)#router bgp 100
RouterA(config-router)#network 192.1.24.0 mask 255.255.252.0
```

Remember that the route will not install a prefix into the BGP table until a matching IGP prefix exists in the IP routing table. BGP assumes that networks defined with the network command are existing networks. This statement can be verified by checking the routing table. If an exact match is not found in the routing table, the network will not be loaded in the BGP table.

Display the BGP table on RouterA with the command **show ip bgp**. Notice that no networks are present.

```
RouterA#show ip bgp
```

In order to get this network into the BGP table, we must define a static route (so the network appears in the IP routing table). This task is accomplished by defining a static route to a null interface 0.

```
RouterA#configure terminal
RouterA(config)#ip route 192.1.24.0 255.255.252.0 null 0
```

Display the BGP table on RouterA with the command **show ip bgp**. Notice that the supernet 192.1.24.0 / 22 is now present.

```
RouterA#show ip bgp
BGP table version is 28, local router ID is 1.1.1.1
Status codes: s suppressed, d damped, h history, * valid, > best, i - internal
Origin codes: i - IGP, e - EGP, ? - incomplete

   Network          Next Hop          Metric    LocPrf      Weight      Path
*> 192.1.24.0/22    0.0.0.0              0                   32768 i
```

BGP Aggregation

Aggregation applies to routes that exist in the BGP routing table, which is different from the network command discussed earlier (which applied to routes that were in the IP routing table). Aggregation can be performed if at least one more-specific route of the aggregate appears in the BGP table.

In Figure 10–14, RouterB is aggregating the routes from AS 100 and AS 200 into one continuous block of addresses to be advertised to AS 400 and beyond. When aggregates are generated from more specific routes received from different neighbors, the router that performs the aggregation is the originator of the new route. Because aggregation causes a loss of information, BGP has defined an AS-SET—a mathematical set consisting of all elements that are contained in the paths that are being summarized.

For example, the aggregate advertised from RouterB would be:

```
              ↓ AS SET
192.1.24.0 /22 300[100 200]i
```

Notice that the route is now originating from AS 300; however, with AS-SET, the aggregate contains a set of all attributes (AS numbers) that existed in the individual routes being summarized.

To test this process, we need to add an additional router to the testbed and make some changes to the configuration of RouterA and RouterB. RouterC will remain unchanged. Attach a new router (RouterD) serially to RouterB with a crossover cable. RouterD will act as the DCE, supplying clock to RouterB. All IP addresses are as shown in Figure 10–15.

Figure 10–14
BGP route
aggregation

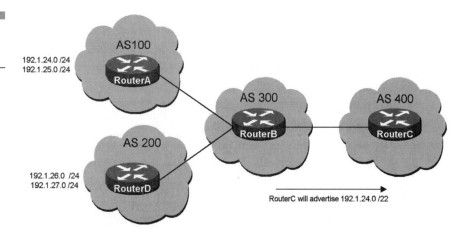

192.1.24.0 /24
192.1.25.0 /24

AS100
RouterA

AS 300
RouterB

AS 400
RouterC

AS 200
192.1.26.0 /24
192.1.27.0 /24
RouterD

RouterC will advertise 192.1.24.0 /22

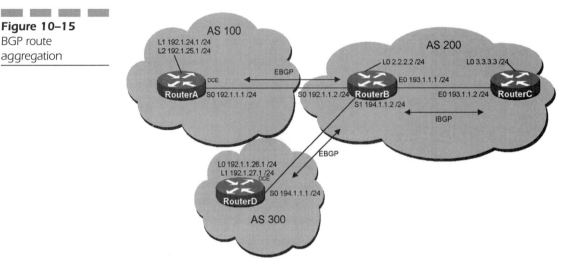

Figure 10–15
BGP route
aggregation

Router Configurations

The configurations for the three routers follows (key BGP configurations
are highlighted in bold):

RouterA

```
version 11.2
no service udp-small-servers
no service tcp-small-servers
!
hostname RouterA
!
interface Loopback0
 ip address 1.1.1.1 255.255.255.0

!
interface Loopback1
 ip address 192.1.24.1 255.255.255.0
!
interface Loopback2
 ip address 192.1.25.1 255.255.255.0
!
!
interface Serial0
 ip address 192.1.1.1 255.255.255.0
 no fair-queue
!
```

```
router bgp 100←Configures a BGP process for autonomous system 200.
  network 192.1.24.0←Specify the list of networks for the BGP routing process
                     to advertise.
  network 192.1.25.0
  neighbor 192.1.1.2 remote-as 200←Specifies the neighboring router and the
                                   autonomous system it is in
!
no ip classless
!
line con 0
line 1 16
line aux 0
line vty 0 4
 login
!
end
```

RouterB

```
!
version 11.2
no service udp-small-servers
no service tcp-small-servers
!
hostname RouterB
!
!interface Loopback0
 ip address 2.2.2.2 255.255.255.0
!
interface Ethernet0/0
 ip address 193.1.1.1 255.255.255.0
!
interface Serial0/0
 ip address 192.1.1.2 255.255.255.0
!
interface Serial0/1
 ip address 194.1.1.2 255.255.255.0
!
!
router bgp 200←Configures a BGP process for autonomous system 200.
  neighbor 192.1.1.1 remote-as 100←Specifies the neighboring router and the
                                   autonomous system it is in
  neighbor 193.1.1.2 remote-as 200←IBGP neighbor
neighbor 194.1.1.1 remote-as 300←IBGP neighbor
!
no ip classless
!
line con 0
line aux 0
line vty 0 4
 login
!
end
```

RouterD

```
Current configuration:
!
version 11.2
no service password-encryption
no service udp-small-servers
no service tcp-small-servers
!
hostname RouterD
!
interface Loopback0
 ip address 4.4.4.4 255.255.255.0
!
interface Loopback1
 ip address 192.1.26.1 255.255.255.0
!
interface Loopback2
 ip address 192.1.27.1 255.255.255.0
!
interface Serial0
 clockrate 500000←Acts as DCE providing clock
!
!
router bgp 300←Configures a BGP process for autonomous system 300.

  network 192.1.26.0←Specify the list of networks for the BGP routing process
                     to advertise.
  network 192.1.27.0
  neighbor 194.1.1.2 remote-as 200←Specifies the neighboring router and the
                                   autonomous system it is in

!
no ip classless
!
line con 0
line aux 0
line vty 0 4
 login
!
end
```

Monitoring and Testing the Configuration

Display the BGP table on RouterC with the command **show ip bgp**. The following example shows the output from the command. Notice that RouterC has learned about all four networks via IBGP from RouterB. Also note that the next-hop address is 193.1.1.1, because we have the next-hop self command under RouterB's BGP process.

```
RouterC#show ip bgp
BGP table version is 5, local router ID is 3.3.3.3
Status codes: s suppressed, d damped, h history, * valid, > best, i - internal
Origin codes: i - IGP, e - EGP, ? - incomplete

   Network        Next Hop     Metric    LocPrf    Weight     Path
*>i192.1.24.0     193.1.1.1       0        100        0       100 i
*>i192.1.25.0     193.1.1.1       0        100        0       100 i
*>i192.1.26.0     193.1.1.1       0        100        0       300 i
*>i192.1.27.0     193.1.1.1       0        100        0       300 i
```

Now, let's aggregate these four networks into one advertisement from RouterB. On RouterB, add the following command under the BGP process:

```
RouterB(config)#router bgp 200
RouterB(config-router)#aggregate-address 192.1.24.0 255.255.252.0 as-set
```

Display the BGP table on RouterC with the command **show ip bgp.** The following example shows the output from this command. Notice that RouterC has learned the aggregate address from RouterB. The {100,300} is the AS-SET information, which tells the router about all elements contained in all paths that are being summarized.

```
RouterC# show ip bgp
BGP table version is 6, local router ID is 3.3.3.3
Status codes: s suppressed, d damped, h history, * valid, > best, i - internal
Origin codes: i - IGP, e - EGP, ? - incomplete

   Network         Next Hop    Metric    LocPrf    Weight     Path
*>i192.1.24.0      193.1.1.2      0        100        0       100 i
*>i192.1.24.0/22   193.1.1.2               100        0       {100,300} i
*>i192.1.25.0      193.1.1.2      0        100        0       100 i
*>i192.1.26.0      193.1.1.2      0        100        0       300 i
*>i192.1.27.0      193.1.1.2      0        100        0       300 i
```

In this example, RouterC is receiving the aggregate address—as well as all of the specific addresses. This process is usually used when a customer is multi-homed to a single provider. The provider would use the more specific routes to send traffic to the customer. The more specific routes enable the provider to make better routing decisions. The aggregate would only be sent towards the Internet, reducing the number of routes sent.

To only send the aggregate and suppress the more specific routes, the optional parameter **summary-only** is added to the aggregate command. This parameter is used when more specific routes do not add any extra benefit, such as making better decisions in forwarding traffic (as discussed earlier in the multi-homed situation).

On RouterB, add the following command under the BGP process:

```
RouterB(config)#router bgp 200
RouterB(config-router)#aggregate-address 192.1.24.0 255.255.252.0 summary-only as-set
```

From RouterC, reset the BGP connection with the command **clear ip bgp 193.1.1.1**. This command will reset only the specified neighbor. If you wish to reset all of the routers' BGP neighbors, you could use the command **clear ip bgp ***.

Display the BGP table on RouterC with the command **show ip bgp**. The following example shows the output from this command. Notice that RouterC is now only receiving the aggregate address.

```
RouterC#show ip bgp
BGP table version is 14, local router ID is 3.3.3.3
Status codes: s suppressed, d damped, h history, * valid, > best, i - internal
Origin codes: i - IGP, e - EGP, ? - incomplete

   Network          Next Hop      Metric     LocPrf     Weight      Path
*>i192.1.24.0/22    193.1.1.2                  100         0      {100,300} i
```

LAB #42: BGP Route Reflectors

Equipment Needed

The following equipment is needed to perform this lab exercise:

- Two Cisco routers with one serial port
- Two Cisco routers with two serial ports
- Cisco IOS 10.0 or higher
- A PC running a terminal emulation program for connecting to the console port of the router
- Two Cisco DTE/DCE crossover cables
- One Cisco rolled cable

Route Reflector Overview

To prevent routing loops within an AS, BGP will not advertise to internal BGP peer routes that it has learned via other internal BGP peers. In Figure 10–16, RouterA will advertise all the routes it has learned via EBGP to RouterB. These routes will not be advertised to RouterC, because RouterB will not pass IBGP routes between RouterA and RouterC. In order for RouterC to learn about these routes, an IBGP connection between RouterA and RouterC is needed.

The full-mesh requirement for IBGP creates the need for neighbor statements to be defined for each IBGP router. In an AS of 100 routers, this situation would require 100 neighbor statements to be defined. As you can see, this situation does not scale well.

To get around this problem, a concept of a route reflector has been defined. A route reflector acts as a concentration router, or focal point, for all internal BGP (IBGP) sessions. Routers that peer with the route reflector are called route reflector clients. The clients peer with the route reflector and exchange routing information. The route reflector then exchanges, or "reflects," this information to all clients—thereby eliminating the need for a fully meshed environment.

In Figure 10–17, RouterA receives updates via EBGP and passes them to RouterB. RouterB is configured as a route reflector with two clients:

Figure 10–16
IBGP full-mesh
requirement

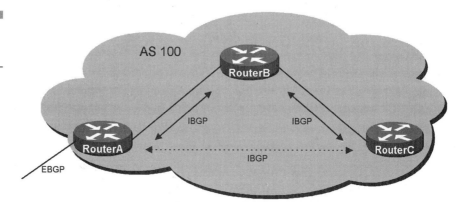

Figure 10–17
A BGP route reflector

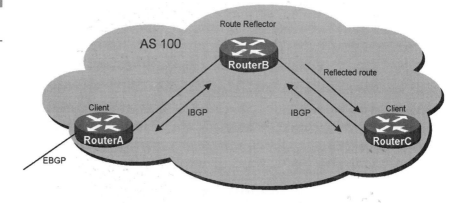

RouterA and RouterC. When RouterB receives the routing updates from RouterA, the router reflects the information to RouterC. An IBGP connection is not needed between RouterA and RouterC, because RouterB is propagating (or reflecting) the information to RouterC.

Configuration Overview

This configuration will use route reflectors to propagate routing information across an AS. All routers will be configured for BGP and OSPF. RouterA is in AS 100 and will be external BGP neighbors with RouterB, which is in AS 200. RouterC and RouterD are also in AS 200, and RouterC will act as the route reflector with two clients: RouterB and RouterD.

All routers are connected serially via crossover cables. RouterB will act as the DCE, supplying clock to RouterA and RouterC. RouterD will act as the DCE, supplying clock for RouterC. The IP addresses are assigned as per Figure 10–18. All routers are configured for BGP and have loopback addresses defined. RouterA will advertise network 1.0.0.0.

Router Configurations

The configurations for the four routers in this example are as follows (key BGP configurations are highlighted in bold):

Figure 10–18
BGP route reflector

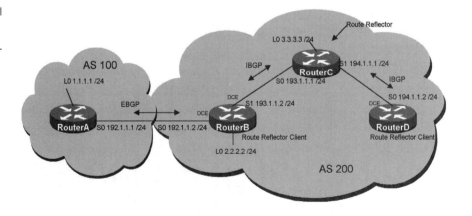

RouterA

```
!
version 11.2
no service udp-small-servers
no service tcp-small-servers
!
hostname RouterA
!
interface Loopback0
 ip address 1.1.1.1 255.255.255.0
!
interface Serial0
 ip address 192.1.1.1 255.255.255.0
 no fair-queue
!
router bgp 100←Configures a BGP process for autonomous system 100.
 network 1.0.0.0←Specify the list of networks for the BGP routing process to
                 advertise.

 neighbor 192.1.1.2 remote-as 200←Specifies the neighboring router and the
                                   autonomous system it is in

!
no ip classless
!
line con 0
line 1 16
line aux 0
line vty 0 4
!
end
```

RouterB

```
version 11.2
service udp-small-servers
service tcp-small-servers
!
hostname RouterB
!
interface Loopback0
 ip address 2.2.2.2 255.255.255.0
!
interface Ethernet0/0
 no ip address
 shutdown
!
interface Serial0/0
```

```
  ip address 192.1.1.2 255.255.255.0
  clockrate 500000←Acts as DCE providing clock

!
interface Serial0/1
  ip address 193.1.1.2 255.255.255.0
  clockrate 500000←Acts as DCE providing clock

!
router ospf 64
  network 0.0.0.0 255.255.255.255 area 0
!
router bgp 200←Configures a BGP process for autonomous system 200
  neighbor 192.1.1.1 remote-as 100
  neighbor 193.1.1.1 remote-as 200←Specifies the neighboring router and the
                                  autonomous system it is in

!
no ip classless
!
line con 0
line aux 0
line vty 0 4
  login
!
end
```

RouterC

```
version 11.2
service udp-small-servers
service tcp-small-servers
!
hostname RouterC
!
!
!
interface Loopback0
  ip address 3.3.3.3 255.255.255.0
!
interface Ethernet0
  no ip address
  shutdown
!
interface Serial0
  ip address 193.1.1.1 255.255.255.0
!
interface Serial1
  ip address 194.1.1.1 255.255.255.0
```

```
!
router ospf 64
 network 0.0.0.0 255.255.255.255 area 0
!
router bgp 200←Configures a BGP process for autonomous system 200
 neighbor 193.1.1.2 remote-as 200
 neighbor 194.1.1.2 remote-as 200←Specifies the neighboring router and the
                                  autonomous system it is in

!
no ip classless
!
line con 0
line aux 0
line vty 0 4
 login
!
end
```

RouterD

```
!
version 11.2
no service password-encryption
no service udp-small-servers
no service tcp-small-servers
!
hostname RouterD
!
interface Loopback0
 ip address 4.4.4.4 255.255.255.0
!
interface Ethernet0
 no ip address
 shutdown
!
interface Serial0
 ip address 194.1.1.2 255.255.255.0
 clockrate 500000←Acts as DCE providing clock

!
router ospf 64
network 0.0.0.0 255.255.255.255 area 0
!
router bgp 200←Configures a BGP process for autonomous system 100
 neighbor 194.1.1.1 remote-as 200←Specifies the neighboring router and the
                                  autonomous system it is in

!
```

```
no ip classless
!
line con 0
line aux 0
line vty 0 4
 login
!
end
```

Monitoring and Testing the Configuration

From RouterB, display the BGP table with the command **show ip bgp**. The following example shows the output from this command. Note that RouterB has learned about network 1.0.0.0.

```
RouterB#show ip bgp
BGP table version is 49, local router ID is 2.2.2.2
Status codes: s suppressed, d damped, h history, * valid, > best, i - internal
Origin codes: i - IGP, e - EGP, ? - incomplete

   Network      Next Hop     Metric    LocPrf    Weight    Path
*> 1.0.0.0      192.1.1.1      0                    0      100 I
```

From RouterC, display the BGP table with the command **show ip bgp**. The output from the command is shown as follows. Note that RouterC also has learned about network 1.0.0.0.

```
RouterC#show ip bgp
BGP table version is 2, local router ID is 3.3.3.3
Status codes: s suppressed, d damped, h history, * valid, > best, i - internal
Origin codes: i - IGP, e - EGP, ? - incomplete

   Network      Next Hop     Metric    LocPrf    Weight    Path
*>i1.0.0.0      192.1.1.1      0         100        0      100 I
```

Display the routing table on RouterC with the command **show ip route**. The output from the command is shown as follows. Notice that RouterC has not loaded the route into the IP routing table.

```
RouterC#show ip route
Codes: C - connected, S - static, I - IGRP, R - RIP, M - mobile, B - BGP
       D - EIGRP, EX - EIGRP external, O - OSPF, IA - OSPF inter area
       E1 - OSPF external type 1, E2 - OSPF external type 2, E - EGP
       i - IS-IS, L1 - IS-IS level-1, L2 - IS-IS level-2, * - candidate default
       U - per-user static route
```

```
Gateway of last resort is not set

        2.0.0.0/32 is subnetted, 1 subnets
O          2.2.2.2 [110/65] via 193.1.1.2, 00:13:17, Serial0
        3.0.0.0/24 is subnetted, 1 subnets
C          3.3.3.0 is directly connected, Loopback0
        4.0.0.0/32 is subnetted, 1 subnets
O          4.4.4.4 [110/65] via 194.1.1.2, 00:13:18, Serial1
O        192.1.1.0/24 [110/128] via 193.1.1.2, 00:13:18, Serial0
C        193.1.1.0/24 is directly connected, Serial0
C        194.1.1.0/24 is directly connected, Serial1
```

The IGP (in this case, OSPF) has not learned about the route, because we are not redistributing the BGP-learned routes on RouterB into OSPF. Remember that BGP must be synchronized with the IGP. To disable synchronization, add the command **no synchronization** under the BGP process.

```
RouterC#configure terminal
Enter configuration commands, one per line. End with CNTL/Z.
RouterC(config)#router bgp 200
RouterC(config-router)#no synchronization
```

In order for the changes to take effect, the BGP neighbors must be reset. To do this task, use the command **clear ip bgp ***, which causes the TCP session between neighbors to be reset—restarting the neighbor negotiations from scratch and invalidating the cache.

```
RouterC#clear ip bgp *
```

Now, display the routing table on RouterC. Note that network 1.0.0.0 is now present.

```
RouterC#show ip route
Codes: C - connected, S - static, I - IGRP, R - RIP, M - mobile, B - BGP
       D - EIGRP, EX - EIGRP external, O - OSPF, IA - OSPF inter area
       E1 - OSPF external type 1, E2 - OSPF external type 2, E - EGP
       i - IS-IS, L1 - IS-IS level-1, L2 - IS-IS level-2, * - candidate default
       U - per-user static route

Gateway of last resort is not set

B      1.0.0.0/8 [200/0] via 192.1.1.1, 00:02:45
        2.0.0.0/32 is subnetted, 1 subnets
O          2.2.2.2 [110/65] via 193.1.1.2, 00:26:28, Serial0
        3.0.0.0/24 is subnetted, 1 subnets
C          3.3.3.0 is directly connected, Loopback0
        4.0.0.0/32 is subnetted, 1 subnets
O          4.4.4.4 [110/65] via 194.1.1.2, 00:26:29, Serial1
O        192.1.1.0/24 [110/128] via 193.1.1.2, 00:26:29, Serial0
C        193.1.1.0/24 is directly connected, Serial0
C        194.1.1.0/24 is directly connected, Serial1
```

From RouterD, display the BGP table with the command **show ip bgp.** The output from the command is shown as follows. Note that RouterD has not learned about any network via BGP.

```
RouterD#show ip bgp
```

RouterB does not have an IBGP connection with RouterD, and RouterC cannot advertise a route via IBGP that was learned from another IBGP neighbor.

There are two ways to fix this problem: Establish an IBGP connection from RouterD to RouterB through the neighbor command, or make RouterC a route reflector. To make RouterC a route reflector for RouterB and RouterD, add the following commands to RouterC:

```
RouterC#conf terminal
RouterC(config)#router bgp 200
RouterC(config-router)#neighbor 193.1.1.2 route-reflector-client
RouterC(config-router)#neighbor 194.1.1.2 route-reflector-client
```

In order for the changes to take effect, the BGP neighbors must be reset. To do this task, use the command **clear ip bgp ***, which causes the TCP session between neighbors to be reset—restarting the neighbor negotiations from scratch and invalidating the cache.

```
RouterC#clear ip bgp *
```

Display the BGP neighbor information on RouterC with the command **show ip bgp neighbor 194.1.1.2**. Following is the truncated output. Notice that neighbor 194.1.1.2 is now a route reflector client.

```
RouterC#show ip bgp neighbors 194.1.1.2
BGP neighbor is 194.1.1.2,  remote AS 200, internal link
 Index 0, Offset 0, Mask 0x0
  Route-Reflector Client
  BGP version 4, remote router ID 4.4.4.4
  BGP state = Established, table version = 11, up for 00:11:41
  Last read 00:00:41, hold time is 180, keepalive interval is 60 seconds
  Minimum time between advertisement runs is 5 seconds
  Received 78 messages, 0 notifications, 0 in queue
  Sent 79 messages, 0 notifications, 0 in queue
  Connections established 9; dropped 8
```

From RouterD, display the BGP table with the command **show ip bgp.** Following is the output from the command. Notice that RouterD's BGP process has now learned about network 1.0.0.0; however, the route will not get loaded into the IP routing table until synchronization is turned off.

```
RouterD#show ip bgp
BGP table version is 3, local router ID is 4.4.4.4
Status codes: s suppressed, d damped, h history, * valid, > best, i - internal
Origin codes: i - IGP, e - EGP, ? - incomplete

   Network      Next Hop      Metric      LocPrf      Weight      Path
*>i1.0.0.0      192.1.1.1        0          100          0        100 i
```

LAB #43: Manipulating BGP Path Selection

Equipment Needed

The following equipment is needed to perform this lab exercise:

- Four Cisco routers, each with two serial ports
- Cisco IOS 10.0 or higher
- A PC running a terminal emulation program for connecting to the console port of the router
- Four Cisco DTE/DCE crossover cables
- One Cisco rolled cable

BGP Path Selection Overview

BGP uses a set of parameters (attributes) that describe the characteristics of a route. The attributes are sent in the BGP update packets with each route. The router uses these attributes to select the best route to the destination. In this lab, we will explore the manipulation of these attributes to control BGP path selections.

It is important to understand the BGP decision process in order to correctly manipulate path selection. The following list is the order of the BGP decision process used by the router in path selection:

1. If the next-hop is unreachable, do not consider the next-hop.
2. Prefer the path that has the largest weight.
3. If the routes have the same weight, use the route with the highest local preference.

4. If the routes have the same local preference, prefer the route that was originated by BGP on this router.

5. If no route was originated, prefer the route with the shortest AS path.

6. If all paths are of the same AS length, prefer the route with lowest origin code (IGP < EGP < INCOMPLETE).

7. If the origin codes are the same, prefer the path with the lowest *Multi-Exit Discriminator* (MED).

8. If the MEDs are the same, prefer external paths over internal paths.

9. If the MEDs are the same, prefer the path through the closest IGP neighbor.

10. If the MEDs are still the same, prefer the path with the lowest BGP router ID.

Configuration Overview

This lab will demonstrate how an administrator can manipulate route selection through the use of BGP attributes. All routers will be configured for BGP. OSPF will be used as the IGP within AS 200. RouterA is in AS 100 and will be external BGP neighbors with RouterB and RouterC, which are in AS 200. RouterB and RouterC will run IBGP to RouterD, which is also in AS 200.

All routers are connected serially via crossover cables. RouterB will act as the DCE, supplying clock to RouterA and RouterD. RouterC will also act as the DCE, supplying clock for RouterD and RouterA. The IP addresses are assigned as per Figure 10–19. All routers are configured for BGP and have loopback addresses defined. RouterA's and RouterD's loopback addresses will be advertised via BGP.

Router Configurations

The configurations for the four routers in this example are as follows (key BGP configurations are highlighted in bold):

Figure 10–19
BGP path selection

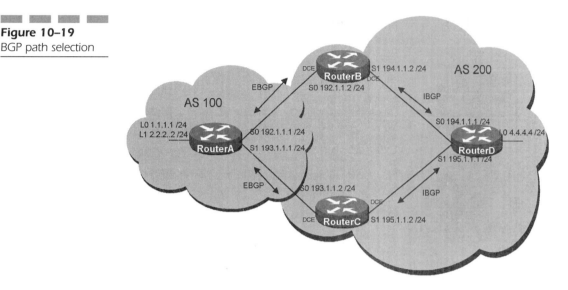

RouterA

```
version 11.2
no service udp-small-servers
no service tcp-small-servers
!
hostname RouterA
!
!
interface Loopback0
 ip address 1.1.1.1 255.255.255.0
!
interface Loopback1
 ip address 2.2.2.2 255.255.255.0
!
interface Ethernet0/0
 no ip address
 shutdown
!
interface Serial0/0
 ip address 192.1.1.1 255.255.255.0
!
interface Serial0/1
 ip address 193.1.1.1 255.255.255.0
!
router bgp 100←Configures a BGP process for autonomous system 100
 network 1.0.0.0
 network 2.0.0.0←Specify the list of networks for the BGP routing process to
                 advertise.
 neighbor 192.1.1.2 remote-as 200
```

```
neighbor 193.1.1.2 remote-as 200←Specifies the neighboring router and the
                                   autonomous system it is in

!
no ip classless
!
line con 0
line aux 0
line vty 0 4
 login
!
end
```

RouterB

```
version 11.2
no service udp-small-servers
no service tcp-small-servers
!
hostname RouterB
!
interface Ethernet0/0
 no ip address
 shutdown
!
interface Serial0/0
 ip address 192.1.1.2 255.255.255.0
 clockrate 500000←Acts as DCE providing clock


!
interface Serial0/1
 ip address 194.1.1.2 255.255.255.0
 clockrate 500000←Acts as DCE providing clock
!
router ospf 64
 passive-interface Serial0/0
 network 194.1.1.0 0.0.0.255 area 0
 network 192.1.1.0 0.0.0.255 area 0
!
router bgp 200←Configures a BGP process for autonomous system 100
no synchronization←Disables synchronization between BGP and your IGP.
neighbor 192.1.1.1 remote-as 100
 neighbor 194.1.1.1 remote-as 200
 neighbor 195.1.1.2 remote-as 200←Specifies the neighboring router and the
                                   autonomous system it is in

!
no ip classless
```

```
!
line con 0
line aux 0
line vty 0 4
 login
!
end
```

RouterC

```
version 11.2
no service udp-small-servers
no service tcp-small-servers
!
hostname RouterC
!
interface Ethernet0/0
 no ip address
 shutdown
!
interface Serial0/0
 ip address 193.1.1.2 255.255.255.0
 clockrate 500000←Acts as DCE providing clock

!
interface Serial0/1
 ip address 195.1.1.2 255.255.255.0
 clockrate 500000←Acts as DCE providing clock

!
router ospf 64
 passive-interface Serial0/0
 network 195.1.1.0 0.0.0.255 area 0
 network 193.1.1.0 0.0.0.255 area 0
!
router bgp 200←Configures a BGP process for autonomous system 200.
no synchronization←Disables synchronization between BGP and your IGP.
 neighbor 193.1.1.1 remote-as 100
 neighbor 194.1.1.2 remote-as 200
 neighbor 195.1.1.1 remote-as 200←Specifies the neighboring router and the
                                  autonomous system it is in

!
no ip classless
!
line con 0
line aux 0
line vty 0 4
 login
!
end
```

RouterD

```
version 11.2
no service udp-small-servers
no service tcp-small-servers
!
hostname RouterD
!
interface Loopback0
 ip address 4.4.4.4 255.255.255.0
!
interface Ethernet0/0
 no ip address
 shutdown
!
interface Serial0/0
 ip address 194.1.1.1 255.255.255.0
!
interface Serial0/1
 ip address 195.1.1.1 255.255.255.0
!
router ospf 64
 network 194.1.1.0 0.0.0.255 area 0
 network 195.1.1.0 0.0.0.255 area 0
 network 4.4.4.0 0.0.0.255 area 0
!
router bgp 200←Configures a BGP process for autonomous system 200
 no synchronization←Disables synchronization between BGP and your IGP.

 neighbor 194.1.1.2 remote-as 200
 neighbor 195.1.1.2 remote-as 200←Specifies the neighboring router and the
                                    autonomous system it is in

!
!
no ip classless
!
line con 0
line aux 0
line vty 0 4
 login
!
end
```

Monitoring and Testing the Configuration

Display the BGP table on RouterD with the command **show ip bgp**. Following is the output from the command. RouterD is learning about network 1.0.0.0 and 2.0.0.0 via BGP from both RouterB and RouterC.

```
RouterD# show ip bgp
BGP table version is 11, local router ID is 4.4.4.4
Status codes: s suppressed, d damped, h history, * valid, > best, i - internal
Origin codes: i - IGP, e - EGP, ? - incomplete

    Network           Next Hop        Metric       LocPrf      Weight        Path
RouterB*>i1.0.0.0     192.1.1.1          0           100          0          100 i
* i                   193.1.1.1          0           100          0          100 i
RouterB*>i2.0.0.0     192.1.1.1          0           100          0          100 i
* i         .         193.1.1.1          0           100          0          100 I
```

Notice the best path (which is indicated by the >) is through RouterB (192.1.1.0). Remember the 10 decision steps that BGP goes through to select the best path. Because all other things were equal, the route from the router with the lowest RouterID is used (RouterB).

This can be verified through the command show ip bgp neighbors. Notice that RouterB's router ID is 194.1.1.2, and RouterC's router ID is 195.1.1.2.

```
RouterD#show ip bgp neighbors
BGP neighbor is 194.1.1.2,  remote AS 200, internal link←RouterB
  Index 0, Offset 0, Mask 0x0
   BGP version 4, remote router ID 194.1.1.2
   BGP state = Established, table version = 11, up for 00:11:56
   Last read 00:00:56, hold time is 180, keepalive interval is 60 seconds
   Minimum time between advertisement runs is 5 seconds
   Received 91 messages, 0 notifications, 0 in queue
   Sent 83 messages, 0 notifications, 0 in queue
   Connections established 6; dropped 5
Connection state is ESTAB, I/O status: 1, unread input bytes: 0
Local host: 194.1.1.1, Local port: 179
Foreign host: 194.1.1.2, Foreign port: 11006

BGP neighbor is 195.1.1.2,  remote AS 200, internal link←RouterC
  Index 0, Offset 0, Mask 0x0
   BGP version 4, remote router ID 195.1.1.2
   BGP state = Established, table version = 11, up for 00:11:40
   Last read 00:00:40, hold time is 180, keepalive interval is 60 seconds
   Minimum time between advertisement runs is 5 seconds
   Received 103 messages, 0 notifications, 0 in queue
   Sent 91 messages, 0 notifications, 0 in queue
   Connections established 8; dropped 7
Connection state is ESTAB, I/O status: 1, unread input bytes: 0
Local host: 195.1.1.1, Local port: 179
Foreign host: 195.1.1.2, Foreign port: 11031
```

Local Preference Attribute

The local preference attribute is a degree of preference given to a BGP route to compare it with other routes to the same destination. This attribute is the second-highest attribute used in the BGP decision process (the Cisco proprietary weight parameter is first). The local preference attribute is local to the AS and does not get passed to EBGP neighbors. The higher the local preference, the more preferred the route.

In this exercise, we will configure RouterC to set the local preference for network 1.0.0.0, learned from RouterA to 200. Because the default local preference is 100, all routers in AS 200 will prefer the path through RouterC to reach network 1.0.0.0.

In order to manipulate the local preference, we need to define which routes will be manipulated through the use of an access list, define the policy that will be applied to those routes through a route map, then assign the route map to a BGP neighbor.

1. Add access-list 1 to RouterC, permitting network 1.0.0.0

```
RouterC#configure terminal

RouterC(config)#access-list 1 permit 1.0.0.0 0.255.255.255
```

2. Define a route map named **localpref** that sets the local preference of the route to 200 if it matches access list 1—and 100 if it does not.

```
RouterC#configure terminal
RouterC(config)#route-map localpref 10←If the IP address matches access-list 1
                                       the local preference is set to 200.
RouterC(config-route-map)#match ip address 1
RouterC(config-route-map)#set local-preference 200
RouterC(config-route-map)route-map localpref permit 20←If the IP address does
                                                        not match access-list
                                                        1, the local preference
                                                        is set to 100.
RouterC(config)# set local-preference 100
```

3. Apply the route map to inbound traffic from BGP neighbor 193.1.1.1 (RouterA).

```
RouterC#configure terminal
RouterC(config)#router bgp 200
RouterC(config-router)#neighbor 193.1.1.1 route-map localpref in
```

In order for the changes to take effect, the BGP neighbors must be reset. To do this task, use the command **clear ip bgp** *. This command causes the TCP session between neighbors to be reset, restarting the neighbor negotiations from scratch and invalidating the cache.

```
RouterC#clear ip bgp *
```

Display the BGP table on RouterD with the command **show ip bgp**. The following shows the output from the command. Notice that the local preference of the route learned from RouterC is now 200 and is the best route (indicated by the > sign).

```
RouterD#show ip bgp
BGP table version is 11, local router ID is 4.4.4.4
Status codes: s suppressed, d damped, h history, * valid, > best, i - internal
Origin codes: i - IGP, e - EGP, ? - incomplete

   Network        Next Hop     Metric    LocPrf    Weight    Path
*>i1.0.0.0        193.1.1.1       0        200        0      100 i←Route learned
                                                                    from RouterC
*  i2.0.0.0       193.1.1.1       0        100        0      100 i
*>i               192.1.1.1       0        100        0      100 i
```

Display the BGP table on RouterB with the command **show ip bgp**. The output from the command is shown as follows. Notice that RouterB is also using the route advertised from RouterC to reach network 1.0.0.0.

```
RouterB#show ip bgp
BGP table version is 20, local router ID is 194.1.1.2
Status codes: s suppressed, d damped, h history, * valid, > best, i - internal
Origin codes: i - IGP, e - EGP, ? - incomplete

   Network        Next Hop     Metric    LocPrf    Weight    Path
*>i1.0.0.0        193.1.1.1       0        200        0      100 i←Route learned
                                                                    from RouterC
*                 192.1.1.1       0                   0      100 i
*  i2.0.0.0       193.1.1.1       0        100        0      100 i
*>                192.1.1.1       0                   0      100 I
```

The Multi-Exit Discriminator (MED) Attribute

The MED attribute is the external metric of a route. Unlike the local preference attribute, the MED is exchanged between autonomous systems; however, the MED that comes into an AS does not leave. As shown in the last section, local preference was used by the AS to influence its own outbound decision processes. The MED can be used to influence the outbound decision of another AS. The lower the MED, the more preferred the route. In Figure 10–20, RouterA sets the MED attribute for network 1.0.0.0 to 50 before advertising it to RouterC—and to 100 before advertising it to RouterB.

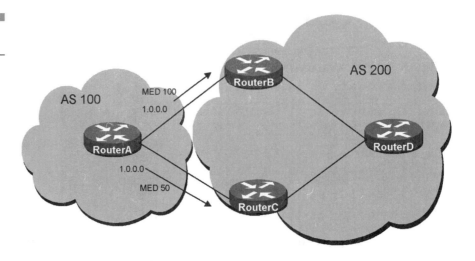

The routers in AS 200 will prefer the route through RouterC, because this route has the lowest MED.

In order to manipulate the MED, we need to identify what networks will be manipulated through the use of an access list. We also need to define a policy that will be applied to those routes through a route map, then assign the route map to a BGP neighbor.

Remove the map statement on RouterC:

```
RouterC#conf terminal
RouterC(config)#router bgp 200
RouterC(config-router)#no neighbor 193.1.1.1 route-map localpref in
```

1. Add access-list 1 to RouterA, permitting network 1.0.0.0.

```
RouterA#configure terminal

RouterA(config)#access-list 1 permit 1.0.0.0 0.255.255.255
```

2. Define two route maps: one named set_med_50, and the other named set_med_100. The first route map sets the MED attribute for network 1.0.0.0 to 50, whereas the latter sets the MED attribute to 100.

```
RouterA#configuration terminal
RouterA(config)#route-map set_med_50 10←The MED attribute for network 1.0.0.0
                                         is set to 50.
RouterA(config-route-map)#match ip address 1
RouterA(config-route-map)#set metric 50
```

```
RouterA(config-route-map)#exit
RouterA(config)#route-map set_med_50 20←The MED attribute for all other
                                 networks is not set.
RouterA(config-route-map)#set metric
RouterA(config-route-map)#exit
RouterA(config)#route-map set_med_100 10←The MED attribute for network 1.0.0.0
                                 is set to 100.
RouterA(config-route-map)#match ip address 1
RouterA(config-route-map)#set metric 100
RouterA(config-route-map)#exit
RouterA(config)#route-map set_med_100 20←The MED attribute for all other
                                 networks is not set.
RouterA(config-route-map)#set metric
```

Apply route map **set_med_50** on outbound routing updates to RouterC (193.1.1.2) and route map **set_med_100** on outbound routing updates to RouterB (192.1.1.2).

```
RouterA#configure terminal
RouterA(config)#router bgp 100
RouterA(config-router)#neighbor 193.1.1.2 route-map set_med_50 out
RouterA(config-router)#neighbor 192.1.1.2 route-map set_med_100 out
```

In order for the changes to take effect, the BGP neighbors must be reset. To do this task, use the command **clear ip bgp ***. This command causes the TCP session between neighbors to be reset, restarting the neighbor negotiations from scratch and invalidating the cache.

```
RouterC#clear ip bgp *
```

Display the BGP table on RouterB with the command **show ip bgp.** The output from the command is shown as follows. Notice that the route to network 1.0.0.0 learned via 193.1.1.1 has a local preference of 50 and is the preferred route.

```
RouterB#show ip bgp
BGP table version is 30, local router ID is 194.1.1.2
Status codes: s suppressed, d damped, h history, * valid, > best, i - internal
Origin codes: i - IGP, e - EGP, ? - incomplete
```

Network	Next Hop	Metric	LocPrf	Weight	Path	
*>i1.0.0.0	193.1.1.1	50	100	0	100 i	←Preferred route
*	192.1.1.1	100		0	100 i	
* i2.0.0.0	193.1.1.1	0	100	0	100 i	
*>	192.1.1.1	0		0	100 I	

From RouterA, display the route maps that are being used with the command **show route-maps**. This command tells which access list is used by the match clause, which set clause is applied, and how many times it has been used. This command is useful in troubleshooting possible route-map problems.

```
RouterA#show route-map
route-map set_med_50, permit, sequence 10
  Match clauses:
    ip address (access-lists): 1
  Set clauses:
    metric 50
  Policy routing matches: 0 packets, 0 bytes
route-map set_med_50, permit, sequence 20
  Match clauses:
  Set clauses:
  Policy routing matches: 0 packets, 0 bytes
route-map set_med_100, permit, sequence 10
  Match clauses:
    ip address (access-lists): 1
  Set clauses:
    metric 100
  Policy routing matches: 0 packets, 0 bytes
route-map set_med_100, permit, sequence 20
  Match clauses:
  Set clauses:
  Policy routing matches: 0 packets, 0 bytes
route-map med, permit, sequence 10
  Match clauses:
    ip address (access-lists): 1
  Set clauses:
  Policy routing matches: 0 packets, 0 bytes
```

AS Path Manipulation

BGP always prefers the route with the shortest AS path. In this exercise, we will configure RouterA to prepend two extra AS path numbers to network 1.0.0.0 (AS 300 and AS 400) before advertising this network to RouterC and RouterB.

In order to manipulate the AS path information, we need to identify which routes will be manipulated through the use of an access list. We also need to define a policy that will be applied to those routes through a route map, then assign the route map to a BGP neighbor.

1. Add access-list 1 to RouterA, permitting network 1.0.0.0.

```
RouterA#configure terminal

RouterA(config)#access-list 1 permit 1.0.0.0 0.255.255.255
```

2. Define a route map named **AS_Path** that prepends two additional AS path numbers (AS300 and AS400) to the route if it matches access list 1.

```
RouterA(config)#route-map AS_Path permit 10
RouterA(config-route-map)#match ip address 1
RouterA(config-route-map)#set as-path prepend 300 400
RouterA(config-route-map)#exit
RouterA(config)#route-map AS_Path 20
RouterA(config-route-map)#set as-path prepend
RouterA(config-route-map)#exit
```

Apply the route map to outbound routing updates to BGP neighbor 193.1.1.2 (RouterC) and neighbor 192.1.1.2 (RouterB).

```
RouterA#configure terminal
RouterA(config)#router bgp 200
RouterA(config-router)#neighbor 193.1.1.2 route-map AS_Path out
RouterA(config-router)#neighbor 192.1.1.2 route-map AS_Path out
```

In order for the changes to take effect, the BGP neighbors must be reset. To do this task, use the command **clear ip bgp** *. This command causes the TCP session between neighbors to be reset, restarting the neighbor negotiations from scratch and invalidating the cache.

```
RouterA#clear ip bgp *
```

Display the BGP table on RouterB with the command **show ip bgp.** The following example shows the output from the command. Notice that the route to network 1.0.0.0 now has an AS path of [100 300 400].

```
RouterB#show ip bgp
BGP table version is 68, local router ID is 194.1.1.2
Status codes: s suppressed, d damped, h history, * valid, > best, i - internal
Origin codes: i - IGP, e - EGP, ? - incomplete

    Network        Next Hop      Metric      LocPrf      Weight      Path
*  i1.0.0.0       193.1.1.1        0          100          0      100 300 400 i
*>                192.1.1.1        0                       0      100 300 400 i
*  i2.0.0.0       193.1.1.1        0          100          0          100 i
*>                192.1.1.1        0                       0          100 i
```

Route Filtering Based on Network Number

The router can filter routing updates to and from a particular neighbor based on the network number. The filter is made up of an access list that is applied to all BGP updates that are sent to or received from a particular neighbor.

In this exercise, we will configure a distribute list on RouterA to prevent prefix 1.0.0.0 / 8 from being advertised into AS 200.

In order to filter routes based on network address, we need to identify network addresses through the use of an access list and apply that list to a BGP neighbor using a distribute list.

1 Define the access list on RouterA to deny network 1.0.0.0 / 8.

```
RouterA#configure terminal
RouterA(config)#no access-list 1←Removes the old access list
RouterA(config)#access-list 1 deny 1.0.0.0 0.255.255.255
RouterA(config)#access-list 1 permit any
```

2. Apply the distribution list to both BGP neighbors.

```
RouterA(config)#router bgp 100
RouterA(config-router)#neighbor 193.1.1.2 distribute-list 1 out
RouterA(config-router)#neighbor 192.1.1.2 distribute-list 1 out
```

In order for the changes to take effect, the BGP neighbors must be reset. To do this task, use the command **clear ip bgp ***. This command causes the TCP session between neighbors to be reset, restarting the neighbor negotiations from scratch and invalidating the cache.

```
RouterA#clear ip bgp *
```

Display the routes that are being advertised via BGP to neighbor 193.1.1.2 with the command **show ip bgp neighbors 193.1.1.2 advertised-routes**. The output from the command is shown as follows. Notice that RouterA is now only advertising network 2.0.0.0.

```
RouterA#show ip bgp neighbors 193.1.1.2 advertised-routes
BGP table version is 3, local router ID is 5.5.5.5
Status codes: s suppressed, d damped, h history, * valid, > best, i - internal
Origin codes: i - IGP, e - EGP, ? - incomplete

   Network       Next Hop      Metric    LocPrf    Weight     Path
*> 2.0.0.0       0.0.0.0         0                 32768 i
```

Display the BGP table on RouterB with the command **show ip bgp**. The output from the command is as follows. Notice that the route to network 1.0.0.0 is no longer in the BGP table.

```
RouterB#show ip bgp
BGP table version is 78, local router ID is 194.1.1.2
Status codes: s suppressed, d damped, h history, * valid, > best, i - internal
Origin codes: i - IGP, e - EGP, ? - incomplete
```

```
       Network      Next Hop     Metric       LocPrf      Weight     Path
*> 2.0.0.0       192.1.1.1      0                         0     100 300 400 i
*  i             193.1.1.1      0            100          0     100 300 400 i
```

BGP Soft Configuration

BGP soft configuration enables policies to be configured and activated without resetting the BGP and TCP session. This feature enables the new policy to take effect without significantly affecting the network. Without BGP, soft configuration BGP is required to reset the neighbor TCP connection in order for the new changes to take effect. This task is accomplished using the **clear ip bgp** command, which was used throughout this chapter.

There are two types of BGP soft reconfiguration; Outbound reconfiguration which will make the new local outbound policy take effect without resetting the BGP session and inbound soft reconfiguration which enables the new inbound policy to take effect.

The problem with inbound reconfiguration is that in order to generate new, inbound updates without resetting the BGP session, all inbound updates (whether accepted or rejected) need to be stored by the router. This process is memory intensive and should be avoided wherever possible.

To avoid the memory overhead needed for inbound soft reconfiguration, the same outcome could be achieved by doing an outbound soft reconfiguration at the other end of the connection.

Outbound soft reconfiguration can be triggered with the following command:

clear ip bgp [*|address | peer-group] [**soft out**]

For inbound soft reconfiguration an additional router command needs to be added before a soft reconfiguration can be issued. The reason is this command tells the router to start storing the received updates.

neighbor [address | peer-group] **soft-reconfiguration inbound**

Inbound soft reconfiguration can than be triggered with the following command:

clear ip bgp [*|address | peer-group] [**soft in**]

Regular Expressions

In the previous section, we looked at identifying routes based on IP address. In this section, we will use regular expressions to identify routes based on AS path information. A regular expression is a pattern to match against an input string. When a regular expression is created, the expression specifies the pattern that a string must match. The following list describes keyboard characters that have special meaning when used in regular expressions.

Character	Symbol	Meaning
Period	.	Match any character, including white space
Asterisk	*	Match zero or more sequences of the pattern
Plus sign	+	Match one or more sequences of the pattern
Question mark	?	Matches zero or one occurrences of the pattern
Caret	^	Begins with
Dollar sign	$	Ends with
Underscore	_	Match the following
Brackets	[ ]	Match a single value in range
Hyphen	-	Separates the end points of a range

Filtering Based on AS Path

For this exercise, let's configure a regular expression in conjunction with a filter list on RouterC that will prevent any network that passes through AS 300 from being sent via BGP to RouterD. Filtering routes based on AS path information can be useful when all routes from a particular AS need to be filtered. If filtering based on AS path was not used, the administrator would have to list each route one-by-one or potentially filter on a prefix. AS path filtering provides an efficient alternative to this process.

In order to filter routes based on AS path information, we need to identify the AS path based on the defined regular expression and apply this information to a BGP neighbor through a filter list.

1. Define the regular expression to deny any route that passed through AS 300.

```
RouterC#configure terminal
RouterC(config)#ip as-path access-list 1 deny _300←Deny any route that passes
                                                    through AS 300.
RouterC(config)#ip as-path access-list 1 permit .*
```

Use the **show ip bgp regexp** command to see which routes the regular expression matches. The following example shows the output from the command. Note that network 2.0.0.0 is the only route that matches the regular expression (_300_). This command is useful in verifying that the regular expression covers the routes that you intend for it to cover.

```
RouterC#show ip bgp regexp _300_
BGP table version is 19, local router ID is 195.1.1.2
Status codes: s suppressed, d damped, h history, * valid, > best, i - internal
Origin codes: i - IGP, e - EGP, ? - incomplete

   Network       Next Hop      Metric      LocPrf      Weight      Path
*> 2.0.0.0       193.1.1.1        0                        0      100 300 400 i
*  i             192.1.1.1        0          100           0      100 300 400 i
```

2. Apply the filter list to BGP neighbor 195.1.1.1.

```
RouterC(config)#router bgp 200
RouterC(config-router)#neighbor 195.1.1.1 filter-list 1 out
```

In order for the changes to take effect, the BGP neighbor must be reset. To do this task, use the command **clear ip bgp ***. This command causes the TCP session between neighbors to be reset, restarting the neighbor negotiations from scratch and invalidating the cache.

```
RouterC#clear ip bgp *
```

Display the AS path access list on RouterC with the command **show ip as-path-access-list**. The following example shows the output from the command. This command is useful in quickly determining which strings will be permitted or denied.

```
RouterC#show ip as-path-access-list
AS path access list 1
    deny _300_
    permit .*
```

Display the BGP filter list configured on RouterC with the command **show ip bgp filter-list 1**. The following example shows the output from the command. This command shows which routes conform to a specified filter list (and therefore will be passed).

```
RouterC#show ip bgp filter-list 1
BGP table version is 5, local router ID is 195.1.1.2
Status codes: s suppressed, d damped, h history, * valid, > best, i - internal
Origin codes: i - IGP, e - EGP, ? - incomplete
```

```
   Network      Next Hop     Metric       LocPrf      Weight      Path
*> 2.0.0.0      193.1.1.1      0                        0         100 i
*  i            192.1.1.1      0            100         0         100 i
```

Display the BGP table on RouterD with the command **show ip bgp**. The following example shows the output from the command. Notice that the route to network 1.0.0.0 via RouterC is no longer present in the routing table.

```
RouterD#show ip bgp
BGP table version is 5, local router ID is 4.4.4.4
Status codes: s suppressed, d damped, h history, * valid, > best, i - internal
Origin codes: i - IGP, e - EGP, ? - incomplete
   Network      Next Hop     Metric       LocPrf      Weight      Path
*>i1.0.0.0      192.1.1.1      0            100         0         100 300 400 i
*  i2.0.0.0     193.1.1.1      0            100         0         100 i
*>i             192.1.1.1      0            100         0         100 I
```

The following list shows the regular expressions and their significance:

Expression	Significance
_300_	Match any routes that pass via AS 300.
_300$	Match any routes that originated in AS 300.
^300_	Only matches routes received.
^300$	Only routes that originated from AS 300 and did not pass through any other AS.
.*	All routes.

Troubleshooting BGP

The Cisco IOS provides many tools for troubleshooting routing protocols. The following example shows a list of key commands, along with a sample output from each, that will aid in troubleshooting BGP.

{show ip bgp} This exec command displays all the entries in the BGP routing table. This command is helpful in determining whether a route has been learned by the BGP process.

```
RouterA#show ip bgp
          ↓Internal version number of the table. This number is incremented
          whenever the table changes.
BGP table version is 3, local router ID is 5.5.5.5←IP address of the router.
Status codes: s suppressed, d damped, h history, * valid, > best, i - internal
Origin codes: i - IGP, e - EGP, ? - incomplete
```

```
     Network      Next Hop      Metric      LocPrf     Weight      Path
*> 1.0.0.0       0.0.0.0        0                                  32768 i
*> 2.0.0.0       0.0.0.0        0                                  32768 i
```

{show ip bgp filter-list}   This exec command displays all routes that conform to a specified filter list. The following example shows a sample output from the command:

```
RouterC#show ip bgp filter-list 1
BGP table version is 5, local router ID is 195.1.1.2
Status codes: s suppressed, d damped, h history, * valid, > best, i - internal
Origin codes: i - IGP, e - EGP, ? - incomplete

     Network      Next Hop      Metric      LocPrf     Weight      Path
*> 2.0.0.0       193.1.1.1      0                      0          100 i
*  i              192.1.1.1     0           100        0          100 i
```

{show ip bgp neighbors)   This exec command displays information about the TCP and BGP connections to neighbors. This command can be used with the argument **received routes or advertised-routes**, which displays all updates that are sent to or received from a particular neighbor. In order to display the received routes, Inbound soft reconfiguration must be configured on the router.

```
RouterC#show ip bgp neighbors 193.1.1.1 received-routes
BGP table version is 3, local router ID is 195.1.1.2
Status codes: s suppressed, d damped, h history, * valid, > best, i - internal
Origin codes: i - IGP, e - EGP, ? - incomplete

     Network      Next Hop      Metric      LocPrf     Weight      Path
*> 2.0.0.0       193.1.1.1      0                      0          100 300 400 I
```

```
RouterA#show ip bgp neighbors 193.1.1.2 advertised-routes
BGP table version is 5, local router ID is 5.5.5.5
Status codes: s suppressed, d damped, h history, * valid, > best, i - internal
Origin codes: i - IGP, e - EGP, ? - incomplete

     Network      Next Hop      Metric      LocPrf     Weight      Path
*> 2.0.0.0       0.0.0.0        0                                  32768 I
```

{show ip bgp paths}   This exec command displays all BGP paths in the database and the number of routes using each path. A regular expression can be added to the command to search for a particular AS or string of autonomous systems.

```
RouterB#show ip bgp paths 400
Address         Hash        Refcount      Metric        Path
0x6069719C      219         1             0            100 300 400 i
0x60764F18      219         1             0            100 300 400 I
```

{show ip bgp regexp}   This exec command displays all routes matching the regular expression. This command can quickly tell you whether your regular expression is matching the routes that you require.

```
RouterB#show ip bgp regexp  _400_
BGP table version is 12, local router ID is 194.1.1.2
Status codes: s suppressed, d damped, h history, * valid, > best, i - internal
Origin codes: i - IGP, e - EGP, ? - incomplete
   Network        Next Hop       Metric      LocPrf      Weight      Path
*  i2.0.0.0       193.1.1.1       0           100          0      100 300 400 i
*>                192.1.1.1       0                        0      100 300 400 I
```

{show ip bgp summary}   This exec command shows the status of all BGP connections. This command also displays all the neighbor routers that are attached and shows the length of time that the BGP session has been in the Established state (or the current state, if it is not Established).

```
RouterC#show ip bgp summary
BGP table version is 19, main routing table version 19←Indicates last version
                                                        of BGP database that
                                                        was injected into the
                                                        main routing table
1 network entries (2/3 paths) using 260 bytes of memory
2 BGP path attribute entries using 252 bytes of memory
0 BGP route-map cache entries using 0 bytes of memory
1 BGP filter-list cache entries using 16 bytes of memory

Neighbor    V   AS   MsgRcvd    MsgSent    TblVer    InQ    OutQ    Up/Down State
193.1.1.1   4   100   7106       7088       19        0      0       02:01:46
194.1.1.2   4   200   7092       7096       19        0      0       04:17:33
195.1.1.1   4   200   7072       7093       19        0      0       04:17:36
```

Conclusion

BGP is an *Exterior Gateway Protocol* (EGP), which means that BGP performs routing between multiple autonomous systems or domains. BGP was developed to replace EGP. BGP solves serious problems that were present with EGP and scales to Internet growth more efficiently. BGP has been deployed extensively on routers within the Internet today.

11

Route Redistribution

Topics Covered in This Chapter

- Redistributing RIP and IGRP
- Redistributing IGRP and EIGRP
- Redistributing RIP and OSPF
- Redistributing IGRP and OSPF
- Detailed troubleshooting examples

Introduction

Route redistribution is required when networks running multiple routing protocols need to be integrated. This chapter covers the interaction of RIP, IGRP, EIGRP, and OSPF routing protocols—as well as how to successfully redistribute routes from one protocol to another.

Commands Discussed in This Chapter

- **area** area-id **range** address mask
- **default-metric** number
- **default-metric** bandwidth delay reliability loading mtu
- **distribute-list** access-list-number | name **in** [type number]
- **distribute-list** access-list-number | name **out** [type number]
- **redistribute protocol** [process-id] {level-1 | level-1-2 | level-2} [metric metric-value]
- **show ip protocols**
- **summary-address** address mask {level-1 | level-1-2 | level-2} prefix mask [not-advertise]

Definitions

area range: This router configuration command is used to consolidate and summarize routes at an *Area Border Router* (ABR).

default-metric: This router configuration command is used to set the metric value for all routes being redistributed into IGRP, EIGRP, BGP, EGP, and OSPF. The default-metric command is used in conjunction with the redistribute router configuration command, setting the metric to the same value for all redistributed routes.

distribute-list in: This router configuration command is used to filter networks received in routing updates.

distribute-list out: This router configuration command is used to suppress networks sent out in routing updates.

redistribute protocol: This router configuration command is used to redistribute routes from one routing domain into another routing domain.

show ip protocols: This exec command will display the parameters and current state of all active routing protocol processes.

summary-address: This router configuration command is used to create aggregate addresses for IS-IS or OSPF. This command enables multiple groups of addresses to be summarized by an ASBR in one advertisement.

IOS Requirements

All of the labs in this chapter were done using IOS 11.2.

Lab #44: Redistributing RIP and IGRP

Equipment Needed

The following equipment is needed to perform this lab exercise:

- Four Cisco routers, two with one serial port and two with two serial ports
- Cisco IOS 10.0 or higher
- A PC running a terminal emulation program
- Three DTE/DCE crossover cables
- A Cisco rolled cable used for console port access

Configuration Overview

This configuration will demonstrate redistribution between two Distance Vector Routing protocols: RIP and IGRP. NetworkA has just been acquired by NetworkB, and the two networks are running different routing protocols. NetworkA is running RIP on RouterA and RouterB, and NetworkB is running IGRP on RouterC and RouterD. In order for the two networks to communicate, RIP is run between RouterB and RouterC.

All routers are connected serially via a crossover cable. RouterB will act as the DCE, supplying clock to RouterA and RouterC. RouterC will act as the DCE, supplying clock to RouterD. The IP addresses are assigned as per Figure 11–1.

Router Configurations

The configurations for the four routers in this example are as follows (key routing configurations commands are highlighted in bold):

RouterA

```
Version 11.2
no service udp-small-servers
no service tcp-small-servers
!
hostname RouterA
!
interface Loopback0
 ip address 1.1.1.1 255.255.255.0
!
interface Ethernet0
 no ip address
 shutdown
!
interface Serial0
 ip address 192.1.1.1 255.255.255.0
!
interface Serial1
 no ip address
 shutdown
!
```

Figure 11–1
Redistributing RIP and IGRP

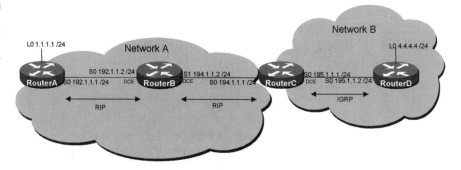

```
router rip←Enables RIP on the Router
 network 192.1.1.0
 network 1.0.0.0
!
no ip classless
!
line con 0
line 1 16
line aux 0
line vty 0 4
!
end
```

RouterB

```
Current configuration:
!
version 11.2
service udp-small-servers
service tcp-small-servers
!
hostname RouterB
!
!
interface Ethernet0
 no ip address
 shutdown
!
interface Serial0
 ip address 192.1.1.2 255.255.255.0
 no fair-queue
 clockrate 500000←Acts as DCE providing clock

!
interface Serial1
 ip address 194.1.1.2 255.255.255.0
 clockrate 500000←Acts as DCE providing clock

!
router rip←Enables the RIP routing process on the router.
 network 192.1.1.0←Specifies what interfaces will receive and send RIP routing
                   updates. It also specifies what networks will be advertised.
network  194.1.1.0
!
line con 0
line aux 0
 transport input all
line vty 0 4
 login
!
end
```

RouterC

```
Current configuration:
!
version 11.2
service udp-small-servers
service tcp-small-servers
!
hostname RouterC
!
!
!
interface Ethernet0
 no ip address
 shutdown
!
interface Serial0
 ip address 194.1.1.1 255.255.255.0
!
interface Serial1
 ip address 195.1.1.1 255.255.255.0
 clockrate 500000←Acts as DCE providing clock

!
router rip←Enables the RIP routing process on the router.
 network  194.1.1.0←Specifies what interfaces will receive and send RIP
                    routing updates. It also specifies what networks will be
                    advertised.
!
router igrp 100←Enables the RIP routing process on the router
 network 195.1.1.0←Specifies what interfaces will receive and send RIP routing
                    updates. It also specifies what networks will be advertised.
!
no ip classless
!
line con 0
line 1 16
line aux 0
line vty 0 4
 login
!
end
```

RouterD

```
version 11.2
no service udp-small-servers
no service tcp-small-servers
!
hostname RouterD
!
```

```
!
interface Loopback0
 ip address 4.4.4.4 255.255.255.0
!
interface Ethernet0
 no ip address
 shutdown
!
interface Serial0
 ip address 195.1.1.2 255.255.255.0
!
interface Serial1
 no ip address
 shutdown
!
router igrp 100←Enables the RIP routing process on the router
 network 195.1.1.0
 network 4.0.0.0←Specifies what interfaces will receive and send RIP routing
                 updates. It also specifies what networks will be advertised.
!
no ip classless
!
line con 0
line 1 16
line aux 0
line vty 0 4
!
end
```

Monitoring and Testing the Configuration

Display the IP routing table on RouterC with the command **show ip route**. The following example shows the output from this command. Notice that RouterC has learned all of NetworkA's routes via RIP.

```
RouterC#show ip route
Codes: C - connected, S - static, I - IGRP, R - RIP, M - mobile, B - BGP
       D - EIGRP, EX - EIGRP external, O - OSPF, IA - OSPF inter area
       E1 - OSPF external type 1, E2 - OSPF external type 2, E - EGP
       i - IS-IS, L1 - IS-IS level-1, L2 - IS-IS level-2, * - candidate default
       U - per-user static route

Gateway of last resort is not set

R    1.0.0.0/8 [120/2] via 194.1.1.2, 00:00:02, Serial0
I    4.0.0.0/8 [100/8976] via 195.1.1.2, 00:00:51, Serial1
R    192.1.1.0/24 [120/1] via 194.1.1.2, 00:00:02, Serial0
C    194.1.1.0/24 is directly connected, Serial0
C    195.1.1.0/24 is directly connected, Serial1
```

Display the IP routing table on RouterB with the command **show ip route**. The following example shows the output from the command. Notice that RouterB has not learned any routes from NetworkB, because RouterB and RouterC are running RIP between them—not IGRP. If they were running IGRP, we would see the exact opposite. RouterB would see all of NetworkB's routes, and RouterC or RouterD would not see any of NetworkA's routes.

```
RouterB#show ip route
Codes: C - connected, S - static, I - IGRP, R - RIP, M - mobile, B - BGP
       D - EIGRP, EX - EIGRP external, O - OSPF, IA - OSPF inter area
       E1 - OSPF external type 1, E2 - OSPF external type 2, E - EGP
       i - IS-IS, L1 - IS-IS level-1, L2 - IS-IS level-2, * - candidate default

Gateway of last resort is not set

R    1.0.0.0 [120/1] via 192.1.1.1, 00:00:05, Serial0
C    192.1.1.0 is directly connected, Serial0
C    194.1.1.0 is directly connected, Serial1
```

Remove RIP from network 194.1.1.0 on RouterB and RouterC.

```
RouterB#configure terminal
RouterB(config)#router rip
RouterB(config-router)#no network 194.1.1.0

RouterC#configure terminal
RouterC(config)#router rip
RouterC(config-router)#no network 194.1.1.0
```

Enable IGRP on network 194.1.1.0 on both RouterB and RouterC.

```
RouterB#configure terminal
RouterB(config)#router igrp 100
RouterB(config-router)#network 194.1.1.0

RouterC#configure terminal
RouterC(config)#router igrp 100
RouterC(config-router)#network 194.1.1.0
```

Display the IP routing table on RouterC with the command **show ip route**. The following example shows the output from the command. Notice that RouterC no longer has any of NetworkA's routes.

```
RouterC#show ip route
Codes: C - connected, S - static, I - IGRP, R - RIP, M - mobile, B - BGP
       D - EIGRP, EX - EIGRP external, O - OSPF, IA - OSPF inter area
       E1 - OSPF external type 1, E2 - OSPF external type 2, E - EGP
```

```
        i - IS-IS, L1 - IS-IS level-1, L2 - IS-IS level-2, * - candidate default
        U - per-user static route

Gateway of last resort is not set

I     4.0.0.0/8 [100/8976] via 195.1.1.2, 00:00:56, Serial1
C     194.1.1.0/24 is directly connected, Serial0
C     195.1.1.0/24 is directly connected, Serial1
```

Display the IP routing table on RouterB with the command **show ip route**. The following example shows the output from the command. Notice that RouterB has now learned NetworkB's routes via IGRP, because RouterB is now participating in the IGRP domain.

```
RouterB#show ip route
Codes: C - connected, S - static, I - IGRP, R - RIP, M - mobile, B - BGP
       D - EIGRP, EX - EIGRP external, O - OSPF, IA - OSPF inter area
       E1 - OSPF external type 1, E2 - OSPF external type 2, E - EGP
       i - IS-IS, L1 - IS-IS level-1, L2 - IS-IS level-2, * - candidate default

Gateway of last resort is not set

R     1.0.0.0 [120/1] via 192.1.1.1, 00:00:26, Serial0
I     4.0.0.0 [100/10976] via 194.1.1.1, 00:00:04, Serial1
C     192.1.1.0 is directly connected, Serial0
C     194.1.1.0 is directly connected, Serial1
I     195.1.1.0 [100/10476] via 194.1.1.1, 00:00:04, Serial1
```

In order for RouterC and RouterD to learn the RIP routers from RouterA, we must use route redistribution. Route redistribution is the process of taking routes learned from one routing protocol, such as RIP, and injecting them into a different routing protocol (such as IGRP).

Because RouterB has all of the IGRP routes from NetworkB, we only need to redistribute the RIP-learned routes on RouterB into IGRP. This process is referred to as one-way redistribution, versus mutual redistribution—where both routing protocols are redistributed into one another.

On RouterB, enable the redistribution of RIP into IGRP.

```
RouterB(config)#router igrp 100
RouterB(config-router)#redistribute rip
```

Display the routing table on RouterC with the command **show ip route**. The output from the command is shown as follows. Notice that RouterC still does not see network 1.0.0.0. Why?

```
RouterC#show ip route
Codes: C - connected, S - static, I - IGRP, R - RIP, M - mobile, B - BGP
       D - EIGRP, EX - EIGRP external, O - OSPF, IA - OSPF inter area
       E1 - OSPF external type 1, E2 - OSPF external type 2, E - EGP
```

```
      i - IS-IS, L1 - IS-IS level-1, L2 - IS-IS level-2, * - candidate default
      U - per-user static route

Gateway of last resort is not set

I    4.0.0.0/8 [100/8976] via 195.1.1.2, 00:00:07, Serial1
I    192.1.1.0/24 [100/10476] via 194.1.1.2, 00:00:47, Serial0
C    194.1.1.0/24 is directly connected, Serial0
C    195.1.1.0/24 is directly connected, Serial1
```

From RouterC, display the IGRP routing updates with the command **debug ip igrp transactions**. The output from this command is shown as follows. Notice that RouterC is receiving an IGRP update for network 1.0.0.0. The route is marked inaccessible, however, which is why the route is not being loaded into the IP routing table.

```
RouterC#
IGRP: received update from 194.1.1.2 on Serial0
      network 1.0.0.0, metric -1 (inaccessible)
      network 192.1.1.0, metric 10476 (neighbor 8476)
IGRP: received update from 195.1.1.2 on Serial1
      network 4.0.0.0, metric 8976 (neighbor 501)
```

The reason that the route is being advertised as inaccessible from RouterB is metrics. RIP and IGRP use totally different metrics to convey route preference. When we redistribute RIP into IGRP, we need to tell the router what the metric will be. Otherwise, the router marks the route as inaccessible.

We need to tell RouterB what the setting for the metric should be when the router redistributes RIP routes into IGRP. There are several ways that this task can be done. The first and simplest method is to set a default metric that will be applied to any route that is distributed into IGRP. To do this task, add the following command to RouterB:

```
RouterB(config)#router igrp 100
RouterB(config-router)#default-metric 10000 100 255 1 1500
```

IGRP uses five metrics to calculate the cost of the route: bandwidth, delay, reliability, load, and MTU.

Display the routing table on RouterC with the command **show ip route**. The output from the command is shown as follows. Notice that all of RouterA's routes are being learned via IGRP.

```
RouterC#show ip route
Codes: C - connected, S - static, I - IGRP, R - RIP, M - mobile, B - BGP
       D - EIGRP, EX - EIGRP external, O - OSPF, IA - OSPF inter area
       E1 - OSPF external type 1, E2 - OSPF external type 2, E - EGP
```

```
        i - IS-IS, L1 - IS-IS level-1, L2 - IS-IS level-2, * - candidate default
        U - per-user static route

Gateway of last resort is not set

I     1.0.0.0/8 [100/8576] via 194.1.1.2, 00:01:22, Serial0
I     4.0.0.0/8 [100/8976] via 195.1.1.2, 00:00:55, Serial1
I     192.1.1.0/24 [100/10476] via 194.1.1.2, 00:01:22, Serial0
C     194.1.1.0/24 is directly connected, Serial0
C     195.1.1.0/24 is directly connected, Serial1
```

The problem with using the default metric command is that the command assigns this metric to all redistributed routes—regardless of which protocol they originated from or how far away they actually are. The default metric can be set on a per-protocol basis by adding the metric to the end of the redistribution command. For example, if we only wanted to set the default metric for RIP routes being redistributed into IGRP, we would use the redistribute command as shown:

```
RouterB#configure terminal
RouterB(config)#router igrp 100
RouterB(config-router)#redistribute rip metric 10000 100 255 1 1500←Default metric
```

This approach provides more flexibility, enabling each protocol that is being redistributed to have different metrics. For each protocol, however, we are assigning the same metric to every redistributed route. To get around this, Route Maps can be used to assign different metrics to routes learned from the same routing protocol. For example, we can assign a different metric for network 1.0.0.0 and network 192.1.1.0.

From RouterB, remove the default metric from the IGRP routing process.

```
RouterB#configure terminal
RouterB(config)#router igrp 100
RouterB(config-router)#no default-metric 10000 100 255 1 1500
```

Setting the metric for a particular route is a three-step process. We need to identify the network through the use of an access list, define the metric that will be applied to the routes through a route map, and assign the route map to a redistribution statement.

1. Add access-list 1 to RouterB, permitting network 1.0.0.0.

```
RouterB#configure terminal

RouterB(config)#access-list 1 permit 1.0.0.0
```

2. Define a route map named **rip_to_igrp** that sets the five IGRP metrics of the route to (56 100 255 1 1500) if it matches access list 1 and (10000 100 255 1 1500) if no match exists.

```
RouterB#configure terminal

RouterB(config)#route-map
RouterB(config)#route-map rip_to_igrp 10
RouterB(config-route-map)#match ip address 1
RouterB(config-route-map)#set metric 56 100 255 1 1500
RouterB(config-route-map)#exit
RouterB(config)#route-map rip_to_igrp 20
RouterB(config-route-map)#set metric  10000 100 255 1 1500
```

3. Apply the route map to routes being redistributed from RIP to IGRP.

```
RouterB#configure terminal
RouterB(config)#router igrp 100
RouterB(config-router)#redistribute rip route-map rip_to_igrp
```

When a RIP route is redistributed into IGRP, the route map, rip_to_igrp, is consulted. If the route matches access list 1 (1.0.0.0), then the metrics are set to (56 100 255 1 1500). If no match exists, the metrics are set to (10000 100 255 1 1500).

Display the IP routing table on RouterC. Notice that the metrics have changed for network 1.0.0.0 but have remained the same for network 192.1.1.0.

```
RouterC#show ip route
Codes: C - connected, S - static, I - IGRP, R - RIP, M - mobile, B - BGP
       D - EIGRP, EX - EIGRP external, O - OSPF, IA - OSPF inter area
       E1 - OSPF external type 1, E2 - OSPF external type 2, E - EGP
       i - IS-IS, L1 - IS-IS level-1, L2 - IS-IS level-2, * - candidate default
       U - per-user static route

Gateway of last resort is not set

I     1.0.0.0/8 [100/180671] via 194.1.1.2, 00:00:05, Serial0
I     4.0.0.0/8 [100/8976] via 195.1.1.2, 00:00:05, Serial1
I     192.1.1.0/24 [100/8576] via 194.1.1.2, 00:00:05, Serial0
C     194.1.1.0/24 is directly connected, Serial0
C     195.1.1.0/24 is directly connected, Serial1
```

Up until this point, we have only been dealing with one-way redistribution. The next topic to be covered is mutual redistribution. Mutual redistribution is defined as each routing protocol being redistributed into the other. In this example, RIP is redistributed into IGRP, and IGRP is redistributed into RIP on RouterB. In order for RouterA to have visibility to NetworkB, RouterB must redistribute the IGRP routes into RIP.

Redistribute the IGRP routes into RIP on RouterB with the following commands:

```
RouterB#configure terminal
RouterB(config)#router rip
RouterB(config-router)#redistribute igrp 100 metric 3
```

Display the IP routing table on RouterA. Notice that RouterA is now receiving all routes via RIP.

```
RouterA#show ip route
Codes: C - connected, S - static, I - IGRP, R - RIP, M - mobile, B - BGP
       D - EIGRP, EX - EIGRP external, O - OSPF, IA - OSPF inter area
       N1 - OSPF NSSA external type 1, N2 - OSPF NSSA external type 2
       E1 - OSPF external type 1, E2 - OSPF external type 2, E - EGP
       i - IS-IS, L1 - IS-IS level-1, L2 - IS-IS level-2, * - candidate default
       U - per-user static route, o - ODR

Gateway of last resort is not set

     1.0.0.0/24 is subnetted, 1 subnets
C       1.1.1.0 is directly connected, Loopback0
R     4.0.0.0/8 [120/3] via 192.1.1.2, 00:00:10, Serial0
C     192.1.1.0/24 is directly connected, Serial0
R     194.1.1.0/24 [120/3] via 192.1.1.2, 00:00:10, Serial0
R     195.1.1.0/24 [120/3] via 192.1.1.2, 00:00:10, Serial0
```

Care must be taken when using mutual redistribution, because routing loops can occur. For example, RouterB is advertising network 4.0.0.0 (which it learned via IGRP) to RouterA via RIP. What would happen if RouterA advertised the route back to RouterB?

The rule of split-horizons prevents this situation from occurring. What if split-horizons were disabled on RouterA, however? RouterB would redistribute the RIP-learned route into IGRP and cause a routing loop.

Lab #45: Redistributing IGRP and EIGRP

Equipment Needed

The following equipment is needed to perform this lab exercise:

- Four Cisco routers, two with one serial port and two with two serial ports
- Cisco IOS 10.0 or higher

- A PC running a terminal emulation program
- Three DTE/DCE crossover cables
- A Cisco rolled cable used for console port access

Configuration Overview

This configuration will demonstrate redistribution between two Cisco proprietary protocols: EIGRP and IGRP. NetworkB has just been acquired by NetworkA, and the two networks are running different routing protocols. NetworkA is running EIGRP on RouterA and RouterB, and NetworkB is running IGRP on RouterC and RouterD. In order for the two networks to communicate, EIGRP must be run between RouterB and RouterC.

All routers are connected serially via a crossover cable. RouterB will act as the DCE, supplying clock to RouterA and RouterC. RouterC will act as the DCE, supplying clock to RouterD. The IP addresses are assigned as per Figure 11–2.

Router Configurations

The configurations for the four routers in this example are as follows (key routing configuration commands are highlighted in bold):

RouterA

```
Current configuration:
!
version 11.2
no service udp-small-servers
```

Figure 11–2
Redistribution
between EIGRP
and IGRP

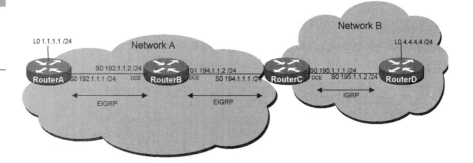

```
no service tcp-small-servers
!
hostname RouterA
!
interface Loopback0
 ip address 1.1.1.1 255.255.255.0
!
!
interface Serial0
 ip address 192.1.1.1 255.255.255.0
!
router eigrp 100
 network 192.1.1.0
 network 1.0.0.0
!
no ip classless
!
line con 0
line 1 16
line aux 0
line vty 0 4
!
end
```

RouterB

```
Current configuration:
!
version 11.2
service udp-small-servers
service tcp-small-servers
!
hostname RouterB
!
!
interface Ethernet0
 no ip address
 shutdown
!
interface Serial0
 ip address 192.1.1.2 255.255.255.0
 no fair-queue
 clockrate 500000←Acts as DCE providing clock
!
interface Serial1
 ip address 194.1.1.2 255.255.255.0
 clockrate 500000←Acts as DCE providing clock
!
router eigrp 100
 network 192.1.1.0
 network  194.1.1.0
```

```
!
line con 0
line aux 0
 transport input all
line vty 0 4
 login
!
end
```

RouterC

```
Current configuration:
!
version 11.1
service udp-small-servers
service tcp-small-servers
!
hostname RouterC
!
!
!
interface Ethernet0
 no ip address
 shutdown
!
interface Serial0
 ip address 194.1.1.1 255.255.255.0
!
interface Serial1
 ip address 195.1.1.1 255.255.255.0
 clockrate 500000←Acts as DCE providing clock
!
router eigrp 100
 network 194.1.1.0
!
router igrp 200
 network 195.1.1.0
!
no ip classless
!
line con 0
line 1 16
line aux 0
line vty 0 4
 login
!
end
```

RouterD

```
version 11.2
no service udp-small-servers
no service tcp-small-servers
!
hostname RouterD
!
!
interface Loopback0
 ip address 4.4.4.4 255.255.255.0
!
interface Ethernet0
 no ip address
 shutdown
!
interface Serial0
 ip address 195.1.1.2 255.255.255.0
!
!
router igrp 200
 network 195.1.1.0
 network 4.0.0.0
!
no ip classless
!
line con 0
line 1 16
line aux 0
line vty 0 4
!
end
```

Monitoring and Testing the Configuration

Display the IP routing table on RouterC with the command **show ip
route**. The following example shows the output from this command.
Notice that RouterC has learned all of NetworkA's routes via EIGRP.

```
RouterC#show ip route
Codes: C - connected, S - static, I - IGRP, R - RIP, M - mobile, B - BGP
       D - EIGRP, EX - EIGRP external, O - OSPF, IA - OSPF inter area
       E1 - OSPF external type 1, E2 - OSPF external type 2, E - EGP
       i - IS-IS, L1 - IS-IS level-1, L2 - IS-IS level-2, * - candidate default
       U - per-user static route

Gateway of last resort is not set

D    1.0.0.0/8 [90/2809856] via 194.1.1.2, 00:02:07, Serial0
I    4.0.0.0/8 [100/8976] via 195.1.1.2, 00:00:10, Serial1
D    192.1.1.0/24 [90/2681856] via 194.1.1.2, 00:02:07, Serial0
```

```
C     194.1.1.0/24 is directly connected, Serial0
C     195.1.1.0/24 is directly connected, Serial1
```

Display the IP routing table on RouterB with the command **show ip route**. The output from the command is shown as follows. Notice that RouterB has not learned any routes from NetworkB.

```
RouterB#show ip route
Codes: C - connected, S - static, I - IGRP, R - RIP, M - mobile, B - BGP
       D - EIGRP, EX - EIGRP external, O - OSPF, IA - OSPF inter area
       E1 - OSPF external type 1, E2 - OSPF external type 2, E - EGP
       i - IS-IS, L1 - IS-IS level-1, L2 - IS-IS level-2, * - candidate default

Gateway of last resort is not set

D     1.0.0.0 [90/2297856] via 192.1.1.1, 00:02:47, Serial0
C     192.1.1.0 is directly connected, Serial0
C     194.1.1.0 is directly connected, Serial1
```

Display the IP routing table on RouterD with the command **show ip route**. The output from the command is shown as follows. Notice that RouterD has not learned any routes from NetworkA.

```
RouterD#show ip route
Codes: C - connected, S - static, I - IGRP, R - RIP, M - mobile, B - BGP
       D - EIGRP, EX - EIGRP external, O - OSPF, IA - OSPF inter area
       N1 - OSPF NSSA external type 1, N2 - OSPF NSSA external type 2
       E1 - OSPF external type 1, E2 - OSPF external type 2, E - EGP
       i - IS-IS, L1 - IS-IS level-1, L2 - IS-IS level-2, * - candidate default
       U - per-user static route, o - ODR

Gateway of last resort is not set

      4.0.0.0/24 is subnetted, 1 subnets
C        4.4.4.0 is directly connected, Loopback0
C     195.1.1.0/24 is directly connected, Serial0
```

Why does this situation occur? Shouldn't IGRP and EIGRP redistribute automatically, because they are similar protocols? The reason that the redistribution is not occurring automatically is because the AS numbers are not the same. In order for mutual redistribution to be automatic, both EIGRP and IGRP must have the same AS number.

Change the AS number for the IGRP process on RouterC and RouterD to 100.

```
RouterC#conf terminal
RouterC(config)#no router igrp 200
RouterC(config)#router igrp 100
RouterC(config-router)#network 195.1.1.0
```

```
RouterD#conf terminal
RouterD(config)#no router igrp 200
RouterD(config)#router igrp 100
RouterD(config-router)#network 195.1.1.0
RouterD(config-router)# network 4.0.0.0
```

Display the IP routing table on RouterD with the command **show ip route**. The output from the command is shown as follows. Notice that RouterD has now learned all of the routes on NetworkA.

```
RouterD#show ip route
Codes: C - connected, S - static, I - IGRP, R - RIP, M - mobile, B - BGP
       D - EIGRP, EX - EIGRP external, O - OSPF, IA - OSPF inter area
       N1 - OSPF NSSA external type 1, N2 - OSPF NSSA external type 2
       E1 - OSPF external type 1, E2 - OSPF external type 2, E - EGP
       i - IS-IS, L1 - IS-IS level-1, L2 - IS-IS level-2, * - candidate default
       U - per-user static route, o - ODR

Gateway of last resort is not set

I    1.0.0.0/8 [100/12976] via 195.1.1.1, 00:00:09, Serial0
     4.0.0.0/24 is subnetted, 1 subnets
C       4.4.4.0 is directly connected, Loopback0
I    192.1.1.0/24 [100/12476] via 195.1.1.1, 00:00:09, Serial0
I    194.1.1.0/24 [100/10476] via 195.1.1.1, 00:00:09, Serial0
```

We could have left the AS numbers different; however, we would have had to use the redistribution command under the routing process.

Lab #46: Redistributing RIP and OSPF

Equipment Needed

The following equipment is needed to perform this lab exercise:

■ Four Cisco routers, two with one serial port and two with two serial ports

■ Cisco IOS 10.0 or higher

■ A PC running a terminal emulation program

■ Three DTE/DCE crossover cables

■ A Cisco rolled cable used for console port access

Figure 11–3
Redistribution
between OSPF
and RIP

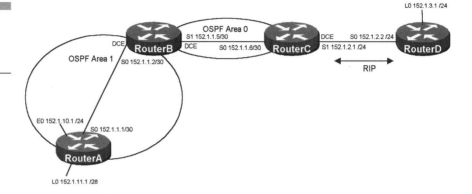

Configuration Overview

This configuration will demonstrate redistribution between a Link State routing protocol (OSPF) and a Distance Vector routing protocol (RIP). NetworkB (RouterD) has just been acquired by NetworkA (RoutersA, B, C), but the two networks are running different routing protocols. NetworkA is running OSPF on RouterA, RouterB, and RouterC, and NetworkB is running RIP on RouterD. In order for the two networks to communicate, RIP must be executed between RouterC and RouterD.

All routers are connected serially via a crossover cable. RouterB will act as the DCE, supplying clock to RouterA and RouterC. RouterC will act as the DCE, supplying clock to RouterD.

RouterA's serial and Ethernet interfaces are in OSPF area 1, along with RouterB's interface S0. RouterC's interface S0 is in OPSF area 0, along with interface S1 on RouterB. RouterD is running RIP on all networks, and RouterC is performing mutual redistribution between OSPF and RIP. The IP addresses are assigned as per Figure 11–3.

Router Configurations

The configurations for the four routers in this example are as follows (key routing configuration commands are highlighted in bold):

RouterA

```
Current configuration:
!
version 11.2
no service udp-small-servers
```

```
no service tcp-small-servers
!
hostname RouterA
!
interface Loopback0
 ip address 152.1.11.1 255.255.255.240
!
interface Ethernet0
 ip address 152.1.10.1 255.255.255.0
 no keepalive
!
interface Serial0
 ip address 152.1.1.1 255.255.255.252
!
router ospf 64
network 152.1.1.0 0.0.0.3 area 1
 network 152.1.10.1 0.0.0.16 area 1
!
no ip classless
!
line con 0
line 1 16
line aux 0
line vty 0 4
!
end
```

RouterB

```
version 11.2
service udp-small-servers
service tcp-small-servers
!
hostname RouterB
!
!
interface Serial0
 ip address 152.1.1.2 255.255.255.252
 no fair-queue
 clockrate 500000←Acts as DCE providing clock
!
interface Serial1
 ip address 152.1.1.5 255.255.255.252
 clockrate 500000←Acts as DCE providing clock
!
!
router ospf 64
 network 152.1.1.0 0.0.0.3 area 1
 network 152.1.1.4 0.0.0.3 area 0
!
line con 0
line aux 0
 transport input all
```

```
line vty 0 4
 login
!
end
```

RouterC

```
version 11.2
service udp-small-servers
service tcp-small-servers
!
hostname RouterC
!
!
!
!
interface Serial0
 ip address 152.1.1.6 255.255.255.252
!
interface Serial1
 ip address 152.1.2.1 255.255.255.0
 clockrate 500000←Acts as DCE providing clock
!
router ospf 64
 redistribute rip
network 152.1.1.4 0.0.0.3 area 0
 default-metric 64
!
router rip
 redistribute ospf 64←Redistributes ospf 64 router RIP
passive-interface Serial0
network 152.1.0.0
 default-metric 2←Sets the metric to 2 on any routes that are redistributed
                    into RIP.
!
no ip classless
!
line con 0
line 1 16
line aux 0
line vty 0 4
 login
!
end
```

RouterD

```
Current configuration:
!
version 11.2
no service udp-small-servers
```

```
no service tcp-small-servers
!
hostname RouterD
!
!
interface Loopback0
 ip address 152.1.3.1 255.255.255.0

!
interface Serial0
 ip address 152.1.2.2 255.255.255.0
!
!
router rip
 network 152.1.0.0
!
no ip classless
!
line con 0
line 1 16
line aux 0
line vty 0 4
 login
!
end
```

Monitoring and Testing the Configuration

Display the IP routing table on RouterC. The following example shows the output from the command. Note that RouterC has learned about network 152.1.3.0, which is the loopback interface of RouterD via RIP. The router has also learned about network 152.1.10.0 / 24 and network 152.1.1.0 / 30 via OSPF. The routes are OSPF inter-area routes, because they originated from OSFP area 1.

RouterC has not learned about network 152.1.11.0 / 28, which is the loopback interface on RouterA, because the network is not configured for OSPF (so the network is not being advertised).

```
RouterC#show ip route
Codes: C - connected, S - static, I - IGRP, R - RIP, M - mobile, B - BGP
       D - EIGRP, EX - EIGRP external, O - OSPF, IA - OSPF inter area
       E1 - OSPF external type 1, E2 - OSPF external type 2, E - EGP
       i - IS-IS, L1 - IS-IS level-1, L2 - IS-IS level-2, * - candidate default
       U - per-user static route

Gateway of last resort is not set

     152.1.0.0/16 is variably subnetted, 5 subnets, 2 masks
O IA    152.1.10.0/24 [110/138] via 152.1.1.5, 00:02:36, Serial0←OSPF inter
                                                                   area route
```

```
O IA     152.1.1.0/30 [110/128] via 152.1.1.5, 00:05:39, Serial0
R        152.1.3.0/24 [120/1] via 152.1.2.2, 00:00:05, Serial1
C        152.1.2.0/24 is directly connected, Serial1
C        152.1.1.4/30 is directly connected, Serial0
```

To fix this problem, we could simply include the network under the OSPF process, then the network would be advertised. The other option is to redistribute connected subnets on RouterA into OSPF.

Add the following commands to the OSPF process on RouterA:

```
RouterA#configure terminal
RouterA(config)#router ospf 64
RouterA(config-router)#redistribute connected subnets
```

Now, display the IP routing table on RouterC. The following example shows the output from this command. Note that RouterC now sees the route. The route is an OSPF external route because the route was redistributed into the domain.

```
RouterC#show ip route
Codes: C - connected, S - static, I - IGRP, R - RIP, M - mobile, B - BGP
       D - EIGRP, EX - EIGRP external, O - OSPF, IA - OSPF inter area
       E1 - OSPF external type 1, E2 - OSPF external type 2, E - EGP
       i - IS-IS, L1 - IS-IS level-1, L2 - IS-IS level-2, * - candidate default
       U - per-user static route

Gateway of last resort is not set

     152.1.0.0/16 is variably subnetted, 6 subnets, 3 masks
O E2    152.1.11.0/28 [110/20] via 152.1.1.5, 00:01:43, Serial0
O IA    152.1.10.0/24 [110/138] via 152.1.1.5, 00:09:21, Serial0
O IA    152.1.1.0/30 [110/128] via 152.1.1.5, 00:09:21, Serial0
R       152.1.3.0/24 [120/1] via 152.1.2.2, 00:00:16, Serial1
C       152.1.2.0/24 is directly connected, Serial1
C       152.1.1.4/30 is directly connected, Serial0
```

Now, display the IP routing table on RouterA. The output from the command is shown as follows. Note that RouterA is not receiving the route to network 152.1.3.0 / 24.

```
RouterA#show ip route
Codes: C - connected, S - static, I - IGRP, R - RIP, M - mobile, B - BGP
       D - EIGRP, EX - EIGRP external, O - OSPF, IA - OSPF inter area
       N1 - OSPF NSSA external type 1, N2 - OSPF NSSA external type 2
       E1 - OSPF external type 1, E2 - OSPF external type 2, E - EGP
       i - IS-IS, L1 - IS-IS level-1, L2 - IS-IS level-2, * - candidate default
       U - per-user static route, o - ODR

Gateway of last resort is not set
```

```
      152.1.0.0/16 is variably subnetted, 4 subnets, 3 masks
C        152.1.11.0/28 is directly connected, Ethernet0
C        152.1.10.0/24 is directly connected, Loopback0
C        152.1.1.0/30 is directly connected, Serial0
O IA     152.1.1.4/30 [110/128] via 152.1.1.2, 00:01:53, Serial0
```

The RIP-learned routes have not been successfully redistributed into OSPF, because with the current configuration on RouterC, only routes with a 16-bit mask (class B) will be redistributed into OSPF. The networks on RouterD have been subnetted using a 24-bit mask.

In order to have the subnet redistributed, you must specify this action in the configuration. Add the following command under the OSPF routing process on RouterC:

```
RouterC#configure terminal
RouterC(config)#router ospf 64
RouterC(config-router)#redistribute rip subnets
```

Display the IP routing table on RouterA. Notice that RouterA now has a route to networks 152.1.2.0 and 152.1.3.0. Also note that the routes are OSPF external routes (O E2), because they were learned from another domain.

```
RouterA#show ip route
Codes: C - connected, S - static, I - IGRP, R - RIP, M - mobile, B - BGP
       D - EIGRP, EX - EIGRP external, O - OSPF, IA - OSPF inter area
       N1 - OSPF NSSA external type 1, N2 - OSPF NSSA external type 2
       E1 - OSPF external type 1, E2 - OSPF external type 2, E - EGP
       i - IS-IS, L1 - IS-IS level-1, L2 - IS-IS level-2, * - candidate default
       U - per-user static route, o - ODR

Gateway of last resort is not set

      152.1.0.0/16 is variably subnetted, 6 subnets, 3 masks
C        152.1.11.0/28 is directly connected, Loopback0
C        152.1.10.0/24 is directly connected, Ethernet0
C        152.1.1.0/30 is directly connected, Serial0
O E2     152.1.3.0/24 [110/64] via 152.1.1.2, 00:01:05, Serial0
O E2     152.1.2.0/24 [110/64] via 152.1.1.2, 00:01:05, Serial0
O IA     152.1.1.4/30 [110/128] via 152.1.1.2, 00:18:54, Serial0
```

Display the IP routing table on RouterD. The following example shows the output. Note that RouterD has only learned about one network: 152.1.10.0 / 24, because all of the other networks are subnetted past the 24-bit boundary. Remember that RIP is a classful protocol and will not pass subnet information.

```
RouterD#show ip route
Codes: C - connected, S - static, I - IGRP, R - RIP, M - mobile, B - BGP
       D - EIGRP, EX - EIGRP external, O - OSPF, IA - OSPF inter area
```

```
          N1 - OSPF NSSA external type 1, N2 - OSPF NSSA external type 2
          E1 - OSPF external type 1, E2 - OSPF external type 2, E - EGP
          i - IS-IS, L1 - IS-IS level-1, L2 - IS-IS level-2, * - candidate default
          U - per-user static route, o - ODR

Gateway of last resort is not set

      152.1.0.0/16 is variably subnetted, 4 subnets, 2 masks
R         152.1.10.0/24 [120/2] via 152.1.2.1, 00:00:27, Serial0
C         152.1.3.0/24 is directly connected, Loopback0
C         152.1.2.0/24 is directly connected, Serial0
C         152.1.4.0/28 is directly connected, Loopback1
```

In order to get these routes redistributed into RIP, we can either create static routes using a 24-bit mask to the two networks and redistribute the routes into RIP—or we can summarize the routes in OSPF.

Let's examine the first option. Create two static routes on RouterC using a 24-bit mask.

```
RouterC#configure terminal
RouterC(config)#ip route 152.1.11.0 255.255.255.0 s0
RouterC(config)#ip route 152.1.1.0 255.255.255.0 s0
```

Redistribute the static routes into RIP on RouterC.

```
RouterC#configure terminal
RouterC(config-router)#redistribute static
```

Display the IP routing table on RouterD. Notice that RouterD now has a route to both networks.

```
RouterD#show ip route
Codes: C - connected, S - static, I - IGRP, R - RIP, M - mobile, B - BGP
       D - EIGRP, EX - EIGRP external, O - OSPF, IA - OSPF inter are
       N1 - OSPF NSSA external type 1, N2 - OSPF NSSA external type 2
       E1 - OSPF external type 1, E2 - OSPF external type 2, E - EGP
       i - IS-IS, L1 - IS-IS level-1, L2 - IS-IS level-2, * - candidate default
       U - per-user static route, o - ODR

Gateway of last resort is not set

      152.1.0.0/16 is variably subnetted, 6 subnets, 2 masks
R         152.1.11.0/24 [120/1] via 152.1.2.1, 00:00:14, Serial0
R         152.1.10.0/24 [120/2] via 152.1.2.1, 00:00:14, Serial0
R         152.1.1.0/24 [120/1] via 152.1.2.1, 00:00:14, Serial0
C         152.1.3.0/24 is directly connected, Loopback0
C         152.1.2.0/24 is directly connected, Serial0
C         152.1.4.0/28 is directly connected, Loopback1
```

Now, remove the static routes and the redistribute static command from RouterC.

```
RouterC#conf terminal
RouterC(config)#no ip route 152.1.1.0 255.255.255.0 Serial0
RouterC(config)#no ip route 152.1.11.0 255.255.255.0 Serial0
RouterC(config-router)#no redistribute static
```

Now, let's examine option two—summarizing the routes to a 24-bit mask in OSPF. To do this task, we need to use the OSPF area range command and the OSPF summary address command. Remember from Chapter 8, *"Open Shortest Path First (OSPF),"* that the OSPF area range command is used to summarize routes from non-backbone OSPF areas into area 0. The OSPF summary address command is used to summarize external routes on an ASBR.

For this lab, we have both types. Network 152.1.11.0 / 28 is an external route because the route was redistributed into the OSPF process. Network 152.1.1.0 / 30 is a non-backbone OSPF area (area1).

NOTE: *The summary-address command summarizes only routes from other routing protocols that are being redistributed into OSPF. The area range command is used for route summarization between OSPF areas. The area range command is used on* Area Border Routers *(ABR), and the summary address command is used on* Autonomous System Border Routers *(ASBR).*

Add the OSPF summary address command under the OSPF process on RouterA. The command will be used to summarize network 152.1.11.0 / 28 to 152.1.11.0 / 24, so the network will be propagated to RouterD.

```
RouterA#conf terminal
RouterA(config)#router ospf 64
RouterA(config-router)#summary-address 152.1.11.0 255.255.255.0
```

Display the IP routing table on RouterD. Note that RouterD now has a route to network 152.1.11.0 / 24.

```
RouterD#show ip route
Codes: C - connected, S - static, I - IGRP, R - RIP, M - mobile, B - BGP
       D - EIGRP, EX - EIGRP external, O - OSPF, IA - OSPF inter area
       N1 - OSPF NSSA external type 1, N2 - OSPF NSSA external type 2
       E1 - OSPF external type 1, E2 - OSPF external type 2, E - EGP
       i - IS-IS, L1 - IS-IS level-1, L2 - IS-IS level-2, * - candidate default
       U - per-user static route, o - ODR

Gateway of last resort is not set

     152.1.0.0/16 is variably subnetted, 5 subnets, 2 masks
R       152.1.11.0/24 [120/2] via 152.1.2.1, 00:00:02, Serial0
R       152.1.10.0/24 [120/2] via 152.1.2.1, 00:00:02, Serial0
C       152.1.3.0/24 is directly connected, Loopback0
```

```
C          152.1.2.0/24 is directly connected, Serial0
C          152.1.4.0/28 is directly connected, Loopback1
```

Add the OSPF area range command under the OSPF process on RouterB. The command will be used to summarize network 152.1.1.0 / 30 to 152.1.1.0 / 24, so the network will be propagated to RouterD.

```
RouterB#configure terminal
RouterB(config)#router ospf 64
RouterB(config-router)#area 1 range 152.1.1.0 255.255.255.0
```

Display the IP routing table on RouterD. Note that RouterD now has a route to network 152.1.1.0 / 24.

```
RouterD#show ip route
Codes: C - connected, S - static, I - IGRP, R - RIP, M - mobile, B - BGP
       D - EIGRP, EX - EIGRP external, O - OSPF, IA - OSPF inter area
       N1 - OSPF NSSA external type 1, N2 - OSPF NSSA external type 2
       E1 - OSPF external type 1, E2 - OSPF external type 2, E - EGP
       i - IS-IS, L1 - IS-IS level-1, L2 - IS-IS level-2, * - candidate default
       U - per-user static route, o - ODR

Gateway of last resort is not set

     152.1.0.0/16 is variably subnetted, 6 subnets, 2 masks
R        152.1.11.0/24 [120/2] via 152.1.2.1, 00:00:02, Serial0
R        152.1.10.0/24 [120/2] via 152.1.2.1, 00:00:02, Serial0
R        152.1.1.0/24 [120/2] via 152.1.2.1, 00:00:02, Serial0
C        152.1.3.0/24 is directly connected, Loopback0
C        152.1.2.0/24 is directly connected, Serial0
C        152.1.4.0/28 is directly connected, Loopback1
```

Care must be taken when using mutual redistribution in order to prevent routing loops. Metrics and split-horizons will help to prevent routing loops, but it is a good idea to configure distribution lists so the router cannot advertise invalid routes. To demonstrate this process, disable split-horizons on RouterC's interface s1.

```
RouterC#configure terminal
RouterC(config-if)#no ip split-horizon
```

Display the RIP update packets from RouterC with the **debug ip rip** command on RouterD. The following example shows the output from the command. Notice that RouterC is now advertising network 152.1.3.0, which is a directly connected network on RouterD. Although RouterD will not install this route in its routing table, because it prefers the directly connected network, it is good design to filter out the route using a distribute list on RouterC.

```
RouterD#
RIP: received v1 update from 152.1.2.1 on Serial0
      152.1.11.0 in 2 hops
      152.1.10.0 in 2 hops
      152.1.1.0 in 2 hops
      152.1.3.0 in 2 hops
      152.1.2.0 in 1 hops
```

Add a distribute list to RouterC, only permitting networks 152.1.11.0, 152.1.1.0, and 152.1.10.0 to be advertised via RIP. This process involves two steps. First, an access list must be set up to identify (and permit or deny) a network based on network address. Then, the access list must be applied to routing updates through the use of a distribute list.

1. Define an access list on RouterC, permitting networks 152.1.11.0, 152.1.1.0, and 152.1.10.0.

```
RouterC#configure terminal
RouterC(config)#access-list 1 permit 152.1.1.0 0.0.0.255
RouterC(config)#access-list 1 permit 152.1.11.0 0.0.0.255
RouterC(config)#access-list 1 permit 152.1.10.0 0.0.0.255
```

2. Apply the access list to routing updates through the use of a distribute list.

```
RouterC#configure terminal
RouterC(config-router)#distribute-list 1 out
```

Display the RIP update packets from RouterC with the **debug ip rip** command on RouterD. The output from the command is shown below. Notice that RouterC is now only advertising the three networks.

```
RIP: received v1 update from 152.1.2.1 on Serial0
      152.1.11.0 in 2 hops
      152.1.10.0 in 2 hops
      152.1.1.0 in 2 hops
```

Lab #47: Redistributing IGRP and OSPF

Equipment Needed

The following equipment is needed to perform this lab exercise:

- Four Cisco routers, two with one serial port and two with two serial ports
- Cisco IOS 10.0 or higher

- A PC running a terminal emulation program
- Three DTE/DCE crossover cables
- A Cisco rolled cable for console port access

Configuration Overview

This configuration will demonstrate redistribution between a Link State routing protocol (OSPF) and a Distance Vector routing protocol (IGRP). NetworkB (RouterD) has just been acquired by NetworkA (RoutersA, B, C), but the two networks are running different routing protocols. NetworkA is running OSPF on RouterA, RouterB, and RouterC, and NetworkB is running IGRP on RouterD. In order for the two networks to communicate, IGRP must be run between RouterC and RouterD.

All routers are connected serially via a crossover cable. RouterB will act as the DCE, supplying clock to RouterA and RouterC. RouterC will act as the DCE, supplying clock to RouterD.

RouterA's serial and Ethernet interfaces are in OSPF area 1, along with RouterB's interface S0. RouterC's interface S0 is in OPSF area 0, along with interface S1 on RouterB. RouterD is running IGRP on all networks, and RouterC is performing mutual redistribution between OSPF and IGRP. The IP addresses are assigned as per Figure 11–4:

Router Configurations

The configurations for the four routers in this example are as follows (key routing configuration commands are highlighted in bold):

Figure 11–4
Redistribution between OSPF and IGRP

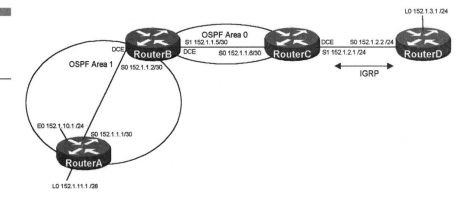

RouterA

```
version 11.2
no service udp-small-servers
no service tcp-small-servers
!
hostname RouterA
!
interface Loopback0
 ip address 152.1.11.1 255.255.255.240
!
interface Ethernet0
 ip address 152.1.10.1 255.255.255.0
 no keepalive
!
interface Serial0
 ip address 152.1.1.1 255.255.255.252
!
!
router ospf 64
 network 152.1.1.0 0.0.0.3 area 1
 network 152.1.10.1 0.0.0.16 area 1
!
no ip classless
!
line con 0
line 1 16
line aux 0
line vty 0 4
!
end
```

RouterB

```
version 11.2
service udp-small-servers
service tcp-small-servers
!
hostname RouterB
!
interface Serial0
 ip address 152.1.1.2 255.255.255.252
 no fair-queue
 clockrate 500000←Acts as DCE providing clock
!
interface Serial1
 ip address 152.1.1.5 255.255.255.252
 clockrate 500000←Acts as DCE providing clock
!
!

router ospf 64
 network 152.1.1.0 0.0.0.3 area 1
```

```
 network 152.1.1.4 0.0.0.3 area 0
!
line con 0
line aux 0
 transport input all
line vty 0 4
 login
!
end
```

RouterC

```
version 11.1
service udp-small-servers
service tcp-small-servers
!
hostname RouterC
!
interface Ethernet0
 no ip address
 shutdown
!
interface Serial0
 ip address 152.1.1.6 255.255.255.252
!
interface Serial1
 ip address 152.1.2.1 255.255.255.0
 clockrate 500000←Acts as DCE providing clock
!
router ospf 64
redistribute igrp 100←Redistributes IGRP 100 into OSPF
network 152.1.1.4 0.0.0.3 area 0
default-metric 64←Sets the metric on any routes that are redistributed into
                   OSPF.

!
router igrp 100
 redistribute ospf 64←Redistributes OSPF into IGRP.
 network 152.1.0.0
 default-metric 1000 10 1 255 1500←Sets the metric to on any routes that are
                                     redistributed into IGRP.

!
no ip classless
!
line con 0
line 1 16
line aux 0
line vty 0 4
 login
!
end
```

RouterD

```
Current configuration:
!
version 11.2
no service udp-small-servers
no service tcp-small-servers
!
hostname RouterD
!
!
interface Loopback0
 ip address 152.1.3.1 255.255.255.0
!
!
interface Serial0
 ip address 152.1.2.2 255.255.255.0
!
interface Serial1
 no ip address
!
router igrp 100
 network 152.1.0.0
!
no ip classless
!
line con 0
line 1 16
line aux 0
line vty 0 4
 login
!
end
```

Monitoring and Testing the Configuration

Display the IP routing table on RouterC. The output from the command is shown as follows. Note that RouterC has learned about network 152.1.3.0, which is the loopback interface of RouterD via IGRP. The router also has learned about network 152.1.10.0 / 24 and network 152.1.1.0 / 30 via OSPF. The routes are OSPF inter-area routes, because they originated from OSFP area 1.

RouterC has not learned about network 152.1.11.0 / 28, which is the loopback interface on RouterA, because the network is not configured for OSPF—so the network is not being advertised.

```
RouterC#show ip route
Codes: C - connected, S - static, I - IGRP, R - RIP, M - mobile, B - BGP
       D - EIGRP, EX - EIGRP external, O - OSPF, IA - OSPF inter area
       E1 - OSPF external type 1, E2 - OSPF external type 2, E - EGP
       i - IS-IS, L1 - IS-IS level-1, L2 - IS-IS level-2, * - candidate default
       U - per-user static route

Gateway of last resort is not set

     152.1.0.0/16 is variably subnetted, 5 subnets, 2 masks
O IA    152.1.10.0/24 [110/138] via 152.1.1.5, 00:00:33, Serial0
O IA    152.1.1.0/30 [110/128] via 152.1.1.5, 00:00:33, Serial0
I       152.1.3.0/24 [100/8976] via 152.1.2.2, 00:00:21, Serial1
C       152.1.2.0/24 is directly connected, Serial1
C       152.1.1.4/30 is directly connected, Serial0
```

To fix this problem, we could simply run OSPF on the network, and then the network would be advertised. The other option is to redistribute connected subnets on RouterA into OSPF.

Add the following command to the OSPF process on RouterA:

```
RouterA#configure terminal
RouterA(config)#router ospf 64
RouterA(config-router)#redistribute connected subnets
```

Now, display the IP routing table on RouterC. The following example shows the output from the command. Note that RouterC now sees the route; however, the route is OSPF external because it was redistributed into the domain.

```
RouterC#show ip route
Codes: C - connected, S - static, I - IGRP, R - RIP, M - mobile, B - BGP
       D - EIGRP, EX - EIGRP external, O - OSPF, IA - OSPF inter area
       E1 - OSPF external type 1, E2 - OSPF external type 2, E - EGP
       i - IS-IS, L1 - IS-IS level-1, L2 - IS-IS level-2, * - candidate default
       U - per-user static route

Gateway of last resort is not set

     152.1.0.0/16 is variably subnetted, 6 subnets, 3 masks
O E2    152.1.11.0/28 [110/20] via 152.1.1.5, 00:00:13, Serial0
O IA    152.1.10.0/24 [110/138] via 152.1.1.5, 00:00:14, Serial0
O IA    152.1.1.0/30 [110/128] via 152.1.1.5, 00:00:14, Serial0
I       152.1.3.0/24 [100/8976] via 152.1.2.2, 00:01:14, Serial1
C       152.1.2.0/24 is directly connected, Serial1
C       152.1.1.4/30 is directly connected, Serial0
```

Now, display the IP routing table on RouterA. The following example shows the output from the command. Note that RouterA is not receiving the route to network 152.1.3.0 / 24.

```
RouterA#show ip route
Codes: C - connected, S - static, I - IGRP, R - RIP, M - mobile, B - BGP
       D - EIGRP, EX - EIGRP external, O - OSPF, IA - OSPF inter area
       N1 - OSPF NSSA external type 1, N2 - OSPF NSSA external type 2
       E1 - OSPF external type 1, E2 - OSPF external type 2, E - EGP
       i - IS-IS, L1 - IS-IS level-1, L2 - IS-IS level-2, * - candidate default
       U - per-user static route, o - ODR

Gateway of last resort is not set

     152.1.0.0/16 is variably subnetted, 4 subnets, 3 masks
C       152.1.11.0/28 is directly connected, Loopback0
C       152.1.10.0/24 is directly connected, Ethernet0
C       152.1.1.0/30 is directly connected, Serial0
O IA    152.1.1.4/30 [110/128] via 152.1.1.2, 00:01:02, Serial0
```

The IGRP-learned routes have not been successfully redistributed into OSPF, because with the current configuration on RouterC, only routes with a 16-bit mask (class B) will be redistributed into OSPF. The networks on RouterD have been subnetted using a 24-bit mask.

In order to have the subnet redistributed, you must specify this event in the configuration. Add the following command under the OSPF routing process on RouterC:

```
RouterC#configure terminal
RouterC(config)#router ospf 64
RouterC(config-router)# redistribute igrp 100 subnets
```

Display the IP routing table on RouterA. The output of the command is shown as follows. Notice that RouterA now has a route to networks 152.1.2.0 and 152.1.3.0. Also note that the routes are OSPF external routes (O E2), because they were learned from another domain.

```
RouterA#show ip route
Codes: C - connected, S - static, I - IGRP, R - RIP, M - mobile, B - BGP
       D - EIGRP, EX - EIGRP external, O - OSPF, IA - OSPF inter area
       N1 - OSPF NSSA external type 1, N2 - OSPF NSSA external type 2
       E1 - OSPF external type 1, E2 - OSPF external type 2, E - EGP
       i - IS-IS, L1 - IS-IS level-1, L2 - IS-IS level-2, * - candidate default
       U - per-user static route, o - ODR

Gateway of last resort is not set

     152.1.0.0/16 is variably subnetted, 6 subnets, 3 masks
C       152.1.11.0/28 is directly connected, Loopback0
C       152.1.10.0/24 is directly connected, Ethernet0
C       152.1.1.0/30 is directly connected, Serial0
O E2    152.1.3.0/24 [110/64] via 152.1.1.2, 00:00:04, Serial0
O E2    152.1.2.0/24 [110/64] via 152.1.1.2, 00:00:04, Serial0
O IA    152.1.1.4/30 [110/128] via 152.1.1.2, 00:00:04, Serial0
```

Display the IP routing table on RouterD. The example below shows the output of this command. Note that RouterD has only learned about one network—152.1.10.0 / 24—because all the other networks are subnetted past the 24-bit boundary. Remember that IGRP is a classful protocol and will not pass subnet information.

```
RouterD#show ip route
Codes: C - connected, S - static, I - IGRP, R - RIP, M - mobile, B - BGP
       D - EIGRP, EX - EIGRP external, O - OSPF, IA - OSPF inter area
       N1 - OSPF NSSA external type 1, N2 - OSPF NSSA external type 2
       E1 - OSPF external type 1, E2 - OSPF external type 2, E - EGP
       i - IS-IS, L1 - IS-IS level-1, L2 - IS-IS level-2, * - candidate default
       U - per-user static route, o - ODR

Gateway of last resort is not set

     152.1.0.0/24 is subnetted, 3 subnets
I       152.1.10.0 [100/12000] via 152.1.2.1, 00:00:31, Serial0
C       152.1.3.0 is directly connected, Loopback0
C       152.1.2.0 is directly connected, Serial0
```

In order to get the routes redistributed into IGRP, we can either create static routes using a 24-bit mask to the two networks and redistribute the routes into IGRP, or we can summarize the routes in OSPF.

Let's examine the first option. Create two static routes on RouterC using a 24-bit mask.

```
RouterC#configure terminal
RouterC(config)#ip route 152.1.11.0 255.255.255.0 s0
RouterC(config)#ip route 152.1.1.0 255.255.255.0 s0
```

Redistribute the static routes into IGRP on RouterC.

```
RouterC#configure terminal
RouterC(config-router)#redistribute static
```

Display the IP routing table on RouterD. Notice that RouterD now has a route to both networks.

```
RouterD#sho ip route
Codes: C - connected, S - static, I - IGRP, R - RIP, M - mobile, B - BGP
       D - EIGRP, EX - EIGRP external, O - OSPF, IA - OSPF inter area
       N1 - OSPF NSSA external type 1, N2 - OSPF NSSA external type 2
       E1 - OSPF external type 1, E2 - OSPF external type 2, E - EGP
       i - IS-IS, L1 - IS-IS level-1, L2 - IS-IS level-2, * - candidate default
       U - per-user static route, o - ODR

Gateway of last resort is not set

     152.1.0.0/24 is subnetted, 5 subnets
```

```
I      152.1.11.0 [100/12000] via 152.1.2.1, 00:00:03, Serial0
I      152.1.10.0 [100/12000] via 152.1.2.1, 00:00:03, Serial0
I      152.1.1.0 [100/12000] via 152.1.2.1, 00:00:03, Serial0
C      152.1.3.0 is directly connected, Loopback0
C      152.1.2.0 is directly connected, Serial0
```

Now, remove the static routes and the redistribute static command from the IGRP routing process on RouterC.

```
RouterC#conf terminal
RouterC(config)#no ip route 152.1.1.0 255.255.255.0 Serial0
RouterC(config)#no ip route 152.1.11.0 255.255.255.0 Serial0
RouterC(config-router)#no redistribute static
```

Now, let's examine option two, which involves summarizing the routes to a 24-bit mask in OSPF. To do this task, we need to use the OSPF area range command and the OSPF summary address command. Remember from Chapter 8 that the OSPF area range command is used to summarize routes from non-backbone OSPF areas into area 0, and the OSPF summary address command is used to summarize external routes on an ASBR.

For this lab, we have both types. Network 152.1.11.0 / 28 is an external route, because the route was redistributed into the OSPF process. Network 152.1.1.0 / 30 is in a non-backbone OSPF area (area1).

NOTE: *The summary-address command only summarizes routes from other routing protocols that are being redistributed into OSPF. The area range command is used for route summarization between OSPF areas. The area range command is used on ABRs, and the summary address command is used on ASBRs.*

Add the OSPF summary address command under the OSPF process on RouterA. The command will be used to summarize network 152.1.11.0 / 28 to 152.1.11.0 / 24, so the network will be propagated to RouterD.

```
RouterA#conf terminal
RouterA(config)#router ospf 64
RouterA(config-router)#summary-address 152.1.11.0 255.255.255.0
```

Display the IP routing table on RouterD. The output of this command is shown as follows. Note that RouterD now has a route to network 152.1.11.0 / 24.

```
RouterD#show ip route
Codes: C - connected, S - static, I - IGRP, R - RIP, M - mobile, B - BGP
       D - EIGRP, EX - EIGRP external, O - OSPF, IA - OSPF inter area
       N1 - OSPF NSSA external type 1, N2 - OSPF NSSA external type 2
       E1 - OSPF external type 1, E2 - OSPF external type 2, E - EGP
       i - IS-IS, L1 - IS-IS level-1, L2 - IS-IS level-2, * - candidate default
       U - per-user static route, o - ODR

Gateway of last resort is not set

     152.1.0.0/24 is subnetted, 4 subnets
I       152.1.11.0 [100/12000] via 152.1.2.1, 00:00:09, Serial0
I       152.1.10.0 [100/12000] via 152.1.2.1, 00:00:09, Serial0
C       152.1.3.0 is directly connected, Loopback0
C       152.1.2.0 is directly connected, Serial0
```

Add the OSPF area range command under the OSPF process on RouterB. The command will be used to summarize network 152.1.1.0 / 30 to 152.1.11.0 / 24, so the network will be propagated to RouterD.

```
RouterB#configure terminal
RouterB(config)#router ospf 64
RouterB(config-router)#area 1 range 152.1.1.0 255.255.255.0
```

Display the IP routing table on RouterD. The output of the command is shown as follows. Note that RouterD now has a route to network 152.1.1.0 / 24.

```
RouterD#show ip route
Codes: C - connected, S - static, I - IGRP, R - RIP, M - mobile, B - BGP
       D - EIGRP, EX - EIGRP external, O - OSPF, IA - OSPF inter area
       N1 - OSPF NSSA external type 1, N2 - OSPF NSSA external type 2
       E1 - OSPF external type 1, E2 - OSPF external type 2, E - EGP
       i - IS-IS, L1 - IS-IS level-1, L2 - IS-IS level-2, * - candidate default
       U - per-user static route, o - ODR

Gateway of last resort is not set

     152.1.0.0/24 is subnetted, 5 subnets
I       152.1.11.0 [100/12000] via 152.1.2.1, 00:00:02, Serial0
I       152.1.10.0 [100/12000] via 152.1.2.1, 00:00:02, Serial0
I       152.1.1.0 [100/12000] via 152.1.2.1, 00:00:02, Serial0
C       152.1.3.0 is directly connected, Loopback0
C       152.1.2.0 is directly connected, Serial0
```

Care must be taken when using mutual redistribution (in order to prevent routing loops). Metrics and split-horizons will help to prevent routing loops, but it is a good idea to configure distribution lists so the router cannot advertise invalid routes. To demonstrate this process, disable split-horizons on RouterC's interface s1.

```
RouterC#configure terminal
RouterC(config-if)#no ip split-horizon
```

Display the IGRP update packets being sent from RouterC with the **debug ip igrp transactions** command. The following example shows the output from the command. Notice that RouterC is now advertising network 152.1.3.0, which is a directly connected network on RouterD. Although RouterD will not install this route in its routing table, because it prefers the directly connected network, it is good design practice to filter out the route using a distribute list on RouterC.

```
RouterC#
IGRP: sending update to 255.255.255.255 via Serial1 (152.1.2.1)
      subnet 152.1.11.0, metric=10000
      subnet 152.1.10.0, metric=10000
      subnet 152.1.1.0, metric=10000
      subnet 152.1.3.0, metric=8976
      subnet 152.1.2.0, metric=8476
```

Add a distribute list to RouterC, permitting only networks 152.1.11.0, 152.1.1.0, and 152.1.10.0 to be advertised via IGRP. This process involves two steps. First, an access-list must be set up to identify (and permit or deny) a network based on network address. Then, the access list must be applied to routing updates through the use of a distribute list.

1. Define an access list on RouterC, permitting networks 152.1.11.0, 152.1.1.0, and 152.1.10.0.

```
RouterC#configure terminal
RouterC(config)#access-list 1 permit 152.1.1.0 0.0.0.255
RouterC(config)#access-list 1 permit 152.1.11.0 0.0.0.255
RouterC(config)#access-list 1 permit 152.1.10.0 0.0.0.255
```

2. Apply the access list to routing updates through the use of a distribute list under the IGRP routing process.

```
RouterC#configure terminal
RouterC(config-router)#distribute-list 1 out
```

Display the IGRP update packets being sent from RouterC with the **debug ip igrp transactions** command on RouterD. The output from the command is shown as follows. Notice that RouterC is now advertising only the three networks.

```
RouterC#
IGRP: sending update to 255.255.255.255 via Serial1 (152.1.2.1)
      subnet 152.1.11.0, metric=10000
      subnet 152.1.10.0, metric=10000
      subnet 152.1.1.0, metric=10000
```

Troubleshooting Route Redistribution

{**show ip protocols**}   This exec command displays the parameters and current state of the active routing protocol process. The output shows the routing protocol used, the timer information, the inbound and outbound filter information, the protocols being redistributed, and the networks for which the protocol is routing. This command is useful in quickly determining which routing protocols are running, which (if any) protocols are being redistributed, and what the redistribution metric is.

```
Routing Protocol is "ospf 64"
  Sending updates every 0 seconds
  Invalid after 0 seconds, hold down 0, flushed after 0
  Outgoing update filter list for all interfaces is not set
  Incoming update filter list for all interfaces is not set
  Default redistribution metric is 64
  Redistributing: ospf 64, igrp 100
  Routing for Networks:
    152.1.1.4/30
  Routing Information Sources:
    Gateway          Distance       Last Update
    152.1.11.1          110         00:15:27
    152.1.1.5           110         00:15:27
  Distance: (default is 110)
```

{**debug ip igrp transactions**}   This exec command displays transaction information on IGRP routing transactions. The information contains the source and destination of each update, the routes that are received or being advertised, and the metric of each route.

```
RouterA#debug ip igrp transactions
IGRP: sending update to 255.255.255.255 via Ethernet0 (148.1.1.1)
      network 10.0.0.0, metric=501
      network 152.1.0.0, metric=10576
      network 192.1.1.0, metric=8476
      network 193.1.1.0, metric=10476
```

{**debug ip rip**}   This exec command displays information on RIP routing transactions. The output shows whether the router is sending or receiving an update, the networks that are contained in the update, and the metric or hop count for each.

```
RIP: sending v1 update to 255.255.255.255 via Ethernet0 (148.1.1.1)
 network 10.0.0.0, metric 1
 network 192.1.1.0, metric 1
network 148.1.0.0, metric 1
RIP: received v1 update from 192.1.1.2 on Serial0
193.1.1.0 in 1 hops
```

{`show ip access-list`} This privileged exec command displays the contents of all current IP access lists. The command can also display specific access lists by number.

```
RouterA#show ip access-lists 1
Standard IP access list 1
permit 150.1.1.0, wildcard bits 0.0.0.255
```

Conclusion

Redistributing routes between protocols can be tricky. In order to be successful, you need to have a complete understanding of the protocols and how they interact. Also understand how route distribution and route advertisement can be controlled with distribute lists, route maps, and passive interfaces. Remember that mutual redistribution can cause routing loops, so care must be taken.

CHAPTER 12

IP Access Lists

Topics Covered in This Chapter

- Detailed overview
- Access list terminology
- Standard IP access lists
- Extended IP access lists
- Extended access lists with the Established option
- Dynamic IP access lists
- How lock-and-key works
- Controlling VTY access
- Detailed troubleshooting examples

Introduction

A router uses access lists to police traffic that comes into or leaves a specified interface. The following list shows some of the ways that access lists can be used:

1. To deny or permit ingress or egress traffic from crossing specified interfaces

2. To define interesting traffic for DDR applications

3. To filter contents of routing updates

4. To control virtual terminal line access

5. To provide traffic flow control

This chapter will explore how to control packet movement through the router by using static and dynamic access lists.

Overview

Access lists, or access control lists, provide basic traffic filtering capabilities. Access lists can be used to control access into or out of the network—or to filter packets at ingress and egress router ports.

Access lists filter network traffic by determining whether a packet should be forwarded or dropped by the router, based on predefined criteria. This criteria is defined by an access list, which in turn is applied to an interface.

Depending on the access list defined, the match criteria can be quite simple (standard access) or fairly complex (extended access-list). Access lists provide a means of examining packets at the ingress and egress router ports, enabling the router to manipulate these packets based on certain criteria.

Access List Terminology

When dealing with access lists on a Cisco router, you should understand the terminology used.

■ **Wildcard mask:** A wildcard mask specifies which bits in an IP address should be ignored when comparing that address with another IP address. A one in the wildcard mask means to ignore that bit position when comparing another IP address, and a zero specifies that the bit position must match.

For example, the following access list (access list 1) specifies that in order for traffic to be permitted, the first three octets must match (150.1.1). This access list permits hosts 1–255 on network 150.1.1.0.

```
access-list 1 permit 150.1.1.0 0.0.0.255
```

150	1	1	0	←IP address
10010110	00000001	00000001	00000000	←Binary representation of IP address
00000000	00000000	00000000	11111111	←Binary representation of Wildcard mask
10010110	00000001	00000001	xxxxxxx	
↑	↑	↑	↑	
150	1	1	x	← When comparing IP addresses, match the first three octets and ignore the last octet.

- **Inbound and outbound**:   When applying an access list to an interface, the user specifies whether the access list is applied to inbound or outbound traffic (or both). By default, the access list is applied to outbound traffic.

The direction of traffic flow is relative to the router interface. For example, in Figure 12–1, RouterA wishes to deny all traffic from host 150.1.1.2 destined for PCA (152.1.1.2). There are two places that an access list could be applied on RouterA. An inbound access list could be applied on the serial interface, or an outbound access list could be applied to the Ethernet interface. It is good design to apply the access lists closest to the traffic that will be denied.

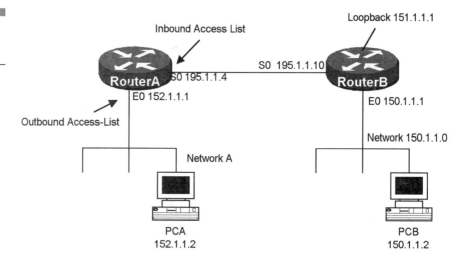

Figure 12–1
Access list
terminology

Commands Discussed in This Chapter

- **access-class** access-list-number {in | out}
- **access-enable** [host] [timeout minutes]
- **access-list** access-list-number {deny | permit} source [source-wildcard]
- **access-list** access-list-number {deny | permit}protocol source source-wildcard destination destination-wildcard [precedence precedence] [tos tos] [log]
- **access-list** access-list-number [**dynamic** dynamic-name [timeout minutes]]
- **access-template** [access-list-number | name] [dynamic-name] [source] [destination] [timeout minutes]
- **autocommand**
- **clear access-list counters** {access-list-number | name}
- **clear access-template** [access-list-number | name] [dynamic-name] [source] [destination]
- **ip access-group** {access-list-number | name}{in | out}
- **ip telnet source-interface**
- **show access-lists** [access-list-number | name]
- **show ip access-list** [access-list-number | name]
- **username** [name] **password** [password]

Definitions

access-class: The access-class command is used to restrict incoming and outgoing VTY connections between a particular VTY line on a Cisco router and a specific address defined by the access-list. This line configuration command applies a specific access list [1–99] to a VTY line. Incoming connections are restricted using the keyword "in," and outgoing connections are restricted using the keyword "out."

access-enable: This exec command is used to create a temporary access list entry in a dynamic access list, based on predefined criteria. The host keyword tells the IOS only to permit access for the particular host which originated the telnet session. The timeout keyword specifies an idle timeout period. If the access list entry is not used within this period of time, the access entry is deleted. If the entry is deleted, the user will have to reauthenticate in order to gain access to the network.

access-list [1–99]: An access list defined with a number ranging from 1 to 99 is a standard access list. A standard access list is used to permit or deny packets solely based on source IP address. The source address is the number of the network or host from which the packet is being sent. The source address is followed by a wildcard mask, which is used to specify the bit positions that are ignored and which positions must match. The wildcard mask is defined in more detail later in this chapter. This command is a global configuration command.

access-list [100–199]: An access list defined with a number ranging from 100–199 is an extended access list. An extended access list can be configured to be dynamic or static. Static is the default and can be changed using the keyword "dynamic." Both static and dynamic access lists will be covered in detail later in this chapter. An extended access list is used to permit or deny packets based on multiple factors (protocol, source IP address, destination IP address, precedence, TOS, and port number), providing much more granularity then a standard access list. The extended access list permits logging, which creates an informational logging message about any packet that matches the list. This option is useful when troubleshooting extended access lists.

access-list [100–199] [dynamic]: An access list defined with a number ranging from 100–199 using the "dynamic" keyword is a dynamic extended access list. A dynamic extended access list, also referred to as lock-and-key security, permits access on a per-user basis to a specific source/destination address through the use of authentication. This command is a global configuration command.

access-template: This exec command enables you to manually place a temporary, dynamic access list on the router.

autocommand: This global configuration command is used to automatically execute a command when a user connects to a particular line. This command will be used later in this chapter when configuring dynamic access-lists.

clear access-list counters: This exec command clears all access list counters. Some access lists keep counters on the number of packets that match each line of a particular list. The access list name or number can be specified. By default, the system will clear all counters.

clear access-template: This exec command clears dynamic access list entries.

ip access-group: The ip access-group command is used to permit or deny incoming or outgoing packets on a particular interface, based on criteria defined in the access list. This interface configuration command applies a specific access list [1–199] to a router interface. Incoming packets are filtered using the keyword "in," and outgoing connections are filtered using the keyword "out."

ip telnet source-interface: This global configuration command enables the user to select an address of an interface as the source address for telnet connections. By default, the source address is the address of the closest interface to the destination.

show access-lists: This exec command displays the contents of current access lists. The access list number can be specified. By default, the system displays all access lists.

show ip access-list: This exec command displays the contents of all current IP access lists. The access list number can be specified. By default, the system displays all extended and standard access lists.

username: This global configuration command is used to define a user-based authentication system.

IOS Requirements

Access lists first appeared in IOS 10.0; however, some of the commands described in this chapter require later IOS versions.

Lab #48: Standard IP Access Lists

Equipment Needed

The following equipment is needed to perform this lab exercise:

- Two Cisco routers, each having one Ethernet port and one serial port
- Cisco IOS 10.0 or higher
- A PC running a terminal emulation program
- One Cisco DTE/DCE crossover cable
- A Cisco rolled cable

Configuration Overview

This configuration will demonstrate packet filtering using standard access lists. As per Figure 12–2, RouterA will permit all traffic from network 150.1.1.0 and will deny traffic from all other networks.

RouterA and RouterB are connected serially via a crossover cable. RouterB will act as the DCE, supplying clock to RouterA. The IP addresses are assigned as per Figure 12–2. RouterB has a loopback interface (IP address 151.1.1.1) defined to provide a test point.

An inbound access list will be applied to the serial interface of RouterA, permitting packets from network 150.1.1.0. All other packets will be denied. RouterB will ping RouterA's serial interface (195.1.1.4) using the extended ping command to source the packet from multiple IP addresses.

NOTE: *Access lists are a sequential collection of permit and deny statements that apply to IP addresses. The router checks addresses against the access list conditions one-by-one. The order of the conditions is critical, because the first match in an access list is used (after which the router stops testing conditions). If no match is found, the packet is denied because of the* implicit deny all *at the end of each access list.*

Figure 12–2
Basic Access lists

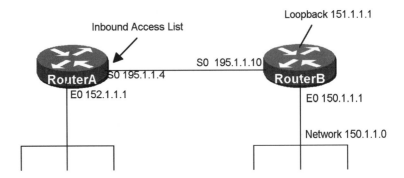

Router Configurations

The configurations for the two routers in this example are as follows (key access list configurations for RouterA are highlighted in bold):

RouterA

```
!
version 11.2
no service udp-small-servers
no service tcp-small-servers
!
hostname RouterA
!
!interface Ethernet0
 ip address 152.1.1.1 255.255.255.0
 no keepalive←Disables the keepalive on the ethernet interface, allows the
               interface to stay up when it is not attached to a hub.
!
interface Serial0
 ip address 195.1.1.4 255.255.255.0
 ip access-group 1 in←Applies access-list 1 to all inbound traffic on serial 0.
!
no ip classless
ip route 150.1.1.0 255.255.255.0 Serial0←Static route is used because no
                                          dynamic routing protocol is
                                          configured.
Ip route 151.1.1.1 255.255.255.255 Serial0←Static route is used because no
                                            dynamic routing protocol is
                                            configured
access-list 1 permit 150.1.1.0 0.0.0.255←Defines access-list 1 permitting
               Wildcard mask ↑            traffic from network 150.1.1.0.
 (Note: all other access implicitly denied)←All access-lists end with an
                                             implied deny all.
!
```

```
line con 0
line vty 0 4
 login
!
end
```

RouterB

```
Current configuration:
!
version 11.1
service udp-small-servers
service tcp-small-servers
!
hostname RouterB
!
interface Loopback0←Defines a virtual interface that will be used as a test
                    point.
  ip address 151.1.1.1 255.255.255.0
!
interface Ethernet0/0
  ip address 150.1.1.1 255.255.255.0
  no keepalive←Disables the keepalive on the ethernet interface, allows the
               interface to stay up when it is not attached to a hub.
!
interface Serial0/0
  ip address 195.1.1.10 255.255.255.0
  clockrate 500000←Acts as DCE providing clock
!
no ip classless
!
line con 0
line aux 0
line vty 0 4
 login
!
end
```

Monitoring and Testing the Configuration

To test the configuration, ping RouterA (195.1.1.4) using the extended ping command on RouterB, and source the packet from the loopback interface (151.1.1.1). To use this command, simply type **ping** at the privileged level.

```
routerB#ping
Protocol [ip]:
Target IP address: 195.1.1.4
Repeat count [5]:
```

```
Datagram size [100]:
Timeout in seconds [2]:
Extended commands [n]: y
Source address or interface: 151.1.1.1
Type of service [0]:
Set DF bit in IP header? [no]:
Validate reply data? [no]:
Data pattern [0xABCD]:
Loose, Strict, Record, Timestamp, Verbose[none]:
Sweep range of sizes [n]:
```

Monitor incoming packets on RouterA using the **debug ip packet** command. The output from this command is shown as follows. Notice that the packet is being denied, and an ICMP host unreachable message is sent back to RouterB.

```
IP: s=151.1.1.1 (Serial0), d=195.1.1.4, len 100, access denied
IP: s=195.1.1.4 (local), d=151.1.1.1 (Serial0), len 56, sending←Host unreachable
                                                             message.
```

The output from the command **show access-list 1** on RouterA is shown as follows. Note that the wildcard mask permits all hosts on network 150.1.1.0.

```
RouterA#show ip access-lists 1
Standard IP access list 1
permit 150.1.1.0, wildcard bits 0.0.0.255
```

Lab #49: Extended IP Access List

Equipment Needed

The following equipment is need to perform this lab exercise:

■ Two Cisco routers, each having one Ethernet port and one serial port

■ Cisco IOS 10.0 or higher

■ A PC running a terminal emulation program

■ One Cisco DTE/DCE crossover cable

■ A Cisco rolled cable

Configuration Overview

This configuration will demonstrate packet filtering using extended access lists. RouterA will permit all traffic from PCC (150.1.1.2) to PCA (152.1.1.2) and will deny all traffic from PCC (150.1.1.2) to PCB (152.1.1.3). An extended access list is used, because we are filtering on both source and destination IP addresses.

RouterA and RouterB are connected serially via a crossover cable. RouterB will act as the DCE, supplying clock to RouterA. The IP addresses are assigned as per Figure 12–3. RouterA and RouterB have secondary IP addresses defined on their Ethernet interfaces, which will be used as test points.

An inbound access list will be applied to the serial interface of RouterA, permitting packets from PCC 150.1.1.2 destined to PCA and denying packets from PCC to PCB.

NOTE: When creating an access list, all entries are sequentially placed in the order in which they are entered. Any subsequent entries are placed at the end of the list. When creating an access list, it is a good idea to edit it offline and either cut and paste them to a router configuration or TFTP them from a server.

Router Configurations

The configurations for the two routers in this example are as follows (key access list configurations for RouterA are highlighted in bold):

Figure 12–3
Extended IP
access list

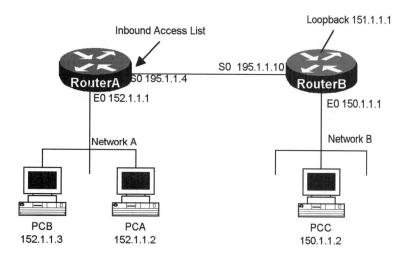

RouterA

```
Current configuration:
!
version 11.2
no service udp-small-servers
no service tcp-small-servers
!
hostname RouterA
!
interface Ethernet0
ip address 152.1.1.2 255.255.255.0 secondary←Secondary IP addresses are used
                                               as test points
 ip address 152.1.1.3 255.255.255.0 secondary
 ip address 152.1.1.1 255.255.255.0
 no keepalive←Disables the keepalive on the ethernet interface,  allows the
              interface to stay up when it is not attached to a hub.
!
interface Serial0
 ip address 195.1.1.4 255.255.255.0
 ip access-group 100 in←Applies access-list 100 to all inbound traffic on
                        serial 0.
!
no ip classless
ip route 150.1.1.0 255.255.255.0 Serial0←Static route is used because no dynamic
                                          routing protocol is configured.
ip route 151.1.1.1 255.255.255.255 Serial0
```

```
                                             Host specific is the same as
                                          ↓wildcard mask 0.0.0.0
access-list 100 permit ip host 150.1.1.2 host 152.1.1.2 log←Generates an
                ↑Permit any IP packet     informational logging message
                 from 150.1.1.2 to        about any packet that matches the
                 152.1.1.2                 entry

access-list 100 deny  ip host 150.1.1.2 host 152.1.1.3 log←Generates an
!               ↑Deny any IP packet       informational logging message
                 from 150.1.1.2 to        about any packet that matches the
                 152.1.1.3                 entry

(Note: all other access implicitly denied)←All access-lists end with an
                                            implied deny all.
!
!
line con 0
line vty 0 4
 login
!
end
```

RouterB

```
version 11.2
service udp-small-servers
service tcp-small-servers
!
hostname RouterB
!
!interface Loopback0
 ip address 151.1.1.1 255.255.255.0←Virtual interface used as a test point
!
interface Ethernet0/0
 ip address 150.1.1.2 255.255.255.0 secondary←Secondary IP addresses are used
                                            as test points
 ip address 150.1.1.1 255.255.255.0
 no keepalive←Disables the keepalive on the ethernet interface, allows the
             interface to stay up when it is not attached to a hub.
!
interface Serial0/0
 clockrate 500000←Acts as DCE providing clock
!
no ip classless
ip route 152.1.1.0 255.255.255.0 Serial0/0←Static route is used, because no
                                           dynamic routing protocol is
                                           configured.
!
line con 0
line aux 0
line vty 0 4
 login
!
end
```

Monitoring and Testing the Configuration

The following examples all use the extended ping command on RouterB to source the packets from the secondary IP addresses defined in the configuration. This command is used instead of multiple PCs on RouterB's LAN.

1. From RouterB, ping 152.1.1.3 using source address 150.1.1.2.

From the output of the **debug ip packet** command on RouterA, we see that the packet is being denied and that an ICMP host unreachable message is being sent.

```
IP: s=150.1.1.2 (Serial0), d=152.1.1.3, len 100, access denied
IP: s=195.1.1.4 (local), d=150.1.1.2 (Serial0), len 56, sending←ICMP host
                                                              unreachable
```

The following example shows the output from the **show ip access-list** command. Notice that the output shows which access lists are defined and the number of matches against each one.

```
RouterA#show ip access-lists
Extended IP access list 100
permit ip host 150.1.1.2 host 152.1.1.2 log (5 matches)
deny ip host 150.1.1.2 host 152.1.1.3 log (105 matches)
```

The following example shows the output from the **log** option, which generates an informational logging message about any packet that matches the extended access list. The logging option is a keyword that can be added to the end of each access list statement. The information-logging message is an excellent tool to use when troubleshooting access lists.

```
SEC-6-IPACCESSLOGDP: list 100 denied icmp 150.1.1.2 -> 152.1.1.3 (0/0), 4 packets
```

2. From RouterB, ping 152.1.1.3 using source address 150.1.1.2.

From the output of the **debug ip packet** command on RouterA, we see that the packet is being permitted.

```
IP: s=150.1.1.2 (Serial0), d=152.1.1.2, len 100, rcvd 7
```

The following example shows the output from the **show ip access-list** command. Notice that the output shows which access lists are defined and the number of matches against each.

```
RouterA#show ip access-lists
Extended IP access list 100
    permit ip host 150.1.1.2 host 152.1.1.2 log (308 matches)
    deny   ip host 150.1.1.2 host 152.1.1.3 log
```

Lab #50: Extended Access List with Established Option

Equipment Needed

The following equipment is needed to perform this lab exercise:

- Two Cisco routers with one Ethernet port and one serial port
- Cisco IOS 10.0 or higher
- A PC running a terminal emulation program

■ One Cisco DTE/DCE crossover cable

■ One Cisco rolled cable

Overview

An extended access list with the keyword established enables inside users to connect to the outside network while still denying outside users from accessing the inside network. This feature is not possible with a standard access list or an extended access list that does not use the established keyword.

The problem is that a standard access list and a basic extended access list will deny all traffic that matches the access list criteria—even if the packet is a response. In Figure 12–4, a standard access list is applied to the serial interface of RouterA, denying all outside traffic from establishing a connection with PCA. Although this process is secure, the process prevents PCA from making a connection to any server on the Internet. The response packets back to PCA will be denied by the access list on RouterA.

NOTE: *When creating a standard or extended access list, remember that by default, an implicit deny all is placed at the end—which means that any packet that does not match the conditions of the entries in the access list is denied.*

An extended access list using the keyword Established enables return packets from an established connection to be permitted through the access

Figure 12–4
Established
connections

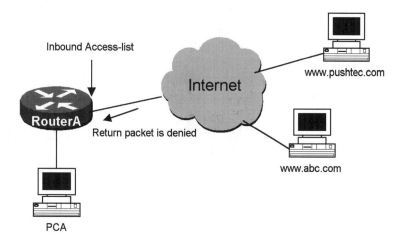

list. The router looks at the TCP datagram, and if the ACK or RST bits are set, the packet is permitted.

1. PCA sends an HTTP packet to server www.pushtec.com.

2. Server www.pushtec.com responds.

3. RouterA applies the access list against the packet. If the return packet has the ACK or RST bit set, the packet is permitted.

If server www.pushtec.com is trying to establish a connection to PCA, the SYN bit would be set, and the packet would be denied. The SYN-chronizing segment is the first segment sent by the TCP protocol and is used to synchronize the two ends of a connection in preparation for opening a new connection.

Configuration Overview

This configuration will demonstrate extended access lists using the Established keyword. The access list on RouterA will deny all non-established IP traffic destined for NetworkA.

RouterA and RouterB are connected serially via a crossover cable. RouterB will act as the DCE, supplying clock to RouterA. The IP addresses are assigned as per Figure 12–5. An inbound access list will be applied to the serial interface of RouterA.

Router Configurations

The configurations for the two routers in this example are as follows (key access list configurations for RouterA are highlighted in bold):

Figure 12–5
Extended access list
with Established
option

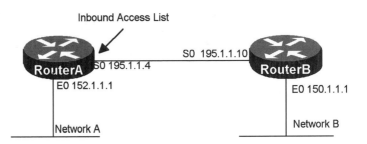

Inbound Access List

RouterA S0 195.1.1.4   S0 195.1.1.10   RouterB

E0 152.1.1.1   E0 150.1.1.1

Network A   Network B

RouterA

```
Current configuration:
!
version 11.2
no service password-encryption
no service udp-small-servers
no service tcp-small-servers
!
hostname RouterA
!
ip telnet source-interface Ethernet0←Sources all Telnet packets from E0 ip add
                                      152.1.1.1
!
interface Ethernet0
 ip address 152.1.1.1 255.255.255.0
 no keepalive←Disables the keepalive on the ethernet interface; enables the
              interface to stay up when it is not attached to a hub
!
interface Serial0
 ip address 195.1.1.4 255.255.255.0
 ip access-group 100 in←Applies access-list 100 to all inbound traffic on
                        serial 0.
 no fair-queue
!
interface Serial1
 no ip address
 shutdown
!

ip route 150.1.1.0 255.255.255.0 Serial0←Static route is used because no
                                         dynamic routing protocol is configured
ip route 151.1.1.1 255.255.255.255 Serial0←Static route is used because no
                                           dynamic routing protocol is configured
access-list 100 permit tcp any host 152.1.1.1 established log←Permit any traffic
                                                              destined for
                                                              152.1.1.1 with the
                                                              ACK or RST bit set.
access-list 100 deny ip any log←This statement is not needed. By default, all
                                traffic is denied. By adding this statement,
                                however, we can monitor how many packets
                                matched the access-list and were denied.
(Note: all other access implicitly denied)←All access lists end with an
                                            implied deny all.
!
!
line con 0
line aux 0
line vty 0 4
login
!
end
```

RouterB

```
!
version 11.2
service udp-small-servers
service tcp-small-servers
!
hostname RouterB
!
interface Ethernet0
   ip address 150.1.1.1 255.255.255.0
 no keepalive←Disables the keepalive on the Ethernet interface; allows the
              interface to stay up when it is not attached to a hub
!
interface Serial0
 ip address 195.1.1.10 255.255.255.0
clockrate 500000←Acts as DCE, providing clock

!
interface Serial1
 no ip address
 shutdown
!
ip route 152.1.1.0 255.255.255.0 Serial0←Static route is used because no dynamic
                                     routing protocol is configured

!
!
line con 0
line aux 0
line vty 0 4
 login←Allows telnet access to the router.
!
end
```

Monitoring and Testing the Configuration

To test this configuration, establish a telnet connection from RouterA to
RouterB. RouterA is configured to use the IP address of the Ethernet
interface to source all telnet packets. This configuration is accomplished
using the command **(ip telnet source-interface e0)** on RouterA.

1. Use the **debug ip packet detailed** command to monitor IP
   packets coming into or leaving RouterA.

2. Telnet from RouterA (152.1.1.1) to RouterB (150.1.1.1).

The following example shows the output from the **debug ip packet
detailed** command on RouterA. Note that all the packets from 150.1.1.1
to 152.1.1.1 have the ACK or RST bit set.

```
IP: s=152.1.1.1 (local), d=150.1.1.1 (Serial0), len 44, sending
    TCP src=11004, dst=23, seq=682801374, ack=0, win=4288 SYN
IP: s=150.1.1.1 (Serial0), d=152.1.1.1, len 44, rcvd 4
    TCP src=23, dst=11004, seq=426675527, ack=682801375, win=2144 ACK SYN
IP: s=152.1.1.1 (local), d=150.1.1.1 (Serial0), len 40, sending
    TCP src=11004, dst=23, seq=682801375, ack=426675528, win=4288 ACK
    TCP src=11004, dst=23, seq=682801375, ack=426675528, win=4288 ACK PSH
IP: s=152.1.1.1 (local), d=150.1.1.1 (Serial0), len 40, sending
    TCP src=11004, dst=23, seq=682801384, ack=426675528, win=4288 ACK
IP: s=150.1.1.1 (Serial0), d=152.1.1.1, len 52, rcvd 4
    TCP src=23, dst=11004, seq=426675528, ack=682801375, win=2144 ACK PSH
```

The following example shows the output from the **log** option, which generates an informational logging message about any packet that matches the extended access list. The response packet from 150.1.1.1 matched access list 100 and is permitted.

```
%SEC-6-IPACCESSLOGP: list 100 permitted tcp 150.1.1.1(23) -> 152.1.1.1(11002),
                                                     1 packet
```

3. Use the **show ip access-list** command to display which access lists are configured and how many packets match the criteria. The output from the command is shown as follows. Note that six packets were permitted, and one packet was denied. This command is useful in troubleshooting access lists, enabling you to quickly see which (if any) line in the access list the packets matched.

```
RouterA#show ip access-lists
Extended IP access list 100
    permit tcp any host 152.1.1.1 established log (6 matches)
    deny   ip any any log (1 match)
```

4. Now, let's try to establish a telnet connection in the opposite direction, from RouterB (150.1.1.1) to RouterA (152.1.1.1). RouterB is configured to use the IP address of the Ethernet interface to source all telnet packets.

5. Use the **debug ip packet detailed** command to monitor IP packets coming into or leaving RouterA. The following example shows the output from the command. Notice that the SYN bit is set. The access list only permits established connections, which are determined by RouterA if the ACK or RST bit is set in the TCP header. The SYNchronizing segment is the first segment sent by the TCP protocol and is used to synchronize the two ends

of a connection in preparation for opening a new connection. The ACKnowledgement bit is set by the receiver to indicate to the sender that information was received successfully. The RST bit (or reset bit) indicates when to reset the connection.

```
IP: s=150.1.1.1 (Serial0), d=152.1.1.2, len 44, access denied
    TCP src=11004, dst=23, seq=2826185914, ack=0, win=2144 SYN
IP: s=195.1.1.4 (local), d=150.1.1.1 (Serial0), len 56, sending
    ICMP type=3, code=13
```

Lab #51: Dynamic IP Access Lists

Equipment Needed

The following equipment is needed to perform this lab exercise:

- Two Cisco routers with one Ethernet port and one serial port
- Cisco IOS 11.1 or higher
- A PC running a terminal emulation program
- One Cisco DTE/DCE crossover cable
- One Cisco rolled cable

Overview

Dynamic access lists (referred to as Lock-and-Key security) permit or deny traffic based on user authentication. For a user to gain access to a host through a router, the user must first telnet to the router and be authenticated. After the user is authenticated, a temporary access list is created that enables the user to reach the destination host.

With Lock-and-Key security, you specify which users are permitted access to which source/destination hosts, as shown in Figure 12–6. Based on user authentication, a temporary entry is created in the access list.

How Lock-and-Key Works

1. PCB telnets to RouterA, connecting via the virtual terminal port.
2. RouterA opens the telnet session and prompts for a username and password. If the user passes the authentication process, then access through the router is permitted.

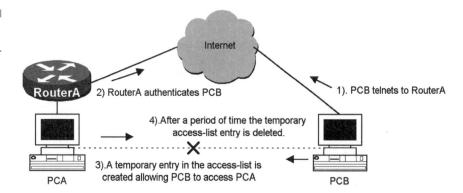

Figure 12–6
Lock-and-key security

3. PCB is then automatically logged out of the telnet session, and a temporary entry is created in the dynamic access list. The temporary access list entry is based on user authentication and is predefined in the configuration. For example, you can configure the list so that PCB only has telnet access to PCA, with all other access being denied.

4. Traffic from PCB can then pass through RouterA.

5. The router deletes the temporary access list after a predefined timeout period. Once the temporary access list is deleted, the user must be reauthenticated by RouterA before passing traffic.

Configuration Overview

This configuration, shown in Figure 12–7, will demonstrate lock-and-key security using a dynamic extended access list. RouterA will authenticate incoming telnet sessions based on username and password. When RouterB logs into RouterA and is authenticated, a five-minute temporary access list entry is created—enabling RouterB (150.1.1.1) to telnet to RouterA (152.1.1.1).

RouterA and RouterB are connected serially via a crossover cable. RouterB will act as the DCE, supplying clock to RouterA. The IP addresses are assigned as per Figure 12–7. An inbound access list will be applied to the serial interface of RouterA.

Router Configurations

The configurations for the two routers in this example are as follows (key access list configurations for RouterA are highlighted in bold):

Figure 12–7
Lock-and-key security

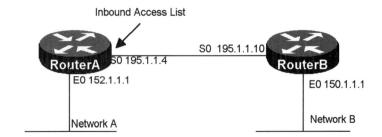

RouterA

```
version 11.2
no service password-encryption
no service udp-small-servers
no service tcp-small-servers
!
hostname RouterA
!
!
username pcb password 0 pcb←Establish a username-based authentication system
               Causes the specified command to be issued automatically
             ↓after the user logs in
username pcb autocommand access-enable timeout 5←If the access list entry is
                      ↑Adds the              not accessed within 5
                      temporary entry        minutes, it is automatically
                      to access-list.        deleted and requires the user
                                             to authenticate again.

ip telnet source-interface Ethernet0←Sources all telnet packets from E0 ip add
                      152.1.1.1

!
interface Ethernet0
 ip address 152.1.1.1 255.255.255.0
no keepalive←Disables the keepalive on the Ethernet interface and enables the
             interface to stay up when it is not attached to a hub

!
interface Serial0
 ip address 195.1.1.4 255.255.255.0
 ip access-group 100 in←Applies access-list 100 to all inbound traffic on
                      serial 0

 no fair-queue
!
interface Serial1
 no ip address
 shutdown
```

```
!
no ip classless
ip route 150.1.1.0 255.255.255.0 Serial0←Static route is used because no dynamic
                                          routing protocol is configured
                       ↓dynamic-name
access-list 100 dynamic tempaccess permit tcp host 150.1.1.1 host 152.1.1.1 eq
    telnet log                                  ↑Only permit telnet
                                                  traffic between
                                                  150.1.1.1 and 152.1.1.1
access-list 100 permit tcp any host 195.1.1.4 eq telnet log←Telnet access must be
                                                  allowed to enable user
                                                  authentication.
access-list 100 deny ip any any log←This statement is not needed. By default, all
                                    traffic is denied. By adding this statement,
                                    however, we can monitor how many packets
                                    matched the access-list and were denied.

(Note: All other access implicitly denied)←All access lists end with an
                                            implied deny all.
!
line con 0
line aux 0
line vty 0 4
   login local←Enables local password checking at login
!
end
```

RouterB

```
Current configuration:
!
version 11.1
service udp-small-servers
service tcp-small-servers
!
hostname RouterB
!
interface Ethernet0
   ip address 150.1.1.1 255.255.255.0
 no keepalive←Disables the keepalive on the Ethernet interface; enables the
              interface to stay up when it is not attached to a hub

!
interface Serial0
 ip address 195.1.1.10 255.255.255.0
 clockrate 500000←Acts as the DCE, providing clock

!
interface Serial1
 no ip address
 shutdown
!
```

```
ip route 152.1.1.0 255.255.255.0 Serial0←Static route is used because no dynamic
                                          routing protocol is configured
!
line con 0
line aux 0
line vty 0 4
login←Enables telnet access to the router
!
end
```

Monitoring and Testing the Configuration

To test this configuration, establish a telnet connection from RouterB to RouterA (195.1.1.4). Log in to RouterA with username pcb and password pcb. The following sample display is what users will see if they are authenticated. Notice that the telnet connection is closed immediately after the password is entered. After authentication, RouterA creates a temporary entry in access list 100.

```
RouterB#telnet 195.1.1.4
Trying 195.1.1.4 ... Open
User Access Verification
Username: pcb
Password: pcb
[Connection to 195.1.1.4 closed by foreign host]
```

The following sample is from the **show ip access-list** command on RouterA. Notice that the temporary entry has been added to access list 100.

```
RouterA#show ip access-lists
Extended IP access list 100
    Dynamic tempaccess permit tcp host 150.1.1.1 host 152.1.1.1 eq telnet log
        permit tcp host 150.1.1.1 host 152.1.1.1 eq telnet log idle-time 5 min.
    permit tcp any host 195.1.1.4 eq telnet log (72 matches)
    deny    ip any any log (1 match)
```

Establish a telnet connection from RouterB (150.1.1.1) to 152.1.1.1. RouterB is configured to use the IP address of the Ethernet interface to source all telnet packets. This task is accomplished using the command **(ip telnet source-interface e0)** on RouterA.

The following example is a sample of the output from the access list log command on RouterA. The log command is an option which is added to the access list during configuration. The log keyword generates an informational logging message about any packet that matches the extended access list. The telnet packet from 150.1.1.1 matched the temporary entry added to access list 100.

```
%SEC-6-IPACCESSLOGP: list 100 permitted tcp 150.1.1.1(11010) -> 152.1.1.1(23), 1
 packet
```

The telnet session was permitted. Now, on RouterA, remove the temporary entry from the access list with the following exec command:

```
clear access-template 100 tempaccess 150.1.1.1 0.0.0.0 152.1.1.1 0.0.0
```

Use the **show ip access-list** command to display which access lists are configured and how many packets matched the criteria. The output from the command is shown as follows. Notice that the temporary entry has been removed from the dynamic access list.

```
RouterA#show ip access-lists
Extended IP access list 100
    Dynamic tempaccess permit tcp host 150.1.1.1 host 152.1.1.1 eq telnet log
    permit tcp any host 195.1.1.4 eq telnet log (124 matches)
    deny   ip any any log (1 match)
```

Telnet from RouterB (150.1.1.1) to 152.1.1.1. Notice that this time, the connection has failed. PCB will have to reauthenticate with RouterA in order to gain telnet access to 152.1.1.1.

```
RouterB#telnet 152.1.1.1
Trying 152.1.1.1 ...
% Destination unreachable; gateway or host down
```

LAB #52: Controlling VTY Access

Equipment Needed

The following equipment is needed to perform this lab exercise:

- Two Cisco routers with one Ethernet port and one serial port
- Cisco IOS 10.0 or higher
- A PC running a terminal emulation program
- One Cisco DTE/DCE crossover cable
- One Cisco rolled cable

Overview

This lab demonstrates how to use access lists to control VTY connections to the router. In a production environment, it is imperative to limit router access to authorized personnel only. This task can be accomplished using password authentication and access control lists.

Access control lists enable you to specify which stations are able to gain telnet access to your router, based on source IP address. Router access should be limited to specific work stations. It is good design to set up a bastion host and only permit specific IP address VTY access to all of your routers. Network administrators telnet to the bastion host and then out to the specific router. A bastion host is a computer that forms part of a security firewall and runs applications that communicate with computers outside an organization.

Configuration Overview

This configuration will demonstrate controlling VTY access to a router using a standard access list. RouterA will only permit VTY access from host 150.1.1.1. All other VTY sessions will be denied.

RouterA and RouterB are connected serially via a crossover cable. RouterB will act as the DCE, supplying clock to RouterA. The IP addresses are assigned as per Figure 12–8. An inbound access list will be applied to the serial interface of RouterA.

Router Configurations

The configurations for the two routers in this example are as follows (key access list configurations for RouterA are highlighted in bold):

Figure 12–8
VTY access control

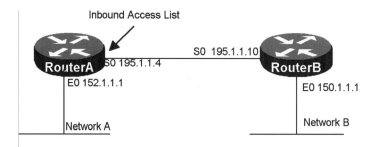

Inbound Access List

RouterA S0 195.1.1.4

S0 195.1.1.10 RouterB

E0 152.1.1.1

E0 150.1.1.1

Network A

Network B

RouterA

```
version 11.2
no service password-encryption
no service udp-small-servers
no service tcp-small-servers
!
hostname RouterA
!
interface Ethernet0
  ip address 152.1.1.1 255.255.255.0
 no keepalive←Disables the keepalive on the Ethernet interface; allows the
             interface to stay up when it is not attached to a hub
!
interface Serial0
 ip address 195.1.1.4 255.255.255.0
 no fair-queue
!
interface Serial1
 no ip address
 shutdown
!
no ip classless
ip route 150.1.1.0 255.255.255.0 Serial0←Static route is used because no dynamic
                                        routing protocol is configured
access-list 1 permit 150.1.1.1←Standard access list permits access from host
                       150.1.1.1.
(Note: all other access implicitly denied)←All access lists end with an
                                         implied deny all.

!
line con 0
line aux 0
line vty 0 4
 access-class 1 in←Applies standard access list 1 to all inbound VTY
                  connections
 password cisco
 login
!
end
```

RouterB

```
version 11.2
service udp-small-servers
service tcp-small-servers
!
hostname RouterB
!
ip telnet source-interface Ethernet0
!
interface Ethernet0
  ip address 150.1.1.1 255.255.255.0
```

```
no keepalive←Disables the keepalive on the Ethernet interface;  permits the
              interface to stay up when it is not attached to a hub

!
interface Serial0
 ip address 195.1.1.10 255.255.255.0
 clockrate 500000←Acts as DCE providing clock

!
interface Serial1
 no ip address
 shutdown
!
ip route 152.1.1.0 255.255.255.0 Serial0←The static route is used, because no
                                         dynamic routing protocol is
                                         configured.
!
line con 0
line aux 0
line vty 0 4
!
end
```

Monitoring and Testing the Configuration

To test this configuration, establish a telnet connection from RouterB to RouterA (195.1.1.4). The source address of the telnet packet is 150.1.1.1, which is defined on RouterB using the command (**ip telnet source-interface Ethernet0**).

The following sample shows what the user will see if the telnet connection is successful.

```
RouterB#telnet 195.1.1.4
Trying 195.1.1.4 ... Open

User Access Verification
Password:
```

On RouterB, edit the configuration so that all telnet packets are sourced from the serial interface. To do this task, perform the following actions in global configuration mode:

```
RouterA(config)#
no ip telnet source-interface Ethernet0
ip telnet source-interface serial0
```

Now, from RouterB, telnet to RouterA (195.1.1.4). The connection is refused, because the source address of the telnet packet does not match the access control list on RouterA.

```
RouterB#telnet 152.1.1.1
Trying 152.1.1.1 ...
% Connection refused by remote host
```

Troubleshooting IP Access Lists

The Cisco IOS provides many tools for troubleshooting access lists. A list of key commands, along with sample output from each, is shown as follows.

{show access-lists} This privileged exec command displays the contents of all current access lists. The command can also display specific access lists by number.

```
RouterA# show access-lists 1
Standard IP access list 1
    permit 150.1.1.1
```

{show ip access-list} This privileged exec command displays the contents of all current IP access lists. The command can also display specific access lists by number.

```
RouterA#show ip access-lists 1
Standard IP access list 1
permit 150.1.1.0, wildcard bits 0.0.0.255
```

{clear access list counters} Some access lists keep counters that count the number of packets that pass each line of an access list. Use the **clear access list counters** command to reset the counters to zero for a particular access list.

```
RouterA#clear access-list counters
```

{debug ip packet} This exec command displays information about packets that are received, generated, or forwarded by the router. When access lists are applied to the router, the output from the debug command will tell you whether the packet was permitted or denied.

```
RouterA#Debug ip packet
IP: s=150.1.1.2 (Serial0), d=152.1.1.3, len 100, access denied
IP: s=195.1.1.4 (local), d=150.1.1.2 (Serial0), len 56, sending
```

Conclusion

Access lists are an integral part of the Cisco IOS, enabling the router to make decisions based on defined criteria. This chapter explores filtering packets and controlling access to the router using standard and extended access lists. Access lists are used for many other things not covered in this chapter, however, such as filtering router updates and determining DDR interesting traffic and flow control, to name a few. These advanced topics will be covered in their respective chapters.

13

Policy-Based Routing

Topics Covered in This Chapter

- Detailed policy routing overview
- Policy routing terminology
- Policy routing based on source IP address
- Policy routing based on packet size
- Policy routing based on application
- Load balancing across default routes
- Access list terminology
- Detailed troubleshooting examples

Introduction

Policy-based routing provides network administrators with greater control over packet forwarding and routing, which goes beyond the capabilities of traditional routing protocols. Traditionally, routers forward packets based on destination addresses using routing tables derived from routing protocols (such as OSPF or RIP).

Policy-based routing goes far beyond traditional routing, enabling network administrators to select forwarding paths not only based on destination addresses but on protocol type, packet size, application, or source address. Policies can be defined to load-balance traffic across multiple routers or provide *Quality of Service* (QOS) by forwarding packets over various links based on traffic profiles. Policy-based routing provides the network administrator with a mechanism to specify what path a packet will take. This freedom is greatly needed in today's high-performance and complex internetworks.

This chapter will explore controlling packet forwarding through a router using policy-based routing.

Policy Routing Overview

Policy routing provides a mechanism for forwarding packets based on criteria defined by the network administrator. Policy-based routing uses **match** and **set** clauses to achieve path selection.

In Figure 13–1, all traffic from PCA destined for the order entry server will go over the ISDN link, and all other traffic from PCA—as well as other nodes—will be routed over the 512K leased line.

RouterA's policy would be quite simple. Any traffic from PCA to the order entry system will have the next-hop set to RouterB. All other traffic

Figure 13–1
Policy-based routing

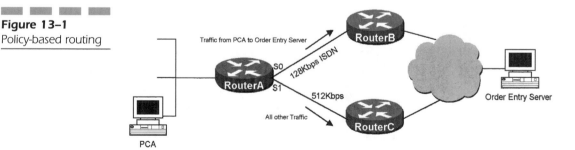

will not match the criteria and will therefore be routed according to the entries in the routing table. The routing table will use the 512Kbps link, because the routers are using OSPF as their routing protocol. Because OSPF uses bandwidth as its metric for selecting the best path, the 512Kbps link will be preferred over the 128Kpbs ISDN link.

NOTE: *Policy routing is set on the interface that receives the packet, not on the interface on which the packet is sent. In Figure 13–1, the policy is applied to RouterA's Ethernet interface.*

Policy Routing Terminology

Match Clause: The match clause evaluates packets on the ingress router port. The match criteria can be as simple as matching a source and destination address using an ACL—or as complex as matching packet size based on specified minimum and maximum packet lengths.

Multiple match clauses can be used to provide even more granularity in route selection. The match clauses are serviced in order, and all must match for the set clause to be applied. If no match is found or if the policy is made to deny instead of permit, then the packet is routed based on the destination address using an entry from the routing table.

Set Clause: The set clause defines the route that the packet will traverse if the match clause is met. Multiple set clauses can be used and are evaluated in the following order. If the first one is not available (i.e., the interface is down), then the next one is tried until the end of the list is reached.

1. Next-hop interfaces
2. Next-hop IP address
3. Next-hop default interfaces
4. Next-hop default IP address

If the end of the list is reached and no set clause is applied, then the packet is routed using the normal destination-based routing process.

NOTE: *Packet forwarding based on policy routing will override packet forwarding based on routing table entries to the same destination.*

Commands Discussed in This Chapter

- **ip local policy route-map** map-tag
- **ip policy route-map** [map-tag]
- **match ip address** {access-list-number | name} [access-list-number]
- **match length** min max
- **route-map** map-tag [permit | deny] [sequence-number]
- **set default interface** type number
- **set interface** type number
- **set ip default next-hop** ip-address
- **set ip next-hop** ip-address [... ip-address]
- **show ip policy**
- **show route-map command**

Definitions

ip local policy route-map: Packets that are generated by the router are not normally policy routed. This global configuration command enables the router to policy route locally generated packets.

ip policy route-map: This interface configuration command enables policy routing on a particular interface and identifies the route map that will be applied to the packet.

match ip address: This route map configuration command bases the policy match condition on a predefined access list.

match length: This route map configuration command bases the policy-match condition on layer 3 packet length. This criteria is often used to direct interactive traffic, which tends to be small-sized packets over different links, rather than large-sized bulk traffic.

route-map: This global configuration command defines the name of the route map and indicates whether the packet matching the criteria is policy routed. If the match criteria are met for the route map and the permit keyword is specified, the packet is policy routed. If the match criteria are met and the deny keyword is specified, then the packet is not policy routed. Several route maps can be defined using the same name. An optional number can be placed at the end of the route map, indicating the order in which the route map will be checked. In this example, two route maps are defined with the name "lab1." One is defined with the item number 10, and the other is defined with the item number 20. An incoming packet is checked against item 10 of route map lab1. If the packet does not match the IP address, then the packet is checked against item 20.

```
route-map lab1 permit 10←Item 10 of route-map lab1.
match ip address 1
set interface Serial0
!
route-map lab1 permit 20←Item 20 of route-map lab1.
match ip address 2
set interface Serial1
```

set default interface: This route-map configuration command indicates which default interface packets that pass the match clause are sent too. This command gives certain packets a different default route. If the router has no explicit route in the routing table for the destination address, then the router will forward the packets out the set default interface.

set interface: This route-map configuration command indicates to which output interface packets that pass the match clause are sent. Multiple output interfaces can be configured. If the first interface is down, then the optionally specified interface, are tried in turn.

set ip default next-hop: This route map configuration command sets the default next-hop. If the router has no explicit route for the destination, then the router will route the packet to the set default next-hop. This process is often used to load-balance between two different service providers. When using the default next-hop set command, the routing table will always be used first to route the packet. If an explicit route does not exist in the routing table, then the packet is forwarded using the policy set default.

set ip next-hop: This route-map configuration command indicates the next-hop IP address to which output packets passing the match clause are forwarded. Multiple next-hop addresses can be configured if the first next-hop specified is down. The optionally specified IP addresses are tried in turn.

show ip policy: This exec command displays which policies are applied to which interfaces.

show route-map: This exec command displays the match and set conditions for all configured route maps. The command can also be used to display a specific route map (by specifying the route map name after the command).

NOTE: *Multiple match commands can be used, but all match commands must "pass" to cause the packet to be routed according to the set actions given with the set commands.*

IOS Requirements

Policy-based routing first appeared in IOS 11.0; however, IOS 11.2 was used for all configurations.

Lab #53: Policy Routing Based on Source IP Address

Equipment Needed

The following equipment is needed to perform this lab exercise:

- Two Cisco routers, each having one Ethernet port and two serial ports
- Cisco IOS 11.0 or higher
- A PC running a terminal emulation program for connecting to the console port of the routers
- Two Cisco DTE/DCE crossover cables
- A Cisco rolled cable

Configuration Overview

This configuration will demonstrate routing packets based on source IP address using policy-based routing. As per Figure 13–2, RouterA will route all traffic from 192.1.1.1 out interface S0, and all traffic from 192.1.1.2 will be routed out interface S1.

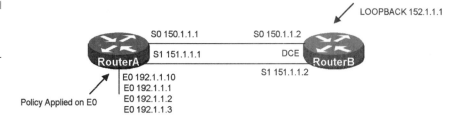

Figure 13–2
Source address policy
routing

RouterA and RouterB are connected serially via two crossover cables. RouterB will act as the DCE, supplying clock to RouterA. The IP addresses are assigned as per Figure 13–2. RouterB has a loopback interface (IP address 152.1.1.1) defined to provide a test point. RouterA has multiple secondary interfaces defined on Ethernet 0, which will also be used as test points. Both RouterA and RouterB will be configured for RIP.

The ip policy route-map **lab1** will be applied to the Ethernet interface of RouterA, setting the next-hop interface to S0 for packets originating from 192.1.1.1 and setting the next-hop interface to S1 for packets originating from 192.1.1.2. All other packets will be routed using the normal, destination-based routing process.

Router Configurations

The configurations for the two routers in this example are as follows (key policy routing configurations are highlighted in bold):

RouterA

```
version 11.2
no service udp-small-servers
no service tcp-small-servers
!
hostname RouterA
!
!
interface Ethernet0
  ip address 192.1.1.1 255.255.255.0 secondary( Secondary IP addresses are used
     as test points )
  ip address 192.1.1.2 255.255.255.0 secondary
  ip address 192.1.1.3 255.255.255.0 secondary
  ip address 192.1.1.10 255.255.255.0
  ip policy route-map lab1←Enables policy routing on interface E0 and
                        identifies the route map lab1, which will be applied
                        to all incoming packets
```

```
no keepalive←Disables the keepalive on the Ethernet interface; enables the
           interface to stay up when it is not attached to a hub

!
interface Serial0
 ip address 150.1.1.1 255.255.255.0
 no fair-queue
!
interface Serial1
 ip address 151.1.1.1 255.255.255.0
!
router rip←Enables the RIP routing process on the router
 network 192.1.1.0←Specifies what interfaces will receive and send RIP routing
           updates. It also specifies what networks will be advertised.
 network 150.1.0.0
 network 151.1.0.0
!
ip local policy route-map lab1←Packets that are generated by the router are not
           normally policy routed. This command enables the
           router to policy route packets that are sourced
           from the router.
no ip classless
access-list 1 permit 192.1.1.1←Access list defines the source IP address of
           192.1.1.1
access-list 2 permit 192.1.1.2
route-map lab1 permit 10←Defines the route map lab1, the number specifies the
           order of the route maps. This information is referred
           to as item 10 of route map lab1.

 match ip address 1←The match criteria is the IP address from access list 1.
 set interface Serial0←The set clause sets the next-hop interface to S0.
!
route-map lab1 permit 20←Defines the route map lab1, the number specifies the
           order of the route maps. This information is referred
           to as item 20 of route map lab1.

 match ip address 2←The match criteria is the IP address from access list 2.
 set interface Serial1←The set clause sets the next hop interface to S1.
!
line con 0
line aux 0
line vty 0 4
 login
!
end
```

RouterB

```
version 11.2
service udp-small-servers
service tcp-small-servers
!
interface Loopback0←Defines a virtual interface that will be used as a test
           point.
```

```
 ip address 152.1.1.1 255.255.255.0
!
interface Ethernet0
 no ip address
 shutdown
!
interface Serial0
 ip address 150.1.1.2 255.255.255.0
 clockrate 500000
!
interface Serial1
 ip address 151.1.1.2 255.255.255.0
 clockrate 500000←Acts as the DCE, providing clock

!
router rip←Enables the RIP routing process on the router

 network 152.1.0.0←Specifies what interfaces will receive and send RIP routing
                   updates. It also specifies what networks will be advertised.
 network 151.1.0.0
 network 150.0.0.0
!
!
line con 0
line 1 16
 transport input all
line aux 0
 transport input all
line vty 0 4
 login
!
end
```

Monitoring and Testing the Configuration

To test the configuration, trace the route to 152.1.1.1 from RouterA using the extended traceroute command to source the packets from 192.1.1.1. To use this command, simply type **traceroute ip** at the privileged router prompt.

```
RouterA#traceroute ip

Target IP address: 152.1.1.1
Source address: 192.1.1.2
Numeric display [n]:
Timeout in seconds [3]:
Probe count [3]:
Minimum Time to Live [1]:
Maximum Time to Live [30]:
Port Number [33434]:
Loose, Strict, Record, Timestamp, Verbose[none]:
Type escape sequence to abort.
Tracing the route to 152.1.1.1
```

The output from the traceroute command is shown as follows. Note that the packet was sent out RouterA's S0 interface, connected to 150.1.1.2.

```
RouterA#
Tracing the route to 152.1.1.1

  1 150.1.1.2 8 msec 8 msec *
```

Now, perform another traceroute, sourcing the packet from 192.1.1.2.

```
RouterA#
Tracing the route to 152.1.1.1

  1 151.1.1.2 8 msec 8 msec *
```

Notice that the packet was sent out interface S1, which is exactly how the policy is defined.

On RouterA, monitor the policy routing with the **debug ip policy** privileged command. From RouterA, ping 152.1.1.1 using the extended ping command to source the packet from 192.1.1.1. To use this command, simply type ping at the privileged level.

```
routerB#ping
Protocol [ip]:
Target IP address: 152.1.1.1
Repeat count [5]:
Datagram size [100]:
Timeout in seconds [2]:
Extended commands [n]: y
Source address or interface: 192.1.1.1
Type of service [0]:
Set DF bit in IP header? [no]:
Validate reply data? [no]:
Data pattern [0xABCD]:
Loose, Strict, Record, Timestamp, Verbose[none]:
Sweep range of sizes [n]:
```

The output from the debug command is shown as follows. Notice that the packet matched item10 of route map **lab1** and was forwarded via interface S0.

```
RouterA#
IP: s=192.1.1.1 (local), d=152.1.1.1, len 100, policy match
IP: route map lab1, item 10, permit
IP: s=192.1.1.1 (local), d=152.1.1.1 (Serial0), len 100, policy routed
IP: local to Serial0 152.1.1.1
```

From RouterA, ping 152.1.1.1—now sourcing the packet from 192.1.1.2. The output from the debug command is shown as follows. Notice that the packet matched item 20 of route map **lab1** and was forwarded via interface S1.

```
 RouterA#
IP: s=192.1.1.2 (local), d=152.1.1.1, len 100, policy match
IP: route map lab1, item 20, permit
IP: s=192.1.1.2 (local), d=152.1.1.1 (Serial1), len 100, policy routed
IP: local to Serial1 151.1.1.2
```

From RouterA, ping 152.1.1.1—sourcing the packet from 192.1.1.3, which is not defined in the match criteria. The output from the debug command is shown as follows. Note that the match criteria was not met, so the router forwarded the packet using a normal destination-based routing process.

```
RouterA#
IP: s=192.1.1.10 (local), d=255.255.255.255 (Ethernet0), len 92, policy rejected
                                                   normal forwarding
```

Now, on RouterA, remove the set clause for item 10 of route map lab1 with the following commands:

```
RouterA(config)#route-map lab1 permit 10
RouterA(config-route-map)#no set interface Serial0
```

From RouterA, ping 152.1.1.1—sourcing the packet from 192.1.1.1. The output from the debug command is shown as follows. Note that the source address matches item 10 of route-map lab1. Because there is no set policy defined, however, the packet is rejected—and the router forwards the packet normally.

```
RouterA#
IP: s=192.1.1.1 (local), d=152.1.1.1, len 100, policy match
IP: route map lab1, item 10, permit
IP: s=192.1.1.1 (local), d=152.1.1.1, len 100, policy rejected - normal forwarding
```

Lab #54: Policy Routing Based on Packet Size

Equipment Needed

The following equipment is needed to perform this lab exercise:

- Two Cisco routers, each having one Ethernet port and two serial ports
- Cisco IOS 11.0 or higher
- A PC running a terminal emulation program for connecting to the console port of the routers
- Two Cisco DTE/DCE crossover cables
- A Cisco rolled cable

Figure 13–3
Packet size policy
routing

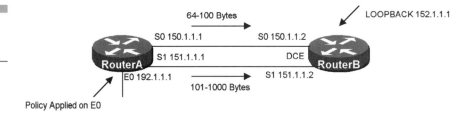

Configuration Overview

This configuration will demonstrate routing packets based on packet size using policy-based routing. As per Figure 13–3, RouterA will route all traffic with a datagram size from 64 to 100 bytes out interface S0, and all packets with a datagram size of 101 to 1000 bytes will be routed out interface S1. All other packet sizes will be routed normally.

RouterA and RouterB are connected serially via crossover cables. RouterB will act as the DCE, supplying clock to RouterA. The IP addresses are assigned as per Figure 13–3. RouterB has a loopback interface (IP address 152.1.1.1) defined to provide a test point. Both RouterA and RouterB will be configured using RIP as their routing protocol.

The ip policy route-map **lab1** will be applied to the Ethernet interface of RouterA. This policy will set the next-hop IP address to 150.1.1.2 for packets with a datagram size from 64 to 100 bytes, and the next-hop IP address will be set to 151.1.1.2 for packets coming with a datagram size from 101 to 1000 bytes. All other packets will be routed through the normal destination-based routing process.

Router Configurations

The configurations for the two routers in this example are as follows (key policy routing configurations are highlighted in bold):

RouterA

```
Current configuration:
!
version 11.2
no service udp-small-servers
no service tcp-small-servers
!
```

```
hostname RouterA
!
!
interface Ethernet0
 ip address 192.1.1.1 255.255.255.0
 ip policy route-map lab1←Enables policy routing on interface E0 and identifies
                         the route map lab1, which will be applied to the packet.
 no keepalive←Disables the keepalive on the Ethernet interface, allows the
              interface to stay up when it is not attached to a hub.

!
interface Serial0
 ip address 150.1.1.1 255.255.255.0
 no fair-queue
!
interface Serial1
 ip address 151.1.1.1 255.255.255.0
!
router rip←Enables the RIP routing process on the router
 network 192.1.1.0←Specifies what interfaces will receive and send RIP routing
                   updates. It also specifies what networks will be advertised.
 network 150.1.0.0
 network 151.1.0.0
!
ip local policy route-map lab1←Packets that are generated by the router are
                               not normally policy routed. This command
                               enables the router to policy route packets
                               that are sourced from the router.
no ip classless
route-map lab1 permit 10←Defines the route map lab1, the number specifies the
                         order of the route maps. This is referred to as item
                         10 of route map lab1.

match length 3 100←The match criteria is the packet length.
set ip next-hop 150.1.1.2←The set clause sets the next hop IP address.
!
route-map lab1 permit 20←Defines the route map lab1, the number specifies the
                         order of the route maps. This is referred to as item
                         20 of route map lab1.
match length 101 1000←The match criteria is the packet length.
set ip next-hop 151.1.1.2←The set clause sets the next hop IP address.
!
line con 0
line aux 0
line vty 0 4
 login
!
end
```

RouterB

```
version 11.2
service udp-small-servers
service tcp-small-servers
```

```
!
hostname routerb
interface Loopback0←Defines a virtual interface that will be used as a test
                     point.
 ip address 152.1.1.1 255.255.255.0
!
interface Ethernet0
 no ip address
 shutdown
!
interface Serial0
 ip address 150.1.1.2 255.255.255.0
 clockrate 500000
!
interface Serial1
 ip address 151.1.1.2 255.255.255.0
 clockrate 500000←Acts as DCE providing clock

!
router rip←Enables the RIP routing process on the router.

 network 152.1.0.0←Specifies what interfaces will receive and send RIP routing
                   updates. It also specifies what networks will be advertised.
 network 151.1.0.0
 network 101.0.0.0
!
!
line con 0
line 1 16
 transport input all
line aux 0
 transport input all
line vty 0 4
 login
!
end
```

Monitoring and Testing the Configuration

From RouterA, monitor the policy routing using the **debug ip policy** command. Using the extended ping command on RouterA, change the ping packet size to 64 bytes and ping 152.1.1.1. The output from the debug command is shown as follows. Note that the 64-byte packet matched item 10 of route map lab1 and was forwarded to 150.1.1.2.

```
RouterA#
IP: s=151.1.1.1 (local), d=152.1.1.1, len 64, policy match
IP: route map lab1, item 10, permit
IP: s=151.1.1.1 (local), d=152.1.1.1 (Serial0), len 64, policy routed
IP: local to Serial0 150.1.1.2
```

From RouterA, ping 152.1.1.1—increasing the packet size to 101 bytes. This packet will match item 20 of route map lab1. The output from the debug command is shown as follows. Note that the 101-byte packet matches item 20 and was forwarded to 151.1.1.2.

```
RouterA#
IP: s=151.1.1.1 (local), d=152.1.1.1, len 101, policy match
IP: route map lab1, item 20, permit
IP: s=151.1.1.1 (local), d=152.1.1.1 (Serial1), len 101, policy routed
IP: local to Serial1 151.1.1.2
```

From RouterA, ping 152.1.1.1—increasing the packet size to 1001 bytes. This packet will not match any items in route map lab1. The output from the debug command is shown as follows. Note that the 1001-byte packet does not match any clauses, so the router forwarded the packet normally.

```
RouterA#
IP: s=151.1.1.1 (local), d=152.1.1.1, len 1001, policy rejected — normal forwarding
IP: s=151.1.1.1 (local), d=152.1.1.1, len 1001, policy rejected — normal forwarding
```

Lab #55: Policy Routing Based on Application

Equipment Needed

The following equipment is needed to perform this lab exercise:

- Two Cisco routers, each having one Ethernet port and two serial ports
- Cisco IOS 11.0 or higher
- A PC running a terminal emulation program for connecting to the router console port
- Two Cisco DTE/DCE crossover cables
- A Cisco rolled cable

Configuration Overview

This configuration will demonstrate routing packets based on application-level data (i.e., FTP, WWW) using policy-based routing. As per Figure 13–4,

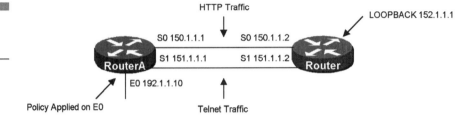

Figure 13–4
Application-level
policy routing

RouterA will route all Web traffic (port 80) out interface S0 and all telnet packets (port 23) out interface S1. All other packet types will be routed normally.

RouterA and RouterB are connected serially via crossover cables. RouterB will act as the DCE, supplying clock to RouterA. The IP addresses are assigned as per Figure 13–4. RouterB has a loopback interface (IP address 152.1.1.1) defined to provide a test point.

The ip policy route-map **lab1** will be applied to the Ethernet interface of RouterA, setting the next-hop IP address to 150.1.1.2 for HTTP packets and the next-hop IP address to 151.1.1.2 for telnet packets. All other packets will be routed through the normal destination-based routing process.

Router Configurations

The configurations for the two routers in this example are as follows (key policy routing configurations are highlighted in bold):

RouterA

```
!
version 11.2
service udp-small-servers
service tcp-small-servers
!
hostname RouterA
!

interface Ethernet0
  ip address 192.1.1.1 255.255.255.0
    ip policy route-map lab1←Enables policy routing on interface E0 and identifies
                      the route map lab1, which will be applied to the packet
  no keepalive←Disables the keepalive on the Ethernet interface, allows the
              interface to stay up when it is not attached to a hub.
!
interface Serial0
```

```
 ip address 150.1.1.1 255.255.255.0
 no fair-queue
!
interface Serial1
 ip address 151.1.1.1 255.255.255.0
!
router rip←Enables the RIP routing process on the router
 network 192.1.1.0←Specifies what interfaces will receive and send RIP routing
                   updates. It also specifies what networks will be advertised.
 network 150.1.0.0
 network 151.1.0.0
!
ip local policy route-map lab1←Packets that are generated by the router are
                               not normally policy routed. This command
                               enables the router to policy route packets
                               that are sourced from the router.

no ip classless
access-list 101 permit tcp any any eq www←Access list 101 sets the match
                                          criteria to WWW traffic.
access-list 102 permit tcp any any eq telnet←Access list 102 sets the match
                                             criteria to telnet traffic.
route-map lab1 permit 10←Defines the route map lab1, the number specifies the
                         order of the route maps. This is referred to as item
                         10 of route map lab1.

 match ip address 101←This defines the match criteria which is tied to access
                      list 101
 set ip next-hop 150.1.1.2←Sets the next hop IP address.
!
route-map lab1 permit 20←Defines the route map lab1, the number specifies the
                         order of the route maps. This is referred to as item
                         20 of route map lab1.

 match ip address 102←This defines the match criteria which is tied to access
                      list 102.
 set ip next-hop 151.1.1.2←Sets the next hop IP address.
!
line con 0
line aux 0
line vty 0 4
 login
!
end
```

RouterB

```
!
version 11.2
service udp-small-servers
service tcp-small-servers
!
```

```
hostname routerb
interface Loopback0←Defines a virtual interface that will be used as a test
                    point
 ip address 152.1.1.1 255.255.255.0
!
interface Ethernet0
 no ip address
 shutdown
!
interface Serial0
 ip address 150.1.1.2 255.255.255.0
 clockrate 500000←Acts as a DCE, providing clock
!
interface Serial1
 ip address 151.1.1.2 255.255.255.0
 clockrate 500000←Acts as a DCE, providing clock
!
router rip←Enables the RIP routing process on the router

 network 152.1.0.0←Specifies what interfaces will receive and send RIP routing
                   updates. It also specifies what networks will be advertised.
 network 151.1.0.0
 network 101.0.0.0

!
line con 0
line 1 16
 transport input all
line aux 0
 transport input all
line vty 0 4
 login
!
end
```

Monitoring and Testing the Configuration

From RouterA, monitor the policy routing using the **debug ip policy** command. Telnet from RouterA to 152.1.1.1. The output from the debug command is shown as follows. Note that the telnet packet matched item 20 of route map lab1 and was forwarded to 151.1.1.2.

```
IP: s=151.1.1.1 (local), d=152.1.1.1, len 44, policy match
IP: route map lab1, item 20, permit
IP: s=151.1.1.1 (local), d=152.1.1.1 (Serial1), len 44, policy routed
IP: local to Serial1 151.1.1.2
```

From RouterA, use the extended telnet command to send an HTTP packet to 152.1.1.2. To use this command, simply type **Telnet 152.1.1.1 www** at the privileged level. The output from the debug command is shown as follows. Note that the HTTP packet matched item 10 of route map lab1 and was forwarded to 150.1.1.2.

```
IP: s=151.1.1.1 (local), d=152.1.1.1, len 44, policy match
IP: route map lab1, item 10, permit
IP: s=151.1.1.1 (local), d=152.1.1.1 (Serial0), len 44, policy routed
IP: local to Serial0 150.1.1.2
```

Lab #56: Load Balancing across Default Routes

Equipment Needed

The following equipment is needed to perform this lab exercise:

- Two Cisco routers, each having one Ethernet port and two serial ports
- One Cisco router with one Ethernet port
- Cisco IOS 11.0 or higher
- A PC running a terminal emulation program for connecting to the console port of the routers
- Two Cisco DTE/DCE crossover cables
- A Cisco rolled cable
- One Ethernet crossover cable, or an Ethernet hub and two straight-through Ethernet cables

Configuration Overview

This configuration provides two end users with equal access to two different service providers. As per Figure 13–5, RouterA will route packets arriving on Ethernet 0 from the source 192.1.1.11 to default interface S0 (if no explicit route for the packet's destination is in the routing table). Packets arriving from 192.1.1.12 are sent to default interface S1 if the router has no explicit route for the packet's destination.

This lab uses the default interface command, which differs from the next-hop interface and next-hop ip address set commands that we used in previous labs. The next-hop set commands send the matching packet out that interface or to that specific ip address, regardless of the routing table. The default interface command only sends the packet out that particular interface if there is no explicit route in the routing table.

Figure 13-5
Load balancing
across default routes

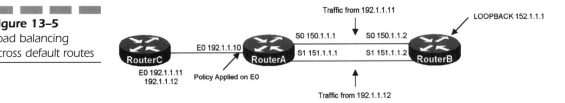

> **NOTE:** When using the default interface set command, the router will first check the routing table for an explicit route. If there is no explicit route available to the destination address of the packet being considered for policy routing, then the router will route the packet out the default interface.

Router Configurations

The configurations for the three routers in this example are as follows (key policy routing configurations are highlighted in bold):

RouterA

```
version 11.2
service udp-small-servers
service tcp-small-servers
!
hostname RouterA
!
!
interface Ethernet0
ip address 192.1.1.10 255.255.255.0
 ip policy route-map lab1←Enables policy routing on interface E0 and identifies
                      the route map lab1, which will be applied to the packet
!
interface Serial0
 ip address 150.1.1.1 255.255.255.0
 no fair-queue
!
interface Serial1
 ip address 151.1.1.1 255.255.255.0
!
router rip
 network 150.1.0.0
 network 151.1.0.0
 network 192.1.1.0
!
no ip classless
```

```
access-list 1 permit 192.1.1.11
access-list 2 permit 192.1.1.12
route-map lab1 permit 10←Defines the route map lab1, the number specifies the
                         order of the route maps. This is referred to as item
                         10 of route map lab1.
 match ip address 1←This defines the match criteria which is tied to access
                    list 1.
 set default interface Serial0←Sets the default interface to S0.
!
route-map lab1 permit 20←Defines the route map lab1, the number specifies the
                         order of the route maps. This is referred to as item
                         10 of route map lab1.
 match ip address 2←This defines the match criteria which is tied to access
                    list 1.
 set default interface Serial1←Sets the default interface to S0.
!
!
line con 0
line aux 0
line vty 0 4
 login
!
end
```

RouterB

```
version 11.2
service udp-small-servers
service tcp-small-servers
!
hostname routerb
!
!
!
interface Loopback0
 ip address 152.1.1.1 255.255.255.0
!
interface Ethernet0
 no ip address
 shutdown
!
interface Serial0
 ip address 150.1.1.2 255.255.255.0
 clockrate 500000←Acts as DCE providing clock

!
interface Serial1
 ip address 151.1.1.2 255.255.255.0
 clockrate 500000←Acts as DCE providing clock
!
router rip
 passive-interface Serial0←Prevents RIP updates from being sent to RouterA
 passive-interface Serial1
 network 152.1.0.0
```

```
 network 151.1.0.0
 network 150.1.0.0
 !
 !
 line con 0
 line 1 16
  transport input all
 line aux 0
  transport input all
 line vty 0 4
  login
 !
 end
```

RouterC

```
version 11.2
service udp-small-servers
service tcp-small-servers
!
hostname routerc
!
interface Ethernet0
  ip address 192.1.1.12 255.255.255.0 secondary
  ip address 192.1.1.11 255.255.255.0
!
interface Serial0
no ip address
shutdown
!
ip route 0.0.0.0 0.0.0.0 192.1.1.10←Sets the default route.
!
!
line con 0
line 1 16
line aux 0
line vty 0 4
  login
!
end
```

Monitoring and Testing the Configuration

When using the default interface set command, the router will first check the routing table for an explicit route. RouterA does not have an explicit route to 152.1.1.1, because RouterB suppresses RIP updates with the passive interface command.

From RouterA, monitor the policy routing using the **debug ip policy** command. From RouterC, ping 152.1.1.1 using the extended ping command to source the packet from 192.1.1.11. The output from the debug command on RouterA is shown as follows. Note that the source address 192.1.1.11 matched item 10 of route map lab1 and was forwarded out interface Serial 0.

```
IP: s=192.1.1.11 (Ethernet0), d=152.1.1.1, len 100, policy match
IP: route map lab1, item 10, permit
IP: s=192.1.1.11 (Ethernet0), d=152.1.1.1 (Serial0), len 100, policy routed
IP: Ethernet0 to Serial0 152.1.1.1
```

From RouterA, ping 152.1.1.1—sourcing the packet from 192.1.1.12. The output from the debug command on RouterA is shown as follows. Note that the source address 192.1.1.12 matched item 20 of route map lab1 and was forwarded out interface Serial 1.

```
IP: s=192.1.1.12 (Ethernet0), d=152.1.1.1, len 100, policy match
IP: route map lab1, item 20, permit
IP: s=192.1.1.12 (Ethernet0), d=152.1.1.1 (Serial1), len 100, policy routed
IP: Ethernet0 to Serial1 152.1.1.1
```

On RouterB, remove the passive interface commands to enable RIP updates to be sent to RouterA. Now that RouterA has a route for 152.1.1.1 learned via RIP, the router will not policy-route the packet. Remember that when using the default interface set command, the router will first check the routing table for an explicit route. If the router has a route to the destination, the packet is forwarded using that route. If there is no explicit route available to the destination address, then the router will route the packet out the default interface—which is set using policy routing.

```
routerb(config)#router rip
routerb(config-router)#no passive-interface s0
routerb(config-router)#no passive-interface s1
```

From RouterC, ping 152.1.1.1. The following example shows the output from the **debug ip policy** command on RouterA. Note that the packet matched item 20 in route map lab1. The set policy was rejected, however, because the routing table has an explicit route to 152.1.1.1.

```
IP: s=192.1.1.12 (Ethernet0), d=152.1.1.1, len 100, policy match
IP: route map lab1, item 20, permit
IP: s=192.1.1.12 (Ethernet0), d=152.1.1.1 (Serial1), len 100, policy rejected —
                                                            normal forwarding
```

Troubleshooting Policy Routing

The Cisco IOS provides many tools for troubleshooting policy routing. A list of key commands, along with sample output from each, is shown as follows.

{show ip policy} This privileged exec command displays which route map is used on which interface.

```
RouterA#show ip policy
Interface       Route map
Ethernet0       lab1
```

{show route-map} This privileged exec command displays configured route maps. This command enables you to view the policies defined by each route map. The command also shows how many packets matched the policy clauses.

```
RouterA#show route-map
route-map lab1, permit, sequence 10
  Match clauses:
    ip address (access-lists): 1
  Set clauses:
    default interface Serial0
  Policy routing matches: 129 packets, 14526 bytes
route-map lab1, permit, sequence 20
  Match clauses:
    ip address (access-lists): 2
  Set clauses:
    default interface Serial1
  Policy routing matches: 205 packets, 23370 bytes
```

{debug ip policy} This exec command helps you determine what policy routing is doing. The command displays information about whether a packet matches the criteria—and if so, the command displays the resulting routing information for the packet. The first line indicates that a packet matched the policy. The second line indicates the item of the route map that the packet matched. In this case, the packet matches item 20 in route map lab1. Line three indicates that the packet was policy-routed out interface S0.

```
IP: s=192.1.1.11 (Ethernet0), d=152.1.1.1, len 100, policy match
IP: route map lab1, item 10, permit
IP: s=192.1.1.11 (Ethernet0), d=152.1.1.1 (Serial0), len 100, policy routed
IP: Ethernet0 to Serial0 152.1.1.1
```

{**show ip local policy**} This exec command displays any route maps used for local policy routing. By default, packets that are generated by the router are not policy-routed. Local policy routing must be enabled on the router using the ip local policy route-map command.

```
RouterA#show ip local policy
Local policy routing is enabled, using route map lab1
route-map lab1, permit, sequence 10
  Match clauses:
    ip address (access-lists): 1
  Set clauses:
    default interface Serial0
  Policy routing matches: 129 packets, 14526 bytes
route-map lab1, permit, sequence 20
  Match clauses:
    ip address (access-lists): 2
  Set clauses:
    default interface Serial1
  Policy routing matches: 205 packets, 23370 bytes
```

Conclusion

Policy-based routing provides network administrators a way to implement packet forwarding based on other criteria—other than traditional, destination-based routing. The following are some of the potential applications for policy routing:

■ Carrier selection for WAN transmissions or internal data path selection for Internet access

■ *Internet Service Providers* (ISPs) can use policy routing to provide equal access to multiple-carrier networks.

■ Policy-based routing can be used to set either the precedence or type-of-service bits in an IP datagram, which can be used to provide QOS across the backbone.

■ Policy-based routing can be used to separate high- and low-priority traffic over separate links.

14

Cisco Discovery
Protocol

Topics Covered in This Chapter

- CDP overview
- Cisco CDP WAN configuration
- Cisco CDP LAN configuration
- CDP troubleshooting

Introduction

Cisco Discovery Protocol (CDP) is a Cisco proprietary protocol that is used for neighbor discovery. CDP is supported across the entire Cisco product line. CDP is helpful in debugging situations. For example, CDP can be used to verify that a given router is connected to the proper port number on its neighbor. This chapter will examine CDP in detail.

Cisco Discovery Protocol Overview

CDP runs on all Cisco routers and switches and can run over any physical media or protocol. Unlike a routing protocol, which shows a next-hop destination port for all known networks, CDP will only show information for directly connected neighbors. CDP is most useful for verifying that a router is connected to the proper port of its neighbor.

Figure 14–1 gives an overview of the information that CDP can provide. A CDP-enabled router can learn directly connected neighbor port and hostname information. Additional information, such as the neighbor's hardware model number and capabilities, are also reported.

How Does CDP Work?

A CDP-enabled router sends out a periodic multicast packet containing a CDP update. The time between these CDP updates is determined by the **cdp timer** command. The timer value default is 60 seconds.

A *Network Associates Sniffer* (NAS) was put on an Ethernet LAN which also had several Cisco routers connected to it. As can be seen from the packet trace on the next page, the router sending the packet includes important information, including the following data:

Figure 14–1
CDP overview

1) Who is my neighbor ?
2) What kind of device are you ?
3) What neighbor port am I connected to ?

1) I am a Cisco 3620
2) I am a router
3) You are connected to port S0/0

S0/0   3620

- Router hostname (Cisco1)
- Router port information (Ethernet 0/0)
- IOS version information (11.2(7a)P)
- IOS platform information (C3620-I-M)
- Hardware version information (Cisco 3600)

Although neighbor router IOS version, IOS platform, and hardware version are not critical pieces of information, neighbor router hostname and neighbor router port information is critical for debug purposes. The use of the **cdp neighbor** command is most useful in debug situations, where one needs to verify to which router and router port a given router is connected.

```
Packet 1 captured at 12/21/1998 12:19:37 AM; Packet size is 318(0x13e)bytes
        Relative time: 000:00:35.858
        Delta time: 0.000.000
    ETHER: Address: 00-E0-1E-5B-0A-81 --->01-00-0C-CC-CC-CC
    Logical Link Control
        SSAP Address: 0xAA, CR bit = 0 (Command)
        DSAP Address: 0xAA, IG bit = 0 (Individual address)
        Unnumbered frame: UI
    SubNetwork Access Protocol
        Organization code: 0x00000c
        Type: Custom Defined
    Data:
    0000: 01 b4 aa 2b 00 01 00 0a 43 69 73 63 6f 31 00 02 | ..a+....Cisco1..
    0010: 00 11 00 00 00 01 01 01 cc 00 04 c1 01 01 01 00 | ........I..A....
    0020: 03 00 0f 45 74 68 65 72 6e 65 74 30 2f 30 00 04 | ...Ethernet0/0..
    0030: 00 08 00 00 00 01 00 05 00 e4 43 69 73 63 6f 20 | .........aCisco
    0040: 49 6e 74 65 72 6e 65 74 77 6f 72 6b 20 4f 70 65 | Internetwork Ope
    0050: 72 61 74 69 6e 67 20 53 79 73 74 65 6d 20 53 6f | rating System So
    0060: 66 74 77 61 72 65 20 0a 49 4f 53 20 28 74 6d 29 | ftware .IOS (tm)
    0070: 20 33 36 30 30 20 53 6f 66 74 77 61 72 65 20 28 |  3600 Software (
    0080: 43 33 36 32 30 2d 49 2d 4d 29 2c 20 56 65 72 73 | C3620-I-M), Vers
    0090: 69 6f 6e 20 31 31 2e 32 28 37 61 29 50 2c 20 53 | ion 11.2(7a)P, S
    00a0: 48 41 52 45 44 20 50 4c 41 54 46 4f 52 4d 2c 20 | HARED PLATFORM,
    00b0: 52 45 4c 45 41 53 45 20 53 4f 46 54 57 41 52 45 | RELEASE SOFTWARE
    00c0: 20 28 66 63 31 29 0a 43 6f 70 79 72 69 67 68 74 |  (fc1).Copyright
    00d0: 20 28 63 29 20 31 39 38 36 2d 31 39 39 37 20 62 |  (c) 1986-1997 b
    00e0: 79 20 63 69 73 63 6f 20 53 79 73 74 65 6d 73 2c | y cisco Systems,
    00f0: 20 49 6e 63 2e 0a 43 6f 6d 70 69 6c 65 64 20 57 |  Inc..Compiled W
    0100: 65 64 20 30 32 2d 4a 75 6c 2d 39 37 20 30 38 3a | ed 02-Jul-97 08:
    0110: 32 35 20 62 79 20 63 63 61 69 00 06 00 0e 63 69 | 25 by ccai....ci
    0120: 73 63 6f 20 33 36 32 30                         | sco 3620
```

Commands Discussed in This Chapter

- **cdp enable**
- **cdp run**
- **cdp timer**
- **clear cdp counters**
- **clear cdp table**
- **show cdp interface**
- **show cdp neighbor**
- **show cdp traffic**
- **debug cdp [packets] [ip] [adjacency] [events]**

Definitions

cdp enable: This command is used to enable CDP on a particular interface. Because CDP is enabled by default, this command will not be shown in the router configuration. This command is an interface command.

cdp run: This command enables CDP on the entire router. Using the **no cdp run** command will disable any CDP activity on the router. Because CDP is enabled by default, the cdp run command will not show in the router configuration. This command is a global command.

cdp timer: This command specifies how often the router sends CDP updates. The default time between CDP updates is 60 seconds. This command is a global command.

clear cdp counters: This command causes the router's CDP traffic counters to be reset. This command is a privileged exec command.

clear cdp table: This command causes the router's CDP table to be cleared. When this situation occurs, the **show cdp neighbor** command will not show any information until another CDP update is received from a neighbor router. This command is a privileged exec command.

show cdp interface: This command will show the status of CDP for each interface on the router. This command is a privileged exec command.

show cdp neighbor: This command causes the router to display neighbor information for all directly attached routers. This command is a privileged exec command.

show cdp traffic: This command will show how many CDP packets have been sent and received by the router. The command also shows how many errored CDP packets have been received. This command is a privileged exec command.

debug cdp [packets] [ip] [adjacency] [events]: This debug command will cause the router to display debugging information for a variety of CDP events.

IOS Requirements

CDP is supported in Cisco IOS releases 10.3 and higher.

Lab #57: Cisco CDP WAN Example

Equipment Needed

The following equipment is needed to perform this lab exercise:

- Three Cisco routers, one of which must have two serial ports. The other two routers can have just one serial port.
- Cisco IOS 10.3 or higher
- A PC running a terminal emulation program. The PC should be connected to one of the three routers using a Cisco rolled cable.
- Two Cisco DTE/DCE crossover cables. If no crossover cables are available, you can make a crossover cable by connecting a standard Cisco DTE cable to a standard Cisco DCE cable.

Configuration Overview

This configuration will demonstrate the basics of CDP and will enable us to see the difference between information supplied by CDP and information supplied by a routing protocol (such as RIP).

The three routers are serially connected, as shown in Figure 14–2. RouterB will act as the DCE, supplying clock to RouterA and RouterC. A PC running a terminal emulation program should be connected to the console port of one of the three routers using a Cisco rolled cable.

NOTE: *Keep in mind that CDP will only supply information for directly connected neighbors, which is in contrast to a routing protocol such as RIP. A routing protocol such as RIP will provide information that enables the router to determine the next interface hop to all known networks.*

Router Configuration

The configurations for the three routers in this example are as follows. Notice that because CDP is enabled by default, there are no specific CDP commands in the configuration.

RouterA

```
Current configuration:
!
version 11.2
no service udp-small-servers
no service tcp-small-servers
!
hostname RouterA
!
enable password cisco
!
interface Serial0/0
 ip address 192.1.1.1 255.255.255.0
 encapsulation ppp
!
router rip
 network 192.1.1.0
!
no ip classless
!
```

Figure 14–2
CDP WAN example

s0/0	s0/0	s0/1	s0/0
192.1.1.1	192.1.1.2	196.1.1.2	196.1.1.3

RouterA   Serial Link   RouterB   Serial Link   RouterC

```
line con 0
line aux 0
line vty 0 4
 password cisco
 login
!
end
```

RouterB

```
Current configuration:
!
version 11.2
no service udp-small-servers
no service tcp-small-servers
!
hostname RouterB
!
enable password cisco
!
interface Serial0/0
 ip address 192.1.1.2 255.255.255.0
 encapsulation ppp
 clockrate 500000
!
interface Serial0/1
 ip address 196.1.1.2 255.255.255.0
 encapsulation ppp
 clockrate 19200
!
router rip
 network 192.1.1.0
 network 196.1.1.0
!
no ip classless
!
line con 0
line aux 0
line vty 0 4
 password cisco
 login
!
end
```

RouterC

```
Current configuration:
!
version 11.2
```

```
no service udp-small-servers
no service tcp-small-servers
!
hostname RouterC
!
enable password cisco
!
interface Serial0/0
 ip address 196.1.1.3 255.255.255.0
 encapsulation ppp
!
router rip
 network 196.1.1.0
!
no ip classless
!
line con 0
line aux 0
line vty 0 4
 password cisco
 login
!
end
```

Monitoring and Testing the Configuration

Let's examine some commands which enable us to monitor the status and results of CDP. The first important command is **show cdp traffic**. This command displays the number of CDP packets that have been received and sent by the router since the last **clear cdp counter** command:

```
RouterA#sh cdp traffic
CDP counters :
        Packets output: 16, Input: 11
        Hdr syntax: 0, Chksum error: 0, Encaps failed: 4
        No memory: 0, Invalid packet: 0, Fragmented: 0
```

The **show cdp** command will display how often CDP updates are sent (60 seconds), as well as how long CDP incoming information is kept until discarded (180 seconds).

```
RouterB#sh cdp
Global CDP information:
        Sending CDP packets every 60 seconds
        Sending a holdtime value of 180 seconds
```

The **show cdp neighbor** command will display information on directly connected neighbors of the router—provided that CDP is enabled on these interfaces. In the following example, we see that interface S0/0 on RouterA is connected to interface S0/0 on RouterB.

```
RouterA#sh cdp neigh
Capability Codes: R - Router, T - Trans Bridge, B - Source Route Bridge
                  S - Switch, H - Host, I - IGMP, r - Repeater

Device ID       Local Intrfce    Holdtme    Capability  Platform  Port ID
RouterB         Ser 0/0          120        R           3620      Ser 0/0
```

Notice how the **show cdp neighbor** command output for RouterB shows two directly connected neighbors: RouterA and RouterC.

```
RouterB#show cdp neighbor
Capability Codes: R - Router, T - Trans Bridge, B - Source Route Bridge
                  S - Switch, H - Host, I - IGMP, r - Repeater

Device ID       Local Intrfce    Holdtme    Capability  Platform  Port ID
RouterA         Ser 0/0          174        R           3620      Ser 0/0
RouterC         Ser 0/1          125        R           3620      Ser 0/0
```

The **show cdp neighbor detail** command provides additional information, such as which IOS version and platform the neighboring device is running.

```
RouterA#sh cdp neighbor detail
-----------------------------------
Device ID: RouterB
Entry address(es):
  IP address: 192.1.1.2
Platform: cisco 3620,   Capabilities: Router
Interface: Serial0/0,   Port ID (outgoing port): Serial0/0
Holdtime : 174 sec

Version :
Cisco Internetwork Operating System Software
IOS (tm) 3600 Software (C3620-I-M), Version 11.2(7a)P, SHARED PLATFORM, RELEASE
SOFTWARE (fc1)
Copyright (c) 1986-1997 by cisco Systems, Inc.
Compiled Wed 02-Jul-97 08:25 by ccai
```

You can use the **show cdp interface** command to verify that CDP is enabled on the desired interfaces. If an interface does not have CDP enabled, the interface will not have an entry when using the following commands:

```
RouterA#sh cdp interface
Ethernet0/0 is administratively down, line protocol is down
  Encapsulation ARPA
  Sending CDP packets every 60 seconds
  Holdtime is 180 seconds
Serial0/0 is up, line protocol is up
  Encapsulation PPP
  Sending CDP packets every 60 seconds
```

```
   Holdtime is 180 seconds
Serial0/1 is administratively down, line protocol is down
   Encapsulation HDLC
   Sending CDP packets every 60 seconds
   Holdtime is 180 seconds
```

Once again, keep in mind the advantages and limitations of CDP. CDP will only show directly connected neighbors. Recall that in this example, the **show cdp neighbor** command issued on RouterA only shows RouterB as being directly connected. The following **show ip route** output shows that the routing protocol RIP also has learned about the 196.1.1.0 network (which is RouterC).

```
RouterA#sh ip route
Codes: C - connected, S - static, I - IGRP, R - RIP, M - mobile, B - BGP
       D - EIGRP, EX - EIGRP external, O - OSPF, IA - OSPF inter area
       N1 - OSPF NSSA external type 1, N2 - OSPF NSSA external type 2
       E1 - OSPF external type 1, E2 - OSPF external type 2, E - EGP
       i - IS-IS, L1 - IS-IS level-1, L2 - IS-IS level-2, * - candidate default
       U - per-user static route, o - ODR

Gateway of last resort is not set

     192.1.1.0/24 is variably subnetted, 2 subnets, 2 masks
C       192.1.1.0/24 is directly connected, Serial0/0
C       192.1.1.2/32 is directly connected, Serial0/0
R    196.1.1.0/24 [120/1] via 192.1.1.2, 00:00:08, Serial0/0
```

CDP Debug Commands

Several debug commands are available for advanced monitoring and troubleshooting of CDP. The following screen print shows all CDP debugging enabled:

```
RouterC#sh debug
CDP:
  CDP packet info debugging is on
  CDP events debugging is on
  CDP neighbor info debugging is on
  CDP IP info debugging is on
```

CDP debug packet events will show packets being sent out and received by the router. The CDP debug information will indicate which router sent traffic to the router being monitored by the debug command. The following example shows a CDP packet being received from RouterB. Notice that the information being received is already known to the router (signified by the line, "Entry found in cache").

```
CDP-PA: Packet received from RouterB on interface Serial0/0
**Entry  found in cache**
```

The following example shows what occurs when the router sends out a CDP packet:

```
CDP-PA: Packet sent out on Serial0/0
```

The reader of this book can try an interesting experiment that will highlight the details of how CDP functions. Using the current three router configuration, turn on CDP debugging with the debug cdp command. Then, pull the cable on serial 0/0 on RouterA. The following screen print should be similar to what you will see (remember to use the **term mon** command to direct output to the screen if you are not connected to the console connector on the router). First, you will see the router declare the line protocol and the interface down:

```
%LINEPROTO-5-UPDOWN: Line protocol on Interface Serial0/0, changed state to down
%LINK-3-UPDOWN: Interface Serial0/0, changed state to down
```

CDP will then declare the interface to be in a failed state:

```
Dec 27 09:14:05: CDP-AD: Interface Serial0/0 going down
Dec 27 09:14:05: CDP-EV: Encapsulation on interface Serial0/0 failed
```

Try typing the **show cdp neighbor** command every few seconds. You will notice that the neighbor information does not change, although the interface is down. This result occurs because of the holdtime value used by CDP. By default, CDP will hold an incoming packet's information for 180 seconds before discarding the information. The following screen print shows that there are still 24 seconds remaining before the CDP process on RouterA will delete the neighbor entry for RouterB.

```
RouterA#sh cdp neigh
Capability Codes: R - Router, T - Trans Bridge, B - Source Route Bridge
                  S - Switch, H - Host, I - IGMP, r - Repeater

Device ID        Local Intrfce    Holdtme    Capability  Platform  Port ID
RouterB          Ser 0/0          24         R           3620      Ser 0/0
```

As shown in the following example, the holdtime will eventually decrease to zero:

```
RouterA#sh cdp neigh
Capability Codes: R - Router, T - Trans Bridge, B - Source Route Bridge
                  S - Switch, H - Host, I - IGMP, r - Repeater
```

Device ID	Local Intrfce	Holdtme	Capability	Platform	Port ID
RouterB	Ser 0/0	**0**	R	3620	Ser 0/0

When the holdtime expires, the router will then age out the entry. Notice in the following screen print that there is no longer an entry for any neighbor routers:

```
RouterA#sh cdp neigh
Capability Codes: R - Router, T - Trans Bridge, B - Source Route Bridge
                  S - Switch, H - Host, I - IGMP, r - Repeater

Device ID        Local Intrfce      Holdtme    Capability  Platform  Port ID
```

CDP will alert you to an aged entry via the following message:

```
Dec 27 09:16:33: CDP-AD: Aging entry for RouterB, on interface Serial0/0
```

When you reconnect the cable going to interface serial 0/0 on RouterA, you will see the interface go to an up state. CDP will start to send out packets. Notice that the first entry received will not be found in the CDP cache, because the old entry was already aged out.

```
%LINK-3-UPDOWN: Interface Serial0/0, changed state to up
%LINEPROTO-5-UPDOWN: Line protocol on Interface Serial0/0, changed state to up
Dec 27 09:17:06: CDP-AD: Interface Serial0/0 coming up
Dec 27 09:17:06: CDP-PA: Packet sent out on Serial0/0
Dec 27 09:17:06: CDP-PA: Packet received from Cisco2 on interface Serial0/0
Dec 27 09:17:06: **Entry NOT found in cache**
```

The **show cdp neighbor** command will now show an entry for neighbor RouterB (which is directly connected):

```
RouterA#sh cdp neigh
Capability Codes: R - Router, T - Trans Bridge, B - Source Route Bridge
                  S - Switch, H - Host, I - IGMP, r - Repeater
```

Device ID	Local Intrfce	Holdtme	Capability	Platform	Port ID
RouterB	Ser 0/0	171	R	3620	Ser 0/0

Lab #58: Cisco CDP LAN Example

Equipment Needed

The following equipment is needed to perform this lab exercise:

■ Three Cisco routers, each having an Ethernet port
■ Cisco IOS 10.3 or higher

- A PC running a terminal emulation program
- Three Ethernet cables
- An Ethernet hub
- An optional LAN sniffer to trace the CDP packets

Configuration Overview

This configuration will show how CDP works on a shared media Ethernet LAN.

The three routers are all connected to the same Ethernet hub, as shown in Figure 14–3. An optional LAN sniffer can also be connected to the Ethernet hub. The LAN sniffer can be used to capture the CDP packets.

NOTE: *Keep in mind that CDP will only supply information for directly connected neighbors, which is in contrast to a routing protocol (such as RIP). A routing protocol such as RIP will provide information that enables the router to determine the next interface hop to all known networks.*

Router Configuration

The configurations for the three routers in this example are as follows. Notice that because CDP is enabled by default, there are no specific CDP commands in the configuration.

Figure 14–3
CDP LAN example

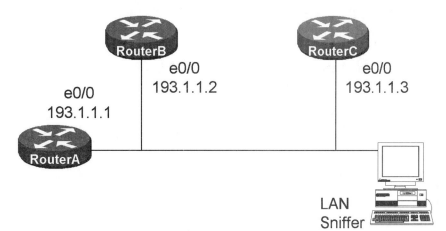

RouterA

```
Current configuration:
!
version 11.2
no service udp-small-servers
no service tcp-small-servers
!
hostname RouterA
!
enable password cisco
!
!
interface Ethernet0/0
 ip address 193.1.1.1 255.255.255.0
!
interface Serial0/0
 shutdown
!
router rip
 network 192.1.1.0
!
no ip classless
!
line con 0
line aux 0
line vty 0 4
 password cisco
 login
!
end
```

RouterB

```
Current configuration:
!
version 11.2
no service udp-small-servers
no service tcp-small-servers
!
hostname RouterB
!
enable password cisco
!
!
interface Ethernet0/0
 ip address 193.1.1.2 255.255.255.0
!
interface Serial0/0
 ip address 192.1.1.2 255.255.255.0
 encapsulation ppp
```

```
  shutdown
  clockrate 500000
!
interface Serial0/1
  shutdown
!
router rip
  network 192.1.1.0
  network 196.1.1.0
!
no ip classless
!
line con 0
line aux 0
line vty 0 4
  password cisco
  login
!
end
```

RouterC

```
Current configuration:
!
version 11.2
no service udp-small-servers
no service tcp-small-servers
!
hostname RouterC
!
enable password cisco
!
!
interface Ethernet0/0
  ip address 193.1.1.3 255.255.255.0
!
interface Serial0/0
  shutdown
!
router rip
  network 196.1.1.0
!
no ip classless
!
line con 0
line aux 0
line vty 0 4
  password cisco
  login
!
end
```

Monitoring and Testing the Configuration

The key CDP monitoring and debug commands were covered in the previous section. Because all the routers in this configuration are connected to the same LAN, each of the three routers will display the same neighbor table as shown in the following **show cdp neighbor** command:

```
RouterA#sh cdp neigh
Capability Codes: R - Router, T - Trans Bridge, B - Source Route Bridge
                  S - Switch, H - Host, I - IGMP, r - Repeater

Device ID        Local Intrfce    Holdtme    Capability  Platform  Port ID
RouterC              Eth 0/0       121           R         3620     Eth 0/0
RouterB              Eth 0/0       177           R         3620     Eth 0/0
```

Conclusion

In this chapter, we examined CDP a media- and protocol-independent, proprietary protocol used for neighbor discovery. CDP does not replace a routing protocol; rather, it will only show information on directly connected neighbors. CDP is particularly useful in determining the neighbor router and port to which a given router is connected.

15

Network Address Translation (NAT)

Topics Covered in This Chapter

- Detailed NAT overview
- NAT terminology
- Static inside source address translation
- Dynamic inside source address translation
- Overloading an inside global address
- Translating overlapping addresses
- Destination address rotary translation
- Changing translation timeouts
- Detailed troubleshooting examples

Introduction

Network Address Translation (NAT) is a router function that provides the translation from one IP address to another. Address translation is required for customers who have private (or unregistered) addresses and wish to access a public service (where publicly registered addresses are used). This chapter will explore NAT capabilities available through the Cisco IOS.

Network Address Translation Overview

One of the greatest problems facing the Internet today is the issue of address depletion. NAT promises to relieve some of this pressure by enabling organizations to reuse globally unique, registered IP addresses in other parts of their network.

NAT will enable organizations to reuse registered IP addresses within multiple domains, as long as the addresses are translated to globally unique Internet registered addresses before they leave that domain. Figure 15–1 shows how basic NAT works. Both stub networks are using the class A address 10.0.0.0 for their internal network. Each organization is assigned an Internet registered unique class C address. This address is used when traffic wishes to flow off the private intranet onto the public Internet.

Figure 15–1
Network Address
Translation (NAT)

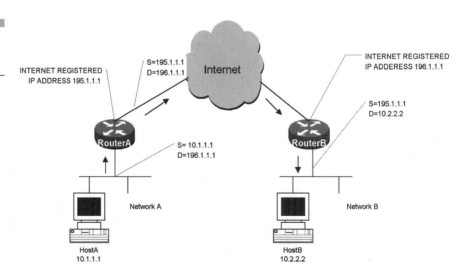

In Figure 15–1, when HostA (10.1.1.1) wishes to send a packet to HostB (10.2.2.2), HostA uses HostB's globally unique address 196.1.1.1 as the packet's destination. When the packet arrives at RouterA, the source address of 10.1.1.1 is translated to the globally unique address of 195.1.1.1. When the packet arrives at RouterB, the destination address is translated to the unregistered IP address 10.2.2.2. Likewise, packets on the return path go through similar address translation.

This process requires no additional configuration to hosts on the internal network. As far as HostA is concerned, 196.1.1.1 is the IP address of HostB (10.2.2.2) on NetworkB. As far as HostB is concerned, 195.1.1.1 is the IP address of HostA (10.1.1.1) on network A.

NAT Terminology

When dealing with NAT on a Cisco router, you should understand the terminology used (as shown in Figure 15–2).

- **Inside local address**:   The IP address that is assigned to a host on the inside network. This address is probably not an IP address assigned by the *Network Information Center* (NIC) or service provider.

- **Inside global address**:   An NIC-registered IP address that is used to represent one or more inside local IP addresses to the outside world

Figure 15–2
NAT terminology

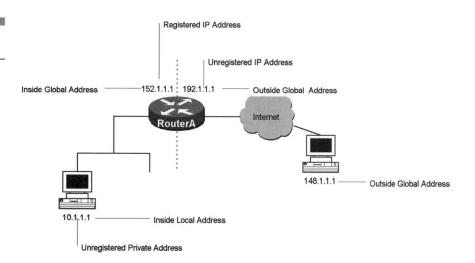

■ **Outside local address**: The IP address of an outside host as it appears to the inside network; not necessarily a legitimate address, but allocated from address space that was routable on the inside

■ **Outside global address**: The IP address assigned to a host on the outside network by the host's owner. The address was allocated from a globally routable address or network space.

Commands Discussed in This Chapter

■ **clear ip nat translations**

■ **debug ip nat**

■ **ip nat** {inside | outside}

■ **ip nat inside destination list** {access-list-number | name} pool name

■ **ip nat inside source** {list {access-list-number | name} pool name [overload] | static local-ip global-ip}

■ **ip nat outside source** {list {access-list-number | name} pool name | static global-ip local-ip}

■ **ip nat pool name** start-ip end-ip {netmask | prefix-length prefix-length} [type rotary]

■ **ip nat translation** {timeout | udp-timeout | dns-timeout | tcp-timeout | finrst-timeout} seconds

■ **show ip nat statistics**

■ **show ip nat translations**

Definitions

clear ip nat: This exec command is used to clear all (or specific) active NAT translations.

ip nat: This command is used to enable NAT for packets originating from (inside) or destined to (outside) interfaces.

ip nat inside destination list: This global command enables NAT for the inside destination address. This command can be configured for both dynamic and static address translations.

ip nat inside source: This global command enables NAT for the inside source address. This command can be configured for both dynamic and static address translations.

ip nat outside source: This global command enables NAT of outside source addresses. This command can be configured for both dynamic and static address translations.

ip nat pool name: This global command defines a pool of IP addresses used for network translations. The pool could define either an inside global pool, an outside local pool, or a rotary pool.

ip nat translation: This global command is used to change the amount of time after which NAT times out.

show ip nat statistics: This command is used to display NAT statistics.

show ip nat translations: This command displays all active NAT translations.

IOS Requirements

NAT first became available in IOS 11.2.

Lab #59: Static Inside Source Address Translation

Equipment Needed

The following equipment is needed to perform this lab exercise:

- Two Cisco routers with one Ethernet port and one serial port
- Cisco IOS 11.2 or higher
- A PC running a terminal emulation program
- A PC with an Ethernet NIC or additional router with an Ethernet interface
- Two Ethernet cables and an Ethernet hub
- A Cisco DTE/DCE crossover cable

Configuration Overview

This configuration will demonstrate NAT for an unregistered, inside IP address to a globally unique, outside address. RouterA will translate the inside source address of 10.1.1.1 to the globally unique address of 195.1.1.1, as shown in Figure 15–3.

RouterA and RouterB are connected serially via a crossover cable. RouterA will act as the DCE, supplying clock to RouterB. The IP addresses are assigned as per Figure 15–4. A PC with an Ethernet NIC (or an additional router) is connected to an Ethernet LAN attached to RouterA. RouterA is configured for NAT and will translate source IP address 10.1.1.1 to 195.1.1.1.

Router Configurations

The configurations for the two routers in this example are as follows (key NAT configurations for RouterA are highlighted in bold):

Figure 15–3
Inside source address translation

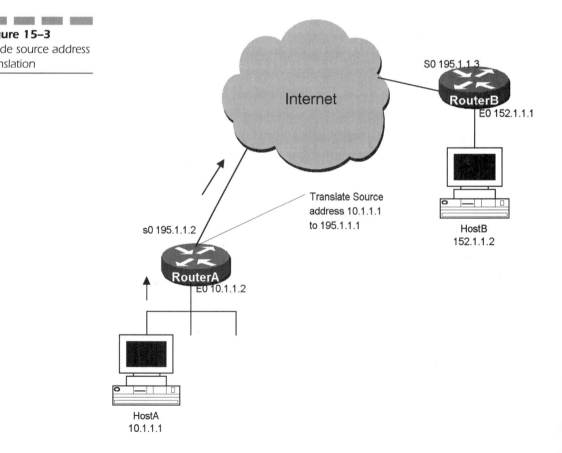

Figure 15–4
Inside source address
translation

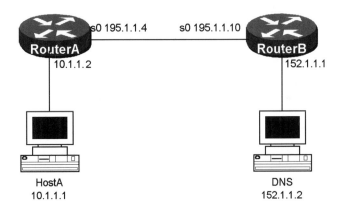

RouterA

```
version 11.2
no service udp-small-servers
no service tcp-small-servers
!
hostname routerA
!
ip nat inside source static 10.1.1.1 195.1.1.1←Translates the inside source
                                                address 10.1.1.1 to 195.1.1.1
!
interface Ethernet0
  ip address 10.1.1.2 255.255.255.0
 ip nat inside←Marks the interface as connected to the inside.
 !
interface Serial0
  ip address 195.1.1.2 255.255.255.0
 ip nat outside←Marks the interface as connected to the outside.
Clock rate 500000
 !
no ip classless
ip route 152.1.1.1 255.255.255.255 Serial0
!
line con 0
line vty 0 4
 login
!
end
```

RouterB

```
Current configuration:
!
version 11.1
service udp-small-servers
service tcp-small-servers
!
hostname RouterB
!
enable password cisco
!
interface Ethernet0/0
  ip address 152.1.1.1 255.255.255.0
!
interface Serial0/0
 ip address 195.1.1.3 255.255.255.0
 !
line con 0
line aux 0
line vty 0 4
 password cisco
 login
```

Monitoring and Testing the Configuration

From HostA, ping HostB (152.1.1.2). Analyze the packets coming into RouterB with the **debug ip packet** command. The output from the command is shown as follows. Note that the source address of the ICMP ping packet is 195.1.1.1.

```
IP: s=195.1.1.1 (Serial0/0), d=152.1.1.1, len 104, rcvd 4←ICMP ECHO
IP: s=152.1.1.1 (local), d=195.1.1.1 (Serial0/0), len 104←ICMP ECHO REPLY
```

From the **debug ip nat** output on RouterA, we can see that the source IP address 10.1.1.1 has been translated to 195.1.1.1, which is a two-way process. The return packet, which is destined for 195.1.1.1 destination IP address, is changed back to 10.1.1.1.

```
NAT: s=10.1.1.1->195.1.1.1, d=152.1.1.1 [2542]
NAT*: s=152.1.1.1, d=195.1.1.1->10.1.1.1 [2542]
```

In the earlier section, we covered a one-to-one mapping between an inside local address and an inside global address. This method is inefficient and does not scale, because each registered IP address can only be used by one endstation. Static translation is most often used when a host on the inside needs to be accessed by a fixed IP address from the outside world.

Figure 15–5 shows an example of when static address mapping is required. HostA wishes to access files on the FTP server; however, the FTP

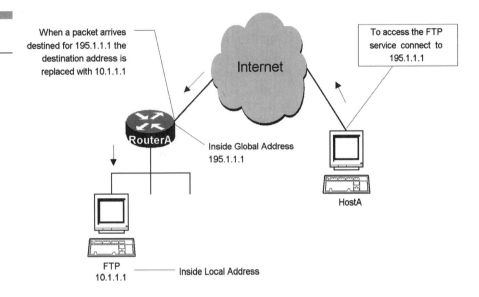

Figure 15–5
Static mapping

When a packet arrives destined for 195.1.1.1 the destination address is replaced with 10.1.1.1

Internet

To access the FTP service connect to 195.1.1.1

RouterA

Inside Global Address
195.1.1.1

HostA

FTP
10.1.1.1 — Inside Local Address

server resides on an inside network and does not have a unique, globally significant IP address. Static mapping is used to define the globally significant address of 195.1.1.1 to the locally significant address of 10.1.1.1.

Lab #60: Dynamic Inside Source Address Translation

Equipment Needed

The following equipment is needed to perform this lab exercise:

■ Two Cisco routers with one Ethernet port and one serial port
■ Cisco IOS 11.2 or higher
■ One PC running a terminal emulation program
■ One Cisco DTE/DCE crossover cable

Overview

The other type of inside address translation is dynamic translation, which establishes a mapping between a group of inside local addresses and a pool of global addresses. This translation is useful when you have a large group of unregistered users who wish to access off-net services.

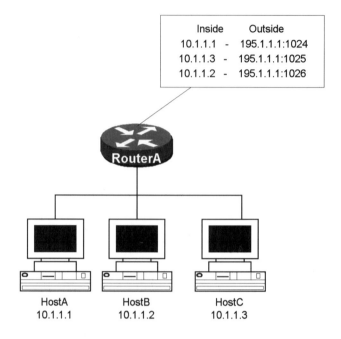

Figure 15–6
Dynamic address
translation

Dynamic inside address translation dynamically translates an unregistered IP address to a registered IP address using a predefined pool. This relationship is one-to-one. As an outside connection is requested, an IP address is used from the pool. When the connection is finished, the globally significant IP address is released back into the pool—where the address can be used for another connection. Dynamic address translation is efficient, because the same global IP address can be used over and over as needed by multiple endstations. In contrast, with the previous static translation, only one particular endstation can use the global address.

Figure 15–6 shows three workstations on a LAN, all of which need access to the outside network. As packets arrive at RouterA, the source address is translated to an Internet-registered address using the predefined pool. This process still involves one-to-one mapping. You need an Internet-registered IP address for each workstation that wishes to communicate outside the private network. Not all PCs will access the Internet at the same time, however. For example, depending on the traffic pattern, 10 registered IP addresses could service 40 PCs.

NOTE: *Although dynamic address translation is more scalable, more efficient, and easier to administer, outside users cannot access inside addresses because there is no static mapping between IP address. After*

each session is closed, the global IP address is released back into the pool—where the address can be used by other sessions. Each endstation can and most likely will be mapped to a different global address when it opens a new connection. Therefore, it is impossible to reference a particular inside address with a global address.

This problem can be avoided by using a combination of dynamic and static translations. All hosts that need to be accessed by outside users, such as FTP and HTTP servers, will be configured using static translations. All other endstations will use dynamic translations.

Configuration Overview

This configuration will demonstrate dynamic translation of inside source addresses to outside global addresses. RouterA will translate any source address within the range of 10.1.1.1 to 10.1.1.3 to any of the three global addresses defined in the address pool "globalpool."

Two Cisco routers are connected serially. RouterA is connected to RouterB via a crossover cable. RouterB acts as the DCE, providing clock for RouterA. A PC running a terminal emulation program is connected to the console port of RouterA. All IP addresses are in the following form (see Figure 15–7):

RouterA is configured for NAT and will dynamically translate any inside source address within the range specified by access-list 1 to a unique, Internet-registered global address—which is predefined by the pool "globalpool."

Router Configurations

The configurations for the two routers in this example are as follows (key NAT commands are highlighted in bold):

Figure 15–7
Dynamic address
translation

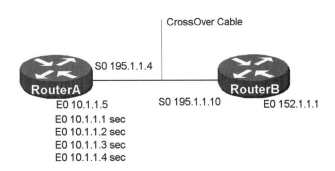

RouterA

```
version 11.2
no service udp-small-servers
no service tcp-small-servers
!
hostname routerA
!
                      ↓Name of the pool
ip nat pool globalpool 195.1.1.1 195.1.1.3 netmask 255.255.255.0←Defines the pool
                                                                of address
                       List 1 reference access-list 1 and defines which
                  ↓addresses will be translated
ip nat inside source list 1 pool globalpool←Globalpool references the pool of
                                          addresses defined in the previous line.
!
interface Ethernet0
 ip address 10.1.1.1 255.255.255.0 secondary
 ip address 10.1.1.2 255.255.255.0 secondary
 ip address 10.1.1.3 255.255.255.0 secondary→Secondary IP addresses are used
                                           as test points
 ip address 10.1.1.4 255.255.255.0 secondary
 ip address 10.1.1.5 255.255.255.0
 ip nat inside→Defines the inside interface
!
interface Serial0
 ip address 195.1.1.4 255.255.255.0
 ip nat outside→Defines the outside interface
!
no ip classless
ip route 152.1.1.1 255.255.255.255 Serial0
access-list 1 permit 10.1.1.2
access-list 1 permit 10.1.1.3
access-list 1 permit 10.1.1.1→Access list 1 defines which inside source
                              addresses will be translated
access-list 1 permit 10.1.1.4
!
line con 0
line vty 0 4
 login
!
end
```

RouterB

```
Current configuration:
!
version 11.1
service udp-small-servers
service tcp-small-servers
```

```
!
hostname RouterB
!
enable password cisco
!
interface Ethernet0/0
   ip address 152.1.1.1 255.255.255.0
!
interface Serial0/0
  ip address 195.1.1.10 255.255.255.0
  clock rate 500000←Defines the clock rate for the DCE interface

  !
line con 0
line aux 0
line vty 0 4
  password cisco
  login
```

Monitoring and Testing the Configuration

To test the configuration, use the extended ping command on RouterA. This command will enable you to source the ping packet from any active IP address on the router. To use this command, simply type ping at the privileged level.

```
routerA#ping
Protocol [ip]:
Target IP address: 152.1.1.1
Repeat count [5]:
Datagram size [100]:
Timeout in seconds [2]:
Extended commands [n]: y
Source address or interface: 10.1.1.2
Type of service [0]:
Set DF bit in IP header? [no]:
Validate reply data? [no]:
Data pattern [0xABCD]:
Loose, Strict, Record, Timestamp, Verbose[none]:
Sweep range of sizes [n]:
```

The following examples all use the extended ping command on RouterA to source the packets from the secondary IP addresses defined in the configuration. This setup is used instead of multiple PCs on RouterA's LAN.

1. From RouterA, ping 152.1.1.1 using source address 10.1.1.2.

2. From RouterA, ping 152.1.1.1 using source address 10.1.1.1.

3. From RouterA, ping 152.1.1.1 using source address 10.1.1.3.

From the **debug ip nat** translations output on RouterA, we see that the source address 10.1.1.2 has been translated to 195.1.1.1, which is the first address in the pool. The global IP addresses from the pool are assigned in the order that they are requested.

```
NAT: s=10.1.1.2->195.1.1.1, d=152.1.1.1 [20]
NAT: s=10.1.1.1->195.1.1.2, d=152.1.1.1 [25]
NAT: s=10.1.1.3->195.1.1.3, d=152.1.1.1 [35]
```

The following output from the **debug ip nat translation** command on RouterA shows what happens when a fourth endstation wishes to access the outside network, but all of the global addresses are being used.

```
NAT: translation failed (L), dropping packet s=10.1.1.4 d=152.1.1.1
```

From these examples, you can see that although dynamic address translation provides more efficient use of global addresses than static translations, each translation still requires its own address. Therefore, the network administrator must accurately gauge the amount of off-net traffic and define the address pool accordingly.

Lab #61: Overloading an Inside Global Address

Equipment Needed

The following equipment is needed to perform this lab exercise:

- Two Cisco routers with one Ethernet port and one serial port
- Cisco IOS 11.2 or higher
- One PC running a terminal emulation program
- A Cisco DTE/DCE crossover cable

Overview

The Cisco IOS enables you to overload a global address, thereby bypassing the need for a one-to-one mapping between the local address and the global address. This feature greatly reduces the number of registered IP addresses needed.

When overloading is configured, the router maintains enough information from higher-level protocols (for example, TCP or UDP port numbers) to translate the global address back to the correct local address. When multiple local addresses map to one global address, the TCP or UDP port numbers of each inside host are used to distinguish between the local addresses.

In Figure 15–8, all of the local addresses on the LAN are translated to one global IP address: 195.1.1.1. The router reuses the inside global address for each translation and uses the TCP or UDP port number to differentiate between endstations.

The following steps are taken by RouterA when overloading is enabled:

1. HostA (10.1.1.1) opens a connection to Host 152.1.1.1 on the Internet.

2. The first packet that RouterA receives from HostA causes the router to check its NAT table.

3. If no translation exists, RouterA replaces the source address with the global address of 195.1.1.1.

4. When the router receives a packet from Host 152.1.1.1 that is destined for 195.1.1.1, the router performs a NAT table lookup using the protocol, inside global address and port number, and

Figure 15–8
Overloading an
inside global address

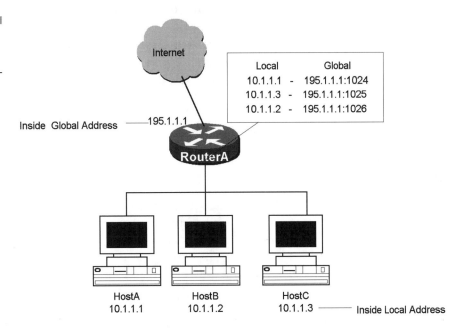

outside address and port number as a key. With this key, RouterA is able to translate the destination address 195.1.1.1 to inside local address 10.1.1.1 and forwards the packet to Host 10.1.1.1.

The following example shows the output from the **show ip nat translations** command on RouterA. Notice the port number after the address. The port number 1029 after the inside global address is the ephemeral port that HostA chooses. Port number 23 after the outside address is the well-known port for Telnet.

```
routerA# show ip nat translations

Pro I     inside global    Inside local      Outside local     Outside global
icmp      195.1.1.1:256    10.1.1.1:256      152.1.1.1:256     152.1.1.1:256
tcp       195.1.1.1:1029   10.1.1.1:1029     152.1.1.1:23      152.1.1.1:23
```

Configuration Overview

This configuration will demonstrate overloading one outside global address. RouterA will translate any source address within the range of 10.1.1.1 to 10.1.1.3 to the global address 195.1.1.1.

Two Cisco routers are connected serially. RouterA is connected to RouterB via a crossover cable. RouterB acts as the DCE, providing clock for RouterA. A PC running a terminal emulation program is connected to the console port of RouterA. All IP addresses are assigned as per Figure 15–9.

RouterA is configured for NAT and will dynamically translate any inside source address within the range specified to the unique, Internet-registered, global address 195.1.1.1.

Figure 15–9
Overloading an inside global address

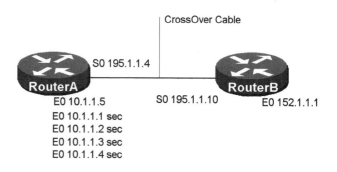

Router Configurations

The configurations for the two routers in this example are as follows (key NAT configurations for RouterA are highlighted in bold):

RouterA

```
version 11.2
no service udp-small-servers
no service tcp-small-servers
!
hostname routerA
!
                    ↓Name of the pool
ip nat pool globalpool 195.1.1.1 195.1.1.1 netmask 255.255.255.0←Defines range of
                                                                 pool; in this
                                                                 case, there is
                                                                 only one address
                                                                 in the pool
                        List 1 references access list 1 and defines which
                   ↓address will be translated.
ip nat inside source list 1 pool globalpool overload←Allows multiple inside
!                                    ↑Defines what    local addresses to be
                                     global address   translated to one
                                     to use           outside global address.

!
interface Ethernet0
  ip address 10.1.1.1 255.255.255.0 secondary
  ip address 10.1.1.2 255.255.255.0 secondary
  ip address 10.1.1.3 255.255.255.0 secondary→Secondary IP addresses are used
                                              as test points.
  ip address 10.1.1.4 255.255.255.0 secondary
  ip address 10.1.1.5 255.255.255.0
  ip nat inside→Defines the inside interface
!
interface Serial0
  ip address 195.1.1.4 255.255.255.0
  ip nat outside←Defines the outside interface
  !
no ip classless
ip route 152.1.1.1 255.255.255.255 Serial0
access-list 1 permit 10.1.1.2
access-list 1 permit 10.1.1.3
access-list 1 permit 10.1.1.1→Access list 1 defines which inside source
                              addresses that will be translated
access-list 1 permit 10.1.1.4
!
line con 0
line vty 0 4
  login
!
end
```

RouterB

```
Current configuration:
!
version 11.1
service udp-small-servers
service tcp-small-servers
!
hostname RouterB
!
enable password cisco
!
interface Ethernet0/0
  ip address 152.1.1.1 255.255.255.0
!
interface Serial0/0
 ip address 195.1.1.10 255.255.255.0
clock rate 500000
!
line con 0
line aux 0
line vty 0 4
 password cisco
 login
```

Monitoring and Testing the Configuration

To test the configuration, ping RouterB (195.1.1.3) using the extended ping command on RouterA. Source the packet from 10.1.1.1 and 10.1.1.2. Monitor the translation using the command **debug ip nat**.

The output from the command is shown as follows. Notice that both the inside source addresses 10.1.1.1 and 10.1.1.2 have been translated to 195.1.1.1.

```
NAT: s=10.1.1.1->195.1.1.1, d=195.1.1.3 [5]
NAT: s=10.1.1.2->195.1.1.1, d=195.1.1.3 [10]
```

Now, show the NAT table using the command **show ip nat translations**. The output from the command is shown as follows. Notice the port number after each IP address. This port number, along with the address, is used as a key to map return packets to the correct inside local IP address.

```
RouterA#show ip nat translations
Pro Inside global        Inside local        Outside local        Outside global
icmp 195.1.1.1:9         10.1.1.2:4          195.1.1.3:4          195.1.1.3:9
icmp 195.1.1.1:8         10.1.1.2:3          195.1.1.3:3          195.1.1.3:8
icmp 195.1.1.1:7         10.1.1.2:2          195.1.1.3:2          195.1.1.3:7
icmp 195.1.1.1:6         10.1.1.2:1          195.1.1.3:1          195.1.1.3:6
icmp 195.1.1.1:5         10.1.1.2:0          195.1.1.3:0          195.1.1.3:5
```

Lab #62: Translating Overlapping Addresses

Equipment Needed

The following equipment is needed to perform this lab exercise:

- Two Cisco routers with one Ethernet port and one serial port
- Cisco IOS 11.2 or higher
- One PC running a terminal emulation program
- Two PCs with Ethernet network interface cards. One PC should be running a DNS server daemon.
- Four Ethernet cables and two Ethernet hubs, plus one Cisco DTE/DCE crossover cable

Overview

Overlapping occurs when an inside local address overlaps with an address of the destination that you are trying to reach. In Figure 15–10, HostA (148.1.1.1) opens a connection to HostB by name, requesting a name-to-address lookup from the DNS server. The DNS server responds with the address of HostB (148.1.1.1). The inside local address overlaps with the outside address.

The Cisco IOS solves this problem by translating the outside global address to an outside local address.

The following steps are taken by RouterA:

1. HostA opens a connection to HostB using its name. A request is sent to the DNS server for a name-to-address resolution.

2. The DNS server responds, resolving HostB to IP address 148.1.1.1.

3. RouterA intercepts the packet and translates the global source address to a local address from the outside local address pool.

4. RouterA keeps a simple table, mapping the global address to the outside local address.

5. When HostA sends a packet to HostB, the destination IP address is the outside local address.

6. When RouterA receives a packet destined for the outside local address, the router translates the local address back to the global address.

Figure 15–10
IP address
overlapping

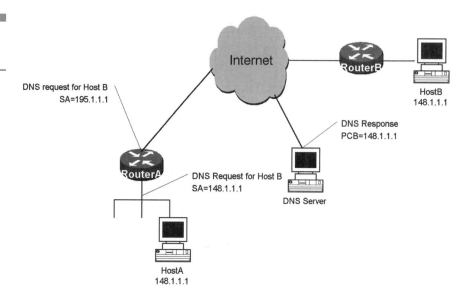

The following example shows the output from the **show ip nat translations** command on RouterA. The outside global address 148.1.1.1 is mapped to outside local address of 2.2.2.2, which is defined in the router configuration.

```
routerA#show ip nat translations

Pro  Inside global      Inside local     Outside local     Outside global
-- --        --                           2.2.2.2           148.1.1.1
tcp  195.1.1.1:1071     10.1.1.1:1071    148.1.1.1:23      148.1.1.1:23
```

Configuration Overview

This configuration demonstrates outside global address translation. RouterA monitors all DNS responses, and if the resolved address overlaps with the inside local address (10.1.1.1), RouterA translates that address to 2.2.2.2.

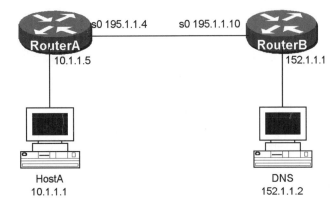

Figure 15-11
IP address
overlapping

Two Cisco routers are connected serially. RouterA is connected to RouterB via a crossover cable. RouterB acts as the DCE, providing clock for RouterA. A PC running a terminal emulation program is connected to the console port of RouterA. All IP address are as shown in figure 15-11.

HostA is configured with a default route of 10.1.1.5 and a DNS entry of 152.1.1.2. RouterA is configured for NAT and will monitor all DNS responses. If the resolved address overlaps with 10.1.1.1, it will statically translate the address of the resolved host to 2.2.2.2.

The second workstation is configured as a DNS and will resolve the name HostB to 10.1.1.1.

Router Configurations

The following configuration defines a static mapping between the outside global address of 10.1.1.1 and the outside local address of 2.2.2.2.

RouterA

```
!
version 11.2
no service udp-small-servers
no service tcp-small-servers
!
hostname routerA
!
!
ip nat pool globalpool 195.1.1.1 195.1.1.3 netmask 255.255.255.0
```

```
ip nat inside source list 1 pool globalpool overload
ip nat outside source static 10.1.1.1 2.2.2.2←Defines translation from the outside
                                                global address 10.1.1.1 to the outside
                                                local address of 2.2.2.2
!
interface Ethernet0
 ip address 10.1.1.2 255.255.255.0 secondary
 ip address 10.1.1.3 255.255.255.0 secondary
 ip address 10.1.1.4 255.255.255.0 secondary
 ip address 10.1.1.5 255.255.255.0
 ip nat inside←Defines the inside interface
 !
interface Serial0
 ip address 195.1.1.4 255.255.255.0
 ip nat outside←Defines the outside interface
 !
no ip classless
ip route 152.1.1.1 255.255.255.255 Serial0
access-list 1 permit 10.1.1.2
access-list 1 permit 10.1.1.3
access-list 1 permit 10.1.1.1
access-list 1 permit 10.1.1.4
!
line con 0
line vty 0 4
 login
!
end
```

RouterB

```
Current configuration:
!
version 11.1
service udp-small-servers
service tcp-small-servers
!
hostname RouterB
!
enable password cisco
!
interface Ethernet0/0
   ip address 152.1.1.1 255.255.255.0
!
interface Serial0/0
 ip address 195.1.1.10 255.255.255.0
clock rate 500000
!
line con 0
line aux 0
line vty 0 4
 password cisco
 login
```

The following configuration defines a dynamic mapping between a pool
of outside local addresses to a group of outside global addresses defined
by an access list.

RouterA

```
Current configuration:
!
version 11.2
no service udp-small-servers
no service tcp-small-servers
!
hostname routerA
!
!ip nat pool globalpool 195.1.1.1 195.1.1.3 netmask 255.255.255.0
                    ↓ Pool Name
ip nat pool outsidelocal 2.2.2.1 2.2.2.4 netmask 255.255.255.0
                            ↑ Pool Range
ip nat inside source list 1 pool globalpool overload

                        ↓References the outside local pool
ip nat outside source list 2 pool outsidelocal←(If the outside global source
                    ↑Specifies what          address matches access list 1
                     addresses should        change to one of the addresses
                     be changed              defined in pool outsidelocal)
!
interface Ethernet0
 ip address 10.1.1.1 255.255.255.0 secondary
 ip address 10.1.1.2 255.255.255.0 secondary
 ip address 10.1.1.3 255.255.255.0 secondary
 ip address 10.1.1.4 255.255.255.0 secondary
 ip address 10.1.1.5 255.255.255.0
 ip nat inside←Defines the inside interface
 !
interface Serial0
 ip address 195.1.1.4 255.255.255.0
 ip nat outside←Defines the outside interface
 !
no ip classless
ip route 152.1.1.1 255.255.255.255 Serial0
access-list 2 permit 10.1.1.1
access-list 2 permit 10.1.1.2←If the outside global source address matches one
                            of these changes
access-list 2 permit 10.1.1.3
access-list 2 permit 10.1.1.4
no cdp run
!
line con 0
line vty 0 4
 login
!
```

RouterB

```
Current configuration:
!
version 11.1
service udp-small-servers
service tcp-small-servers
!
hostname RouterB
!
enable password cisco
!
interface Ethernet0/0
  ip address 152.1.1.1 255.255.255.0
!
interface Serial0/0
 ip address 195.1.1.10 255.255.255.0
clock rate 500000
!
line con 0
line aux 0
line vty 0 4
 password cisco
 login
```

Monitoring and Testing the Configuration

To test the configuration, ping HostB from HostA using the domain name. Use the **debug ip nat** command and the **show ip nat translations** command to verify that the translation is working properly.

The output from the **debug ip nat** command is shown as follows. Note that the DNS response is translated to 2.2.2.2.

```
r3#deb ip nat
01:04:23: NAT: i: udp (10.1.1.1, 1082) -> (10.10.3.111, 53) [62735]
01:04:23: NAT: s=10.1.1.1->195.1.1.1, d=10.10.3.111 [62735]
01:04:23: NAT: o: udp (10.10.3.111, 53) -> (195.1.1.1, 1082) [9227]
01:04:23: NAT: DNS resource record 10.1.1.1 -> 2.2.2.2
01:04:23: NAT: s=10.10.3.111, d=195.1.1.1->10.1.1.1 [9227]
01:04:23: NAT: o: icmp (10.1.1.100, 256) -> (10.1.1.1, 256) [21]
01:04:24: NAT: o: icmp (10.1.1.100, 256) -> (10.1.1.1, 256) [22]
01:04:25: NAT: o: icmp (10.1.1.100, 256) -> (10.1.1.1, 256) [23]
01:04:26: NAT: o: icmp (10.1.1.100, 256) -> (10.1.1.1, 256) [24]
```

The output from the **show ip nat translations** command on RouterA is shown as follows. Note that the overlapping outside global address of 10.1.1.1 is translated to 2.2.2.2.

```
r3#show ip nat translations
Pro Inside global    Inside local       Outside local      Outside global
-- 195.1.1.1         10.1.1.1           --                  --
-- --                --                  2.2.2.2             10.1.1.1
```

Lab #63: Destination Address Rotary Translation

Equipment Needed

The following equipment is needed to perform this lab exercise:

- Two Cisco routers with one Ethernet port and one serial port
- Cisco IOS 11.2 or higher
- One PC running a terminal emulation program
- One Cisco DTE/DCE crossover cable

Overview

Network Address Rotary translation can be used as a means to provide load sharing among multiple, highly utilized hosts. Figure 15–12 illustrates this feature. For example, Company X has multiple FTP servers that are accessed by customers to download software. The NAT translation is transparent to the user. They simply FTP to the virtual IP address 152.1.1.10.

When RouterA receives a packet destined for the virtual IP address, the router translates the destination address to the first FTP server. When the next FTP connection is established to the virtual IP address, RouterA translates the destination address to the second FTP server. These translations occur in a round-robin fashion, providing equal load balancing across multiple FTP servers.

RouterA takes the following steps when translating a rotary address:

1. Host A (148.1.1.100) establishes a connection to virtual host 152.1.1.10.

2. RouterA receives the packet destined for the virtual host 152.1.1.10 and translates the destination address to the next "real" host from the pool (in this case, FTP server 152.1.1.1).

3. FTP server 152.1.1.1 receives the packet and responds.

Figure 15–12
Load balancing
using NAT

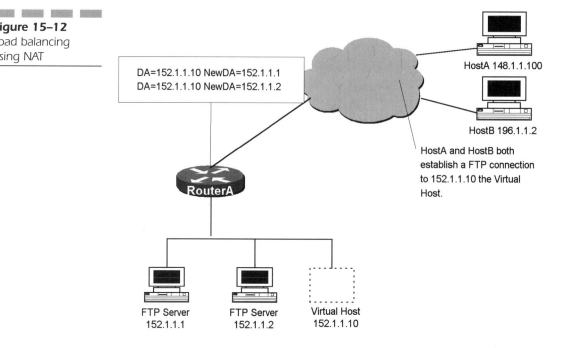

4. RouterA receives the response packet from FTP server 152.1.1.1 and performs a NAT table lookup using the inside local address and port number (and the outside address and port number as the key).

5. RouterA then translates the source address to the address of the virtual host and forwards the packet.

6. Host B (196.1.1.2) establishes a connection to virtual host 152.1.1.10.

7. RouterA receives the packet destined for virtual host 152.1.1.10 and translates the destination address to next "real" host from the pool (in this case, FTP server 152.1.1.2).

8. RouterA receives the response packet from FTP server 152.1.1.2, performs the NAT lookup, translates the source address to the virtual address, and forwards the packet.

Configuration Overview

This configuration will demonstrate load sharing using destination address rotary translation. RouterA will translate destination addresses of any packet that matches access list 2 using real host addresses from the rotary pool "loadsharing."

The pool defines the addresses of the real hosts, and the access list defines the virtual address. If a translation does not already exist, TCP packets from serial 0 (the outside interface), whose destination address matches access list 2, are translated to an address from the pool.

RouterA and RouterB are connected serially via a crossover cable. RouterB will act as the DCE, supplying clock to RouterA. The IP addresses are assigned as per Figure 15–13. Secondary IP addresses are used on RouterA as test points only.

RouterA is configured for destination address rotary translation. From RouterB, telnet to virtual host 152.1.1.10. Instead of using multiple PCs off the router's Ethernet, configure secondary IP addresses. RouterA will also be configured to enable VTY sessions—so that we can establish a Telnet session to the secondary IP address on RouterA.

Router Configuration

The configurations for the two routers in this example are as follows (key NAT configurations for RouterA are highlighted in bold):

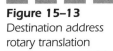

Figure 15–13
Destination address
rotary translation

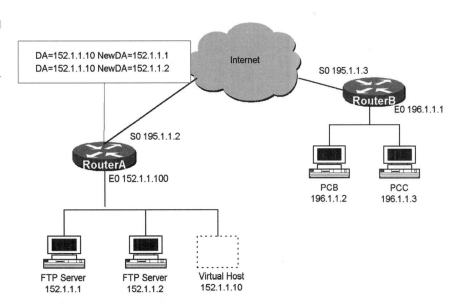

DA=152.1.1.10 NewDA=152.1.1.1
DA=152.1.1.10 NewDA=152.1.1.2

Internet

S0 195.1.1.3

RouterB

E0 196.1.1.1

S0 195.1.1.2

RouterA

E0 152.1.1.100

PCB
196.1.1.2

PCC
196.1.1.3

FTP Server
152.1.1.1

FTP Server
152.1.1.2

Virtual Host
152.1.1.10

RouterA

```
Current configuration:
!
version 11.2
no service udp-small-servers
no service tcp-small-servers
!
hostname RouterA
!
!
```
                                                                              Defines
                                                                              the pool
              ↓ Pool Name   ↓ Pool Range   ↓ as rotary
```
ip nat pool loadsharing 152.1.1.1 152.1.1.2 prefix-length 24 type rotary
ip nat inside destination list 2 pool loadsharing←If the destination address
!                                    ↑ References access      matches access list 2,
                                     list 2                   replace with an IP
                                                              address  from pool
                                                              "loadsharing."
```
```
!
interface Ethernet0
  ip address 152.1.1.1 255.255.255.0 secondary←Secondary IP address used for
                                                      test point
  ip address 152.1.1.2 255.255.255.0 secondary←Secondary IP address used for
                                                      test point
  ip address 152.1.1.100 255.255.255.0
  ip nat inside←Defines the inside interface
!
interface Serial0
  ip address 195.1.1.2 255.255.255.0
  ip nat outside←Defines the Outside interface
!
no ip classless
access-list 2 permit 152.1.1.10←Defines what destination address will be
                                     translated
!
line con 0
line vty 0 4
  password cisco←Sets the VTY password to cisco
  login←Allows telnet access into the router
!
end
```

RouterB

```
Current configuration:
!
version 11.1
service udp-small-servers
service tcp-small-servers
!
hostname RouterB
!
```

```
enable password cisco
!
!
interface Ethernet0/0
  ip address 196.1.1.1 255.255.255.0
 !
interface Serial0/0
 ip address 195.1.1.3 255.255.255.0
 clockrate 500000←Acts as DCE, providing clock
```

Monitoring and Testing the Configuration

Perform the following steps to test the configuration:

1. On RouterA, issue the command **debug ip nat**.

2. On RouterB, telnet to IP address 152.1.1.10.

The following example shows the output from the **debug ip nat** command on RouterA. The first line is the translation from destination 152.1.1.10 to the first address of the pool 152.1.1.1. The next line is the return packet from 152.1.1.1. Note that RouterA translated the source address to the virtual IP address 152.1.1.10 before forwarding the packet to RouterB.

```
NAT: s=195.1.1.3, d=152.1.1.10->152.1.1.1 [0]
NAT: s=152.1.1.1->152.1.1.10, d=195.1.1.3 [0]
```

3. On RouterB, telnet again to IP address 152.1.1.10.

The following example shows the output from the **debug ip nat** command on RouterA. Note that this time, destination address 152.1.1.10 is translated to the second address in the pool (152.1.1.2).

```
NAT: s=195.1.1.3, d=152.1.1.10->152.1.1.2 [0]
NAT: s=195.1.1.3, d=152.1.1.10->152.1.1.2 [0]
```

4. Show the NAT table on RouterA using the command **show ip nat translations**. The following example shows the output from the command. Note that after each address is the port number. This number combined with the protocol type is used as a key to translate the return packet.

```
Pro Inside global      Inside local       Outside local        Outside global
tcp 152.1.1.10:23      152.1.1.2:23       195.1.1.3:26658      195.1.1.3:26658
tcp 152.1.1.10:23      152.1.1.1:23       195.1.1.3:26146      195.1.1.3:26146
```

Change Translation Timeouts

Dynamic translation will time out after a period of inactivity. By default, simple translation not configured for overloading will time out after 24 hours. To change the default timeout period, perform the following command in global configuration mode:

```
ip nat translation timeout { seconds}←Command changes the timeout value for
                                         dynamic address translations that do not
                                         use overloading
```

When overloading is configured, Cisco IOS enables finer control over translation entry timeouts. Each entry contains more information about the traffic that is using the entry. The UDP, TCP, DNS, and finish timers can be changed with the following global configuration commands:

```
ip nat translation udp-timeout {seconds}←Changes the UDP timeout value. The
                                           default is five minutes.
ip nat translation dns-timeout {seconds}←Changes the DNS timeout value. The
                                           default is one minute.
ip nat translation tcp-timeout (seconds)←Changes the TCP timeout value (the
                                           default is 24 hours)
ip nat translation finrst-timeout (seconds)←Changes the finish and reset
                                             timeouts; the default is one minute
```

Troubleshooting NAT

The Cisco IOS provides many tools for troubleshooting NAT. A list of commands, along with a sample output from each, is shown as follows.

{show ip nat statistics} This command displays the number of active translations, along with the number of translations that have expired. An expired translation is a translation that has been inactive for a period of time and has been removed from the table. The command also shows the inside and outside configured interfaces.

```
RouterA#show ip nat statistics
Total active translations: 0 (0 static, 0 dynamic; 0 extended)
Outside interfaces: Serial0
Inside interfaces: Ethernet0
Hits: 20  Misses: 20
Expired translations: 20
Dynamic mappings:
-- Inside Source
access-list 1 pool pool refcount 0
```

```
pool pool: netmask 255.255.255.0
        start 195.1.1.1 end 195.1.1.1
        type generic, total addresses 1, allocated 0 (0%), misses 0
```

{**show ip nat translations**}   This command displays all active translations: the translated protocol of the packet, the inside local address, the inside global address, the outside local address, and the outside global address.

From the following output, we can see that a ping packet (protocol icmp) with the inside local address of 10.1.1.1 has been translated to the inside global address of 195.1.1.1. The number after the IP address is the port number, which is used in this particular translation because the router is configured for overloading.

```
RouterA#show ip nat translations
Pro  Inside global      Inside local      Outside local      Outside global
icmp 195.1.1.1:4        10.1.1.1:4        195.1.1.3:4        195.1.1.3:4
icmp 195.1.1.1:3        10.1.1.1:3        195.1.1.3:3        195.1.1.3:3
icmp 195.1.1.1:2        10.1.1.1:2        195.1.1.3:2        195.1.1.3:2
icmp 195.1.1.1:1        10.1.1.1:1        195.1.1.3:1        195.1.1.3:1
icmp 195.1.1.1:0        10.1.1.1:0        195.1.1.3:0        195.1.1.3:0
```

{**show ip nat translations verbose**}   This command is an extension of the previous command and displays more detailed information about how long ago the translation was created and how long ago the translation was last used.

From the following output, we can see that the translation was created one minute and 31 seconds ago and was last used 31 seconds ago.

```
RouterA#show ip nat translations verbose
Pro  Inside global    Inside local    Outside local    Outside global
icmp 195.1.1.1:4      10.1.1.1:4      195.1.1.3:4      195.1.1.3:4
    create 00:01:31, use 00:00:31, left 00:00:28, flags: extended
icmp 195.1.1.1:3      10.1.1.1:3      195.1.1.3:3      195.1.1.3:3
    create 00:00:31, use 00:00:31, left 00:00:28, flags: extended
```

{**clear ip nat translation**}   This command is used to clear all (or specific) active translations. The following list shows some extensions that can be used with this command.

*   The asterisk clears all dynamic translations.

Inside   Clears specific inside address and port translations

Outside   Clears specific outside address and port translations

TCP   Clears specific inside address by protocol

UDP   Clears specific inside address by protocol

{clear ip nat statistics}   This command is used to clear the counters for all NAT statistics.

{debug ip nat}   This command is used to verify the operation of the NAT feature by displaying information about every packet that is translated by the router. The command will also display information about certain errors or exceptional conditions, such as the failure to allocate a global address.

From the following output of the command, we can see that the source address 10.1.1.1 has been translated to the global address 195.1.1.1.

```
NAT: s=10.1.1.1->195.1.1.1, d=195.1.1.3 [35]
```

Conclusion

This chapter explores *Network Address Translation* (NAT). NAT enables the addresses inside one stub domain to be reused by any other stub domain. NAT also enables organizations to appear as if they are using different IP address space than what is actually being used—thereby reducing the need for unique, registered IP addresses. NAT can also save private network administrators from having to renumber hosts and routers that do not conform to global IP addressing. NAT is defined in RFC 1631.

16

Hot Standby Router Protocol (HSRP)

Topics Covered in This Chapter

- Detailed HSRP Overview
- Basic HSRP Configuration (One HSRP Group)
- Basic HSRP Configuration Using the Track Option
- Multi-group HSRP Configuration
- Detailed Troubleshooting Examples

Introduction

This chapter will explore the configuration and troubleshooting of Cisco's *Hot Standby Router Protocol* (HSRP). HSRP provides high network availability by protecting against a single router failure. Without HSRP, the failure of a single default gateway router could isolate all hosts.

Overview

The majority of today's TCP/IP LAN networks rely on the use of a default gateway (which is statically configured in the host) in order to route packets to hosts on other networks. The default gateway is usually a router connected to the Internet or a company's intranet. Each host on the LAN is configured to forward packets to this destination if the host it is trying to reach is not on the same network. This process provides for a single point of failure on the network. If the gateway is down, all the hosts on the LAN are isolated from the rest of the network. To combat this problem, many companies install redundant gateways. The problem with this method is that the user host is pointed at one gateway. If this router should fail, then the user must change his or her statically configured default gateway.

HSRP resolves this problem by enabling the network administrator to configure a set of routers to work together, to present the appearance of a single default gateway. The routers in an HSRP group share a virtual Mac address and IP address. This address is used by hosts on the LAN as the default gateway. The HSRP protocol selects which router is active, and the active router receives and routes packets that are destined for the group's Mac address.

HSRP uses multicast, UDP-based hello packets to communicate with other routers that are part of the same HSRP group. Each router in the group watches for hello packets from the active and standby routers. If the active router becomes unavailable, the standby will assume the active role and route the packets for the network.

Commands Discussed in This Chapter

- **debug standby**
- **show standby**
- **standby** [*group-number*] **ip** [*ip-address* [**secondary**]]
- **standby** [*group-number*] **priority** *priority-number*

■ **standby** [*group-number*] **timers** *hellotime holdtime* **standby** [*group-number*] **preempt**

■ **standby** [*group-number*] **track** *type number* [interface-priority]

Definitions

standby ip: Used to activate HSRP

standby priority: Used to set the HSRP priority on an interface. The HSRP member with the highest standby priority (assuming preemption is enabled) becomes the active router.

standby timers: Used to configure the time between hello packets (hello time) and the amount of time after not hearing a hello packet from a HSRP neighbor that the router declares the neighbor down (holdtime).

standby preempt: Indicates that when the local router's standby priority is higher than the current active router, the local router should attempt to assume control as the active router.

standby track: Used to configure an interface to change its HSRP priority, based on the availability of another interface

IOS Requirements

The HSRP feature set was first introduced in IOS 10.0.

LAB #64: Basic HSRP Configuration (One HSRP Group)

Equipment Needed

The following equipment is needed to perform this lab exercise:

■ Two Cisco Routers

■ Cisco IOS 10.0 or higher

■ A PC with an Ethernet NIC running a TCP/IP protocol stack

■ One Ethernet hub

■ Ethernet cables

Figure 16–1
One HSRP group

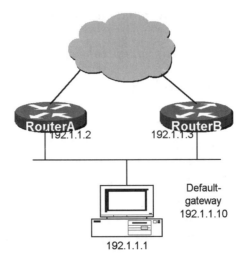

Default-
gateway
192.1.1.10

192.1.1.1

Figure 16–1 shows a basic HSRP design, where RouterA and RouterB are in one HSRP group. The hosts on the LAN use the default gateway of 192.1.1.10, which is a virtual IP address.

The object of this configuration is to enable HSRP on both routers. If the active router fails, the standby router should take over and route for the 192.1.1.X network. No reconfiguration is needed on the hosts.

Router Configuration

The following example shows the configurations for RouterA and RouterB (key HSRP commands are highlighted in bold):

RouterA

```
!
version 11.2
no service udp-small-servers
no service tcp-small-servers
!
hostname RouterA
!
!
interface Ethernet0
 ip address 192.1.1.2 255.255.255.0
 no ip redirects
 standby priority 200
 standby preempt
 standby ip 192.1.1.10
```

```
!
interface Serial0
 no ip address
 shutdown
 no fair-queue
!
no ip classless
!
line con 0
line 1 16
line aux 0
line vty 0 4
!
end
```

RouterB

```
Current configuration:
!
version 11.1
service udp-small-servers
service tcp-small-servers
!
hostname RouterB
!
!
interface Ethernet0
 ip address 192.1.1.3 255.255.255.0
 no ip redirects
 standby priority 150
 standby preempt
 standby ip 192.1.1.10
!
interface Serial0
 no ip address
 shutdown
!
no ip classless
!
line con 0
line aux 0
line vty 0 4
 login
!
end
```

Monitoring and Testing the Configuration

In this configuration, RouterA is the active router—because the priority is set to 200. If the standby router does not receive a hello packet from the active router in 10 seconds (which is the default holdtime), the standby router becomes active. To test this configuration, remove the Ethernet cable from RouterA. The following example shows the output from the command **debug standby** on RouterB. Notice that the last incoming hello message was received from RouterA at 00:31:52. Ten seconds after this transmission, at 00:32:02, RouterB becomes the active router.

```
00:31:52: SB0:Ethernet0 Hello in 192.1.1.2 Active pri 200 hel 3 hol 10 ip 192.1.1.10
00:31:52: SB0:Ethernet0 Hello out 192.1.1.3 Standby pri 150 hel 3 hol 10 ip 192.1.1.10
00:31:55: SB0:Ethernet0 Hello out 192.1.1.3 Standby pri 150 hel 3 hol 10 ip 192.1.1.10
00:31:58: SB0:Ethernet0 Hello out 192.1.1.3 Standby pri 150 hel 3 hol 10 ip 192.1.1.10
00:32:01: SB0:Ethernet0 Hello out 192.1.1.3 Standby pri 150 hel 3 hol 10 ip 192.1.1.10
00:32:02: SB0: Ethernet0 state Standby -> Active
00:32:02: SB: Ethernet0 changing MAC address to 0000.0c07.ac00
```

Basic HSRP Configuration Using the Track Option

The Track option under HSRP enables the router to track other interfaces, so if one of the other interfaces goes down, the device's Hot Standby priority is lowered. When the priority is lowered below that of the router in Standby, the Standby router becomes active. This event is critical if the primary router loses its connection to the Internet or the company's intranet. Without tracking, the primary router would still receive packets from the hosts on the LAN—although the router does not have a route to the outside world. If the two routers are running an IGP, the primary router will route the packets via the secondary router. No ICMP redirects will occur, however. If not, the packets will be dropped.

Figure 16–2 shows a basic HSRP design, where RouterA and RouterB are in one HSRP group. RouterA is monitoring the status of its serial interface with the use of the Track command. When the interface goes down, RouterA lowers its priority, and RouterB becomes the active router.

Router Configuration

The following example shows the configuration that RouterA uses to track the serial interfaces in case of failure.

Figure 16–2
Basic HSRP

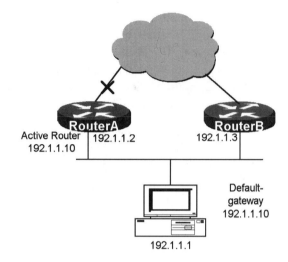

RouterA

```
Current configuration:
!
version 11.2
no service udp-small-servers
no service tcp-small-servers
!
hostname RouterA
!
interface Ethernet0
 ip address 192.1.1.2 255.255.255.0
 no ip redirects
 standby priority 200
 standby preempt
 standby ip 192.1.1.10
 standby track Serial0 51
!
interface Serial0
 ip address 172.1.1.1 255.255.255.252
 no fair-queue
!
no ip classless
!
line con 0
line 1 16
line aux 0
line vty 0 4
 login
!
end
```

The **standby track serial 0 51** decreases the priority of RouterA by 51 if the serial interface should go down. Remember from the previous configuration that the priority of RouterA was set 50 points higher than RouterB. The following debug output (**debug standby**) shows what will happen when the serial 0 on RouterA fails.

At time 00:15:50, the serial interface on RouterA goes down. At time 00:15:52, RouterA decreases the HSRP priority by 50 points, making the priority 149, and RouterA resigns as the active speaker.

```
 SB0:Ethernet0 Hello out 192.1.1.2 Active pri 200 hel 3 hol 10 ip 192.1.1.10
00:15:48: SB0:Ethernet0 Hello in 192.1.1.3 Standby pri 150 hel 3 hol 10 ip 192.1.1.10
%LINEPROTO-5-UPDOWN: Line protocol on Interface Serial0, changed state to down
00:15:51: SB0:Ethernet0 Hello out 192.1.1.2 Active pri 200 hel 3 hol 10 ip 192.1.1.10
00:15:51: SB0:Ethernet0 Hello in 192.1.1.3 Standby pri 150 hel 3 hol 10 ip 192.1.1.10
%LINK-3-UPDOWN: Interface Serial0, changed state to down
00:15:52: SB0: Ethernet0 Now 0/1 tracked interfaces up
00:15:52: SB0: Ethernet0 Priority was 200 now 149, configured as 200
00:15:52: SB0:Ethernet0 Hello out 192.1.1.2 Active pri 149 hel 3 hol 10 ip 192.1.1.10
00:15:52: SB0:Ethernet0 Coup in 192.1.1.3 Standby pri 150 hel 3 hol 10 ip 192.1.1.10
00:15:52: SB0: Ethernet0 state Active -> Speak
00:15:52: SB0:Ethernet0 Resign out 192.1.1.2 Speak pri 149 hel 3 hol 10 ip 192.1.1.10
```

LAB #65: Multi-Group HSRP Configuration

Equipment Needed

The following equipment is needed to perform this lab exercise:

- Two Cisco routers
- Cisco IOS 10.0 or higher
- Two PCs with Ethernet NICs running a TCP/IP protocol stack
- One Ethernet hub
- Ethernet cables

Overview

The router can be in multiple HSRP groups at one time. This feature enables the LAN administrator to load-balance across all of the routers, while still providing redundancies in case of a failure. In Figure 16–3, each PC on the LAN uses a different default gateway. HostA uses default gateway 192.1.1.10, which is the Virtual IP address of HSRP group 1. HostB uses 192.1.1.11, which is the Virtual IP address of HSRP group 2.

Figure 16–3
Multiple HSRP groups

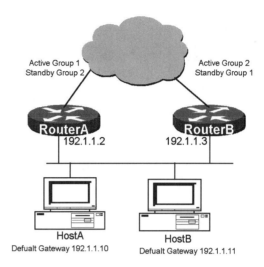

When there are no failures, the traffic on the LAN is split equally between both routers. When a failure occurs, however, the standby router becomes active for that group, and all traffic is routed to that interface.

Figure 16–3 shows two routers each in two standby groups, RouterA is active for group one and standby for group 2, RouterB is active for group two and standby for group one.

Router Configuration

The following are the configurations for RouterA and RouterB (key HSRP commands are highlighted in bold):

RouterA

```
Current configuration:
!
version 11.2
no service udp-small-servers
no service tcp-small-servers
!
hostname RouterA
!
!
interface Ethernet0
 ip address 192.1.1.2 255.255.255.0
 no ip redirects
```

```
 standby preempt
 standby 1 priority 200
 standby 1 ip 192.1.1.10
 standby 2 priority 150
 standby 2 ip 192.1.1.11
!
interface Serial0
 no ip address
 shutdown
 no fair-queue
!
no ip classless
!
line con 0
line 1 16
line aux 0
line vty 0 4
!
end
```

RouterB

```
Current configuration:
!
version 11.1
service udp-small-servers
service tcp-small-servers
!
hostname RouterB
!
interface Ethernet0
 ip address 192.1.1.3 255.255.255.0
 no ip redirects
   standby preempt
   standby 1 priority 150
 standby 1 ip 192.1.1.10
 standby 2 priority 200
 standby 2 ip 192.1.1.11

!
interface Serial0
 no ip address
 shutdown
!
no ip classless
!
line con 0
line aux 0
line vty 0 4
 login
!
end
```

Monitoring and Testing the Configuration

The following example shows the output from the **show standby** command on RouterA. Notice that RouterA's state is active for group 1 and is standby for group 2.

```
RouterA#sho standby
Ethernet0/0 - Group 1
  Local state is Active, priority 200
  Hellotime 3 holdtime 10
  Next hello sent in 00:00:02.496
  Hot standby IP address is 192.1.1.10 configured
  Active router is local
  Standby router is 192.1.1.3 expires in 00:00:08
Ethernet0/0 - Group 2
  Local state is Standby, priority 150
  Hellotime 3 holdtime 10
  Next hello sent in 00:00:02.496
  Hot standby IP address is 192.1.1.11 configured
  Active router is 192.1.1.3 expires in 00:00:07
  Standby router is local
```

Troubleshooting HSRP

HSRP has only one debug command: **debug standby**. The output of this command, however, will tell you a lot.

{debug standby} From the Cisco command line, enter the **debug standby** command. The following example is a sample output from this command. The debug shows the source of the hello packet, whether the packet was received or sent, and on what interface the packet was sent. The debug also shows the active and standby routers, as well as priority, hello, and hold timers.

From this debug message, you can tell that RouterA is the active router with a priority of 200 and that RouterB is the standby router with a priority of 150.

```
RouterA#debug standby
Hot standby protocol debugging is on
SB0:Ethernet1/0 Hello out 192.1.1.2 Active pri 200 hel 3 hol 10 ip 192.1.1.10
SB0:Ethernet1/0 Hello in 192.1.1.3 Standby pri 150 hel 3 hol 10 ip 192.1.1.10
```

{show standby} From the Cisco command line, enter the **show standby** command. The following example is a sample output from this command. The command shows the local state of the router, whether the router is active or standby, the router's priority, and whether or not the router can preempt. The command also shows the hello, holdtime, standby ip address, and the address of the standby router.

```
RouterA#sho standby
Ethernet1/0 - Group 0
  Local state is Active, priority 200, may preempt
  Hellotime 3 holdtime 10
  Next hello sent in 00:00:01
  Hot standby IP address is 192.1.1.10 configured
  Active router is local
  Standby router is 192.1.1.3 expires in 00:00:09
```

Conclusion

HSRP provides high network availability and is useful for hosts that do not support routing protocols and cannot automatically switch to a new default gateway (router) if the primary router fails.

17

Network Time Protocol (NTP)

Topics Covered in This Chapter

- NTP technology overview
- Configuring a Cisco router as an NTP time server
- Configuring NTP peers
- Cisco NTP authentication
- Configuring Cisco NTP for LAN broadcasts

Introduction

Network Time Protocol (NTP) is a TCP/IP protocol designed to distribute accurate time throughout a network. NTP uses UDP as its transport mechanism. This chapter will explore the NTP capabilities available through the Cisco IOS.

NTP Overview

Every Cisco router has a system clock that can store the current date and time. NTP addresses the problem of how to synchronize all routers in a network to a common clock source. In addition to synchronizing all routers, NTP can be used to synchronize all system clocks in a given network. This feature applies to all workstations, as well as any other systems that have a system clock. NTP client software is available for a wide variety of workstations and servers. There are several reasons why it is important that all routers in a network share a common time:

- Debug and event timestamps—Debug and event timestamps collected from several different routers are meaningless, unless they are all referenced to a common time.
- Transaction processing—These types of transactions need to be accurately timestamped.
- Simulation—Complex transactions are often divided between multiple systems. Common clocks are needed between these multiple systems to ensure a proper sequence of events.
- System maintenance—Performing a function such as reloading all routers in a network at the same time requires a common clock across the entire network.

NTP will usually be able to synchronize all system clocks within 10 milliseconds of each other over a WAN.

How Does NTP Work?

This section will give a high-level, simplified overview of how NTP works. NTP is fully described in RFC 1305.

NTP addresses the basic problem shown in Figure 17–1. Two routers, RouterA and RouterB, are connected via a serial link. Both RouterA and

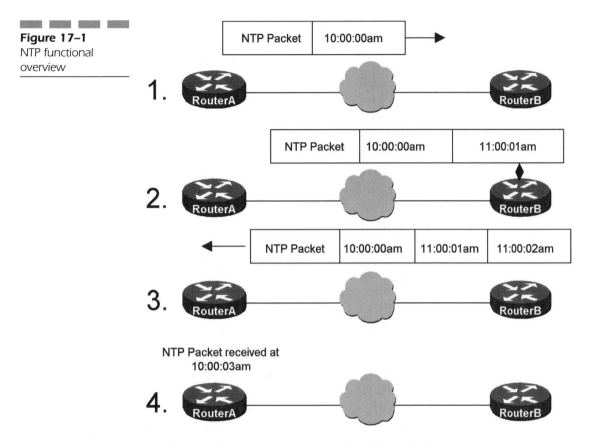

Figure 17-1
NTP functional
overview

RouterB have independent system clocks. How can we devise a protocol
to automatically synchronize the system clocks of both routers?
Let's assume the following:

■ Before RouterA and RouterB synchronize their system clocks,
RouterA's clock is set for 10 a.m.—and RouterB's clock is set for 11
a.m.

■ RouterB will be our time server, meaning that RouterA will set its
clock to match the clock of RouterB.

■ The delay in getting a packet from RouterA to RouterB is one
second in each direction.

■ The delay in getting a packet through RouterB is also one second.
Clock synchronization occurs in the following way:

1. RouterA sends an NTP packet to RouterB, which has a timestamp corresponding to the time the packet left RouterA. This timestamp will be 10:00:00 a.m.

2. RouterB provides a timestamp when the packet arrives. This timestamp will be 11:00:01 a.m.

3. RouterB provides another timestamp when the packet leaves for RouterA. This timestamp will be 11:00:02 a.m.

4. When the response packet is received at RouterA, RouterA provides another timestamp. This timestamp will be 10:00:03 a.m.

RouterA now has enough information to calculate two important items:

■ The round-trip delay of the packet exchange

■ The difference in clocks between RouterA and RouterB

RouterA will now be able to set its clock to agree with RouterB's clock. One should keep in mind that this example is just a high-level overview of how NTP works. As outlined in RFC 1305, NTP uses complex algorithms to ensure clock accuracy.

NTP Implementation

In a real-world application, you would usually not use a router as an NTP server. The accuracy of the clock on a router is far lower than can be achieved using commercial time products. One such product is the DATUM Tymserve 2000 Network Time Server. This device is a combination of a GPS receiver and an NTP server. The product receives Stratum 1 clocking signals from the GPS network. The Tymserve is connected to an Ethernet LAN, where the device can respond to NTP requests from peers and clients.

The low cost of these types of devices can also allow for distributed clocking systems (where a Tymeserve 2000 is located locally, for example, such as on a college campus)—eliminating the need for clock synchronization over the wide area.

Commands Discussed in This Chapter

■ **ntp access-group {query-only | serve-only | serve | peer }** *access-list number*

■ **ntp authenticate**

- **ntp authentication-key** *number* **md5** *value*
- **ntp broadcast** [**version** *number*]
- **ntp broadcast client**
- **ntp broadcast delay** *microseconds*
- **ntp clock period** *value*
- **ntp disable**
- **ntp master** [*stratum*]
- **ntp peer** *ip-address* [**version** *number*] [**key** *keyid*] [**source** *interface*] [**prefer**]
- **ntp server** *ip-address* [**version** *number*] [**key** *keyid*] [**source** *interface*] [**prefer**]
- **ntp source** *type number*
- **ntp trusted-key** *key-number*
- **ntp update-calendar**
- **show ntp status**
- **show ntp association**
- **show ntp association detail**

Definitions

ntp access-group: This global command is used to control access to the router's NTP services.

ntp authenticate: Use this global command to enable NTP authentication.

ntp authentication-key: This global command defines an authentication key for use with NTP.

ntp broadcast: This interface command is used to specify that a specific interface should send NTP broadcast packets.

ntp broadcast client: This interface command enables the router to receive NTP broadcast packets on the specified interface.

ntp broadcast delay: This global command is used to set the estimated round-trip delay between the router and the NTP server.

ntp clock-period: THIS GLOBAL COMMAND SHOULD NOT BE ENTERED. THE ROUTER WILL AUTOMATICALLY GENERATE THIS COMMAND WHEN NTP SYNCHRONIZES THE SYSTEM.

ntp disable: This interface command Prevents the specified interface from receiving NTP packets.

ntp master: This global command is used to configure the router as an NTP clock master. This command should only be used when an external NTP source is not available (or for test purposes).

ntp peer: This global command causes the router's system clock to synchronize to a peer (or to synchronize a peer).

ntp server: This global command causes the router's system clock to be synchronized by a time server.

ntp source: This global command will force the router to use a particular source address in its NTP packets.

ntp trusted-key: This global command is used to authenticate the router to a specific authentication key.

ntp update-calendar: This global command causes NTP to periodically update the calendar on a Cisco 7XXX series router.

show ntp status: This exec command is used to display NTP information for the router. This command can show whether the router is synchronized to an NTP peer or to an NTP server.

show ntp association [detail]: This exec command displays NTP information, such as polling cycles.

IOS Requirements

The labs in this chapter were done using IOS Version 11.2. Most of the NTP functionality that is discussed in this chapter can be tested using IOS 10.0 and later. The reader should check the Cisco Web site bug reports for their particular IOS. Some IOS versions have NTP functionality issues.

Lab #66: Cisco NTP Using Time Servers

Equipment Needed

The following equipment is needed to perform this lab exercise:

- Three Cisco routers, one having two serial ports
- Cisco IOS 10.0 or higher
- A PC running a terminal emulation program
- Two Cisco DTE/DCE crossover cables. If no crossover cables are available, you can make a crossover cable by connecting a standard Cisco DTE cable to a standard Cisco DCE cable.

Configuration Overview

This configuration will demonstrate two Cisco routers synchronizing their time clocks to a Cisco router acting as an NTP time server. Three Cisco routers are connected serially. RouterA is connected to RouterB via a crossover cable. RouterB is connected to RouterC via a crossover cable.

RouterB acts as a DCE, supplying clock to both RouterA and RouterC. IP addresses are assigned as per the following diagram (see Figure 17–2). A PC running a terminal emulation program is connected to the console port of RouterA.

RouterA is configured as the NTP clock master. Both RouterB and RouterC are configured to synchronize to RouterA via the NTP server statement.

NOTES: *NTP convergence can take up to half an hour, which means that when changing the system clock on the NTP master, it can take up to half an hour for all other clocks in the configuration to synchronize. This situation is caused by NTP viewing a clock change as an instability in the clocking system. NTP waits for a stable system before synchronizing and propagating any changes.*

A Cisco router will not have a valid date and time set when it is powered on. After power on, the clock is set to March 1, 1993. The clock must be given a valid setting before NTP takes effect. The clock can be set via the clock set command, whose syntax is as follows:

```
clock set hh:mm:ss day month year
```

Figure 17–2
NTP time server lab

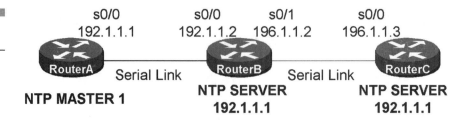

Router Configuration

The configurations for the three routers in this example are as follows (key NTP commands are highlighted in bold):

RouterA

```
Current configuration:
!
version 11.2
no service udp-small-servers
no service tcp-small-servers
!
hostname RouterA
!
enable password cisco
!
no ip domain-lookup
!
interface Ethernet0/0
 ip address 10.10.3.100 255.255.255.0
!
interface Serial0/0
 ip address 192.1.1.1 255.255.255.0
 encapsulation ppp
!
router rip
 network 10.0.0.0
 network 192.1.1.0
!
ip classless
!
line con 0
 exec-timeout 120 0
 password cisco
 login
line aux 0
 password cisco
 login
```

```
line vty 0 4
 exec-timeout 120 0
 password cisco
 login
!
ntp master 1
end
```

RouterB

```
Current configuration:
!
version 11.2
no service udp-small-servers
no service tcp-small-servers
!
hostname RouterB
!
enable password cisco
!
no ip domain-lookup
!
interface Serial0/0
 ip address 192.1.1.2 255.255.255.0
 encapsulation ppp
 clockrate 500000
!
interface Serial0/1
 ip address 196.1.1.2 255.255.255.0
 encapsulation ppp
 clockrate 19200
!
router rip
 network 192.1.1.0
 network 196.1.1.0
!
ip classless
!
line con 0
 password cisco
 login
line aux 0
 password cisco
 login
line vty 0 4
 exec-timeout 120 0
 password cisco
 login
!
ntp clock-period 17179866
ntp server 192.1.1.1
end
```

RouterC

```
Current configuration:
!
version 11.2
no service udp-small-servers
no service tcp-small-servers
!
hostname RouterC
!
!
no ip domain-lookup
!
interface Serial0/0
 ip address 196.1.1.3 255.255.255.0
 encapsulation ppp
!
router rip
 network 196.1.1.0
!
no ip classless
!
line con 0
 password cisco
 login
line aux 0
 password cisco
 login
line vty 0 4
 exec-timeout 30 0
 password cisco
 login
!
ntp clock-period 17179864
ntp server 192.1.1.1
end
```

Monitoring the Configuration

After RouterA has converged and stabilized its new clock time, the router will start to propagate its clock settings. The **show ntp status** command can be used to monitor the synchronization state of each router.

The **show ntp status** output from RouterA shows that the router is synchronized. Notice that the reference is listed as being local, because this router is configured as a clock master. Because we had the command **ntp master 1** on RouterA, the router declares itself as a stratum 1 source.

```
RouterA#sh ntp status
Clock is synchronized, stratum 1, reference is .LOCL.
nominal freq is 250.0000 Hz, actual freq is 250.0000 Hz, precision is 2**24
reference time is BA879B74.9051655D (11:28:52.563 UTC Wed Mar 3 1999)
clock offset is 0.0000 msec, root delay is 0.00 msec
root dispersion is 0.02 msec, peer dispersion is 0.02 msec
RouterA#
```

The **show ntp status** output from RouterB and RouterC is identical. Notice that both routers are in a synchronized state. Each router is reported to be operating at stratum 2. This information is correct, because they are synchronized to a stratum 1 source. Finally, notice that the clock reference is listed as being 192.1.1.1. This address is the interface address of RouterA, our NTP master.

```
RouterB#sh ntp status
Clock is synchronized, stratum 2, reference is 192.1.1.1
nominal freq is 250.0000 Hz, actual freq is 250.0000 Hz, precision is 2**24
reference time is BA879BA3.91C82791 (11:29:39.569 UTC Wed Mar 3 1999)
clock offset is -2.0598 msec, root delay is 1.97 msec
root dispersion is 3.02 msec, peer dispersion is 0.93 msec

RouterC#sh ntp status
Clock is synchronized, stratum 2, reference is 192.1.1.1
nominal freq is 250.0000 Hz, actual freq is 250.0000 Hz, precision is 2**24
reference time is BA879B9C.90A0FB53 (11:29:32.564 UTC Wed Mar 3 1999)
clock offset is -0.7317 msec, root delay is 74.55 msec
root dispersion is 2.52 msec, peer dispersion is 1.75 msec
```

Another useful command is the **show ntp associations** command. The output for this command is shown as follows for each of the three routers. This command shows how often the router sends/receives NTP updates. The command also shows when the last update was received. RouterB, for example, last received an NTP update 14 seconds ago.

```
RouterA#sh ntp associations

      address    ref clock    st    when    poll    reach    delay   offset    disp
*~127.127.7.1    .LOCL         0      43      64      377     0.0     0.00      0.0
 * master (synced), # master (unsynced), + selected, - candidate, ~ configured


RouterB#sh ntp associations

      address    ref clock    st    when    poll    reach    delay   offset    disp
*~192.1.1.1      LOCL          1      14      64      377     2.0     -2.06     0.9
 * master (synced), # master (unsynced), + selected, - candidate, ~ configured
```

```
RouterC#sh ntp assoc

      address    ref clock   st    when    poll   reach   delay   offset   disp
*~192.1.1.1       LOCL        1     39      64     377     74.6    -0.73    1.8
 * master (synced), # master (unsynced), + selected, - candidate, ~ configured
```

Lab #67: Cisco NTP Using Time Servers and Peers

Equipment Needed

The following equipment is needed to perform this lab exercise:

- Three Cisco routers, one having two serial ports
- Cisco IOS 10.0 or higher
- A PC running a terminal emulation program
- Two Cisco DTE/DCE crossover cables. If no crossover cables are available, you can make a crossover cable by connecting a standard Cisco DTE cable to a standard Cisco DCE cable.

Configuration Overview

This configuration will demonstrate one Cisco router synchronizing its time clock to a Cisco router NTP time server. A second Cisco router will synchronize its clock to the Cisco NTP server as a peer connection. Three Cisco routers are connected serially. RouterA is connected to RouterB via a crossover cable. RouterB is connected to RouterC via a crossover cable. RouterB acts as a DCE, supplying clock to both RouterA and RouterC. IP addresses are assigned as per the following diagram (see Figure 17–3). A PC running a terminal emulation program is connected to the console port of RouterA.

RouterA is configured as the NTP clock master. RouterB is configured to synchronize to RouterA via the NTP server statement. RouterC is configured to synchronize to RouterB as a peer. Because RouterB is already synchronized to RouterA, RouterC will always synchronize to RouterB.

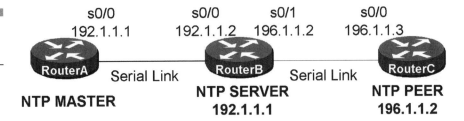

Figure 17–3
NTP server and
peer lab

>
>
> ***NOTES:*** *NTP convergence can take up to half an hour, which means*
> *that when changing the system clock on the NTP master, it can take up*
> *to half an hour for all other clocks in the configuration to synchronize.*
> *This situation is caused by NTP viewing a clock change as an instability*
> *in the clocking system. NTP waits for a stable system before*
> *synchronizing and propagating any changes.*

>
>
> *A Cisco router will not have a valid date and time set when it is powered*
> *on. After power on, the clock is set to March 1, 1993. The clock must be*
> *given a valid setting before NTP takes effect. The clock can be set via the*
> *clock set command, whose syntax is as follows:*

```
clock set hh:mm:ss day month year
```

Router Configuration

The configurations for the three routers in this example are as follows
(key NTP commands are highlighted in bold):

RouterA

```
Current configuration:
!
version 11.2
no service udp-small-servers
no service tcp-small-servers
!
hostname RouterA
!
enable password cisco
!
no ip domain-lookup
!
interface Ethernet0/0
 ip address 10.10.3.100 255.255.255.0
!
```

```
interface Serial0/0
 ip address 192.1.1.1 255.255.255.0
 encapsulation ppp
!
router rip
 network 10.0.0.0
 network 192.1.1.0
!
ip classless
!
line con 0
 exec-timeout 120 0
 password cisco
 login
line aux 0
 password cisco
 login
line vty 0 4
 exec-timeout 120 0
 password cisco
 login
!
ntp master 1
end
```

RouterB

```
Current configuration:
!
version 11.2
no service udp-small-servers
no service tcp-small-servers
!
hostname RouterB
!
enable password cisco
!
no ip domain-lookup
!
interface Serial0/0
 ip address 192.1.1.2 255.255.255.0
 encapsulation ppp
 clockrate 500000
!
interface Serial0/1
 ip address 196.1.1.2 255.255.255.0
 encapsulation ppp
 clockrate 19200
!
router rip
 network 192.1.1.0
 network 196.1.1.0
!
```

```
ip classless
!
line con 0
 password cisco
 login
line aux 0
 password cisco
 login
line vty 0 4
 exec-timeout 120 0
 password cisco
 login
!
ntp clock-period 17179854
ntp server 192.1.1.1
end
```

RouterC

```
Current configuration:
!
version 11.2
no service udp-small-servers
no service tcp-small-servers
!
hostname RouterC
!
!
no ip domain-lookup
!
interface Serial0/0
 ip address 196.1.1.3 255.255.255.0
 encapsulation ppp
!
router rip
 network 196.1.1.0
!
no ip classless
!
line con 0
 password cisco
 login
line aux 0
 password cisco
 login
line vty 0 4
 exec-timeout 30 0
 password cisco
 login
!
ntp clock-period 17179866
ntp peer 196.1.1.2
end
```

Monitoring the Configuration

After RouterA has converged and stabilized its new clock time, the router will start to propagate its clock settings. The **show ntp status** command can be used to monitor the synchronization state of each router.

The **show ntp status** output from RouterA shows that the router is synchronized. Notice that the reference is listed as being local, because this router is configured as a clock master. Because we had the command **ntp master 1** on RouterA, the router declares itself as a stratum 1 source.

```
RouterA#sh  ntp status
Clock is synchronized, stratum 1, reference is .LOCL.
nominal freq is 250.0000 Hz, actual freq is 250.0000 Hz, precision is 2**24
reference time is BA879FB4.904CEDDC (11:47:00.563 UTC Wed Mar 3 1999)
clock offset is 0.0000 msec, root delay is 0.00 msec
root dispersion is 0.02 msec, peer dispersion is 0.02 msec
```

Notice that the **show ntp status** output from RouterB and RouterC are not identical. RouterB is synchronized to RouterA. RouterB is listed as being a stratum 2 source. Its reference is 192.1.1.1 (RouterA). RouterC is listed as a stratum 3 source because of RouterC synchronizing to RouterB. Notice that RouterC is using RouterB as its reference (196.1.1.2).

```
RouterB#sh ntp status
Clock is synchronized, stratum 2, reference is 192.1.1.1
nominal freq is 250.0000 Hz, actual freq is 250.0002 Hz, precision is 2**24
reference time is BA879FA0.8FD33F2F (11:46:40.561 UTC Wed Mar 3 1999)
clock offset is -2.7416 msec, root delay is 1.94 msec
root dispersion is 4.50 msec, peer dispersion is 1.72 msec


RouterC#sh ntp status
Clock is synchronized, stratum 3, reference is 196.1.1.2
nominal freq is 250.0000 Hz, actual freq is 250.0000 Hz, precision is 2**24
reference time is BA879FE4.8DF8FEFE (11:47:48.554 UTC Wed Mar 3 1999)
clock offset is -0.8742 msec, root delay is 70.74 msec
root dispersion is 4.84 msec, peer dispersion is 0.31 msec
```

Let's take a look at the **show ntp associations** command as shown in the following screen prints. This command shows how often the router sends/receives NTP updates and shows when the last update was received. RouterC, for example, last received an NTP update 10 seconds ago.

```
RouterA#sh ntp associations

        address   ref clock   st    when    poll   reach   delay   offset    disp
*~127.127.7.1     LOCL       0      25      64     377     0.0     0.00      0.0
  * master (synced), # master (unsynced), + selected, - candidate, ~ configured
```

```
RouterB#sh ntp associations

      address    ref clock   st     when    poll    reach   delay   offset   disp
*~192.1.1.1      LOCL.       1      61      64      377     1.9     -2.74    1.7
 * master (synced), # master (unsynced), + selected, - candidate, ~ configured


RouterC#sh ntp associations

      address    ref clock   st     when    poll    reach   delay   offset   disp
*~196.1.1.2      .192.1.1.1  2      10      64      377     68.8    -0.87    0.3
 * master (synced), # master (unsynced), + selected, - candidate, ~ configured
```

Lab #68: Cisco NTP with Authentication

Equipment Needed

The following equipment is needed to perform this lab exercise:

- Two Cisco routers, each having one serial port
- Cisco IOS 10.0 or higher
- A PC running a terminal emulation program
- A Cisco DTE/DCE crossover cable. If no crossover cables are available, you can make a crossover cable by connecting a standard Cisco DTE cable to a standard Cisco DCE cable.

Configuration Overview

This configuration will demonstrate the authentication features of NTP. Cisco's NTP implementation includes powerful authentication capabilities, which ensure that NTP updates are being sent from a trusted source.

Two Cisco routers are connected serially. RouterA is connected to RouterB via a crossover cable. RouterB acts as a DCE, supplying clock to RouterA. IP addresses are assigned as per the following diagram (see Figure 17–4). A PC running a terminal emulation program is connected to the console port of RouterA.

RouterA is configured as the NTP clock master. RouterB is configured to synchronize to RouterA via the NTP server statement. RouterA and RouterB are configured for NTP authentication. This authentication uses MD5 security to ensure the validity of NTP packets being sent between the two routers.

NOTES: *NTP convergence can take up to half an hour, which means that when changing the system clock on the NTP master, it can take up to half an hour for all other clocks in the configuration to synchronize. This situation is caused by NTP viewing a clock change as an instability in the clocking system. NTP waits for a stable system before synchronizing and propagating any changes. Next, change the two authentication keys to a similar value for both routers and verify that the two routers do synchronize their time via NTP.*

This exercise should be tried in two steps. First, enter the configurations for RouterA and RouterB with both RouterA and RouterB having a different authentication key value. The command syntax is

```
ntp authentication-key number md5 value.
```

As an example, enter the command for RouterA as follows: ntp authentication-key 1 md5 cisco. Then, enter the command for RouterB as follows: ntp authentication-key 1 md5 bay. Entering this information will cause the authentication to fail between the two routers. This result will demonstrate how an authentication failure will cause NTP to not work between the two routers. The authentication key will appear encrypted as soon as it is entered, which will cause a clear-text key such as cisco to appear in the following manner when viewing the configuration via the show run command:

```
ntp authentication-key 1 md5 045802150C2E 7
```

A Cisco router will not have a valid date and time set when it is powered on. After power on, the clock is set to March 1, 1993. The clock must be given a valid setting before NTP takes effect. The clock can be set via the clock set command, whose syntax is as follows:

```
clock set hh:mm:ss day month year
```

Figure 17–4
NTP authentication

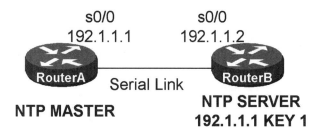

Router Configuration

The configurations for the two routers in this example are as follows (key NTP commands are highlighted in bold):

RouterA

```
Current configuration:
!
version 11.2
no service udp-small-servers
no service tcp-small-servers
!
hostname RouterA
!
enable password cisco
!
no ip domain-lookup
!
interface Ethernet0/0
 ip address 10.10.3.100 255.255.255.0
!
interface Serial0/0
 ip address 192.1.1.1 255.255.255.0
 encapsulation ppp
!
router rip
 network 192.1.1.0
!
ip classless
!
line con 0
 exec-timeout 120 0
 password cisco
 login
line aux 0
 password cisco
 login
line vty 0 4
 exec-timeout 120 0
 password cisco
 login
!
ntp authentication-key 1 md5 045802150C2E 7
ntp authenticate
ntp trusted-key 1
ntp master
end
```

RouterB

```
Current configuration:
!
version 11.2
no service udp-small-servers
no service tcp-small-servers
!
hostname RouterB
!
enable password cisco
!
no ip domain-lookup
!
interface Ethernet0/0
 ip address 10.10.3.101 255.255.255.0
!
interface Serial0/0
 ip address 192.1.1.2 255.255.255.0
 encapsulation ppp
 clockrate 500000
!
interface Serial0/1
 ip address 196.1.1.2 255.255.255.0
 encapsulation ppp
 clockrate 19200
!
router rip
 network 192.1.1.0
 network 196.1.1.0
!
ip classless
!
line con 0
 password cisco
 login
line aux 0
 password cisco
 login
line vty 0 4
 exec-timeout 120 0
 password cisco
 login
!
ntp authentication-key 1 md5 121A0C041104 7
ntp authenticate
ntp trusted-key 1
ntp clock-period 17179827
ntp server 192.1.1.1 key 1
end
```

Monitoring the Configuration

After RouterA has converged and stabilized its new clock time, the router will start to propagate its clock settings. The **show ntp status** command can be used to monitor the synchronization state of each router.

The **show ntp status** output from RouterA shows that the router is synchronized. Notice that the reference is listed as being local, because this router is configured as a clock master. RouterA declares itself as a stratum 8 source, because we did not specify any stratum in the **ntp master** command.

```
RouterA#sh ntp status
Clock is synchronized, stratum 8, reference is 127.127.7.1
nominal freq is 250.0000 Hz, actual freq is 250.0000 Hz, precision is 2**24
reference time is BA2DE8FD.D1BC0A57 (10:35:41.819 UTC Fri Dec 25 1998)
clock offset is 0.0000 msec, root delay is 0.00 msec
root dispersion is 0.02 msec, peer dispersion is 0.02 msec
```

RouterB is also synchronized as a stratum 9 source, because the router is referenced to RouterA, which is a stratum 8 source.

```
RouterB#sh ntp status
Clock is synchronized, stratum 9, reference is 192.1.1.1
nominal freq is 250.0000 Hz, actual freq is 250.0006 Hz, precision is 2**24
reference time is BA2DE912.F26F9533 (10:36:02.947 UTC Fri Dec 25 1998)
clock offset is 0.1931 msec, root delay is 0.73 msec
root dispersion is 1.79 msec, peer dispersion is 1.57 msec
```

Let's take a look at the **show ntp associations** command, as shown in the following screen prints. This command shows how often the router sends/receives NTP updates and also shows when the last update was received. RouterB, for example, last received an NTP update 27 seconds ago.

```
RouterA#sh ntp assoc

      address      ref clock     st    when   poll   reach   delay   offset    disp
*~127.127.7.1   127.127.7.1    7     20     64     377    0.0     0.00      0.0
 * master (synced), # master (unsynced), + selected, - candidate, ~ configured


RouterB#sh ntp assoc

      address      ref clock     st    when   poll   reach   delay   offset    disp
*~192.1.1.1     127.127.7.1    8     27     128    377    0.0     0.19      1.6
 * master (synced), # master (unsynced), + selected, - candidate, ~ configured
```

The **ntp association detail** command contains additional important information regarding the current NTP status. For example, the following screen print shows the time that is being broadcast to other systems (highlighted in bold).

```
RouterA#sh ntp assoc detail
127.127.7.1 configured, our_master, sane, valid, stratum 7
ref ID 127.127.7.1, time BA2DE8FD.D1BC0A57 (10:35:41.819 UTC Fri Dec 25 1998)
our mode active, peer mode passive, our poll intvl 64, peer poll intvl 64
root delay 0.00 msec, root disp 0.00, reach 377, sync dist 0.015
delay 0.00 msec, offset 0.0000 msec, dispersion 0.02
precision 2**24, version 3
org time BA2DE8FD.D1BC0A57 (10:35:41.819 UTC Fri Dec 25 1998)
rcv time BA2DE8FD.D1BC0A57 (10:35:41.819 UTC Fri Dec 25 1998)
xmt time BA2DE8FD.D1BDEB65 (10:35:41.819 UTC Fri Dec 25 1998)
filtdelay =     0.00     0.00     0.00     0.00     0.00     0.00     0.00     0.00
filtoffset =    0.00     0.00     0.00     0.00     0.00     0.00     0.00     0.00
filterror =     0.02     0.99     1.97     2.94     3.92     4.90     5.87     6.85
Reference clock status:  Running normally
Timecode:
```

Lab #69: Cisco NTP Using LAN Broadcasts

Equipment Needed

The following equipment is needed to perform this lab exercise:

- Three Cisco routers, each having one Ethernet port
- Cisco IOS 10.0 or higher
- A PC running a terminal emulation program
- An Ethernet hub
- Three Ethernet cables connecting each router to the Ethernet hub
- An optional LAN sniffer, which is connected into the Ethernet hub. This device will enable traces to be taken, which will show the NTP packets being sent on the network.

Configuration Overview

This configuration demonstrates the broadcast capabilities of NTP. NTP updates will be broadcast on an Ethernet LAN to two Cisco routers. We will see that the broadcast configuration is less complex than the previous configurations, due to the fact that NTP peer and server IP addresses are no longer needed.

Three Cisco routers are all connected to the same Ethernet LAN. All three routers' IP addresses reside on the same network. IP addresses are assigned as per the following diagram (see Figure 17–5). A PC running a terminal emulation program is connected to the console port of RouterA. An optional LAN sniffer can be connected on the LAN to allow for capture and analysis of the NTP packets.

NOTES: *NTP convergence can take up to half an hour, which means that when changing the system clock on the NTP master, it can take up to half an hour for all other clocks in the configuration to synchronize. This situation is caused by NTP viewing a clock change as an instability in the clocking system. NTP waits for a stable system before synchronizing and propagating any changes.*

A Cisco router will not have a valid date and time set when it is powered on. After power on, the clock is set to March 1, 1993. The clock must be given a valid setting before NTP takes effect. The clock can be set via the **clock set** *command, whose syntax is as follows:*

```
clock set hh:mm:ss day month year
```

Due to IOS issues, the NTP broadcast statement under the Ethernet interface of RouterA must be reentered every time the clock is changed.

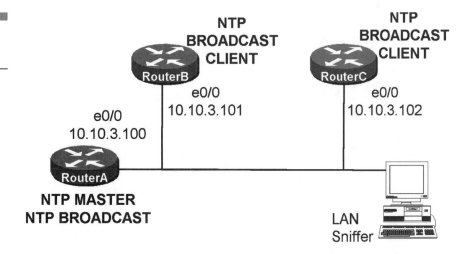

Figure 17–5
NTP LAN broadcast lab

NTP Packet Capture

The following trace was taken with a Network Associates analyzer. The trace shows a completely decoded NTP packet that was sent on the LAN of this example.

```
Packet 5 captured at 11/28/1998 11:35:30 PM; Packet size is 90(0x5a)bytes
        Relative time: 000:00:49.927
        Delta time: 37.671.943
    Ethernet Version II
        Address: 00-E0-1E-5B-0A-81 --->FF-FF-FF-FF-FF-FF
        Ethernet II Protocol Type: IP
    Internet Protocol
        Version(MSB 4 bits): 4
        Header length(LSB 4 bits): 5 (32-bit word)
        Service type: 0x00
                000. .... = 0 - Routine
                ...0 .... = Normal delay
                .... 0... = Normal throughput
                .... .0.. = Normal reliability
        Total length: 76 (Octets)
        Fragment ID: 1278
        Flags summary: 0x00
                0... .... = Reserved
                .0.. .... = May be fragmented
                ..0. .... = Last fragment
                Fragment offset(LSB 13 bits): 0 (0x00)
        Time to live: 255 seconds/hops
        IP protocol type: UDP (0x11)
        Checksum: 0xA935
        IP address 10.10.3.100 ->BROADCAST
        No option
    User Datagram Protocol
        Port Network Time Protocol --> Network Time Protocol
        Total length: 56 (Octets)
        Checksum: 0xF9EF
    Network Time Protocol
        Leap Indicator: 0 - No Warning
        Version Number: 3
        Mode: 5 - Broadcast
        Stratum: 8 - Secondary Reference
        Poll Interval: 6 (Sec)
        Precision: 232 (Sec)
        Root Delay: 0.0 (Sec.200PicoSec)
        Root Dispersion: 0.2 (Sec.200PicoSec)
        Reference Source Address: 127.127.7.1
        Reference Timestamp: 3121240502.2318470671 (Sec.200PicoSec)
        Originate Timestamp: 0.0 (Sec.200PicoSec)
        Receive Timestamp: 0.0 (Sec.200PicoSec)
        Transit Timestamp: 3121240534.2318467748 (Sec.200PicoSec)
```

Router Configuration

The configurations for the three routers in this example are as follows (key NTP commands are highlighted in bold):

RouterA

```
Current configuration:
!
version 11.2
no service udp-small-servers
no service tcp-small-servers
!
hostname RouterA
!
enable password cisco
!
no ip domain-lookup
!
interface Ethernet0/0
 ip address 10.10.3.100 255.255.255.0
 ntp broadcast
!
interface Serial0/0
 ip address 192.1.1.1 255.255.255.0
 encapsulation ppp
!
router rip
 network 10.0.0.0
 network 192.1.1.0
!
ip classless
!
line con 0
 exec-timeout 120 0
 password cisco
 login
line aux 0
 password cisco
 login
line vty 0 4
 exec-timeout 120 0
 password cisco
 login
!
ntp master
end
```

RouterB

```
Current configuration:
!
version 11.2
no service udp-small-servers
no service tcp-small-servers
!
hostname RouterB
!
enable password cisco
!
no ip domain-lookup
!
interface Ethernet0/0
 ip address 10.10.3.101 255.255.255.0
 ntp broadcast client
!
interface Serial0/0
 ip address 192.1.1.2 255.255.255.0
 encapsulation ppp
 clockrate 500000
!
interface Serial0/1
 ip address 196.1.1.2 255.255.255.0
 encapsulation ppp
 clockrate 19200
!
router rip
 network 192.1.1.0
 network 196.1.1.0
!
ip classless
!
line con 0
 password cisco
 login
line aux 0
 password cisco
 login
line vty 0 4
 exec-timeout 120 0
 password cisco
 login
!
end
```

RouterC

```
Current configuration:
!
version 11.2
no service udp-small-servers
no service tcp-small-servers
!
hostname RouterC
!
!
no ip domain-lookup
!
interface Ethernet0/0
 ip address 10.10.3.102 255.255.255.0
 ntp broadcast client
!
interface Serial0/0
 ip address 196.1.1.3 255.255.255.0
 encapsulation ppp
!
router rip
 network 196.1.1.0
!
no ip classless
!
line con 0
 password cisco
 login
line aux 0
 password cisco
 login
line vty 0 4
exec-timeout 30 0
 password cisco
 login
!
end
```

Monitoring the Configuration

After RouterA has converged and stabilized its new clock time, the router will start to propagate its clock settings. The **show ntp status** command can be used to monitor the synchronization state of each router.

The **show ntp status** output from RouterA shows that the router is synchronized.

```
RouterA#sh ntp status
Clock is synchronized, stratum 8, reference is 127.127.7.1
nominal freq is 250.0000 Hz, actual freq is 250.0000 Hz, precision is 2**24
reference time is BA374A04.95680411 (13:20:04.583 UTC Fri Jan 1 1999)
clock offset is 0.0000 msec, root delay is 0.00 msec
root dispersion is 0.02 msec, peer dispersion is 0.02 msec

RouterB#sh ntp status
Clock is synchronized, stratum 9, reference is 10.10.3.100
nominal freq is 250.0000 Hz, actual freq is 250.0000 Hz, precision is 2**24
reference time is BA374A2B.9511C731 (13:20:43.582 UTC Fri Jan 1 1999)
clock offset is 3.4407 msec, root delay is 0.93 msec
root dispersion is 382.71 msec, peer dispersion is 379.24 msec

RouterC#sh ntp status
Clock is synchronized, stratum 9, reference is 10.10.3.100
nominal freq is 250.0000 Hz, actual freq is 250.0000 Hz, precision is 2**24
reference time is BA374A2B.96B65B60 (13:20:43.588 UTC Fri Jan 1 1999)
clock offset is -4.7316 msec, root delay is 0.78 msec
root dispersion is 134.98 msec, peer dispersion is 130.20 msec
```

Let's take a look at the **show ntp associations** command, as shown in the following screen prints. This command shows how often the router sends/receives NTP updates. The command also shows when the last update was received. RouterC, for example, last received an NTP update 52 seconds ago.

```
RouterC#sh ntp assoc

      address   ref clock    st    when   poll  reach  delay  offset   disp
* 10.10.3.100 127.127.7.1    8      52     64    376    0.8   -4.73   130.2
  * master (synced), # master (unsynced), + selected, - candidate, ~ configured
```

The **ntp association detail** command contains additional important information regarding the current NTP status. For example, the following screen print shows the time that is being broadcast to other systems (highlighted in bold).

```
RouterC#sh ntp assoc detail
10.10.3.100 dynamic, our_master, sane, valid, stratum 8
ref ID 127.127.7.1, time BA374A04.95680411 (13:20:04.583 UTC Fri Jan 1 1999)
our mode bdcast client, peer mode bdcast, our poll intvl 64, peer poll intvl 64
root delay 0.00 msec, root disp 0.03, reach 376, sync dist 130.615
delay 0.78 msec, offset -4.7316 msec, dispersion 130.20
precision 2**24, version 3
org time BA374A2B.9562442A (13:20:43.583 UTC Fri Jan 1 1999)
rcv time BA374A2B.96B65B60 (13:20:43.588 UTC Fri Jan 1 1999)
xmt time BA374983.F15A0680 (13:17:55.942 UTC Fri Jan 1 1999)
filtdelay =    0.78    0.78    2.43    0.78    2.73    1.17    3.08    0.00
filtoffset =  -4.73   -0.25   -7.38   -0.27   -7.28   -0.11   -7.15    0.00
filterror =    0.99    1.97    2.58    2.59    2.61    2.62    2.64 16000.0
```

Conclusion

This chapter explores *Network Time Protocol* (NTP). NTP is used to synchronize all systems in a network to the same clock. There are several reasons why clock synchronization is important, such as being able to debug and timestamp events at the same time for all systems in a network.

NTP is defined in RFC 1305 and uses a simple method to determine the round-trip delay between two systems, as well as the time difference between two systems.

This chapter contains detailed lab exercises using Cisco as an NTP server. NTP servers, peers, authentication, and broadcasting are presented.

In the real world, a standalone, GPS-referenced, NTP server can be used to provide network synchronization.

18

Novell Internetwork Packet Exchange (IPX)

Topics Covered in This Chapter

- IPX technology overview
- IPX configuration using RIP/SAP
- Configuring EIGRP on an IPX network
- Static SAP entries
- SAP access lists
- Troubleshooting IPX

Introduction

Novell *Internetwork Packet Exchange* (IPX), although less popular then it once was, is still a widely deployed networking protocol. This chapter will explore the IPX protocol and will examine how the protocol is supported by the Cisco IOS.

Novell IPX Overview

Novell Netware is both an operating system and a networking protocol. Novell IPX is based on the *Xerox Network System* (XNS) protocols. When we use the term IPX, we refer to the entire Novell protocol stack, just as we use IP to refer to the entire TCP/IP suite.

IPX Addressing

Addressing in a Novell IPX network is different then addressing in an IP network. An IPX address is in the format of network.node.socket, as shown in Figure 18–1. The three parts of the IPX address are the following:

- Network portion—Every IPX network is assigned a globally unique, 32-bit network number.
- Node portion—Each IPX device (usually a workstation, router, or server) is assigned a 48-bit node address. This 48-bit address is taken from the MAC address of the device itself. This address is an attractive feature of IPX. Having the node address of an IPX device use the device's MAC address means that IPX will not need *Address Resolution Protocol* (ARP). An IPX-enabled device wishing to send a datagram to another IPX device only needs to know the IPX address of the endstation, because the MAC address of the endstation is embedded in the IPX address. The sending station has enough information to create an Ethernet or token ring frame, because the destination MAC address is already known. With IP, you know an end device's IP address, but you do not know the end device's MAC address that is needed to build the Ethernet, token ring, or FDDI datalink frame. IP uses ARP to find the MAC address of a destination device or network whose IP address is already known.

▪ Socket portion—The socket is a 16-bit number that identifies a software process using IPX in the endstation. Some socket numbers are reserved, and some are available for use by the endstation.

We see in Figure 18–1 that the network address is 32 bits, the node address is 48 bits, and the socket number is 16 bits. A complete IPX address is a 96-bit number expressed as a 12-byte hexadecimal number.

IPX Protocol Stack

Figure 18–2 shows the IPX protocol stack. The key portions of the protocol stack can be described as follows:

IPX Network Layer

IPX (Internetwork Packet Exchange) provides network-layer, connectionless datagram delivery to support Novell Netware. The minimum IPX packet size is 30 bytes, and the maximum packet size is 65,535 bytes. An IPX packet has a 30-byte header, as shown in Figure 18–3.

IPX Transport Layer

Novell IPX uses SPX as its transport-layer protocol. SPX is a connection-oriented protocol. No data transfer can take place between two endstations using SPX until a connection has been built.

Service Advertising Protocol (SAP)

A SAP is used to advertise and distribute Novell server information. Netware servers and routers broadcast a SAP message every 60 seconds. This message advertises which services they provide.

Figure 18–1
IPX addressing

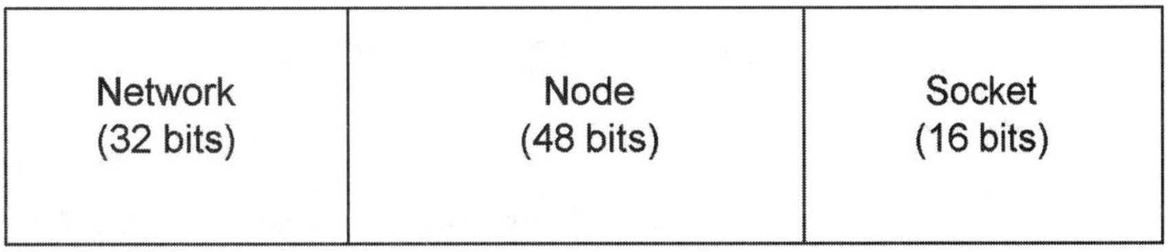

Network (32 bits)	Node (48 bits)	Socket (16 bits)

Figure 18–2
IPX protocol stack

Session	SAP
Transport	SPX
Network	IPX / RIP / NLSP / EIGRP
Data-Link	802.2 MAC / 802.2 LLC
Physical	Ethernet / TokenRing / FDDI

There are three types of SAP packets:

1. **Periodic updates**—A periodic update is used by a server when it has a service to advertise. The server sends a SAP broadcast with the service's name, service type, and full IPX address (network.node.socket). Routers listen to and store these broadcasts. Routers periodically broadcast these updates to all directly connected neighbors.

2. **Service queries**—A service query is used by a Netware client to locate a server. This kind of query is often referred to as a *Get Nearest Server* (GNS) query. This service query is a broadcast and does not go off the local network. The query will be answered by the local router, which has stored the periodic updates that it has received from servers on the network.

3. **Service responses**—A service response is a response to a service query. This response is usually from a router.

IPX Routing Protocols

IPX uses three different routing protocols to propagate routing information:

1. IPX RIP—A distance vector protocol that has many similarities to IP RIP. IPX RIP differs from IP RIP because the IPX

Figure 18–3
IPX packet structure

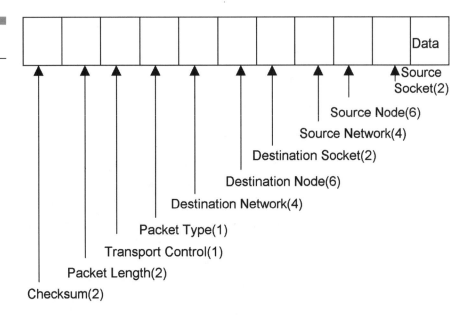

endstation requests route information, whereas with an IP network, the endstation will have a default route to the nearest router. IPX updates are broadcast every 60 seconds. IPX RIP uses two metrics. The first metric is delay, referred to as ticks. The second metric is hop count. The route with the lowest delay will be given preference over the route with the lowest hop count. If two routes exist with the same tick value, then the router will use the hop count of each route to determine the best route.

2. NLSP—A link state protocol that provides load balancing across equal cost paths and features much faster convergence times then IPX RIP.

3. EIGRP—This protocol is the Cisco proprietary Enhanced IGRP. This routing protocol features automatic redistribution between RIP/SAP and EIGRP.

RIP/SAP Operation

RIP and SAP work closely together in an IPX network. Figure 18–4 shows how an IPX endstation locates a server and finds a route to that server.

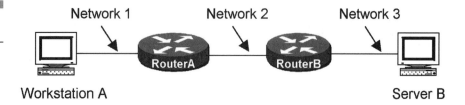

Figure 18–4
SAP operation

1. Workstation A sends a GNS request to find a server.

2. RouterA has cached a SAP update from RouterB, advertising ServerB. RouterA sends a SAP reply to Workstation A.

3. Workstation A now has the IPX address of ServerB. Workstation A knows that ServerB is on Network 3. Workstation A now needs to find a route to Network 3.

4. RouterA knows about Network 3 via RIP updates. RouterA sends a RIP response packet to Workstation A.

IPX Encapsulation Types

Figure 18–5 shows the different IPX Ethernet encapsulation types.

When running on a LAN, IPX runs on Ethernet, Token Ring, and FDDI. IPX can use four different Ethernet encapsulation types on a LAN, which means that four different MAC frames can be used on an IPX network. If two workstations on a NetWare LAN use different Ethernet encapsulation types, they cannot talk to each other directly—and their traffic has to go through a router.

The four Ethernet encapsulation types are:

1. Ethernet II—This encapsulation type is referred to by Cisco as ARPA encapsulation.

2. 802.2—This encapsulation type is referred to by Cisco as SAP encapsulation.

3. 802.3—This encapsulation type is referred to by Cisco as Novell-Ether encapsulation and is the default encapsulation on a Cisco Ethernet interface.

4. SNAP—This encapsulation type is referred to by Cisco as SNAP encapsulation.

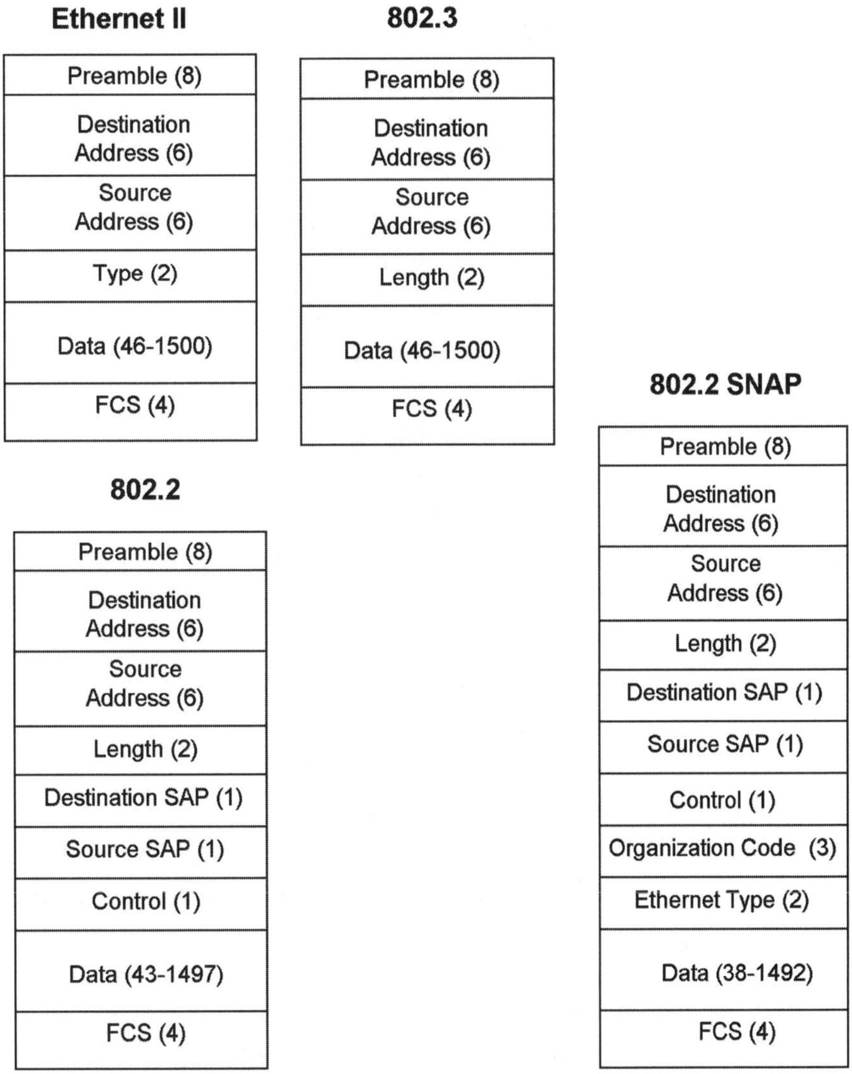

Figure 18–5

IPX Ethernet
encapsulation types

Ethernet II

Preamble (8)
Destination Address (6)
Source Address (6)
Type (2)
Data (46-1500)
FCS (4)

802.3

Preamble (8)
Destination Address (6)
Source Address (6)
Length (2)
Data (46-1500)
FCS (4)

802.2

Preamble (8)
Destination Address (6)
Source Address (6)
Length (2)
Destination SAP (1)
Source SAP (1)
Control (1)
Data (43-1497)
FCS (4)

802.2 SNAP

Preamble (8)
Destination Address (6)
Source Address (6)
Length (2)
Destination SAP (1)
Source SAP (1)
Control (1)
Organization Code (3)
Ethernet Type (2)
Data (38-1492)
FCS (4)

IPX supports two different Token Ring encapsulation types:

1. Cisco SAP, which is the default

2. Cisco SNAP

IPX supports three different FDDI encapsulation types:

1. Cisco SNAP

2. Cisco SAP

3. Novell-FDDI Raw

Commands Discussed in This Chapter

- **access-list** *access-list-number* **[deny|permit]** *network*[*.node*] [*network-mask.node-mask*] [*service-type*[*server-name*]]
- **debug ipx routing activity**
- **debug ipx routing events**
- **debug ipx sap activity**
- **debug ipx sap events**
- **distribute-list in**
- **distribute-list out**
- **ipx network** *network* [**encapsulation** *encapsulation-type* [**secondary**]]
- **ipx output-sap-filter** *access-list-number*
- **ipx router [eigrp** *autonomous-system-number* | **nlsp** [*tag*] | **rip]**
- **ipx routing** [*node*]
- **ipx sap** *service-type name network.node socket hop-count*
- **network** [*network-number*] |**all**]
- **ping [ipx]** [*network.node*]
- **show access-list**
- **show ipx eigrp interfaces** [*type number*] [*as-number*]
- **show ipx eigrp neighbors [servers]** [*autonomous-system-number* | *interface*]
- **show ipx interface** [*type number*]
- **show ipx interface brief**
- **show ipx route** [*network*] **[default] [detailed]**
- **show ipx servers [unsorted** | **[sorted [name** | **net** | **type**]] **[regexp** *name*]
- **show ipx traffic**

Definitions

access-list: This global configuration command defines access lists for SAP filters, route filters, and NLSP filters.

debug ipx routing activity: This debug command displays information on IPX routing activity.

debug ipx routing events: This debug command displays information on IPX routing activity.

debug ipx sap activity, debug ipx sap events: These debug commands provide information on IPX SAP packets.

distribute-list in: This router configuration command filters IPX network information as the information comes into a router.

distribute-list out: This router configuration command filters IPX network information as the information leaves a router.

ipx network: This interface configuration command enables IPX routing on the selected interface. The command can also be used to select the encapsulation type on a LAN interface.

ipx router: This global configuration command is used to specify which type of routing protocol to use. Valid options are RIP, EIGRP, and NLSP.

ipx routing: This global configuration command enables IPX routing on a router. You can optionally set the IPX node number for this router.

ipx sap: This global configuration command creates static SAP entries in the router's IPX server table.

network: This router configuration command specifies which networks should be included in routing updates.

ping ipx: This exec command is used to verify IPX network reachability.

show access-list: This exec command displays information on access lists that have been defined on the router.

show ipx eigrp interfaces: This exec command displays information on any interfaces that have been enabled for the EIGRP routing protocol.

show ipx eigrp neighbor: This exec command will display information on neighbor routers that have been discovered by EIGRP.

show ipx interface: This exec command displays information on router interfaces that have been configured for the IPX protocol.

show ipx interface brief: This exec command provides a summary of all router interfaces that have been configured for the IPX protocol.

show ipx route: This exec command displays the IPX route table for the router.

show ipx servers: This exec command displays all IPX servers that have either been discovered through SAP advertisements or have been statically configured.

show ipx traffic: This exec command shows information on transmitted and received IPX protocol packets. The output is sorted by IPX packet type, such as RIP, EIGRP, SAP, etc.

IOS Requirements

These labs were done using IOS 11.2.

Lab #70: IPX Configuration with IPX RIP/SAP

Equipment Needed

The following equipment is needed to perform this lab exercise:

■ Three Cisco routers. One of the routers must have two serial interfaces; the other two routers must have one serial interface and one Ethernet interface.

■ Two Cisco crossover cables. If a Cisco crossover cable is not available, then you can use a Cisco DTE cable connected to a Cisco DCE cable.

■ A Cisco rolled cable for console port connection to the routers

■ A Cisco IOS image that supports the IPX protocol

Configuration Overview

This lab will demonstrate IPX configuration and monitoring. As shown in Figure 18–6, this lab defines five IPX networks. RouterA, RouterB, and RouterC are each given IPX node numbers a.a.a, b.b.b, and c.c.c, respectively. The three routers are connected, as shown in Figure 18–6. RouterB acts as a DCE and supplies clocking to RouterA and RouterC.

Figure 18-6
IPX with RIP/SAP

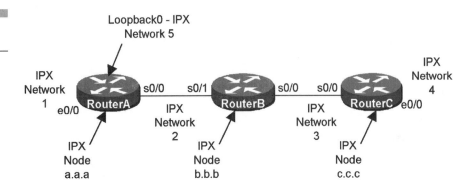

Router Configuration

The configurations for the three routers in this example are as follows
(key IPX commands are highlighted in bold):

RouterA

```
Current configuration:
!
version 11.2
no service password-encryption
no service udp-small-servers
no service tcp-small-servers
!
hostname RouterA
!
!
ipx routing 000a.000a.000a←Enable IPX routing. Define the IPX node to be 000a.000a.000a.
!
interface Loopback0
 no ip address
 ipx network 5←Make this interface IPX network 5
!
interface Ethernet0/0
 no ip address
 no keepalive
 ipx network 1←Make this interface IPX network 1
!
interface Serial0/0
 no ip address
 encapsulation ppp
 ipx network 2←Make this interface IPX network 2
 no fair-queue
!
no ip classless
```

```
!
line con 0
line aux 0
line vty 0 4
 login
!
end
```

RouterB

```
Current configuration:
!
version 11.2
no service password-encryption
no service udp-small-servers
no service tcp-small-servers
!
hostname RouterB
!
!
```
ipx routing 000b.000b.000b←Enable IPX routing. Define the IPX node to be 000b.000b.000b
```
!
interface Serial0/0
 no ip address
 encapsulation ppp
```
 ipx network 3←Make this interface IPX network 3
```
 no fair-queue
 clockrate 64000
!
interface Serial0/1
 no ip address
 encapsulation ppp
```
 ipx network 2←Make this interface IPX network 2
```
 clockrate 64000
!
no ip classless
!
line con 0
line aux 0
line vty 0 4
 login
!
end
```

RouterC

```
Current configuration:
!
version 11.2
no service password-encryption
no service udp-small-servers
```

```
no service tcp-small-servers
!
hostname RouterC
!
!
ipx routing 000c.000c.000c←Enable IPX routing. Define the IPX node to be 000c.000c.000c
!
interface Ethernet0/0
 no ip address
 no keepalive
 ipx network 4←Make this interface IPX network 4
!
interface Serial0/0
 no ip address
 encapsulation ppp
 ipx network 3←Make this interface IPX network 3
 no fair-queue
!
no ip classless
!
line con 0
line aux 0
line vty 0 4
 login
!
end
```

Notice that there are no routing protocols explicitly configured for any of the three routers, because with the IPX protocol, IPX RIP is enabled by default.

Monitoring and Testing the Configuration

Let's start by connecting to RouterA. Type the **show ipx interface brief** command to display the status of all interfaces on the router. We see that there are three interfaces on this router that are running the IPX protocol. These interfaces are: Ethernet0/0 on IPX network 1, Serial0/0 on IPX network 2, and the Loopback 0 interface on IPX network 5. We see that each of these interfaces are in an up/up state. Notice that the encapsulation on the Ethernet0/0 interface is set to NOVELL-ETHER. Recall from the introduction section in this chapter that the default encapsulation on an Ethernet interface is NOVELL-ETHER.

```
RouterA#show ipx interface brief
Interface       IPX Network Encapsulation Status                  IPX State
Ethernet0/0     1           NOVELL-ETHER   up                      [up]
Serial0/0       2           PPP            up                      [up]
BRI0/0          unassigned  not config'd   administratively down   n/a
BRI0/0:1        unassigned  not config'd   administratively down   n/a
```

```
BRI0/0:2        unassigned    not config'd   administratively down   n/a
Ethernet1/0     unassigned    not config'd   administratively down   n/a
Serial1/0       unassigned    not config'd   administratively down   n/a
Serial1/1       unassigned    not config'd   administratively down   n/a
Loopback0       5             UNKNOWN        up                      [up]
```

Type the **show ipx route** command to display the routing table for this router. The routing table shows us that three IPX networks are directly connected. Network 1 is on Ethernet0; Network 2 is on Serial 0; and Network 5 is on Loopback 0. RouterA has learned about two networks via the IPX RIP routing protocol. Network 3 is one hop and seven ticks away, and Network 4 is two hops and 13 ticks away.

```
RouterA#show ipx route
Codes: C - Connected primary network,    c - Connected secondary network
       S - Static, F - Floating static, L - Local (internal), W - IPXWAN
       R - RIP, E - EIGRP, N - NLSP, X - External, A - Aggregate
       s - seconds, u - uses

5 Total IPX routes. Up to 1 parallel paths and 16 hops allowed.

No default route known.

C            1 (NOVELL-ETHER),  Et0/0
C            2 (PPP),           Se0/0
C            5 (UNKNOWN),       Lo0
```

```
             Tick Count          Next hop address
                ↓                   ↓
R            3 [07/01] via       2.000b.000b.000b,   49s, Se0/0
                  ↑
             Hop Count to destination network
```

```
             Tick Count          Next hop address
                ↓                   ↓
R            4 [13/02] via       2.000b.000b.000b,   50s, Se0/0
                  ↑
             Hop Count to destination network
```

The show interface s 0/0 command usually shows an IP address. Because there is no IP enabled on this router, the show command does not display a network address. We see that IPXCP is opened, which is the IPX Network Control Protocol.

```
RouterA#show int s 0/0
Serial0/0 is up, line protocol is up
  Hardware is QUICC Serial
  MTU 1500 bytes, BW 1544 Kbit, DLY 20000 usec, rely 255/255, load 1/255
  Encapsulation PPP, loopback not set, keepalive set (10 sec)
  LCP Open
```

```
Open: CDPCP, IPXCP←No IP is enabled on this interface
Last input 00:00:01, output 00:00:01, output hang never
Last clearing of "show interface" counters never
Queueing strategy: fifo
Output queue 0/40, 0 drops; input queue 0/75, 0 drops
5 minute input rate 0 bits/sec, 0 packets/sec
5 minute output rate 0 bits/sec, 0 packets/sec
    99 packets input, 3888 bytes, 0 no buffer←Packets input
    Received 99 broadcasts, 0 runts, 0 giants, 0 throttles
    0 input errors, 0 CRC, 0 frame, 0 overrun, 0 ignored, 0 abort
    100 packets output, 3902 bytes, 0 underruns←Packets output
    0 output errors, 0 collisions, 16 interface resets
    0 output buffer failures, 0 output buffers swapped out
    31 carrier transitions
    DCD=up   DSR=up   DTR=up   RTS=up   CTS=up
```

Specific IPX information for the interface can be displayed with the **show ipx int** command.

```
RouterA#show ipx int s 0/0
Serial0/0 is up, line protocol is up
  IPX address is 2.000a.000a.000a [up]←IPX address
```

                                    A WAN interface has a default IPX
                                    delay of 6
                                         ↓

```
Delay of this IPX network, in ticks is 6 throughput 0 link delay 0
IPXWAN processing not enabled on this interface.
IPX SAP update interval is 1 minute(s)
IPX type 20 propagation packet forwarding is disabled
Incoming access list is not set
Outgoing access list is not set
IPX helper access list is not set
SAP GNS processing enabled, delay 0 ms, output filter list is not set
SAP Input filter list is not set
SAP Output filter list is not set
SAP Router filter list is not set
Input filter list is not set
Output filter list is not set
Router filter list is not set
Netbios Input host access list is not set
Netbios Input bytes access list is not set
Netbios Output host access list is not set
Netbios Output bytes access list is not set
Updates each 60 seconds, aging multiples RIP: 3 SAP: 3
SAP interpacket delay is 55 ms, maximum size is 480 bytes
RIP interpacket delay is 55 ms, maximum size is 432 bytes
Watchdog processing is disabled, SPX spoofing is disabled, idle time 60
IPX accounting is disabled
IPX fast switching is configured (enabled)
RIP packets received 9, RIP packets sent 9←RIP is running on this interface
SAP packets received 1, SAP packets sent 1←SAP is running on this interface
```

Type the **show interface e 0/0** command to display information about the Ethernet interface of the router. There are two important items to note here:

1. There is no IP address on this interface, because the IP protocol is not configured on this router.

2. The MAC address of the interface is 00e0.1e5b.2601. The interface did not take the 000a.000a.000a MAC address that has been assigned to the Serial0 interface of this router by the command **IPX Routing 000A.000A.000A** in the router's configuration.

```
RouterA#show int e 0/0
Ethernet0/0 is up, line protocol is up
  Hardware is AmdP2, address is 00e0.1e5b.2601 (bia 00e0.1e5b.2601)
  MTU 1500 bytes, BW 10000 Kbit, DLY 1000 usec, rely 128/255, load 1/255
  Encapsulation ARPA, loopback not set, keepalive not set
  ARP type: ARPA, ARP Timeout 04:00:00
  Last input never, output 00:00:54, output hang never
  Last clearing of "show interface" counters never
  Queueing strategy: fifo
  Output queue 0/40, 0 drops; input queue 0/75, 0 drops
  5 minute input rate 0 bits/sec, 0 packets/sec
  5 minute output rate 0 bits/sec, 0 packets/sec
     0 packets input, 0 bytes, 0 no buffer
     Received 0 broadcasts, 0 runts, 0 giants, 0 throttles
     0 input errors, 0 CRC, 0 frame, 0 overrun, 0 ignored, 0 abort
     0 input packets with dribble condition detected
     576 packets output, 96038 bytes, 0 underruns
     576 output errors, 0 collisions, 1 interface resets
     0 babbles, 0 late collision, 0 deferred
     576 lost carrier, 0 no carrier
     0 output buffer failures, 0 output buffers swapped out
```

Specific IPX information for the interface can be displayed with the **show ipx int e 0/0** command.

```
RouterA#show ipx int e 0/0
Ethernet0/0 is up, line protocol is up
  IPX address is 1.00e0.1e5b.2601, NOVELL-ETHER [up]←default IPX encapsulation

                              A LAN interface has a default IPX
                              delay of 1
                                   ↓
Delay of this IPX network, in ticks is 1 throughput 0 link delay 0
  IPXWAN processing not enabled on this interface.
  IPX SAP update interval is 1 minute(s)
  IPX type 20 propagation packet forwarding is disabled
  Incoming access list is not set
```

```
Outgoing access list is not set
IPX helper access list is not set
SAP GNS processing enabled, delay 0 ms, output filter list is not set
SAP Input filter list is not set
SAP Output filter list is not set
SAP Router filter list is not set
Input filter list is not set
Output filter list is not set
Router filter list is not set
Netbios Input host access list is not set
Netbios Input bytes access list is not set
Netbios Output host access list is not set
Netbios Output bytes access list is not set
Updates each 60 seconds, aging multiples RIP: 3 SAP: 3
SAP interpacket delay is 55 ms, maximum size is 480 bytes
RIP interpacket delay is 55 ms, maximum size is 432 bytes
IPX accounting is disabled
IPX fast switching is configured (enabled)
RIP packets received 0, RIP packets sent 200
SAP packets received 0, SAP packets sent 166
```

RouterB and RouterC should be reachable from RouterA. IPX has limited test functionality compared to IP. With IPX, you can only ping another IPX interface.

```
RouterA#ping ipx 2.b.b.b←ping RouterB

Type escape sequence to abort.
Sending 5, 100-byte IPX cisco Echoes to 2.000b.000b.000b, timeout is 2 seconds:
!!!!!
Success rate is 100 percent (5/5), round-trip min/avg/max = 28/29/32 ms
```

Using the IPX ping command verify that you can reach RouterC.

```
RouterA#ping ipx 3.c.c.c←ping RouterC

Type escape sequence to abort.
Sending 5, 100-byte IPX cisco Echoes to 3.000c.000c.000c, timeout is 2 seconds:
!!!!!
Success rate is 100 percent (5/5), round-trip min/avg/max = 56/56/60 ms
```

Now, connect to RouterC. Type the **show ipx route** command to display the IPX routing table for RouterC. We see that RouterC has two directly connected IPX networks: Network 3 and Network 4. Three networks have been learned via IPX RIP: Network 1, Network 2, and Network 4. All of these RIP routes have a next-hop address of RouterB.

```
RouterC#show ipx route
Codes: C - Connected primary network,    c - Connected secondary network
       S - Static, F - Floating static, L - Local (internal), W - IPXWAN
       R - RIP, E - EIGRP, N - NLSP, X - External, A - Aggregate
       s - seconds, u - uses

5 Total IPX routes. Up to 1 parallel paths and 16 hops allowed.

No default route known.

C          3 (PPP),          Se0/0
C          4 (NOVELL-ETHER), Et0/0


                           The next hop address for all remote networks
                           is RouterB
                              ↓
R          1 [13/02] via    3.000b.000b.000b,   57s, Se0/0
R          2 [07/01] via    3.000b.000b.000b,   58s, Se0/0
R          5 [13/02] via    3.000b.000b.000b,   58s, Se0/0
```

Type the **show ipx interface brief** command to display the status of each interface on the router. We see that RouterC has two IPX networks configured. Network 4 is assigned to interface Ethernet0/0, and Network 3 is assigned to interface S0/0. We see that both networks are in an up/up status.

```
RouterC#show ipx interface brief
Interface         IPX Network Encapsulation Status                IPX State
Ethernet0/0       4           NOVELL-ETHER  up                    [up]
Serial0/0         3           PPP           up                    [up]
BRI0/0            unassigned  not config'd  administratively down n/a
BRI0/0:1          unassigned  not config'd  administratively down n/a
BRI0/0:2          unassigned  not config'd  administratively down n/a
```

Both RouterB and RouterA should be reachable via an IPX ping. Try to ping Network 3 on RouterB.

```
RouterC#ping ipx 3.b.b.b

Type escape sequence to abort.
Sending 5, 100-byte IPX cisco Echoes to 3.000b.000b.000b, timeout is 2 seconds:
!!!!!
Success rate is 100 percent (5/5), round-trip min/avg/max = 28/29/32 ms
```

Make sure that both interfaces on IPX Network 2 are also reachable.

```
RouterC#ping ipx 2.b.b.b←ping RouterB

Type escape sequence to abort.
Sending 5, 100-byte IPX cisco Echoes to 2.000b.000b.000b, timeout is 2 seconds:
!!!!!
```

```
Success rate is 100 percent (5/5), round-trip min/avg/max = 28/29/32 ms

RouterC#ping ipx 2.a.a.a←ping RouterA

Type escape sequence to abort.
Sending 5, 100-byte IPX cisco Echoes to 2.000a.000a.000a, timeout is 2 seconds:
!!!!!
Success rate is 100 percent (5/5), round-trip min/avg/max = 56/56/56 ms
```

The **show ipx traffic** command is useful. The command gives detailed information on the number of IPX packets that have been sent or received on the router.

```
RouterC#show ipx traffic
System Traffic for 0.0000.0000.0001 System-Name: RouterC
Rcvd:    36 total, 0 format errors, 0 checksum errors, 0 bad hop count,
         0 packets pitched, 36 local destination, 0 multicast
Bcast:   16 received, 29 sent
Sent:    50 generated, 0 forwarded
         0 encapsulation failed, 0 no route
SAP:     1 SAP requests, 0 SAP replies, 0 servers
         0 SAP Nearest Name requests, 0 replies
         0 SAP General Name requests, 0 replies
         5 SAP advertisements received, 4 sent
         2 SAP flash updates sent, 0 SAP format errors
RIP:     1 RIP requests, 0 RIP replies, 5 routes
         9 RIP advertisements received, 18 sent
         2 RIP flash updates sent, 0 RIP format errors
Echo:    Rcvd 5 requests, 15 replies
         Sent 15 requests, 5 replies
         0 unknown: 0 no socket, 0 filtered, 0 no helper
         0 SAPs throttled, freed NDB len 0
Watchdog:
         0 packets received, 0 replies spoofed
Queue lengths:
         IPX input: 0, SAP 0, RIP 0, GNS 0
         SAP throttling length: 0/(no limit), 0 nets pending lost route reply
         Delayed process creation: 0
EIGRP:   Total received 0, sent 0
         Updates received 0, sent 0
         Queries received 0, sent 0
         Replies received 0, sent 0
         SAPs received 0, sent 0
NLSP:    Level-1 Hellos received 0, sent 0
         PTP Hello received 0, sent 0
         Level-1 LSPs received 0, sent 0
         LSP Retransmissions: 0
         LSP checksum errors received: 0
         LSP HT=0 checksum errors received: 0
         Level-1 CSNPs received 0, sent 0
         Level-1 PSNPs received 0, sent 0
         Level-1 DR Elections: 0
         Level-1 SPF Calculations: 0
         Level-1 Partial Route Calculations: 0
```

Now, let's connect to RouterB. Use the **show ipx interface brief** command to display a summary of all interfaces on the router. We see that there are two IPX networks on this router—S0/0 and S0/1—both of which are in an up/up state.

```
RouterB#show ipx interface brief
Interface          IPX Network  Encapsulation Status                 IPX State
Ethernet0/0        unassigned   not config'd  administratively down  n/a
Serial0/0          3            PPP           up                     [up]
Serial0/1          2            PPP           up                     [up]
```

The **show ipx route** command will display the routing table information for RouterB. We see that RouterB has two directly connected networks: Network 2 and Network 3. Networks 1, 4, and 5 have been learned via IPX RIP.

```
RouterB#show ipx route
Codes: C - Connected primary network,    c - Connected secondary network
       S - Static, F - Floating static, L - Local (internal), W - IPXWAN
       R - RIP, E - EIGRP, N - NLSP, X - External, A - Aggregate
       s - seconds, u - uses

5 Total IPX routes. Up to 1 parallel paths and 16 hops allowed.

No default route known.

C         2 (PPP),           Se0/1
C         3 (PPP),           Se0/0
R         1 [07/01] via      2.000a.000a.000a,    30s, Se0/1←RIP route
R         4 [07/01] via      3.000c.000c.000c,    31s, Se0/0←RIP route
R         5 [07/01] via      2.000a.000a.000a,    31s, Se0/1←RIP route
```

Using the IPX ping command, verify that you can reach RouterC and RouterA.

```
RouterB#ping ipx 3.c.c.c←ping RouterC

Type escape sequence to abort.
Sending 5, 100-byte IPX cisco Echoes to 3.000c.000c.000c, timeout is 2 seconds:
!!!!!
Success rate is 100 percent (5/5), round-trip min/avg/max = 28/29/32 ms

RouterB#ping ipx 2.a.a.a←ping RouterA

Type escape sequence to abort.
Sending 5, 100-byte IPX cisco Echoes to 2.000a.000a.000a, timeout is 2 seconds:
!!!!!
Success rate is 100 percent (5/5), round-trip min/avg/max = 28/29/32 ms
```

Let's try to telnet to RouterC. Issue the telnet command, and when prompted for a host, enter 3.c.c.c. We see that RouterB issues an error message, saying that it is unable to find a computer address. Telnet is an IP protocol application. IPX does not use Telnet, nor does it have an equivalent. The only test tool that is available when running IPX on a network is the IPX ping. This is why it is important to always run the IP protocol on your network.

```
RouterB#telnet
Host: ?3.c.c.c←try to telnet to an IPX address
Translating "3.c.c.c"...domain server (255.255.255.255)
% Unknown command or computer name, or unable to find computer address
       ↑
       Telnet can only be used with the IP protocol. IPX does not support
       telnet
```

Let's examine how the IPX RIP routing protocol works. Enable IPX RIP debugging with the **debug ipx routing activity** and **debug ipx routing events** commands. If you are not connected to the console port of the router, be sure to also issue the **terminal monitor** command to send all debug output to your terminal session.

```
RouterB#debug ipx routing activity
IPX routing debugging is on

RouterB#debug ipx routing events
IPX routing events debugging is on
```

IPX RIP has many similarities to IP RIP in terms of how updates are sent and received. Every 60 seconds, a router will send an update to each directly connected neighbor. The update consists of all routes that the router can reach and the distance to those routes. With IP RIP, there is one metric (hop-count). With IPX RIP, there are two metrics. The first metric is hop-count. The second metric is delay. By default, the delay on a WAN interface is six, and the delay on a LAN interface is one. The following two show interface outputs for a Ethernet and a serial interface show that the delay is listed in the output of the **show ipx interface** command:

```
RouterA#show ipx int e 0/0
Ethernet0/0 is up, line protocol is up
  IPX address is 1.00e0.1e5b.2601, NOVELL-ETHER [up]

                              A LAN interface has a default IPX delay
                              of 1
                              ↓
Delay of this IPX network, in ticks is 1 throughput 0 link delay 0
```

```
RouterA#show ipx int s 0/0
Serial0/0 is up, line protocol is up
  IPX address is 2.000a.000a.000a [up]
```

```
                                        A WAN interface has a default IPX
                                        delay of 6
                                        ↓
  Delay of this IPX network, in ticks is 6 throughput 0 link delay 0
```

IPX RIP will prefer a route with lower delay over a route with a lower hop-count.

The **debug ipx routing** output, shown as follows, displays the updates sent out from and received on RouterB. The first update is sent from RouterB to RouterC. The update informs RouterC that RouterB has a route to IPX network 5, IPX network 1, and IPX network 2.

```
RouterB sends an update to RouterC
↓
IPXRIP: positing full update to 3.ffff.ffff.ffff via Serial0/0 (broadcast)
IPXRIP: src=3.000b.000b.000b, dst=3.ffff.ffff.ffff, packet sent
     network 5, hops 2,   delay 13
     network 1, hops 2,   delay 13
     network 2, hops 1,   delay 7
```

Next, RouterB receives an update from RouterC. RouterC informs RouterB that it has a route to IPX network 4.

```
RouterB receives an update from RouterC
↓
IPXRIP: update from 3.000c.000c.000c
     4 in 1 hops, delay 7
```

RouterB then sends an update to RouterA. RouterB tells RouterA that it has a route to IPX network 4 and IPX network 3.

```
RouterB sends an update to RouterA
↓
IPXRIP: positing full update to 2.ffff.ffff.ffff via Serial0/1 (broadcast)
IPXRIP: src=2.000b.000b.000b, dst=2.ffff.ffff.ffff, packet sent
     network 4, hops 2,   delay 13
     network 3, hops 1,   delay 7
```

Finally, RouterB receives an update from RouterA. RouterA informs RouterB that it has a route to IPX network 1 and IPX network 5.

```
RouterB receives an update from RouterA
↓
IPXRIP: update from 2.000a.000a.000a
    1 in 1 hops, delay 7
    5 in 1 hops, delay 7
```

This process repeats itself every 60 seconds.

Lab #71: IPX EIGRP

Equipment Needed

The following equipment is needed to perform this lab exercise:

■ Three Cisco routers. One of the routers must have two serial interfaces, and the other two routers must have one serial interface and one Ethernet interface.

■ Two Cisco crossover cables. If a Cisco crossover cable is not available, then you can use a Cisco DTE cable connected to a Cisco DCE cable.

■ A Cisco rolled cable for console port connection to the routers

■ A Cisco IOS image that supports the IPX protocol

Configuration Overview

This lab will demonstrate IPX routing protocols. By default, IPX RIP is enabled on all interfaces. EIGRP can also be used as a routing protocol for IPX networks. EIGRP has several advantages over RIP, such as the following:

■ Faster convergence

■ Less network traffic dedicated to routing updates (EIGRP only sends out periodic updates of its routing table)

■ Lower CPU utilization

■ Better scaling in large networks

■ Automatic redistribution with IPX RIP

In this lab, we will be running IPX RIP on the LAN interfaces and EIGRP on all other interfaces. Because IPX RIP is enabled on all interfaces by default, we will be explicitly turning it off on those interfaces where we want to run EIGRP.

As shown in Figure 18–7, this lab defines five IPX networks. RouterA, RouterB, and RouterC are each given IPX node numbers: a.a.a, b.b.b, and c.c.c, respectively. The three routers are connected, as shown in the figure. RouterB acts as a DCE and supplies clocking to RouterA and RouterC.

Router Configuration

The configurations for the three routers in this example are as follows (key IPX commands are highlighted in bold):

RouterA

```
Current configuration:
!
version 11.2
no service password-encryption
no service udp-small-servers
no service tcp-small-servers
!
hostname RouterA
!
!
ipx routing 000a.000a.000a←Enable IPX routing. Define the IPX node to be 000a.000a.000a
!
interface Loopback0
 no ip address
 ipx network 5←Make this interface IPX network 5
!
interface Ethernet0/0
 no ip address
 no keepalive
```

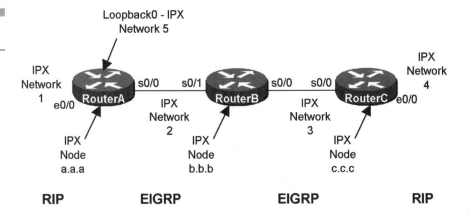

Figure 18–7
IPX EIGRP

Loopback0 - IPX
Network 5

IPX
Network
1
e0/0 **RouterA** s0/0   s0/1 **RouterB** s0/0   s0/0 **RouterC** e0/0

IPX
Network
2

IPX
Network
3

IPX
Network
4

IPX
Node
a.a.a

IPX
Node
b.b.b

IPX
Node
c.c.c

RIP   **EIGRP**   **EIGRP**   **RIP**

```
 ipx network 1
!
interface Serial0/0
 no ip address
 encapsulation ppp
 ipx network 2←Make this interface IPX network 2
 no fair-queue
!
no ip classless
!
!
ipx router eigrp 1←Enable IPX EIGRP autonomous system 1
 network 2←Include IPX network 2 in EIGRP updates
!
!
ipx router rip←Enable IPX RIP on this router
 no network 2←Do not advertise IPX network 2 in RIP updates
!
line con 0
line aux 0
line vty 0 4
 login
!
end
```

RouterB

```
Current configuration:
!
version 11.2
no service password-encryption
no service udp-small-servers
no service tcp-small-servers
!
hostname RouterB
!
!
ipx routing 000b.000b.000b←Enable IPX routing. Define the IPX node to be 000b.000b.000b
!
interface Serial0/0
 no ip address
 encapsulation ppp
 ipx network 3←Make this interface IPX network 3
no fair-queue
 clockrate 64000
!
interface Serial0/1
 no ip address
 encapsulation ppp
 ipx network 2←Make this interface IPX network 2
clockrate 64000
!
no ip classless
```

```
!
!
ipx router eigrp 1←Enable IPX EIGRP autonomous system 1
 network all←Advertise all IPX networks on this router in EIGRP updates
!
!
no ipx router rip←Do not enable IPX RIP on this router
!
!
line con 0
line aux 0
line vty 0 4
 login
!
end
```

RouterC

```
Current configuration:
!
version 11.2
no service password-encryption
no service udp-small-servers
no service tcp-small-servers
!
hostname RouterC
!
!
ipx routing 000c.000c.000c←Enable IPX routing. Define the IPX node to be 000c.000c.000c
!
interface Ethernet0/0
 no ip address
 no keepalive
 ipx network 4←Make this interface IPX network 4
!
interface Serial0/0
 no ip address
 encapsulation ppp
 ipx network 3←Make this interface IPX network 3
 no fair-queue
!
no ip classless
!
!
ipx router eigrp 1←Enable IPX EIGRP autonomous system 1
 network 3←Include IPX network 3 in EIGRP updates
!
!
ipx router rip←Enable IPX RIP on this router
 no network 3←Do not advertise IPX network 3 in RIP updates
!
line con 0
line aux 0
```

```
line vty 0 4
 login
!
end
```

Notice that IPX RIP/SAP has to be turned off on those interfaces where we do not want it to run.

Monitoring and Testing the Configuration

Let's start by connecting to RouterA. Verify that all IPX interfaces are up and active with the **show ipx interface brief** command.

```
RouterA#show ipx interface brief
Interface          IPX Network Encapsulation Status               IPX State
Ethernet0/0        1           NOVELL-ETHER  up                   [up]
Serial0/0          2           PPP           up                   [up]
BRI0/0             unassigned  not config'd  administratively down n/a
BRI0/0:1           unassigned  not config'd  administratively down n/a
BRI0/0:2           unassigned  not config'd  administratively down n/a
Ethernet1/0        unassigned  not config'd  administratively down n/a
Serial1/0          unassigned  not config'd  administratively down n/a
Serial1/1          unassigned  not config'd  administratively down n/a
Loopback0          5           UNKNOWN       up                   [up]
```

The **show ipx route** command shows us that we have three directly connected networks (Network 1, Network 2, and Network 5). Two remote networks have been learned via EIGRP: Networks 3 and 4. Notice that there are no RIP-learned routes in this routing table.

```
RouterA#show ipx route
Codes: C - Connected primary network,    c - Connected secondary network
       S - Static, F - Floating static, L - Local (internal), W - IPXWAN
       R - RIP, E - EIGRP, N - NLSP, X - External, A - Aggregate
       s - seconds, u - uses

5 Total IPX routes. Up to 1 parallel paths and 16 hops allowed.

No default route known.

C        1 (NOVELL-ETHER),  Et0/0
C        2 (PPP),           Se0/0
C        5 (UNKNOWN),       Lo0

EIGRP learned route
↓
E        3 [2681856/0] via          2.000b.000b.000b, age 02:08:01,
```

EIGRP learned route
↓
```
E              4 [2707456/1] via          2.000b.000b.000b, age 02:07:52,
                         385u, Se0/0
```

The **show ipx eigrp neighbor** command will display information on which neighboring EIGRP routers have been discovered.

```
RouterA#show ipx eigrp neigh

IPX EIGRP Neighbors for process 1
H   Address                   Interface      Hold Uptime   SRTT      RTO    Q    Seq
                                             (sec)         (ms)             Cnt  Num
0   2.000b.000b.000b          Se0/0          13 02:10:19   53        318    0    38
    ↑
       RouterB, interface S0/1 is an EIGRP neighbor
```

The **show ipx eigrp interfaces** command will show which router interfaces are running EIGRP. Notice that only interface S0/0 of RouterA is an EIGRP interface. Interface E0/0 on RouterA is still running IPX RIP.

```
RouterA#show ipx eigrp interfaces

IPX EIGRP Interfaces for process 1

                        Xmit Queue     Mean   Pacing Time    Multicast     Pending
Interface     Peers     Un/Reliable    SRTT   Un/Reliable    Flow Timer    Routes
Se0/0         1         0/0            53     0/15           263           0
↑
Only interface S0/0 is running EIGRP. Interface E0/0 is still running EIGRP.
```

Now, let's connect to RouterB. The **show ipx interface brief** command should show us that all interfaces are up and active.

```
RouterB#show ipx interface brief
Interface          IPX Network Encapsulation Status                      IPX State
Ethernet0/0        unassigned  not config'd  administratively down       n/a
Serial0/0          3           PPP           up                          [up]
Serial0/1          2           PPP           up                          [up]
```

The **show ipx route** command should show EIGRP routes to three IPX networks: 1, 4, and 5.

```
RouterB#show ipx route
Codes: C - Connected primary network,    c - Connected secondary network
       S - Static, F - Floating static, L - Local (internal), W - IPXWAN
       R - RIP, E - EIGRP, N - NLSP, X - External, A - Aggregate
       s - seconds, u - uses
```

```
5 Total IPX routes. Up to 1 parallel paths and 16 hops allowed.

No default route known.

C            2 (PPP),            Se0/1
C            3 (PPP),            Se0/0
E            1 [2195456/1] via         2.000a.000a.000a, age 02:08:28,
                       392u, Se0/1
E            4 [2195456/1] via         3.000c.000c.000c, age 02:08:28,
                       3u, Se0/0
E            5 [2297856/1] via         2.000a.000a.000a, age 02:08:28,
                       1u, Se0/1
```

There should be two discovered EIGRP neighbors: IPX Network 2 and IPX Network 3. Verify this status with the **show ipx eigrp neighbor** command.

```
RouterB#show ipx eigrp neigh

IPX EIGRP Neighbors for process 1
H   Address                  Interface      Hold Uptime   SRTT      RTO   Q   Seq
                                            (sec)         (ms)            Cnt Num


       EIGRP neighbor RouterA
       ↓
1   2.000a.000a.000a         Se0/1          10 02:11:10   22        200   0   20


       EIGRP neighbor RouterC
       ↓
0   3.000c.000c.000c         Se0/0          14 02:11:41   43        258   0   22
```

Verify with the **show ipx eigrp interfaces** command that both serial interfaces on RouterB are running EIGRP.

```
RouterB#show ipx eigrp interfaces

IPX EIGRP Interfaces for process 1

                        Xmit Queue   Mean   Pacing Time   Multicast    Pending
Interface    Peers      Un/Reliable  SRTT   Un/Reliable   Flow Timer   Routes
Se0/0        1          0/0          43     0/15          207          0
Se0/0        1          0/0          22     0/15          103          0
↑
```
Both serial interfaces on RouterB are using EIGRP for their routing protocol.

The **show ipx eigrp traffic** command is a useful command that shows how much EIGRP traffic has been sent and received on the router.

```
RouterB#show ipx eigrp traffic
IP-EIGRP Traffic Statistics for process 1
  Hellos sent/received: 3433/3430
  Updates sent/received: 11/11
  Queries sent/received: 10/7
  Replies sent/received: 7/10
  Acks sent/received: 37/33
  Input queue high water mark 2, 0 drops
```

Now, connect to RouterC. Verify that all IPX interfaces are active with the **show ipx interface brief** command.

```
RouterC#show ipx interface brief
Interface          IPX Network Encapsulation Status                IPX State
Ethernet0/0        4           NOVELL-ETHER  up                     [up]
Serial0/0          3           PPP           up                     [up]
BRI0/0             unassigned  not config'd  administratively down  n/a
BRI0/0:1           unassigned  not config'd  administratively down  n/a
BRI0/0:2           unassigned  not config'd  administratively down  n/a
```

The **show ipx route** command should reveal that there are three networks that have been learned via EIGRP. These should be Networks 1, 2, and 5.

```
RouterC#show ipx route
Codes: C - Connected primary network,    c - Connected secondary network
       S - Static, F - Floating static, L - Local (internal), W - IPXWAN
       R - RIP, E - EIGRP, N - NLSP, X - External, A - Aggregate
       s - seconds, u - uses

5 Total IPX routes. Up to 1 parallel paths and 16 hops allowed.

No default route known.

C          3 (PPP),          Se0/0
C          4 (NOVELL-ETHER),  Et0/0
E          1 [2707456/1] via          3.000b.000b.000b, age 02:09:47,
                         4u, Se0/0
E          2 [2681856/0] via          3.000b.000b.000b, age 02:09:47,
                         1u, Se0/0
E          5 [2809856/1] via          3.000b.000b.000b, age 02:09:47,
                         1u, Se0/0
```

The **show ipx eigrp interfaces** command should show that there is one interface on this router that is running EIGRP: Serial0/0.

```
RouterC#show ipx eigrp interfaces

IPX EIGRP Interfaces for process 1
```

Interface	Peers	Xmit Queue Un/Reliable	Mean SRTT	Pacing Time Un/Reliable	Multicast Flow Timer	Pending Routes
Se0/0	1	0/0	20	0/15	95	0

Lab #72: Static SAP Entries and SAP Access Lists

Equipment Needed

The following equipment is needed to perform this lab exercise:

- Three Cisco routers. One of the routers must have two serial interfaces, and the other two routers must have one serial interface and one Ethernet interface.

- Two Cisco crossover cables. If a Cisco crossover cable is not available, then you can use a Cisco DTE cable connected to a Cisco DCE cable.

- A Cisco rolled cable for console port connection to the routers

- A Cisco IOS image that supports the IPX protocol

Configuration Overview

This lab will demonstrate how SAP advertisements work on a Cisco router. We will define static SAPs on our routers and explore how these work. SAP updates can take up a lot of bandwidth on an IPX network. The Cisco IOS enables static SAP entries to be created. Finally, we will demonstrate how a Cisco router can filter SAP updates.

As shown in Figure 18–8, this lab defines five IPX networks. RouterA, RouterB, and RouterC are each given IPX node numbers: a.a.a, b.b.b, and c.c.c, respectively.

The three routers are connected, as shown in the figure. RouterB acts as a DCE and supplies clocking to RouterA and RouterC.

NOTE: *Although we are not running IPX RIP/SAP on the WAN, we will see that SAP updates are still propagated throughout the network.*

Router Configuration

The configurations for the three routers in this example are as follows (key IPX commands are highlighted in bold):

Figure 18–8
IPX SAP

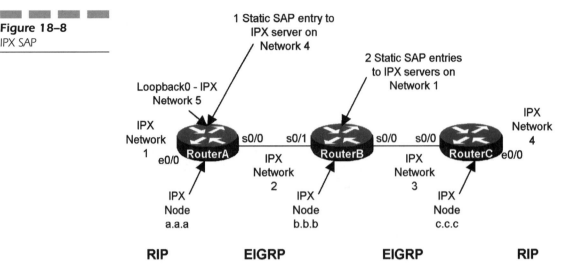

RouterA

```
Current configuration:
!
version 11.2
no service password-encryption
no service udp-small-servers
no service tcp-small-servers
!
hostname RouterA
!
!
ipx routing 000a.000a.000a←Enable IPX routing. Define the IPX node to be 000a.000a.000a
!
interface Loopback0
 no ip address
 ipx network 5←Make this interface IPX network 5
!
interface Ethernet0/0
 no ip address
 no keepalive
 ipx network 1←Make this interface IPX network 1
!
interface Serial0/0
 no ip address
 encapsulation ppp
 ipx network 2←Make this interface IPX network 2
 no fair-queue
!
no ip classless
!
```

```
!
ipx router eigrp 1←Enable IPX EIGRP autonomous system 1
 network 2←Include IPX network 2 in EIGRP updates
!
!
ipx router rip←Enable IPX RIP on this router
 no network 2←Do not advertise IPX network 2 in RIP updates
!
!
ipx sap 4 Server4 4.00e0.1e5b.0a81 451 2←Define a static SAP entry on this
                                            router
!
!
line con 0
line aux 0
line vty 0 4
 login
!
end
```

RouterB

```
Current configuration:
!
version 11.2
no service password-encryption
no service udp-small-servers
no service tcp-small-servers
!
hostname RouterB
!
!
ipx routing 000b.000b.000b←Enable IPX routing. Define the IPX node to be 000b.000b.000b
!
interface Serial0/0
 no ip address
 encapsulation ppp
 ipx network 3←Make this interface IPX network 3
 no fair-queue
 clockrate 64000
!
interface Serial0/1
 no ip address
 encapsulation ppp
 ipx network 2
 clockrate 64000
!
no ip classless
!
!
ipx router eigrp 1←Enable IPX EIGRP autonomous system 1
 network all←Include all IPX networks in EIGRP advertisements
!
```

```
!
no ipx router rip←Do not enable IPX RIP on this router
!
ipx sap 4 Server1 1.00e0.1e5b.2601 451 1←Define a static SAP entry on this
                                            router
ipx sap 7 Server2 1.00e0.1e5b.2601 451 1←Define a static SAP entry on this
                                            router
!
!
line con 0
line aux 0
line vty 0 4
 login
!
end
```

RouterC

```
Current configuration:
!
version 11.2
no service password-encryption
no service udp-small-servers
no service tcp-small-servers
!
hostname RouterC
!
!
ipx routing 000c.000c.000c←Enable IPX routing. Define the IPX node to be 000c.000c.000c
!
interface Ethernet0/0
 no ip address
 no keepalive
 ipx network 4←Make this interface IPX network 4
!
interface Serial0/0
 no ip address
 encapsulation ppp
 ipx network 3←Make this interface IPX network 3
 no fair-queue
!
no ip classless
!
!
ipx router eigrp 1←Enable IPX EIGRP autonomous system 1
 network 3←Include IPX network 3 in EIGRP updates
!
!
ipx router rip←Enable IPX RIP on this router
 no network 3←Do not advertise IPX network 3 in RIP updates
!
line con 0
line aux 0
```

```
line vty 0 4
 login
!
end
```

Monitoring and Testing the Configuration

Looking at the configurations of our three routers, we see that we have defined three static SAP entries.

1. RouterA has a static SAP entry to a server (Server4) that is located on IPX Network 4.

2. RouterB has a static SAP entry to a server (Server1) that is located on IPX Network 1.

3. RouterB has a second static SAP entry to a server (Server2) that is also located on IPX Network 1.

Let's connect to RouterA. We can view the known IPX servers with the **show ipx servers** command. Notice that RouterA only knows about one IPX server: Server4. This server is the one that we have statically defined on RouterA. Why does RouterA not know about the two servers (Server1 and Server2) that we statically defined on RouterB? The answer requires an understanding of RIP/SAP split-horizon. RIP/SAP split-horizon says that a router will never advertise RIP routing or SAP server information out the same interface from which it learned the information. In this case, the static SAP entry on RouterB, which points to two servers on RouterA, will never be broadcast to RouterA. RouterB treats the static entry as if the entry had been learned from RouterA. Thus, RouterA should not have an entry for the two servers that were statically defined on RouterB.

```
RouterA#show ipx servers
Codes: S - Static, P - Periodic, E - EIGRP, N - NLSP, H - Holddown, + = detail
1 Total IPX Servers

Table ordering is based on routing and server info

    Type  Name              Net     Address   Port    Route Hops  Itf
S    4    Server4           4.00e0.1e5b.0a81:0451     2707456/01   2
Se0/0
```

Now, connect to RouterB. Use the **show ipx servers** command to view all IPX servers known to RouterB. RouterB knows about two IPX servers. These are the two servers (Server1 and Server2) that we statically defined on RouterB. Why does RouterB not know about the IPX server (Server4) that is statically defined on RouterA? Once again, the answer is split-horizon. The static SAP entry on RouterA points to IPX Network 4. The static SAP entry on RouterA is treated as if it were learned from RouterB, because RouterB is the next-hop toward IPX Network 4. Thus, RouterA will not send the static SAP entry to RouterB, because the router thinks that the entry came from RouterB in the first place.

```
RouterB#show ipx servers
Codes: S - Static, P - Periodic, E - EIGRP, N - NLSP, H - Holddown, + = detail
2 Total IPX Servers

Table ordering is based on routing and server info

    Type  Name                  Net      Address     Port   Route Hops   Itf
S   4     Server1               1.00e0.1e5b.2601:0451       2195456/01   1  Se0/1
S   7     Server2               1.00e0.1e5b.2601:0451       2195456/01   1  Se0/1
```

Now, let's connect to RouterC. The **show ipx servers** command shows us that RouterC knows about two IPX servers (Server1 and Server2). These are the two servers that were statically defined on RouterB. RouterB will advertise these server entries to RouterC, because RouterB treats the static entries as if they were learned from RouterA. Thus, RouterB is allowed to send the static SAP entries to RouterC without violating the split-horizon rule.

```
RouterC#show ipx servers
Codes: S - Static, P - Periodic, E - EIGRP, N - NLSP, H - Holddown, + = detail
2 Total IPX Servers

Table ordering is based on routing and server info

    Type  Name                  Net      Address     Port   Route Hops   Itf
E   4     Server1               1.00e0.1e5b.2601:0451       2707456/01   2  Se0/0
E   7     Server2               1.00e0.1e5b.2601:0451       2707456/01   2  Se0/0
```

Let's turn on SAP debugging with the **debug ipx sap events** and **debug ipx sap activity** commands. Remember to also use the **term mon** command to direct the debug output to your terminal if you are not connected to the console port of the router.

```
RouterC#debug ipx sap activity
IPX service debugging is on

RouterC#debug ipx sap events
IPX service events debugging is on
```

The following output will be repeated every 60 seconds. We see that RouterC is sending a SAP update to IPX Network 4, telling the network about two IPX servers (Server1 and Server2). Notice that we do not see any SAP updates coming into RouterC from RouterB, because we are running EIGRP on the WAN link between RouterC and RouterB, not RIP/SAP.

```
                         RouterC broadcasts the SAP updates to the Ethernet
                         LAN on Ethernet0/0
                                      ↓
IPXSAP: positing update to 4.ffff.ffff.ffff via Ethernet0/0 (broadcast) (full)
IPXSAP: Update type 0x2 len 160 src:4.00e0.1e5b.0a81 dest:4.ffff.ffff.ffff(452)
  type 0x4, "Server1", 1.00e0.1e5b.2601(451), 2 hops←RouterC advertises two IPX
                                                      servers to IPX network 4
  type 0x7, "Server2", 1.00e0.1e5b.2601(451), 2 hops
```

Cisco supports extensive IPX filtering capabilities. One of the Cisco IPX features is the capability to filter outgoing or incoming SAP updates. This feature is frequently used for security purposes, where you do not want certain users or networks to know about specific servers. Let's change the configuration of RouterB so that RouterB only sends an IPX SAP server update to RouterC for Server1 (and not Server2). Enter configuration mode with the **config term** command. Enter the global command **access-list 1000 deny -1 7 Server2** and **access-list 1000 permit -1**. Then, go into interface configuration mode using the **int s 0/0** command and enter the command **ipx output-sap-filter 1000**. We have now configured an access list on RouterB that will not send out any updates for an IPX server named Server2 that is a SAP type 7.

```
RouterB#config term
Enter configuration commands, one per line. End with CNTL/Z.
RouterB(config)#access-list 1000 deny -1 7 Server2
RouterB(config)#access-list 1000 permit -1
RouterB(config)#
RouterB(config)#int s 0/0
RouterB(config-if)#ipx output-sap-filter 1000
RouterB(config-if)#exit
RouterB(config)#exit
RouterB#
```

After entering the earlier access list commands on RouterB, quickly connect to RouterC. IPX SAP debugging should still be enabled on RouterC. The following debug output will be seen on RouterC. Notice how RouterC deletes the entry to Server2 by first declaring the server unreachable (advertises the server with a hop-count of 16). Then, RouterC no longer advertises the server.

```
IPXEIGRP: Sending EIGRP SAP flash
IPXEIGRP: Received EIGRP SAP from 3.000b.000b.000b←EIGRP update received from
                                                    RouterB

IPXSAP: positing update to 4.ffff.ffff.ffff via Ethernet0/0 (broadcast) (full)
IPXSAP: Update type 0x2 len 160 src:4.00e0.1e5b.0a81 dest:4.ffff.ffff.ffff(452)
 type 0x4, "Server1", 1.00e0.1e5b.2601(451), 2 hops
 type 0x7, "Server2", 1.00e0.1e5b.2601(451), 16 hops←RouterC advertises
                                                      Server2 as being 16 hops
                                                      away. This means that it
                                                      is unreachable.
IPXSAP: server type 7 named Server2 metric 255 being deleted
IPX: SAP queue-hash deleted for type 7, count 2

IPXSAP: positing update to 4.ffff.ffff.ffff via Ethernet0/0 (broadcast) (full)
IPXSAP: Update type 0x2 len 96 src:4.00e0.1e5b.0a81 dest:4.ffff.ffff.ffff(452)
 type 0x4, "Server1", 1.00e0.1e5b.2601(451), 2 hops←RouterC no longer
                                                     advertises Server2

IPXSAP: positing update to 4.ffff.ffff.ffff via Ethernet0/0 (broadcast) (full)
IPXSAP: Update type 0x2 len 96 src:4.00e0.1e5b.0a81 dest:4.ffff.ffff.ffff(452)
 type 0x4, "Server1", 1.00e0.1e5b.2601(451), 2 hops←RouterC no longer
                                                     advertises Server2
```

Turn off all debugging output with the **undebug all** command.

```
RouterC#undebug all
All possible debugging has been turned off
```

The **show ipx server** command should now only show one server, Server1.

```
RouterC#show ipx server
Codes: S - Static, P - Periodic, E - EIGRP, N - NLSP, H - Holddown, + = detail
1 Total IPX Servers

Table ordering is based on routing and server info

   Type Name               Net     Address     Port   Route Hops  Itf
E    4  Server1            1.00e0.1e5b.2601:0451       2707456/01  2  Se0/0
```

Let's reconnect to RouterB. Use the show ipx server command to display all known servers. We see that RouterB still knows about two servers—Server1 and Server2—although the router is filtering any updates related to Server2 to RouterC.

```
RouterB#show ipx server
Codes: S - Static, P - Periodic, E - EIGRP, N - NLSP, H - Holddown, + = detail
2 Total IPX Servers
```

```
Table ordering is based on routing and server info

      Type Name                    Net     Address      Port   Route Hops  Itf
S     4    Server1                 1.00e0.1e5b.2601:0451       2195456/01  1   Se0/1
S     7    Server2                 1.00e0.1e5b.2601:0451       2195456/01  1   Se0/1
```

The **show access-list** command can be used to verify that RouterB has an active access list.

```
RouterB#show access-list
IPX SAP access list 1000←Access List 1000
     deny FFFFFFFF 7 Server2←Do not send any updates to any network regarding
                             IPX Server2 with a server type of 7
     permit FFFFFFFF←Permit SAP updates to all other networks
```

Now, let's remove the output-sap-filter from RouterB. Enter configuration mode and under interface s 0/0, type the command **no ipx output-sap-filter 1000**.

```
RouterB#config term
Enter configuration commands, one per line. End with CNTL/Z.
RouterB(config)#int s 0/0
RouterB(config-if)#no ipx output-sap-filter 1000
RouterB(config-if)#exit
RouterB(config)#exit
```

Now, connect to RouterC. After a few seconds, the entry for Server2 will reappear in the **show ipx server** output.

```
RouterC#show ipx server
Codes: S - Static, P - Periodic, E - EIGRP, N - NLSP, H - Holddown, + = detail
2 Total IPX Servers

Table ordering is based on routing and server info

      Type Name                    Net     Address      Port   Route Hops  Itf
E     4    Server1                 1.00e0.1e5b.2601:0451       2707456/01  2   Se0/0
E     7    Server2                 1.00e0.1e5b.2601:0451       2707456/01  2   Se0/0
                ↑
        The entry for Server2 will now be back in the IPX server list
```

Now, we are going to add an input SAP filter on RouterC. An input SAP filter will filter out SAP updates that come into a router. Enter router configuration mode and enter the following **access-list** and **ipx input-sap-filter** statements.

```
RouterC#config term
Enter configuration commands, one per line. End with CNTL/Z.
RouterC(config)#access-list 1000 deny -1 4 Server1
RouterC(config)#access-list 1000 permit -1
RouterC(config)#exit
RouterC(config)#int s 0/0
RouterC(config-if)#ipx input-sap-filter 1000←Deny any incoming SAP advertisements
                                             that are for server type 4 and for a
                                             server named Server1.
RouterC(config-if)#exit
RouterC#
```

Now, view the IPX server list for RouterC with the **show ipx server** command. After a few minutes, the entry for Server1 will no longer be listed. RouterC is now filtering out these incoming SAP advertisements.

```
RouterC#sh ipx server
Codes: S - Static, P - Periodic, E - EIGRP, N - NLSP, H - Holddown, + = detail
1 Total IPX Servers

Table ordering is based on routing and server info

     Type Name                  Net    Address      Port   Route Hops  Itf
E       7 Server2               1.00e0.1e5b.2601:0451      2707456/01  2 Se0/0
```

The Cisco IOS also provides extensive route filtering capabilities. Output route filters prevent routes to selected networks from being advertised to other routers. Input route filters prevent advertised routes from being entered into the IPX routing table. Let's start off with an output route filter. View the IPX routing table of RouterC with the **show ipx route** command. We see that RouterC has learned about IPX Networks 1, 2, and 5 via EIGRP.

```
RouterC#show ipx route
Codes: C - Connected primary network,    c - Connected secondary network
       S - Static, F - Floating static, L - Local (internal), W - IPXWAN
       R - RIP, E - EIGRP, N - NLSP, X - External, A - Aggregate
       s - seconds, u - uses

5 Total IPX routes. Up to 1 parallel paths and 16 hops allowed.

No default route known.

C          3 (PPP),          Se0/0
C          4 (NOVELL-ETHER),  Et0/0

Routes to networks 1, 2, and 5 are learned via EIGRP
↓
E          1 [2707456/1] via        3.000b.000b.000b, age 00:03:23,
                         4u,  Se0/0
```

```
E          2 [2681856/0] via         3.000b.000b.000b, age 00:03:24,
                                 1u, Se0/0
E          5 [2809856/1] via         3.000b.000b.000b, age 00:03:24,
                                 1u, Se0/0
```

Connect to RouterA and enter configuration mode. Enter the following access list and distribute-list command. A distribute-list command is used with EIGRP to filter routes. The access list will deny RouterA from advertising any information on IPX Network 5.

```
RouterA#config term
Enter configuration commands, one per line. End with CNTL/Z.
RouterA(config)#access-list 810 deny 5←Do not advertise IPX network 5
RouterA(config)#access-list 810 permit -1←Advertise all other IPX networks
RouterA(config)#
RouterA(config)#router eigrp 1
RouterA(config-ipx-router)#distribute-list 810 out
RouterA(config-ipx-router)#exit
RouterA(config)#exit
```

Now, connect to RouterC. After a short period, the **show ipx route** command will reveal that the entry for a route to IPX Network 5 is no longer in the routing table.

```
RouterC#sh ipx route
Codes: C - Connected primary network,     c - Connected secondary network
       S - Static, F - Floating static, L - Local (internal), W - IPXWAN
       R - RIP, E - EIGRP, N - NLSP, X - External, A - Aggregate
       s - seconds, u - uses

4 Total IPX routes. Up to 1 parallel paths and 16 hops allowed.

No default route known.

C          3 (PPP),            Se0/0
C          4 (NOVELL-ETHER),   Et0/0
E          1 [2707456/1] via         3.000b.000b.000b, age 00:00:34,
                                 2u, Se0/0
E          2 [2681856/0] via         3.000b.000b.000b, age 00:09:09,
                                 1u, Se0/0
```

Now, connect to RouterB. Use the **show ipx route** command to examine the routing table. Notice that the route to IPX Network 5 has also been deleted from RouterB's routing table. RouterA is no longer advertising IPX Network 5 to either RouterB or RouterC.

```
RouterB#sh ipx route
Codes: C - Connected primary network,     c - Connected secondary network
       S - Static, F - Floating static, L - Local (internal), W - IPXWAN
       R - RIP, E - EIGRP, N - NLSP, X - External, A - Aggregate
       s - seconds, u - uses

4 Total IPX routes. Up to 1 parallel paths and 16 hops allowed.

No default route known.

C          2 (PPP),          Se0/1
C          3 (PPP),          Se0/0
E          1 [2195456/1] via          2.000a.000a.000a, age 00:01:52,
                     15u, Se0/1
E          4 [2195456/1] via          3.000c.000c.000c, age 00:01:53,
                     7u, Se0/0
```

Now, we will add an input route filter. Enter router configuration mode on RouterC. Add the following access-list and distribute-list command. This access list will filter any incoming advertisements for IPX Network 1 that come into RouterC.

```
RouterC#config term
Enter configuration commands, one per line. End with CNTL/Z.
RouterC(config)#access-list 820 deny 1←Filter out any routing updates for IPX
                                                 network 1
RouterC(config)#access-list 820 permit -1
RouterC(config)#
RouterC(config)#ipx router eigrp 1
RouterC(config-ipx-router)#distribute-list 820 in
RouterC(config-ipx-router)#exit
RouterC(config)#exit
```

Now, take a look at the IPX routing table for RouterC with the **show ipx route** command. The routing entry to IPX Network 1 has been removed from the routing table.

```
RouterC#sh ipx route
Codes: C - Connected primary network,     c - Connected secondary network
       S - Static, F - Floating static, L - Local (internal), W - IPXWAN
       R - RIP, E - EIGRP, N - NLSP, X - External, A - Aggregate
       s - seconds, u - uses

3 Total IPX routes. Up to 1 parallel paths and 16 hops allowed.

No default route known.

C          3 (PPP),          Se0/0
C          4 (NOVELL-ETHER),  Et0/0
E          2 [2681856/0] via          3.000b.000b.000b, age 00:00:08,
                     1u, Se0/0
```

Connect to RouterB and use the **show ipx route** command to view the routing table. We see that the route to IPX Network 1 is still in the routing table, because we are filtering this route as it comes into RouterC. The route is not filtered to RouterB.

```
RouterB#sh ipx route
Codes: C - Connected primary network,    c - Connected secondary network
       S - Static, F - Floating static, L - Local (internal), W - IPXWAN
       R - RIP, E - EIGRP, N - NLSP, X - External, A - Aggregate
       s - seconds, u - uses

4 Total IPX routes. Up to 1 parallel paths and 16 hops allowed.

No default route known.

C        2 (PPP),           Se0/1
C        3 (PPP),           Se0/0
E        1 [2195456/1] via        2.000a.000a.000a, age 00:03:40,
                   27u, Se0/1
E        4 [2195456/1] via        3.000c.000c.000c, age 00:00:23,
                   2u, Se0/0
```

IPX Monitoring and Troubleshooting Commands

This section will discuss key IPX monitoring and troubleshooting commands.

{**show ipx interface brief**}   This command can be used to get a quick snapshot of the state of all interfaces on a router that are running the IPX protocol.

```
RouterA#show ipx interface brief
Interface            IPX Network Encapsulation Status              IPX State
Ethernet0/0          1           NOVELL-ETHER  up                  [up]
Serial0/0            2           PPP           up                  [up]
BRI0/0               unassigned  not config'd  administratively down  n/a
BRI0/0:1             unassigned  not config'd  administratively down  n/a
BRI0/0:2             unassigned  not config'd  administratively down  n/a
Ethernet1/0          unassigned  not config'd  administratively down  n/a
Serial1/0            unassigned  not config'd  administratively down  n/a
Serial1/1            unassigned  not config'd  administratively down  n/a
Loopback0            5           UNKNOWN       up                  [up]
```

{**show ipx route**}   This command displays the routing table for this router. The routing table shows us that three IPX networks are directly connected. Network 1 is on Ethernet0, Network 2 is on Serial 0, and Network 5 is on Loopback 0. RouterA has learned about two networks via the IPX RIP routing protocol. Network 3 is one hop and seven ticks away, and Network 4 is two hops and 13 ticks away.

```
RouterA#show ipx route
Codes: C - Connected primary network,    c - Connected secondary network
       S - Static, F - Floating static, L - Local (internal), W - IPXWAN
       R - RIP, E - EIGRP, N - NLSP, X - External, A - Aggregate
       s - seconds, u - uses

5 Total IPX routes. Up to 1 parallel paths and 16 hops allowed.

No default route known.

C             1 (NOVELL-ETHER),    Et0/0
C             2 (PPP),             Se0/0
C             5 (UNKNOWN),         Lo0
```

```
              Tick Count          Next hop address
                  ↓                    ↓
R             3 [07/01] via        2.000b.000b.000b,    49s, Se0/0
                        ↑
              Hop Count to destination network
```

```
              Tick Count          Next hop address
                  ↓                    ↓
R             4 [13/02] via        2.000b.000b.000b,    50s, Se0/0
                        ↑
              Hop Count to destination network
```

{show interface}   The **show interface** command will show which link control protocols have been negotiated and opened. Traffic information and lead state status for the interface will also be displayed.

```
RouterA#show int s 0/0
Serial0/0 is up, line protocol is up
  Hardware is QUICC Serial
  MTU 1500 bytes, BW 1544 Kbit, DLY 20000 usec, rely 255/255, load 1/255
  Encapsulation PPP, loopback not set, keepalive set (10 sec)
  LCP Open
  Open: CDPCP, IPXCP←No IP is enabled on this interface
  Last input 00:00:01, output 00:00:01, output hang never
  Last clearing of "show interface" counters never
  Queueing strategy: fifo
  Output queue 0/40, 0 drops; input queue 0/75, 0 drops
  5 minute input rate 0 bits/sec, 0 packets/sec
  5 minute output rate 0 bits/sec, 0 packets/sec
     99 packets input, 3888 bytes, 0 no buffer←Packets input
```

```
           Received 99 broadcasts, 0 runts, 0 giants, 0 throttles
           0 input errors, 0 CRC, 0 frame, 0 overrun, 0 ignored, 0 abort
           100 packets output, 3902 bytes, 0 underruns←Packets output
           0 output errors, 0 collisions, 16 interface resets
           0 output buffer failures, 0 output buffers swapped out
           31 carrier transitions
           DCD=up  DSR=up  DTR=up  RTS=up  CTS=up
```

{show ipx interface}   Specific IPX information for an interface running the IPX protocol can be displayed with the **show ipx int s** command. This command shows the IPX address of the interface, as well as IPX routing, filtering, and SAP information.

```
RouterA#show ipx int s 0/0
Serial0/0 is up, line protocol is up
  IPX address is 2.000a.000a.000a [up]←IPX address

                                  A WAN interface has a default IPX
                                  delay of 6.
                                        ↓
Delay of this IPX network, in ticks is 6 throughput 0 link delay 0
IPXWAN processing not enabled on this interface.
IPX SAP update interval is 1 minute(s)
IPX type 20 propagation packet forwarding is disabled
Incoming access list is not set
Outgoing access list is not set
IPX helper access list is not set
SAP GNS processing enabled, delay 0 ms, output filter list is not set
SAP Input filter list is not set
SAP Output filter list is not set
SAP Router filter list is not set
Input filter list is not set
Output filter list is not set
Router filter list is not set
Netbios Input host access list is not set
Netbios Input bytes access list is not set
Netbios Output host access list is not set
Netbios Output bytes access list is not set
Updates each 60 seconds, aging multiples RIP: 3 SAP: 3
SAP interpacket delay is 55 ms, maximum size is 480 bytes
RIP interpacket delay is 55 ms, maximum size is 432 bytes
Watchdog processing is disabled, SPX spoofing is disabled, idle time 60
IPX accounting is disabled
IPX fast switching is configured (enabled)
RIP packets received 9, RIP packets sent 9←RIP is running on this interface
SAP packets received 1, SAP packets sent 1←SAP is running on this interface
```

{ping ipx}   IPX is limited in its diagnostic capabilities compared to IP. With IPX, the only tool available to test network connectivity is the **ping ipx** command.

```
RouterA#ping ipx 2.b.b.b←ping RouterB

Type escape sequence to abort.
Sending 5, 100-byte IPX cisco Echoes to 2.000b.000b.000b, timeout is 2 seconds:
!!!!!
Success rate is 100 percent (5/5), round-trip min/avg/max = 28/29/32 ms
```

{show ipx traffic}   The **show ipx traffic** command displays IPX traffic information for all interfaces on the router. User traffic, routing protocols, and SAP statistics are also displayed.

```
RouterC#show ipx traffic
System Traffic for 0.0000.0000.0001 System-Name: RouterC
Rcvd:     36 total, 0 format errors, 0 checksum errors, 0 bad hop count,
          0 packets pitched, 36 local destination, 0 multicast
Bcast:    16 received, 29 sent
Sent:     50 generated, 0 forwarded
          0 encapsulation failed, 0 no route
SAP:      1 SAP requests, 0 SAP replies, 0 servers
          0 SAP Nearest Name requests, 0 replies
          0 SAP General Name requests, 0 replies
          5 SAP advertisements received, 4 sent
          2 SAP flash updates sent, 0 SAP format errors
RIP:      1 RIP requests, 0 RIP replies, 5 routes
          9 RIP advertisements received, 18 sent
          2 RIP flash updates sent, 0 RIP format errors
Echo:     Rcvd 5 requests, 15 replies
          Sent 15 requests, 5 replies
          0 unknown: 0 no socket, 0 filtered, 0 no helper
          0 SAPs throttled, freed NDB len 0
Watchdog:
          0 packets received, 0 replies spoofed
Queue     lengths:
          IPX input: 0, SAP 0, RIP 0, GNS 0
          SAP throttling length: 0/(no limit), 0 nets pending lost route reply
          Delayed process creation: 0
EIGRP:    Total received 0, sent 0
          Updates received 0, sent 0
          Queries received 0, sent 0
          Replies received 0, sent 0
          SAPs received 0, sent 0
NLSP:     Level-1 Hellos received 0, sent 0
          PTP Hello received 0, sent 0
          Level-1 LSPs received 0, sent 0
          LSP Retransmissions: 0
          LSP checksum errors received: 0
```

```
        LSP HT=0 checksum errors received: 0
        Level-1 CSNPs received 0, sent 0
        Level-1 PSNPs received 0, sent 0
        Level-1 DR Elections: 0
        Level-1 SPF Calculations: 0
        Level-1 Partial Route Calculations: 0
```

{show ipx eigrp neighbor}   This command will display information on which neighboring EIGRP routers have been discovered.

```
RouterA#show ipx eigrp neigh

IPX EIGRP Neighbors for process 1
H    Address                   Interface      Hold Uptime    SRTT      RTO    Q   Seq
                                              (sec)          (ms)           Cnt Num
0    2.000b.000b.000b          Se0/0          13 02:10:19    53        318    0   38
```

{show ipx eigrp interfaces}   This command will show which router interfaces are running EIGRP.

```
RouterA#show ipx eigrp interfaces

IPX EIGRP Interfaces for process 1

                      Xmit Queue     Mean   Pacing Time    Multicast     Pending
Interface    Peers    Un/Reliable    SRTT   Un/Reliable    Flow Timer    Routes
Se0/0          1         0/0          53       0/15           263           0
↑
```
Interface S0/0 is running EIGRP.

{show ipx eigrp traffic}   This command shows how much EIGRP traffic has been sent and received on the router.

```
RouterB#show ipx eigrp traffic
IP-EIGRP Traffic Statistics for process 1
  Hellos sent/received: 3433/3430
  Updates sent/received: 11/11
  Queries sent/received: 10/7
  Replies sent/received: 7/10
  Acks sent/received: 37/33
  Input queue high water mark 2, 0 drops
```

{show ipx servers} This command displays any servers that have either been statically defined on the router or learned via SAP updates.

```
RouterA#show ipx servers
Codes: S - Static, P - Periodic, E - EIGRP, N - NLSP, H - Holddown, + = detail
1 Total IPX Servers

Table ordering is based on routing and server info

     Type  Name               Net      Address      Port   Route Hops  Itf
S     4   Server4             4.00e0.1e5b.0a81:0451        2707456/01  2
Se0/0
```

{show access-list} This command is used to display information on access lists that have been defined on the router.

```
RouterB#show access-list
IPX SAP access list 1000←Access List 1000
    deny FFFFFFFF 7 Server2←Do not send any updates to any network regarding
                         IPX Server2 with a server type of 7
    permit FFFFFFFF←Permit SAP updates to all other networks
```

{debug ipx routing activity}
{debug ipx routing events} These commands display information on IPX RIP routing protocol activity.

```
RouterB#debug ipx routing activity
IPX routing debugging is on

RouterB#debug ipx routing events
IPX routing events debugging is on
```

{debug ipx sap activity}
{debug ipx sap events} The **debug ipx sap activity** and **debug ipx sap events** commands will display information SAP packets being sent or received on the router.

```
RouterC#debug ipx sap activity
IPX service debugging is on

RouterC#debug ipx sap events
IPX service events debugging is on
```

Conclusion

This chapter explored the Novell IPX networking protocol. Although Novell IPX is declining in popularity, it is still in widespread use. The hands-on labs in this chapter explored key Novell IPX topics such as the following:

- Basic IPX configuration and monitoring
- IPX EIGRP configuration
- IPX static SAP entries
- IPX SAP and router filtering capabilities

19

Appletalk

Topics Covered in This Chapter

- Appletalk technology overview
- Cisco Appletalk support
- Appletalk EIGRP configuration
- Appletalk GRE tunnels
- Appletalk traffic filtering
- Appletalk zone filtering
- Troubleshooting Appletalk networks

Introduction

Appletalk is a networking protocol developed by Apple Computer to provide networking services for its Macintosh computers. Appletalk is the most automatic of all the desktop protocols, but Appletalk is also the chattiest. For example, the default routing protocol for Appletalk is RTMP. RTMP sends routing updates every 10 seconds to all directly connected neighbors.

Appletalk Terminology

An Appletalk node can be any device that is connected to an Appletalk network and is assigned an Appletalk address. Nodes can be Macintosh computers, printers, or any other device that resides on the network and is addressable.

An Appletalk network can be thought of as a physical LAN or WAN, which contains one or more Appletalk nodes.

An Appletalk zone is a logical group of networks. A zone will usually consist of Appletalk nodes that reside in different physical locations. Zones are similar in concept to a virtual LAN. In Figure 19–1, we see an example of how Appletalk zones can work. Figure 19–1 also shows an Appletalk network with three Ethernet segments. The Ethernet segment on RouterA and RouterB are both in zone Engineering. When a Macintosh user on the Ethernet LAN connected to RouterC wants to access resources in the Engineering zone, he is given access to the LAN on RouterA and RouterB. Zones enable you to functionally group network resources without any regard to their actual physical location.

Appletalk Addressing

Early Appletalk networks were referred to as Phase I or non-extended networks. Phase I networks had a limited address space. Each LAN or WAN segment was permitted to have up to 127 hosts and up to 127 servers. Each LAN or WAN segment could only be assigned a single Appletalk network number.

Appletalk Phase II networks are much more flexible in their network addressing. A Phase II network permits multiple network numbers to exist on each network segment, which means that a LAN can contain multiple Appletalk networks. The range of network numbers that exists on a network segment is referred to as the cable range of the segment. The

Figure 19–1
Improper Appletalk
address range

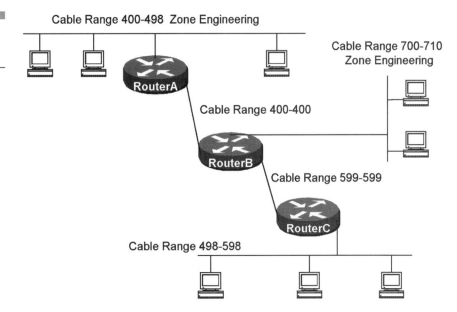

Cable Range 400-498 Zone Engineering

Cable Range 700-710
Zone Engineering

RouterA

Cable Range 400-400

RouterB

Cable Range 599-599

RouterC

Cable Range 498-598

cable range must be unique and cannot overlap with other router inter-faces. Figure 19–1 shows an example of an Appletalk network with improperly assigned cable range numbers. In the case of Figure 19–1, there is an address conflict, because Network 498 has been assigned to both Ethernet LANs. Figure 19–2 shows a properly configured Appletalk network with no address overlaps.

Appletalk node address assignment is designed to minimize the amount of configuration needed on a Macintosh computer. When a Macintosh is first powered on, the computer sends a broadcast to any routers on the same network segment—asking about the cable range of the network segment. Once a router responds, the Macintosh chooses a network number within the cable range. The Macintosh then picks a node number. Before the Appletalk node uses the network.node combination it has picked, the computer queries the network to see whether the network.node combination is already in use. If the address is already used, the Macintosh will continue to choose new addresses until an unused address has been found.

As shown in Figure 19–3, an Appletalk address is 24 bits long. The address is written in a network.node format. The first 16 bits are the network number, and the last eight bits are the node number. This situation means that all Appletalk networks will be numbered less then 65,536, and all Appletalk nodes will be numbered less then 256. Node numbers 0 and 255 are reserved (255 is used as a network broadcast address). An Appletalk network can therefore have 254 nodes per network.

Figure 19–2
Proper Appletalk
address assignment

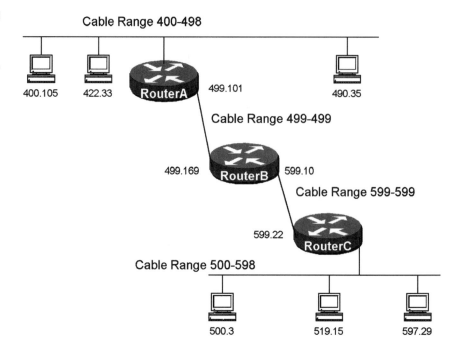

Figure 19–3
Appletalk address
structure

Appletalk Protocol Stack

Figure 19–4 shows the Appletalk stack and its relationship to the OSI stack.

Physical and Datalink Layers

In addition to being supported on WAN links such as Frame-Relay and
ISDN, Appletalk is supported on four major LAN platforms:

■ EtherTalk—Apple's version of Ethernet
■ TokenTalk—Apple's version of Token Ring

Figure 19–4
Appletalk stack and
its relationship to
the OSI stack

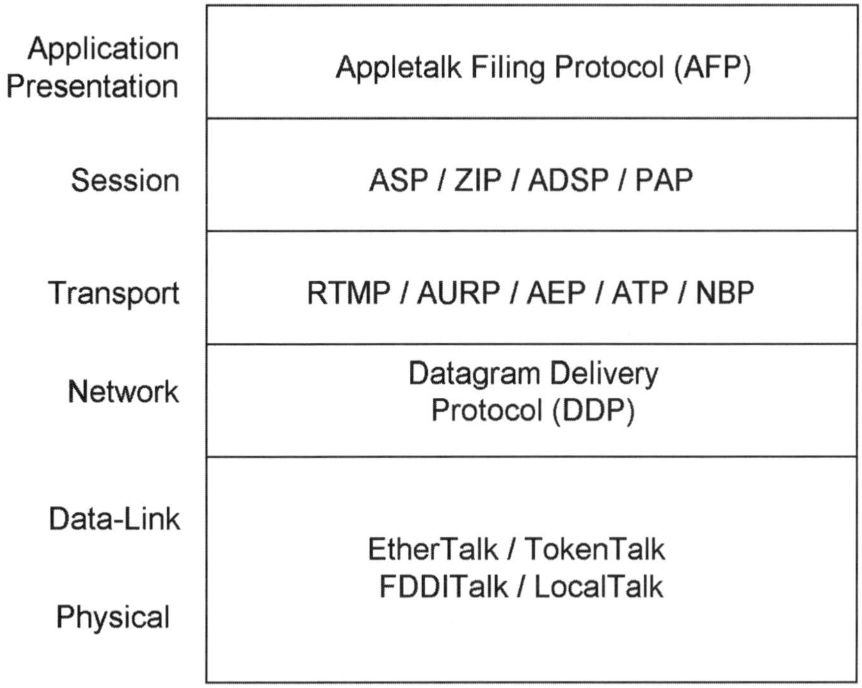

OSI Layer	Appletalk Protocol
Application Presentation	Appletalk Filing Protocol (AFP)
Session	ASP / ZIP / ADSP / PAP
Transport	RTMP / AURP / AEP / ATP / NBP
Network	Datagram Delivery Protocol (DDP)
Data-Link Physical	EtherTalk / TokenTalk FDDITalk / LocalTalk

- FDDITalk—Apple's version of FDDI
- Appletalk—An Apple proprietary serial link that runs at 230 Kbits/second

Network Layer

Appletalk uses the *Datagram Delivery Protocol* (DDP) at the network layer for routing packets in a network. Appletalk is a routable protocol because it has a network layer address associated with each Appletalk node. DDP is a connectionless network protocol. Figure 19–5 shows the DDP packet header in more detail.

Transport Layer

Several protocols exist in the Appletalk transport layer:

- *Routing Table Maintenance Protocol* (RTMP)—A distance vector routing protocol that is similar to IP RIP. RTMP is chatty and sends out a routing update to all connected neighbors every 10 seconds.

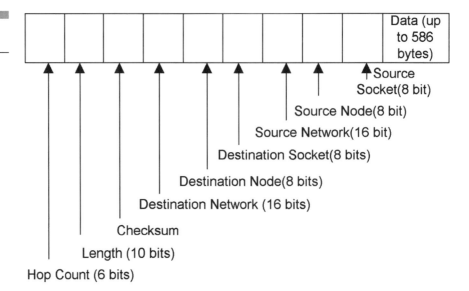

Figure 19–5
DDP packet

- *Appletalk Echo Protocol* (AEP)—AEP is a simple protocol, generating packets that can be used to test the reachability of various network nodes.
- *Appletalk Transaction Protocol* (ATP)—ATP provides connection-based data transfer for Appletalk traffic. ATP functions in a similar mode to TCP in an IP network. ATP provides for data acknowledgment, retransmission, packet sequencing, and fragmentation and reassembly.
- NBP—The *Name Binding Protocol* (NBP) associates an Appletalk name with an address.

Session Layer

Appletalk supports several upper-layer protocols:

- *Appletalk Session Protocol* (ASP)—ASP establishes and maintains sessions between an Appletalk client and a server.
- *Zone Information Protocol*—The Zone Information Protocol maintains network number to zone name mappings in zone information tables. ZIP uses RTMP routing tables to keep up with network topology changes. When ZIP finds a routing table entry that is not in the ZIP, it creates a new ZIP entry.
- *Appletalk Printer Access Protocol* (PAP)—PAP is a connection-oriented protocol that establishes and maintains connections between clients and printers.

Application/Presentation Layer

The *Appletalk Filing Protocol* (AFP) helps clients share server files across a network.

Appletalk Routing Protocols

Cisco supports three routing protocols for Appletalk networks:

■ RTMP—The Routing Table Maintenance Protocol is enabled by default on an Appletalk network. RTMP is a distance vector routing protocol, which uses hop-count as its metric. The update period for RTMP is every 10 seconds, regardless of whether there was a change in the network. This frequent update has the effect of producing a large amount of routing traffic on an Appletalk network.

■ AURP—*Appletalk Update-Based Routing Protocol* (AURP). This routing protocol is similar to RTMP in that it is a distance vector routing protocol with a maximum hop-count of 15 hops. AURP differs from RTMP in that it only sends routing updates when a change has occurred in the network, whereas RTMP sends updates every 10 seconds. AURP is also a tunneling protocol, which enables Appletalk to be tunneled in TCP/IP—thus enabling two Appletalk networks to be connected over a TCP/IP network. The TCP/IP connection is called a tunnel and is counted as one network hop. The router that connects an Appletalk network to a tunnel is referred to as an exterior router.

■ EIGRP—Appletalk EIGRP is used mainly for WAN links in an Appletalk network. Appletalk EIGRP uses the same composite metric that IP and IPX EIGRP use. Appletalk EIGRP also uses the same DUAL routing algorithm, only sending out routing updates when a change has occurred in the network. Appletalk EIGRP differs from IP and IPX EIGRP in that the AS number used to start the routing process must be unique for each router. Appletalk EIGRP features automatic redistribution with the RTMP routing protocol.

Appletalk Zones

An Appletalk zone is a grouping of similar resources and is similar in concept to a *Virtual Lan* (VLAN). Each Appletalk network must be defined as a member of one or more zones. The Appletalk ZIP maintains a list of all zone names and associated Appletalk network numbers for the entire network. Members of a particular zone can be located anywhere in the entire network. Let's look at what will happen when an Appletalk node, such as an Apple Macintosh, needs a service such as a printer:

- The Macintosh chooser will send a request to the local router for a list of all zones.
- The Macintosh looks in the list of zones for the appropriate service.
- If the appropriate service is found, the Macintosh will send a request to each of the cable numbers in the selected zone.
- The local router sends this request as a multicast to the selected zones.
- The services in the selected zones will reply to the router that sent the multicast.
- The router that sent the multicast will forward these replies to the originating Macintosh node.
- The Macintosh node can now select the appropriate service.

Commands Discussed in This Chapter

- **access-list** *access-list-number* [**deny** | **permit**] **cable-range** | **zones** | **additional-zones** | **other-access**
- **appletalk access-group** *access-list-number*
- **appletalk cable-range** *cable-range* [*network.node*]
- **appletalk distribute list** *access-list-number* **out**
- **appletalk protocol** [**aurp** | **eigrp** | **rtmp**]
- **appletalk route-redistribution**
- **appletalk routing** [**eigrp** *route-number*]
- **appletalk zip-reply-filter** *access-list-number*
- **appletalk zone** *zone-name*
- **debug apple zip**
- **ping appletalk** *[network.node]*
- **show appletalk access-lists**
- **show appletalk eigrp interfaces** *[type number]*
- **show appletalk eigrp neighbors** *[interface]*

- **show appletalk eigrp traffic**
- **show appletalk globals**
- **show appletalk interface [brief]** *[type number]*
- **show appletalk neighbors** *[neighbor-address]*
- **show appletalk route** *[network | type number]*
- **show appletalk traffic**
- **show appletalk zone** *[zone-name]*
- **tunnel destination**
- **tunnel source** *[ip-address | type number]*

Definitions

access-list: This global configuration command defines the actions that the router should take for various data, route, zone, and other Appletalk access lists.

appletalk access-group: This interface configuration command assigns an access list to an interface.

appletalk cable-range: This interface configuration command defines an extended Appletalk network.

appletalk distribute list: This interface configuration command is used to filter routing updates.

appletalk protocol: This interface configuration command specifies which routing protocol to use on a particular interface. The default Appletalk routing protocol is RTMP.

appletalk route-redistribution: This global configuration command causes RTMP routes to be redistributed into EIGRP and EIGRP routes to be redistributed into RTMP.

appletalk routing: This global configuration command is used to enable Appletalk routing on a router. The command can optionally enable the EIGRP routing protocol on the router.

appletalk zip-reply-filter: This interface command is used with an access list to limit the number of zones that are visible on an Appletalk network.

appletalk zone: This interface command sets the zone name for an Appletalk network.

debug apple zip: This debug command enables Appletalk ZIP debug.

ping appletalk: This exec command is used to verify host reachability.

show appletalk access-lists: This exec command displays all Appletalk access lists that are defined on the router.

show appletalk eigrp interfaces: This exec command displays information about router interfaces that are configured for the EIGRP routing protocol.

show appletalk eigrp neighbors: This exec command will display information on any EIGRP neighbor routers.

show appletalk globals: This exec command displays information about how Appletalk is configured to operate on the router.

show appletalk interface: This exec command displays the status of interfaces that are running Appletalk.

show appletalk neighbors: This exec command displays information on directly connected routers that are running Appletalk.

show appletalk route: This exec command displays all entries in the Appletalk routing table.

show appletalk traffic: This exec command shows information about the amount of Appletalk traffic that is flowing through the router.

show appletalk zone: This exec command displays the contents of the Appletalk ZIP table.

tunnel destination: This interface configuration command sets the destination IP address for an Appletalk tunnel.

tunnel source: This interface configuration command sets the source interface for an Appletalk tunnel.

IOS Requirements

These labs were done using IOS 11.1.

Lab #73: Basic Appletalk Configuration

Equipment Needed

The following equipment is needed to perform this lab exercise:

- Three Cisco routers. One of the routers must have two serial interfaces; the other two routers must have one serial interface and one Ethernet interface.
- Two Cisco crossover cables. If a Cisco crossover cable is not available, then you can use a Cisco DTE cable connected to a Cisco DCE cable.
- A Cisco rolled cable for console port connection to the routers
- A Cisco IOS image that supports the Appletalk protocol

Configuration Overview

This lab will demonstrate basic Appletalk configuration and monitoring. A three-node Appletalk network will be set up. The RTMP dynamic routing protocol will be used to learn all routes in the network.

The three routers are connected, as shown in Figure 19–6. RouterB acts as a DCE and supplies clocking to both RouterA and RouterC.

NOTE: *Making changes to Appletalk routing parameters will sometimes require the router to be reloaded. Make sure to save the configuration before reloading the router.*

Figure 19–6
Basic Appletalk connectivity

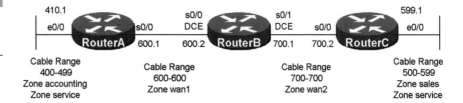

Router Configuration

The configurations for the three routers in this example are as follows (Appletalk commands are highlighted in bold):

RouterA

```
Current configuration:
!
version 11.1
no service udp-small-servers
no service tcp-small-servers
!
hostname RouterA
!
appletalk routing←Enable Appletalk routing on this router
!
interface Ethernet0/0
 no ip address
 no keepalive
 appletalk cable-range 400-499 410.1←Define a cable range for this interface
                                      and an address of 410.1
 appletalk zone accounting←Define the primary Appletalk zone to be accounting
 appletalk zone service←Define the secondary Appletalk zone to be service
!
interface Serial0/0
 no ip address
 encapsulation ppp
 appletalk cable-range 600-600 600.1←Define a cable range for this interface
                                     and an address of 600.1
 appletalk zone wan1←Define the primary Appletalk zone to be wan1
!
no ip classless
logging buffered
!
line con 0
line aux 0
line vty 0 4
 login
!
end
```

RouterB

```
Current configuration:
!
version 11.1
no service udp-small-servers
no service tcp-small-servers
!
hostname RouterB
!
enable password cisco
!
appletalk routing←Enable Appletalk routing on this router
!
interface Serial0/0
 no ip address
 encapsulation ppp
 appletalk cable-range 600-600 600.2←Define a cable range for this interface
                                  and an address of 600.2
 appletalk zone wan1←Define the Appletalk zone to be wan1
 no fair-queue
!
interface Serial0/1
 no ip address
 encapsulation ppp
 appletalk cable-range 700-700 700.1←Define a cable range for this interface
                                  and an address of 700.1
 appletalk zone wan2←Define the Appletalk zone to be wan2
 clockrate 64000←Provide clocking to neighbor router
!
no ip classless
logging buffered
!
line con 0
line aux 0
line vty 0 4
 password cisco
 login
!
end
```

RouterC

```
Current configuration:
!
version 11.1
no service udp-small-servers
```

```
no service tcp-small-servers
!
hostname RouterC
!
!
appletalk routing←Enable Appletalk routing on this router
!
interface Ethernet0/0
 no ip address
 no keepalive
 appletalk cable-range 500-599 599.1←Define a cable range for this interface
                                    and an address of 599.1
 appletalk zone sales←Define the primary Appletalk zone to be sales
 appletalk zone service←Define the secondary Appletalk zone to be service
!
interface Serial0/0
 no ip address
 encapsulation ppp
 appletalk cable-range 700-700 700.2←Define a cable range for this interface
                                    and an address of 700.2.
 appletalk zone wan2←Define the primary Appletalk zone to be wan2
 no fair-queue
!
no ip classless
logging buffered
!
line con 0
line aux 0
line vty 0 4
 login
!
end
```

Monitoring and Testing the Configuration

Let's start by connecting to RouterA and typing the **show appletalk route** command. This command will display the contents of the Appletalk routing table. We see that RouterA has two directly connected Appletalk networks: 400-499 (which is located on E0/0) and 600-600 (which is located on S0/0). Two networks have been learned via the Appletalk RTMP routing protocol. These are Networks 500-599 (which is located on

E0/0 of RouterC) and 700-700 (which is the serial link between RouterB and RouterC). We see that the Appletalk routing table shows the zones that are associated with each network.

```
RouterA#show appletalk route
Codes: R - RTMP derived, E - EIGRP derived, C - connected, A - AURP
       S - static  P - proxy
4 routes in internet

The first zone listed for each entry is its default (primary) zone.

C Net 400-499 directly connected, Ethernet0/0, zone accounting
                Additional zones: 'service'
R Net 500-599 [2/G] via 600.2, 8 sec, Serial0/0, zone sales
                Additional zones: 'service'
C Net 600-600 directly connected, Serial0/0, zone wan1
R Net 700-700 [1/G] via 600.2, 8 sec, Serial0/0, zone wan2
```

The **show appletalk zone** command will display all zones that are on the network. Notice that the service zone exists on both RouterA and RouterC.

```
RouterA#show appletalk zone
Name               Network(s)
wan1               600-600
wan2               700-700
accounting         400-499
service            500-599 400-499←This zone exists on two different
                                   Appletalk networks
sales              500-599
Total of 5 zones
```

Another useful command is **show appletalk globals**. This command provides a summary of the entire Appletalk network. We see from the following output that there are a total of four routes and five zones in our network. We also see that our RTMP routing protocol will send an update every 10 seconds, mark a route as bad after 20 seconds, and discard a route after 60 seconds.

```
RouterA#show appletalk globals
Appletalk global information:
   Internet is incompatible with older, AT Phase1, routers.
   There are 4 routes in the internet.
   There are 5 zones defined.
   Logging of significant Appletalk events is disabled.
   ZIP resends queries every 10 seconds.
   RTMP updates are sent every 10 seconds.
   RTMP entries are considered BAD after 20 seconds.
   RTMP entries are discarded after 60 seconds.
   AARP probe retransmit count: 10, interval: 200 msec.
   AARP request retransmit count: 5, interval: 1000 msec.
```

```
DDP datagrams will be checksummed.
RTMP datagrams will be strictly checked.
RTMP routes may not be propagated without zones.
Routes will not be distributed between routing protocols.
Routing between local devices on an interface will not be performed.
IPTalk uses the udp base port of 768 (Default).
Appletalk EIGRP is not enabled.
Alternate node address format will not be displayed.
Access control of any networks of a zone hides the zone.
```

The **show appletalk traffic** command shows all Appletalk traffic that has been received or sent from the router. Traffic statistics are broken up into specific Appletalk protocols, such as routing, Appletalk echo (similar to an IP ping), and ZIP.

```
RouterA#show appletalk traffic
Appletalk statistics:
  Rcvd:      74 total, 0 checksum errors, 0 bad hop count
        74 local destination, 0 access denied
        0 for MacIP, 0 bad MacIP, 0 no client
        7 port disabled, 0 no listener
        0 ignored, 0 martians
  Bcast:     0 received, 143 sent
  Sent:      145 generated, 0 forwarded, 0 fast forwarded, 0 loopback
        0 forwarded from MacIP, 0 MacIP failures
        0 encapsulation failed, 0 no route, 0 no source
  DDP: 74 long, 0 short, 0 macip, 0 bad size
  NBP: 15 received, 0 invalid, 0 proxies
          0 replies sent, 20 forwards, 15 lookups, 0 failures
  RTMP:      60 received, 0 requests, 0 invalid, 0 ignored
        127 sent, 0 replies
  AURP:      0 Open Requests, 0 Router Downs
        0 Routing Information sent, 0 Routing Information received
        0 Zone Information sent, 0 Zone Information received
        0 Get Zone Nets sent, 0 Get Zone Nets received
        0 Get Domain Zone List sent, 0 Get Domain Zone List received
        0 bad sequence
  ATP: 0 received
  ZIP: 9 received, 8 sent, 0 netinfo
Appletalk statistics:
  Echo:      0 received, 0 discarded, 0 illegal
        0 generated, 0 replies sent
  Responder: 0 received, 0 illegal, 0 unknown
          0 replies sent, 0 failures
  AARP:      0 requests, 0 replies, 0 probes
        0 martians, 0 bad encapsulation, 0 unknown
        10 sent, 0 failures, 0 delays, 0 drops
  Lost:      0 no buffers
  Unknown: 0 packets
  Discarded: 0 wrong encapsulation, 0 bad SNAP discriminator
```

Notice that the **show interface e 0/0** command does not display any Appletalk-specific information. The command only shows the MAC address of the interface and high-level input and output traffic information.

```
RouterA#show interface e 0/0←There is no Appletalk specific information shown
                                in this commands output
Ethernet0/0 is up, line protocol is up
  Hardware is AmdP2, address is 00e0.1e5b.0d21 (bia 00e0.1e5b.0d21)
  MTU 1500 bytes, BW 10000 Kbit, DLY 1000 usec, rely 164/255, load 1/255
  Encapsulation ARPA, loopback not set, keepalive not set
  ARP type: ARPA, ARP Timeout 04:00:00
  Last input never, output 00:00:06, output hang never
  Last clearing of "show interface" counters never
  Queueing strategy: fifo
  Output queue 0/40, 0 drops; input queue 0/75, 0 drops
  5 minute input rate 0 bits/sec, 0 packets/sec
  5 minute output rate 0 bits/sec, 0 packets/sec
    0 packets input, 0 bytes, 0 no buffer
    Received 0 broadcasts, 0 runts, 0 giants
    0 input errors, 0 CRC, 0 frame, 0 overrun, 0 ignored, 0 abort
    0 input packets with dribble condition detected
    77 packets output, 7574 bytes, 0 underruns
    77 output errors, 0 collisions, 3 interface resets
    0 babbles, 0 late collision, 0 deferred
    77 lost carrier, 0 no carrier
    0 output buffer failures, 0 output buffers swapped out
```

To see Appletalk information for a specific interface, you need to use the **show appletalk interface** command. Type **show appletalk interface e 0/0** to display the Appletalk information for the Ethernet 0/0 port on RouterA. The output of this command gives us important Appletalk interface information, such as the cable range of this interface, the interface address, and zone information.

```
RouterA#show appletalk interface e 0/0
Ethernet0/0 is up, line protocol is up
  Appletalk cable range is 400-499←Network cable range information
  Appletalk address is 410.1, Valid←Interface address information
  Appletalk primary zone is "accounting"←Primary zone
  Appletalk additional zones: "service"←Secondary zone
  Appletalk address gleaning is disabled
  Appletalk route cache is enabled
```

A serial interface running Appletalk can also have port information displayed with two different commands. The **show interface s 0/0** command shows general interface information. The only indication that this interface is running Appletalk is the atalkcp LCP that is indicated as open. This situation occurs as part of the PPP negotiation process and tells us that Appletalk traffic can be carried across this serial link.

```
RouterA#show interface s 0/0
Serial0/0 is up, line protocol is up
  Hardware is QUICC Serial
  MTU 1500 bytes, BW 1544 Kbit, DLY 20000 usec, rely 255/255, load 1/255
  Encapsulation PPP, loopback not set, keepalive set (10 sec)
  LCP Open
```

Appletalk control protocol has been negotiated and open
↓

```
  Open: atalkcp, cdp
  Last input 00:00:02, output 00:00:02, output hang never
  Last clearing of "show interface" counters never
  Input queue: 0/75/0 (size/max/drops); Total output drops: 0
  Queueing strategy: weighted fair
  Output queue: 0/64/0 (size/threshold/drops)
     Conversations  0/1 (active/max active)
     Reserved Conversations 0/0 (allocated/max allocated)
  5 minute input rate 0 bits/sec, 0 packets/sec
  5 minute output rate 0 bits/sec, 0 packets/sec
     185 packets input, 7207 bytes, 0 no buffer
     Received 185 broadcasts, 0 runts, 0 giants
     5 input errors, 0 CRC, 5 frame, 0 overrun, 0 ignored, 0 abort
     185 packets output, 6968 bytes, 0 underruns
     0 output errors, 0 collisions, 14 interface resets
     0 output buffer failures, 0 output buffers swapped out
     0 carrier transitions
     DCD=up  DSR=up  DTR=up  RTS=up  CTS=up
```

Specific Appletalk information can be displayed for the serial interface with the **show appletalk interface** s 0/0 command. As with the Ethernet interface, this command will show us Appletalk information for the serial interface of this router.

```
RouterA#show appletalk interface s 0/0
Serial0/0 is up, line protocol is up
  Appletalk cable range is 600-600
  Appletalk address is 600.1, Valid
  Appletalk zone is "wan1"
  Appletalk port configuration verified by 600.2
  Appletalk address gleaning is not supported by hardware
  Appletalk route cache is enabled
```

The **show appletalk neighbors** command can be used to verify that you are connected to the proper neighbors. The output of this command shows us that we are connected to a neighbor at Appletalk address 600.2, which is the s0/0 interface of RouterB.

```
RouterA#show appletalk neighbors
Appletalk neighbors:
  600.2             Serial0/0, uptime 00:08:10, 0 secs
                Neighbor is reachable as a RTMP peer
```

Appletalk supports a ping command which can be used to test for network reachability. Let's make sure that the s0/0 interface of RouterC is active. Type **ping appletalk 700.2**. This command will send an Appletalk echo request to RouterC at Appletalk address 700.2. The ping should be successful, as shown here.

```
RouterA#ping appletalk 700.2

Type escape sequence to abort.
Sending 5, 100-byte Appletalk Echoes to 700.2, timeout is 2 seconds:
!!!!!
Success rate is 100 percent (5/5), round-trip min/avg/max = 56/56/60 ms
```

Make sure that the Ethernet interface of RouterC is also reachable. Use the **ping appletalk 599.1** command to verify that the interface is active.

```
RouterA#ping appletalk 599.1

Type escape sequence to abort.
Sending 5, 100-byte Appletalk Echoes to 599.1, timeout is 2 seconds:
!!!!!
Success rate is 100 percent (5/5), round-trip min/avg/max = 56/58/60 ms
```

The only network connectivity/reachability aid that Appletalk supports is the ping command. Try to telnet to RouterC at Appletalk address 599.1. We see that the telnet was not successful, because Telnet is a TCP/IP application. You should always run the TCP/IP protocol on your network. Network access and SNMP are vital to a successful network, and TCP/IP is key to these functions.

```
RouterA#telnet 599.1
% Unknown command or computer name, or unable to find computer address
```

Now, let's connect to RouterB and examine its Appletalk status. Type **show appletalk route** to display the Appletalk routing table. We see that RouterB has two directly connected Appletalk networks: 600-600 (serial connection to RouterA) and 700-700 (serial connection to RouterC). Two networks are being learned via the Appletalk RTMP routing protocol. These are 400-499 (Ethernet port on RouterA) and 500-599 (Ethernet port on RouterC).

```
RouterB#sh appletalk route
Codes: R - RTMP derived, E - EIGRP derived, C - connected, A - AURP
       S - static  P - proxy
4 routes in internet

The first zone listed for each entry is its default (primary) zone.
```

```
R Net 400-499 [1/G] via 600.1, 9 sec, Serial0/0, zone accounting
               Additional zones: 'service'
R Net 500-599 [1/G] via 700.2, 7 sec, Serial0/1, zone sales
               Additional zones: 'service'
C Net 600-600 directly connected, Serial0/0, zone wan1
C Net 700-700 directly connected, Serial0/1, zone wan2
```

The show appletalk zone command reveals a zone table that is identical to the zone table of RouterA. Assuming that no zone filters are in effect, the zone table of all routers on a network should be identical.

```
RouterB#show appletalk zone
Name                              Network(s)
wan1                              600-600
wan2                              700-700
accounting                        400-499
service                           400-499 500-599
sales                             500-599
Total of 5 zones
```

Now, let's connect to RouterC. Display the Appletalk routing table with the **show appletalk route** command. We see that RouterC has two directly connected Appletalk networks. The first directly connected network is 500-599 (Ethernet interface of RouterC), and the second directly connected network is 700-700 (serial connection between RouterC and RouterA).

```
RouterC#show appletalk route
Codes: R - RTMP derived, E - EIGRP derived, C - connected, A - AURP
       S - static  P - proxy
4 routes in internet

The first zone listed for each entry is its default (primary) zone.

R Net 400-499 [2/G] via 700.1, 3 sec, Serial0/0, zone accounting
               Additional zones: 'service'
C Net 500-599 directly connected, Ethernet0/0, zone sales
               Additional zones: 'service'
R Net 600-600 [1/G] via 700.1, 3 sec, Serial0/0, zone wan1
C Net 700-700 directly connected, Serial0/0, zone wan2
```

As with the zone tables, the zone information on RouterC is identical to the zone information on RouterA.

```
RouterC#show appletalk zone
Name                              Network(s)
wan1                              600-600
wan2                              700-700
accounting                        400-499
service                           400-499 500-599
sales                             500-599
Total of 5 zones
```

Verify that RouterC has network connectivity with RouterA by using the ping command to verify that RouterC is active.

```
RouterC#ping appletalk 410.1

Type escape sequence to abort.
Sending 5, 100-byte Appletalk Echoes to 410.1, timeout is 2 seconds:
!!!!!
Success rate is 100 percent (5/5), round-trip min/avg/max = 56/58/60 ms
```

Lab #74: Appletalk EIGRP Configuration

Equipment Needed

The following equipment is needed to perform this lab exercise:

- Three Cisco routers. One of the routers must have two serial interfaces; the other two routers must have one serial interface and one Ethernet interface.
- Two Cisco crossover cables. If a Cisco crossover cable is not available, then you can use a Cisco DTE cable connected to a Cisco DCE cable.
- A Cisco rolled cable for console port connection to the routers
- A Cisco IOS image that supports the Appletalk protocol

Configuration Overview

This lab will demonstrate Appletalk EIGRP. Like IP EIGRP, Appletalk EIGRP has many advantages over Appletalk RTMP—such as less traffic overhead and faster convergence times. As shown in Figure 19–7, each of the three routers will be configured to run Appletalk EIGRP on the wide-area portion of our test network. The Ethernet interfaces on both RouterA and RouterC will still run RTMP. Appletalk features automatic redistribution between RTMP and EIGRP.

NOTE: *Making changes to Appletalk routing parameters will sometimes require the router to be reloaded. Make sure to save the configuration before reloading the router.*

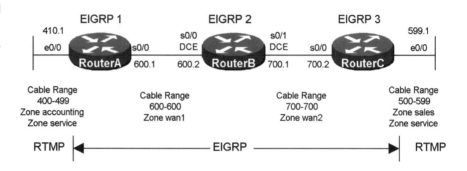

The three routers are connected, as shown in Figure 19–7. RouterB acts as a DCE and supplies clocking to RouterA and RouterC.

 NOTE: *Every router that runs Appletalk EIGRP must have a unique EIGRP process number, which is the opposite of IP EIGRP—where all routers must have the same EIGRP process number.*

Router Configuration

The configurations for the three routers in this example are as follows (key Appletalk commands are highlighted in bold):

RouterA

```
Current configuration:
!
version 11.1
no service udp-small-servers
no service tcp-small-servers
!
hostname RouterA
!
appletalk routing eigrp 1←Enable EIGRP Routing. Each Appletalk router must
                          have a different EIGRP process number
appletalk route-redistribution←This command is automatically added when
                                Appletalk EIGRP is enabled
!
interface Ethernet0/0
 no ip address
 no keepalive
 appletalk cable-range 400-499 410.1←Define a cable range for this interface
                                     and an address of 410.1
```

```
 appletalk zone accounting←Define the primary Appletalk zone to be accounting
 appletalk zone service←Define the secondary Appletalk zone to be service
!
interface Serial0/0
 no ip address
 encapsulation ppp
 appletalk cable-range 600-600 600.1←Define a cable range for this interface
                                  and an address of 600.1

 appletalk zone wan1←Define the primary Appletalk zone to be wan1
 appletalk protocol eigrp←Enable EIGRP on this interface
 no appletalk protocol rtmp←Disable RTMP on this interface
!
line con 0
line aux 0
line vty 0 4
 login
!
end
```

RouterB

```
Current configuration:
!
version 11.1
no service udp-small-servers
no service tcp-small-servers
!
hostname RouterB
!
enable password cisco
!
appletalk routing eigrp 2←Enable EIGRP Routing. Each Appletalk router must
                       have a different EIGRP process number
appletalk route-redistribution←This command is automatically added when
                           Appletalk EIGRP is enabled
!
interface Serial0/0
 no ip address
 encapsulation ppp
 appletalk cable-range 600-600 600.2←Define a cable range for this interface
                                  and an address of 600.1
 appletalk zone wan1←Define the primary Appletalk zone to be wan1
 appletalk protocol eigrp←Enable EIGRP on this interface
 no appletalk protocol rtmp←Disable RTMP on this interface
```

```
 no fair-queue
 clockrate 64000←Provide clocking to neighbor router
!
interface Serial0/1
 no ip address
 encapsulation ppp
 appletalk cable-range 700-700 700.1←Define a cable range for this interface
                                   and an address of 700.1
 appletalk zone wan2←Define the primary Appletalk zone to be wan2
 appletalk protocol eigrp←Enable EIGRP on this interface
 no appletalk protocol rtmp←Disable RTMP on this interface
 clockrate 64000←Provide clocking to neighbor router
!
no ip classless
logging buffered
!
line con 0
line aux 0
line vty 0 4
 password cisco
 login
!
end
```

RouterC

```
Current configuration:
!
version 11.1
no service udp-small-servers
no service tcp-small-servers
!
hostname RouterC
!
!
appletalk routing eigrp 3←Enable EIGRP Routing. Each Appletalk router must
                        have a different EIGRP process number
appletalk route-redistribution←This command is automatically added when
                             Appletalk EIGRP is enabled
!
interface Ethernet0/0
 no ip address
 no keepalive
 appletalk cable-range 500-599 599.1←Define a cable range for this interface
                                   and an address of 599.1

 appletalk zone sales←Define the primary Appletalk zone to be sales
 appletalk zone service←Define the primary Appletalk zone to be service
!
interface Serial0/0
```

```
 no ip address
 encapsulation ppp
 appletalk cable-range 700-700 700.2←Define a cable range for this interface
                                    and an address of 700.2

 appletalk zone wan2←Define the primary Appletalk zone to be wan2
 appletalk protocol eigrp←Enable EIGRP on this interface
 no appletalk protocol rtmp←Disable RTMP on this interface
 no fair-queue
!
no ip classless
logging buffered
!
line con 0
line aux 0
line vty 0 4
 login
!
end
```

Monitoring and Testing the Configuration

Let's start by connecting to RouterA. Type the **show appletalk route** command to display the Appletalk routing table. We see that we have two directly connected networks and two networks that are being learned via EIGRP. Recall from the previous lab that these EIGRP-learned networks were previously RTMP-learned networks.

```
RouterA#show appletalk route
Codes: R - RTMP derived, E - EIGRP derived, C - connected, A - AURP
       S - static  P - proxy
4 routes in internet

The first zone listed for each entry is its default (primary) zone.

C Net 400-499 directly connected, Ethernet0/0, zone accounting
                Additional zones: 'service'
E Net 500-599 [2/G] via 600.2, 2153 sec, Serial0/0, zone sales
                Additional zones: 'service'
C Net 600-600 directly connected, Serial0/0, zone wan1
E Net 700-700 [1/G] via 600.2, 2200 sec, Serial0/0, zone wan2
```

Verify that you can ping the Ethernet interface of RouterC with the **ping appletalk 599.1** command. This command should be 100 percent successful, indicating that the entire network is up and active.

```
RouterA#ping appletalk 599.1

Type escape sequence to abort.
Sending 5, 100-byte Appletalk Echoes to 599.1, timeout is 2 seconds:
!!!!!
Success rate is 100 percent (5/5), round-trip min/avg/max = 56/56/56 ms
```

There are several important EIGRP commands. Type the command **show appletalk eigrp interface** to display interfaces on RouterA that are running EIGRP. Notice that on RouterA, only the S0/0 interface is running EIGRP. The Ethernet interface (E0/0) is still running the Appletalk RTMP routing protocol.

```
RouterA#show appletalk eigrp interface
AT/EIGRP Neighbors for process 1, router id 1

                   Xmit Queue    Mean    Pacing Time   Multicast    Pending
Interface   Peers  Un/Reliable   SRTT    Un/Reliable   Flow Timer   Routes
Se0/0         1       0/0         21        0/10          98           0
```

The **show appletalk eigrp neighbor** command will display active EIGRP neighbor routers. RouterB at Appletalk address 600.2 is the only EIGRP neighbor of RouterA.

```
RouterA#show appletalk eigrp neighbor
AT/EIGRP Neighbors for process 1, router id 1
H    Address                  Interface   Hold Uptime    SRTT    RTO   Q   Seq
                                          (sec)          (ms)          Cnt Num
0    600.2                    Se0/0         14 00:37:29   21      200   0   8
```

The **show appletalk eigrp traffic** command can be used to display EIGRP traffic that passes through a router. We see from this command output that RouterA is actively passing EIGRP hello messages.

```
RouterA#show appletalk eigrp traffic
AT-EIGRP Traffic Statistics
  Hellos sent/received: 499/488
  Updates sent/received: 6/4
  Queries sent/received: 0/2
  Replies sent/received: 2/0
  Acks sent/received: 5/6
  Input queue high water mark 1, 0 drops
```

Another way to verify that EIGRP is running on a particular interface is to use the **show appletalk interface** command. Type the command for the s0/0 interface. Notice from the following command output that the routing protocol for the interface is EIGRP.

```
RouterA#show appletalk interface s 0/0
Serial0/0 is up, line protocol is up
  Appletalk cable range is 600-600
  Appletalk address is 600.1, Valid
  Appletalk zone is "wan1"
  Routing protocols enabled: EIGRP
  Appletalk port configuration verified by 600.2
  Appletalk address gleaning is not supported by hardware
  Appletalk route cache is enabled
```

Now, connect to RouterB. The routing table can be displayed with the **show appletalk route** command. RouterB has two directly connected networks and two networks that have been learned via EIGRP. Notice that there are no RTMP-learned routes on RouterB.

```
RouterB#show appletalk route
Codes: R - RTMP derived, E - EIGRP derived, C - connected, A - AURP
       S - static  P - proxy
4 routes in internet

The first zone listed for each entry is its default (primary) zone.

E Net 400-499 [1/G] via 600.1, 2299 sec, Serial0/0, zone accounting
                Additional zones: 'service'
E Net 500-599 [1/G] via 700.2, 2240 sec, Serial0/1, zone sales
                Additional zones: 'service'
C Net 600-600 directly connected, Serial0/0, zone wan1
C Net 700-700 directly connected, Serial0/1, zone wan2
```

The **show appletalk interface** command can be used to verify that EIGRP is running on both serial interfaces of RouterB.

```
RouterB#show appletalk interface s 0/0
Serial0/0 is up, line protocol is up
  Appletalk cable range is 600-600
  Appletalk address is 600.2, Valid
  Appletalk zone is "wan1"
  Routing protocols enabled: EIGRP
  Appletalk port configuration verified by 600.1
  Appletalk address gleaning is not supported by hardware
  Appletalk route cache is enabled


RouterB#show appletalk interface s 0/1
Serial0/1 is up, line protocol is up
  Appletalk cable range is 700-700
  Appletalk address is 700.1, Valid
  Appletalk zone is "wan2"
  Routing protocols enabled: EIGRP
```

```
Appletalk port configuration verified by 700.2
Appletalk address gleaning is not supported by hardware
Appletalk route cache is enabled
```

The EIGRP routing status for the serial interfaces on RouterB can also be verified with the **show appletalk eigrp interface** command.

```
RouterB#show appletalk eigrp interface
AT/EIGRP Neighbors for process 1, router id 2

                    Xmit Queue    Mean    Pacing Time   Multicast    Pending
Interface   Peers   Un/Reliable   SRTT    Un/Reliable   Flow Timer   Routes
Se0/0         1        0/0        285        0/10          1418        0
Se0/1         1        0/0         28        0/10            50        0
```

RouterB's EIGRP neighbors can be displayed with the **show appletalk eigrp neighbor** command. Neighbor 700.2 is the serial interface of RouterC, and Neighbor 600.1 is the serial interface of RouterA.

```
RouterB#show appletalk eigrp neighbor
AT/EIGRP Neighbors for process 1, router id 2
H   Address                Interface    Hold Uptime    SRTT    RTO    Q   Seq
                                        (sec)          (ms)         Cnt  Num
1   700.2                  Se0/1         14 00:37:41     28    200    0   2
0   600.1                  Se0/0         12 00:38:39    285   1710    0   8
```

Now, connect to RouterC. Display the router's routing table with the **show appletalk route** command. We see that RouterC has learned two networks via the EIGRP routing protocol.

```
RouterC#show appletalk route
Codes: R - RTMP derived, E - EIGRP derived, C - connected, A - AURP
       S - static  P - proxy
4 routes in internet

The first zone listed for each entry is its default (primary) zone.

E Net 400-499 [2/G] via 700.1, 2299 sec, Serial0/0, zone accounting
               Additional zones: 'service'
C Net 500-599 directly connected, Ethernet0/0, zone sales
               Additional zones: 'service'
E Net 600-600 [1/G] via 700.1, 2299 sec, Serial0/0, zone wan1
C Net 700-700 directly connected, Serial0/0, zone wan2
```

Display the interfaces on RouterC that are running EIGRP with the **show appletalk eigrp interface** command. We see that only the serial interface on the router is running EIGRP.

```
RouterC#show appletalk eigrp interface
AT/EIGRP Neighbors for process 1, router id 3

                 Xmit Queue    Mean    Pacing Time    Multicast   Pending
Interface  Peers Un/Reliable   SRTT    Un/Reliable    Flow Timer  Routes
Se0/0      1     0/0           24      0/10           50          0
```

RouterC's EIGRP neighbors can be displayed with the **show appletalk eigrp neighbor** command. RouterB at Appletalk address 700.1 is the only EIGRP neighbor to RouterC.

```
RouterC#show appletalk eigrp neighbor
AT/EIGRP Neighbors for process 1, router id 3
H   Address                 Interface   Hold Uptime    SRTT   RTO  Q  Seq
                                             (sec)     (ms)       Cnt Num
0   700.1                   Se0/0       13 00:38:46    24     200  0  7
```

Let's see what happens if two neighbor routers have the same Appletalk EIGRP process ID. Connect to RouterB and enter router configuration mode. Enter the command **appletalk routing eigrp 3**.

```
RouterB#config term
Enter configuration commands, one per line. End with CNTL/Z.
RouterB(config)#appletalk routing eigrp 3
RouterB(config)#exit
RouterB#
```

After this command is entered, both RouterB and RouterC will have the same EIGRP process ID. The following output will be seen. RouterB is telling us that RouterC (Appletalk address 700.2) has the same router ID as itself.

```
%AT-5-COMPATERR4: Appletalk EIGRP neighbor incompatibility; 700.2 has same route
r ID (3)
%AT-5-COMPATERR4: Appletalk EIGRP neighbor incompatibility; 700.2 has same route
r ID (3)
%AT-5-COMPATERR4: Appletalk EIGRP neighbor incompatibility; 700.2 has same route
r ID (3)
%AT-5-COMPATERR4: Appletalk EIGRP neighbor incompatibility; 700.2 has same route
r ID (3)
%AT-5-COMPATERR4: Appletalk EIGRP neighbor incompatibility; 700.2 has same route
r ID (3)


RouterB#config term
Enter configuration commands, one per line. End with CNTL/Z.
RouterB(config)#appletalk routing eigrp 2
RouterB(config)#exit
```

Lab #75: Appletalk GRE Tunnel

Equipment Needed

The following equipment is needed to perform this lab exercise:

■ Three Cisco routers. One of the routers must have two serial interfaces; the other two routers must have one serial interface and one Ethernet interface.

■ Two Cisco crossover cables. If a Cisco crossover cable is not available, then you can use a Cisco DTE cable connected to a Cisco DCE cable.

■ A Cisco rolled cable for console port connection to the routers

■ A Cisco IOS image that supports the Appletalk protocol

Configuration Overview

This lab will show how to configure an Appletalk GRE tunnel. This Cisco feature enables a network to run Appletalk on the end-router nodes. Routers that connect the Appletalk end nodes run a GRE tunnel to tunnel any Appletalk traffic in an IP packet.

Figure 19–8 shows the logical representation of this lab. As far as Appletalk is concerned, RouterA and RouterB are directly connected via Network 600. The tunnel makes the intermediate router (RouterB) invisible to the two Appletalk routers (RouterA and RouterB).

The three routers are connected, as shown in Figure 19–9. RouterA and RouterC are running both Appletalk and IP on each of their interfaces. RouterB is only configured for IP. RouterB acts as a DCE and supplies clocking to RouterA and RouterC.

Figure 19–8
Appletalk GRE/IP
tunnel logical
representation

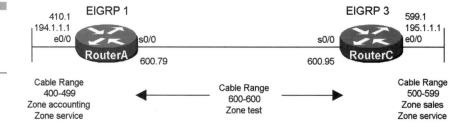

Figure 19–9
Appletalk GRE/IP tunnel

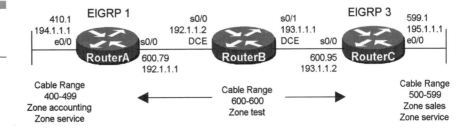

NOTE: *Notice that RouterB is only running TCP/IP. There is no Appletalk routing being run on RouterB. All Appletalk traffic that is being generated on RouterA and RouterC is being encapsulated in TCP/IP. Also, making changes to Appletalk routing parameters will sometimes require the router to be reloaded. Make sure to save the configuration before reloading the router.*

Router Configuration

The configurations for the three routers in this example are as follows (key Appletalk commands are highlighted in bold):

RouterA

```
Current configuration:
!
version 11.1
no service udp-small-servers
no service tcp-small-servers
!
hostname RouterA
!
appletalk routing eigrp 1←Enable EIGRP Routing. Each Appletalk router must
                     have a different EIGRP process number
appletalk route-redistribution←This command is automatically added when
                     Appletalk EIGRP is enabled
!
interface Tunnel1
 no ip address
 appletalk cable-range 600-600 600.79←Define a cable range for this interface
                     and an address of 600.79

 appletalk zone test←Define the primary Appletalk zone to be tested
 appletalk protocol eigrp←Enable EIGRP on this interface
 tunnel source Ethernet0/0←Define a tunnel source interface
```

```
 tunnel destination 195.1.1.1←Define a tunnel destination address
!
interface Ethernet0/0
 ip address 194.1.1.1 255.255.255.0
 no keepalive
 appletalk cable-range 400-499 410.1←Define a cable range for this interface
                                 and an address of 410.1

 appletalk zone accounting←Define the primary Appletalk zone to be accounting
 appletalk zone service←Define the secondary Appletalk zone to be service
!
interface Serial0/0
 ip address 192.1.1.1 255.255.255.0
 encapsulation ppp
!
router rip
 network 192.1.1.0
 network 194.1.1.0
!
line con 0
line aux 0
line vty 0 4
 login
!
end
```

RouterB

```
Current configuration:
!
version 11.1
no service udp-small-servers
no service tcp-small-servers
!
hostname RouterB
!
enable password cisco
!
interface Serial0/0
 ip address 192.1.1.2 255.255.255.0
 encapsulation ppp
 no fair-queue
 clockrate 64000←Provide clocking to neighbor router
!
interface Serial0/1
 ip address 193.1.1.1 255.255.255.0
 encapsulation ppp
 clockrate 64000←Provide clocking to neighbor router
!
router rip
 network 193.1.1.0
 network 192.1.1.0
```

```
!
line con 0
line aux 0
line vty 0 4
 password cisco
 login
!
end
```

RouterC

```
Current configuration:
!
version 11.1
no service udp-small-servers
no service tcp-small-servers
!
hostname RouterC
!
!
appletalk routing eigrp 3←Enable EIGRP Routing. Each Appletalk router must
                        have a different EIGRP process number
appletalk route-redistribution←This command is automatically added when
                        Appletalk EIGRP is enabled
!
interface Tunnel1
 no ip address
 appletalk cable-range 600-600 600.95←Define a cable range for this interface
                        and an address of 600.95
 appletalk zone test←Define the primary Appletalk zone to be tested
 appletalk protocol eigrp←Enable EIGRP on this interface
 tunnel source Ethernet0/0←Define a tunnel source interface
 tunnel destination 194.1.1.1←Define a tunnel destination address
!
interface Ethernet0/0
 ip address 195.1.1.1 255.255.255.0
 no keepalive
 appletalk cable-range 500-599 599.1←Define a cable range for this interface
                        and an address of 599.1
 appletalk zone sales←Define the primary Appletalk zone to be sales
 appletalk zone service←Define the secondary Appletalk zone to be service
!
interface Serial0/0
 ip address 193.1.1.2 255.255.255.0
 encapsulation ppp
 no fair-queue
!
router rip
 network 193.1.1.0
 network 195.1.1.0
!
```

```
line con 0
line aux 0
line vty 0 4
 login
!
end
```

Monitoring and Testing the Configuration

Let's start by connecting to RouterA and displaying the routing table with the **show appletalk route** command. Notice that there are a total of three routes in the Appletalk network. Recall from the two previous labs that there were four Appletalk routes before we added the tunnel interface. The tunnel between RouterA and RouterC is a single Appletalk network. Note that the EIGRP routing protocol is running over the tunnel, and Network 500-599 on RouterC is being learned via EIGRP.

```
RouterA#show appletalk route
Codes: R - RTMP derived, E - EIGRP derived, C - connected, A - AURP
       S - static  P - proxy
3 routes in internet

The first zone listed for each entry is its default (primary) zone.

C Net 400-499 directly connected, Ethernet0/0, zone accounting
               Additional zones: 'service'
E Net 500-599 [1/G] via 600.95, 523 sec, Tunnel1, zone sales
               Additional zones: 'service'
C Net 600-600 directly connected, Tunnel1, zone test
```

Display the zones on the network with the **show appletalk zone** command. We see that the tunnel zone is displayed as zone test at Network 600-600.

```
RouterA#show appletalk zone
Name                           Network(s)
test                           600-600
accounting                     400-499
service                        500-599 400-499
sales                          500-599
Total of 4 zones
```

Display the active EIGRP interfaces on RouterA with the **show appletalk eigrp interface** command. We see that the only EIGRP interface on RouterA is the tunnel interface.

```
RouterA#show appletalk eigrp interface
AT/EIGRP Neighbors for process 1, router id 1

                   Xmit Queue      Mean    Pacing Time    Multicast    Pending
Interface   Peers  Un/Reliable     SRTT    Un/Reliable    Flow Timer   Routes
Tu1          1       0/0           436      58/1100        3212          0
```

We can verify end-to-end network connectivity with the **ping appletalk 599.1** command. This command will send a ping to the Ethernet interface of RouterC. The ping should be 100 percent successful.

```
RouterA#ping appletalk 599.1

Type escape sequence to abort.
Sending 5, 100-byte Appletalk Echoes to 599.1, timeout is 2 seconds:
!!!!!
Success rate is 100 percent (5/5), round-trip min/avg/max = 72/72/72 ms
```

The tunnel interface status can be displayed with the **show interface tunnel1** command. This command will show us how much traffic has passed through the tunnel. The command also shows us the tunnel source and destination, as well as the tunnel protocol and transport—which is GRE and IP.

```
RouterA#show interface tunnel1
Tunnel1 is up, line protocol is up
  Hardware is Tunnel
  MTU 1500 bytes, BW 9 Kbit, DLY 500000 usec, rely 255/255, load 1/255
  Encapsulation TUNNEL, loopback not set, keepalive set (10 sec)
  Tunnel source 194.1.1.1 (Ethernet0/0), destination 195.1.1.1
  Tunnel protocol/transport GRE/IP, key disabled, sequencing disabled
  Checksumming of packets disabled,  fast tunneling enabled
  Last input 00:00:00, output 00:00:04, output hang never
  Last clearing of "show interface" counters never
  Queueing strategy: fifo
  Output queue 0/0, 0 drops; input queue 0/75, 0 drops
  5 minute input rate 0 bits/sec, 0 packets/sec
  5 minute output rate 0 bits/sec, 0 packets/sec
     250 packets input, 14254 bytes, 0 no buffer
     Received 0 broadcasts, 0 runts, 0 giants
     0 input errors, 0 CRC, 0 frame, 0 overrun, 0 ignored, 0 abort
     5298 packets output, 284287 bytes, 0 underruns
     0 output errors, 0 collisions, 0 interface resets
     0 output buffer failures, 0 output buffers swapped out
```

Because we are running an IP tunnel between the Ethernet interfaces of RouterA and RouterC, we are not running any Appletalk protocol on the serial interface of RouterA. This status can be verified with the **show appletalk interface s 0/0** command. As in the following example, there is no Appletalk running on this interface.

```
RouterA#show appletalk interface s 0/0
Serial0/0 is up, line protocol is up
  Appletalk protocol processing disabled
```

Use the **show appletalk interface e 0/0** command to verify that the Ethernet interface of RouterA is running Appletalk.

```
RouterA#show appletalk interface e 0/0
Ethernet0/0 is up, line protocol is up
  Appletalk cable range is 400-499
  Appletalk address is 410.1, Valid
  Appletalk primary zone is "accounting"
  Appletalk additional zones: "service"
  Appletalk address gleaning is disabled
  Appletalk route cache is enabled
```

Now, let's connect to RouterB. RouterB is not running any Appletalk protocols on any of its interfaces. The tunnel that runs from RouterA to RouterC is only using RouterB as a TCP/IP transit node. We can verify that we are not running any Appletalk protocols on RouterB with the **show appletalk global**, **show appletalk route**, and **show appletalk zone** commands. Each of the outputs from these commands should indicate that no Appletalk is running on RouterB.

```
RouterB#show appletalk global
% Appletalk not running
```

```
RouterB#show appletalk route
% Appletalk not running
```

```
RouterB#show appletalk zone
% Appletalk not running
```

Display the IP routing table on RouterB with the **show ip route** command. We see that RouterB has two directly connected networks and two networks that have been learned via the RIP routing protocol. IP is enabled and is running on all routers in our network. The IP routing table shows us that the entire network is reachable, from the Ethernet interface of RouterA (194.1.1.1) to the Ethernet interface of RouterC (195.1.1.1).

```
RouterB#show ip route
Codes: C - connected, S - static, I - IGRP, R - RIP, M - mobile, B - BGP
       D - EIGRP, EX - EIGRP external, O - OSPF, IA - OSPF inter area
       E1 - OSPF external type 1, E2 - OSPF external type 2, E - EGP
       i - IS-IS, L1 - IS-IS level-1, L2 - IS-IS level-2, * - candidate default
       U - per-user static route
```

```
Gateway of last resort is not set

     192.1.1.0/24 is variably subnetted, 2 subnets, 2 masks
C       192.1.1.0/24 is directly connected, Serial0/0
C       192.1.1.1/32 is directly connected, Serial0/0
     193.1.1.0/24 is variably subnetted, 2 subnets, 2 masks
C       193.1.1.0/24 is directly connected, Serial0/1
C       193.1.1.2/32 is directly connected, Serial0/1
R       194.1.1.0/24 [120/1] via 192.1.1.1, 00:00:24, Serial0/0
R       195.1.1.0/24 [120/1] via 193.1.1.2, 00:00:13, Serial0/1
```

Now, let's connect to RouterC. Verify that you can reach RouterA with the **ping appletalk 410.1** command.

```
RouterC#ping appletalk 410.1

Type escape sequence to abort.
Sending 5, 100-byte Appletalk Echoes to 410.1, timeout is 2 seconds:
!!!!!
Success rate is 100 percent (5/5), round-trip min/avg/max = 72/83/108 ms
```

Display the Appletalk routing table with the **show appletalk route** command. As we saw on RouterA, there are only three routes in our Appletalk network.

```
RouterC#show appletalk route
Codes: R - RTMP derived, E - EIGRP derived, C - connected, A - AURP
       S - static  P - proxy
3 routes in internet

The first zone listed for each entry is its default (primary) zone.

E Net 400-499 [1/G] via 600.79, 652 sec, Tunnel1, zone accounting
               Additional zones: 'service'
C Net 500-599 directly connected, Ethernet0/0, zone sales
               Additional zones: 'service'
C Net 600-600 directly connected, Tunnel1, zone test
```

Verify that the output of the **show appletalk zone** command matches the show appletalk zone output on RouterA. Every router on an Appletalk network should have an identical list of zones (assuming that there are no zone filters in effect).

```
RouterC#show appletalk zone
Name                            Network(s)
test                            600-600
accounting                      400-499
service                         400-499 500-599
sales                           500-599
Total of 4 zones
```

The **show appletalk interface s 0/0** command reveals that the serial interface on RouterC is not running any Appletalk routing. The Appletalk traffic is being tunneled into IP once it leaves the Ethernet interface of RouterC.

```
RouterC#show appletalk interface s 0/0
Serial0/0 is up, line protocol is up
  Appletalk protocol processing disabled
```

The **show appletalk interface e 0/0** command will verify that the Appletalk protocol is being run on the Ethernet interface of RouterC.

```
RouterC#show appletalk interface e 0/0
Ethernet0/0 is up, line protocol is up
  Appletalk cable range is 500-599
  Appletalk address is 599.1, Valid
  Appletalk primary zone is "sales"
  Appletalk additional zones: "service"
  Appletalk address gleaning is disabled
  Appletalk route cache is enabled
```

Display the status of the IP tunnel on RouterC with the **show interface tunnel1** command. The tunnel should be in an up/up state. Notice how the command displays the source and destination of the tunnel.

```
RouterC#show interface tunnel1
Tunnel1 is up, line protocol is up
  Hardware is Tunnel
  MTU 1500 bytes, BW 9 Kbit, DLY 500000 usec, rely 255/255, load 1/255
  Encapsulation TUNNEL, loopback not set, keepalive set (10 sec)
  Tunnel source 195.1.1.1 (Ethernet0/0), destination 194.1.1.1
  Tunnel protocol/transport GRE/IP, key disabled, sequencing disabled
  Checksumming of packets disabled,  fast tunneling enabled
  Last input 00:00:01, output 00:00:00, output hang never
  Last clearing of "show interface" counters never
  Queueing strategy: fifo
  Output queue 0/0, 0 drops; input queue 0/75, 0 drops
  5 minute input rate 0 bits/sec, 0 packets/sec
  5 minute output rate 0 bits/sec, 0 packets/sec
     250 packets input, 14459 bytes, 0 no buffer
     Received 0 broadcasts, 0 runts, 0 giants
     0 input errors, 0 CRC, 0 frame, 0 overrun, 0 ignored, 0 abort
     5386 packets output, 289355 bytes, 0 underruns
     0 output errors, 0 collisions, 0 interface resets
     0 output buffer failures, 0 output buffers swapped out
```

Lab #76: Appletalk Traffic and Zone Filtering

Equipment Needed

The following equipment is needed to perform this lab exercise:

- Three Cisco routers. One of the routers must have two serial interfaces; the other two routers must have one serial interface and one Ethernet interface.
- Two Cisco crossover cables. If a Cisco crossover cable is not available, then you can use a Cisco DTE cable connected to a Cisco DCE cable.
- A Cisco rolled cable for console port connection to the routers
- A Cisco IOS image that supports the Appletalk protocol

Configuration Overview

This lab will demonstrate several types of Appletalk filters:

1. Appletalk Zone filters—This type of filter will prevent selected zones from appearing in the zone list of a router.
2. Appletalk data packet filters—This type of filter will prevent traffic from reaching selected Appletalk nodes.
3. Appletalk routing filters—This type of filter will prevent Appletalk routing updates from being sent out of a router.

The three routers are connected, as shown in Figure 19–10. RouterB acts as a DCE and supplies clocking to RouterA and RouterC.

Router Configuration

The configurations for the three routers in this example are as follows (key Appletalk commands are highlighted in bold):

Figure 19–10
Appletalk filtering

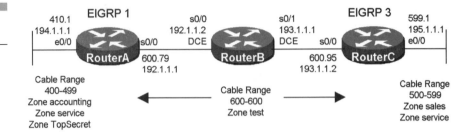

RouterA

```
Current configuration:
!
version 11.1
no service udp-small-servers
no service tcp-small-servers
!
hostname RouterA
!
appletalk routing eigrp 1←Enable EIGRP Routing. Each Appletalk router must
                          have a different EIGRP process number
appletalk route-redistribution←This command is automatically added when
                              Appletalk EIGRP is enabled
!
interface Tunnel1
 no ip address
 appletalk cable-range 600-600 600.79←Define a cable range for this interface
                                    and an address of 600.79
 appletalk zone test←Define the primary Appletalk zone to be tested
 appletalk protocol eigrp←Enable EIGRP on this interface
 tunnel source Ethernet0/0←Define a tunnel source interface
 tunnel destination 195.1.1.1←Define a tunnel destination address
!
interface Ethernet0/0
 ip address 194.1.1.1 255.255.255.0
 no keepalive
 appletalk cable-range 400-499 410.1←Define a cable range for this interface
                                    and an address of 410.1
 appletalk zone accounting←Define the primary Appletalk zone to be accounting
 appletalk zone service←Define the secondary Appletalk zone to be service
 appletalk zone TopSecret←Define the secondary Appletalk zone to be TopSecret
!
interface Serial0/0
 ip address 192.1.1.1 255.255.255.0
 encapsulation ppp
!
router rip
 network 192.1.1.0
 network 194.1.1.0
!
```

```
line con 0
line aux 0
line vty 0 4
 login
!
end
```

RouterB

```
Current configuration:
!
version 11.1
no service udp-small-servers
no service tcp-small-servers
!
hostname RouterB
!
enable password cisco
!
interface Serial0/0
 ip address 192.1.1.2 255.255.255.0
 encapsulation ppp
 no fair-queue
 clockrate 64000←Provide clocking to neighbor router
!
interface Serial0/1
 ip address 193.1.1.1 255.255.255.0
 encapsulation ppp
 clockrate 64000←Provide clocking to neighbor router
!
router rip
 network 193.1.1.0
 network 192.1.1.0
!
line con 0
line aux 0
line vty 0 4
 password cisco
 login
!
end
```

RouterC

```
Current configuration:
!
version 11.1
```

```
no service udp-small-servers
no service tcp-small-servers
!
hostname RouterC
!
!
appletalk routing eigrp 3←Enable EIGRP Routing. Each Appletalk router must
                          have a different EIGRP process number
appletalk route-redistribution←This command is automatically added when
                               Appletalk EIGRP is enabled
!
interface Tunnel1
 no ip address
 appletalk cable-range 600-600 600.95←Define a cable range for this interface
                                      and an address of 600.95
 appletalk zone test←Define the primary Appletalk zone to be test
 appletalk protocol eigrp←Enable EIGRP on this interface
 tunnel source Ethernet0/0←Define a tunnel source interface
 tunnel destination 194.1.1.1←Define a tunnel destination address
!
interface Ethernet0/0
 ip address 195.1.1.1 255.255.255.0
 no keepalive
 appletalk cable-range 500-599 599.1←Define a cable range for this interface
                                     and an address of 599.1
 appletalk zone sales←Define the primary Appletalk zone to be sales
 appletalk zone service←Define the secondary Appletalk zone to be service
!
interface Serial0/0
 ip address 193.1.1.2 255.255.255.0
 encapsulation ppp
 no fair-queue
!
router rip
 network 193.1.1.0
 network 195.1.1.0
!
line con 0
line aux 0
line vty 0 4
 login
!
end
```

Monitoring and Testing the Configuration

Let's start by connecting to RouterA and making sure that our test network is up and active with the **show appletalk route** command. RouterA should have two directly connected networks and one network that is being learned via the EIGRP routing protocol.

```
RouterA#show appletalk route
Codes: R - RTMP derived, E - EIGRP derived, C - connected, A - AURP
       S - static  P - proxy
3 routes in internet

The first zone listed for each entry is its default (primary) zone.

C Net 400-499 directly connected, Ethernet0/0, zone accounting
             Additional zones: 'TopSecret','service'
E Net 500-599 [1/G] via 600.95, 1958 sec, Tunnel1, zone sales
             Additional zones: 'service'
C Net 600-600 directly connected, Tunnel1, zone test
```

Verify that RouterA has all our network zones in its zone table with the **show appletalk zone** command.

```
RouterA#show appletalk zone
Name                              Network(s)
TopSecret                         400-499
test                              600-600
accounting                        400-499
service                           500-599 400-499
sales                             500-599
Total of 5 zones
```

Now, connect to RouterC and display its route table using the **show appletalk route** command. Make sure that Network 400-499 is in the route table.

```
RouterC#show appletalk route
Codes: R - RTMP derived, E - EIGRP derived, C - connected, A - AURP
       S - static  P - proxy
3 routes in internet

The first zone listed for each entry is its default (primary) zone.

E Net 400-499 [1/G] via 600.79, 2010 sec, Tunnel1, zone accounting
             Additional zones: 'service','TopSecret'
C Net 500-599 directly connected, Ethernet0/0, zone sales
             Additional zones: 'service'
C Net 600-600 directly connected, Tunnel1, zone test
```

Display the zone list on RouterC with the **show appletalk zone** command. The list of zones on RouterC should match the list of zones on RouterA. We see that these two zone lists do match, and both RouterC and RouterA have five zones in their zone tables.

```
RouterC#show appletalk zone
Name                            Network(s)
TopSecret                       400-499
test                            600-600
accounting                      400-499
service                         400-499 500-599
sales                           500-599
Total of 5 zones
```

If you have not already saved the configuration on RouterC, do so now with the **write mem** command.

Reconnect to RouterA. We are going to reload RouterC while we monitor the Appletalk ZIP protocol on RouterA. We will see how RouterC requests a zone list from RouterA when RouterC reboots. Enable appletalk ZIP debug with the **debug apple zip** command. Make sure that you are connected to the console port of RouterA. If you are not connected to the console port, issue the **term mon** command to send all debug output to the screen.

```
RouterA#debug apple zip
Appletalk ZIP Packets debugging is on
```

While still connected to RouterA, power off RouterC and then power it on again. After RouterC finishes booting and loading the IOS, you will see the following debug output on RouterA:

```
1  AT: Recvd ZIP cmd 5 from 600.95-6
2  AT: Answering ZIP GetNetInfo rcvd from 600.95 via Tunnel1
3  AT: Sent GetNetInfo reply to 600.95 via Tunnel1
4  AT: Recvd ZIP cmd 1 from 600.95-6
5  AT: 1 networks in ZIPquery pkt from 600.95
6  AT: Sent ZIP answer with 3 nets to 600.95
7  AT: NextNbrZipQuery: [500-599] zoneupdate 0 gw: 600.95 n: 600.95
8  AT: NextNbrZipQuery: r->rpath.gwptr: 606BA174, n: 606BA174
9  AT: maint_SendNeighborQueries, sending 1 queries to 600.95
10 AT: 1 query packet sent to neighbor 600.95
11 AT: Recvd ZIP cmd 2 from 600.95-6
12 AT: 2 zones in ZIPreply pkt, src 600.95
13 AT: net 500, zonelen 5, name sales
14 AT: net 500, zonelen 7, name service
15 AT: in CancelZoneRequest, cancelling req on 500-599...succeeded
16 AT: atZip_GC() called.
```

The first line of the debug output shows RouterA receiving a ZIP request from RouterC (600.95 is the tunnel interface Appletalk address of RouterC). Line 2 shows us that this request is a ZIP GetNetInfo request. The sixth line of the debug output (AT: Sent ZIP answer with 3 nets to 600.95) shows RouterA sending RouterC zone information on three Appletalk networks. Line 10 shows RouterA sending a ZIP query packet to RouterC at Appletalk address 600.95. Line 12 shows RouterC sending a ZIP reply back to RouterA. Notice that RouterC sends RouterA information on two zones. Line 13 and line 14 show the two zones that RouterC sends to RouterA. These are the sales and service zones.

Reconnect to RouterC and verify that the zone table is correct using the **show appletalk zone** command. We see that three networks (TopSecret, accounting, and service) are defined on the 400-499 network, which is located on RouterA. These are the three zones that RouterA sent to RouterC in the ZIP reply.

```
RouterC#show appletalk zone
Name                              Network(s)
TopSecret                         400-499
test                              600-600
accounting                        400-499
service                           500-599 400-499
sales                             500-599
Total of 5 zones
```

Now, reconnect to RouterA. We are going to add a zone access list on RouterA. The access list will deny any zone reply packets to be sent from RouterA that refer to the TopSecret zone.

Enter router configuration mode with the **config term** command. Enter the global access-list commands shown as follows. Then, enter interface configuration mode and enter the appletalk zip-reply-filter 600 statement under the tunnel 1 interface.

```
RouterA#config term
Enter configuration commands, one per line. End with CNTL/Z.
RouterA(config)#access-list 600 deny zone TopSecret
RouterA(config)#access-list 600 permit additional-zones
RouterA(config)#access-list 600 permit other-access
RouterA(config)#int tunnel1
RouterA(config-if)#appletalk zip-reply-filter 600
RouterA(config-if)#exit
RouterA(config)#exit
RouterA#
```

The access list that was just entered on RouterA can be confirmed with the **show apple access 600** command.

```
RouterA#sh apple access 600
Appletalk access list 600:
```
   deny zone TopSecret
   permit additional-zones
   permit other-access

RouterA now has an Appletalk zone reply filter that will restrict any ZIP reply packets from being sent out of the tunnel 1 interface that reference the zone TopSecret. Verify that Appletalk ZIP debug is still enabled with the **show debug** command.

```
RouterA#sh debug
Appletalk:
```
   Appletalk ZIP Packets debugging is on

Now that the ZIP access list is on RouterA, power off RouterC and power it on again. While RouterC is reloading, monitor RouterA to see what debug activity takes place. The following debug output should be seen:

```
RouterA#
```

```
1  AT: Recvd ZIP cmd 5 from 600.95-6
2  AT: Answering ZIP GetNetInfo rcvd from 600.95 via Tunnel1
3  AT: Sent GetNetInfo reply to 600.95 via Tunnel1
4  AT: Recvd ZIP cmd 1 from 600.95-6
5  AT: 1 networks in ZIPquery pkt from 600.95
6  AT: Sent ZIP answer with 2 nets to 600.95
7  AT: NextNbrZipQuery: [500-599] zoneupdate 0 gw: 600.95 n: 600.95
8  AT: NextNbrZipQuery: r->rpath.gwptr: 606BA174, n: 606BA174
9  AT: maint_SendNeighborQueries, sending 1 queries to 600.95
10 AT: 1 query packet sent to neighbor 600.95
11 AT: Recvd ZIP cmd 2 from 600.95-6
12 AT: 2 zones in ZIPreply pkt, src 600.95
13 AT: net 500, zonelen 5, name sales
14 AT: net 500, zonelen 7, name service
15 AT: in CancelZoneRequest, cancelling req on 500-599.succeeded
16 AT: atzip_GC() called
```

Notice in lines 1 and 2 that RouterC sends a ZIP GetNetInfo query to RouterA. In line 6, RouterA responds with only two networks. Recall from our previous trace that RouterA responded with three networks when we did not have a ZIP reply filter.

Verify that all zones are visible on RouterA with the **show appletalk zone** command.

```
RouterA#show appletalk zone
Name                                Network(s)
TopSecret                           400-499
test                                600-600
accounting                          400-499
service                             500-599 400-499
sales                               500-599
Total of 5 zones
```

Now, connect to RouterC and display the zone listings with the **show appletalk zone** command. We see that while RouterA knows about five zones, RouterC only knows about four zones. Compare the zone listing of RouterA with the zone listing of RouterC. Notice that RouterC does not have an entry for the TopSecret zone because of the ZIP reply filter that we added on RouterA. RouterA is no longer telling RouterC about the TopSecret zone.

```
RouterC#show appletalk zone
Name                                Network(s)
test                                600-600
accounting                          400-499
service                             500-599 400-499
sales                               500-599
Total of 4 zones
```

From RouterC, try to ping the Ethernet interface of RouterA at Appletalk address 410.1. The ping should be successful. The 400-499 Appletalk network is still accessible from RouterC, although we have an active zone filter and the zone corresponding to Network 410 is not in the zone list.

```
RouterC#ping apple 410.1

Type escape sequence to abort.
Sending 5, 100-byte Appletalk Echoes to 410.1, timeout is 2 seconds:
!!!!!
Success rate is 100 percent (5/5), round-trip min/avg/max = 72/72/72 ms
```

Now, we will add an Appletalk data packet filter to RouterA. The data packet filter will deny any traffic that is destined for the network associated with the zone TopSecret. As follows, from the configuration of RouterA, we still we have access list 600 defined.

```
access-list 600 deny zone TopSecret
access-list 600 permit additional-zones
access-list 600 permit other-access
```

Enter router configuration mode with the **config term** command. Enter interface configuration mode and type the **appletalk access-group 600** command. This command will take the existing access list #600 and apply it to a data packet filter on RouterA. Any traffic that is sent out the tunnel 1 interface of RouterA that has a source Appletalk address associated with the zone TopSecret will be discarded.

```
RouterA#config term
Enter configuration commands, one per line. End with CNTL/Z.
RouterA(config)#
RouterA(config)#interface tunnel1
RouterA(config-if)#appletalk access-group 600
RouterA(config-if)#exit
RouterA(config)#exit
```

Now, connect to RouterC. Try to ping RouterA at Appletalk address 410.1. The ping will not be successful, due to the data packet filter that we have added to RouterA.

```
RouterC#ping 410.1

Type escape sequence to abort.
Sending 5, 100-byte Appletalk Echoes to 410.1, timeout is 2 seconds:
.....
Success rate is 0 percent (0/5)
```

Reconnect to RouterA and remove the data packet filter with the **no appletalk access-group 600** command entered in router interface configuration mode.

```
RouterA#config term
Enter configuration commands, one per line. End with CNTL/Z.
RouterA(config)#int tunnel 1
RouterA(config-if)#no appletalk access-group 600
RouterA(config-if)#exit
RouterA(config)#exit
```

Now, connect to RouterC and try to ping RouterA at Appletalk address 410.1. The ping should now be successful.

```
RouterC#ping 410.1

Type escape sequence to abort.
Sending 5, 100-byte Appletalk Echoes to 410.1, timeout is 2 seconds:
!!!!!
Success rate is 100 percent (5/5), round-trip min/avg/max = 72/72/72 ms
```

Now, we are going to add an outgoing routing table update filter on RouterA. A routing table update filter will control which routes RouterA advertises to RouterC. We will change our routing protocol between RouterA and RouterC from EIGRP to RTMP. RTMP sends 10-second updates, and that makes it easier to demonstrate how this lab should work.

Let's start by adding the access list and disabling EIGRP on RouterA. We will not activate the access list at this time.

```
RouterA#config term
Enter configuration commands, one per line. End with CNTL/Z.
RouterA(config)#access-list 601 deny cable-range 400-499
RouterA(config)#access-list 601 deny other-access
RouterC(config)#int tunnel1
RouterC(config-if)#no appletalk protocol eigrp
RouterC(config-if)#exit
RouterA(config)#exit
```

The access list that was just entered on RouterA can be confirmed with the **show apple access 601** command.

```
RouterA#sh apple access 601
Appletalk access list 601:
  deny cable-range 400-499
  deny other-access
```

Connect to RouterC, enter configuration mode, and remove the EIGRP routing protocol from the tunnel 1 interface.

```
RouterC#config term
Enter configuration commands, one per line. End with CNTL/Z.
RouterC(config)#int tunnel1
RouterC(config-if)#no appletalk protocol eigrp
RouterC(config-if)#exit
RouterC(config)#exit
```

Reconnect to RouterA and display the routing table with the **show appletalk route** command. Notice that the 500-599 network is now being learned via RTMP instead of EIGRP. RTMP updates are sent every 10 seconds. The following screen print shows us that the last RTMP update from RouterC was received nine seconds ago.

```
RouterA#sh appletalk route
Codes: R - RTMP derived, E - EIGRP derived, C - connected, A - AURP
       S - static  P - proxy
3 routes in internet

The first zone listed for each entry is its default (primary) zone.

C Net 400-499 directly connected, Ethernet0/0, zone accounting
               Additional zones: 'TopSecret','service'
```

```
R Net 500-599 [1/G] via 600.95, 9 sec, Tunnel1, zone sales
               Additional zones: 'service'
C Net 600-600 directly connected, Tunnel1, zone test
```

Type the **show appletalk route** command several more times. Watch how the RTMP 10-second counter resets itself to zero seconds every 10 seconds. This activity proves that RouterA is actively receiving RTMP updates from RouterC.

```
RouterA#sh appletalk route
Codes: R - RTMP derived, E - EIGRP derived, C - connected, A - AURP
       S - static  P - proxy
3 routes in internet

The first zone listed for each entry is its default (primary) zone.

C Net 400-499 directly connected, Ethernet0/0, zone accounting
               Additional zones: 'TopSecret','service'
R Net 500-599 [1/G] via 600.95, 2 sec, Tunnel1, zone sales
               Additional zones: 'service'
C Net 600-600 directly connected, Tunnel1, zone test
```

Now, connect to RouterC. Let's verify that RouterC is learning about RouterA via RTMP and that the RTMP updates are being received every 10 seconds. Type the **show appletalk route** command to view the Appletalk routing table. The following screen print shows us that an RTMP update was received from RouterC nine seconds ago.

```
RouterC#show appletalk route
Codes: R - RTMP derived, E - EIGRP derived, C - connected, A - AURP
       S - static  P - proxy
3 routes in internet

The first zone listed for each entry is its default (primary) zone.

R Net 400-499 [1/G] via 600.79, 9 sec, Tunnel1, zone accounting
               Additional zones: 'service','TopSecret'
C Net 500-599 directly connected, Ethernet0/0, zone sales
               Additional zones: 'service'
C Net 600-600 directly connected, Tunnel1, zone test
```

Type the **show appletalk route** command several more times. Watch how the RTMP 10-second counter resets itself to zero seconds every 10 seconds. This activity shows us that RouterC is actively receiving RTMP updates from RouterA.

```
RouterC#show appletalk route
Codes: R - RTMP derived, E - EIGRP derived, C - connected, A - AURP
       S - static  P - proxy
3 routes in internet

The first zone listed for each entry is its default (primary) zone.

R Net 400-499 [1/G] via 600.79, 0 sec, Tunnel1, zone accounting
                Additional zones: 'service','TopSecret'
C Net 500-599 directly connected, Ethernet0/0, zone sales
                Additional zones: 'service'
C Net 600-600 directly connected, Tunnel1, zone test
```

Now, connect to RouterA. We will now activate the routing table update access list. Enter configuration mode with the **config term** command. Under interface configuration mode, enter the command **appletalk distribute-list 601 out** under the tunnel1 interface.

```
RouterA#config term
Enter configuration commands, one per line. End with CNTL/Z.
RouterA(config)#int tunnel1
RouterA(config-if)#appletalk distribute-list 601 out
RouterA(config-if)#exit
RouterA(config)#exit
```

Now, connect to RouterC. Enter the **show appletalk route** command a few times. You will shortly notice that RTMP updates are no longer being sent from RouterA to RouterC. The following screen print shows us that the last RTMP update was received 15 seconds ago from RouterA.

```
RouterC#show appletalk route
Codes: R - RTMP derived, E - EIGRP derived, C - connected, A - AURP
       S - static  P - proxy
3 routes in internet

The first zone listed for each entry is its default (primary) zone.

R Net 400-499 [1/G] via 600.79, 15 sec, Tunnel1, zone accounting
                Additional zones: 'service','TopSecret'
C Net 500-599 directly connected, Ethernet0/0, zone sales
                Additional zones: 'service'
C Net 600-600 directly connected, Tunnel1, zone test
```

As seen in the following screen print, the last RTMP update was received from RouterA 76 seconds ago.

```
RouterC#show appletalk route
Codes: R - RTMP derived, E - EIGRP derived, C - connected, A - AURP
       S - static  P - proxy
3 routes in internet

The first zone listed for each entry is its default (primary) zone.

R Net 400-499 [31/B] via 600.79, 76 sec, zone accounting
                Additional zones: 'service','TopSecret'
C Net 500-599 directly connected, Ethernet0/0, zone sales
                Additional zones: 'service'
C Net 600-600 directly connected, Tunnel1, zone test
```

The RTMP route to RouterA will eventually be deleted from the routing table. We see as follows that we no longer have the route in our table. The only entries in the routing table are the two networks that are directly connected to RouterC.

```
RouterC#show appletalk route
Codes: R - RTMP derived, E - EIGRP derived, C - connected, A - AURP
       S - static  P - proxy
2 routes in internet

The first zone listed for each entry is its default (primary) zone.

C Net 500-599 directly connected, Ethernet0/0, zone sales
                Additional zones: 'service'
C Net 600-600 directly connected, Tunnel1, zone test
```

Now, let's reconnect to RouterA and delete the routing table update access list. Enter router configuration mode with the **config term** command, and in interface configuration mode, enter the command **no appletalk distribute-list 601 out**.

```
RouterA#config term
Enter configuration commands, one per line. End with CNTL/Z.
RouterA(config)#int tunnel1
RouterA(config-if)#no appletalk distribute-list 601 out
RouterA(config-if)#exit
RouterA(config)#exit
```

Reconnect to RouterC and display the Appletalk routing table with the **show appletalk route** command. We see that Network 400–499 is once again visible via an RTMP-learned route.

```
RouterC#show appletalk route
Codes: R - RTMP derived, E - EIGRP derived, C - connected, A - AURP
       S - static  P - proxy
3 routes in internet

The first zone listed for each entry is its default (primary) zone.

R Net 400-499 [1/G] via 600.79, 9 sec, Tunnel1, zone accounting
                Additional zones: 'service','TopSecret'
C Net 500-599 directly connected, Ethernet0/0, zone sales
                Additional zones: 'service'
C Net 600-600 directly connected, Tunnel1, zone test
```

After several seconds, type the **show appletalk route** command again. We see that the counters are once again resetting themselves every ten seconds.

```
RouterC#show appletalk route
Codes: R - RTMP derived, E - EIGRP derived, C - connected, A - AURP
       S - static  P - proxy
3 routes in internet

The first zone listed for each entry is its default (primary) zone.

R Net 400-499 [1/G] via 600.79, 0 sec, Tunnel1, zone accounting
                Additional zones: 'service','TopSecret'
C Net 500-599 directly connected, Ethernet0/0, zone sales
                Additional zones: 'service'
C Net 600-600 directly connected, Tunnel1, zone test
```

Appletalk Monitoring and Troubleshooting Commands

This section will discuss key Appletalk monitoring and troubleshooting commands.

{show appletalk route} This command displays the contents of the Appletalk routing table. In the following example, we see that RouterA has two directly connected Appletalk networks: 400-499 (which is located on E0/0) and 600-600 (which is located on S0/0). Two networks have been learned via the Appletalk RTMP routing protocol: Networks 500-599 and 700-700. We see that the Appletalk routing table shows the zones that are associated with each network.

```
RouterA#show appletalk route
Codes: R - RTMP derived, E - EIGRP derived, C - connected, A - AURP
       S - static  P - proxy
4 routes in internet

The first zone listed for each entry is its default (primary) zone.
```

C Net 400-499 directly connected, Ethernet0/0, zone accounting
                Additional zones: 'service'
R Net 500-599 [2/G] via 600.2, 8 sec, Serial0/0, zone sales
                Additional zones: 'service'
C Net 600-600 directly connected, Serial0/0, zone wan1
R Net 700-700 [1/G] via 600.2, 8 sec, Serial0/0, zone wan2

{**show appletalk zone**}   This command displays all zones that are on the network. Notice that the service zone exists on two different Appletalk networks.

```
RouterA#show appletalk zone
Name                              Network(s)
wan1                              600-600
wan2                              700-700
accounting                        400-499
```
**service   500-599 400-499←This zone exists on
                                          two different Appletalk
                                          networks**
```
sales                             500-599
Total of 5 zones
```

{**show appletalk globals**}   This command provides a summary of the entire Appletalk network. We see that there are a total of four routes and five zones in this example network. We also see that the RTMP routing protocol will send an update every 10 seconds, mark a route as bad after 20 seconds, and discard a route after 60 seconds.

```
RouterA#show appletalk globals
Appletalk global information:
   Internet is incompatible with older, AT Phase1, routers.
```
   There are 4 routes in the internet.
   There are 5 zones defined.
```
   Logging of significant Appletalk events is disabled.
   ZIP resends queries every 10 seconds.
```
   RTMP updates are sent every 10 seconds.
   RTMP entries are considered BAD after 20 seconds.
   RTMP entries are discarded after 60 seconds.
```
   AARP probe retransmit count: 10, interval: 200 msec.
   AARP request retransmit count: 5, interval: 1000 msec.
   DDP datagrams will be checksummed.
```

```
RTMP datagrams will be strictly checked.
RTMP routes may not be propagated without zones.
Routes will not be distributed between routing protocols.
Routing between local devices on an interface will not be performed.
IPTalk uses the udp base port of 768 (Default).
Appletalk EIGRP is not enabled.
Alternate node address format will not be displayed.
Access control of any networks of a zone hides the zone.
```

{show apple access} This command displays Appletalk access lists that have been defined on the router. If the command includes a specific access list number, only that numbered access list will be displayed.

```
RouterA#sh appletalk access
Appletalk access list 600:
  deny zone TopSecret
  permit additional-zones
  permit other-access
Appletalk access list 601:
  deny cable-range 400-499
  deny other-access

RouterA#sh apple access 600
Appletalk access list 600:
  deny zone TopSecret
  permit additional-zones
  permit other-access
```

{show appletalk traffic} This command shows all Appletalk traffic that has been received or sent from the router. Traffic statistics are broken up into specific Appletalk protocols, such as routing, echo, and ZIP.

```
RouterA#show appletalk traffic
Appletalk statistics:
  Rcvd: 74 total, 0 checksum errors, 0 bad hop count
        74 local destination, 0 access denied
        0 for MacIP, 0 bad MacIP, 0 no client
        7 port disabled, 0 no listener
        0 ignored, 0 martians
  Bcast: 0 received, 143 sent
  Sent: 145 generated, 0 forwarded, 0 fast forwarded, 0 loopback
        0 forwarded from MacIP, 0 MacIP failures
        0 encapsulation failed, 0 no route, 0 no source
  DDP: 74 long, 0 short, 0 macip, 0 bad size
  NBP: 15 received, 0 invalid, 0 proxies
        0 replies sent, 20 forwards, 15 lookups, 0 failures
```

```
RTMP: 60 received, 0 requests, 0 invalid, 0 ignored
       127 sent, 0 replies
AURP:    0 Open Requests, 0 Router Downs
         0 Routing Information sent, 0 Routing Information received
         0 Zone Information sent, 0 Zone Information received
         0 Get Zone Nets sent, 0 Get Zone Nets received
         0 Get Domain Zone List sent, 0 Get Domain Zone List received
         0 bad sequence
ATP: 0 received
ZIP: 9 received, 8 sent, 0 netinfo
Appletalk statistics:
  Echo:      0 received, 0 discarded, 0 illegal
             0 generated, 0 replies sent
  Responder: 0 received, 0 illegal, 0 unknown
          0 replies sent, 0 failures
  AARP:      0 requests, 0 replies, 0 probes
             0 martians, 0 bad encapsulation, 0 unknown
             10 sent, 0 failures, 0 delays, 0 drops
  Lost: 0 no buffers
  Unknown: 0 packets
  Discarded: 0 wrong encapsulation, 0 bad SNAP discriminator
```

{**show interface**}   The standard **show interface** commands do not display any Appletalk-specific information. In the following example, the **show interface e 0/0** command only shows the MAC address of the port and high-level input and output traffic information.

```
RouterA#show interface e 0/0←There is no Appletalk specific information shown
                                in this command's output
Ethernet0/0 is up, line protocol is up
  Hardware is AmdP2, address is 00e0.1e5b.0d21 (bia 00e0.1e5b.0d21)
  MTU 1500 bytes, BW 10000 Kbit, DLY 1000 usec, rely 164/255, load 1/255
  Encapsulation ARPA, loopback not set, keepalive not set
  ARP type: ARPA, ARP Timeout 04:00:00
  Last input never, output 00:00:06, output hang never
  Last clearing of "show interface" counters never
  Queueing strategy: fifo
  Output queue 0/40, 0 drops; input queue 0/75, 0 drops
  5 minute input rate 0 bits/sec, 0 packets/sec
  5 minute output rate 0 bits/sec, 0 packets/sec
     0 packets input, 0 bytes, 0 no buffer
     Received 0 broadcasts, 0 runts, 0 giants
     0 input errors, 0 CRC, 0 frame, 0 overrun, 0 ignored, 0 abort
     0 input packets with dribble condition detected
     77 packets output, 7574 bytes, 0 underruns
     77 output errors, 0 collisions, 3 interface resets
     0 babbles, 0 late collision, 0 deferred
     77 lost carrier, 0 no carrier
     0 output buffer failures, 0 output buffers swapped out
```

{**show appletalk interface**}   Appletalk information for a specific port can be displayed with the **show appletalk interface** command. The output of this command gives us important Appletalk interface information, such as the cable range of this interface, the interface address, and zone information.

```
RouterA#show appletalk interface e 0/0
Ethernet0/0 is up, line protocol is up
  Appletalk cable range is 400-499←Network cable range information
  Appletalk address is 410.1, Valid←Interface address information
  Appletalk primary zone is "accounting"←Primary zone
  Appletalk additional zones: "service"←Secondary zone
  Appletalk address gleaning is disabled
  Appletalk route cache is enabled
```

A serial interface running Appletalk can also have port information displayed with two different commands. The **show interface** command shows general interface information. The only indication that this interface is running Appletalk is the atalkcp LCP that is indicated as open. This situation occurs as part of the PPP negotiation process and tells us that Appletalk traffic can be carried across this serial link.

```
RouterA#show interface s 0/0
Serial0/0 is up, line protocol is up
  Hardware is QUICC Serial
  MTU 1500 bytes, BW 1544 Kbit, DLY 20000 usec, rely 255/255, load 1/255
  Encapsulation PPP, loopback not set, keepalive set (10 sec)
  LCP Open

Appletalk control protocol has been negotiated and open
                 ↓
  Open: atalkcp, cdp
  Last input 00:00:02, output 00:00:02, output hang never
  Last clearing of "show interface" counters never
  Input queue: 0/75/0 (size/max/drops); Total output drops: 0
  Queueing strategy: weighted fair
  Output queue: 0/64/0 (size/threshold/drops)
     Conversations  0/1 (active/max active)
     Reserved Conversations 0/0 (allocated/max allocated)
  5 minute input rate 0 bits/sec, 0 packets/sec
  5 minute output rate 0 bits/sec, 0 packets/sec
     185 packets input, 7207 bytes, 0 no buffer
     Received 185 broadcasts, 0 runts, 0 giants
     5 input errors, 0 CRC, 5 frame, 0 overrun, 0 ignored, 0 abort
     185 packets output, 6968 bytes, 0 underruns
     0 output errors, 0 collisions, 14 interface resets
     0 output buffer failures, 0 output buffers swapped out
     0 carrier transitions
     DCD=up  DSR=up  DTR=up  RTS=up  CTS=up
```

Specific Appletalk information can be displayed for the serial interface with the **show appletalk interface** command. As with the Ethernet interface, this command will show us Appletalk information for the serial interface of this router.

```
RouterA#show appletalk interface s 0/0
Serial0/0 is up, line protocol is up
  Appletalk cable range is 600-600
  Appletalk address is 600.1, Valid
  Appletalk zone is "wan1"
  Appletalk port configuration verified by 600.2
  Appletalk address gleaning is not supported by hardware
  Appletalk route cache is enabled
```

{**show appletalk neighbors**}   This command can be used to verify that you are connected to the proper neighbors. The output of this command shows us that we are connected to a neighbor at Appletalk address 600.2.

```
RouterA#show appletalk neighbors
Appletalk neighbors:
  600.2             Serial0/0, uptime 00:08:10, 0 secs
            Neighbor is reachable as a RTMP peer
```

{**show appletalk eigrp interface**}   When running Appletalk EIGRP, there are several important commands used to monitor the network. The **show appletalk eigrp interface** command is used to display interfaces on a router that is running EIGRP.

```
RouterA#show appletalk eigrp interface
AT/EIGRP Neighbors for process 1, router id 1
```

Interface	Peers	Xmit Queue Un/Reliable	Mean SRTT	Pacing Time Un/Reliable	Multicast Flow Timer	Pending Routes
Se0/0	1	0/0	21	0/10	98	0

{**show appletalk eigrp neighbor**}   This command displays active EIGRP neighbor routers. In the following example, RouterA has an EIGRP neighbor at Appletalk address 600.2.

```
RouterA#show appletalk eigrp neighbor
AT/EIGRP Neighbors for process 1, router id 1
H    Address                    Interface    Hold Uptime   SRTT    RTO   Q  Seq
                                              (sec)         (ms)          Cnt Num
0    600.2                      Se0/0        14 00:37:29   21      200   0   8
```

{show appletalk eigrp traffic}   This command can be used to display EIGRP traffic that passes through a router. We see from this command output that RouterA is actively passing EIGRP hello messages.

```
RouterA#show appletalk eigrp traffic
AT-EIGRP Traffic Statistics
   Hellos sent/received: 499/488
   Updates sent/received: 6/4
   Queries sent/received: 0/2
   Replies sent/received: 2/0
   Acks sent/received: 5/6
   Input queue high water mark 1, 0 drops
```

Another way to verify that EIGRP is running on a particular interface is to use the **show appletalk interface** command. Notice from the following command output that the routing protocol for the interface is EIGRP.

```
RouterA#show appletalk interface s 0/0
Serial0/0 is up, line protocol is up
   Appletalk cable range is 600-600
   Appletalk address is 600.1, Valid
   Appletalk zone is "wan1"
   Routing protocols enabled: EIGRP
   Appletalk port configuration verified by 600.2
   Appletalk address gleaning is not supported by hardware
   Appletalk route cache is enabled
```

{show interface tunnel1}   An Appletalk GRE/IP tunnel interface can have its status displayed with the **show interface tunnel1** command. This command will show us how much traffic has passed through the tunnel. The command also shows us the tunnel source and destination, as well as the tunnel protocol and transport (which is GRE and IP).

```
RouterA#show interface tunnel1
Tunnel1 is up, line protocol is up
   Hardware is Tunnel
   MTU 1500 bytes, BW 9 Kbit, DLY 500000 usec, rely 255/255, load 1/255
   Encapsulation TUNNEL, loopback not set, keepalive set (10 sec)
   Tunnel source 194.1.1.1 (Ethernet0/0), destination 195.1.1.1
   Tunnel protocol/transport GRE/IP, key disabled, sequencing disabled
```

```
Checksumming of packets disabled,  fast tunneling enabled
Last input 00:00:00, output 00:00:04, output hang never
Last clearing of "show interface" counters never
Queueing strategy: fifo
Output queue 0/0, 0 drops; input queue 0/75, 0 drops
5 minute input rate 0 bits/sec, 0 packets/sec
5 minute output rate 0 bits/sec, 0 packets/sec
    250 packets input, 14254 bytes, 0 no buffer
    Received 0 broadcasts, 0 runts, 0 giants
    0 input errors, 0 CRC, 0 frame, 0 overrun, 0 ignored, 0 abort
    5298 packets output, 284287 bytes, 0 underruns
    0 output errors, 0 collisions, 0 interface resets
    0 output buffer failures, 0 output buffers swapped out
```

Conclusion

This chapter explored the Appletalk networking protocol. Appletalk requires the least amount of configuration on end systems but has one drawback: it is the chattiest of all desktop protocols. We explored several ways to reduce the amount of overhead on an Appletalk network, such as running EIGRP on the WAN or using a GRE tunnel. We also demonstrated the Cisco IOS support for Appletalk routing access lists, data access lists, and ZIP access lists.

CHAPTER 20

Catalyst 5000 Switches

Topics Covered in This Chapter

- LAN switching overview
- Catalyst product line
- VLAN configuration on the Catalyst Switch
- Configuring Catalyst Switches for port security
- Configuring an ISL trunk on a Catalyst Switch
- Routing between VLANs
- Troubleshooting Catalyst Switches

Introduction

This chapter will discuss Cisco Systems LAN switching products, specifically the Catalyst 5000 family of switches. The Catalyst is much more than just a high-speed switching hub. The equipment supports multiple *Virtual Local Area Networks* (VLANs), advanced router functionality, and ATM LAN emulation.

Catalyst 5000 Series Overview

The Catalyst 5000 series of switches consists of four different switch models. The different models can be summarized as follows:

Switch	Slots	Overview
Catalyst 5002	2	• Supports a single supervisor module • Can accommodate a single switching module
Catalyst 5000	5	• Supports a single supervisor module • Can accommodate up to four switching modules • Supports the route switch module
Catalyst 5505	5	• Supports a single supervisor module • Can accommodate a redundant supervisor module • Can accommodate up to four additional switching modules • Supports the route switch module
Catalyst 5500	13	• Supports a single supervisor module • Can accommodate a redundant supervisor module • Can accommodate up to 12 additional switching modules • Supports Lightstream ATM modules • Supports the route switch module

Catalyst 5500 Product Overview

The Catalyst 5500 is a 13-slot, high-performance switch. Highlights of the 5500 include the following features:

■ A 3.6Gb/sec switch fabric

■ Up to 528 switched 10Mb/s Ethernet ports

- Up to 264 switched 100Mb/s Ethernet ports
- Up to 132 switched 100Mb/s fiber Ethernet ports
- Up to eight ATM OC-12 ports
- Up to 32 ATM OC-3 ports
- Up to 32 DS3 ATM interfaces
- Up to 96 25Mb/s ATM ports
- Up to seven route switch modules
- Up to seven ATM LANE modules
- Up to 11 FDDI modules
- Capability for dual redundant supervisor engines
- Hot swappable modules
- Hot swappable power supplies
- Hot swappable fan assemblies

Catalyst Components

Figure 20–1 shows the types of cards that can populate a Catalyst 5000 series switch.

Figure 20–1
Catalyst switch components

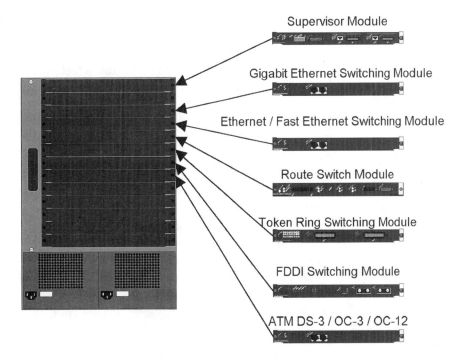

Supervisor Module

Gigabit Ethernet Switching Module

Ethernet / Fast Ethernet Switching Module

Route Switch Module

Token Ring Switching Module

FDDI Switching Module

ATM DS-3 / OC-3 / OC-12

- Supervisor Engine—The Supervisor Engine is the main processor for the Catalyst switch. The Catalyst 5500 can accommodate up to two Supervisor Engines. If one Supervisor Engine fails, then the other will take over for the failed unit. The Supervisor II only supports 1.2Gb/sec of backplane bandwidth. The Supervisor III supports 3.6Gbit/sec of backplane bandwidth, as well as fast Etherchannel links up to 400Mbits/sec.

- Route Switch Module—This module provides routing functionality to the Catalyst switch. The RSM runs the traditional Cisco Router IOS and is comparable in performance to a Cisco 7500 router. The RSM does not have any physical interfaces; rather, it uses the concept of logical interfaces to route traffic between different VLANs.

- Ethernet/Token Ring/FDDI switching modules—The Catalyst supports a variety of LAN switching modules. In addition, the Catalyst supports Fast EtherChannel links at speeds up to 800Mb/s full duplex using multiple 100Mb/s Ethernet links grouped into a single, logical link.

VLANs

In order to fully understand the concept of a VLAN, we must first review the various ways of connecting hosts on a LAN.

Figure 20–2 shows the traditional way of connecting six workstations to a non-switched Ethernet network. Each of the six workstations connects to a basic Ethernet hub. The hub effectively connects all six workstations onto the same Ethernet cable. The entire hub constitutes a single collision domain (only one workstation can transmit at a time) and a single broadcast domain (all workstations will receive all traffic that is sent by any other workstation). All six workstations reside in the same collision and broadcast domain.

Figure 20–3 shows a bridge device. Three workstations reside on two different LANs. The two LANs are connected by the bridge device. Each LAN connected to the bridge is a separate collision domain, but all six workstations reside on a single broadcast domain.

Figure 20–4 shows a router device. Three workstations reside on two different LANs. The two LANs are connected by the router. Each LAN resides in its own collision domain and its own broadcast domain.

Figure 20–5 shows a LAN switch that supports VLANs. All six workstations are connected to the same LAN switch.

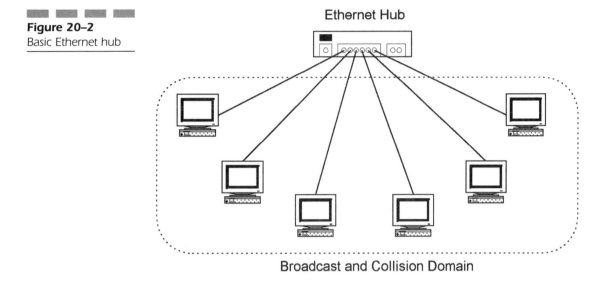

Figure 20–2
Basic Ethernet hub

Ethernet Hub

Broadcast and Collision Domain

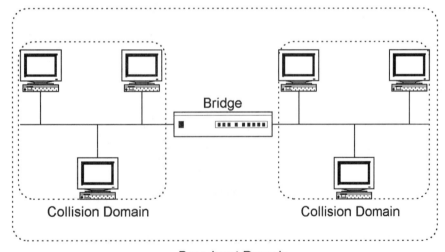

Figure 20–3
Bridge example

Bridge

Collision Domain

Collision Domain

Broadcast Domain

A VLAN is an administratively defined broadcast domain. All endstations that reside in a common VLAN will receive broadcast packets that are sent by other endstations that reside on the VLAN. A VLAN may sound similar to a traditional LAN switch, but the key difference is that in a VLAN, the endstations do not need to be in the same physical location.

The three workstations that reside in each VLAN are all in a single-broadcast domain. Each of the six workstations are in their own collision domain.

Figure 20–4
Router example

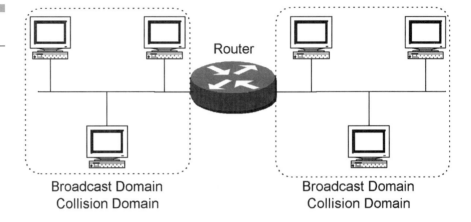

Broadcast Domain   Broadcast Domain
Collision Domain   Collision Domain

Figure 20–5
LAN switch example

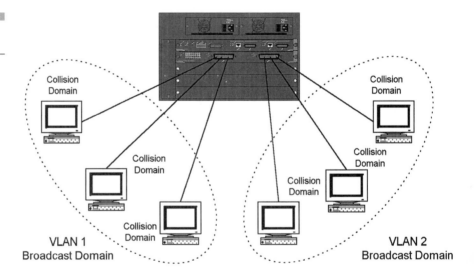

Routing Between VLANs

Two routers that reside in separate VLANs encounter the same issue that two routers residing on two different LANs have. How do you route between the VLANs? The catalyst switch can accomplish this task in one of two ways:

1. The catalyst has the capability to connect to a router via a 100Mb/s Ethernet link using *Interswitch Link* (ISL) encapsulation. The router that is connected to the catalyst uses subinterfaces to route between the VLANs. Each VLAN is

assigned to a separate subinterface on the router. This concept is shown in Figure 20–6.

2. Use a *Route Switch Module* (RSM). The Catalyst RSM is a Cisco 7500 class router that is packaged in a Catalyst card form factor. The RSM does not have any physical interfaces; rather, it uses virtual interfaces to route between VLANs.

Accessing the Catalyst

Every Catalyst 5000 family switch has an internal logical interface referred to as the SC0 interface. The SC0 interface is used to provide an active IP address that can be used to telnet into the Catalyst for configuration and monitoring. The SC0 interface is usually in VLAN 1 but can be moved to any VLAN. Without an active SC0 interface, the Catalyst switch would need to be accessed via the console or Aux port on the Supervisor Engine. The Catalyst also supports SLIP connections. The Catalyst SLIP IP address is configured by defining the SL0 interface on the switch.

Figure 20–6
Routing between
VLANs

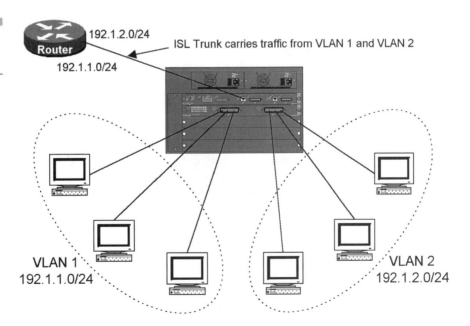

Catalyst Trunks

Catalyst user ports can also be defined as trunks. These trunks can be used to connect a Catalyst switch to other Catalyst switches or to a router.

Catalyst Configuration

Configuring a Cisco Catalyst switch is different then configuring a Cisco router in several ways:

- The router has a separate configuration mode. With the Catalyst, you type the configuration commands at the enable prompt command line. On both the Catalyst and router, changes take effect immediately.

- A Cisco router has several modes of operation, such as exec, debug, configuration, etc. The Catalyst switch only has normal and privileged modes.

- The router has two types of configuration memory: running and startup. The running configuration is the configuration that is currently active on the router. The startup configuration is the configuration that is stored in NVRAM. When you make a configuration change on the router, the running configuration changes—but the startup configuration does not change. With the Catalyst, there is only one configuration memory, and it gets changed as soon as a configuration change is made.

- The **show run** command on the router will display the currently running configuration. The Cisco router configuration is usually short, only showing commands that have been entered and that are not the default commands. The Catalyst switch configuration is long and shows every parameter for the switch, whether or not it has been configured by the user. Following are some lines from a Catalyst switch configuration.

```
#module 5 : 12-port 10/100BaseTX Ethernet
set module name    5
set module enable  5
set VLAN 1     5/1-10
set VLAN 2     5/11-12
set port channel 5/1-12 off
set port channel 5/1-12 auto
set port enable    5/1-12
set port level     5/1-12  normal
```

```
set port speed        5/1-12   auto
set port trap         5/1-12   disable
set port name         5/11 RouterB
set port name         5/12 RouterA
set port name         5/1-10
set port security     5/1-12   disable
set port broadcast    5/1-12   0
set port membership   5/1-12   static
set cdp enable        5/1-12
set cdp interval 5/1-12 60
set trunk 5/1   auto 1-1005
set trunk 5/2   auto 1-1005
set trunk 5/3   auto 1-1005
set trunk 5/4   auto 1-1005
set trunk 5/5   auto 1-1005
set trunk 5/6   auto 1-1005
set trunk 5/7   auto 1-1005
set trunk 5/8   auto 1-1005
set trunk 5/9   auto 1-1005
set trunk 5/10  auto 1-1005
set trunk 5/11  auto 1-1005
set trunk 5/12  off 1-1005
set spantree portfast      5/1-12 disable
set spantree portcost      5/1   100
set spantree portcost      5/2   100
set spantree portcost      5/3   100
set spantree portcost      5/4   100
set spantree portcost      5/5   100
set spantree portcost      5/6   100
set spantree portcost      5/7   100
set spantree portcost      5/8   100
set spantree portcost      5/9   100
set spantree portcost      5/10 100
set spantree portcost      5/11 100
set spantree portcost      5/12 100
set spantree portpri       5/1-12 32
set spantree portvlanpri 5/1   0
set spantree portvlanpri 5/2   0
set spantree portvlanpri 5/3   0
set spantree portvlanpri 5/4   0
set spantree portvlanpri 5/5   0
set spantree portvlanpri 5/6   0
set spantree portvlanpri 5/7   0
set spantree portvlanpri 5/8   0
set spantree portvlanpri 5/9   0
set spantree portvlanpri 5/10 0
set spantree portvlanpri 5/11 0
set spantree portvlanpri 5/12 0
set spantree portvlancost 5/1   cost 99
set spantree portvlancost 5/2   cost 99
set spantree portvlancost 5/3   cost 99
set spantree portvlancost 5/4   cost 99
set spantree portvlancost 5/5   cost 99
set spantree portvlancost 5/6   cost 99
```

```
set spantree portvlancost 5/7   cost  99
set spantree portvlancost 5/8   cost  99
set spantree portvlancost 5/9   cost  99
set spantree portvlancost 5/10  cost  99
set spantree portvlancost 5/11  cost  99
set spantree portvlancost 5/12  cost  99
```

Commands Discussed in This Chapter

- **clear config all**
- **ping** *host [packet_size] [packet_count]*
- **set interface sc0** *[ip_addr [netmask [broadcast]]]*
- **set ip permit {enable | disable} / set ip permit** *ip_addr [mask]*
- **set port name** *mod_num / port_num [name_string]*
- **set port security** *mod_num / port_num* **{enable | disable}** *[mac_addr]*
- **set trunk** *mod_num / port_num* **[on | off | desirable | auto]** *[vlan_range]*
- **set vlan** *vlan_num mod_num / port_num*
- **set vtp domain** *name*
- **show cam dynamic**
- **show interface**
- **show ip permit**
- **show mac** *[mod_num / [port_num]]*
- **show module** *mod_num*
- **show port** *[mod_num / port_num]*
- **show system**
- **show trunk** *[mod_num[/ port_num]]*
- **show version**
- **show vlan** *[vlan]*
- **show vtp domain**

Definitions

clear config all: This privileged command clears the Catalyst configuration and resets the switch.

ping: This normal mode command sends ICMP echo request packets to the selected node.

set interface: This privileged command sets the sc0 interface for inband telnet and SNMP access. The command can also be used to set the sl0 interface for SLIP telnet and SNMP access.

set ip permit: This privileged command enables or disables the IP permit list and creates an entry in the IP permit list.

set port name: This privileged command sets the name of a Catalyst switch port.

set port security: This privileged command enables or disables MAC-level port security on the switch.

set trunk: This privileged command configures a Catalyst port to become a trunk.

set vlan: This privileged command configures VLAN options on the switch.

set vtp domain: This privileged command sets the VTP domain name.

show cam dynamic: This normal command shows the contents of the CAM table.

show interface: This normal command displays information about the Catalyst switch interfaces.

show ip permit: This normal command displays information on IP permit lists that are defined on the switch.

show mac: This normal command displays information on MAC level statistics on the switch.

show module: This normal command displays module information for the switch.

show port: This normal command displays port level statistics for the switch.

show system: This normal command displays system information for the switch.

show trunk: This normal command shows trunking information for the switch.

show version: This normal command shows hardware and software version information for the switch.

show vlan: This normal command displays VLAN information for the switch.

show vtp domain: This normal command displays VTP domain information for the switch.

IOS Requirements

These labs were done using Cisco IOS 11.2. ISL trunks are supported in IOS 11.2 and higher. The Catalyst switch was running Version 3.1.

Lab #77: Basic Catalyst Configuration, VLANs, and Port Security

Equipment Needed

The following equipment is needed to perform this lab exercise:

- Two Cisco routers with Ethernet interfaces
- A Catalyst switch with 10 Mb/s or 10/100 Mb/s Ethernet ports
- Two Ethernet cables
- A Cisco rolled cable for console port connection to the routers
- A straight-through cable for console port connection to the Catalyst switch

Configuration Overview

This lab will demonstrate how to configure a Catalyst 5500 for basic LAN switching. Two routers, RouterA and RouterB, will be connected to a Catalyst switch as shown in Figure 20–7. The two routers will both reside in the same VLAN. Two Catalyst security features will also be demonstrated: IP permit and MAC filtering.

Figure 20–7
Catalyst configuration with port security

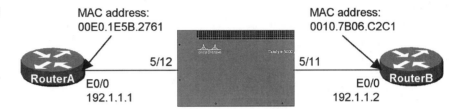

MAC address:
00E0.1E5B.2761

MAC address:
0010.7B06.C2C1

5/12

5/11

RouterA E0/0
192.1.1.1

E0/0 RouterB
192.1.1.2

- IP permit—This feature permits up to 10 IP addresses to be entered into the Catalyst. When IP permit is enabled, the Catalyst will only accept telnet and SNMP traffic from the 10 predefined IP addresses. If an unauthorized address attempts to send telnet or SNMP traffic to the switch, the traffic is rejected—and the Catalyst records the source address of the rejected traffic.

- MAC filtering—The Catalyst can be configured to reject incoming traffic on a port that does not have a source MAC address that matches a predefined MAC address that has been entered into the switch.

NOTES: *Cisco makes many models of LAN switches. Although this lab was done using a Catalyst 5500 switch, there are other LAN switches in the Cisco product line that could be used. For example, the Catalyst 1924 Enterprise Edition switch is a low-cost switch that is capable of doing VLANs and can also have a 100Mb/s ISL trunk.*

The Catalyst does not use the same IOS as a Cisco router. You will notice that the command set is different. Many items that are taken for granted on the router, such as being able to use the Tab key to complete a command, are not available on the Catalyst switch. Catalyst ports are referred to by slot and port number. For example, in this lab, we are connected to the 11th and 12th port of Card 5. The Catalyst will refer to these ports as 5/11 and 5/12, respectively.

Router Configuration

The configurations for the two routers in this example are as follows:

RouterA

```
Current configuration:
!
version 11.2
no service password-encryption
no service udp-small-servers
no service tcp-small-servers
!
hostname RouterA
!
interface Ethernet0/0
 ip address 192.1.1.1 255.255.255.0←Define the IP address for the interface
                                     connected to the Catalyst switch
!
no ip classless
!
line con 0
line aux 0
line vty 0 4
 exec-timeout 30 0
 login
!
end
```

RouterB

```
Current configuration:
!
version 11.2
no service password-encryption
no service udp-small-servers
no service tcp-small-servers
!
hostname RouterB
!
interface Ethernet0/0
 ip address 192.1.1.2 255.255.255.0←Define the IP address for the interface
                                     connected to the Catalyst switch
!
no ip classless
!
line con 0
line aux 0
line vty 0 4
 exec-timeout 30 0
 login
!
end
```

Monitoring and Testing the Configuration

Let's start by connecting to the Catalyst 5500. We will clear the entire configuration on the Catalyst so we are sure that we are starting with a known configuration. Use the command **clear config all** to set the Catalyst back to its factory default state.

```
Console> (enable) clear config all
This command will clear all configuration in NVRAM.
This command will cause ifIndex to be reassigned on the next system startup.
Do you want to continue (y/n) [n]? y
.......
...........................
................
...........................
...........................
...................

System configuration cleared.
```

After the Catalyst has been reset, all ports are defined to be on a single VLAN: VLAN 1. The Catalyst acts as a large multiport LAN switch. The Catalyst will automatically sense that an active LAN is connected to one of its ports and will set the corresponding port parameters correctly. We see from the **show port** output that ports 5/11 and 5/12 have been automatically configured. Their status is connected, they are both in VLAN 1, and they are both running 10Mb/s, half-duplex Ethernet. Keep in mind that we did not have to configure ports 5/11 and 5/12 after we reset the Catalyst to factory default state.

```
Console> (enable) sh port
Port   Name    Status      Vlan    Level   Duplex    Speed   Type
----   ------  ---------   -----   ------  -------   -----   -------------
 5/11          connected   1       normal  a-half    a-10    10/100BaseTX
 5/12          connected   1       normal  a-half    a-10    10/100BaseTX
```

More detailed port status is available by adding the port number after the show port command. Type **show port 5/11** to view the status for port 5/11. We see that additional data, such as MAC-level security information and Ethernet collision and error statistics, are listed.

```
Console> (enable) sh port 5/11
Port   Name    Status      Vlan    Level   Duplex    Speed   Type
----   ------  ---------   -----   ------  -------   -----   -------------
 5/11          connected   1       normal  a-half    a-10    10/100BaseTX
```

```
Port   Security        Secure-Src-Addr      Last-Src-Addr   Shutdown   Trap
-----  ---------       ----------------     -------------   ---------  ------------
 5/11  disabled                                             No         disabled

Port   Broadcast-Limit      Broadcast-Drop
-----  ---------------      --------------
 5/11  -                    0
Port   Status          Channel     Channel     Neighbor          Neighbor
                       mode        status      device            port
-----  ---------       -------     ---------   ----------------  ----------------
 5/11  connected       auto        not channel

Port   Align-Err       FCS-Err     Xmit-Err    Rcv-Err    UnderSize
-----  ---------       --------    ---------   --------   ----------
 5/11  0               0           0           0          0

Port   Single-Col   Multi-Coll  Late-Coll   Excess-Col  Carri-Sen  Runts  Giants
-----  ----------   ----------  ---------   ----------  ---------  -----  ------
 5/11  0            0           0           0           0          0      0

Last-Time-Cleared
-------------------------
Sun May 16 1999, 02:25:04
```

Catalyst ports can be given names to make them easier to identify. Use the **set port name** command to give a name to ports 5/11 and 5/12.

```
Console> (enable) set port name 5/11 RouterB
Port 5/11 name set.
Console> (enable) set port name 5/12 RouterA
Port 5/12 name set.
```

We see from the **show port 5/12** command that the port name has been set to RouterA.

```
Console> (enable) sh port 5/12
Port   Name      Status      Vlan    Level    Duplex    Speed   Type
----   ------    ---------   -----   ------   -------   -----   -------------
 5/12  RouterA   connected   1       normal   a-half    a-10    10/100BaseTX

Port   Security        Secure-Src-Addr      Last-Src-Addr   Shutdown   Trap
-----  ---------       ----------------     -------------   ---------  ------------
 5/12  disabled                                             No         disabled

Port   Broadcast-Limit      Broadcast-Drop
-----  ---------------      --------------
 5/12  -                    0
Port   Status          Channel     Channel     Neighbor          Neighbor
                       mode        status      device            port
-----  ---------       -------     ---------   ----------------  ----------------
 5/12  connected       auto        not channel
```

```
Port    Align-Err    FCS-Err    Xmit-Err    Rcv-Err    UnderSize
-----   ---------    --------   ---------   --------   ----------
 5/12   0            0          0           0          0

Port    Single-Col   Multi-Coll Late-Coll   Excess-Col Carri-Sen  Runts  Giants
-----   ----------   ---------- ---------   ---------- ---------  -----  ------
 5/12   0            0          0           0          0          0      0

Last-Time-Cleared
--------------------------
Sun May 16 1999, 02:25:04
```

Now, connect to RouterB. Verify that you can ping RouterA at IP address 192.1.1.1. Remember that both RouterA and RouterB were automatically put into VLAN 1 when we reset the Catalyst switch.

```
RouterB#ping 192.1.1.1

Type escape sequence to abort.
Sending 5, 100-byte ICMP Echos to 192.1.1.1, timeout is 2 seconds:
!!!!!
Success rate is 100 percent (5/5), round-trip min/avg/max = 1/2/4 ms
```

The Catalyst switch can be assigned an internal IP address that is used for SNMP and Telnet access. The IP address can be verified with the **show interface** command. As follows, we see that there are no IP addresses set for the switch:

```
Console> (enable) sh interface
sl0: flags=51<UP,POINTOPOINT,RUNNING>
        slip 0.0.0.0 dest 128.73.35.160
sc0: flags=63<UP,BROADCAST,RUNNING>
        VLAN 1 inet 0.0.0.0 netmask 0.0.0.0 broadcast 0.0.0.0
```

The IP address for inband access can be entered into the switch with the **set interface sc0** command. Enter an sc0 IP address of 192.1.1.3 as follows. Notice that this address is on the same network as the IP addresses of RouterA (192.1.1.1) and RouterB (192.1.1.2).

```
Console> (enable) set interface sc0 192.1.1.3
Interface sc0 IP address set.
```

The show interface command will now indicate that the sc0 IP address has been set to 192.1.1.3.

```
Console> (enable) sh interface
sl0: flags=51<UP,POINTOPOINT,RUNNING>
        slip 0.0.0.0 dest 128.73.35.160
sc0: flags=63<UP,BROADCAST,RUNNING>
        VLAN 1 inet 192.1.1.3 netmask 255.255.255.0 broadcast 192.1.1.255
```

Once the sc0 address has been set, verify that it is active by pinging the sc0 address.

```
Console> (enable) ping 192.1.1.3
192.1.1.3 is alive
```

We will be also be able to ping RouterA and RouterB.

```
Console> (enable) ping 192.1.1.1
192.1.1.1 is alive


Console> (enable) ping 192.1.1.2
192.1.1.2 is alive
```

Both RouterA and RouterB should be able to ping the sc0 interface of the Catalyst switch. We see as follows that RouterA is able to ping the Catalyst.

```
RouterA#ping 192.1.1.3

Type escape sequence to abort.
Sending 5, 100-byte ICMP Echos to 192.1.1.3, timeout is 2 seconds:
!!!!!
Success rate is 100 percent (5/5), round-trip min/avg/max = 1/3/4 ms
```

IP Permit Lists

The Catalyst switch has powerful security features. One such feature is the IP permit capability of the switch. The IP permit feature of the Catalyst enables the user to define up to 10 IP addresses that are allowed inbound SNMP and telnet access to the switch. The permit list can be displayed with the **show ip permit** command. We see as follows that there are no IP addresses in the permit list of the switch.

```
Console> (enable) show ip permit
IP permit list feature disabled.
Permit List      Mask
------------     ---------------

Denied IP Address    Last Accessed Time    Type
------------------   -------------------   ------
```

Let's add an IP address to the permit list of the switch with the **set ip permit 192.1.1.1** command. This command will provide RouterA with inbound SNMP and telnet access to the Catalyst switch.

```
Console> (enable) set ip permit 192.1.1.1
192.1.1.1 added to IP permit list.
```

The **show ip permit** command will now indicate that 192.1.1.1 is on the permit list. Notice that the IP permit list feature has been disabled. This state is the default state of the IP permit list.

```
Console> (enable) show ip permit
IP permit list feature disabled.
Permit List        Mask
------------       ----------------
192.1.1.1

Denied IP Address      Last Accessed Time      Type
------------------     ------------------      ------
```

After the IP permit list has been defined, the list must be enabled with the **set ip permit enable** command.

```
Console> (enable) set ip permit enable
IP permit list enabled.
```

Now, let's connect to RouterB. The IP address of RouterB's Ethernet interface that is connected to the Catalyst switch is 192.1.1.2. This address is not on the IP permit list of the Catalyst switch. Let's try to ping the sc0 interface of the Catalyst switch from RouterB. We see that the ping is successful. Remember that the IP permit list only denies inbound SNMP and Telnet access to the switch.

```
RouterB#ping 192.1.1.3

Type escape sequence to abort.
Sending 5, 100-byte ICMP Echos to 192.1.1.3, timeout is 2 seconds:
!!!!!
Success rate is 100 percent (5/5), round-trip min/avg/max = 4/4/4 ms
```

Let's try to telnet to the Catalyst switch at IP address 192.1.1.3. We see that the Catalyst switch rejects the Telnet session, because RouterB's address of 192.1.1.2 is not on the IP permit list.

```
RouterB#telnet 192.1.1.3
Trying 192.1.1.3 ... Open
Access not permitted. Closing connection...

[Connection to 192.1.1.3 closed by foreign host]
```

Now, connect to the Catalyst switch and display the IP permit list with the **show ip permit** command. We see that the denied IP address list now has an entry for the telnet session that we just tried to initiate from RouterB.

```
Console> (enable) show ip permit
IP permit list feature enabled.
Permit List      Mask
------------     ----------------
192.1.1.1

Denied IP Address     Last Accessed Time     Type
-----------------     ------------------     ------
192.1.1.2             05/25/99,14:25:50      Telnet
```

Disable the IP permit list with the **set ip permit disable** command.

```
Console> (enable) set ip permit disable
IP permit list disabled.
```

Now, reconnect to RouterB and try to Telnet to the Catalyst switch. We see that the telnet is now successful, because the IP permit list has been disabled.

```
RouterB#telnet 192.1.1.3
Trying 192.1.1.3 ... Open

Cisco Systems Console

Enter password:
Console> ena
Enter password:
Console> (enable)
Console> (enable) exit

[Connection to 192.1.1.3 closed by foreign host]
```

Secure Port Filtering

The Catalyst switch can be configured to only permit inbound traffic on a switch port that contains a MAC address that has been entered into the Catalyst switch. This feature is called Secure Port filtering. We see from the following output of the **show port 5/12** command that there are no entries under the MAC Source Address fields on the interface.

```
Console> (enable) sh port 5/12
Port   Name     Status      Vlan    Level   Duplex    Speed    Type
----   ------   ---------   -----   ------  -------   -----    -------------
5/12   RouterA  connected   1       normal  a-half    a-10     10/100BaseTX

Port   Security    Secure-Src-Addr    Last-Src-Addr   Shutdown   Trap
-----  ---------   ----------------   -------------   ---------  ------------
5/12   disabled                                       No         disabled

Port   Broadcast-Limit      Broadcast-Drop
-----  --------------       --------------
5/12   -                    0
Port   Status      Channel   Channel    Neighbor          Neighbor
                   mode      status     device            port
-----  ---------   -------   ---------  ----------------  ----------------
5/12   connected   auto      not channel

Port   Align-Err   FCS-Err    Xmit-Err   Rcv-Err   UnderSize
-----  ---------   --------   ---------  --------  ----------
5/12   0           0          0          0         0

Port   Single-Col  Multi-Coll Late-Coll  Excess-Col Carri-Sen  Runts  Giants
-----  ----------  ---------- ---------  ---------- ---------  -----  ------
5/12   0           0          0          0          0          0      0

Last-Time-Cleared
--------------------------
Sun May 16 1999, 02:25:04
```

We will now configure the Catalyst to only permit inbound Ethernet packets on port 5/12 that contain a specific source MAC address. In order for us to configure Secure Port Filtering on the Catalyst, we will need to know the MAC address of the host that is connected to port 5/12. RouterA's E0/0 interface is connected to port 5/12 on the Catalyst switch. Connect to RouterA, and use the **show interface e0/0** command to view the MAC address for the Ethernet interface of the router. We see that the MAC address for this interface is 00e0.1e5b.2761.

```
RouterA#sh int e 0/0
Ethernet0/0 is up, line protocol is up
   Hardware is AmdP2, address is 00e0.1e5b.2761 (bia 00e0.1e5b.2761)
   Internet address is 192.1.1.1/24
   MTU 1500 bytes, BW 10000 Kbit, DLY 1000 usec, rely 255/255, load 1/255
   Encapsulation ARPA, loopback not set, keepalive set (10 sec)
   ARP type: ARPA, ARP Timeout 04:00:00
   Last input 00:00:22, output 00:00:07, output hang never
   Last clearing of "show interface" counters never
   Queueing strategy: fifo
   Output queue 0/40, 0 drops; input queue 0/75, 0 drops
   5 minute input rate 0 bits/sec, 0 packets/sec
   5 minute output rate 0 bits/sec, 0 packets/sec
      18672 packets input, 17647218 bytes, 0 no buffer
```

```
Received 3662 broadcasts, 0 runts, 0 giants, 0 throttles
0 input errors, 0 CRC, 0 frame, 0 overrun, 0 ignored, 0 abort
0 input packets with dribble condition detected
24112 packets output, 18236637 bytes, 0 underruns
118 output errors, 0 collisions, 1 interface resets
0 babbles, 0 late collision, 1 deferred
118 lost carrier, 0 no carrier
0 output buffer failures, 0 output buffers swapped out
```

Now, connect to the Catalyst switch. Use the **set port security** command shown as follows to define which MAC address will be accepted when traffic comes into the Catalyst switch.

```
Console> (enable) set port security 5/12 enable 00-e0-1e-5b-27-62
Port 5/12 port security enabled with 00-e0-1e-5b-27-62 as the secure mac address
Trunking disabled for Port 5/12 due to Security Mode
```

Reconnect to RouterA. Try to ping the sc0 interface of the Catalyst at IP address 192.1.1.3. We see that the ping fails.

```
RouterA#ping 192.1.1.3

Type escape sequence to abort.
Sending 5, 100-byte ICMP Echos to 192.1.1.3, timeout is 2 seconds:
.....
Success rate is 0 percent (0/5)
```

Connect to the Catalyst switch. We see that the status of the port is shutdown. The reason for the port being shutdown is shown under the **Secure-Src-Addr** and **Last-Src-Addr** columns. These two columns show which MAC addresses will be allowed into the switch port and what the last MAC address sent to the port was. Notice that the Last-Src-Addr does not match the Secure-Src-Addr.

```
Console> (enable) show port 5/12
```

Port	Name	Status	Vlan	Level	Duplex	Speed	Type
5/12	RouterA	shutdown	1	normal	a-half	a-10	10/100BaseTX

Port	Security	**Secure-Src-Addr**	**Last-Src-Addr**	Shutdown	Trap
5/12	enabled	**00-e0-1e-5b-27-62**	**00-e0-1e-5b-27-61**	Yes	Disabled

Port	Broadcast-Limit	Broadcast-Drop
5/12	-	0

Port	Status	Channel mode	Channel status	Neighbor device	Neighbor port
5/12	shutdown	auto	not channel		

```
Port    Align-Err   FCS-Err    Xmit-Err    Rcv-Err    UnderSize
-----   ---------   --------   ---------   --------   ----------
 5/12   0           0          0           0          0

Port    Single-Col  Multi-Coll Late-Coll   Excess-Col Carri-Sen  Runts   Giants
-----   ----------  ---------- ---------   ---------- ---------  -----   ------
 5/12   0           0          0           0          0          0       0

Last-Time-Cleared
--------------------------
Sun May 16 1999, 02:25:04
```

Disable port security on port 5/12 with the command **set port security 5/12 disable**.

```
Console> (enable) set port security 5/12 disable
Port 5/12 port security disabled.
```

Use the show port 5/12 command to view the port status. We see that the status is now connected.

```
Console> (enable) sh port 5/12
Port   Name       Status       Vlan    Level   Duplex    Speed   Type
----   ------     ---------    -----   ------  -------   -----   -------------
 5/12  RouterA    connected    1       normal  a-half    a-10    10/100BaseTX

Port   Security   Secure-Src-Addr    Last-Src-Addr       Shutdown   Trap
-----  ---------  ---------------    -----------------   ---------  -----------
 5/12  disabled                                          No         disabled

Port   Broadcast-Limit    Broadcast-Drop
-----  --------------     --------------
 5/12  -                  0
Port   Status      Channel     Channel     Neighbor           Neighbor
                   mode        status      device             port
-----  ---------   ---------   ---------   ----------------   ----------------
 5/12  connected   auto        not channel

Port    Align-Err   FCS-Err    Xmit-Err    Rcv-Err    UnderSize
-----   ---------   --------   ---------   --------   ----------
 5/12   0           0          0           0          0

Port    Single-Col  Multi-Coll Late-Coll   Excess-Col Carri-Sen  Runts   Giants
-----   ----------  ---------- ---------   ---------- ---------  -----   ------
 5/12   0           0          0           0          0          0       0

Last-Time-Cleared
--------------------------
Sun May 16 1999, 02:25:04
```

Connect to RouterA. You should once again be able ping RouterB at IP address 192.1.1.2.

```
RouterA#ping 192.1.1.2

Type escape sequence to abort.
Sending 5, 100-byte ICMP Echos to 192.1.1.2, timeout is 2 seconds:
!!!!!
Success rate is 100 percent (5/5), round-trip min/avg/max = 4/7/8 ms
```

Now, we are going to move both RouterA and RouterB to VLAN 2. Remember that when we reset the Catalyst, we said that the switch resets in a state where all ports are in VLAN 1. The Catalyst switch must have a domain name before it can use VLAN numbers other than one. We see in the **show vtp domain** output that the domain name has not been set on this switch.

```
Console> (enable) sh vtp domain
```

Domain Name	Domain Index	VTP Version	Local Mode	Password
	1	2	server	-

Vlan-count	Max-vlan-storage	Config Revision	Notifications
5	1023	0	disabled

Last Updated	V2 Mode	Pruning	PruneEligible on Vlans
0.0.0.0	disabled	disabled	2-1000

Set the vtp domain name with the command **set vtp domain CCIE_STUDY_GUIDE**.

```
Console> (enable) set vtp domain CCIE_STUDY_GUIDE
VTP domain CCIE_STUDY_GUIDE modified


Console> (enable) show vtp domain
```

Domain Name	Domain Index	VTP Version	Local Mode	Password
CCIE_STUDY_GUIDE	1	2	server	-

Vlan-count	Max-vlan-storage	Config Revision	Notifications
5	1023	0	disabled

Last Updated	V2 Mode	Pruning	PruneEligible on Vlans
0.0.0.0	disabled	disabled	2-1000

Use the **set VLAN 2 5/11** command to move port 5/11 to VLAN 2. Notice that the switch automatically modifies VLAN 1 and removes port 5/11 from VLAN 1.

```
Console> (enable) set VLAN 2 5/11
VLAN 2   configuration successful
VLAN 2   modified.
VLAN 1   modified.
VLAN    Mod/Ports
----    -------------------
2       5/11
```

Use the **set VLAN 2 5/12** command to move port 5/12 to VLAN 2.

```
Console> (enable) set VLAN 2 5/12
VLAN 2   modified.
VLAN 1   modified.
VLAN    Mod/Ports
----    -------------------
2       5/11-12
```

Activate the VLAN with the command **set VLAN 2**.

```
Console> (enable) set VLAN 2
VLAN 2 configuration successful
```

The **show VLAN 2** command will now indicate that VLAN 2 is active and contains two ports: 5/11 and 5/12.

```
Console> (enable) sh VLAN 2
VLAN Name                                  Status      Mod/Ports, Vlans
---------------------------------------    ----------  ------------------------
2    VLAN0002                              active      5/11-12


VLAN Type  SAID    MTU   Parent RingNo  BrdgNo  Stp  BrdgMode  Trans1  Trans2
---- ----  ------  ----  ------ ------  ------  ---  --------  ------  ------
2    enet  100002  1500  -      -       -       -    -         0       0


VLAN    AREHops    STEHops   Backup CRF
-----   -------    -------   ----------
```

The VLAN status can also be displayed using the **show vlan** command. We see that all of the other Ethernet ports still reside in the default VLAN 1.

```
Console> (enable) sh vlan
VLAN Name                                  Status      Mod/Ports, Vlans
---------------------------------------    ----------  ------------------------
1    default                               active      2/1-2
                                                       3/1-24
                                                       5/1-10
                                                       7/1-24
                                                       10/1-24
```

```
2     VLAN0002                          active    5/11-12
1002  fddi-default                      active
1003  token-ring-default                active    12/1-16
1004  fddinet-default                   active
1005  trnet-default                     active


VLAN  Type  SAID   MTU   Parent RingNo BrdgNo Stp  BrdgMode Trans1 Trans2
----  ----  ------ ----  ------ ------ ------ ---  -------- ------ ------
1     enet  100001 1500  -      -      -      -    -        0      0
2     enet  100002 1500  -      -      -      -    -        0      0
1002  fddi  101002 1500  -      0x0    -      -    -        0      0
1003  trcrf 101003 1500  0      0x0    -      -    -        0      0
1004  fdnet 101004 1500  -      -      0x0    ieee -        0      0
1005  trbrf 101005 1500  -      -      0x0    ibm  -        0      0


VLAN  AREHops  STEHops  Backup CRF
----- -------  -------  ----------
1003  7        7        off
```

We can verify that VLAN 2 is active by connecting to RouterA and trying to ping RouterB at IP address 192.1.1.2. We see from the following output that the ping was successful. RouterA and RouterB are now both on VLAN 2.

```
RouterA#ping 192.1.1.2

Type escape sequence to abort.
Sending 5, 100-byte ICMP Echos to 192.1.1.2, timeout is 2 seconds:
!!!!!
Success rate is 100 percent (5/5), round-trip min/avg/max = 4/7/8 ms
```

Lab #78: ISL Trunk with Routing between VLANs

Equipment Needed

The following equipment is needed to perform this lab exercise:

- Two Cisco routers with Ethernet interfaces
- One Cisco router with a 100Mb/s Ethernet interface
- A Catalyst switch
- Three Ethernet cables

■ A Cisco rolled cable for console port connection to the routers

■ A straight-through cable for console port connection to the Catalyst switch

Configuration Overview

This lab will demonstrate how to route between two VLANs. As shown in Figure 20–8, RouterA will reside in VLAN 1, and RouterB will reside in VLAN 2. Both VLAN 1 and VLAN 2 reside on different IP networks. Because the Catalyst is a layer 2 switch, it is unable to route between the two VLANs. A layer 3 router is needed to perform this function. The solution is to define a high-speed trunk between the Catalyst switch and a router. This trunk is referred to as an *Interswitch Link* (ISL) and runs over a 100Mb/s Ethernet interface.

 NOTES: Cisco makes many models of LAN switches. Although this lab was done using a Catalyst 5500 switch, there are other LAN switches in the Cisco product line that could be used. For example, the Catalyst 1924 Enterprise Edition is a low-cost switch that is capable of doing VLANs and can also have a 100Mb/s ISL trunk.

 The Catalyst does not use the same IOS as a Cisco router. You will notice that the command set is different. Many items that are taken for granted on the router, such as being able to use the Tab key to complete a command, are not available on the Catalyst Switch. Also, Catalyst ports

Figure 20–8
Routing between
two VLANs

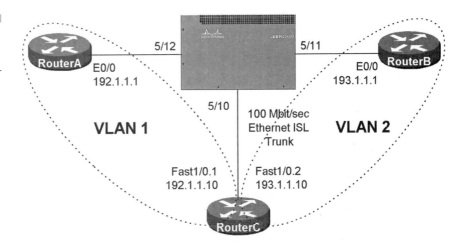

are referred to by slot and port number. For example, in this lab, we are connected to the 11th and 12th port of Card 5. The Catalyst will refer to these ports as 5/11 and 5/12, respectively.

Router Configuration

The configurations for the three routers in this example are as follows:

RouterA

```
Current configuration:
!
version 11.2
no service password-encryption
no service udp-small-servers
no service tcp-small-servers
!
hostname RouterA
!
interface Ethernet0/0
 ip address 192.1.1.1 255.255.255.0←Define the IP address for the interface
                                    connected to the Catalyst switch
!
router rip
 network 192.1.1.0
!
no ip classless
!
line con 0
line aux 0
line vty 0 4
 exec-timeout 30 0
 login
!
end
```

RouterB

```
Current configuration:
!
version 11.2
no service password-encryption
no service udp-small-servers
no service tcp-small-servers
!
```

```
hostname RouterB
!
!
!
interface Ethernet0/0
 ip address 193.1.1.1 255.255.255.0←Define the IP address for the interface
                                    connected to the Catalyst switch
!
router rip
 network 193.1.1.0
!
no ip classless
!
line con 0
line aux 0
line vty 0 4
 exec-timeout 30 0
 login
!
end
```

RouterC

```
Current configuration:
!
version 11.2
no service password-encryption
no service udp-small-servers
no service tcp-small-servers
!
hostname RouterC
!
interface FastEthernet1/0←This 100Mb/s interface connects to the Catalyst
                          trunk port
 no ip address
 no logging event subif-link-status
!
interface FastEthernet1/0.1←This subinterface accepts traffic from VLAN 1
 encapsulation isl 1←Define ISL encapsulation and accept traffic from VLAN 1
 ip address 192.1.1.10 255.255.255.0←IP address for this subinterface
 no ip redirects
!
interface FastEthernet1/0.2←This subinterface accepts traffic from VLAN 2
 encapsulation isl 2←Define ISL encapsulation and accept traffic from VLAN 2
 ip address 193.1.1.10 255.255.255.0←IP address for this subinterface
 no ip redirects
!
router rip←We need to dynamically route between VLAN 1 and VLAN 2. Our routes
            will be learned via RIP
 network 192.1.1.0←Propagate RIP for the network on VLAN 1
 network 193.1.1.0←Propagate RIP for the network on VLAN 2
!
```

```
no ip classless
!
!
line con 0
line aux 0
line vty 0 4
 login
!
end
```

Monitoring and Testing the Configuration

Let's start by setting the Catalyst 5500 to its factory default setting with the **clear config all** command. Remember from the previous lab that after the Catalyst has been reset, all of the Ethernet ports will be assigned to VLAN 1.

```
Console> (enable) clear config all
This command will clear all configuration in NVRAM.
This command will cause ifIndex to be reassigned on the next system startup.
Do you want to continue (y/n) [n]? y
.......
............................
...............
............................
............................
..................

System configuration cleared.
```

Because we will be assigning Catalyst ports to multiple VLANs, we must set the VTP domain name of the switch with the **set vtp domain** command.

```
Console> (enable) set vtp domain CCIE_LAB
VTP domain CCIE_LAB modified
```

Port 5/12 is in VLAN 1 for this lab. We do not need to enter any commands to place port 5/12 into VLAN 1, because this state is the default state of the Catalyst switch. Port 5/11 will be assigned to VLAN 2 for this lab. To assign port 5/11 to VLAN 2, we use the **set VLAN 2 5/11** command.

```
Console> (enable) set VLAN 2 5/11
VLAN 2 configuration successful
VLAN 2 modified.
VLAN 1 modified.
VLAN   Mod/Ports
----   ---------
2      5/10-11
```

Enable VLAN 2 with the **set VLAN 2** command.

```
Console> (enable) set VLAN 2
VLAN 2 configuration successful
```

Port 5/10 will be the trunk port for this lab. Port 5/10 will connect to our Cisco router. We will see shortly that port 5/10 will transmit all VLAN traffic to the Cisco router. The Cisco router will then be able to route between our two VLANs. We need to set port 5/10 to trunk mode with the **set trunk 5/10 on** command.

```
Console> (enable) set trunk 5/10 on
Port(s) 5/10 trunk mode set to on.
```

The status of port 5/10 can be viewed with the **show port 5/10** command. We see that the port is active and is now defined as a trunk port. Notice that the port is running at 100Mb/s full duplex.

```
Console> (enable) sh port 5/10
Port    Name      Status       Vlan     Level    Duplex    Speed    Type
----    ------    ---------    -----    ------    -------   -----    -------------
 5/10             connected    trunk    normal    a-full    a-100    10/100BaseTX

Port    Security   Secure-Src-Addr    Last-Src-Addr    Shutdown   Trap
-----   ---------  ----------------   -------------    ---------  -----------
 5/10   disabled                                       No         disabled

Port    Broadcast-Limit    Broadcast-Drop
-----   ---------------    --------------
 5/10   -                  -
Port    Status     Channel    Channel      Neighbor            Neighbor
                   mode       status       device              port
-----   ---------  --------   ----------   ----------------    ----------------
 5/10   connected  auto       not channel

Port    Align-Err   FCS-Err    Xmit-Err    Rcv-Err    UnderSize
-----   ---------   --------   ---------   --------   ----------
 5/10   0           0          0           0          0

Port    Single-Col  Multi-Coll Late-Coll  Excess-Col Carri-Sen  Runts   Giants
-----   ----------  ---------- ---------   ---------- ---------  -----   ------
 5/10   0           0          0           0          0          0       -

Last-Time-Cleared
-------------------------
Sun May 16 1999, 02:25:04
```

Verify that the ports connected to RouterA and RouterB (5/12 and 5/11) are connected. Notice that port 5/11 (RouterB) is in VLAN 2, while port 5/12 (RouterA) is in VLAN 1.

```
Console> (enable) sh port 5/11
Port   Name   Status      Vlan    Level   Duplex    Speed   Type
----   ----   ---------   -----   ------  -------   -----   ------------
 5/11         connected   2       normal  a-half    a-10    10/100BaseTX


Console> (enable) sh port 5/12
Port   Name   Status      Vlan    Level   Duplex    Speed   Type
----   ----   ---------   -----   ------  -------   -----   ------------
 5/12         connected   1       normal  a-half    a-10    10/100BaseTX
```

The **show trunk** command gives us specific information on our trunk, showing us which VLANs are permitted on the trunk and which VLANs are active on the trunk. We see that in our case, all traffic from all VLANs is permitted on trunk 5/10.

```
Console> (enable) sh trunk
Port   Mode   Status
----   ----   ----------
 5/10  on     trunking

Port   Vlans allowed on trunk
----   ----------------------------------------------------------------
 5/10  1-1005

Port   Vlans allowed and active in management domain
----   ----------------------------------------------------------------
 5/10  1-2,1003,1005

Port   Vlans in spanning tree forwarding state and not pruned
----   ----------------------------------------------------------------
 5/10  1-2,1003,1005
```

Now, let's connect to RouterA and view the routing table with the **show ip route** command. We see that we are learning a route to the 193.1.1.0 network. The 193.1.1.0 network connects RouterB to the Catalyst switch on VLAN 2. The routing table on RouterA tells us that RouterC is working properly and is routing between two VLANs.

```
RouterA#sh ip route
Codes: C - connected, S - static, I - IGRP, R - RIP, M - mobile, B - BGP
       D - EIGRP, EX - EIGRP external, O - OSPF, IA - OSPF inter area
       N1 - OSPF NSSA external type 1, N2 - OSPF NSSA external type 2
       E1 - OSPF external type 1, E2 - OSPF external type 2, E - EGP
       i - IS-IS, L1 - IS-IS level-1, L2 - IS-IS level-2, * - candidate default
       U - per-user static route, o - ODR

Gateway of last resort is not set

C    192.1.1.0/24 is directly connected, Ethernet0/0
R    193.1.1.0/24 [120/1] via 192.1.1.10, 00:00:26, Ethernet0/0
```

Make sure that we have end-to-end connectivity by trying to ping RouterB at IP address 193.1.1.1. The ping should be successful.

```
RouterA#ping 193.1.1.1

Type escape sequence to abort.
Sending 5, 100-byte ICMP Echos to 193.1.1.1, timeout is 2 seconds:
!!!!!
Success rate is 100 percent (5/5), round-trip min/avg/max = 4/4/4 ms
```

Now, let's connect to RouterB. View the routing table on RouterB with the **show ip router** command. We see that RouterB has learned a route to RouterA via RIP.

```
RouterB#sh ip route
Codes: C - connected, S - static, I - IGRP, R - RIP, M - mobile, B - BGP
       D - EIGRP, EX - EIGRP external, O - OSPF, IA - OSPF inter area
       N1 - OSPF NSSA external type 1, N2 - OSPF NSSA external type 2
       E1 - OSPF external type 1, E2 - OSPF external type 2, E - EGP
       i - IS-IS, L1 - IS-IS level-1, L2 - IS-IS level-2, * - candidate default
       U - per-user static route, o - ODR

Gateway of last resort is not set

R    192.1.1.0/24 [120/1] via 193.1.1.10, 00:00:10, Ethernet0/0
C    193.1.1.0/24 is directly connected, Ethernet0/0
```

Make sure that we can ping RouterA at IP address 192.1.1.1.

```
RouterB#ping 192.1.1.1

Type escape sequence to abort.
Sending 5, 100-byte ICMP Echos to 192.1.1.1, timeout is 2 seconds:
!!!!!
Success rate is 100 percent (5/5), round-trip min/avg/max = 4/6/8 ms
```

Now, connect to RouterC and view its routing table with the **show ip route** command. We see that RouterC has two directly connected networks. Each of these networks is coming into RouterC on the same physical 100Mb/s Ethernet circuit. The Ethernet circuit has defined two subinterfaces. VLAN 1 is associated with subinterface FastEthernet 1/0.1, and VLAN 2 is assigned to subinterface FastEthernet 1/0.2.

```
RouterC#sh ip route
Codes: C - connected, S - static, I - IGRP, R - RIP, M - mobile, B - BGP
       D - EIGRP, EX - EIGRP external, O - OSPF, IA - OSPF inter area
       N1 - OSPF NSSA external type 1, N2 - OSPF NSSA external type 2
       E1 - OSPF external type 1, E2 - OSPF external type 2, E - EGP
       i - IS-IS, L1 - IS-IS level-1, L2 - IS-IS level-2, * - candidate default
       U - per-user static route, o - ODR

Gateway of last resort is not set

C    192.1.1.0/24 is directly connected, FastEthernet1/0.1
C    193.1.1.0/24 is directly connected, FastEthernet1/0.2
```

From RouterC, ping RouterA and RouterB to verify that the circuit is active.

```
RouterC#ping 192.1.1.1

Type escape sequence to abort.
Sending 5, 100-byte ICMP Echos to 192.1.1.1, timeout is 2 seconds:
!!!!!
Success rate is 100 percent (5/5), round-trip min/avg/max = 4/4/4 ms


RouterC#ping 193.1.1.1

Type escape sequence to abort.
Sending 5, 100-byte ICMP Echos to 193.1.1.1, timeout is 2 seconds:
!!!!!
Success rate is 100 percent (5/5), round-trip min/avg/max = 1/3/4 ms
```

Troubleshooting

{show version}   The **show version** command displays important system-level information, including the version of system firmware, firmware level and serial number for each card installed in the switch, system memory, and uptime statistics.

```
Console> (enable) show ver
WS-C5500 Software, Version McpSW: 3.1(1) NmpSW: 3.1(1)
Copyright (c) 1995-1997 by Cisco Systems
NMP S/W compiled on Dec 31 1997, 18:36:38
MCP S/W compiled on Dec 31 1997, 18:33:15

System Bootstrap Version: 3.1(2)

Hardware Version: 1.3  Model: WS-C5500  Serial #: 069028115
```

```
Module    Ports    Model      Serial #     Hw    Fw       Fw1      Sw
------    -----    -------    ----------   ---   ----     ----     -------------
2         2        WS-X5530   008167898    1.8   3.1(2)   4.1(1)   3.1(1)
3         24       WS-X5224   008161402    1.3   3.1(1)            3.1(1)
5         12       WS-X5203   008451509    1.1   3.1(1)            3.1(1)
7         24       WS-X5224   008161009    1.3   3.1(1)            3.1(1)
10        24       WS-X5224   008161288    1.3   3.1(1)            3.1(1)
12        16       WS-X5030   007380744    1.0   1.0(117  2.2(4)   3.1(1)


          DRAM                     FLASH                   NVRAM
Module    Total    Used    Free    Total   Used    Free   Total   Used   Free
------    -----    ----    ----    -----   ----    ----   -----   ----   ----
2         32640K   11854K  20786K  8192K   3224K   4968K  512K    106K   406K

Uptime is 5 days, 20 hours, 14 minutes
```

{show module}   The show module command shows which type of card is inserted into each slot of the Catalyst switch.

```
Console> (enable) show module
Mod Module-Name    Ports   Module-Type          Model       Serial-Num  Status
---------------    ------  --------------------  --------    ----------  ------
2                  2       10/100BaseTX Supervis WS-X5530    008167898   ok
3                  24      10/100BaseTX Ethernet WS-X5224    008161402   ok
5                  12      10/100BaseTX Ethernet WS-X5203    008451509   ok
7                  24      10/100BaseTX Ethernet WS-X5224    008161009   ok
10                 24      10/100BaseTX Ethernet WS-X5224    008161288   ok
12                 16      Token Ring            WS-X5030    007380744   ok

Mod MAC-Address(es)                                 Hw     Fw       Sw
--- ---------------------------------------------   ----   ----     ----------------
2   00-90-f2-a7-c1-00 thru 00-90-f2-a7-c4-ff        1.8    3.1(2)   3.1(1)
3   00-10-7b-2e-ca-e8 thru 00-10-7b-2e-ca-ff        1.3    3.1(1)   3.1(1)
5   00-10-7b-09-9a-50 thru 00-10-7b-09-9a-5b        1.1    3.1(1)   3.1(1)
7   00-10-7b-3d-be-f0 thru 00-10-7b-3d-bf-07        1.3    3.1(1)   3.1(1)
10  00-10-7b-3d-be-c0 thru 00-10-7b-3d-be-d7        1.3    3.1(1)   3.1(1)
12  00:05:77:05:86:42 thru 00:05:77:05:86:52        1.0    1.0(117  3.1(1)

Mod    Sub-Type    Sub-Model    Sub-Serial    Sub-Hw
----   --------    ---------    ----------    -------
2      EARL 1+     WS-F5520     0008157389    1.1
2      uplink      WS-U5531     0008577601    1.1
```

{show mac}   The show mac command displays detailed statistics on traffic passing through the Catalyst switch. The following screen print has been truncated to just show the statistics for three ports on a Catalyst switch. Notice the detailed reporting statistics for each port, including total received and transmitted frames, multicast, unicast, and broadcast statistics, error statistics, and total octets transmitted and received.

```
Console> (enable) show mac
MAC      Rcv-Frms    Xmit-Frms    Rcv-Multi    Xmit-Multi    Rcv-Broad    Xmit-Broad
---      --------    ---------    ---------    ----------    ---------    ----------
 5/10    30948       251858       14649        251758        108               0
 5/11    44490       166061        4953        145105         96            5774
 5/12    43857       166409        4438        145408         15            5823


MAC      Dely-Exced    MTU-Exced    In-Discard    Lrn-Discrd    In-Lost    Out-Lost
---      ----------    ---------    ----------    ----------    -------    --------
 5/10    0             0            38            0             0          0
 5/11    0             0            61            0             0          0
 5/12    2             0            73            0             0          0


Port     Rcv-Unicast    Rcv-Multicast    Rcv-Broadcast
----     -----------    -------------    -------------
 5/10    16192          14649            108
 5/11    39441           4953             96
 5/12    39405           4438             15


Port     Xmit-Unicast    Xmit-Multicast    Xmit-Broadcast
----     ------------    --------------    --------------
 5/10     100            251764                  0
 5/11    15182           145107               5774
 5/12    15178           145410               5823


Port     Rcv-Octet     Xmit-Octet
----     ----------    ----------
 5/10    3183207       23975586
 5/11    20334264      27851660
 5/12    20290059      27865755


Last-Time-Cleared
-------------------------
Sun May 16 1999, 02:25:04
```

{clear config all}   The **clear config all** command causes the switch to be reset to its factory default state. In this state, all ports reside in VLAN 1, and the Catalyst acts as a large switching hub.

```
Console> (enable) clear config all
This command will clear all configuration in NVRAM.
This command will cause ifIndex to be reassigned on the next system startup.
Do you want to continue (y/n) [n]? y
.......
............................
................
............................
............................
...................

System configuration cleared.
```

{show port} The **show port** command displays statistics on port-level configuration on the Catalyst switch. The Catalyst can automatically sense speed and duplex on each port of the switch. For example, we see in the following output that ports 5/11 and 5/12 have been automatically configured. Their status is connected, they are both in VLAN 1, and they are both running 10Mb/s, half-duplex Ethernet.

```
Console> (enable) sh port
Port  Name              Status    Vlan  Level  Duplex  Speed  Type
----  ----------------  --------  ----  -----  ------  -----  -----------
5/1                     notconnect 1    normal auto    auto   10/100BaseTX
5/2                     notconnect 1    normal auto    auto   10/100BaseTX
5/3                     notconnect 1    normal auto    auto   10/100BaseTX
5/4                     notconnect 1    normal auto    auto   10/100BaseTX
5/5                     notconnect 1    normal auto    auto   10/100BaseTX
5/6                     notconnect 1    normal auto    auto   10/100BaseTX
5/7                     notconnect 1    normal auto    auto   10/100BaseTX
5/8                     notconnect 1    normal auto    auto   10/100BaseTX
5/9                     notconnect 1    normal auto    auto   10/100BaseTX
5/10                    notconnect 1    normal auto    auto   10/100BaseTX
5/11                    connected  1    normal a-half  a-10   10/100BaseTX
5/12                    connected  1    normal a-half  a-10   10/100BaseTX
```

{show port *slot/port*} More detailed port status is available by adding the port number after the show port command. In the following example, we see that additional data, such as MAC-level security information and Ethernet collision and error statistics, are listed for the specified port.

```
Console> (enable) sh port 5/11
Port    Name     Status       Vlan    Level    Duplex    Speed   Type
----    ------   ---------    -----   ------   -------   -----   -------------
 5/11            connected    1       normal   a-half    a-10    10/100BaseTX

Port    Security    Secure-Src-Addr     Last-Src-Addr    Shutdown    Trap
-----   ---------   ----------------    -------------    ---------   ------------
 5/11   disabled                                         No          disabled

Port    Broadcast-Limit      Broadcast-Drop
-----   ---------------      -------------
 5/11   -                    0
Port    Status      Channel    Channel     Neighbor           Neighbor
                    mode       status      device             port
-----   ---------   -------    ----------  ----------------   ----------------
 5/11   connected   auto       not channel

Port    Align-Err   FCS-Err    Xmit-Err    Rcv-Err    UnderSize
-----   ---------   ---------  ---------   --------   ----------
 5/11   0           0          0           0          0

Port    Single-Col  Multi-Coll  Late-Coll  Excess-Col  Carri-Sen  Runts  Giants
-----   ----------  ----------  --------   ----------  ---------  -----  ------
 5/11   0           0           0          0           0          0      0

Last-Time-Cleared
-------------------------
Sun May 16 1999, 02:25:04
```

{show cam dynamic} The **show cam dynamic** command displays connected host MAC addresses that have been learned by the switch.

```
Console> (enable) show cam dynamic
VLAN    Dest MAC/Route Des        Destination Ports or VCs
----    ------------------        ------------------------------------------------
2       00-e0-1e-9c-8e-b0         5/10
1       00-e0-1e-9c-8e-b0         5/10
2       00-10-7b-06-c2-c1         5/11
1       00-e0-1e-5b-27-61         5/12
1       00-00-ff-ff-ff-fb         1/4
Total Matching CAM Entries Displayed = 5
```

{show system} The **show system** command displays system contacts, current and peak traffic utilization, uptime, and thermal information.

```
Console> (enable) show system
PS1-Status   PS2-Status   Fan-Status   Temp-Alarm   Sys-Status   Uptime d,h:m:s   Logout
---------    ---------    ---------    ----------   ---------    -------------    ------
ok           none         ok           off          ok           5,20:14:10       20 min

PS1-Type     PS2-Type     Modem    Baud    Traffic   Peak    Peak-Time
--------     --------     -----    ----    -------   ----    ------------------------
WS-C5508     none         disable  9600    0%        0%      Sun May 16 1999, 02:25:04

System Name                 System Location               System Contact
-------------------         ---------------------         --------------------
```

{set interface}   The **set interface** command is used to set the IP address for inband access to the switch.

```
Console> (enable) set interface sc0 192.1.1.3
Interface sc0 IP address set.
```

{show interface}   The **show interface** command is used to display the internal Catalyst IP addresses for inband access and SLIP access.

```
Console> (enable) sh interface
sl0: flags=51<UP,POINTOPOINT,RUNNING>
        slip 0.0.0.0 dest 128.73.35.160
sc0: flags=63<UP,BROADCAST,RUNNING>
        VLAN 1 inet 192.1.1.3 netmask 255.255.255.0 broadcast 192.1.1.255
```

{set ip permit}   The **set ip permit** command creates an IP permit list, which the Catalyst uses to permit inband Telnet and SNMP access to the switch. Up to 10 IP addresses can be defined.

```
Console> (enable) set ip permit 192.1.1.1
192.1.1.1 added to IP permit list.
```

{show ip permit}   The **show ip permit** command is used to display the IP permit lists for the switch and to see if any invalid IP addresses have tried to access the switch for Telnet or for SNMP access. The IP permit list must be enabled with the **set ip permit enable** command. You can turn off the IP permit list with the **set ip permit disable** command.

```
Console> (enable) show ip permit
IP permit list feature enabled.
Permit List   Mask
-----------   ----
192.1.1.1

Denied IP Address    Last Accessed Time    Type
-----------------    ------------------    -------
192.1.1.2            05/25/99,14:25:50     Telnet
```

{**set port security**}   The **set port security** command is used to define which MAC addresses are permitted to send traffic into the switch on a per-port basis. The following command will cause the switch to only permit inbound traffic on port 5/12 from a host with a MAC address of 00-e0-1e-5b-27-62. Port security can be disabled with the **set port security 5/12 disable** command.

```
Console> (enable) set port security 5/12 enable 00-e0-1e-5b-27-62
Port 5/12 port security enabled with 00-e0-1e-5b-27-62 as the secure mac address
Trunking disabled for Port 5/12 due to Security Mode
```

{**show vtp domain**}   The **show vtp domain** shows key domain information for the switch. The Catalyst switch must have a domain name set before it can use VLAN numbers other than VLAN 1. The vtp domain name is set with the **set vtp domain** command.

```
Console> (enable) sh vtp domain
Domain Name            Domain Index    VTP Version   Local Mode   Password
-------------------    ------------    -----------   ----------   --------
                       1               2             server       -

Vlan-count    Max-vlan-storage    Config Revision    Notifications
----------    ----------------    ---------------    -------------
5             1023                0                  disabled

Last Updated    V2 Mode     Pruning    PruneEligible on Vlans
------------    --------    -------    ----------------------
0.0.0.0         disabled    disabled   2-1000
```

{**set vlan** *vlan_number slot_port*}   The **set vlan** command is used to place a specific port in a VLAN. The example assigns port 5/12 to VLAN 2. The VLAN is activated with the **set vlan** command.

```
Console> (enable) set VLAN 2 5/12
VLAN 2 modified.
VLAN 1 modified.
VLAN    Mod/Ports
----    ----------
2       5/11-12
```

{show vlan}   The **show vlan** command displays information on all of the VLANs defined on the Catalyst switch.

```
Console> (enable) sh vlan
VLAN   Name                             Status    Mod/Ports, Vlans
----   ------------------------------   ------    -----------------
1      default                          active    2/1-2
                                                  3/1-24
                                                  5/1-10
                                                  7/1-24
                                                  10/1-24
2      VLAN0002                         active    5/11-12
1002   fddi-default                     active
1003   token-ring-default               active    12/1-16
1004   fddinet-default                  active
1005   trnet-default                    active


VLAN   Type   SAID    MTU   Parent  RingNo  BrdgNo  Stp   BrdgMode  Trans1 Trans2
----   ----   ------  ----  ------  ------  ------  ----  --------  ------ ------
1      enet   100001  1500  -       -       -       -     -         0      0
2      enet   100002  1500  -       -       -       -     -         0      0
1002   fddi   101002  1500  -       0x0     -       -     -         0      0
1003   trcrf  101003  1500  0       0x0     -       -     -         0      0
1004   fdnet  101004  1500  -       -       0x0     ieee  -         0      0
1005   trbrf  101005  1500  -       -       0x0     ibm   -         0      0


VLAN   AREHops    STEHops    Backup CRF
----   -------    -------    ----------
1003   7          7          off
```

{show vlan *vlan_number*}   When supplied with a specific VLAN number, the **show vlan** command displays information on the specified VLAN. We see as follows that the VLAN name, status, and member ports are some of the statistics that are displayed.

```
Console> (enable) sh VLAN 2
VLAN   Name                     Status    Mod/Ports, Vlans
----   ----------------------   ------    ----------------------------
2      VLAN0002                 active    5/11-12


VLAN   Type   SAID    MTU   Parent  RingNo  BrdgNo  Stp   BrdgMode  Trans1 Trans2
----   ----   ------  ----  ------  ------  ------  ----  --------  ------ ------
2      enet   100002  1500  -       -       -       -     -         0      0


VLAN    AREHops    STEHops    Backup CRF
----    -------    -------    ----------
```

{set trunk}   The **set trunk** command configures a Catalyst port as a trunk port.

```
Console> (enable) set trunk 5/10 on
Port(s) 5/10 trunk mode set to on.
```

{show trunk}   The **show trunk** command displays specific information on Catalyst trunks, such as which VLANs are permitted on the trunk and which VLANs are active on the trunk. We see that in the following screen print, all traffic from all VLANs is permitted on trunk 5/10.

```
Console> (enable) sh trunk
Port      Mode      Status
----      ----      ------
 5/10     on        trunking

Port   Vlans allowed on trunk
----   -------------------------------------------------------------------
 5/10  1-1005

Port   Vlans allowed and active in management domain
----   -------------------------------------------------------------------
 5/10  1-2,1003,1005

Port   Vlans in spanning tree forwarding state and not pruned
----   -------------------------------------------------------------------
 5/10  1-2,1003,1005
```

Conclusion

This chapter has explored the operations and configuration of the Catalyst 5500, one of a family of a broad range of LAN switches sold by Cisco. We have seen that the Catalyst switch combines the capabilities of a switching hub with VLAN capabilities. The Catalyst can accept a router module in the form of a *Route Switch module* (RSM), making the catalyst into a layer 2 switch and a layer 3 router in a single unit.

Several Catalyst capabilities were demonstrated in the labs, including MAC port security, IP permit lists, routing between multiple VLANs, and ISL trunking.

21

Loading the IOS Image on a Router

Topics Covered in This Chapter

- Cisco code load overview
- TFTP server configuration
- Cisco IOS naming conventions
- Run from RAM and run from Flash routers
- Loading IOS from a TFTP server
- Loading an IOS image from another router
- Troubleshooting TFTP transfers on a Cisco router

Introduction

This chapter will explain how to load an IOS image onto a Cisco Router. We will examine the two types of memory platforms on Cisco routers: run from RAM and run from Flash systems. Finally, we will show how to make a Cisco router into a TFTP server so that IOS code can be loaded directly from another router in your network.

Code Load Overview

All Cisco routers store their Operating System, referred to as their Internetwork Operating System (or IOS) in a flash memory located on the router. Any time a new version of IOS needs to be loaded onto the router, the flash memory will need to be upgraded with the new code. Cisco's primary method of loading code on the router is to load the code via TFTP. TFTP is an anonymous (no password required) file transfer protocol that uses UDP for its transport layer. The router that needs the new code requests the code from a TFTP server. A TFTP server is usually a PC or workstation running a TFTP daemon.

The TFTP server software used in this chapter is Exceed by Hummingbird Communications. Exceed runs on Windows 95, Windows 98, and Windows NT platforms. Exceed includes many TCP/IP programs, such as a TFTP Daemon and an FTP Daemon. Exceed is configured by first enabling the TFTP server service, as shown in Figure 21–1.

The TFTP download and upload directories are then defined. As shown in Figure 21–2, TFTP read and write operations will be done from a directory called download. Notice from Figure 21–2 that TFTP uses UDP port 69. Our PC has now been configured to act as a TFTP daemon.

As shown in Figure 21–3, there are four IOS images in the download directory of our workstation. During the labs in this chapter, our Cisco routers will be loading IOS images from this directory using TFTP.

A Cisco router also has the capability to act as a TFTP server. This feature eliminates the need for a PC or workstation on your network that runs a TFTP server program.

Code Load Naming Conventions

Cisco IOS images adhere to a well-defined naming convention. Cisco maintains an online document on its Web page titled, "Software Naming

Figure 21–1
Enabling the TFTP
server service

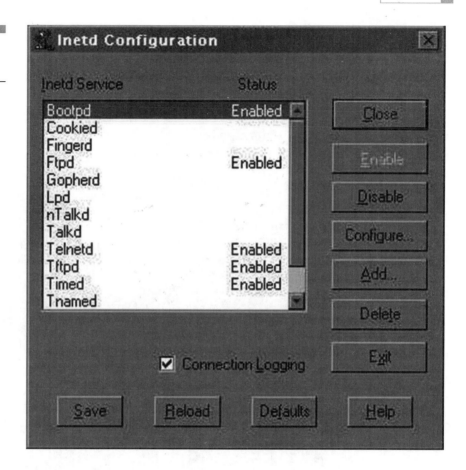

Conventions for IOS." The naming conventions enable you to interpret the meaning of the characters in the filename of an IOS image. As an example, let's look at the IOS filenames for two of the IOS images we will be using during this chapter.

The IOS code filename for the Cisco 3620 is: **c3620-i-mz_113-8_T1.bin**. This filename can be interpreted as follows:

```
Hardware Platform is a Cisco 3620
↓         IP Subset Version
↓            ↓        Run from RAM                    Platform Specific
↓            ↓           ↓                               ↓
c3620  -  i-     m   z_              113-8_     T1.bin
                      ↑                  ↑
                   Zipped            IOS 11.3(8)
```

Figure 21–2
TFTP uses UDP port
69

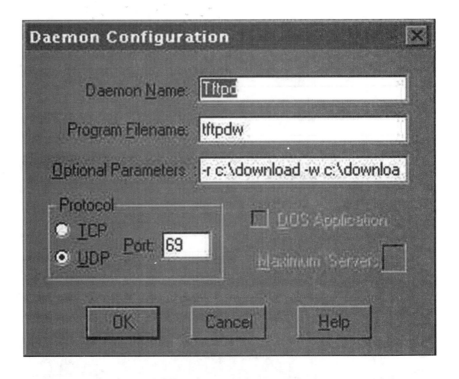

Figure 21–3
IOS images in the
download directory

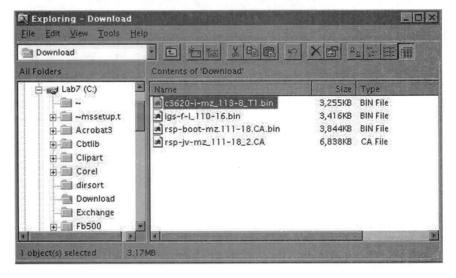

We see that this file is an IOS image for a Cisco 3620 router. This file is an IP subset code load that is compressed and is designed to run from RAM. The IOS version is 11.3(8).

The IOS code filename for the Cisco 2500 is: **igs-g-L_111-24.bin**. This filename can be interpreted as follows:

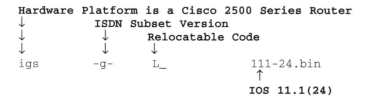

```
Hardware Platform is a Cisco 2500 Series Router
↓              ISDN Subset Version
↓                  ↓        Relocatable Code
↓                  ↓            ↓
igs            -g-          L_                    111-24.bin
                                                      ↑
                                               IOS 11.1(24)
```

We see that this file is an IOS image for a Cisco 2500 router. It is an ISDN and IP code load that is relocatable. The IOS version is 11.1(24).

Following are some more detailed descriptions of the IOS naming conventions:

■ An IOS image name has three parts, and each part is separated by dashes (e.g., aaaa-bbbb-cc, where:

■ aaaa = Platform

■ bbbbb = Feature sets

■ cc = Where the IOS image executes from and if the IOS image is compressed

Platform

The first part of the image name specifies on which platform the image runs.

```
as5200      5200
c1600       1600
c2500       25xx, 3xxx, 5100, AP (11.2 and later only)
c25FX       Fixed Frad platform
c3620       3620
c3640       3640
c3800       3800
c4000       4000    (11.2 and later only)
c4500       4500, 4700
c7000       7000, 7010   (11.2 and later only)
c7200       7200
igs         IGS, 25xx, 3xxx, 5100, AP
```

Feature Sets

The following capabilities are defined:

a - APPN
a2 - ATM
b - Appletalk
boot - used for boot images
c - Comm-server/Remote Access Server (RAS) subset (SNMP, IP, Bridging,
 IPX, Atalk, Decnet, FR, HDLC, PPP, X,25, ARAP, tn3270, PT,
 XRemote, LAT) (non-CiscoPro)
c - CommServer lite (CiscoPro)
c2 - Comm-server/Remote Access Server (RAS) subset (SNMP, IP,
Bridging,
       IPX, Atalk, Decnet, FR, HDLC, PPP, X,25, ARAP, tn3270, PT,
       XRemote, LAT) (CiscoPro)
d - Desktop subset (SNMP, IP, Bridging, WAN, Remote Node, Terminal
       Services, IPX, Atalk, ARAP)
    (11.2 - Decnet)
d2 - reduced Desktop subset(SNMP, IP, IPX, ATALK, ARAP)
diag - IOS based diagnostics images
e - IPeXchange (no longer used in 11.3 and later)
     - StarPipes DB2 Access - Enables Cisco IOS to act as a "Gateway" to
       all IBM DB2 products for downstream clients/servers in 11.3T
eboot - ethernet boot image for mc3810 platform
f - FRAD subset (SNMP, FR, PPP, SDLLC, STUN)
f2 - modified FRAD subset, EIGRP, Pcbus, Lan Mgr removed, OSPF added
g - ISDN subset (SNMP, IP, Bridging, ISDN, PPP, IPX, Atalk)
g2 - gatekeeper proxy, voice and video
h - For Malibu(2910), 8021D, switch functions, IP Host
hdiag - Diagnostics image for Malibu(2910)
i - IP subset (SNMP, IP, Bridging, WAN, Remote Node, Terminal
Services)
i2 - subset similar to IP subset for system controller image (3600)
i3 - reduced IP subset with BGP/MIB, EGP/MIB, NHRP, DIRRESP removed.
j - enterprise subset (formerly bpx, includes protocol translation)
    *** not used until 10.3 ***
k - kitchen sink (enterprise for high-end) (Not used after 10.3)
k2 - high-end enterprise w/CIP2 ucode (Not used after 10.3)
k1 - Baseline Privacy key encryption (On 11.3 and up)
k2 - Triple DES (On 11.3 and up)
k3 - Reserved for future encryption capabilities (On 11.3 and up)
k4 - Reserved for future encryption capabilities (On 11.3 and up)
k5 - Reserved for future encryption capabilities (On 11.3 and up)
k6 - Reserved for future encryption capabilities (On 11.3 and up)
k7 - Reserved for future encryption capabilities (On 11.3 and up)
k8 - Reserved for future encryption capabilities (On 11.3 and up)
k9 - Reserved for future encryption capabilities (On 11.3 and up)
l - IPeXchange IPX, static routing, gateway
m - RMON (11.1 only)
n - IPX
o - Firewall (formerly IPeXchange Net Management)
p - Service Provider (IP RIP/IGRP/EIGRP/OSPF/BGP, CLNS ISIS/IGRP)

p2 - Service Provider w/CIP2 ucode
p3 - as5200 service provider
p4 - 5800 (Nitro) service provider
q - Async
q2 - IPeXchange Async
r - IBM base option (SRB, SDLLC, STUN, DLSW, QLLC) - used with
    i, in, d (See note below.)
r2 - IBM variant for 1600 images
r3 - IBM variant for Ardent images (3810)
r4 - reduced IBM subset with BSC/MIB, BSTUN/MIB, ASPP/MIB, RSRB/MIB
removed.
    s - source route switch (SNMP, IP, Bridging, SRB) (10.2 and following)
s - (11.2 only) additions to the basic subset:
  c1000 - (OSPF, PIM, SMRP, NLSP, ATIP, ATAURP, FRSVC, RSVP, NAT)
  c1005 - (X.25, full WAN, OSPF, PIM, NLSP, SMRP, ATIP, ATAURP,
        FRSVC, RSVP, NAT)
   c1600 - (OSPF, IPMULTICAST, NHRP, NTP, NAT, RSVP, FRAME_RELAY_SVC)
         AT "s" images also have: (SMRP,ATIP,AURP)
         IPX "s" images also have: (NLSP,NHRP)
  c2500 - (NAT, RMON, IBM, MMP, VPDN/L2F)
  c2600 - (NAT, IBM, MMP, VPDN/L2F, VOIP and ATM)
  c3620 - (NAT, IBM, MMP, VPDN/L2F) In 11.3T added VOIP
  c3640 - (NAT, IBM, MMP, VPDN/L2F) In 11.3T added VOIP
  c4000 - (NAT, IBM, MMP, VPDN/L2F)
  c4500 - (NAT, ISL, LANE, IBM, MMP, VPDN/L2F)
  c5200 - (PT, v.120, managed modems, RMON, MMP, VPDN/L2F)
  c5300 - (MMP, VPDN, NAT, Modem Management, RMON, IBM)
  c5rsm - (NAT, LANE and VLANS)
  c7000 - (ISL, LANE, IBM, MMP, VPDN/L2F)
  c7200 - (NAT, ISL, IBM, MMP, VPDN/L2F)
  rsp - (NAT, ISL, LANE, IBM, MMP, VPDN/L2F)
t - (11.2) AIP w/ modified Ucode to connect to Teralink 1000 Data
u - IP with VLAN RIP (Network Layer 3 Switching Software,
    rsrb, srt, srb, sr/tlb)
v - VIP and dual RSP (HSA) support
v2 - Voice V2D
w - Reserved for WBU (remaining characters are specific to WBU)
       i - IISP
       l - LANE & PVC
       p - PNNI
       v - PVC traffic shaping
w2 - Reserved for CiscoAdvantage ED train (remaining characters are
    specific to CiscoAdvantage)
       a - IPX, static routing, gateway
       b - Net Management
       c - FR/X.25
       y - Async
w3 - Reserved for Distributed Director
x - X.25 in 11.1 and earlier releases. FR/X.25 in 11.2 (IPeXchange)
    H.323 Gatekeeper/Proxy in 11.3 releases for 2500, 3620, 3640
y - reduced IP (SNMP, IP RIP/IGRP/EIGRP, Bridging, ISDN, PPP) (C1003/4)
   - reduced IP (SNMP, IP RIP/IGRP/EIGRP, Bridging, WAN - X.25) (C1005)
   (11.2 - includes X.25) (c1005)
y - IP variant (no Kerberos, Radius, NTP, OSPF, PIM, SMRP, NHRP...)

```
    (c1600)
y2 - IP variant (SNMP, IP RIP/IGRP/EIGRP, WAN - X.25, OSPF, PIM)
    (C1005)
y2 - IP Plus variant (no Kerberos, Radius, NTP, ...) (c1600)
y3 - IP/X.31
y4 - reduced IP variant (Cable, Mibs, DHCP, EZHTTP)
z  - managed modems
40 - 40-bit encryption
56 - 56-bit encryption
56i - 56-bit encryption with IPSEC
```

Where the IOS Image Runs

```
f - Flash
m - RAM
r - ROM
1 - relocatable
```

The following command may be added if the image has been "zip" compressed:

```
z - zip compressed
```

Run from RAM and Run from Flash Routers

A Cisco router either executes its IOS from RAM or flash memory. Executing from flash memory is slower.

Run from flash routers are units such as the Cisco 2500 series and some of the Cisco 1600 series routers. The entire IOS is loaded into the flash memory in an uncompressed format. The Cisco IOS runs from the flash memory. Upgrading the IOS becomes an issue. How can you load new code into a flash memory that is currently executing the IOS? Cisco addresses this problem by having a special IOS located in a ROM on the router. A boot helper program reloads the router from the boot ROM. The flash can then be upgraded, and the new IOS image can be run from flash. Most run from flash routers can have dual banks of flash, which will permit an IOS file to be downloaded into one bank of flash at the same time that an IOS image is running out of the second bank of flash.

Run from RAM routers are units such as the Cisco 3600, 4000, 7000, and 7500 series. These routers store a compressed IOS image in flash. When booting, the router copies the IOS from flash into RAM and executes the IOS out of RAM. These run from RAM routers have their IOS upgraded by copying a new file to flash. Because flash is not being used to execute the IOS image, you can simply TFTP the new IOS image to the router's flash.

Commands Discussed in This Chapter

- **copy tftp flash**
- **debug tftp**
- **show flash [all | chips | detailed | err | partition** *number* **[all | chips | detailed | err] | summary]**
- **show version**
- **tftp server flash** [*partition-number*:] *filename*

Definitions

copy tftp flash: This exec command copies a file from a TFTP server to the contents of flash memory on the router.

debug tftp: This debug command provides output showing any TFTP transactions that occur on the router.

show flash: This exec command displays the contents of flash memory.

show version: This exec command displays router information, such as system configuration, IOS level, and the names and sources of configuration files.

tftp server: This global command specifies that the router should act as a TFTP server for the file specified in the command.

IOS Requirements

The copy TFTP command has been available since IOS 10.0. Other features, such as being able to make the Cisco router into a TFTP server, have only been available since IOS 11.0.

Lab #79: Loading an IOS Image from a TFTP Server to a Run from RAM Router

Equipment Needed

The following equipment is needed to perform this lab exercise:

■ One Cisco router with an Ethernet interface

■ A PC running a TFTP daemon with an Ethernet card. The PC should also have a terminal emulation program such as Procomm or HyperTerminal.

■ A Cisco rolled cable for console port connection to the router

■ An Ethernet hub with two Ethernet cables

Configuration Overview

This lab will take a Cisco router that is running IOS 11.2(7) and upgrade it to IOS 11.3(8). This configuration will demonstrate how to load an IOS image on a Cisco router that utilizes a run from RAM architecture. Examples of run from RAM routers are the Cisco 3600 series, the Cisco 4000 series, and the Cisco 7000 series.

A PC running TFTP server software will be connected to the same LAN as a Cisco router. The software used in this lab is Exceed from Hummingbird Communications. The Exceed software package contains many TCP/IP programs, such as a TFTP server, an FTP server, and an X windows server. The new version of the IOS image will reside on the PC and will be transferred to the Cisco router using TFTP. The PC will be acting as the TFTP server, and the Cisco router will be the TFTP client.

RouterA and the PC are connected, as shown in Figure 21–4.

Figure 21–4
Connection between RouterA and the TFTP Server

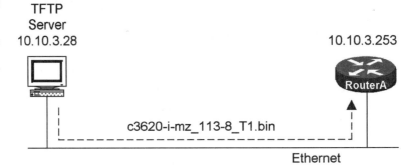

TFTP Server
10.10.3.28

10.10.3.253

c3620-i-mz_113-8_T1.bin

Ethernet

Router Configuration

The configurations for the router in this example are as follows:

RouterA

```
Current configuration:
!
version 11.2
no service udp-small-servers
no service tcp-small-servers
!
hostname RouterA
!
!
!
interface Ethernet0/0
  ip address 10.10.3.253 255.255.255.0←The Ethernet interface is on the same
                                        network as the TFTP server.
!
no ip classless
!
line con 0
line aux 0
line vty 0 4
  login
!
end
```

RouterA will be loading a new IOS image from a TFTP server. RouterA's configuration does not need any special commands to load the IOS image. The only item that needs to be configured on RouterA is the Ethernet interface.

Monitoring and Testing the Configuration

Let's start by connecting to RouterA. Use the **show version** command to find out what version of IOS the router is currently running. We see that the router is running a version of 11.2. The **show version** command also tells us other key information about the router's software image and memory capabilities. We see that the router has 16MB of DRAM. The DRAM is used to run the IOS on a run from RAM router, such as the Cisco 3620 that we are using in this lab. We also see that this router has 16MB of flash memory. The flash memory stores one or more IOS images. The show version output also tells us that the currently running IOS was loaded from flash memory. Finally, we see that our router platform is a 3620 router.

```
RouterA#show version                    Router is running IOS version 11.2(7a)P
Cisco Internetwork Operating System Software  ↓
IOS (tm) 3600 Software (C3620-I-M), Version 11.2(7a)P, SHARED PLATFORM, RELEASE
SOFTWARE (fc1)
Copyright (c) 1986-1997 by cisco Systems, Inc.
Compiled Wed 02-Jul-97 08:25 by ccai
Image text-base: 0x600088E0, data-base: 0x60440000

ROM: System Bootstrap, Version 11.1(7)AX [kuong (7)AX], EARLY DEPLOYMENT
RELEASE SOFTWARE (fc2)

RouterA uptime is 54 minutes      The IOS was loaded from flash memory
System restarted by reload          ↓
System image file is "flash:c3620-i-mz.112-7a.P", booted via flash

This router is a Cisco 3620
↓
cisco 3620 (R4700) processor (revision 0x81) with 12288K/4096K bytes of memory.
Processor board ID 05706232                                  ↑
R4700 processor, Implementation 33, Revision 1.0←The router has 16MB of DRAM.
                                              The DRAM is broken up into
                                              12MB of main memory, used for
                                              processing, and 4MB of shared
                                              memory user for I/O.
Bridging software.
X.25 software, Version 2.0, NET2, BFE and GOSIP compliant.
Basic Rate ISDN software, Version 1.0.
1 Ethernet/IEEE 802.3 interface(s)
1 Serial network interface(s)
1 ISDN Basic Rate interface(s)
DRAM configuration is 32 bits wide with parity disabled.
29K bytes of non-volatile configuration memory.
16384K bytes of processor board System flash (Read/Write)←The router has 16MB
                                                        of flash memory

Configuration register is 0x2102
```

Type the **show flash** command to view the contents of the flash memory on the router. We see that the flash memory contains a single file, c3620-i-mz.112-7a.P. The size of the file is 2,259,976 bytes. The flash memory is 16MB in size.

```
RouterA#show flash

System flash directory:
File  Length    Name/status
  1    2259976   c3620-i-mz.112-7a.P←There is only a single file in flash
                                     memory.
[2260040 bytes used, 14517176 available, 16777216 total]
16384K bytes of processor board System flash (Read/Write)
↑
16MB of flash memory on this router
```

Let's make sure that we can reach our TFTP server at IP address 10.10.3.28 by using a ping command.

```
RouterA#ping 10.10.3.28

Type escape sequence to abort.
Sending 5, 100-byte ICMP Echos to 10.10.3.28, timeout is 2 seconds:
!!!!!
Success rate is 100 percent (5/5), round-trip min/avg/max = 1/3/8 ms
```

Once we are sure we can reach the TFTP server, we can start loading the new IOS image to the router. Use the **copy tftp flash** command to start a TFTP transfer from the PC to the flash memory of RouterA. Notice that we will specify not to erase the current file that resides in the flash memory of the router.

```
RouterA#copy tftp flash

System flash directory:
File   Length    Name/status
  1    2259976   c3620-i-mz.112-7a.P
[2260040 bytes used, 14517176 available, 16777216 total]
Address or name of remote host [10.10.3.28]?←Address of TFTP server
Source file name? c3620-i-mz_113-8_T1.bin←Name of IOS image we want to load
Destination file name [c3620-i-mz_113-8_T1.bin]?
Accessing file 'c3620-i-mz_113-8_T1.bin' on 10.10.3.28...
Loading c3620-i-mz_113-8_T1.bin from 10.10.3.28 (via Ethernet0/0): ! [OK]

Erase flash device before writing? [confirm]n←Do not erase the current file in
                                              the router's flash memory.
Copy 'c3620-i-mz_113-8_T1.bin' from server
  as 'c3620-i-mz_113-8_T1.bin' into Flash WITHOUT erase? [yes/no]y
Loading c3620-i-mz_113-8_T1.bin from 10.10.3.28 (via Ethernet0/0):
!!!!!!!!!!!!!!!!!!!!!!!!!!!!!!!!!!!!!!!!!!!!!!!!!!!!!!!!!!!!!!!!!!!!!!
!!!!!!!!!!!!!!!!!!!O!!!!!!!!!!!!!!!!!!!!!!!!!!!!!!!!!!!!!!!!!!!!!!!!!!!
                   ↑
                   An O means that a TFTP packet was received out of order

!!!!!!!!!!!!!!!!!!!!!!!!!!!!!!!!!!!!!!!!!!!!!!!!!!!!!!!!!!!!!O!!!!!!!!!
!!!!!!!!!!!!!!!!!!!!!!!!!!!!!!!!!!!!!!!!!!!!!!!!!!!!!!!!!!!!!!!!!!!!!!!!
!!!!!!!!!!!!!!!!!!!!!!!!!!!!!!!!!!!!!!!!O!!!!!!!!!!!!!!!!!!!!!!!!!!!!!!!
!!!!!!!!!!!!!!!!!!!!!!!!!!!!!!!!!!!!!!!!!!!!!!!!!!!!!!!!!!!!!!!!!!!!!!!!
!!!!!!!!!!!!!!!!!!!!!!!!O!!!!!!!!!!!!!!!!!!!!!!!!!!!!!!!!!!!!!!!!!!!!!!!
!!!!!!!!!!!!!!!!!!!!!!!!!!!!!!!!!!!!!!!!!!!!!!!!!!!!!!!!!!!!!!!!!!!!!!!!
!!!!!!!O!!!!!!!!!!!!!!!!!!!!!!!!!!!!!!!!!!!!!!!!!!!!!!!!!!!!!!!!!!!!!!!!
!!!!!!!!!!!!!!!!!!!!!!!!!!!!!!!!!!!!!!!!!!!!!
[OK - 3332232/14517176 bytes]

Verifying checksum... OK (0x1837)
Flash device copy took 00:00:35 [hh:mm:ss]
```

After the file download is complete, check the contents of the router's flash memory with the **show flash** command. We see that there are now two files in the flash memory of the router.

```
RouterA#show flash

System flash directory:
File   Length      Name/status
   1    2259976    c3620-i-mz.112-7a.P
   2    3332232    c3620-i-mz_113-8_T1.bin←New file that we just loaded
[5592336 bytes used, 11184880 available, 16777216 total]
16384K bytes of processor board System flash (Read/Write)
```

Because there are two files in the flash memory, we need to tell the router which file to load during its power on sequence. Enter router configuration mode with the **config term** command. Enter the **boot system flash** command shown as follows.

```
RouterA#config term
Enter configuration commands, one per line. End with CNTL/Z.
RouterA(config)#boot system flash c3620-i-mz_113-8_T1.bin
RouterA(config)#exit
```

You can verify that this command has been properly entered with the **show run** command.

```
RouterA#show run
Building configuration...

Current configuration:
!
version 11.2
no service udp-small-servers
no service tcp-small-servers
!
hostname RouterA
!
boot system flash c3620-i-mz_113-8_T1.bin←The router will load this file from
                                          flash memory during its power on
                                          sequence.
!
interface Ethernet0/0
 ip address 10.10.3.253 255.255.255.0
 !
no ip classless
!
line con 0
line aux 0
line vty 0 4
 login
!
end
```

The configuration changes must be written with a **write mem** command, because we have to reload the router.

```
RouterA#write mem
Building configuration...
[OK]

RouterA#reload
Proceed with reload? [confirm]
```

After the router reloads, it will be running IOS version 11.3(8)T1. We see that this file has been loaded from router flash.

```
RouterA#show ver
Cisco Internetwork Operating System Software
IOS (tm) 3600 Software (C3620-I-M), Version 11.3(8)T1, RELEASE SOFTWARE (fc1)
Copyright (c) 1986-1999 by cisco Systems, Inc.
Compiled Thu 11-Feb-99 17:22 by ccai
Image text-base: 0x60008918, data-base: 0x605B8000

ROM: System Bootstrap, Version 11.1(7)AX [kuong (7)AX], EARLY DEPLOYMENT
RELEASE SOFTWARE (fc2)

RouterA uptime is 5 minutes
System restarted by reload
System image file is "flash:c3620-i-mz_113-8_T1.bin", booted via flash

cisco 3620 (R4700) processor (revision 0x81) with 12288K/4096K bytes of memory.
Processor board ID 05706232
R4700 processor, Implementation 33, Revision 1.0
Bridging software.
X.25 software, Version 3.0.0.
Basic Rate ISDN software, Version 1.1.
1 Ethernet/IEEE 802.3 interface(s)
1 Serial network interface(s)
1 ISDN Basic Rate interface(s)
DRAM configuration is 32 bits wide with parity disabled.
29K bytes of non-volatile configuration memory.
16384K bytes of processor board System flash (Read/Write)

Configuration register is 0x2102
```

As an alternative, you can also load an IOS image to the router and erase the contents of the router's flash memory. We see an example as follows, where there are two files in the flash memory of the router.

```
RouterA#show flash

System flash directory:
File  Length     Name/status
   1  2259976    c3620-i-mz.112-7a.P
```

```
  2    3332232  c3620-i-mz_113-8_T1.bin
[5592336 bytes used, 11184880 available, 16777216 total]
16384K bytes of processor board System flash (Read/Write)
```

If you want to load a new IOS image without keeping the old image, use the **copy tftp flash** command and permit the flash device to be erased before writing.

```
RouterA#copy tftp flash

System flash directory:
File  Length    Name/status
  1    2259976  c3620-i-mz.112-7a.P
  2    3332232  c3620-i-mz_113-8_T1.bin
[5592336 bytes used, 11184880 available, 16777216 total]
Address or name of remote host [10.10.3.28]? 10.10.3.28
Source file name? c3620-i-mz_113-8_T1.bin
Destination file name [c3620-i-mz_113-8_T1.bin]?
Accessing file 'c3620-i-mz_113-8_T1.bin' on 10.10.3.28...
Loading c3620-i-mz_113-8_T1.bin from 10.10.3.28 (via Ethernet0/0): ! [OK]

Erase flash device before writing? [confirm]←Pressing enter at this prompt
                                              will cause the flash to be erased
                                              before writing a new file.
Flash contains files. Are you sure you want to erase? [confirm]

Copy 'c3620-i-mz_113-8_T1.bin' from server
   as 'c3620-i-mz_113-8_T1.bin' into Flash WITH erase? [yes/no]y
Erasing device...
eeeeeeeeeeeeeeeeeeeeeeeeeeeeeeeeeeeeeeeeeeeeeeeeeeeeeeeeeeeeee ...erased
↑
The flash is being erased.

Loading c3620-i-mz_113-8_T1.bin from 10.10.3.28 (via Ethernet0/0):
!!!!!!!!!!!!!!!!!!!!!!!!!!!!!!!!O!!!!!!!!!!!!!!!!!!!!!!!!!!!!!!!!!!!!!!!!!!!!O!!!!!!!!
                               ↑
                   An O means that a TFTP packet was received out of order.

!!!!!!!!!!!!!!!!!!!!!!!!!!!!!!!!!!!!!!!!!!!!!!!!!!!!!!!!!!!!!!!O!!!!!!!!!!!!
!!!!!!!!!!!!!!!!!!!!!!!!!!!!!O!!!!!!!!!!!!!!!!!!!!!!!!!!!!!!!!!!!!!!!!!!!!!!!!
!!!!!!!!!!!!!!!!!!!!!!!!!O!!!!!!!!!!!!!!!!!!!!!!!!!!!!!!!!!!!!!!O!!!!!!!!!!!!!!!
!!!!!!!!!!!!!!!!!!!!!!!!!!!!!!!!!!!!!!!!!!!!!!!!!!!!!!!!!!!!!!!O!!!!!!!!!!!!!!!!
!!!!!!!!!!!!!!!!!!!!!O!!!!!!!!!!!!!!!!!!!!!!!!!!!!!!!!!!!!!!!!!!!!!!!!!!!!!!!!
!!!!!!!!!!!!!!!!!!!!!O!!!!!!!!!!!!!!!!!!!!!!!!!!!!!!!!!!!!!O!!!!!!!!!!O!!!!!!!!!!!
!!!!!!!!!!!!!!!!!!!!!!!!!!!!!!!!!!!!!!!!!!!!!!!!!!!!!!!!!!!!O!!!!!!!!!!!!!!!!!!
!!!!!!!!!!!!!!!!!!!!!!O!!
[OK - 3332232/16777216 bytes]

Verifying checksum... OK (0x1837)
Flash device copy took 00:00:34 [hh:mm:ss]
```

After the IOS download is complete, we see that there is only one file in the flash device. We allowed the router to erase the flash before starting the download.

```
RouterA#sh flash

System flash directory:
File  Length    Name/status
  1   3332232   c3620-i-mz_113-8_T1.bin
[3332296 bytes used, 13444920 available, 16777216 total]
16384K bytes of processor board System flash (Read/Write)
```

Lab #80: Loading an IOS Image from a TFTP Server to a Run from FLASH Router

Equipment Needed

The following equipment is needed to perform this lab exercise:

- One Cisco router with an Ethernet interface
- A PC running a TFTP daemon with an Ethernet card. The PC should also have a terminal emulation program such as Procomm or HyperTerminal.
- A Cisco rolled cable for console port connection to the router
- An Ethernet hub with two Ethernet cables

Configuration Overview

This configuration will demonstrate how to load an IOS image on a Cisco router that utilizes a run from flash architecture. Examples of run from flash routers are the Cisco 2500 series and some of the Cisco 1600 series.

A PC running TFTP server software will be connected to the same LAN as a Cisco router. The software used in this lab is Exceed from Hummingbird Communications. The Exceed software package contains many TCP/IP programs, such as a TFTP server, an FTP server, and an X windows server. The new version of the IOS image will reside on the PC and will be transferred to the Cisco router using the TFTP transfer protocol.

The PC will be acting as the TFTP server, and the Cisco router will be the TFTP client.

RouterC and the PC are connected, as shown in Figure 21–5.

Router Configuration

The configurations for the router in this example are as follows:

RouterC

```
Current configuration:
!
version 11.1
service udp-small-servers
service tcp-small-servers
!
hostname RouterC
!
!
interface Ethernet0
ip address 10.10.3.253 255.255.255.0←The Ethernet interface is on the same
network as the TFTP server.
!
no ip classless
!
line con 0
line aux 0
line vty 0 4
  login
!
end
```

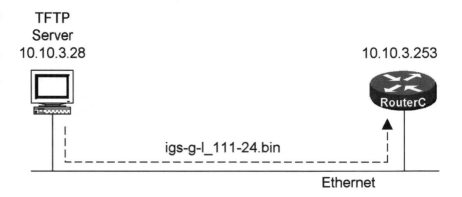

Figure 21–5
Connection between RouterC and the TFTP Server

Monitoring and Testing the Configuration

Let's start by connecting to RouterC. Use the **show version** command to find out which version of IOS the router is currently running. We see that the router is running a version of 11.1. The **show version** command also tells us other key information about the router's software image and memory capabilities. We see that the router has 2MB of DRAM. We also see that this router has 8MB of flash memory. The flash memory stores one or more IOS images. The **show version** output also tells us that the currently running IOS was loaded from flash memory. Finally, we see that our router platform is a 2524 router.

```
RouterC#sh ver                                  Router is running IOS version 11.1(4)
Cisco Internetwork Operating System Software   ↓
IOS (tm) 3000 Software (IGS-I-L), Version 11.1(4), RELEASE SOFTWARE (fc1)
Copyright (c) 1986-1996 by cisco Systems, Inc.
Compiled Mon 17-Jun-96 15:45 by mkamson
Image text-base: 0x0301F2B4, data-base: 0x00001000

ROM: System Bootstrap, Version 11.0(5), SOFTWARE
ROM: 3000 Bootstrap Software (IGS-BOOT-R), Version 11.0(5), RELEASE SOFTWARE
(fc1)

RouterC uptime is 8 minutes          The IOS was loaded from flash memory.
System restarted by reload              ↓
System image file is "flash:igs-i-1.111-4", booted via flash

This router is a Cisco 2524
 ↓
cisco 2524 (68030) processor (revision B) with 1024K/1024K bytes of memory.
                                                   ↑
                                       The router has 2MB of
                                       DRAM. 1MB is used for
                                       processor memory and 1MB
                                       is used for I/O memory.



Processor board ID 03879418, with hardware revision 00000000
Bridging software.
X.25 software, Version 2.0, NET2, BFE and GOSIP compliant.
Basic Rate ISDN software, Version 1.0.
1 Ethernet/IEEE 802.3 interface.
2 Serial network interfaces.
1 ISDN Basic Rate interface.
5-in-1 module for Serial Interface 0
56k 4-wire CSU/DSU for Serial Interface 1
Integrated NT1 for ISDN Basic Rate interface
32K bytes of non-volatile configuration memory.
8192K bytes of processor board System flash (Read ONLY)←The router has 8MB of
                                                          flash memory.


Configuration register is 0x2102
```

Display the contents of the router's flash memory using the **show flash** command. We see that the flash contains a single file.

```
RouterC#show flash

System flash directory:
File   Length    Name/status
  1    3747048   igs-i-1.111-4
[3747112 bytes used, 4641496 available, 8388608 total]
8192K bytes of processor board System flash (Read ONLY)
```

Let's make sure that we can reach our TFTP server at IP address 10.10.3.28 by using a ping command.

```
RouterA#ping 10.10.3.28

Type escape sequence to abort.
Sending 5, 100-byte ICMP Echos to 10.10.3.28, timeout is 2 seconds:
!!!!!
Success rate is 100 percent (5/5), round-trip min/avg/max = 1/3/8 ms
```

Once we verify that we can ping our TFTP server, we can start to download the new IOS image to the router. The Cisco 2524 is a run from flash router, which means that the router's IOS image executes out of the same flash memory in which the IOS image resides. Loading a new IOS to the router is a bit more complex than loading a new IOS image on a router, which runs the IOS from RAM. The router will reload itself and load a small IOS image out of its ROM memory. The router will then load the new IOS image into flash memory.

```
RouterC#copy tftp flash
                 ****  NOTICE  ****
Flash load helper v1.0
This process will accept the copy options and then terminate
the current system image to use the ROM based image for the copy.←The router
                                                              will load
                                                              a special
                                                              ROM-based
                                                              IOS image,
                                                              which will
                                                              write the
                                                              new IOS
                                                              to flash
                                                              memory.
Routing functionality will not be available during that time.
If you are logged in via telnet, this connection will terminate.
Users with console access can see the results of the copy operation.
                 — ******** —
Proceed? [confirm]
```

```
System flash directory:
File    Length     Name/status
   1    3747048    igs-i-1.111-4
[3747112 bytes used, 4641496 available, 8388608 total]
Address or name of remote host [255.255.255.255]? 10.10.3.28←TFTP server
                                                             address
Source file name? igs-g-l_111-24.bin
Destination file name [igs-g-l_111-24.bin]?
Accessing file 'igs-g-l_111-24.bin' on 10.10.3.28...
Loading igs-g-l_111-24.bin from 10.10.3.28 (via Ethernet0): ! [OK]

Erase flash device before writing? [confirm]←Erase the current flash contents?
Flash contains files. Are you sure you want to erase? [confirm]

System configuration has been modified. Save? [yes/no]: y
Building configuration...
[OK]

Copy 'igs-g-l_111-24.bin' from server
   as 'igs-g-l_111-24.bin' into Flash WITH erase? [yes/no]y

%SYS-5-RELOAD: Reload requested
SERVICE_MODULE(1): self test finished: Passed
%SYS-4-CONFIG_NEWER: Configurations from version 11.1 may not be correctly
understood.
%FLH: igs-g-l_111-24.bin from 10.10.3.28 to flash ...

System flash directory:
File    Length     Name/status
   1    3747048    igs-i-1.111-4
[3747112 bytes used, 4641496 available, 8388608 total]
Accessing file 'igs-g-l_111-24.bin' on 10.10.3.28...
Loading igs-g-l_111-24.bin .from 10.10.3.28 (via Ethernet0): ! [OK]

Erasing device... eeeeeeeeeeeeeeeeeeeeeeeeeeeeeeeee ...erased←The router is
erasing the flash memory.
Loading igs-g-l_111-24.bin from 10.10.3.28 (via Ethernet0):
!!!!!!!!!!O!!!!!!!!!!!!!!!!!!!!!!!!!!!!!O!!!!!!!!!!!!O!!!!!!!!!!!!!!!!!!!!!!!!!!O!!!
                                       ↑
                    An O means that a TFTP packet was received out of order.

!!!!!!!!!!O!!!!!!!!!!!!!!!!!!!!!!!!!!!!!O!!!!!!!!!!!!!O!!!!!!!!!!!!!!!!!!!!!!!!!!O!!!!!!!!O!!!
!!!!!!!!!!!!!!!!!!!!!!!!!!!!O!!!!!!!!!!!!!!O!!!!!!!!!!!!!!!!!!!!!!!!!!!!!O!!!!!!!!!!!!!O!!!!!!!!
!!!!!!!!!!!!!!!!!!!!!O!!!!!!!!!!!!!O!!!!!!!!!!!!!!!!!!!!!!!!!!!!!O!!!!!!!!!!!!!O!!!!!!!!!!!
!!!!!!!!!!!!!!O!!!!!!!!!!!!O!!!!!!!!!!!!!!!!!!!!!!!!!!!!O!!!!!!!!!!!!!O!!!!!!!!!!!!!!!!!
!!!!!!!!!!O!!!!!!!!!!!!!O!!!!!!!!!!!!!!!!!!!!!!!!!!!!O!!!!!!!!!!!!!O!!!!!!!!!!!!!!!!!!!
!!!!!!O!!!!!!!!!!!!!O!!!!!!!!!!!!!!!!!!!!!!O!!!!!!!O!!!!!!!!!!!!!!!!!!!O!!!!!!
!!!!!!O!!!!!!!!!!!!!!!!!!!O!!!!!!!!!!!!!O!!!!!!!!!!O!!!!!!!!!!!!!!!!O!!!!!!!!!
!!O!!!!!!!!!!!!!!!!!!!!!!!!!!!!O!!!!!!!!!!!!O!!!!!!!!!!!!!!!!!!!!O!!!!!!!!!!!!!O
!!!!!!!!!!!!!!!!!!!!!!!!!!O!!!!!!!!!!!!!O!!!!!!!!!!!!!!
[OK - 3735976/8388608 bytes]

Verifying checksum... OK (0xB84C)
Flash copy took 0:02:11 [hh:mm:ss]
```

```
%FLH: Re-booting system after download←The router will reload itself before
                                           booting the new IOS image.
```

```
Cisco Internetwork Operating System Software
IOS (tm) 3000 Software (IGS-G-L), Version 11.1(24), RELEASE SOFTWARE (fc1)
Copyright (c) 1986-1999 by cisco Systems, Inc.
Compiled Mon 04-Jan-99 19:14 by richv
Image text-base: 0x0301F310, data-base: 0x00001000

cisco 2524 (68030) processor (revision B) with 1024K/1024K bytes of memory.
Processor board ID 03879418, with hardware revision 00000000
Bridging software.
Basic Rate ISDN software, Version 1.0.
1 Ethernet/IEEE 802.3 interface.
1 ISDN Basic Rate interface.
Integrated NT1 for ISDN Basic Rate interface
32K bytes of non-volatile configuration memory.
8192K bytes of processor board System flash (Read ONLY)
```

After the IOS reloads, use the show version command to verify that the router is running the new system image. We see that the router is now running IOS 11.1(24).

```
RouterC#show version
Cisco Internetwork Operating System Software
IOS (tm) 3000 Software (IGS-G-L), Version 11.1(24), RELEASE SOFTWARE (fc1)
Copyright (c) 1986-1999 by cisco Systems, Inc.
Compiled Mon 04-Jan-99 19:14 by richv
Image text-base: 0x0301F310, data-base: 0x00001000

ROM: System Bootstrap, Version 11.0(5), SOFTWARE
ROM: 3000 Bootstrap Software (IGS-BOOT-R), Version 11.0(5), RELEASE SOFTWARE
(fc1)

RouterC uptime is 0 minutes
System restarted by reload
System image file is "flash:igs-g-l_111-24.bin", booted via flash
```

```
cisco 2524 (68030) processor (revision B) with 1024K/1024K bytes of memory.
Processor board ID 03879418, with hardware revision 00000000
Bridging software.
Basic Rate ISDN software, Version 1.0.
1 Ethernet/IEEE 802.3 interface.
1 ISDN Basic Rate interface.
Integrated NT1 for ISDN Basic Rate interface
32K bytes of non-volatile configuration memory.
8192K bytes of processor board System flash (Read ONLY)

Configuration register is 0x2102
```

Use the **show flash** command to verify that we have the correct file in our router's flash.

```
RouterC#show flash

System flash directory:
File   Length     Name/status
  1    3735976    igs-g-l_111-24.bin
[3736040 bytes used, 4652568 available, 8388608 total]
8192K bytes of processor board System flash (Read ONLY)
```

Lab #81: Loading an IOS Image from Another Router

Equipment Needed

The following equipment is needed to perform this lab exercise:

- Two Cisco routers, each with a single serial interface

- A Cisco V.35 crossover cable. If no crossover cable is available, you can use a Cisco DCE cable connected to a Cisco DTE cable.

- A Cisco rolled cable for console port connection to the router

Configuration Overview

This configuration will demonstrate how a Cisco router can act as a TFTP server. This feature is a powerful capability of the router. Recall from the two previous labs that we needed to have a TFTP server software pack-

Figure 21–6
Connection between
RouterA and RouterB

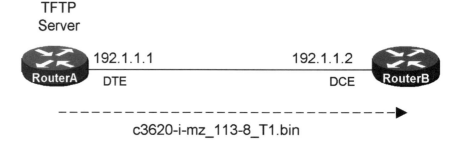

age running on a PC in order to load an IOS image on the router. With the TFTP server capability built into the router, we can load an IOS image from any router in our network from which we have IP connectivity.

RouterA and RouterB will be connected, as shown in Figure 21–6. RouterB will act as a DCE, supplying clock to RouterA.

RouterA will be configured to be a TFTP server. RouterB will be the TFTP client. RouterB will request the file c3620-i-mz_113-8_T1.bin from RouterA.

Router Configuration

The configurations for the two routers in this example are as follows:

RouterA (TFTP Server)

```
Current configuration:
!
version 11.3
service timestamps debug uptime
service timestamps log uptime
no service password-encryption
!
hostname RouterA
!
boot system flash c3620-i-mz_113-8_T1.bin
enable password cisco
!
interface Ethernet0/0
 ip address 10.10.3.253 255.255.255.0
```

```
!
interface Serial0/0
 ip address 192.1.1.1 255.255.255.0
 encapsulation ppp
!
no ip classless
!
tftp-server flash c3620-i-mz_113-8_T1.bin←RouterA is acting as a TFTP server.
                                          The router will only accept requests
                                          for the file c3620-i-mz_113-
                                          8_T1.bin.
!
line con 0
line aux 0
line vty 0 4
 password cisco
 login
!
end
```

RouterB (TFTP Client)

```
Current configuration:
!
version 11.2
no service password-encryption
no service udp-small-servers
no service tcp-small-servers
!
hostname RouterB
!
enable password cisco
!
interface Serial0/0
 ip address 192.1.1.2 255.255.255.0
 encapsulation ppp
 no fair-queue
 clockrate 64000←RouterB acts as a DCE, supplying a clock to RouterA.
!
no ip classless
!
line con 0
line aux 0
line vty 0 4
 password cisco
 login
!
end
```

Monitoring and Testing the Configuration

The **tftp-server flash c3620-i-mz_113-8_T1.bin** command in the configuration of RouterA defines RouterA to be a TFTP server. The command will enable requests for the file **c3620-i-mz_113-8_T1.bin** (IOS version 11.3(8)) to be retrieved from the flash memory of RouterA. Let's check the contents of the flash on RouterA to make sure that the correct file is there. Use the **show flash** command to view the contents of RouterA's flash memory. We see that the file is in the flash memory of RouterA.

```
RouterA#show flash

System flash directory:
File   Length    Name/status
  1    3332232   c3620-i-mz_113-8_T1.bin←RouterA is configured so that only this
                                         file can be requested via TFTP out of
                                         its flash memory.
[3332296 bytes used, 13444920 available, 16777216 total]
16384K bytes of processor board System flash (Read/Write)
```

Now, let's connect to RouterB. Verify that we can reach RouterA by pinging RouterA at IP address 192.1.1.1.

```
RouterB#ping 192.1.1.1

Type escape sequence to abort.
Sending 5, 100-byte ICMP Echos to 192.1.1.1, timeout is 2 seconds:
!!!!!
Success rate is 100 percent (5/5), round-trip min/avg/max = 28/30/32 ms
```

Display the contents of the flash memory on RouterB. We see that RouterB has three IOS images in its flash memory: 11.2(7), 11.3(3), and 11.2(16).

```
RouterB#show flash

System flash directory:
File   Length    Name/status
  1    2259976   c3620-i-mz.112-7a.P←11.2(7)
  2    4568036   c3620-is-mz_113-3a_T.bin←11.3(3)
  3    2972356   c3620-d-mz_112-16_p.bin←11.2(16)
[9800560 bytes used, 6976656 available, 16777216 total]
16384K bytes of processor board System flash (Read/Write)
```

Now, let's copy an IOS image from RouterA to RouterB. We will use the same command as we used in the previous two labs. The only difference here is that a Cisco router is acting as a TFTP server, instead of a PC. Type the **copy tftp flash** command.

```
RouterB#copy tftp flash

System flash directory:
File   Length     Name/status
  1    2259976    c3620-i-mz.112-7a.P
  2    4568036    c3620-is-mz_113-3a_T.bin
  3    2972356    c3620-d-mz_112-16_p.bin
[9800560 bytes used, 6976656 available, 16777216 total]
Address or name of remote host [192.1.1.1]? 192.1.1.1←Address of RouterA (our
                                                                TFTP server)
Source file name? c3620-i-mz_113-8_T1.bin←The IOS file that we want to load
Destination file name [c3620-i-mz_113-8_T1.bin]?
Accessing file 'c3620-i-mz_113-8_T1.bin' on 192.1.1.1...
Loading c3620-i-mz_113-8_T1.bin from 192.1.1.1 (via Serial0/0): ! [OK]

Erase flash device before writing? [confirm]←We will erase the flash before
                                                     loading our new image.
Flash contains files. Are you sure you want to erase? [confirm]

Copy 'c3620-i-mz_113-8_T1.bin' from server
  as 'c3620-i-mz_113-8_T1.bin' into Flash WITH erase? [yes/no]y

Erasing device...               Flash memory is being erased
                                           ↓
eeeeeeeeeeeeeeeeeeeeeeeeeeeeeeeeeeeeeeeeeeeeeeeeeeeeeeeeeeeeeeeee ...erased
Loading c3620-i-mz_113-8_T1.bin from 192.1.1.1 (via Serial0/0):
!!!!!!!!!!!!!!!!!!!!!!!!!!!!!!!!!!!!!!!!!!!!!!!!!!!!!!!!!!!!!!!!!!!!!!!!!!!!!!!
!!!!!!!!!!!!!!!!!!!!!!!!!!!!!!!!!!!!!!!!!!!!!!!!!!!!!!!!!!!!!!!!!!!!!!!!!!!!!!!
!!!!!!!!!!!!!!!!!!!!!!!!!!!!!!!!!!!!!!!!!!!!!!!!!!!!!!!!!!!!!!!!!!!!!!!!!!!!!!!
!!!!!!!!!!!!!!!!!!!!!!!!!!!!!!!!!!!!!!!!!!!!!!!!!!!!!!!!!!!!!!!!!!!!!!!!!!!!!!!
!!!!!!!!!!!!!!!!!!!!!!!!!!!!!!!!!!!!!!!!!!!!!!!!!!!!!!!!!!!!!!!!!!!!!!!!!!!!!!!
!!!!!!!!!!!!!!!!!!!!!!!!!!!!!!!!!!!!!!!!!!!!!!!!!!!!!!!!!!!!!!!!!!!!!!!!!!!!!!!
!!!!!!!!!!!!!!!!!!!!!!!!!!!!!!!!!!!!!!!!!!!!!!!!!!!!!!!!!!!!!!!!!!!!!!!!!!!!!!!
!!!!!!!!!!!!!!!!!!!!!!!!!!!!!!!!!!!!!!!!!!!!!!!!!!!!!!!!!!!!!!!!!!!!!!!!!!!!!!!
!!!!!!!!!!!!!
[OK - 3332232/16777216 bytes]

Verifying checksum... OK (0x1837)
Flash device copy took 00:08:38 [hh:mm:ss]
```

After the TFTP code load is complete, use the **show flash** command to
view the contents of the flash memory on RouterB. We see that the three
original files have been erased, and an IOS image of 11.3(8) is now in the
router.

```
RouterB#show flash

System flash directory:
File   Length     Name/status
  1    3332232    c3620-i-mz_113-8_T1.bin
[3332296 bytes used, 13444920 available, 16777216 total]
16384K bytes of processor board System flash (Read/Write)
```

Reload the router with the **reload** command.

```
RouterB#reload
Proceed with reload? [confirm]
```

The router will reload with IOS version 11.3(8).

```
                              The router will reload with IOS 11.3(8).
Cisco Internetwork Operating System Software    ↓
IOS (tm) 3600 Software (C3620-I-M), Version 11.3(8)T1,   RELEASE SOFTWARE (fc1)
Copyright (c) 1986-1999 by cisco Systems, Inc.
Compiled Thu 11-Feb-99 17:22 by ccai
Image text-base: 0x60008918, data-base: 0x605B8000

cisco 3620 (R4700) processor (revision 0x81) with 12288K/4096K bytes of memory.
Processor board ID 05706229
R4700 processor, Implementation 33, Revision 1.0
Bridging software.
X.25 software, Version 3.0.0.
1 Ethernet/IEEE 802.3 interface(s)
2 Serial network interface(s)
DRAM configuration is 32 bits wide with parity disabled.
29K bytes of non-volatile configuration memory.
16384K bytes of processor board System flash (Read/Write)
```

Troubleshooting TFTP Transfers on a Cisco Router

{**debug tftp**}   The Cisco IOS provides a command, **debug tftp**, which shows the status of TFTP transfers. The following output shows how TFTP sends an acknowledgment packet for every block of traffic sent.

```
RouterA#debug tftp
TFTP Packets debugging is on
RouterA#
02:25:06: TFTP: Sending block 216 (retry 0), socket_id 0x60A3F8E4  ←Block sent
02:25:06: TFTP: Received ACK for block 216, socket_id 0x60A3F8E4  ←Block ACK
02:25:06: TFTP: Sending block 217 (retry 0), socket_id 0x60A3F8E4
02:25:06: TFTP: Received ACK for block 217, socket_id 0x60A3F8E4
02:25:06: TFTP: Sending block 218 (retry 0), socket_id 0x60A3F8E4
02:25:06: TFTP: Received ACK for block 218, socket_id 0x60A3F8E4
02:25:06: TFTP: Sending block 219 (retry 0), socket_id 0x60A3F8E4
02:25:06: TFTP: Received ACK for block 219, socket_id 0x60A3F8E4
02:25:06: TFTP: Sending block 220 (retry 0), socket_id 0x60A3F8E4
02:25:06: TFTP: Received ACK for block 220, socket_id 0x60A3F8E4
02:25:06: TFTP: Sending block 221 (retry 0), socket_id 0x60A3F8E4
02:25:06: TFTP: Received ACK for block 221, socket_id 0x60A3F8E4
02:25:06: TFTP: Sending block 222 (retry 0), socket_id 0x60A3F8E4
02:25:06: TFTP: Received ACK for block 222, socket_id 0x60A3F8E4
02:25:06: TFTP: Sending block 223 (retry 0), socket_id 0x60A3F8E4
```

```
02:25:06: TFTP: Received ACK for block 223, socket_id 0x60A3F8E4
02:25:06: TFTP: Sending block 224 (retry 0), socket_id 0x60A3F8E4
02:25:06: TFTP: Received ACK for block 224, socket_id 0x60A3F8E4
02:25:06: TFTP: Sending block 225 (retry 0), socket_id 0x60A3F8E4
02:25:07: TFTP: Received ACK for block 225, socket_id 0x60A3F8E4
02:25:07: TFTP: Sending block 226 (retry 0), socket_id 0x60A3F8E4
02:25:07: TFTP: Received ACK for block 226, socket_id 0x60A3F8E4
```

{show flash}   The **show flash** command displays all IOS images that are loaded in the flash memory of the router. We see that an image of IOS 11.3(8) is loaded in flash. The **show flash** command also displays how much total flash and available flash there is on the router.

```
RouterB#show flash

System flash directory:
File   Length    Name/status
   1   3332232   c3620-i-mz_113-8_T1.bin←Single IOS image in the router's flash
[3332296 bytes used, 13444920 available, 16777216 total]←16MB flash total,
3.3MB used, 13.4MB available
16384K bytes of processor board System flash (Read/Write)
```

{show version}   The **show version** command displays key information about the router's software image and memory capabilities. We see that the router has 16MB of DRAM. The DRAM is used to run the IOS on a run from RAM router, such as the Cisco 3620. We also see that this router has 16MB of flash memory. The flash memory stores one or more IOS images. The **show version** output also tells us that the currently running IOS was loaded from flash memory.

```
RouterC#sh ver                          Router is running IOS version 11.1(4)
Cisco Internetwork Operating System Software   ↓
IOS (tm) 3000 Software (IGS-I-L), Version 11.1(4), RELEASE SOFTWARE (fc1)
Copyright (c) 1986-1996 by cisco Systems, Inc.
Compiled Mon 17-Jun-96 15:45 by mkamson
Image text-base: 0x0301F2B4, data-base: 0x00001000

ROM: System Bootstrap, Version 11.0(5), SOFTWARE
ROM: 3000 Bootstrap Software (IGS-BOOT-R), Version 11.0(5), RELEASE SOFTWARE
(fc1)

RouterC uptime is 8 minutes        The IOS was loaded from flash memory.
System restarted by reload            ↓
System image file is "flash:igs-i-1.111-4", booted via flash
```

```
This router is a Cisco 2524
  ↓
cisco 2524 (68030) processor (revision B) with 1024K/1024K bytes of memory.
                                                        ↑
                                            The router has 2MB of
                                            DRAM. 1MB is used for
                                            processor memory, and 1MB
                                            is used for I/O memory.
```

Conclusion

The capability to load IOS images to a Cisco router via TFTP is a powerful feature. As we saw in this section, a Cisco router can also act as an TFTP server for a network of routers.

CHAPTER **22**

Cisco Password Recovery

Topics Covered in This Chapter

- Cisco password recovery overview
- Understanding the Cisco configuration register
- Password recovery on a Cisco 3600
- Password recovery on a Cisco 2500
- Password recovery on a Catalyst Switch

Introduction

This chapter provides detailed information on recovering lost or unknown passwords on Cisco routers and Catalyst switches. Password recovery instructions will be given for the Cisco 2500, Cisco 3600, and Catalyst 5000.

Password Recovery Overview

A Cisco router goes through a predefined startup sequence. After power on tests and loading of the IOS image, the router looks to NVRAM for its configuration instructions. These configuration instructions not only contain information on routing protocols and addressing, but they also contain information on the login passwords of the router.

Password recovery involves telling the router to ignore the contents of the NVRAM when the router goes through its startup sequence. This task is done by modifying the router's configuration register, a 16-bit register located in the router's NVRAM. This activity causes the router to load a blank configuration containing no login passwords. After logging into the router without any passwords, the user can then view the passwords in the NVRAM configuration and either use them, delete them, or change them. The router is then rebooted with known passwords.

Password recovery techniques vary by router family, but in general, most observe the following format:

1. Connect a terminal to the console port of the router.
2. If the router is powered on, power it off and back on again. If the router is powered off, power it on.
3. While the router is booting, you must break into the boot sequence and put the router in monitor mode.
4. While in monitor mode, configure the router to boot up without reading the contents of NVRAM.
5. Reload the router.
6. After the router reloads without reading NVRAM, there will not be any privileged or non-privileged passwords. Get into privileged mode and either view, change, or delete the NVRAM passwords.
7. Go into configuration mode and set the router to boot from NVRAM.
8. Reload the router. The passwords are now known.

Configuration Register

A Cisco router has a 16-bit register known as the virtual configuration register. This register resides in NVRAM. The register is used to set several basic features on the router, such as the following:

■ Causing the router to ignore the contents of NVRAM

■ Setting the console baud rate

■ Setting the format of IP broadcast packets

■ Causing the router to boot from ROM, flash, or to use the startup configuration to determine the correct location for the router's IOS image

The first item in the previous list causes the router to ignore the contents of NVRAM (which is used for password recovery).

The 16-bit value of the configuration register is always expressed in hexadecimal format and is always written as 0xVALUE, where VALUE is the register setting. We will see, for example, that a typical configuration register value is 0x2102.

Figure 22–1 shows the meaning of each bit position in the virtual configuration register for a Cisco 3600 router.

Let's look at some of the key fields of the virtual configuration register and examine their possible values:

Bits 0-3—Boot field

These four bits determine whether the router will reload into ROM monitor mode, boot from the first image located in flash, or get its image loading instructions from the configuration located in NVRAM.

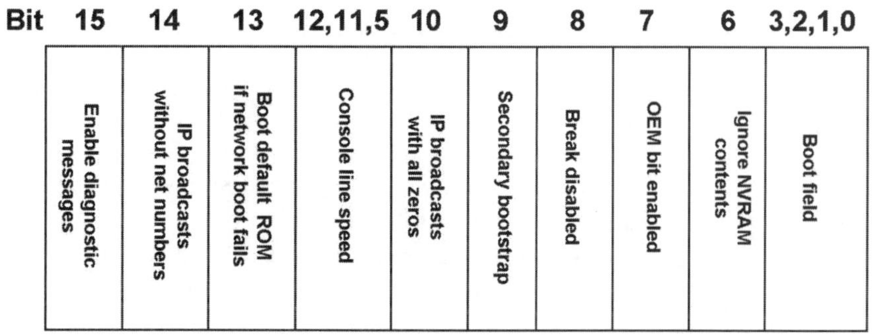

Figure 22–1
Cisco 3600
configuration register

Bit	15	14	13	12,11,5	10	9	8	7	6	3,2,1,0
	Enable diagnostic messages	IP broadcasts without net numbers	Boot default ROM if network boot fails	Console line speed	IP broadcasts with all zeros	Secondary bootstrap	Break disabled	OEM bit enabled	Ignore NVRAM contents	Boot field

Bit 6—NVRAM ignore

When bit 6 is set to a one, the router will ignore the contents of NVRAM when it boots. This bit is the one we set when doing password recovery.

Bit 8—Break disable

Setting this bit to a one causes the router to ignore the break key.

Bits 5&11&12—Console speed

These three bits determine the speed of the router's console. The 3600 console port defaults to 9600 bits/sec but can operate at speeds from 1200 to 115200 bits/sec.

Interpreting the Configuration Register

Let's look at a typical configuration register value of 0x2102 and review how to convert this hexadecimal value to a binary value. Figure 22–2 contains a hexadecimal-to-binary conversion chart.

Conversion from the hexadecimal value of 0x2102 to a binary value is a simple exercise. Each digit of the hexadecimal register value gets converted to four binary bits. The 0x2102 value should be converted one hexadecimal digit at a time. The first hexadecimal digit is a two and gets converted to a 0010. The second hexadecimal digit is a one and gets converted to 0001. The third hexadecimal digit is a zero and gets converted to 0000. The last hexadecimal digit is a two and gets converted to 0010. After converting each individual hexadecimal digit, a 16-bit value can be created. The 16 bit value would be:

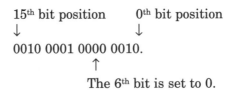

15th bit position 0th bit position

↓   ↓

0010 0001 0000 0010.

↑

The 6th bit is set to 0.

The bit numbers are counted so that the rightmost bit is the 0th bit, and the leftmost bit is the 15th bit.

We see from this example that the 6th bit is set to zero, which means that the contents of NVRAM will not be ignored when the router reboots.

Figure 22–2
Hexadecimal-to-binary conversion chart

Hex	Binary
0	0000
1	0001
2	0010
3	0011
4	0100
5	0101
6	0110
7	0111
8	1000
9	1001
A	1010
B	1011
C	1100
D	1101
E	1110
F	1111

Breaking the Normal Router Startup Sequence

The key to successfully recovering a lost or unknown password is being able to interrupt the normal startup sequence of the router and gain access to monitor mode. This is accomplished by issuing a break signal from your terminal emulator while the router is booting. The break sequence varies on different terminal emulators. The two most popular terminal emulators are Windows 95 HyperTerminal and ProComm. The break sequence for ProComm is generated by pressing the ALT+B keys at the same time. In Windows 95 HyperTerminal the break sequence is generated by pressing the Ctrl+Break keys at the same time.

Commands Discussed in This Chapter

■ **show version**
■ **show running-config**

- show startup-config
- confreg
- reset
- config-register
- i
- o/r
- enable
- config term
- copy startup-config running config
- write erase
- reload
- set pass
- set enablepass

Definitions

show version: An exec command that is used to show the system hardware, IOS version, configuration file, boot image, and contents of the configuration register

show running-config: An exec command that displays the contents of the current executing configuration

show startup-config: An exec command that shows the contents of the saved configuration stored in NVRAM

confreg: A ROM monitor command used to view and change the contents of the configuration register

reset: A ROM monitor command used to reload the router after changing the contents of the configuration register. This command is specific to certain Cisco models, such as the 3600 series.

config-register: A global configuration command used to change the contents of the 16-bit configuration register

i: A ROM monitor command used to reload a router after changing the contents of the configuration register. This command is specific to certain Cisco models, such as the 2500 series.

o/r: A ROM monitor command used to change the contents of the configuration register. This command is specific to certain Cisco models, such as the 2500 series.

enable: An exec command used to place a Cisco router or Catalyst switch into enabled mode

config term: An exec command used to enter router configuration mode

copy startup-config running config: An exec command used to copy the configuration stored in NVRAM to the currently running configuration

write erase: An exec command that causes the configuration stored in NVRAM to be erased

reload: An exec command that causes the IOS to reload

set pass: A Catalyst Switch command used to set the non-enabled password

set enablepass: A Catalyst Switch command used to set the enabled password

IOS Requirements

These password recovery procedures apply to all IOS versions of 10.0 and later.

Lab #82: Cisco 3600 Password Recovery

Equipment Needed

The following equipment is needed to perform this lab exercise:

- A Cisco 3600 series router
- A PC running a terminal emulation program, preferably ProComm or Windows HyperTerminal
- A Cisco rolled cable connecting the router to the PC

Configuration Overview

This section will provide detailed instructions on recovering an unknown password on a Cisco 3600 series router, as shown in Figure 22–3.

NOTES: *Pressing the break sequence too soon after powering on the router can cause the router to lock up. In this case, simply power cycle the router again. Wait to press the break sequence until the router prints a message describing its processor type and main memory configuration.*

Also, keep in mind that terminal emulation programs use different key combinations to generate the break sequence. The two most popular terminal emulators are Windows 95 HyperTerminal and ProComm. The break sequence for ProComm is generated by pressing the ALT+B keys at the same time. In Windows 95 HyperTerminal, the break sequence is generated by pressing the Ctrl+Break keys at the same time.

Password recovery can only be performed with a terminal attached to the console port of the router. These procedures will not work on the Aux port of the router.

Password Recovery Procedures

Before beginning, the router should have an enable password and a login password set. The following configuration shows an example of the enable and login password both set to cisco:

Figure 22–3
Cisco 3600 password
recovery

PC running
Hyperterm

Console
Port

Router

```
Current configuration:
!
version 11.2
no service udp-small-servers
no service tcp-small-servers
!
hostname Cisco3620
!
enable password cisco←Enable password.
!
no ip classless
!
line con 0
 password cisco←Login Password
 login
line aux 0
line vty 0 4
 login
!
end
```

The following **show version** command reveals that the configuration register of the router is set to a value of 0x2102. As described in the previous section, this value will cause the router to use the NVRAM configuration file during the boot process. This register value will be changed during the password recovery process, causing the router to ignore the contents of the NVRAM configuration file during the boot process.

```
Cisco3620#sh ver
Cisco Internetwork Operating System Software
IOS (tm) 3600 Software (C3620-I-M), Version 11.2(8)P, RELEASE SOFTWARE (fc1)
Copyright (c) 1986-1997 by cisco Systems, Inc.
Compiled Mon 11-Aug-97 19:50 by ccai
Image text-base: 0x600088E0, data-base: 0x6044A000

ROM: System Bootstrap, Version 11.1(7)AX [kuong (7)AX], EARLY DEPLOYMENT
RELEASE SOFTWARE (fc2)

Cisco3620 uptime is 1 minute
System restarted by reload
System image file is "flash:c3620-i-mz.112-8.P", booted via flash

cisco 3620 (R4700) processor (revision 0x81) with 12288K/4096K bytes of memory.
Processor board ID 05706480
R4700 processor, Implementation 33, Revision 1.0
Bridging software.
X.25 software, Version 2.0, NET2, BFE and GOSIP compliant.
1 Ethernet/IEEE 802.3 interface(s)
2 Serial network interface(s)
DRAM configuration is 32 bits wide with parity disabled.
29K bytes of non-volatile configuration memory.
```

```
16384K bytes of processor board System flash (Read/Write)
8192K bytes of processor board PCMCIA Slot0 flash (Read/Write)
```
Configuration register is 0x2102

The first step in the password recovery process is to power cycle the router, turning it off and back on again. If the router is already off, then turn the router on. During the first few seconds of the boot process, you will see the following display:

```
System Bootstrap, Version 11.1(7)AX [kuong (7)AX], EARLY DEPLOYMENT RELEASE
SOFTWARE (fc2)
Copyright (c) 1994-1996 by cisco Systems, Inc.
C3600 processor with 16384 Kbytes of main memory
Main memory is configured to 32 bit mode with parity disabled←Press the break
                                                                sequence here.
```

After these messages are displayed, press the proper break sequence. Remember that every terminal emulation program has its own key combinations to force a break. The break sequence for ProComm is generated by pressing the ALT+B keys at the same time. In Windows 95 HyperTerminal, the break sequence is generated by pressing the Ctrl+Break keys at the same time. When the proper break sequence is pressed, the router will go into Rom monitor mode:

```
monitor: command "boot" aborted due to user interrupt
```

At the rommon prompt type the command: **confreg**

```
rommon 1 >
rommon 1 > confreg
```

A current configurations summary will be displayed. You will be asked a series of questions. The proper yes and no responses should be entered for each question. Answer yes to the questions, "Do you wish to change the configuration?", "Ignore system config info?", and "Change the boot characteristics?". Answer no to the other questions. Finally, type a 2 to cause the system to boot the full IOS image upon startup:

```
    Configuration Summary
enabled are:
load rom after netboot fails
console baud: 9600
boot: image specified by the boot system commands
      or default to: cisco2-C3600
do you wish to change the configuration? y/n  [n]:  y
enable  "diagnostic mode"? y/n  [n]:  n
enable  "use net in IP bcast address"? y/n  [n]:  n
disable "load rom after netboot fails"? y/n  [n]:  n
enable  "use all zero broadcast"? y/n  [n]:  n
```

```
enable   "break/abort has effect"? y/n   [n]:   n
enable   "ignore system config info"? y/n    [n]:   y
change console baud rate? y/n   [n]:   n
change the boot characteristics? y/n   [n]:   y
enter to boot:
 0 = ROM Monitor
 1 = the boot helper image
 2-15 = boot system
    [2]:   2
```

A configuration summary will be printed, showing that the router will now ignore the system configuration information (NVRAM) upon startup:

```
    Configuration Summary
enabled are:
load rom after netboot fails
ignore system config info
console baud: 9600
boot: image specified by the boot system commands
      or default to: cisco2-C3600
```

You will again be asked if you want to change the configuration. This time, answer no.

```
do you wish to change the configuration? y/n   [n]:   n
```

The router will display a reminder that it must be reset in order for the changes to take effect. Type the reset command at the monitor prompt:

```
You must reset or power cycle for new config to take effect
rommon 2 >
rommon 2 > reset
```

The router will reload. This time, the router will ignore the configuration information contained in the NVRAM. When the router finishes booting, there will not be a console password or an enable password. Press enter to get into user mode and type **enable** to get into privileged mode:

```
Press RETURN to get started!
```

```
Router>
Router>ena
Router#
```

Use the **show running-configuration** command to view the router's current configuration. You will notice that the configuration contains no passwords of any kind. This configuration is created when the router ignores the contents of NVRAM:

```
Current configuration:
!
version 11.2
no service udp-small-servers
no service tcp-small-servers
!
hostname Router
!
no ip classless
!
line con 0←No passwords
line aux 0
line vty 0 4
 login
!
end
```

The key to password recovery is being able to view, change, or delete the passwords contained in the router's normal startup configuration stored in NVRAM.

Viewing: If you wish to learn the current password and continue to use it, type the **show startup-configuration** command. From the following configuration, you will notice that both the console and enable passwords are set to "cisco." The viewing option will only work if the password is not encrypted. If the password is encrypted, you will either have to change it or delete it.

```
Router#sh start
Using 355 out of 30712 bytes
!
version 11.2
no service udp-small-servers
no service tcp-small-servers
!
hostname Cisco3620
!
enable password cisco←Enable password
!
no ip classless
!
line con 0
 password cisco←Login password
 login
line aux 0
line vty 0 4
 login
!
end
```

Changing: To change the current passwords, you will need to copy the NVRAM configuration to the running configuration. This task is done via the command **copy startup-configuration running-configuration**. Enter configuration mode using the **config term** command. Type the new passwords. Press Ctrl+Z to exit configuration mode when you are done. Type **write mem** to save the new passwords to NVRAM.

Delete: You can erase the passwords by using the **write erase** command.

The final step before reloading is to change the router's configuration register to a value which will cause the router to load its initial configuration from NVRAM. The current configuration register value can be viewed using the **show version** command. The value appears at the end of the command's output. In this case, the value of 0x2142 causes the router to ignore the contents of NVRAM.

```
Router#sh ver
Cisco Internetwork Operating System Software
IOS (tm) 3600 Software (C3620-I-M), Version 11.2(8)P, RELEASE SOFTWARE (fc1)
Copyright (c) 1986-1997 by cisco Systems, Inc.
Compiled Mon 11-Aug-97 19:50 by ccai
Image text-base: 0x600088E0, data-base: 0x6044A000

ROM: System Bootstrap, Version 11.1(7)AX [kuong (7)AX], EARLY DEPLOYMENT
     RELEASE SOFTWARE (fc2)

Router uptime is 0 minutes
System restarted by power-on
System image file is "flash:c3620-i-mz.112-8.P", booted via flash

cisco 3620 (R4700) processor (revision 0x81) with 12288K/4096K bytes of memory.
Processor board ID 05706480
R4700 processor, Implementation 33, Revision 1.0
Bridging software.
X.25 software, Version 2.0, NET2, BFE and GOSIP compliant.
1 Ethernet/IEEE 802.3 interface(s)
2 Serial network interface(s)
DRAM configuration is 32 bits wide with parity disabled.
29K bytes of non-volatile configuration memory.
16384K bytes of processor board System flash (Read/Write)
8192K bytes of processor board PCMCIA Slot0 flash (Read/Write)
Configuration register is 0x2142
```

The router's configuration register value is changed by typing **configure term** at the command prompt. Use the **config-register** command to enter the new register value. In this case, the new register value is 0x2102.

```
Router#config term
Enter configuration commands, one per line. End with CNTL/Z.
Router(config)#config-register 0x2102
Router(config)#exit
```

The **show version** command will now reflect the new setting. Notice that this new setting will not take effect until the router is reloaded.

```
Router#sh ver
Cisco Internetwork Operating System Software
IOS (tm) 3600 Software (C3620-I-M), Version 11.2(8)P, RELEASE SOFTWARE (fc1)
Copyright (c) 1986-1997 by cisco Systems, Inc.
Compiled Mon 11-Aug-97 19:50 by ccai
Image text-base: 0x600088E0, data-base: 0x6044A000

ROM: System Bootstrap, Version 11.1(7)AX [kuong (7)AX], EARLY DEPLOYMENT
     RELEASE SOFTWARE (fc2)

Router uptime is 1 minute
System restarted by power-on
System image file is "flash:c3620-i-mz.112-8.P", booted via flash

cisco 3620 (R4700) processor (revision 0x81) with 12288K/4096K bytes of memory.
Processor board ID 05706480
R4700 processor, Implementation 33, Revision 1.0
Bridging software.
X.25 software, Version 2.0, NET2, BFE and GOSIP compliant.
1 Ethernet/IEEE 802.3 interface(s)
2 Serial network interface(s)
DRAM configuration is 32 bits wide with parity disabled.
29K bytes of non-volatile configuration memory.
16384K bytes of processor board System flash (Read/Write)
8192K bytes of processor board PCMCIA Slot0 flash (Read/Write)
Configuration register is 0x2142 (will be 0x2102 at next reload)
```

Type the **reload** command at the router prompt to reload the router and cause the new configuration register values to take effect. You do not need to save configuration register changes.

```
Router#reload

System configuration has been modified. Save? [yes/no]: n
Proceed with reload? [confirm]
```

The router will now reload, and it will obtain is initial configuration from the contents of NVRAM. The passwords of the router are now known and can be used to access the privileged mode of the router.

Lab #83: Cisco 2500 Password Recovery

Equipment Needed

The following equipment is needed to perform this lab exercise:

- A Cisco 2500 series router
- A PC running a terminal emulation program, preferably ProComm or Windows HyperTerminal
- A Cisco rolled cable connecting the router to the PC

Configuration Overview

This section will provide detailed instructions on recovering an unknown password on a Cisco 2500 series router, as shown in Figure 22–4.

NOTES: *Pressing the break sequence too soon after powering on the router can cause the router to lock up. In this case, simply power cycle the router again. You should wait to press the break sequence until the router prints a message related to the size of the router's main memory.*

Keep in mind that terminal emulation programs use different key combinations to generate the break sequence. The two most popular terminal emulators are Windows 95 HyperTerminal and ProComm. The break sequence for ProComm is generated by pressing the ALT+B keys at the same time. In Windows 95 HyperTerminal, the break sequence is generated by pressing the Ctrl+Break keys at the same time.

Figure 22–4
Cisco 2500 password recovery

Console
Port

2500

PC running
Hyperterm

NOTE: *Password recovery can only be performed with a terminal attached to the console port of the router. These procedures will not work on the Aux port of the router.*

Password Recovery Procedures

Before beginning, the router should have an enable password and a login password set. The following configuration shows an example of the enable and login password both set to cisco:

Router

```
Current configuration:
!
version 11.0
service udp-small-servers
service tcp-small-servers
!
hostname Cisco2500
!
enable password cisco←Enable password
!
line con 0
 password cisco←Login password
 login
line aux 0
 transport input all
line vty 0 4
 login
!
end
```

The following **show version** command reveals that the configuration register of the router is set to a value of 0x2102. As described in the previous section, this value will cause the router to use the NVRAM configuration file during the boot process. This register value will be changed during the password recovery process, causing the router to ignore the contents of the NVRAM configuration file during the boot process.

```
Cisco2500#sh ver
Cisco Internetwork Operating System Software
IOS (tm) 3000 Software (IGS-D-L), Version 11.0(10), RELEASE SOFTWARE (fc3)
Copyright (c) 1986-1996 by cisco Systems, Inc.
Compiled Mon 05-Aug-96 18:19 by loreilly
Image text-base: 0x03025A14, data-base: 0x00001000

ROM: System Bootstrap, Version 5.2(8a), RELEASE SOFTWARE
ROM: 3000 Bootstrap Software (IGS-RXBOOT), Version 10.2(8a), RELEASE SOFTWARE
(fc1)
```

```
Cisco2500 uptime is 2 minutes
System restarted by reload
System image file is "flash:igs-d-1.110-10", booted via flash

cisco 2500 (68030) processor (revision A) with 4096K/2048K bytes of memory.
Processor board ID 01412484, with hardware revision 00000000
Bridging software.
X.25 software, Version 2.0, NET2, BFE and GOSIP compliant.
1 Ethernet/IEEE 802.3 interface.
2 Serial network interfaces.
32K bytes of non-volatile configuration memory.
8192K bytes of processor board System flash (Read ONLY)
```

Configuration register is 0x2102

> The first step in the password recovery process is to power cycle the
> router, turning it off and back on again. If the router is already off, then
> turn it on. During the first few seconds of the boot process, you will see
> the following message displayed:

```
System Bootstrap, Version 5.2(8a), RELEASE SOFTWARE
Copyright (c) 1986-1995 by cisco Systems
2500 processor with 4096 Kbytes of main memory←Press the break sequence here
```

> After these messages are displayed, press the proper break sequence.
> Remember that every terminal emulation program has its own key com-
> binations to force a break. The break sequence for ProComm is generated
> by pressing the ALT+B keys at the same time. In Windows 95 HyperTer-
> minal, the break sequence is generated by pressing the Ctrl+Break keys
> at the same time. When the proper break sequence is pressed, the router
> will go into monitor mode:

```
    Abort at 0x10EA838 (PC)
    >
```

At the > prompt type the command: o/r 0x42

```
    >o/r 0x42
    >
```

Type an i to reboot the router.

```
    >
    >i
```

> The router will reload. This time, it will ignore the configuration infor-
> mation contained in the NVRAM. When the router finishes booting, there
> will not be a console password or an enable password. Press **enter** to get
> into user mode and type **enable** to get into privileged mode:

```
Press RETURN to get started!


Router>
Router>ena
Router#
```

Use the **show running-configuration** command to view the router's current configuration. You will notice that the configuration contains no passwords of any kind. This configuration gets created when the router ignores the contents of NVRAM:

```
Router#sh run


Building configuration...

Current configuration:
!
version 11.0
service udp-small-servers
service tcp-small-servers
!
hostname Router
!
line con 0←No passwords
line aux 0
 transport input all
line vty 0 4
 login
!
end
```

The key to password recovery is being able to view, change, or delete the passwords contained in the router's normal startup configuration stored in NVRAM.

Viewing: If you wish to learn the current password and continue to use it, type the **show startup-configuration** command. From the following configuration, you will notice that both the console and enable passwords are set to "cisco." The viewing option will only work if the password is not encrypted. If the password is encrypted, you will either have to change it or delete it.

```
Router#sh start
Using 348 out of 32762 bytes
!
version 11.0
service udp-small-servers
service tcp-small-servers
!
```

```
hostname Cisco2500
!
enable password cisco←Enable password
!
line con 0
 password cisco←Login password
 login
line aux 0
 transport input all
line vty 0 4
 login
!
end
```

Changing: To change the current passwords, you will need to copy the NVRAM configuration to the running configuration. This task is done via the **copy startup-configuration running-configuration** command. Enter configuration mode using the **config term** command. Type the new passwords. Press Ctrl+Z to exit configuration mode when you are done. Type **write mem** to save the new passwords to NVRAM.

Erase: You can erase the passwords by using the **write erase** command.

The final step before reloading is to change the router's configuration register to a value that will cause the router to load its initial configuration from NVRAM. The current configuration register value can be viewed using the **show version** command. The value appears at the end of the command's output. In this case, the value of 0x2142 causes the router to ignore the contents of NVRAM.

```
Router#sh ver
Cisco Internetwork Operating System Software
IOS (tm) 3000 Software (IGS-D-L), Version 11.0(10), RELEASE SOFTWARE (fc3)
Copyright (c) 1986-1996 by cisco Systems, Inc.
Compiled Mon 05-Aug-96 18:19 by loreilly
Image text-base: 0x03025A14, data-base: 0x00001000

ROM: System Bootstrap, Version 5.2(8a), RELEASE SOFTWARE
ROM: 3000 Bootstrap Software (IGS-RXBOOT), Version 10.2(8a), RELEASE SOFTWARE
(fc1)

Router uptime is 1 minute
System restarted by power-on
System image file is "flash:igs-d-l.110-10", booted via flash

cisco 2500 (68030) processor (revision A) with 4096K/2048K bytes of memory.
Processor board ID 01412484, with hardware revision 00000000
Bridging software.
X.25 software, Version 2.0, NET2, BFE and GOSIP compliant.
1 Ethernet/IEEE 802.3 interface.
```

```
2 Serial network interfaces.
32K bytes of non-volatile configuration memory.
8192K bytes of processor board System flash (Read ONLY)
```

Configuration register is 0x42

The router's configuration register value is changed by typing **config-ure term** at the command prompt. Use the **config-register** command to enter the new register value. In this case, the new register value is 0x2102.

```
Router#config term
Enter configuration commands, one per line. End with CNTL/Z.
Router(config)#conf
Router(config)#config-register 0x2102
Router(config)#exit
```

The **show version** command will now reflect the new setting. Notice that this new setting will not take effect until the router is reloaded.

```
Router#sh ver
Cisco Internetwork Operating System Software
IOS (tm) 3000 Software (IGS-D-L), Version 11.0(10), RELEASE SOFTWARE (fc3)
Copyright (c) 1986-1996 by cisco Systems, Inc.
Compiled Mon 05-Aug-96 18:19 by loreilly
Image text-base: 0x03025A14, data-base: 0x00001000

ROM: System Bootstrap, Version 5.2(8a), RELEASE SOFTWARE
ROM: 3000 Bootstrap Software (IGS-RXBOOT), Version 10.2(8a), RELEASE SOFTWARE
(fc1)

Router uptime is 1 minute
System restarted by power-on
System image file is "flash:igs-d-1.110-10", booted via flash

cisco 2500 (68030) processor (revision A) with 4096K/2048K bytes of memory.
Processor board ID 01412484, with hardware revision 00000000
Bridging software.
X.25 software, Version 2.0, NET2, BFE and GOSIP compliant.
1 Ethernet/IEEE 802.3 interface.
2 Serial network interfaces.
32K bytes of non-volatile configuration memory.
8192K bytes of processor board System flash (Read ONLY)
```

Configuration register is 0x42 (will be 0x2102 at next reload)

Type the **reload** command at the router prompt to reload the router and cause the new configuration register values to take effect. You do not need to save configuration register changes.

```
Router#reload

System configuration has been modified. Save? [yes/no]: n
Proceed with reload? [confirm]
```

> The router will now reload and will obtain its initial configuration from the contents of NVRAM. The passwords of the router are now known and can be used to access the privileged mode of the router.

Lab #84: Cisco Catalyst 5000 Password Recovery

Equipment Needed

The following equipment is needed to perform this lab exercise:

- A Cisco Catalyst 5000 series switch
- A PC running a terminal emulation program, preferably ProComm or Windows 95 HyperTerminal
- A straight cable connecting the switch to the PC

Configuration Overview

This section will provide detailed instructions on recovering an unknown password on a Cisco Catalyst 5000 series switch, as shown in Figure 22–5.

Figure 22–5
Catalyst 5000
password recovery

PC running
Hyperterm

Console
Port

CAT 5000

> *NOTE:*   *Password recovery can only be performed with a terminal attached to the console port of the switch. The Supervisor III module on the Catalyst 5500 has both a console port and an Aux port. Password recovery will only work on the console port of the switch.*

Password Recovery Procedures

The Catalyst Switch follows a different password recovery scheme than the router. The passwords on the Catalyst Switch are not valid for the first 30 seconds after the switch powers up and sends the initial system login prompt. This feature enables you to gain access to the switch by simply pressing **Enter** at the password prompts. The drawback to this feature is that you only have 30 seconds to gain entry to the switch and change the passwords. Changing both system passwords in only 30 seconds can be difficult.

One way around this situation is to type the password change sequence into a text editor and copy the data to the clipboard. When the Catalyst Switch reboots, you can paste this sequence to the screen and send the password change commands to the Catalyst Switch all at once.

The first step in the password recovery process is to power cycle the switch, turning it off and on again. As with a router, you must be connected to the console port. If the switch is already off, then turn it on. During the first few seconds of the boot process, you will see the following information displayed:

```
System Bootstrap, Version 3.1(2)
Copyright (c) 1994-1997 by cisco Systems, Inc.
Processor with 32768 Kbytes of main memory

Autoboot executing command: "boot bootflash:"
CCCCCCCCCCCCCCCCCCCCCCCCCCCCCCCCCCCCCCCCCCCCCCCCCCCCCCCCCCCCCCCCCCCCCCCCCCCCCC
Uncompressing file:
########################################################
##############################################################################
##############################################################################
##############################################################################
##############################################################################
##############################################################################
##############################################################################
##########################################################################
```

```
System Power On Diagnostics
NVRAM Size .. .................512KB
ID Prom Test .................Passed
DPRAM Size ...................16KB
DPRAM Data 0x55 Test .........Passed
DPRAM Data 0xaa Test .........Passed
DPRAM Address Test ...........Passed
Clearing DPRAM ...............Done
System DRAM Memory Size .......32MB
DRAM Data 0x55 Test ..........Passed
DRAM Data 0xaa Test ..........Passed
DRAM Address Test  ...........Passed
Clearing DRAM ................Done
EARL++ .......................Present
EARL RAM Test ................Passed
EARL Serial Prom Test ........Passed
Level2 Cache .................Present
Level2 Cache test.............Passed

Boot image: bootflash:cat5000-sup3.3-1-1.bin

Running System Diagnostics from this Supervisor (Module 2)
This may take up to 2 minutes....please wait
```

When the following console message appears, press the Enter key to log into the switch. Remember that for the next 30 seconds, the switch passwords will not be set—and pressing the Enter key at a password prompt will enable access.

```
Cisco Systems Console←Press the enter key when you see this message.
```

Pressing the enter key the first time will give you access to the switches non-privileged mode:

```
Console>
```

The following sequence can either be typed within the 30-second null password period or can be pasted to the terminal emulation screen. If you wish to paste it to the screen, you must first create the proper password change script in a text editor. The string would be as follows:

```
Ena←ena is the Catalyst command for entering privileged mode. Follow this word
    by pressing enter twice.

set pass←set pass will cause the Catalyst to change the non-privileged mode
        password. Follow this command by pressing the Enter key four times.



set enablepass←set enablepass will cause the Catalyst to change the privileged
            mode password. Follow this command by pressing the Enter key
            four times.
```

After creating this string in the text editor, do a select all and copy the information to the clipboard. When the Catalyst prompt appears, copy this text sequence to the terminal:

```
Console> ena
Enter password:
Console> (enable) set pass
Enter old password:
Enter new password:
Retype new password:
Password changed.
Console> (enable) set enablepass
Enter old password:
Enter new password:
Retype new password:
Password changed.
Console> (enable)
```

The password on the Catalyst had now been set to the Enter key for both the privileged and non-privileged modes. The Catalyst passwords can now be set to any value.

Conclusion

This chapter provided detailed information about recovering lost or unknown passwords on Cisco routers and Catalyst switches. We also saw that recovering the password on a Cisco router involves gaining console access to the router and changing the configuration register, so that the router ignores the contents of NVRAM when it powers up.

Changing the password on the Catalyst 5000 family of switches involves gaining console access to the Catalyst and being able to change the system passwords within 30 seconds of first gaining console access after a power-on of the switch.

23

HTTP Access
with a
Cisco Router

Topics Covered in This Chapter

- ▣ HTTP server overview
- ▣ Configuring a Cisco router as an HTTP server
- ▣ Using access lists to restrict HTTP access to a router
- ▣ Troubleshooting HTTP transfers

Introduction

This Cisco IOS feature enables management access to a router via a standard Web browser, such as Netscape Navigator or Microsoft Internet Explorer. This feature is beneficial to those users who are more comfortable using a Web browser interface than the Cisco command line.

HTTP Overview

HTTP is a client/server application that uses TCP as its transport protocol. A client runs a Web browser application, such as Netscape Navigator or Microsoft Internet Explorer. The Web client makes requests to an HTTP server running an http daemon program. These requests from the Web browser to the httpd server usually occur over TCP port 80. Figure 23–1 shows a simplified HTTP client and server configuration.

Commands Discussed in This Chapter

- **ip http server**
- **ip http port [*number*]**
- **ip http access class [*access-list-number* | *name*]**
- **debug ip http url**
- **debug ip http tokens**
- **debug ip transactions**

Figure 23–1
Basic HTTP
client/server setup

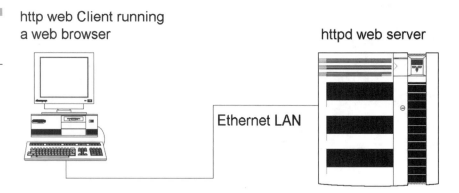

http web Client running
a web browser

httpd web server

Ethernet LAN

Definitions

IP http server: This global command enables the router to respond to HTTP requests from a Web browser.

IP http port: This global command is used to change the TCP port number that the router uses to listen to HTTP requests. By default, HTTP uses TCP port 80.

IP http access class: This global command is used to control which Web browser hosts can access the router via HTTP requests.

IOS Requirements

The HTTP feature was first introduced in IOS version 11.0(6).

Lab #85: Basic Configuration without an Access List

Equipment Needed

The following equipment is needed to perform this lab exercise:

■ Two Cisco routers, each having at least one serial port. One of the two routers must have an Ethernet port.

■ A PC or workstation that is Ethernet-connected to one of the two routers

■ One Cisco DTE/DCE crossover cable. If no crossover cables are available, you can make one by connecting a standard Cisco DTE cable to a standard Cisco DCE cable.

■ Either an Ethernet crossover cable or two Ethernet cables and an Ethernet hub

Configuration Overview

The objective of this lab is to be able to access and manage both Cisco1 and Cisco2 from the Web browser running on the workstation at 10.10.3.77.

Figure 23–2 shows the router connectivity for the examples used in this chapter. A PC/Mac/Unix workstation running a Web browser is Ethernet attached to a gateway Cisco router, Cisco1. Router Cisco1 is serially attached to a second router, Cisco2. IP addresses are as shown in the diagram.

In this lab, the Cisco router will be running an httpd daemon and will be acting as a Web server for a Web browser client application.

Router Configuration

Following are the configurations that should be entered into routers Cisco1 and Cisco2:

Cisco1

```
Current configuration:
!
version 11.2
no service udp-small-servers
no service tcp-small-servers
!
hostname Cisco1
!
enable password cisco
!
no ip domain-lookup
!
interface Ethernet0/0
```

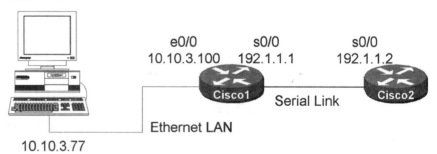

Figure 23–2
Cisco HTTP Web
server setup

http web Client running
a web browser

```
 ip address 10.10.3.100 255.255.255.0
!
interface Serial0/0
 ip address 192.1.1.1 255.255.255.0
!
router rip
 network 10.0.0.0
 network 192.1.1.0
!
ip http server←Enable this router to act as an HTTP server
ip classless
!
line con 0
 exec-timeout 120 0
 password cisco
 login
line aux 0
 password cisco
 login
line vty 0 4
 exec-timeout 120 0
 password cisco
 login
!
end
```

Cisco2

```
Current configuration:
!
version 11.2
no service udp-small-servers
no service tcp-small-servers
!
hostname Cisco2
!
enable password cisco
!
no ip domain-lookup
!
interface Serial0/0
 ip address 192.1.1.2 255.255.255.0
 clockrate 800000
!
interface Serial0/1
 ip address 196.1.1.2 255.255.255.0
 encapsulation ppp
 clockrate 19200
!
router rip
 network 192.1.1.0
 network 196.1.1.0
```

```
!
ip http server←Enable this router to act as an HTTP server
ip classless
!
line con 0
 password cisco
 login
line aux 0
 password cisco
 login
line vty 0 4
 exec-timeout 120 0
 password cisco
 login
!
end
```

The **ip http server** command in each of the configurations enables the router to respond to HTTP requests from a Web client.

Monitoring and Testing the Configuration

After entering the proper configurations into Cisco1 and Cisco2, verify connectivity between the workstation and the two routers by performing a ping on each router from the workstation.

```
C:\TEMP>ping 10.10.3.100

Pinging 10.10.3.100 with 32 bytes of data:

Reply from 10.10.3.100: bytes=32 time=7ms TTL=19
Reply from 10.10.3.100: bytes=32 time=7ms TTL=20
Reply from 10.10.3.100: bytes=32 time=7ms TTL=20
Reply from 10.10.3.100: bytes=32 time=7ms TTL=20
```

Verify connectivity to Cisco2 at address 192.1.1.2 via the same method.

Now, start up the Web browser. As shown in Figure 23–3, enter the address of Cisco2 in the URL field and press **Return**. You should be presented with the initial login screen, as shown in the figure.

Enter a username of "cisco" and a password of "cisco," then click OK.

You should now see the initial screen, as shown in Figure 23–4. Click the **show interfaces** option to view the status of the interfaces on Cisco2. Figure 23–5 depicts the output of this command.

Figure 23–3
Web browser login
screen

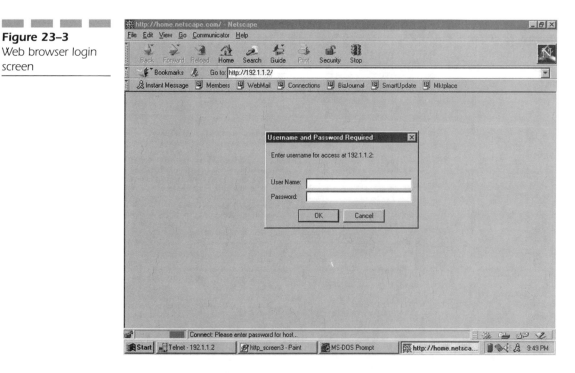

Figure 23–4
Router home screen

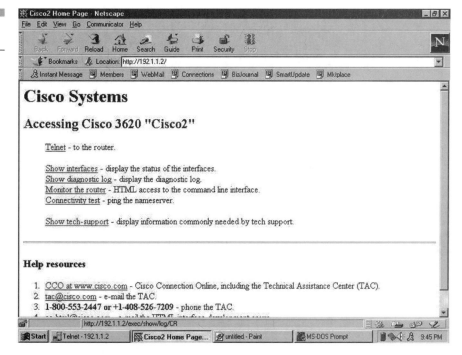

Figure 23–5
Show interfaces
screen

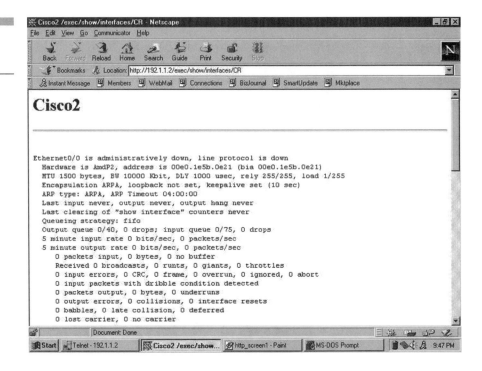

Lab #86: Advanced Configuration with an Access List

Configuration Overview

We will now add an **ip http access class** statement to the configuration we had in Lab #85. This command provides enhanced security, only permitting browsers at allowed IP addresses to access the router via HTTP.

Router Configuration

The configuration for the router in this example is as follows:

Cisco1

```
Current configuration:
!
version 11.2
no service udp-small-servers
no service tcp-small-servers
!
hostname Cisco1
!
enable password cisco
!
no ip domain-lookup
!
interface Ethernet0/0
 ip address 10.10.3.100 255.255.255.0
!
interface Serial0/0
 ip address 192.1.1.1 255.255.255.0
!
router rip
 network 10.0.0.0
 network 192.1.1.0
!
ip http server←Enable this router to act as an HTTP server
ip http access-class 1←Only allow hosts defined by access-list 1 HTTP access
                       to this router
ip classless
access-list 1 deny    10.10.3.77←Define an access-list for allowed HTTP hosts
access-list 1 permit any
!
line con 0
 exec-timeout 120 0
 password cisco
 login
line aux 0
 password cisco
 login
line vty 0 4
 exec-timeout 120 0
 password cisco
 login
!
end
```

The configuration for Cisco2 remains the same.

Monitoring and Testing the Configuration

Try to access router Cisco1 from the Web browser. You will now notice that the Web browser at 10.10.3.77 can no longer access Cisco1. The workstation can still access Cisco2 via the Web browser.

The **ip http access-class 1** command specifies that access list 1 should be applied to any HTTP requests. The **access-list 1 deny 10.10.3.77** specifies that no traffic from 10.10.3.77 will be permitted. The **access-list 1 permit any** statement permits all other traffic.

The **ip http port** command can also be used in this configuration. This command enables the router to listen for HTTP requests on a port other than the default port of 80.

Troubleshooting HTTP

Several debug commands are available to assist in troubleshooting and monitoring HTTP connections to a router network:

{Debug ip http url}   From the cisco command line, enter the **debug ip http url** command:

```
Cisco2#debug ip http url
HTTP URL debugging is on
```

This command will show URL information. In the following example, we see that the Web browser at 10.10.3.77 has accessed the show interfaces screen on the router.

```
HTTP: processing URL '/exec/show/interfaces/CR' from host 10.10.3.77
```

{Debug ip http tokens}   From the cisco command line, enter the **debug ip http tokens** command:

```
Cisco2#debug ip http tokens
HTTP tokens debugging is on
```

When an http request is made to the router, this command will show individual token information parsed by the router.

```
HTTP: token len 3: 'GET'
HTTP: token len 1: ' '
HTTP: token len 1: '/'
HTTP: token len 1: ' '
HTTP: token len 4: 'HTTP'
HTTP: token len 1: '/'
HTTP: token len 1: '1'
HTTP: token len 1: '.'
```

```
HTTP: token len 1: '0'
HTTP: token len 2: '\15\12'
HTTP: token len 10: 'Connection'
HTTP: token len 1: ':'
HTTP: token len 1: ' '
HTTP: token len 4: 'Keep'
HTTP: token len 1: '-'
HTTP: token len 5: 'Alive'
HTTP: token len 2: '\15\12'
HTTP: token len 4: 'User'
HTTP: token len 1: '-'
HTTP: token len 5: 'Agent'
HTTP: token len 1: ':'
HTTP: token len 1: ' '
HTTP: token len 7: 'Mozilla'
HTTP: token len 1: '/'
HTTP: token len 1: '4'
HTTP: token len 1: '.'
```

{Debug ip http transactions}   From the cisco command line, enter the **debug ip http transactions** command:

```
Cisco2#debug ip http transactions
HTTP transactions debugging is on
```

When an http request is made to the router, this command shows the high-level transactions between the Web browser and the router.

```
HTTP: parsed uri '/exec/show/tech-support/cr'
HTTP: client version 1.0
HTTP: parsed extension Referer
HTTP: parsed line  http://192.1.1.2/
HTTP: parsed extension Connection
HTTP: parsed line  Keep-Alive
HTTP: parsed extension User-Agent
HTTP: parsed line  Mozilla/4.05 [en] (Win95; I)
HTTP: parsed extension Host
HTTP: parsed line  192.1.1.2
HTTP: parsed extension Accept
HTTP: parsed line  image/gif, image/x-xbitmap, image/jpeg, image/
HTTP: parsed extension Accept-Language
HTTP: parsed line  en
HTTP: parsed extension Accept-Charset
HTTP: parsed line  iso-8859-1,*,utf-8
HTTP: parsed extension Authorization
HTTP: parsed authorization type Basic
HTTP: received GET 'exec'
```

Conclusion

This chapter demonstrates the httpd server capabilities of the Cisco router. Accessing devices via an HTTP interface is becoming an increasingly popular method of managing a network.

Appendix A

ASCII Conversion Charts

Decimal	HEX	ASCII Character	Meaning	Keyboard Entry
0	0	NUL	Null	Ctrl-@
1	1	SOH	Start of heading	Ctrl-A
2	2	STX	Start of text	Ctrl-B
3	3	ETX	Break/end of text	Ctrl-C
4	4	EOT	End of transmission	Ctrl-D
5	5	ENQ	Enquiry	Ctrl-E
6	6	ACK	Positive acknowledgment	Ctrl-F
7	7	BEL	Bell	Ctrl-G
8	8	BS	Backspace	Ctrl-H
9	9	HT	Horizontal tab	Ctrl-I
10	0A	LF	Line feed	Ctrl-J
11	0B	VT	Vertical tab	Ctrl-K
12	0C	FF	Form feed	Ctrl-L
13	0D	CR	Carriage return	Ctrl-M
14	0E	SO	Shift out	Ctrl-N
15	0F	SI	Shift in/XON (resume output)	Ctrl-O
16	10	DLE	Data link escape	Ctrl-P
17	11	DC1	Device control character 1	Ctrl-Q
18	12	DC2	Device control character 2	Ctrl-R
19	13	DC3	Device control character 3	Ctrl-S
20	14	DC4	Device control character 4	Ctrl-T
21	15	NAK	Negative acknowledgment	Ctrl-U
22	16	SYN	Synchronous idle	Ctrl-V
23	17	ETB	End of transmission block	x

Decimal	HEX	ASCII Character	Meaning	Keyboard Entry
24	18	CAN	Cancel	Ctrl-X
25	19	EM	End of medium	Ctrl-Y
26	1A	SUB	Substitute/end of file	Ctrl-Z
27	1B	ESC	Escape	Ctrl-[
28	1C	FS	File separator	Ctrl-\
29	1D	GS	Group separator	Ctrl-]
30	1E	RS	Record separator	Ctrl-^
31	1F	US	Unit separator	Ctrl-_
32	20	SP	Space	Space
33	21	!	!	!
34	22	"	"	"
35	23	#	#	#
36	24	$	$	$
37	25	%	%	%
38	26	&	&	&
39	27	'	'	'
40	28	(	(	(
41	29	)	)	)
42	2A	*	*	*
43	2B	+	+	+
44	2C	,	,	,
45	2D	-	-	-
46	2E	.	.	.
47	2F	/	/	/
48	30	0	Zero	0
49	31	1	One	1
50	32	2	Two	2
51	33	3	Three	3
52	34	4	Four	4

Decimal	HEX	ASCII Character	Meaning	Keyboard Entry
53	35	5	Five	5
54	36	6	Six	6
55	37	7	Seven	7
56	38	8	Eight	8
57	39	9	Nine	9
58	3A	:	:	:
59	3B	;	;	;
60	3C	<	<	<
61	3D	=	=	=
62	3E	>	>	>
63	3F	?	?	?
64	40	@	@	@
65	41	A	A	A
66	42	B	B	B
67	43	C	C	C
68	44	D	D	D
69	45	E	E	E
70	46	F	F	F
71	47	G	G	G
72	48	H	H	H
73	49	I	I	I
74	4A	J	J	J
75	4B	K	K	K
76	4C	L	L	L
77	4D	M	M	M
78	4E	N	N	N
79	4F	O	O	O
80	50	P	P	P
81	51	Q	Q	Q

Decimal	HEX	ASCII Character	Meaning	Keyboard Entry
82	52	R	R	R
83	53	S	S	S
84	54	T	T	T
85	55	U	U	U
86	56	V	V	V
87	57	W	W	W
88	58	X	X	X
89	59	Y	Y	Y
90	5A	Z	Z	Z
91	5B	[	[	[
92	5C	\	\	\
93	5D	]	]	]
94	5E	^	^	^
95	5F	_	_	_
96	60	'	'	'
97	61	a	a	a
98	62	b	b	b
99	63	c	c	c
100	64	d	d	d
101	65	e	e	e
102	66	f	f	f
103	67	g	g	g
104	68	h	h	h
105	69	i	i	i
106	6A	j	j	j
107	6B	k	k	k
108	6C	l	l	l
109	6D	m	m	m
110	6E	n	n	n

Decimal	HEX	ASCII Character	Meaning	Keyboard Entry
111	6F	o	o	o
112	70	p	p	p
113	71	q	q	q
114	72	r	r	r
115	73	s	s	s
116	74	t	t	t
117	75	u	u	u
118	76	v	v	v
119	77	w	w	w
120	78	x	x	x
121	79	y	y	y
122	7A	z	z	z
123	7B	{	{	{
124	7C						
125	7D	}	}	}
126	7E	~	Tilde	~
127	7F	DEL	Delete	Del

Appendix B

Novell SAP Service List

Decimal	Hex	SAP Description
0	0000	Unknown
1	0001	User
2	0002	User Group
3	0003	Print Queue or Print Group
4	0004	File Server (SLIST source)
5	0005	Job Server
6	0006	Gateway
7	0007	Print Server or Silent Print Server
8	0008	Archive Queue
9	0009	Archive Server
10	000a	Job Queue
11	000b	Administration
15	000F	Novell TI-RPC
23	0017	Diagnostics
32	0020	NetBIOS
33	0021	NAS SNA Gateway
35	0023	NACS Async Gateway or Asynchronous Gateway
36	0024	Remote Bridge or Routing Service
38	0026	Bridge Server or Asynchronous Bridge Server
39	0027	TCP/IP Gateway Server
40	0028	Point to Point (Eicon) X.25 Bridge Server
41	0029	Eicon 3270 Gateway
42	002a	CHI Corp
44	002c	PC Chalkboard

Decimal	Hex	SAP Description
45	002d	Time Synchronization Server or Asynchronous Timer
46	002e	ARCserve 5.0 / Palindrome Backup Director 4.x (PDB4)
69	0045	DI3270 Gateway
71	0047	Advertising Print Server
74	004a	NetBlazer Modems
75	004b	Btrieve VAP/NLM 5.0
76	004c	Netware SQL VAP/NLM Server
77	004d	Xtree Network Version Netware XTree
80	0050	Btrieve VAP 4.11
82	0052	QuickLink (Cubix)
83	0053	Print Queue User
88	0058	Multipoint X.25 Eicon Router
96	0060	STLB/NLM
100	0064	ARCserve
102	0066	ARCserve 3.0
114	0072	WAN Copy Utility
122	007a	TES-Netware for VMS
146	0092	WATCOM Debugger or Emerald Tape Backup Server
149	0095	DDA OBGYN
152	0098	Netware Access Server (Asynchronous gateway)
154	009a	Netware for VMS II or Named Pipe Server
155	009b	Netware Access Server
158	009e	Portable Netware Server or SunLink NVT
161	00a1	Powerchute APC UPS NLM
170	00aa	LAWserve
172	00ac	Compaq IDA Status Monitor
256	0100	PIPE STAIL
258	0102	LAN Protect Bindery
259	0103	Oracle DataBase Server

Decimal	Hex	SAP Description
263	0107	Netware 386 or RSPX Remote Console
271	010f	Novell SNA Gateway
273	0111	Test Server
274	0112	Print Server (HP)
276	0114	CSA MUX (f/Communications Executive)
277	0115	CSA LCA (f/Communications Executive)
278	0116	CSA CM (f/Communications Executive)
279	0117	CSA SMA (f/Communications Executive)
280	0118	CSA DBA (f/Communications Executive)
281	0119	CSA NMA (f/Communications Executive)
282	011a	CSA SSA (f/Communications Executive)
283	011b	CSA STATUS (f/Communications Executive)
286	011e	CSA APPC (f/Communications Executive)
294	0126	SNA TEST SSA Profile
298	012a	CSA TRACE (f/Communications Executive)
299	012b	Netware for SAA
301	012e	IKARUS virus scan utility
304	0130	Communications Executive
307	0133	NNS Domain Server or Netware Naming Services Domain
309	0135	Netware Naming Services Profile
311	0137	Netware 386 Print Queue or NNS Print Queue
321	0141	LAN Spool Server (Vap, Intel)
338	0152	IRMALAN Gateway
340	0154	Named Pipe Server
358	0166	NetWare Management
360	0168	Intel PICKIT Comm Server or Intel CAS Talk Server
369	0171	UNKNOWN
371	0173	Compaq
372	0174	Compaq SNMP Agent

Decimal	Hex	SAP Description
373	0175	Compaq
384	0180	XTree Server or XTree Tools
394	018A	UNKNOWN
432	01b0	GARP Gateway (net research)
433	01b1	Binfview (Lan Support Group)
447	01bf	Intel LanDesk Manager
458	01ca	AXTEC
459	01cb	Shiva NetModem/E
460	01cc	Shiva LanRover/E
461	01cd	Shiva LanRover/T
472	01d8	Castelle FAXPress Server
474	01da	Castelle LANPress Print Server
476	01dc	Castille FAX/Xerox 7033 Fax Server/Excel Lan Fax
496	01f0	LEGATO
501	01f5	LEGATO
563	0233	NMS Agent or Netware Management Agent
567	0237	NMS IPX Discovery or LANtern Read/Write Channel
568	0238	NMS IP Discovery or LANtern Trap/Alarm Channel
570	023a	LABtern
572	023c	MAVERICK
574	023e	UNKNOWN
575	023f	Used by eleven various Novell Servers / Novell SMDR
590	024e	Netware Connect
618	026a	Network Management (NMS) Service Console
619	026b	Time Synchronization Server (Netware 4.x)
632	0278	Directory Server (Netware 4.x)
989	03dd	Banyan ENS for Netware Client NLM
772	0304	Novell SAA Gateway
776	0308	COM or VERMED 1

Decimal	Hex	SAP Description
778	030a	Galacticomm's Worldgroup Server
780	030c	Intel Netport 2 or HP JetDirect or HP Quicksilver
800	0320	Attachmate Gateway
807	0327	Microsoft Diagnostics
808	0328	WATCOM SQL server
821	0335	MultiTech Systems Multisynch Comm Server
835	2101	Performance Technology Instant Internet
853	0355	Arcada Backup Exec
858	0358	MSLCD1
865	0361	NETINELO
894	037e	Twelve Novell file servers in the PC3M family
895	037f	ViruSafe Notify
902	0386	HP Bridge
903	0387	HP Hub
916	0394	NetWare SAA Gateway
923	039b	Lotus Notes
951	03b7	Certus Anti Virus NLM
964	03c4	ARCserve 4.0 (Cheyenne)
967	03c7	LANspool 3.5 (Intel)
983	03d7	Lexmark printer server (type 4033-011)
984	03d8	Lexmark XLE printer server (type 4033-301)
990	03de	Gupta Sequel Base Server or NetWare SQL
993	03e1	Univel Unixware
996	03e4	Univel Unixware
1020	03fc	Intel Netport
1021	03fd	Print Server Queue
1196	04ac	On-Time Scheduler NLM
1034	040A	ipnServer
1035	040B	UNKNOWN

Decimal	Hex	SAP Description
1037	040D	LVERRMAN
1038	040E	LVLIC
1040	0410	UNKNOWN
1044	0414	Kyocera
1065	0429	Site Lock Virus (Brightworks)
1074	0432	UFHELP R
1075	0433	Synoptics 281x Advanced SNMP Agent
1092	0444	Microsoft NT SNA Server
1096	0448	Oracle
1100	044c	ARCserve 5.01
1111	0457	Canon GP55 Running on a Canon GP55 network printer
1114	045a	QMS Printers
1115	045b	Dell SCSI Array (DSA) Monitor
1169	0491	NetBlazer Modems
1200	04b0	CD-Net (Meridian)
1217	04C1	UNKNOWN
1299	0513	Emulux NQA Something from Emulex
1312	0520	Site Lock Checks
1321	0529	Site Lock Checks (Brightworks)
1325	052d	Citrix OS/2 App Server
1343	0535	Tektronix
1344	0536	Milan
1387	056b	IBM 8235 modem server
1388	056c	Shiva LanRover/E PLUS
1389	056d	Shiva LanRover/T PLUS
1408	0580	McAfee's NetShield anti-virus
1466	05BA	Compatible Systems Routers
1569	0621	IBM AntiVirus NLM
1571	0623	UNKNOWN

Decimal	Hex	SAP Description
1900	076C	Xerox
1947	079b	Shiva LanRover/E 115
1958	079c	Shiva LanRover/T 115
2154	086a	ISSC collector NLMs
2175	087f	ISSC DAS agent for AIX
2857	0b29	Site Lock
3113	0c29	Site Lock Applications
3116	0c2c	Licensing Server
9088	2380	LAI Site Lock
9100	238c	Meeting Maker
18440	4808	Site Lock Server or Site Lock Metering VAP/NLM
21845	5555	Site Lock User
25362	6312	Tapeware
28416	6f00	Rabbit Gateway (3270)
30467	7703	MODEM
32770	8002	NetPort Printers (Intel) or LANport
32776	8008	WordPerfect Network Version
34238	85BE	Cisco Enhanced Interior Routing Protocol (EIGRP)
34952	8888	WordPerfect Network Version or Quick Network Management
36864	9000	McAfee's NetShield anti-virus
38404	9604	CSA-NT_MON
46760	b6a8	Ocean Isle Reachout Remote Control
61727	f11f	Site Lock Metering VAP/NLM
61951	f1ff	Site Lock
62723	F503	SCA-NT
64507	fbfb	TopCall III fax server
65535	ffff	Any Service or Wildcard

Appendix C

ISDN CAUSE CODES

Class	Value	Number	Cause
000	0001	1	Unallocated (unassigned) number
000	0010	2	No route to specified transit network
000	0011	3	No route to destination
000	0110	6	Channel Unacceptable
000	0111	7	Call awarded and being delivered in an established channel
001	0000	16	Normal call clearing
001	0001	17	User busy
001	0010	18	No user responding
001	0011	19	No answer from user (user alerted)
001	0101	21	Call Rejected
001	0110	22	Number changed
001	1010	26	Non selected user clearing
001	1011	27	Destination out of order
001	1100	28	Invalid number format
001	1101	29	Facility rejected
001	1110	30	Response to status enquiry
001	1111	31	Normal, unspecified
010	0010	34	No circuit/channel available
010	0110	38	Network out of order
010	1001	41	Temporary failure
010	1010	42	Switching equipment congestion
010	1011	43	Access information discarded
010	1100	44	Requested circuit/channel not available
010	1101	45	Pre-empted
010	1111	47	Resources unavailable, unspecified
011	0001	49	Quality of service unavailable

Class	Value	Number	Cause
011	0010	50	Requested facility not subscribed
011	0100	52	Outgoing calls barred
011	0110	54	Incoming calls barred
011	1001	57	Bearer capability not authorized
011	1010	58	Bearer capability not presently available
011	1111	63	Service or option not available, unspecified
100	0001	65	Bearer capability not implemented
100	0010	66	Channel type not implemented
100	0101	69	Requested facility not implemented
100	0110	70	Only restricted digital information bearer capability is available
100	1111	79	Service or option not implemented, unspecified
101	0001	81	Invalid call reference value
101	0010	82	Identified channel does not exist
101	0011	83	A suspended call exists, but this call identity does not
101	0100	84	Call identity in use
101	0101	85	No call suspended
101	0110	86	Call having the requested call identity has been cleared
101	1000	88	Incompatible destination
101	1011	91	Invalid transit network selection
101	1111	95	Invalid message, unspecified
110	0000	96	Mandatory information element is missing
110	0001	97	Message type nonexistent or not implemented
110	0010	98	Message not compatible with call state or message type nonexistent or not implemented
110	0011	99	Information element nonexistent or not implemented
110	0100	100	Invalid information element contents
110	0101	101	Message not compatible with call state
110	0110	102	Recovery on timer expired
110	1111	111	Protocol error, unspecified
111	1111	127	Interworking, unspecified

INDEX

Get Cisco Certified and Get Ahead
Anne Martinez
007-135258-9
$24.99

Written by the author of the best-selling Get Certified and Get Ahead, this one-stop, Web-enhanced resource answers the most frequently asked questions about Cisco certification and shows you the many opportunities awaiting Cisco certified professionals. This complete guide helps you to choose the right Cisco certification, and develop your own personal training and certification road map. Packed with study aids and test-taking tips this book is your clearest and most cost-effective path to Cisco certification and a more lucrative professional future.

SOFTWARE AND INFORMATION LICENSE

The software and information on this diskette (collectively referred to as the "Product") are the property of The McGraw-Hill Companies, Inc. ("McGraw-Hill") and are protected by both United States copyright law and international copyright treaty provision. You must treat this Product just like a book, except that you may copy it into a computer to be used and you may make archival copies of the Products for the sole purpose of backing up our software and protecting your investment from loss.

By saying "just like a book," McGraw-Hill means, for example, that the Product may be used by any number of people and may be freely moved from one computer location to another, so long as there is no possibility of the Product (or any part of the Product) being used at one location or on one computer while it is being used at another. Just as a book cannot be read by two different people in two different places at the same time, neither can the Product be used by two different people in two different places at the same time (unless, of course, McGraw-Hill's rights are being violated).

McGraw-Hill reserves the right to alter or modify the contents of the Product at any time.

This agreement is effective until terminated. The Agreement will terminate automatically without notice if you fail to comply with any provisions of this Agreement. In the event of termination by reason of your breach, you will destroy or erase all copies of the Product installed on any computer system or made for backup purposes and shall expunge the Product from your data storage facilities.

LIMITED WARRANTY

McGraw-Hill warrants the physical diskette(s) enclosed herein to be free of defects in materials and workmanship for a period of sixty days from the purchase date. If McGraw-Hill receives written notification within the warranty period of defects in materials or workmanship, and such notification is determined by McGraw-Hill to be correct, McGraw-Hill will replace the defective diskette(s). Send request to:

Customer Service
McGraw-Hill
Gahanna Industrial Park
860 Taylor Station Road
Blacklick, OH 43004-9615

The entire and exclusive liability and remedy for breach of this Limited Warranty shall be limited to replacement of defective diskette(s) and shall not include or extend any claim for or right to cover any other damages, including but not limited to, loss of profit, data, or use of the software, or special, incidental, or consequential damages or other similar claims, even if McGraw-Hill has been specifically advised as to the possibility of such damages. In no event will McGraw-Hill's liability for any damages to you or any other person ever exceed the lower of suggested list price or actual price paid for the license to use the Product, regardless of any form of the claim.

THE McGRAW-HILL COMPANIES, INC. SPECIFICALLY DISCLAIMS ALL OTHER WARRANTIES, EXPRESS OR IMPLIED, INCLUDING BUT NOT LIMITED TO, ANY IMPLIED WARRANTY OF MERCHANTABILITY OR FITNESS FOR A PARTICULAR PURPOSE. Specifically, McGraw-Hill makes no representation or warranty that the Product is fit for any particular purpose and any implied warranty of merchantability is limited to the sixty day duration of the Limited Warranty covering the physical diskette(s) only (and not the software or information) and is otherwise expressly and specifically disclaimed.

This Limited Warranty gives you specific legal rights; you may have others which may vary from state to state. Some states do not allow the exclusion of incidental or consequential damages, or the limitation on how long an implied warranty lasts, so some of the above may not apply to you.

This Agreement constitutes the entire agreement between the parties relating to use of the Product. The terms of any purchase order shall have no effect on the terms of this Agreement. Failure of McGraw-Hill to insist at any time on strict compliance with this Agreement shall not constitute a waiver of any rights under this Agreement. This Agreement shall be construed and governed in accordance with the laws of New York. If any provision of this Agreement is held to be contrary to law, that provision will be enforced to the maximum extent permissible and the remaining provisions will remain in force and effect.